JUSTICE AND SCHOOL SYSTEMS

The Role of the Courts in Education Litigation

JUSTICE AND SCHOOL SYSTEMS

The Role of the Courts in Education Litigation

Edited by Barbara Flicker

Temple University Press · Philadelphia

Temple University Press, Philadelphia 19122
Copyright © 1990 by Temple University. All rights reserved
Published 1990
Printed in the United States of America

The paper used in this publication meets the minimum
requirements of American National Standard for
Information Sciences—Permanence of Paper for Printed
Library Materials, ANSI Z39.48-1984 ∞

Library of Congress Cataloging-in-Publication Data
Justice and school systems: the role of the courts in
education litigation / edited by Barbara Flicker.
    p. cm.
    Bibliography: p.
    Includes index.
    ISBN 0-87722-675-X (alk. paper)
    1. Discrimination in education—Law and legislation—
United States—Cases. I. Flicker, Barbara.
KF4154.J67   1990
344.73'0798—dc20
[347.304798]   89-5018
                       CIP

CONTENTS

PREFACE

This book examines the cases brought to enforce the laws against discrimination based on race, gender, disability, or language in the school system and considers the impact of the litigation on the communities in which the cases originated. It is the culmination of a project that began at the Institute of Judicial Administration in 1974 and is a sequel to *Limits of Justice: The Courts' Role in School Desegregation*, edited by Howard I. Kalodner and James J. Fishman and published in 1978. Grants from the Ford Foundation have helped to support the project from its inception.

IJA is one of the first court organizations in the nation. It was founded at the New York University School of Law in 1952 by Arthur T. Vanderbilt, the late Chief Justice of the New Jersey Supreme Court, to study the operation of the courts and to improve the administration of justice. In furtherance of that mission, Paul Nejelski, who was IJA Director in 1974, established the Courts' Role in Desegregation of Education Litigation Project, with Howard Kalodner as Project Director and Jim Fishman as Associate Director. The purpose was to examine the response of the local judicial systems to the challenge of *Brown v. Board of Education*, the 1954 U.S. Supreme Court decision barring racial segregation in the public schools.

Limits of Justice was completed during Howard Kalodner's tenure as IJA Director. He and Jim Fishman then arranged for a new project to be funded by the Ford Foundation. This project would begin by exploring the implementation of the court orders adopted in several of the cases examined in the first volume and would then expand into other aspects of discrimination in the schools.

Subsequently, Professor Kalodner left IJA to become Dean of Western New England College School of Law and Professor Fishman joined the faculty of Pace University Law School. By the time I arrived to assume the duties of IJA Director in 1983, the project had been in abeyance for five years. With invaluable assistance from Howard and Jim, I enthusiastically reactivated the project.

Then, in 1986, as a result of my hectic professional life of constant commuting between New York and Los Angeles, I called upon John Blackmore, IJA Director of Special Projects, for assistance. In 1987 and 1988 John supervised the myriad details of checking citations and communicating with authors, publishers, and copy editors.

I am deeply grateful to the people who contributed to the publication of this volume. Many thanks to Howard, Jim, John, Marya Lenn Yee, Carwina Weng, and R. May Lee for this version of the book. I also am grateful to the law students who worked on the manuscript over the years of the project: Carol Grelecki, Sam Laufer, Kevin Quigley, Nancy Heller, Michael Oshima, Janette Payne, Jean Zimmerman, and Susan Cook. My personal thanks go to the authors, all of whom contributed brilliant essays to this volume; to Paul Nejelski; and to the tireless IJA staff: current IJA Director Margaret Shaw, Gerry Hansen, Fred Oberthal, and Calvin Hudson. And finally, I thank our friends at Temple University Press for their support and counsel, especially Acquisitions Editor Jane Cullen, who gently guided us through many crises since she became interested in this book in 1985; Production Editor Joan Vidal; Managing Editor Doris B. Braendel; and Director David M. Bartlett.

Barbara Flicker

PART I

Introduction

CHAPTER 1

Overview of Judicial Activism in Education Litigation

HOWARD I. KALODNER

TEN YEARS AGO I wrote an introductory essay to the Institute of Judicial Administration's first volume of case histories of school desegregation cases, *Limits of Justice: The Courts' Role in School Desegregation.* In that essay, I expressed concern about the desirability, in the long run, of the active and essentially solitary role of the federal courts in shouldering the burden of school desegregation. While I identified areas in which courts could improve the judicial process in school desegregation cases, I also stated:

> None of these changes could alter the essential character of the role of courts in school desegregation litigation. It is when the court is able to define the constitutional right to an education free of discriminatory school board action—and then confidently to expect the school board, the state commissioner of education, or other state or federal officials or agencies to formulate and implement the requisite changes to implement that right— that the role of courts can be reduced to more traditional proportions. . . .
>
> No political institution can long withstand the punishment of political isolation without an impact on its conduct.

Elsewhere, in that same essay, I recognized the necessity of judicial intervention, "for all of the faults that have characterized adjudication [in school desegregation cases], it is not possible to conceive of a constitutional system in which no institution of government is prepared to declare and enforce constitutional rights."

The contradiction between the judicial need for self-preservation and the societal need for its active involvement in these controversies is still with us today. The essays contained in this volume describe judicial declaration and enforcement of constitutional and statutory rights in the public educational systems. Each of the essays concerns judicial process when parties bring to the court claims of discrimination based on race, gender, handicap, or language. The essays describe particular instances of litigation, and they report on the views of lawyers and judges who have participated in a wide array of litigation brought to enforce constitutional and statutory rights of children in public education.

These are tales of progress and frustration, of creativity and plodding, of judicial activism and of judicial coercion; they are dramatic stories of society being forced through litigation to confront its failure to make available education that does not discriminate because of the race, gender, national origin, or intellectual or physical impairment of the children of our nation. They are worth reading for their individual stories, and even more valuable for what they constitute as a whole, a story of a society that has all too frequently been willing to visit on the children of the minority the prejudices of the adult members of the majority society.

It is not easy to identify the causes of either success or failure in the kinds of litigation described in these essays. It is not even easy to determine whether they are all of one kind, or must be distinguished by whether they rest on constitutional or statutory basis or both, or whether they were brought to vindicate the rights of racial or ethnic minorities or of persons who are physically handicapped or developmentally disabled. Most important, from the point of view of judicial administration, it is not easy to determine the degree to which success or failure is related to legal issues or the social and political setting in which the case is brought, or into which the remedial decree is delivered. But while the answers to these and other questions are not immediately clear, their importance to the legal, adjudicative, and political system is great and the essays in this book contribute significantly toward our understanding of the questions and provide concrete instances against which general hypotheses can be tested.

Readers of these studies will draw their own conclusions from them. I remain of the view that litigation is the last and the least but all too frequently the only recourse of those who suffer discrimination at the hands of those who administer our educational systems. Ingenuity on the part of judges and counsel has increased the effectiveness of litigation only marginally; willingness on the part of some school administrators to treat a loss in litigation as a source of power to bring about effective change resisted by their constituencies has been at the core of litigation that can be regarded as successful. True success will be achieved when those responsible for our educational systems are prepared to respect the dual imperatives of principles of nondiscrimination and of the critical significance to our society of excellence in education. Litigation plays a very small role in this important domain of political morality.

Two of the essays in this volume are reports of surveys of judges and lawyers who have been the participants in school desegregation cases. Barbara Flicker reports that judges who have presided in these cases are, on the whole, pleased with their conduct of the cases and with the results achieved.

They acknowledge that the results are not perfect and tend to attribute the inability to achieve perfect results to white flight, to segregated housing patterns, and to insufficient funds. Each of these observations serves as a useful perspective on the essays describing individual cases throughout this volume.

There is no doubt about the diminished number of white students attending public school in our major cities. From the point of view of formulation of a remedy in a school desegregation suit, anything other than a stable school population creates difficulties in the durability of the remedial decree and necessitates the inclusion of some process by which the decree can be modified to reflect population changes. Even more significant, the very possibility of achieving a desegregated school system can be frustrated by extreme shifts in the school population away from what we had previously regarded as the "majority" school population. The causes of this development are many: Changes in fertility rates and in the desire to live in suburbs and exurbs are certainly among the prime causes. The first is not to be blamed on school desegregation litigation; the second has sometimes been attributed to such litigation, but seems rather to be a further development in population movements that first took America off the farms and to the cities and now take it from the cities to the suburbs. Whether this exodus from the cities has been accelerated by school desegregation we will probably never know. Whether one believes that white children are to be found in the public schools of suburban areas because of white flight from integrated schools or because of an election of life style having little or no relation to issues of desegregation may, from a moral perspective, influence whether one believes that the suburbs should or should not be included in remedial decrees. But from the point of view of the law (as differentiated from the broader sweep of moral judgment), only if the suburban school system participated in intentional segregative acts can the court reach that system in its equitable decree. The use of settlement on threat of litigation can, however, as recorded in these pages, sometimes bring such suburban school systems into the ambit of a settlement in a school desegregation case.

Segregated housing patterns are at the root of the de facto segregated school system. The conjunction of the American preference for neighborhood schools and segregated housing patterns inescapably produces segregated schools. The choices before the court that must craft a decree ending segregation are therefore quite narrow in many cases: Either some children must be transported to a school at some remove from their homes, or the system must attract voluntary attendance by some children at some remove from their homes. Busing children is not regarded as desirable by most American parents; busing children into a neighborhood with a different racial composition is particularly anathema both to parents of majority students and to majority residents of neighborhoods that are the recipients of bused children. The Boston school desegregation case is a particularly disturbing example of such parental and neighborhood response.

Transporting children adds to the expense of a public educational system. Creating schools (frequently called "magnet schools") to attract voluntary attendance in a neighborhood away from one's own adds to the expense of a public educational system. Providing special or remedial education, bilingual teachers, psychologists, and social workers to assist in the educational process adds to the expense of a public educational system, and paying lawyers and other costs of school litigation adds to the cost of public educational systems. While the financial resources of public education or of municipal government are not static, neither are they infinitely expandable. In many of our cities, one of the results of population movement has been to deplete the tax base of the city at the same time as the costs of city government have risen dramatically. It is no wonder that judges report that limited financial resources significantly limit their ability to achieve a perfect result in either school desegregation cases or in the litigation, also reported herein, concerning bilingual education, education of the handicapped, or gender-neutral education.

Barbara Flicker's essay contains a useful review of the literature on the important question of at what point a judge has intervened too far in the administration of a government function. This literature makes assumptions that are not always supported by the evidence of judicial behavior. Other essays in this volume should be examined to determine the degree to which the courts have or have not limited their actions to the proper judicial role described by such observers as Professor (now University of Pennsylvania Law School Dean) Colin Diver, who has written that one inquiry ought to be whether the judge "left room for the exercise of governmental choice in the remedial process."[1] I believe that these essays, and studies previously published by the Institute of Judicial Administration and others, support the conclusion that it is never easy to characterize in quite that way the conduct of judges in these cases. Determination of where persuasion ends and coercion begins is rarely so determinable as Dean Diver's test would seem to require.

Professor Tractenberg conducted a survey of attorneys who had represented parties in school desegregation cases. While the response to his survey of 264 lawyers was modest, the degree of agreement among them on many issues may support a conclusion of greater reliability than the size of the sample would otherwise justify. While many of the issues addressed by the respondents shed light on the attorneys' perspectives about desegregation litigation, one area explored by both the judges' and attorneys' surveys is of particular note. Flicker reports that while only 17 percent of the judges surveyed were "dissatisfied with the results of the cases," "48% were dissatisfied with the results of desegregation cases in general."[2] Professor Tractenberg's survey "indicates that the attorneys ranked litigation fairly low as a remedy for school segregation and could not agree about promising alternative approaches. Overall, most respondents ranked litigation as either one of many solutions or an inadequate solution."[3]

One of the conclusions reached by both the judges who presided over and the attorneys who presented these cases is that the litigation was, within the limited powers of the adjudicative system, an effective tool for the determination of whether or not unlawful segregation existed in the public schools and for the creation of a remedy reasonably designed to remedy the wrong that was found. On the other hand, both judges and attorneys, reflecting on their respective experiences, report a sense of dissatisfaction with, or at least perceived inadequacy of, the adjudicative system. Reading the individual case studies in this volume may provide the basis for an understanding of why this litigation can be, at one and the same time, successful and frustrating for the participants. At the heart of the inquiry into this phenomenon lie two questions: To what extent are the participants in the adjudicative system simply reflecting the inability of the adjudicative process, no matter how structured, to alter the priorities and prejudices of society, and to what extent are the participants reflecting inadequacies in the concepts underlying the litigation?

This volume contains studies of desegregation litigation in Chicago and St. Louis and of litigation involving both desegregation and bilingual education in Denver. The volume includes a description of litigation brought to require the federal government to enforce federal laws and regulations against local school authorities allegedly engaged in discrimination based upon race, gender, or handicap. Finally, the volume includes two case studies, one in New York City and the other in Boston, of litigation designed to force compliance with federal and state law providing for special education for the physically handicapped or developmentally disabled. Some of the authors view the litigation from the standpoint of uninvolved (though certainly not disinterested) observers. Other authors were active participants in the litigation on which they now report. As is true of all history, whether written by lawyers or historians, these histories are excerpts and paraphrases of reality. However, they are necessarily richer and more detailed than those secured from either contemporary accounts in the media on one hand or judicial opinions on the other. They join with case studies previously published by the Institute of Judicial Administration and others and, like them, are published with the hope that the experiences of the attorneys, judges, and most of all the parties in these cases may be of assistance to us in understanding our adjudicative system as it grapples with the reformation of governmental institutions that have failed to meet the standards of conduct set by the federal and state constitutions and laws of the United States.

CHICAGO

The Chicago litigation did not involve a dispute over the issue of whether or not the Chicago school system was in compliance with federal law. The parties agreed that it was not, and the focus was therefore entirely on remedy. While it is true that there is ordinarily a liability phase in the litigation of these education cases, the Chicago litigation is not unique in its absence, as Michael Rebell's description of Boston's experience in *Allen v. McDonough* makes clear (see Chapter 3). What is quite special about the Chicago litigation is how difficult it is to arrive at a solution to the inescapable costs associated with desegregation of a city school system. The cost of the Chicago consent decree and whether it represented an appropriate response to an admission of the need for desegregation is at the very heart of Professor Shoenberger's essay.

The consent decree in the Chicago case was not the first treatment of racial segregation in Chicago's schools. It followed a decade of litigation in which the Chicago school system repeatedly defended itself on the ground that the admittedly substantial number of single-race schools in Chicago was not the result of intentional segregative acts but rather of a segregated housing pattern. While admitting that there was a disproportion in expenditures in white and nonwhite schools, the school Board attributed these differences to the desire of experienced, and therefore more highly compensated, teachers to transfer to the predominantly white schools. In permitting such transfers, and giving priority on the basis of seniority for them, Chicago school policy echoed the policy found in many cities and frequently incorporated into the collective bargaining agreements of teachers.

Nonetheless, the school Board did not desire the continuation of the situation, and when the U.S. Department of Justice, at the request of the U.S. Department of Health, Education and Welfare (then HEW, later to become the U.S. Department of Education) brought suit against the Chicago school Board, the school Board was prepared to agree to a consent order rather than litigate the liability issue. It was clear from statistics maintained by the school system that it suffered from both student and teacher segregation.

In this respect Chicago may represent a forerunner of the urban school system in the United States. Once the remedial plan set 65 percent as the maximum percentage of white students assigned to any school, the result was a reassignment of one-quarter of the white students, leaving only 38,000 white students unassigned. And yet, so few were the white students in the system that approximately 200 schools would have remained entirely black under the plan. Furthermore, the dollar cost of the reassignment (the plan called for busing 25,000 students and reassigning a total of 41,000 students) was higher than the mayor was prepared to accept. Moreover, minority observers were not prepared to accept the degree of segregation that would remain even with the implementation of the plan. Others in the minority community, however, were not eager to involve their children in more substantial transportation.

The response of the school Board was to propose its "Effective Schools Program," a program calling for enriched education in the lowest ranked schools in Chicago. The final student assignment plan relied not upon mandatory busing but upon voluntary student reassignment. The goal was to achieve a maximum representation of 70 percent white students in any one school. Although the plan would leave many single-race schools, and although the burdens of voluntary transportation as conceived by the plan would rest mostly on minorities, the court believed that the plan did not violate the U.S. Constitution. It is not possible to read Professor Shoenberger's essay without concluding that this judgment was as much an acknowledgment of the limits imposed by the reality of Chicago pupil demographics as it was an interpretation of the Constitution. One wonders, of course, whether the court would have viewed the situation in so accepting a manner had there been a liability phase of the suit proving purposeful discrimination by the school Board.

It is with the institution by the school Board in 1983 of an action against the U.S. government that the Chicago story takes a turn unique among the desegregation cases described in this volume. The school Board wished the court to interpret the consent decree signed by the U.S. government as obliging the federal government to provide financial assistance to the school Board in implementing the decree. The U.S. District Court so found, and this judgment was affirmed in principle on appeal to the Seventh Circuit. On remand for further review, the district court judge issued a sharply worded opinion attacking the United States's refusal to fund the plan and ordered the payment of $103 million to the Chicago Board of Education to assist it in implementing the plan contained in the consent decree. Not only was that judgment vacated, but the Seventh Circuit twice reassigned the case to other district court judges, presumably in dissatisfaction with the disposition both by the original judge and his successor selected by the Seventh Circuit. While the Seventh Circuit suggested, presumably to increase the pressure both on the state government and the governments of the cities and towns surrounding Chicago, that cross-district busing or a finding of liability on the part of the state might be necessary, there is little evidence that such liability could have been demonstrated.

Illinois has provided more funding for Chicago's school system, but it remains largely segregated and the enrichment or magnet school program, while representing an improvement in the system, hardly can be described as an integrated, educationally rich public school system.

The Chicago study raises several questions and provides at least some basis for their contemplation. What can be gleaned from the Constitution or laws about the responsibility of a school system whose student population is overwhelmingly minority? Does the Constitution in fact call for a satisfactory quality of education with desegregation simply an efficient but not necessary way of achieving quality? The Supreme Court has certainly not yet said so. But there is little doubt that the goal of an improved school system may be either the priority of minority citizens or at least understood to be possible in situations where integration is not. In Chicago, the school system was ready to implement such a plan. For the legal system, whether the courts have the power to force the allocation of public funds, whether from the federal, state, or local government remains an unanswered question. The issue was of course even more difficult when the possible funding source was the federal government, an entity that had not been found to have engaged in segregative acts in the Chicago school system.

DENVER

In *Limits of Justice: The Courts' Role in School Desegregation*, Jessica and Jeffrey Pearson described in detail the origins and proceedings of *Keyes v. School District No. 1*, the litigation concerning segregation in the Denver, Colorado, school system.[4] In Chapter 5 herein, Professor James Fishman (who was coeditor of *Limits of Justice*) and his coauthor, Lawrence Strauss, return to the Denver school desegregation case to review and update that proceeding. As was true in the Chicago litigation, the U.S. District Court judge chose to exercise his equitable power not by imposing a particular desegregation plan on the school system but by requiring repeated submissions of plans to the court until the plan passed constitutional muster.

Such a vision of the judicial role hardly can be called activist. The court, they write, served as a boundary setter; within those boundaries the school Board was free to create plans designed to bring about the end of segregation to the extent possible. And yet, as Fishman and Strauss carefully document, that reactive rather than dominant role did not avoid the politicization of the school system.

As the authors see it, politicization has its dark cloud and its silver lining. On one hand, the school Board, once politicized, appeared to make judgments based upon political and electoral considerations. Arguably school boards should have as their first priority concern with the quality of education of the students in the system. On the other hand, that same politicization has meant that the attention of the public has been drawn to the school system, and neither malice nor neglect of the system will go unnoticed by the aware electorate.

A second aspect of importance in the Denver case is the effort of the district court judge, ten years after the initiation of the lawsuit, to bring to a close judicial oversight of the school system. That the judge would initiate this effort is worth noting. Even more so is the response of the Board. One segment of the school Board submitted a plan, called the Total Access Plan, which was based on open enrollments and magnet schools. The parallel to the Chicago plan is obvious. But the Board could not agree on that plan and so submitted two plans. The alternative plan still would have restored the concept of neighborhood schools, but it called for restoration of fewer of these and the retention therefore of some pupil transportation. The judge told the Board that it had to devise one plan.

The attempted submission of two plans reflects the dilemma the courts so frequently face in school desegregation cases. While objecting to judicial supervision of the schools, arguing with some justification that it is not the job of the courts to run a school system, school boards wish the court to make the tough and politically unpopular choices that must sometimes be made by those who administer a school system. The response of the court, instructing the Board that it must itself submit one plan, is a response designed to make it clear that a mature and responsible governing body is not free to use the court as its excuse for action or inaction nor as its surrogate to implement unpopular programs.

The court was successful in prevailing upon the Board to present a single plan. But on review, the court decided the plan would most likely lead to re-segregation and was therefore unacceptable. The court did not then presume to develop its own plan; it ordered the Board to present a new plan. Such a course of action is not the most efficient way of creating judicial orders, but it is consistent with the concept that it is the school Board and not the court that must be responsible for selecting a course of action that will both meet the standards of the law and be consistent with the educational goals and policies of the school system.

The Board then submitted a consensus plan, theoretically for one year but continued year-to-year since. Once again in Denver there are racially identifiable schools. The authors suggest that white flight, politicization of the school Board, and bureaucratic inertia have afflicted the Denver school system. They suggest that problems of faculty integration, classroom segregation through ability grouping, and a large number of suspensions of minority students all serve to undercut achievements in student population.

Interwoven with the issues of racial segregation in the Denver case has been the treatment by the school system of Hispanic children, many of whom come to school as Spanish speakers. Hispanics intervened in the Denver case, arguing that the school Board had violated the federal Equal Educational Opportunity Act of 1974, which required local school authorities to "take appropriate action to overcome language barriers that impede equal participation by its students in its instructional program."

There is little doubt that there is at least the potential for conflict between the proposition that there ought to be a cessation of racial segregation and the proposition that appropriate action must be taken to overcome language barriers. There are educational devices available to avoid such conflict, but they involve the allocation of economic and human resources that may be beyond the ability or the willingness of the public to accept.

On the other hand, Fishman and Strauss point out that the school Board more easily formulated plans for children confronting language barriers than it resolved the problems of segregation. They speculate that there are three aspects of the language problem that make resolution easier. First, there is greater moral agreement on the educational need of the children for assistance in overcoming language barriers; second, there is no burden on others in arriving at a resolution, since funding is available from both the state and federal governments; third, the school system felt it did not bear any blame for the problems faced by children without English language skills. These astute observations must be compared with the experiences of Boston and New York in cases involving special education for the handicapped.[5]

It is not possible to avoid commenting on the curious behavior of the Tenth Circuit in its review of district court dispositions in the Denver case. The repeated vacations of judgment and reassignment to different district court judges raises serious questions about the use of the appellate process not to review findings of fact and determinations of law or even to monitor the reasonableness of the exercise of the equitable judgment of the district court judge, but rather to manipulate trial court results through the choice of the trial court judge. This seems on its face at least to be the inappropriate exercise of appellate power. We do not expect our appellate courts to engage in judge-shopping.

ST. LOUIS

D. Bruce La Pierre served as the Special Master in litigation brought to desegregate the public schools of St. Louis. The litigation ultimately involved both the city of St. Louis and St. Louis County. As La Pierre points out, few examples exist in desegregation litigation of interdistrict student transfer plans. In St. Louis, such a plan was adopted as a voluntary settlement. The St. Louis story is worthy of attention for both of these aspects of its remedial order. Equally worthy of attention is the character of the role played by the district court judge and by La Pierre.

This litigation, as is true of the Denver litigation and of so many other examples, has been before the federal courts for many years. The original complaint was filed in 1972. The settlement agreement involving interdistrict transfer and other significant elements was agreed to in 1983, three years after the order of a prior intradistrict remedy. La Pierre demonstrates in his essay that although by 1987 the interdistrict transfer settlement had made numerical improvements in the school populations in St. Louis County, full implementation of the 1983 settlement agreement has not yet been achieved. Thus the still unconcluded St. Louis school desegregation litigation is now 18 years old.

School desegregation could not be achieved in St. Louis by an intra-district order. Population movements and demographic changes in society created a situation in which the intradistrict order of the district court had left two-thirds of the black students in racially identifiable schools. An inter-district remedy was therefore a necessary aspect of the litigation from the plaintiff's point of view.

The achievement of a settlement agreement of interdistrict dimensions seems to be a dramatic example of the ways the existence of litigation, well before a judicial decree arising out of such litigation, can create forces that increase the power of some participants and diminish the power of others. This phenomenon is understood by trial lawyers, of course, but perhaps is less well understood by the general public. It was the pressure of threatened litigation against the school boards of St. Louis County rather than judicial findings and orders that brought these school boards to the bargaining table and gave the Special Master the influence required to achieve agreement.

Since we have seen many cases in which agreement has not been reached in desegregation litigation and many cases in which only the decree of the district court could impose a resolution of a desegregation suit, the example of St. Louis raises directly the issue of why this familiar tool of adjudication has worked there and not elsewhere.

I suggest that in the political setting in which school boards operate, there are almost equal and opposing forces at work at the outset of school de-segregation litigation. Depending on which of these forces triumphs, two contrary outcomes are possible: a school board that must be ordered by the court to do that which it otherwise refuses to do and then must be monitored every day to assure compliance with the judicial decree, or a school board that decides to engage in the acts of negotiation, compromise, and settle-ment that lead to a judicial decree adopted by and with the consent of the litigants.

On the one hand, school boards resist the notion that they have engaged in deliberate acts of segregation. Few in our society would publicly ac-knowledge racism and prejudice let alone racist and unconstitutional acts. Furthermore, the school boards fear the reaction of a constituency in which the majority will oppose desegregation or, at least, will oppose involuntary transportation of children. Finally, the school boards are concerned that the disruption of the educational process that may accompany pupil reassign-ment would be contrary to their obligations to assure the quality of public education in their districts. On the other hand, school boards are increas-ingly risk-averse. They increasingly understand the enormous costs of liti-gation, both in terms of legal fees and the time taken by school personnel involved in the litigation. Furthermore, changing social views make the appearance of racism in many communities even more unacceptable than the appearance of yielding to pressures brought by minorities. It is apparent that the balance of these forces was played out quite differently in the Boston school desegregation case and the St. Louis case.

La Pierre's essay suggests another dynamic force that may provide an alternative or supplementary explanation for the ability to achieve a settlement, and indeed an interdistrict settlement, in St. Louis. That force was the way the court and its Special Master defined their roles in the litigation. Rather than beginning with the details of desegregation, the Special Master's approach was to secure agreement to general principles. These general principles included not only the goal of desegregation but also the goal of a final definition of school Board obligations so that the settlement would represent a conclusive resolution of the case. For the plaintiffs, there had to be the element of promise that desegregation could be achieved; for the defendants, there had to be the element that the settlement would be conclusive. This is familiar to litigating attorneys, but it is not an approach always found in school desegregation litigation. Both sides had something to gain, and it was clear that the cost of gaining it was to provide to the other side its price.

It was, I think, the combination of the balance of forces pressing on the school Board and the approach taken by the court and Special Master that made possible the settlement described by La Pierre. Whether it could be reproduced in another setting is difficult to say. Certainly its techniques are worthy of study.

Although substantial gains have been made in desegregation in St. Louis as a result of the settlement, other aspects of the agreement are both critical and, to some extent, not yet fully implemented. The plan contemplated that there would remain in the city a substantial number of black children in racially identifiable schools. The plan contemplated that there would be improvements in the physical plant of these schools and enrichment of the education offered. Implementation of this aspect of the plan involved, of course, significant expenditures of public funds. The capital improvement program has been priced at $115 million. These costs are in addition to the substantial costs of other elements of the agreement. As has been true in all other desegregation litigation, implementation of the order—whether it originates with the court or, as in St. Louis, by consent of the parties— requires a significant change in the allocation of public funds. Those additional expenditures did not come easily for most American cities in the 1980s.

Even in the core matter of desegregation, problems remain in St. Louis, just as they do in other cities. Paralleling the observations of Fishman and Strauss in Denver, La Pierre observes that there is a high suspension rate of black students attending the county schools and a rather high withdrawal rate of black students from the interdistrict transfer program. While many of the transportation problems have been solved, many of the bused children suffer significant inconvenience, and those burdens are disproportionately experienced by black children. The sharing of the burden by white children has been left to depend upon the development of magnet schools designed to draw the white children into the predominantly black schools. That has yet to occur, and whether the settlement truly can be called a success without that development must be seriously challenged.

ADAMS AND WEAL

The essays in this volume are, in general, descriptions of litigation brought against individual school boards alleging their failures to provide the education or the educational setting guaranteed by the constitutions and laws of the United States or of the individual states. *Adams v. Bennett* and *Women's Educational Action League (WEAL) v. Bennett* are cases brought against an agency of the United States to require that agency to enforce applicable law. If successful, the strategy employed would have a far broader impact than could litigation involving a particular school board. The *WEAL* litigation directed its concern at agency action in connection with gender discrimination. The *Adams* litigation was primarily concerned with agency action in connection with racial segregation. In each case plaintiffs argued that the federal agency charged with the responsibility of investigating school boards in response to complaints of discrimination and conducting periodic reviews to assure compliance had failed to execute its obligations. The approach, then, was narrow. It sought to achieve procedural rather than substantive goals, though it is clear that the plaintiffs believed that if the agency were required to conform its procedural behavior to legal requirements, the substantive results would be to pressure school boards all over the country to end discrimination and segregation. Professor Salomone's description of the political winds that blew through the agency over the decade and a half of the pendency of this litigation necessarily raises the question of whether the traditional lawyers' faith that fair and reasonable process will yield fair and reasonable results is applicable in this context.

As Professor Salomone skillfully develops the background and progress of the litigation, both the problems and promise of the approach taken become clear. Ironically, just as the approach taken by the plaintiffs focused on agency procedure rather than substance, so the defendants' ultimate response was an attack on elements of the procedural setting of the litigation. And for the moment at least, one such procedural element, that of standing, appears to have frustrated the objectives of the plaintiffs.[6]

Professor Salomone's essay is a record of the importance of the philosophy and character of the political party and person in power to the work of a federal agency. Since, as is true of all of the litigation described in this volume, litigation took place over a significant period of time, we see presidents and their staffs come and go, and we see the varying responses of a federal agency affected by the quality and philosophy of those presidents and their staffs.

The U.S. District Court judge who has presided in the *Adams* and *WEAL* litigation has, in the words of Professor Salomone, exercised a "minimalist" role; that is, the judge has restricted his orders to those describing procedures and timetables for action rather than ones designed to affect the outcome of agency action. Of course, to a large extent that posture was dictated by the litigation strategy adopted by the plaintiffs. But even within that strategy, the court had to choose between an active role, a reactive role, or a mediative role. The active role would have the judge develop procedural limits; the reactive role would have the judge require the parties to make suggestions of proposed orders; the mediative role would have the judge encourage the parties to agree on an order that the court would issue. The judge alternated between these last two approaches and abstained from taking the initiative by drafting the order.

Setting to one side the problems of standing, separation of powers, or other procedural challenges to the plaintiff's actions, one must question whether success could have been declared were it not for these issues. The agency now does in fact process complaints more rapidly than it did at the outset of the litigation, and compliance reviews are carried out with greater frequency. But there is at least some evidence that these improvements would contribute to the ultimate objectives of the plaintiffs—the ending of discrimination and desegregation—only when the national leadership determines that it shares the plaintiffs' goals. Viewed, however, not as a matter of success or failure in changing national policy but rather as a way of drawing attention to administrative agency failure, the litigation certainly brought to light the unacceptable behavior of an agency that simply ignored its statutory mandate.

SPECIAL EDUCATION CASES IN NEW YORK CITY AND BOSTON

Michael Rebell, who represented the plaintiff in the New York City case of *Jose P. v. Ambach,* has provided two essays describing litigation involving the education of handicapped or special needs children. One of his essays focuses on *Jose P. v. Ambach;* the other discusses *Allen v. McDonough,* which arose in Boston. These histories of special education cases, together with Rebell's introductory essay, provide not only an enrichment of the reader's understanding of education litigation, but also a perspective on the other school litigation discussed and described both in this and other case studies and commentaries on school litigation, most of which focus on racial desegregation.

Rebell's thesis is that discrimination against the handicapped must be defined as "structural discrimination." This phenomenon is to be distinguished from "intentional discrimination" or even "discriminatory impact." Its hallmark is a failure of an educational system to respond appropriately to legitimate educational needs of a given class of persons. Particularly, his concern is with the educational needs of disabled children. He views the race discrimination cases as involving "intentional discrimination" or "discriminatory impact," thus to be differentiated from the special education cases he describes. State statutes in New York[7] and Massachusetts,[8] a federal statute,[9] and more general provisions of law, including the Fourteenth Amendment to the Constitution of the United States and Section 504 of the Rehabilitation Act of 1973,[10] not only provide in general the basic principle of nondiscrimination but impose the affirmative obligation to provide an appropriate education to the handicapped.

Two critical distinctions emerge between cases alleging unlawful segregation based upon race and cases alleging failure to provide appropriate education for the handicapped. First, the legal standard is quite specific and direct. This contrasts with the more abstract concept of racial discrimination, with its complexities of intention and its inclusion of the concept of causation. Second, ending an existing inadequacy in the education of the handicapped is a goal that the public can accept with little, if any, dissent. The fact that the litigation does not have to ascribe moral failure probably assists the school board in its willingness to work with the plaintiff and with the court to remedy inadequacies found to exist in the education of handicapped children.

On the other hand, there is to be found in this litigation the same potential for intervention or interference with the professional educational structure that is to be found in school desegregation cases. As is true in school desegregation cases, if the board is willing to work with the plaintiff to arrive at a settlement, the judge becomes simply a monitor of the implementation of the settlement, rather than a czar of the school system. If this observation is correct, then the differences between "structural discrimination" and "discriminatory impact" become more difficult to discern. For example, the non-city school boards within St. Louis County, as recounted by La Pierre, did not believe they had engaged in discriminatory practices, but decided, for the reasons made clear in La Pierre's essay, to join in a voluntary agreement in an effort to avoid litigation. With that agreement formed, the role of the court was considerably more like the role of the courts in the education for the handicapped cases than in other cases involving racial desegregation in which the school board defendant remained recalcitrant throughout the litigation.

While a part of this difference in school board action and reaction is undoubtedly related to the legal standards underlying the different forms of
litigation, the ability of the school board to agree to a consent order without
acknowledging intentional discrimination makes the two kinds of litigation
look more alike. Where they continue to differ, of course, is the degree of
political difficulty that the board confronts, or fears it will confront, if it
yields to the pressure of litigation and reaches such a consensual arrange-
ment. Key to the ability of the judge to serve a more acceptable "passive"
role as monitor and reactor, then, is the existence or anticipation of significant public opposition if the board agrees to a settlement. If this observation
is correct, although there is much to be learned from the cases concerning
the education of the handicapped, the differences between this litigation and
desegregation litigation may not be explainable in terms of the difference
between "structural" and other discrimination.[11] While as social observers
we note the difference between the public's reaction to issues of race and
its reaction to issues of handicap, as observers of the law we need to be
concerned with legal standards, legal procedures, and the role of the courts.

Rebell's description of the New York City case, in which he served as
co-counsel to the plaintiff class, stresses the impact on the litigation of the
personality and goals of the particular administrator within the New York
City Board of Education and of the attorney representing the Board. In
this respect, the case description echoes several others contained in this
volume. In his essay on the Boston case involving the education of handicapped children, Rebell points out that the personality of the individual
in charge of monitoring compliance had a significant impact on the implementation of the equitable decree. Perhaps in all litigation personalities
of individual actors, plaintiffs, plaintiffs' attorneys, defendants, defendants'
attorneys, judges, monitors, Special Masters, and others involved in the adjudicative process make a difference in process and even outcome. It may be
that this phenomenon is simply the more striking in the kind of protracted
litigation that is typical of all school litigation, whether it be described as
"structural discrimination" litigation or "intentional discrimination" litigation.

There can be little doubt that litigation concerning education of the
handicapped has been benefited by the degree that the law defining the right
to an appropriate education focuses on the quality of education. This issue
is for many at the crux of the educational crisis in the United States and
is at the heart of most of the litigation brought invoking the intervention of
the courts. School desegregation litigation purports to be focused on the
numerical question of integration, although the character of the remedies,
particularly those arrived at by consent, suggests that the concern for quality
of education is as important in school desegregation cases as it is in cases
involving education of the handicapped.

CONCLUSION

When the Institute of Judicial Administration undertook this further set of case studies with the assistance of funding from the Ford Foundation, we were uncertain whether there was more that such a sequel could
contribute. While we remained confident that the technique of thorough
case study represented a valuable contribution both to lawmakers and to the
general public, we wondered whether our new investigations would simply
be redundant sequels.

We need not have feared. Not only has this volume added to our study
of school litigation cases involving a broader set of issues, including education of the handicapped, bilingual education, and discrimination against
women in our schools; it has reflected an evolving sense of public values
about the obligations of our society to its most needy citizens—an obligation
that goes well beyond the confines of the negative prescript that there shall
be no intentional segregation of the races. Where that obligation is made
explicit by law, for example in the cases involving the handicapped, litigation
is able to serve a beneficial role. As Michael Rebell points out, the power of
the court to threaten with contempt keeps the parties focused on their legal
responsibilities to plan and to execute.

The essays in this volume also demonstrate an evolving understanding
that our judges are more effective when they force the parties to take the
planning initiative wherever possible and thus preserve the role of the court
as one that responds to initiatives (they are initiatives even if under judicial
duress) rather than seize the administrative role directly.

Fortunately, our growing social sense of responsibility has made this more
passive role feasible. If, confronted with findings of constitutional and statutory violations, a school board will respond by submitting a plan that it
honestly believes will remedy the wrong, the court is able to carry out a more
traditional role. This scenario continues to use the courts as bearers of the
burden of public animus either for the result or its cost, but it does not force
the court to bear the burden of direct displacement of public administrative
officials.

In these essays, however, two further problems emerge that confront the
courts, problems for which the legal system provides little help. First, it is
apparent that in those areas in which the legal standard does not directly
address educational quality, an issue that is of grave concern to those who
initiate the litigation, remediation may reach well beyond and be quite different from the definition of the legal right. Such a mismatch, or nonmatch,
of right and remedy is troublesome since we rely upon the definition of
the right to set the boundaries of the remedy. Second, remedies in school
cases necessarily involve reallocation of public funds, whether those funds be
local, state, or federal. The remedies are frequently expensive and someone

must pay. It is perhaps the issue of cost that precipitates most particularly the concern for the relationship between right and remedy, but the issue of cost has its own life and creates its own burden. Were the funds available for education plentiful, this issue would hardly be worth noting, but funds are not plentiful and are not likely to be so at any time in the near future.

Finally, the litigation about desegregation continues to be overwhelmed by events beyond the control of the courts. Demographic changes, particularly in our largest urban centers, white flight, and patterns of one-race neighborhoods all continue to frustrate the legal objective of desegregation. To the extent that the legal standard requires proof of intentionally segregative acts by the school board, these phenomena make such proof even more difficult. Perhaps the next round of litigation will resemble events in Yonkers, New York, described briefly by Barbara Flicker in her essay "The View from the Bench." That case reminds us, of course, that instances of classic school board recalcitrance can still be found, and when they are, the activist judge will necessarily be found. The case also suggests that we may have to broaden the focus of litigation so that it encompasses housing discrimination as well as school segregation if we are to find solutions to our problems of segregation of the races in our society. On the other hand, in that same essay Flicker provides statistical evidence that of 125 school districts sampled by the U.S. Commission on Civil Rights in June 1987, segregation had declined in 117 of the districts, despite the fact that majority enrollment had declined in 74 of the 125 districts. In general, our society has been making progress slowly since the decision of the Supreme Court of the United States in 1954 in *Brown v. Board of Education.* But there remain pockets of deeply rooted problems of racial separation, which have yet to be solved.

In considering the role of adjudication in this setting, it is wise to take note of Flicker's wise advice:

> A judge cannot operate a school or improve the quality of the education that is provided. A judge cannot force a city or a school board to cooperate with grace or enthusiasm. A court is not a political arena and a judge is not a politician. And there is a point at which a judge has to withdraw from the supervisory role, a point at which implementation has occurred.

As we now see emerging a phase of litigation in which the school board attempts to terminate the continuing role of the court, this last comment by Flicker takes on great importance. The essays in this volume only touch on this problem, though Fishman and Strauss consider the problem in their discussion of Denver. It is not difficult to predict that the fact that our legal standards in desegregation cases do not address educational quality will result in the termination of jurisdiction in many cases before any improvement in education has taken place. When all the racial integration that is possible is the intermixture of a token number of whites in predominantly black urban schools, or the intermixture of a token number of blacks or Hispanics in otherwise white suburban schools, we will witness the end, and an unsuccessful end, of our efforts in school desegregation litigation. At least some of the case studies in this volume suggest a richer set of remedies and point toward both desegregation of our schools and enrichment of our educational system. But this work is not primarily for the courts; it is primarily for our legislative and executive branches of government. When they set the standards of quality and provide the financial resources needed, these case studies show the evolution of judicial administrative techniques that will allow the courts to play their role, when needed, in facilitating improvements in our public education system.

The courts still represent the last best hope of each of our citizens when the executive and legislative branches have yielded to the demands of the many against the rights of the few. Where the few are politically able to assert what the majority cannot refuse, though they may have to assert it in the form of adjudication, it is likely that the remedy will approach their adjudicative goals and possible that the remedy can be achieved through judge-assisted settlement. Where the majority is prepared to deny the legitimate right, even though it is declared by the courts, the remedy will almost certainly fall short of the prayer for relief and may fall short of any significant remediation of the wrong. Education remains a moral obligation of our society to all of our children. Only a willingness of the majority to honor that obligation without regard to race, gender, English language skills, or handicap will permit the courts to resolve disputed claims, confident that those judicial resolutions will be honored by public authorities.

NOTES

1. Diver, *The Judge as Political Powerbroker: Superintending Structural Change in Public Institutions*, 65 VA. L. REV. 43 (1979).

2. Flicker, p. 380 in this volume.

3. Tractenberg, p. 411 in this volume.

4. J. FISHMAN AND H. KALODNER, LIMITS OF JUSTICE: THE COURTS' ROLE IN SCHOOL DESEGREGATION (1978).

5. See studies of *Jose P. v. Ambach* and *Allen v. McDonough* in Chapters 2 and 3 in this volume.

6. Adams v. Bell, 675 F. Supp. 668 (D.C. 1987).

7. Laws 1976, ch. 853, codified as N.Y. Ed. Law Art. 89 (McKinney's 1981).

8. 1972 Mass. Acts, ch. 766, § 1 (principally codified as amended at Mass. Gen. Laws Ann., ch. 71B, §§ 1–14 (West 1982 and Supp. 1983).

9. Education for All Handicapped Children's Act of 1975, 20 U.S.C. § 1401 *et seq.*

10. Rehabilitation Act of 1973, § 504, 29 U.S.C. § 794.

11. Rebell interprets my prefatory remarks in *Limits of Justice* as assuming that "extensive resistance experienced by the courts in desegregation cases would necessarily apply to all institutional reform contexts." That preface discussed desegregation cases and reflected the judicial experience in such cases between *Brown v. Board of Education* and the publication of that volume. Rather than disagree, Rebell and I agree, I think, with my statement in that Introduction: "It is when the court is able to define the constitutional right to an education free of discriminatory school board action—and then confidently to expect the school board, the state commissioner of education, or other state or federal officials or agencies to formulate and implement the requisite changes to implement that right—that the role of courts can be reduced to more traditional dimensions." To this observation, Rebell adds primarily the valid point that the court may, in some cases, need to maintain a continuing jurisdiction as both societal facts and educational theory change and may make an impact upon the court's remedial judgment.

PART II

Educational Opportunities for
Children with Handicaps

CHAPTER 2

Jose P. v. Ambach: Special Education Reform in New York City

MICHAEL A. REBELL

THE DRAMATIC ASSERTION in recent years of a right to equal opportunity by the disabled had its origin in *Brown v. Board of Education*,[1] the landmark race desegregation case. Although anti-discrimination concepts regarding the handicapped emerged from race discrimination precedents, the problems of the disadvantaged are, in fact, qualitatively different. As one judge aptly put it, "[A]ttempting to fit the problem of discrimination against the handicapped into the model remedy for race discrimination is akin to fitting a square peg into a round hole."[2]

Legal doctrines dealing with problems of discrimination against the disabled need to be reconsidered to take cognizance of the factors that distinguish this setting from the race discrimination context. This is not to deny, of course, that the handicapped, like racial minorities, have been victims of stigma, stereotyping, and invidious discrimination.[3] Fear of the handicapped, a continuing legacy of historical patterns of abandonment, and exclusion (as well as ignorance of their actual and potential abilities) renders them continuing targets of bigotry and oppression. But beyond this core common experience of prejudice there are at least three fundamental factors that distinguish discrimination against the handicapped from race discrimination.

First is the reality that the very notion of disability or "handicap" implies limitations that in many situations do provide justification for some types of differential treatment of disabled persons.[4] Second is the difficulty of defining precisely who are "the disabled." Unlike racial or cultural minorities, the handicapped do not constitute a coherent group sharing common physical, psychological, or cultural characteristics. Finally, "handicapping" conditions are to a large extent relative, socially defined characteristics rather than absolute criteria. Many disabilities exist, in whole or in part, only in relation to established societal eligibility standards or because of society's reluctance to reorder traditional practices or physical structures so as to permit access for those who are currently excluded.[5]

In essence, the problem of discrimination in many areas affecting the handicapped is less one of overcoming bigotry and invidious prejudice than of redesigning social structures and institutions to make them more responsive to the needs of the disabled. It is, in short, a problem of structural change. Accordingly, a failure to respond in appropriate fashion to the legitimate needs of the disabled for structural change can appropriately be termed "structural discrimination." Structural discrimination is therefore a distinctive legal concept, different from "intentional discrimination" or "discriminatory impact," the main legal standards used in the race discrimination area.

A doctrine of structural discrimination must, of course, be based on an understanding of what is "reasonable" access or "reasonable" accommodation in a particular circumstance. In theory, if sufficient resources were applied, the physical environment—and possibly even the attitudinal environment—could be reshaped totally to permit full participation in all aspects of social life for all categories of the disabled. Realistically, the amount of resources (and the attitudinal commitment) needed for such radical reform are beyond the scope of contemporary political or ethical consensus. On the other hand, some degree of resource commitment and institutional change beyond merely opening the doors to existing institutions is undeniably a contemporary moral imperative. Precisely where to draw the line in meeting the needs of the handicapped without imposing excessive demands on the public fisc and the public psyche is the critical analytic problem posed for the application of structural discrimination theory.

On a broad conceptual level, structural discrimination theory can deal with this problem by delineating certain priority areas in which claims for special accommodation by the disabled should be honored. Conversely, claims in other areas, which have been declared non-priority, will not be enforced, barring unusual circumstances. I have argued elsewhere that education, employment, and architectural barrier removal have, in essence, been designated such priority areas by Congress and the courts while at least one other area, hospitalization benefits provided under Medicaid, can be said to have been declared a non-priority area.[6] Within each of the denominated priority areas, courts and legislatures may also establish certain basic principle or policy parameters. For example, recent decisions of the federal courts have indicated that access to basic public transportation is a priority area and that within this area, equipping buses with wheelchair lifts or providing mini-van paratransit systems for the handicapped is a reasonable accommodation, but that retrofitting of all subway stations is not.[7]

There is, however, a limit to the extent to which abstract legal doctrine can define the extent of appropriate structural change in any particular situation. A theory of structural discrimination must, to a great extent, be contextual, reflecting the needs of each concrete setting. The principled deliberations of the Supreme Court, as well as the public policy debates of the Congress, are often too far removed from the day-to-day problems of the disabled to determine how the competing considerations in the equity balance should be weighed in particular contexts.

Trial level courts are, however, well equipped to undertake this task. Through the judge's personal knowledge of local conditions and the remedial processes that the court can directly monitor, a trial court is able to implement effectively the general principles established in statutes or appellate decisions. In other words, structural discrimination is an "open" doctrine whose broad parameters can be established at the level of principle or overarching public policy, but whose substance can be determined only by a grass-roots-level implementation process.[8]

In the years following *Brown*, the federal courts took on an activist role in implementing their desegregation mandates. This "new model" of institutional reform litigation inspired analogous judicial activism in other social contexts, including the treatment of clients at institutions for the mentally retarded and the education of handicapped students in public schools.[9] Judicial involvement in many of these new model litigations has been criticized, with many of the critics assuming that the extensive resistance experienced by the courts in desegregation cases would also apply to other institutional reform contexts.[10] Judicial initiatives to overcome structural discrimination against the handicapped, however, may raise fewer of these problems because of the qualitative differences in the types of discrimination being remedied. Courts, in fact, may be especially well-suited for formulating and enforcing the rights of the disabled.

The area of educational rights illustrates this point well. The Education of All Handicapped Children's Act of 1975 (the EHA)[11] provides extensive procedures and due process protections geared to guarantee all handicapped children an equal educational opportunity.[12] Its core anti-discrimination standard, the right to an "appropriate education," is, however, ambiguous and undefined.

The Supreme Court wrestled with this issue in *Board of Education v. Rowley*,[13] a case in which the parents of a hearing-impaired second grader claimed an entitlement to the services of a deaf language interpreter, costing approximately $15,000 per year. The Court resolved the immediate issue in the case by declaring that the student was already receiving sufficient "educational benefits" as evidenced by her passing grades. The vague "educational benefits" standard articulated in *Rowley*, however, provides little substantive guidance to courts in future cases.[14] Thus the basic structural discrimination question of precisely how much change a local school district is obligated to undertake to accommodate the needs of the handicapped —and at what cost—has not been answered either by Congress's general "appropriate education" standard or by the Supreme Court's "educational benefits" rubric.

Formulation of meaningful criteria for determining what is an "appropriate education" requires, more than in most areas of law, in-depth case law development. Only through careful consideration of the actual needs of particular disabled children and the resources available in a specific local school district in relation to the comparative educational opportunities given to non-handicapped children, can equity be established. Thus, new model institutional reform litigation takes on added significance in cases involving discrimination against the handicapped because remedial mechanisms are needed here not only to assure compliance with statutory requirements, but also to develop substantive content for abstract liability standards.

Given the enhanced role of trial courts in disability rights cases, case studies of the implementation of court decrees in this area take on special significance. This section presents two parallel case study overviews of judicial implementation of the educational rights of the handicapped. The first, *Jose P. v. Ambach*, is a federal class action involving more than 100,000 special needs children in New York City; the second, *Allen v. McDonough*, covers more than a decade of state court involvement in special education reform in Boston.

These studies show that in New York, court intervention has resulted in extensive administrative reorganization, renovation of more than 50 school buildings to make them accessible to the physically handicapped, and adoption of innovative staff recruitment techniques. In Boston, judicial jurisdiction has led to significant new procedures for parental participation, implementation of a sophisticated data tracking system, and the creation of a monitoring system designed to ensure permanent accountability. In both cities, the number of handicapped students served and the extent of compliance with newly enacted procedural protections have dramatically improved, although in neither locale is the job yet complete.

While the priorities for reform have differed in the two cities, the basic legal process has been remarkably similar. Both New York City's federal action and Boston's state court proceeding have been marked by brief liability stages and lengthy remedial processes. In contrast to the vituperative setting of many desegregation cases, both of the remedial stages here have consisted largely of cooperative endeavors to devise structural solutions to systemic educational problems. The commonality of the basic legal processes in these two special education cases—which took place in different cities and in different court systems—would appear to provide significant empirical support for structural discrimination theory.

Also consistent with structural discrimination theory is the open, evolving nature of the structural reforms actually adopted in each of the two cities. The key task under structural discrimination theory is to define workable parameters for implementing basic entitlements. In the education context, this means providing substantive content for understanding what an "appropriate education" for a student with a disability should be. In New York, the priorities that emerged were decentralization of the service delivery system, "mainstreaming," and improved facilities accessibility. In Boston, more emphasis was placed on administrative reorganization, transportation, and data management systems.

To a large extent then the legal entitlement to an "appropriate education" in New York City and in Boston can be said to mean the extent of services as defined and enforced in the specific court judgments. The abstract statutory right became concrete and meaningful only through these mechanisms. In those areas that emerged as priorities in the particular setting, plaintiffs' needs tended to be fully met regardless of cost, while in other lesser priority areas, defendants' claims of resource limitations tended to be accepted. In some sectors, radical structural innovations were effected; in others, much or all of the status quo was maintained.

Viewing the entitlements in this way provides an answer to the difficult question of whether accommodating the needs of the disabled will require unlimited resource expenditures. If entitlements of the disabled are seen as being essentially defined through the implementation process of an active adversary system, one can conclude that the handicapped have received priority attention and the maximum resource allocations that institutions and political forces sensitized to their needs can reasonably be expected to provide. In short, the extensive set of entitlements created by the EHA, which arguably are unlimited in the abstract, gain appropriate and practical parameters in practice, through the judicial process.

COMMENCEMENT OF THE
NEW YORK LITIGATION

The city of New York boasts the nation's largest—and undoubtedly its most complex—public school system. During the 1970s, New York had more than one million public school students, some 60,000 teachers, and a budget of over $3 billion. The city's approximately 1,000 public schools are governed through a complex system, which divides authority between 32 elected local community school boards (having primary jurisdiction over elementary and junior high schools), and a city-wide chancellor (having primary jurisdiction over high schools and special education matters). Overall supervision and policy making authority is lodged in a central Board of Education, composed of seven members of whom two are appointed by the mayor and one each by the city's borough presidents.[15]

Prior to the early 1970s, New York State, like most other jurisdictions, took a complacent posture toward the educational needs of disabled children. The state's compulsory education law at the time specifically exempted any child "whose mental or physical condition is such that his attendance upon instruction . . . would endanger the health or safety of himself or of others, or who was feeble-minded to the extent that he is unable to benefit from instruction."[16] The statutory scheme, enacted in 1947, assumed that many handicapped children whose parents did deem them capable of an education would be placed in separate private institutions for the handicapped.[17]

OBTAINING FEDERAL COURT JURISDICTION

In the early 1970s, parents of handicapped children and their advocates took a more aggressive stance. They pressed city and state officials repeatedly to expand and improve services. When these efforts proved of no avail they filed federal court challenges against both the statutory ceiling on private school tuitions[18] and against the general inadequacy of services in the public school system.[19] Simultaneous intense lobbying in Albany led to substantial revisions in the statutory scheme covering the education of handicapped children. The authority and responsibility of public school systems to provide classes for the disabled were clearly articulated,[20] specific evaluation and placement requirements were set forth, and detailed due process rights for parents were established.[21]

In 1973, after the federal courts had indicated that plaintiffs should first seek relief under state law,[22] an administrative proceeding was commenced before the Commissioner of Education on behalf of all unserved handicapped children in the city of New York.[23] Over the next few years, the commissioner issued four decisions. Each decision held that in failing promptly to evaluate and place handicapped children in appropriate educational programs, the New York City Board of Education had violated state statutes and commissioner's implementing regulations that required prompt remedial action.[24]

Deeming the Board's 1978 plan to eliminate waiting lists "vague, ambiguous and replete with meaningless generalization,"[25] the *Reid* plaintiffs asked the commissioner to put the Board's Division of Special Education and Pupil Personnel Services into receivership. The commissioner decided instead to deal with the problem in his administrative capacity, and he entered into negotiations with newly installed New York City Schools Chancellor Frank Macchiarola.[26]

On October 22, 1978, Chancellor Macchiarola's staff issued a "Status Report on Evaluation and Placement," which specified that 8,259 handicapped children were awaiting evaluation and 4,449 were awaiting placement. These statistics were accompanied by new commitments to reorganize the Division of Special Education and to provide additional resources in order to expedite the evaluation and placement process. New York State Department of Education Assistant Commissioner Louis Grumet responded to this report by asking for clarification and additional details about the Board's plans—and by indicating that New York City's allotment of EHA federal funding would be held up until the Board submitted "an acceptable plan for the diminution of the waiting list."²⁷

In response to these pressures, the Board, on January 16, 1979, submitted to the commissioner a new plan calling for the elimination of the entire waiting list backlog by August 1, 1979. The State Education Department considered this plan acceptable. Accordingly, on January 19, 1979, Assistant Commissioner Grumet announced that the withheld federal funds would be released. The *Reid* attorneys, however, were not satisfied. On February 16, 1979, they filed a class action suit in the U.S. District Court, Eastern District of New York under the caption *Jose P. v. Ambach*.²⁸

Plaintiffs' complaint and motion for a preliminary injunction in *Jose P.* recounted the long history of administrative findings of waiting list violations, the repeated submission of plans, and the continuing noncompliance. At the time of filing, the waiting list total had risen to over 14,000 students. Plaintiffs' request for relief was succinct and to the point. They asked the Court to

> issue preliminary and permanent injunctions requiring defendants to
> (1) establish and implement an effective plan to insure that all handicapped children in New York City will receive prompt evaluation and placement in free, appropriate public special education, and (2) submit to the Court and counsel for plaintiffs regular periodic reports on the implementation of the plan; . . . appoint a Special Master to monitor on behalf of the Court defendants' implementation of the plan required by the preceding paragraph.²⁹

The defendants' response did not dispute the basic facts, but emphasized instead the inappropriateness of judicial intervention at this time. They argued that "if the Court were to grant the relief requested, it would disrupt the State's efforts to timely evaluate and place children in need of special education and involve a federal court in the continuous supervision of a state function."³⁰

Judge Eugene H. Nickerson, to whom the case was assigned, lost little time in rejecting defendants' procedural objections. After a brief hearing at which the defendants conceded the existence of long waiting lists,³¹ he expressed a willingness to take jurisdiction of the case and to involve the court in attempting to remedy this long-standing problem. Thus, in a decision issued on May 16, 1979, he took note of the long history of noncompliance, despite four remedial orders by the state commissioner and held: "In light of this history, the Commissioner's objection and the argument by city defendants that this Court should abstain in order to give the Board's latest plan a chance to work are not persuasive."³²

Judge Nickerson did not, however, accept plaintiffs' proposed remedial approach. In lieu of the simple call for an order mandating "a quick, effective plan" for immediate compliance, the judge noted that the case raised a type of "polycentric . . . problem [that] cannot easily be resolved through a traditional courtroom-bound adjudicative process."[33] Accordingly, he chose a more far-ranging approach.

In formulating a remedial mechanism, Judge Nickerson also took note of the position of the plaintiffs and *amici* in *United Cerebral Palsy v. Board of Education*, a case filed shortly after *Jose P.* and assigned to him that also attacked the New York City Board of Education's failure to comply with legal mandates concerning the educational rights of handicapped students.[34] The *UCP* complaint raised waiting list claims similar to those in *Jose P.*, but it also alleged a series of substantive educational deficiencies that affected plaintiffs' rights to appropriate education. These included a lack of individualized placement procedures, inadequate preparation of individual education programs (IEP), unavailability of "mainstreaming" opportunities, inaccessibility of facilities to the non-ambulatory, a lack of requisite related services, and inefficiencies in contracting procedures for placement in private school. In order to solve the long-standing evaluation and placement problems, the *UCP* plaintiffs asked the Court to appoint a Special Master whose specific mandate would be "to consider recommendations for appropriate structural and governance reforms for implementation by the Court."[35]

Judge Nickerson agreed to appoint a Special Master and gave him extraordinary legal authority. The May 16, 1979, order in *Jose P.* designated as Special Master Marvin E. Frankel, a recently retired federal judge who not only had an outstanding reputation as a jurist but also possessed detailed knowledge of the workings of the byzantine New York City school system from his experience as the judge in a New York City bilingual education case several years earlier.[36] Judge Frankel's broad mandate was to "make recommendations as he deems appropriate as to what decree the Court should enter to provide the requisite public education to handicapped children in the City of New York."[37]

In sum, the successful initiation of the *Jose P.* litigation can be said to have resulted from the combination of two complementary strategic approaches: the *Jose P.* plaintiffs' emphasis on a quick, decisive liability finding and the *UCP* plaintiffs' urging of broad structural remedial mechanism.[38] From the perspective of structural discrimination analysis, there are two salient points concerning the initial stages of the *Jose P.* litigation. First is the absence of any claims of invidious animus or intentional discrimination among the numerous allegations of educational inadequacies and violations of statutory mandates.[39] Because the Board of Education had never denied its legal obligation to eliminate the waiting lists, there never was any real confrontation concerning plaintiffs' legal entitlements.[40] Indeed, from the first administrative proceedings through the court hearings it was the Board of Education itself that compiled the statistics that established plaintiffs' claims.

Second, the federal district court took jurisdiction of the case with an expectation that its role would be to design innovative approaches to deal with complex educational problems. The court rejected defendants' procedural arguments precisely because it had concluded that the administrative and political routes had proved unsuccessful. The court recognized that if the problem were to be solved, it would need to devise new ways to deal with a difficult "polycentric" problem.

CRAFTING THE JUDGMENT

Fundamental responsibility for shaping an effective remedy to eliminate the extensive waiting lists and restructure the city's special education system, tasks that the State Commissioner of Education and his entire staff had been unable to accomplish despite six years of intensive efforts, now rested with Special Master Marvin Frankel. Frankel immediately convened meetings with the attorneys for the parties, Board of Education staff, and representatives of other groups who expressed interest in participating in the proceedings.[41]

At the initial sessions, Special Master Frankel asked the participants to give their views on what his role should be and what a report to Judge Nickerson should contain. It was decided that the most productive initial undertaking would be an information exchange between the parties.[42] Although this process was initiated by the parties in a cooperative, optimistic atmosphere, by mid-summer relations had deteriorated. The information exchange process had broken down and the *Jose P.* plaintiffs requested the immediate appointment of a receiver to "establish and implement an effective plan."[43]

By the time a meeting on the issue was convened, however, plaintiffs learned that Dr. Jerry Gross, the newly appointed Executive Director of the Division of Special Education, had been considering substantial reforms corresponding to the types of changes plaintiffs had contemplated.[44] At the meeting, Special Master Frankel set aside the dispute on information submissions and directed the parties to submit drafts of proposed judgments, based on Dr. Gross's proposals, before the end of the month.[45]

Dr. Gross's restructuring plan, formally issued on September 10, 1979, reflected his personal commitment to a policy of "decategorization." As a newcomer to the system, his perspective was that the traditional organization of services in the Division of Special Education was archaic and ineffective. The main thrust of the plan[46] was to emphasize the evaluation of needs and the delivery of services at the neighborhood school level and to promote mainstreaming of children in regular classes, with back-up "resource room" assistance. The core of the plan would be the establishment in each school of a school-based support team (SBST) consisting of a psychologist, social worker, special educator, and administrators and teachers from the local school. New York's traditional reliance on "self-contained" special education classes, organized through a centralized administration, was to be dramatically restructured.

Plaintiffs were quick to accept the philosophical premises of Dr. Gross's plan. They insisted, however, that before it would be incorporated into a judicial decree, the court must add specific timelines and resource commitments, explicit procedural protections for the parents, and provisions for periodic reporting and ongoing monitoring to assure compliance.

The judgment negotiated by the parties and adopted by the court in December of 1979 [47] blended the substance of the Board of Education's Special Education in Transition Plan with the specific legal protections sought by the plaintiffs. So, for example, the judgment adopted Dr. Gross's plan for establishment of an SBST in each school but added a timeline mandate specifying that this be accomplished no later than April 15, 1981. [48] To assure that sufficient staff was hired to meet the needs of the new system, defendants were required to "make maximum reasonable efforts" in hiring. They were also committed to enter into contracts with private facilities to conduct evaluations or to provide placements for handicapped children if the Board was unable to meet the evaluation and placement needs through its own resources. [49] Some flexibility was given to the Board to catch up with the waiting list backlogs, but a final deadline of April 1, 1980, was established for their total elimination. [50]

The judgment also contained a detailed plan that would ensure accessibility for the physically handicapped to all facilities housing present programs by September 1980, together with a long-range plan requiring at least one elementary and one junior high school in each of the city's 32 community districts and one high school in each of the six regions to be fully accessible. [51] Detailed reporting requirements called for monthly reports on numbers of students evaluated and numbers placed, as well as additional information on staffing needs, availability of classroom space, and delivery of services to non-English speaking students. [52]

Two key areas, establishing due process procedures for parents and defining a continuum of educational programs and services, required additional time to formulate. The parties agreed to continue negotiations and to produce a further document, to be known as the January Plan, to cover these issues. [53] In addition, the Board's commitments for meeting the staffing needs, classroom space, and specialized instructional material and supplies that were required to implement the programs described in the continuum of services would be set forth in an additional document to be known as the April Plan, which also would be incorporated in the document at a later date. [54]

Barely six months after issuance of the court's basic liability decision, the judgment entered in *Jose P.* committed the Board of Education to re-organize radically its entire approach to providing education to handicapped students. The rapid formulation of such an extensive remedial decree was undoubtedly due in large part to the fortuitous circumstances that brought together an ambitious new Director of Special Education, a group of plain-tiffs willing to accept his expertise as the foundation for a remedial decree, and an astute Special Master who was able to inspire the parties to reach agreement on a complex web of issues needed to provide a legal structure for the agreed educational policy directions.

THE NEGOTIATING PROCESS

The basic judgment in *Jose P.* was formulated relatively quickly be-cause, as in most successful negotiations, a way was found for both sides to obtain their primary goals. Defendants here could take satisfaction from the fact that their educational philosophy, as well as their basic structural reform plan, were adopted as the core of the judgment. Since the judgment provided the specific timelines, resource commitments, and due process procedural protections that were their main concern, plaintiffs also believed that their prime objectives had been achieved.

Actual implementation of the complex, 45-page judicial decree would, however, prove to be more difficult, more time consuming—and perhaps ultimately more successful—than any of the parties at the time could have anticipated. The parties expected some future confrontations over cost issues and deadlines. What the lawyers for both sides did not fully appreciate at the outset, however, was that Dr. Gross's reorganization plan did not constitute a proven educational system that could be fully implemented over time if suf-ficient resources were provided. Rather, it was an imaginative proposal for beginning a structural reform process whose direction and substance would be subject to ongoing reformulation.

Acceptance of the extensive commitments in this judgment constituted a leap of faith by the chancellor and the Board of Education. They had committed themselves, under pain of contempt, to specific timelines for im-plementing an entirely new system that had never been shown to be workable in any large school system, let alone in the complex New York City sys-tem.[55] They were, in fact, embarking on an unprecedented legal course that would involve the parties in an ongoing process of reconsidering and modi-fying the provisions of the judgment to reflect knowledge gained from actual experience in the field.

During the first two years of implementation, this ongoing structural re-form process entailed negotiation of the January Plan and the April Plan called for under the judgment. In regard to the former, the judgment provided that by January 9, 1980 (barely a month after the basic judgment had been entered), city defendants would formulate further plans, subject to the plaintiffs' comments, covering SBST evaluation procedures, standards for the provision of related services, and a detailed description of each program in a full continuum of educational services.[56]

Consistent with their insistence on an explicit commitment of resources necessary to carry out Dr. Gross's bold new plan, plaintiffs had also insisted that defendants provide detailed information on precisely how the continuum of programs and services described in the January Plan actually would be put into effect. Thus, the Board was given an additional four months to assemble the necessary documentation and resource commitments to provide detailed information on staffing, supplies, and classroom space issues.[57] This was the essence of the April Plan.

The scope of the tasks encompassed by the January Plan and the April Plan proved to be far more extensive than the parties had anticipated. The January Plan was completed almost one year late, being approved by the court in January 1981.[58] Negotiation of the April Plan also extended far beyond its original April 1980 schedule. In May 1981, the parties reached agreement on the structure of the April Plan, but many of the open issues were brought to the court for resolution in 1982 and some were still undecided and under negotiation in 1988.[59]

Negotiation of the January Plan and the April Plan evolved into an ongoing process, over a multi-year span, in which the attorneys for both sides, their educational policy advisors and, at times, the Special Master and the court not only filled in the open areas of the basic structural reorganization plans, but also reacted to its ongoing implementation. As feedback was obtained on problems arising in the field, the parties drafted provisions in the follow-up documents that would deal with these realities. In working through their concerns, the parties often agreed on entirely new organizational approaches, with new timelines and resource commitments that would then supersede the original agreements.

The enormity of the enterprise in which the parties were engaged is reflected both in the size of the final January Plan and April Plan documents and in the range and complexity of the issues they covered. The January Plan, as finally adopted by the court and incorporated as an integral part of the judgment, consisted of a 76-page basic plan together with a 185-page appendix. The May 1981 version of the April Plan consisted of a 54-page basic plan, an 85-page supplement, and a 200-page appendix.

The table of contents for the January Plan listed 30 topic areas for which specific policies and procedures were set forth, ranging from procedures for evaluation of students with limited English proficiency to methods for promoting parental attendance at meetings and contracting with non-public schools. The table of contents for the April Plan listed 12 complex subject areas, ranging from projected numbers of personnel needed in future years in each service category to facilities accessibility issues.

As might be expected from the scope and complexity of the issues listed, the negotiating process itself became expansive. The lawyers on both sides brought to the table a range of interested persons and a diversity of resources.[60] At most negotiating sessions, the attorneys were accompanied by various educational consultants and specialists on the particular items under consideration. Other consultants often reviewed drafts of proposals prior to the meetings.

Early on, plaintiffs adopted an informal division of labor. They assigned to particular attorneys, or groups of attorneys, primary initial responsibility for children with a particular category of disability, although the named attorneys in the case were, of course, aware of their overall responsibility for insuring implementation of all aspects of the decree. The defendants, of course, were able to draw upon the resources of the entire Board of Education and State Education Department to ensure that the specialized needs of children across the entire range of handicapping conditions were being considered.

Since literally hundreds of complex issues were being negotiated, there was potential for continuous confrontation and repeated impasses. Under the terms of the judgment, either party was entitled to seek the intervention of the Special Master or the court on virtually any issue. Extensive resort to this formal adjudicative option would have totally undermined the entire process. Paradoxically, it was precisely because the parties were able to avoid constantly calling on the court that the judicial reform agenda could be achieved.

One major reason why extensive confrontations were avoided was the role played by the Special Master, Marvin Frankel. All parties agreed on his unique ability to "lubricate the negotiation process."[61] Judge Frankel moved the process along in a regular pattern. After the parties had negotiated for a number of weeks on certain issues, a status report would be sent to Judge Frankel. The parties would list a dozen or so issues on which negotiating impasses or major problems had surfaced. Judge Frankel would talk these issues through with the parties, usually covering each in no more than 15 or 20 minutes, focusing on the heart of the issue, and often proposing ways to resolve the critical problems. By the end of the session, the outlines of solutions acceptable to all parties would emerge and the negotiating process would continue, without any need for formal decisions from the Special Master or the court. It is significant in this regard that throughout the more than two-year period of intensive negotiations of the basic judgment and the

January Plan and the April Plan, only three substantive aspects of the plans needed to be formally adjudicated by the Special Master, with recommendations sent on to the court.[62]

PROMOTING COMPLIANCE

The Confrontational Stage

While the parties were continuing their negotiations to work out the details of the January Plan and the April Plan, problems of compliance with the provisions to which they had previously agreed began to arise. The compliance concerns, although also the subjects of negotiation and compromise, led to more adversarial confrontations. For example, at the very time that the parties were reaching substantial agreement in the culminating phase of the April Plan negotiations, plaintiffs raised formal complaints with the Special Master and the court on alleged violations of procedures for private school placement for students on waiting lists.[63] They also sought a special summer program to provide compensatory services for students who had been denied services to which they were entitled under the judgment during the school year.[64]

Once the task of negotiating the substance of the January Plan and the April Plan had been substantially completed, the plaintiffs turned their full attention to these compliance problems. The immediate occasion for controversy was the Board's new plan to reduce the waiting lists that were submitted in January 1982.[65] The Board claimed that the waiting lists for evaluation and placement had been reduced to approximately 2,200 and 2,800 respectively by November 1981. The Board considered these reductions to constitute "substantial results," and it committed itself to renewed management initiatives and more extensive hiring efforts to close the existing compliance gaps.[66] Plaintiffs were not impressed. They replied that defendants' plan would not eliminate the waiting list, and they asked the court to order the hiring of 225 new SBST teams and to mandate specific new procedures for teacher hiring, obtaining classroom space, contracting out for related services, and implementing the data retrieval and information systems required under the judgment.[67]

Perhaps not coincidentally, the increasingly adversarial posture of the case occurred shortly after Dr. Jerry Gross, the author of the Special Education in Transition Plan, had resigned as Director of the Division of Special Education. Dr. Gross's resignation was apparently related to criticism he had received for overexpenditure of the education budget and for difficulties in his relationship with the chancellor and the seven members of the Board of Education.[68]

On August 1, 1981, a new Executive Director, Dr. Alan Gartner, assumed office. Gartner, an administrator at the Graduate Center of the City

University, was a close associate of Chancellor Macchiarola and had conducted an extensive evaluation review of the Special Education Division for him several years earlier. Dr. Gartner lacked Dr. Gross's commitment to the Special Education in Transition Plan and the *Jose P.* judgment that had been largely crafted around it. He also had a markedly more negative view of the role of courts in educational policy matters.[69]

Not surprisingly, relations between the defendants and plaintiffs deteriorated rapidly with the change of administrator. Although negotiations continued, both on outstanding aspects of the April Plan and on the noncompliance issues raised by the plaintiffs, Dr. Gartner let it be known that he was impatient with plaintiffs' continuing oversight of his division. Plaintiffs were also informally made aware of the fact that the Board had retained a prestigious Park Avenue law firm to prepare a major motion to vacate the judgment and terminate the court's jurisdiction.

On March 3, 1982, Chancellor Macchiarola filed with the court an unusual affidavit that procedurally had no relevance to any pending issues but whose substance reflected strong feelings concerning the court's role.[70] Macchiarola, who was himself a lawyer as well as an administrator, first acknowledged the unique aspects of this type of lawsuit: "[A] class action lawsuit such as this one is unique in that the interests of the parties are not truly adverse: each side, in the final analysis, has an equal claim and an equal obligation to represent the interests of the handicapped children who constitute the class."[71] He also explained defendants' reasons for negotiating and agreeing to the consent judgment with the plaintiffs:

> City defendants might have raised a range of procedural and substantive defenses to plaintiffs' claims. Instead, we chose to negotiate a plan with plaintiffs and their representatives assuming that the development of such a plan would increase both the quality and the quantity of educational services for children with special needs. We adopted this course of action not because we feared that our legal defenses lacked merit, but because we recognized that protracted litigation, regardless of its outcome, could only delay the implementation of a broad range of needed reforms in special education.[72]

Although he acknowledged the "value" of the efforts undertaken by all concerned to develop the judgment, Chancellor Macchiarola stated, "Now, however, that valuable framework has become an unhealthy fetter."[73] Specifically, he complained that the judgment had imposed rigid timelines that distorted the evaluation process, compelled overly rapid, standardized processing, and funneled into the special educational system thousands of students who might have been served in regular education.[74] In addition, he charged that the judgment impeded administrative flexibility since each proposed change in procedures or organizational structure had to be submitted to the plaintiffs and the court for approval and extensive staff time had to be devoted to meeting with the plaintiffs and satisfying court demands.[75]

Plaintiffs responded to Chancellor Macchiarola's charges by noting that the stringent 60-day time pressures to which the chancellor was objecting came from state law and regulations that the court was merely enforcing. They further indicated, "If the Board feels that the judgment is pressing too hard, the plaintiffs will be happy to sit down, as we have in the past, to deal with these matters."[76]

After the filing of the Macchiarola affidavit, the litigation took on an increasingly confrontational tone. Judge Frankel invoked traditional litigation mechanisms and scheduled evidentiary hearings concerning plaintiffs' litany of noncompliance claims. After the hearings, Frankel issued two reports, one recommending that the court order the creation of 150 more SBST teams[77] and the other recommending that defendants be put on notice that they would be held in contempt if their student placement procedures continued to violate specific provisions in the judgment.[78]

Before Judge Nickerson had an opportunity to consider fully the Special Master's recommendations, however, the Board of Education filed its long-threatened major motion to vacate the judgment. The motion was submitted on October 5, 1982, by Harold R. Tyler, Jr., of Patterson, Belknap, Webb & Tyler. Tyler, formerly a federal judge in New York City, had left the Board to become second-in-command of the Justice Department during the Ford administration. In engaging his talents for this task, the Board of Education had pulled out the heaviest guns. It clearly was determined to terminate the court's involvement in its special education affairs.

The Board's motion argued that it had substantially satisfied the requirements of the judgment because the latest statistics indicated that the waiting list backlog had been virtually eliminated by the summer of 1982. In addition, the Board claimed that the judgment should be vacated as a matter of law because recent decisions of the U.S. Supreme Court had clarified and limited the court's proper role in cases of this sort. Continued application of the 1979 judgment would represent an unjustified intrusion into the management of the local educational system, defendants claimed.[79]

Plaintiffs responded that defendants had manipulated the statistics to create a false impression that waiting lists had been eliminated. Furthermore, they claimed defendants' papers did not even allege compliance with the numerous other substantive requirements of the judgment covering such items as individualized education program (IEP) preparation, mainstreaming, facilities accessibility, and provision of related services. Finally, plaintiffs strongly disputed defendants' interpretation of the recent Supreme Court decisions.[80]

Judge Nickerson rejected defendants' motion to vacate the judgment. In an extensive opinion issued on February 24, 1983, he also upheld plaintiffs' position that defendants were in noncompliance with the judgment and ordered additional measures to compel compliance.[81] In regard to the legal issues, Judge Nickerson held that the Supreme Court in *Rowley*, "did not purport to rule on the issue decided by this Court,"[82] and therefore he saw no reason to reconsider the basic holdings of his prior decisions. On the factual issues, Judge Nickerson agreed with plaintiffs that the defendants' waiting list statistics had adopted a definition of the term "referral" that differed from that embodied in the state regulations and judgment, and that "the interpretation of the City Defendants [was] wholly unjustified."[83] The court also rejected defendants' stance that they need comply only with the "core" waiting list issues raised by the original *Jose P.* complaint: "[N]o consequences follow from the fact that the *Jose P.* case, when filed, was 'about' waiting lists. It is now 'about' everything in the judgment, and as to many of those things, city defendants do not even suggest they are in compliance."[84]

Although he issued strong findings in favor of plaintiffs on all these points, Judge Nickerson declined to follow Judge Frankel's recommendation that the Board be ordered specifically to hire 150 more SBST teams. He also rejected the other detailed relief that the plaintiffs had requested. Instead, accepting the approach of the latest Special Master Report, Judge Nickerson held that the defendants would be required to meet their responsibilities through methods of their own choosing, but under strong contempt pressures from the court.[85] Because Judge Frankel had asked to be relieved from the burdens of the Special Master position he had borne for more than two years, Judge Nickerson appointed as a new Special Master a U.S. magistrate in the Eastern District, John Caden. Caden was authorized to commence hearings "with all appropriate dispatch" in order to make findings "as to the extent to which City Defendants and their agents are now in contempt of this Court's judgment and . . . what measures should be imposed on City Defendants, and on which employees and agents of City Defendants, so as to bring about compliance."[86]

The Cooperative Phase

The contempt hearings called for in Judge Nickerson's order were, however, never held. The court's strongly worded edict paradoxically resulted in a new cooperative phase in the litigation that was more conciliatory than anything that had occurred before. After attending a few initial sessions with Magistrate Caden, the parties quickly agreed to a new round of intensive negotiations in an attempt to resolve all the major outstanding issues.[87]

Progress in the negotiations was aided by two major personnel changes on the Board's side. First was the appointment of Edward Sermier to replace Dr. Gartner, who had resigned shortly after issuance of Judge Nickerson's decision. Sermier was a management-by-objective specialist who had no specific background with special education.[88] His stated mission as Executive Director was to take charge of the organizational problems of the division and to focus its resources in order to achieve, finally, compliance with the court's order. Second was the upgrading of representation by the Corporation Counsel's office by the assignment of Special Assistant Corporation Counsel Jeffrey E. Glen to take personal responsibility for the case. Unlike his predecessors, Glen had personal authority to make commitments on legal matters and had sufficient clout with both the Board and the city officials to be in a position to "sell" settlements he might reach with plaintiffs on controversial issues. Plaintiffs quickly realized that a new opportunity was at hand: They were now dealing with an executive director who was staking his reputation on remedying the long-standing waiting list problems and with a high-level defense attorney whose mandate was to avoid the issuance of contempt citations against the Board.

Given the new conciliatory atmosphere, the parties quickly reached agreement on a far-reaching new stipulation that covered all the outstanding issues in the case. In the stipulation, the defendants committed themselves to hire 613 new teachers and 600 psychologists, social workers, or educational evaluators by September 1983.[89] They also agreed to implement an extensive computerized data system that once and for all would provide accurate waiting list figures.[90] Other key provisions established new procedures to assure that all students on waiting lists would be placed by September,[91] that monthly reports would utilize the definitions of referral and placement approved by the court,[92] that all outstanding triennial evaluations would be completed within one year,[93] and that procedures would be developed to identify and correct missing or incomplete IEP.[94] The parties also agreed to undertake further negotiations on the various outstanding "quality education issues" such as mainstreaming and the continuum of services, consideration of which had been delayed since the original January Plan and April Plan submission dates.[95]

During the following two school years, the negotiating process evolved into a pattern of regular Thursday meetings, where both the deferred long range issues and immediate compliance problems were placed on the agenda. These meetings were generally attended by a core of three to five attorneys on each side, two to three program consultants, and six to 12 program staff on the specific issues that would be negotiated on that day. Plaintiffs' educational and data consultants had ongoing access and contacts with their counterparts at the Board, and plaintiffs' attorneys were invited to visit schools, Committee on the Handicapped headquarters, or central board offices to monitor compliance.[96]

As a result of this process, substantial progress was made on new approaches to architectural accessibility issues, the new continuum of program services, development of a computerized data system, and a number of other items. Agreement was also reached on key aspects of a new set of procedures for the evaluation and placement process that the parties hoped would provide a lasting solution to the perennial waiting list problems.

Although the parties agreed on the thrust of the new evaluation and placement procedures, defendants argued that implementation would, on average, require more than the 60 days permitted by the judgment. Plaintiffs were skeptical of the need to modify the timelines and reluctant to approve permanently the new due process procedures until convinced that they could be implemented fairly in the field. Rather than attempting to reach a lawyer's compromise or litigate these critical questions, the parties agreed to research the problem. The new procedures would be put into effect for the 1984–1985 school year, and an extensive study of their actual implementation would be undertaken. At the end of the school year, the parties would reconsider all aspects of these procedures and particularly whether they should be adopted as a permanent remedy in the present or a modified form.[97]

The results of the study, which was completed in the summer of 1986, were inconclusive. The plaintiffs then returned to court, asking Judge Nickerson to order the hiring of more evaluation staff and specific compliance with the judgment. After defendants submitted a further compliance plan that the plaintiffs had deemed unacceptable, Judge Nickerson remanded the matter to Magistrate Caden to hold hearings on plaintiffs' request for further relief.[98]

On the basis of six days of hearings, Magistrate Caden issued a report in March 1988, which stated that defendants' July 1987 compliance plan "was not viable when it was written and is not viable now."[99] He recommended that the Board be required to hire several hundred additional evaluators, insure that 20 percent of all evaluation staff be bilingual, and provide adequate space, equipment, and supplies for the evaluation teams in each school.

The magistrate's recommendation led to another round of intensive negotiations, which resulted in a new stipulation that called for even more staff (but of differing types) than the magistrate had recommended. In total, New York City was now to have 960 school psychologists (of which one-third were to be bilingual), 960 educational evaluators (one-third bilingual), and 572 social workers (one-half bilingual). This staff was expected to provide, on average, one full-time, professional team in each public school in the city. The stipulation also provided for a lengthening of the timelines for completion of the evaluations, support services for the school-based teams, extensive bilingual recruitment, scholarship and loan forgiveness programs, new medical examination procedures, reforms of the placement process, and a commitment to conclude negotiations on all other outstanding issues within one year.[100] In addition, the parties agreed on specific definitions of "substantial compliance," implemented an extensive monitoring system with 57 full time monitors, and defined conditions for eventual disengagement by the court.

A DECADE OF JUDICIAL ACTIVISM: WHAT HAS IT WROUGHT?

The extensive *Jose P.* litigation has, at the time of this writing, involved the federal district court and a core group of plaintiff attorneys in an ongoing process of designing and implementing a fundamental structural reordering of the entire special education system in New York City for almost ten years. What has resulted from this extensive effort?

Statistics tell an important part of the story. The number of children served in special education has roughly doubled. Specifically, the special education register grew from 59,452 students as of June 1979[101] to 116,000 as of April 1985.[102] Costs of providing these services more than tripled: The overall special education budget rose from $304 million in fiscal year 1979 to $933 million in 1985.[103]

Waiting list figures, the initial thrust of the *Jose P.* case, also tell an important part of the tale. The number of children awaiting placement site offers of over 60 days dramatically declined from approximately 3,000 per month in October 1981 to approximately 600 by October 1987. Similarly, the number of children awaiting counseling services was down from 5,442 in October 1981 to 1,226 in May 1987. Similar figures obtained for occupational therapy (958 in October 1982, to 16 in May 1987), physical therapy (720 to 28), and speech and language therapy (3,994 to 1,046).[104]

Similar impressive compliance statistics were reported in regard to reducing the 1983 backlog of 51,322 mandatory triennial evaluations.[105] By September 1984, the Board reported a 98 percent compliance rate in this area.[106] In terms of the total number of evaluations, however (including initial evaluations, reevaluations, and triennials), such progress has not occurred. In October 1981, the waiting list in this area was 2,944. In October 1987, it was 10,226.[107]

Statistics, however, can tell only part of the story. Although the pressure of the judicial mandates in *Jose P.* clearly has led to a dramatic increase in the number of pupils served and a corresponding reduction in some of the waiting lists, a full assessment of the litigation's impact must also consider the quality of services delivered to the students on the burgeoning special education registers and the extent to which positive and permanent structural changes have been implemented. Although a complete analysis of the institutional reform that has resulted from the ten years of *Jose P.* litigation and its impact on educational services is beyond the scope of the present chapter, an illustrative sense of the structural impact of the lawsuit can be conveyed by describing in some detail how the system responded to judicial compliance pressures in two key areas: staff hiring and student mainstreaming.

Staff Hiring

One of the major reasons for the perennial waiting lists in New York City was a chronic shortage of staff—both teachers and clinicians such as psychologists, social workers, physical therapists, and occupational therapists. The system's staffing requirements to cover accelerating registers as well as annual attrition owing to death, retirement, and voluntary terminations were enormous. For example, at the end of the 1979–1980 school year, there were 7,751 budgeted teaching positions. The projected number of teachers needed to staff fully the anticipated requirements for the next September was 9,974, an increase of 2,223 teachers.[108] The system's needs were even more acute in regard to clinical specialties. As of June 1980, the Board employed only 13 physical therapists and three occupational therapists, although 91 of each of these specialists were the projected numbers needed to meet the requirements of student IEPs for the following September.[109]

Despite an extensive recruitment drive during the spring, summer, and fall of 1980, the Board of Education was unable to fill all the slots. Only 1,762 teachers were hired during the fall of 1981,[110] a shortfall of 561. With clinical staff, the situation was still worse. For example, only seven full-time and 12 part-time physical therapists were on staff to fill the 91 positions needed, and only 14 full-time and six part-time of the 91 occupational therapists.[111] As a result of these staffing shortfalls, thousands of students remained on waiting lists for placement or for related services. Many others were accommodated only by being placed in classes that exceeded normal class size limits set forth in state regulations.[112]

The major causes of the Board's hiring difficulties were beyond dispute: the low starting salaries, onerous licensing requirements imposed by the New York City Board of Examiner procedures,[113] and the undesirability of many of the available assignments or school locations to many potential applicants.[114] Nevertheless, despite these difficulties, plaintiffs claimed that more staff could be hired if an aggressive, well-organized recruitment drive were undertaken. The Board had mounted an intensive advertising campaign in a variety of local and out-of-state newspapers in 1980 and 1981, had conducted on-site recruiting at various colleges and universities, and had held training sessions for the Board of Examiners tests.[115] Plaintiffs argued that still more could be done in each of these areas.

In addition, plaintiffs pressed for a major structural reform that the Board assiduously resisted. The Board's massive recruiting drives held each year at the end of August in hot, un-airconditioned hiring halls had often ended in failure. Plaintiffs said that this system dissuaded potential candidates and gave competing school districts in the metropolitan area four months lead time to hire the best applicants. The obvious solution to this problem, they argued, would be to provide firm job offers to potential candidates in the spring, on an individualized recruitment basis.[116] Defendants considered plaintiffs' position on this point to be totally unrealistic. Union contract requirements, federal staff integration regulations, and the administrative complexities of projecting specific vacancies far in advance in the enormous New York City school system simply made a spring hiring option an impossibility.[117]

After the issuance of Judge Nickerson's February 1983 Order, a renewed recruitment effort was made during the following spring and summer. Although these efforts resulted in the hiring of the full complement of psychologists, social workers, and guidance counselors to which the system had committed itself, substantial problems remained in filling basic teaching and specialized clinical staff positions. As of September 1, 1983, 729 positions were unfilled, 484 of them in classroom teaching spots.[118]

Facing these facts, the plaintiffs and city defendants agreed that hiring problems would be the main priority at their negotiating sessions the next fall. These deliberations resulted in an agreement by the city defendants to intensify their recruitment efforts and to place more responsibility for recruitment of special education staff directly under the Division of Special Education rather than under the Board's central Office of Personnel. The priority focus on hiring problems in the new conciliatory atmosphere also led to a reconsideration—and eventual adoption—of plaintiffs' spring hiring plan.

Harold Coopchik, newly appointed Director of Personnel of the Division of Special Education, agreed to investigate each of the problems that had in the past impeded the possibility of extensive spring hiring. He and members of his staff met with representatives of the teachers union, the Board of Examiners, and the Board's budgeting and personnel placement officials to reconsider union contract, licensing, and vacancy projection issues. Having obtained their tentative commitments to considering a new approach, he drafted a new proposal for spring 1984 staffing. The new approach consisted of a method for identifying vacancies at particular schools and a procedure for allocating an agreed number of spring hiring positions to each geographical region based on historical teacher attrition rates. These allocations would be determined in such a way as not to interfere with contractual transfer rights of experienced teachers.

Plaintiffs saw this approach as a substantial breakthrough and cooperated with the defendants to iron out the details of the project—even to the extent of redrafting letters to potential candidates to improve their "marketability," and visiting recruiting sites to offer suggestions on decor and ambiance.

By early spring, a final version of the new recruitment plan was officially promulgated and its implementation was begun.[119]

The plan operated smoothly during the next few months and as a result most teachers recruited for the fall semester were hired on an individualized basis in the late spring and early summer. The traditional massive hiring drives were not held that August or early September. Although the staffing problem was not fully solved by September, it was substantially improved. As of September 5, 1984, there were 134 teacher vacancies compared with the 484 at the beginning of the previous September.[120] Plaintiffs applauded these efforts but noted that the remaining vacancies were concentrated in a limited number of schools in areas that teacher applicants tended to avoid or that had especially high attrition rates. They pressed the Board to devise new methods to attract and hold teachers in these schools during the spring 1985 recruitment season.

Coopchik and his staff responded also to this suggestion. They devised a Special Educators in Training program that would offer financial support for 12 credits of graduate study and special teacher training assistance to applicants who would commit to assignments in the designated schools.[121] Although plaintiffs were skeptical as to whether this inducement would be sufficient to attract qualified candidates, over 2,000 applications were received in the spring of 1985 for the 168 positions.[122]

The long-standing difficulty in the hiring of certain clinical staff personnel was substantially ameliorated during the 1983–1984 school year by an additional innovative structural reform devised through the *Jose P.* negotiations. The Board's difficulties in hiring occupational and physical therapists stemmed in large part from the fact that these specialized services were in great demand in hospitals and private facilities throughout the metropolitan area. The Board's low salary scale for year-round work schedules, which were tied to municipal contract scales that could not easily be adjusted, as well as the lack of long-range career ladders for professionals in this field, stymied even the most intensive recruitment efforts. Recognizing these factors, the parties agreed to consider seriously an approach that had been proposed by plaintiffs years before but had not ever been actively pursued, namely, contracting out for these services with private agencies.[123]

In the June 1983 stipulation, the defendants committed themselves to developing with plaintiffs an effective method for contracting out both evaluations and related services.[124] Consequently, at the beginning of the new school year, it established a new Office of Related and Contractual Services and passed a resolution authorizing the sum of $4.5 million for contracting with private agencies for both evaluations and related services.[125]

The director of the new office, Stephan Hittman, quickly went about the task of lining up agencies that could provide personnel at the specific school sites on an as-needed basis. By December 1, 1983, 1,062 students were receiving occupational therapy services, 1,017 physical therapy services, and 30,207 speech services through Board of Education staff and the contracted services.[126] Shortly thereafter the basic waiting lists for many of the related services were largely eliminated.[127]

The parties also agreed to an additional innovative procedure, authorizing a voucher mechanism, known as a "related service authorization" (RSA) that would entitle students to obtain necessary therapy or related services on an individual basis if the Board could not provide the service directly or through its master contracts.[128] Under the detailed regulations negotiated by the parties, the Board agreed to pay private clinicians at rates of up to $60 per session plus transportation costs.

Implementation of the voucher system on a wide-ranging basis clearly would have been a dramatic departure from prior practices and very costly to operate. However, owing to the success of increased recruitment efforts and the contracting out system put into effect early in the school year, the waiting lists for related services were substantially reduced, and the RSA procedure, the ultimate fallback mechanism under the June 1983 stipulation, was rarely put into effect.[129] Thus the RSA procedures were considered by all concerned to be one of the most successful innovations of the litigation —precisely because they applied substantial pressure for other remedies to work in their stead and thereby hardly ever needed to be actually used.

Although the New York City school system had substantially improved its recruitment procedures and had ameliorated most shortage areas by 1988, there remained one glaring problem area: lack of bilingual staff. For example, out of 249 needed bilingual psychologists, only 84 were actually on staff in early 1988.[130] Bilingual recruitment therefore became a major priority of the plaintiffs in the negotiations that summer. The stipulation that finally emerged provided $4.5 million for additional recruitment efforts and a three-year, $6 million fund for a scholarship and loan forgiveness program that plaintiffs had put forward as a major proposed remedy during the prior year's litigation.[131]

Mainstreaming

One of the most significant educational policy priorities to be written into the EHA was the requirement that handicapped children be educated in "the least restrictive environment"; that is, to the maximum extent appropriate with non-handicapped children.[132] Although children's educational needs obviously vary in severity, complexity, and duration, these mandates generally have been interpreted to require the placement of handicapped children in regular classrooms whenever possible. Such channeling of handicapped children into regular classes is commonly known as "mainstreaming."

At the time that the original *Jose P.* judgment was being negotiated, the parties noted this strong statutory preference for mainstreaming—and the fact that New York City had done little to move toward that goal.[133] They also recognized that mainstreaming was one of the most complex educational policy issues. It raised special problems in New York City, whose decentralized system placed primary responsibility for regular education in local community school boards and for special education with the central authorities. Mainstreaming therefore would require extensive structural reforms that could not be easily resolved in the drafting of the judgment. Thus it was one of the substantive issues that was left for further development in the January Plan and the April Plan.[134]

In the negotiation of the April Plan, mainstreaming became one of the two contested items that were brought to the attention of the Special Master and ultimately to the court. Plaintiffs had two problems with the mainstreaming aspects of defendants' initial draft of the continuum of services plan. First, they alleged that the opportunities for part-time or eventual full-time mainstreaming in academic classes were set forth in vague, and therefore unenforceable, language. Second, they complained that the opportunity for students in self-contained classes to participate in non-academic activities such as lunch, assembly, or trips was left to the discretion of building principals and local supervisors without any program guidelines or accountability standards.[135]

After the parties agreed to defer the development of the basic continuum of services and with it the issues of academic class mainstreaming, the second issue, that of mainstreaming opportunities in non-academic areas, became the focus of contention. Defendants agreed to rephrase the requirements to provide specifically that all special education students would be integrated with non-handicapped students for lunch, assemblies, trips, and other special school events "unless it is not appropriate for the students to do so."[136] Plaintiffs, however, were not satisfied with this change because it still permitted exceptions at the discretion of the local school officials. As an alternative they suggested that exceptions be permitted only if formally set forth by the Committee on the Handicapped in a student's Individual Education Plan.[137]

The parties could not resolve this issue, and accordingly it was brought before the Special Master. Judge Frankel concluded that the positions of both sides were "somewhat extreme." The plaintiffs, he said, were correct in objecting to granting unfettered discretion to school principals. This was well illustrated by a reported incident in which a school principal barred mainstreaming arrangements simply because he thought them too burdensome. On the other hand, plaintiffs' proposed IEP remedy was too cumbersome.

Therefore, "acknowledging that compromises are not always sound, the

Special Master propose[d] a middle course."[138] His compromise solution was to permit exceptions from the general non-academic mainstreaming requirement for lunch, assemblies, and gym only if included in the IEP or when prescribed in writing, with a brief statement of reasons for the exception by the school principal, teacher, site supervisor, or other staff person. Copies of the forms prescribing the exceptions were to be kept in the school files and made available for inspection by counsel for plaintiffs and *amici*.[139]

Plaintiffs accepted the Special Master's compromise proposal, but city defendants did not. The issue therefore went to the court. In a short, conclusory opinion, Judge Nickerson accepted the Special Master's recommendation.[140]

Over the next few months, attention once again turned to the basic issue of academic class mainstreaming. It was clear that not much academic mainstreaming was taking place, and where it did occur it was not very effective. A State Education Department report of site visits to six high schools summarized the situation as follows:

> The failure of many students to succeed in (or even attend) their mainstream classes attests to the inappropriate nature of some of the mainstream assignments. In one school it was reported that 75% of the students had been scheduled for mainstream classes at the beginning of the year but only 25% were able to remain until the end of the term. This rate of failure would seem to indicate that greater preparation of both students and teachers is required.[141]

Some of the reasons for these difficulties were admitted in a candid report prepared by one of Dr. Gartner's assistants:

> In junior high school, academic mainstreaming is particularly affected by availability of space. Regular education students are programmed first and special education students are placed in remaining space. Several principals raised the problem of possible grievances by regular education teachers concerning violations of contractual limits on class size due to mainstreaming.[142]

Substantial improvement in mainstreaming practices undoubtedly would require a sustained commitment not only by the Division of Special Education but by the entire school system. Extensive institutional impediments posed by the union contract, teacher apathy, administrators' resistance, and space limitations had to be overcome. Meaningful mainstreaming also would require sensitive preparation of children in the regular classes and of the handicapped students and their parents. After the issuance of Judge Nickerson's February 1983 order,[143] the parties returned to the long-delayed task of developing a basic continuum of service and the attendant mainstreaming components.[144] The defendants agreed to meet with plaintiffs' educational experts on a regular basis to discuss issues involved in developing this complex document.

When an initial draft of the new continuum of services plan was presented, plaintiffs complained that, like the first draft of the continuum in the 1980 April Plan, it contained only vague references to providing academic mainstreaming opportunities "as appropriate." Although plaintiffs' suggestions on this score had been rebuffed in 1980, this time the defendants' curriculum experts acknowledged their validity. Dr. Mary Beth Fafard, the prime author of the continuum draft, promised to attempt to include in each program description in her revised draft a specific statement of what "appropriate" mainstreaming should mean in that context, with specific benchmarks and guidelines to motivate teachers to maximize mainstreaming opportunities and to hold them accountable. The working draft of the new continuum document, dated April 1, 1984, carried out that commitment.[145]

The inclusion of specific guidelines in the description of the continuum of services was one critical element of a successful mainstreaming reform. In order for the new approaches actually to be implemented on a system-wide basis, however, serious steps would need to be taken to overcome entrenched institutional impediments. Accordingly, plaintiffs prepared a document listing the structural changes necessary for this task. Among other things, they asked that the chancellor issue a major position paper on mainstreaming that would communicate to all principals and school administrators throughout the system his personal commitment to the enterprise, that the number of special education classes in each building in the city be limited to no more than 25 percent of the student population, and that the enrollment of handicapped children in any particular classroom be limited to 20 percent.[146]

In response to plaintiffs' demands, defendants agreed to form a high level mainstreaming committee whose membership would be representative of the Division of Special Education, the High School Division, and the community school boards. This committee's mandate was to study plaintiffs' recommendations and to develop an action plan for implementing academic classroom mainstreaming throughout the city school system. The committee was chaired by Dr. Charles Schoenhaut, the Superintendent of High Schools in Brooklyn and Queens, who was later to become Deputy Chancellor for the entire school system.

In the fall of 1984, the mainstreaming committee announced that the percentage of special education students placed in any community school would be limited and that the Board would implement a pilot project in three community school districts during the 1984–1985 school year. The community superintendents in the three districts were committed to the proposal, and the union's cooperation had been obtained. After assessing the results of the pilot project, the Board extended this approach to a city-wide basis for the 1985–1986 school year. Plaintiffs accepted this plan as an interim process while continuing to press for more extensive planning and thoroughgoing commitments to mainstreaming reform.

During the 1986–1987 school year the mainstreaming committee was reconstituted under the chairmanship of Robert Mastruzzi, the Manhattan Superintendent of High Schools. In May of 1987, the committee issued a report that set forth basic principles for effective mainstreaming on a school-level basis. These included requiring each principal to formulate a mainstreaming plan for his or her building; establishing a mainstreaming committee; and devising identification procedures, criteria for placement, and consultation and reporting procedures. Support for the plan had been obtained from the teachers' and supervisors' unions that had participated actively in the mainstreaming committee's work. The new approach was well-received by the plaintiffs and was promptly incorporated in an implementation directive of the chancellor, which called for a phase-in of the new plan beginning in September 1987, and for full implementation in every school throughout the system by September 1988.[147]

As the *Jose P.* case neared completion of its tenth year of judicially supervised remedial implementation at the end of 1988, the situation in regard to mainstreaming could be summarized as follows: "Non-academic mainstreaming" for assemblies, lunch, trips, and special events had apparently become the norm throughout the system, except for some programs for the severely handicapped. The more difficult task of implementing comprehensive mainstreaming of the handicapped in academic classrooms had begun to be implemented under an extensive new plan, which met with plaintiffs' approval, although a dispute had arisen as to whether sufficient funds had been allocated to permit full implementation during the 1988–1989 school year.[148]

NOTES

Acknowledgment: I would like to thank, for their helpful comments on this chapter, John Blackmore, Shirley Cohen, Jim Fishman, Barbara Flicker, Marvin Frankel, John C. Gray, Jr., Carolyn Heft, Paula Hepner, Jane Stern, Joseph Viteritti, Marya Yee, and various New York City Board of Education officials and Corporation Counsel attorneys who wish to remain anonymous. This chapter was prepared for the Institute of Judicial Administration as part of the project on the Role of Courts in Education Litigation, under Grant No. 740-0327B from the Ford Foundation.

Note: Since the inception of *Jose P. v. Ambach*, the author has participated in the litigation as co-counsel for the consolidated plaintiff class, a status that has provided an understanding of the depth and range of issues not available to most academic observers. On the other hand, this status also may raise questions of objectivity. We hope that these have been minimized by (1) citing a documentary source for each factual point; (2) circulating drafts of the chapter and obtaining input from a wide variety of individuals involved in the process; and (3) disclosing these facts at the outset.

1. 347 U.S. 483 (1954). The general societal acceptance of the *Brown* doctrine was substantially aided by the passage of Title VI of the 1964 Civil Rights Act, 42 U.S.C. § 200d *et seq.* For a discussion of its legislative history and implementation of Title VI in the educational area, *see* M. REBELL AND A. BLOCK, EQUALITY AND EDUCATION: FEDERAL CIVIL RIGHTS ENFORCEMENT IN THE NEW YORK CITY SCHOOL SYSTEM (University of Chicago 1985).

2. Garrity v. Gallen, 552 F. Supp. 171, 206 (D.N.H. 1981).

3. For discussions of the type of invidious discrimination suffered by the disabled, *see* Kriegel, *Uncle Tom and Tiny Tim: Some Reflections on the Crippled as Negro*, 38 AM. SCH. 412 (1969); UNITED STATES CONSTITUTION ON CIVIL RIGHTS: ACCOMMODATING THE SPECTRUM OF INDIVIDUAL ABILITIES, ch. 2 (1983); S. HERR, RIGHTS AND ADVOCACY FOR RETARDED PEOPLE (1983); City of Cleburne v. Cleburne Living Center, 473 U.S. 432 (1985) (Marshall, J., concurring in part and dissenting in part).

4. The term "disability," which has connotations of physical or intellectual limitations stemming from a medical condition, is preferred by many advocates to the term "handicap," which has greater connotations of inferior status. On the other hand, the term "disability," precisely because of its medical connotations, implies a lesser moral obligation of society at large to eliminate impediments that "handicap" certain individuals. In any event, since most statutes and writings in this area tend to use the terms interchangeably, that practice will also be utilized here, with a preference, where feasible, for the term "disabled."

5. These factors are discussed more fully in Rebell, *Structural Discrimination and the Rights of the Disabled*, 74 GEO. L.J. 1435 (1986), as is the theory of "structural discrimination" upon which the analytic perspective of this section is based.

6. *See* Rebell, *Structural Discrimination, supra* n. 5.

7. *Compare* American Transportation System v. Lewis, 655 F.2d 1272 (D.C. Cir. 1981), with Dopico v. Goldschmidt, 687 F.2d 644 (2d Cir. 1982). *See also Note, Rethinking Equality and Difference: Disability Discrimination in Public Transportation*, 97 YALE L.J. 863, 873–878 (1988) (discussion of current Department of Transportation regulations).

8. "Adjustments hammered out in the real world of budgets, organizational constraints and precious self-interests may tell a good deal more about competing value positions than the abstract purposes of law." Clune and Van Pelt, *A Political Method of Evaluating the Education for All Handicapped Children's Act of 1975 and the Several Gaps of Gap Analysis*, 48 LAW & CON. PROBL. 7, 62 (1985).

9. The classic analytic description of the new model of institutional reform litigation is set forth in Chayes, *The Role of the Judge in Public Law Litigation*, 89 HARV. L. REV. 1281 (1976). *See also* Chayes, *Foreword: Public Law Litigation and the Burger Court*, 96 HARV. L. REV. (1982). For an overview on the literature on institutional reform litigation, *see* M. REBELL AND A. BLOCK, EDUCATIONAL POLICY MAKING AND THE COURTS: AN EMPIRICAL STUDY OF JUDICIAL ACTIVISM, ch. 1 (1982).

10. *See, e.g.,* H. KALODNER AND J. FISHMAN, LIMITS OF JUSTICE: THE COURT'S ROLE IN SCHOOL DESEGREGATION (1978); D. HOROWITZ, THE COURTS AND SOCIAL POLICY (1977); Fletcher, *The Discretionary Constitution: Institutional Remedies and Judi-*

cial Legitimacy, 91 YALE L.J. 635 (1982); Nagel, *Separation of Powers and the Scope of Federal Equitable Remedies*, 20 STAN. L. REV. 661 (1982). The distinction between the judicial role in desegregation and non-desegregation cases is discussed further in EDUCATIONAL POLICY AND THE COURTS, *supra* note 9, ch. 10.

11. 20 U.S.C. § 1401 *et seq.* The EHA largely incorporates concepts of equal educational opportunity articulated by the courts in Mills v. Board of Education, 348 F. Supp. 866 (D.D.C. 1972); Pennsylvania Association for Retarded Children v. Pennsylvania, 334 F. Supp. 1257 (E.D. Pa. 1971), *modified* 343 F. Supp. 279 (E.D. Pa. 1972) (hereinafter PARC). *See generally* Tweedie, *The Politics of Legalization in Special Education Reform*, in SPECIAL EDUCATION POLITICS 3 (J. Chambers and W. Hartman eds. 1983).

12. For example, the Act and its detailed implementing regulations require that an "individualized educational program" (IEP) be formulated for each child 20 U.S.C. § 1401(19); § 1404(a)(5); § 1413(a)(11); § 1414(a)(5), that to the "maximum extent appropriate, handicapped children be educated with the non-handicapped" 20 U.S.C. §§ 1412(5)(B), 1414(a)(1)(C)(iv), and that parents be guaranteed rights to extensive administrative review and court hearings to challenge any decisions of the educational authorities with which they disagree 20 U.S.C. § 1415; 34 C.F.R. §§ 300.500–300.514.

13. 458 U.S. 176 (1982).

14. For a critique of the Supreme Court's *Rowley* decision in relation to structural discrimination theory, *see Structural Discrimination, supra* note 5. The Supreme Court's other major decisions under the EHA, Irving Independent School District v. Tatro, 468 U.S. 883 (1984) (catheterization services are "related services" under the Act) and School Committee of the Town of Burlington v. Department of Education, 471 U.S. 359 (1985) (parents should be reimbursed retroactively for private school enrollments later shown to be warranted) do provide specific guidance to the lower courts in the narrow areas they cover. However, the federal courts continue to be preoccupied with such questions as how to apply in particular situations the broad "mainstreaming" requirements of the EHA (*see, e.g.*, Springdale School District v. Grace, 693 F.2d 41 [8th Cir. 1982]; Roncker v. Walters, 700 F.2d 1058 [6th Cir. 1983]; Visco v. School District of Pittsburgh, 684 F. Supp. 1310 [W.D. Pa. 1988]), and the right to other related services (*see, e.g.*, TG and PG v. Board of Education of Piscataway, N.J., 738 F.2d 420 [3d Cir. 1984], Max M. v. Thompson, 592 F. Supp. 1437 [N.D. Ill. 1984]; Gregory K. v. Longview School District, 811 F.2d 1307 [9th Cir. 1987]). In all of these areas, as with the core anti-discrimination principle, implementation by the district courts based on their knowledge of the particular situation is critical.

15. For general overviews of the New York City school system's history and its governing structure, *see* D. RAVITCH, THE GREAT SCHOOL WARS, NEW YORK CITY 1805–1973 (1974); D. ROGERS, 110 LIVINGSTON STREET: POLITICS AND BUREAUCRACY IN THE NEW YORK CITY SCHOOL SYSTEM (1968); J. VITERITTI, ACROSS THE RIVER: POLITICS AND EDUCATION IN THE CITY (1983). For a discussion of the school decentralization law (N.Y. EDUC. LAW ART. 52-A §§ 2590–2590-n [McKinney 1981]), *see* Rebell, *New York's School Decentralization Law: Two and a Half Years Later*, 2 J. LAW & ED. 1 (1983).

16. Former N.Y. Educ. Law § 3208 (McKinney 1981). *See also,* ¶¶ 18, 19 of Amended Stipulation in Pennsylvania Association for Retarded Children (PARC) v. Pennsylvania, 343 F. Supp. 279, 309–310 (E.D. Pa. 1972) (agreement to cease interpreting analogous Pennsylvania statute, Pa. Stat. Ann. Tit. 24 § 13-1330(2) (Purdon 1962), so as to deny access to a free public education to mentally retarded children).

17. Former N.Y. Educ. Law § 4407, *repealed* by L. 1976, ch. 853 § 2 (authorizing contracts for up to $2,000 in private school tuition for handicapped children).

18. McMillan v. Board of Education, 331 F. Supp. 302 (S.D.N.Y. 1971). Astute legal services attorneys also took advantage of a little-known provision in the Family Court Act, which authorized Family Court judges to provide a "suitable order" for the needs of a handicapped child (Former N.Y. Family Court Act § 232, *repealed* by L. 1976, ch. 853, § 4). They devised a procedure whereby legal services attorneys would obtain orders for "appropriate education" requiring the city, subsequently reimbursed up to 50 percent by the state, to pay tuition costs for the enrollment of these students in non-public schools. *See, e.g.,* Matter of Downey, 72 Misc.2d 772 (N.Y. Fam. Ct. 1973); Matter of Jessup, 85 Misc.2d 575 (N.Y. Fam. Ct. 1975); Matter of Warren A., 53 A.D.2d 400 (2d Dept. 1976); Matter of Kaye, 54 A.D.2d 907 (2d Dept. 1976).

19. Reid v. Board of Education, 453 F.2d 238 (2d Cir. 1971) (challenge by class of brain-injured children to New York City Board's failure to evaluate promptly and to provide special classes for all eligible children); Lora v. Board of Education, 456 F. Supp. 1211 (E.D. N.Y. 1978), *vacated and remanded on other grounds,* 623 F.2d 248 (2d Cir. 1980) (challenge by class of minority students assigned to special day schools for the emotionally handicapped based on both discriminatory placement criteria and inadequacy of facilities, staff, and instructional materials in the special schools).

20. However, school districts were still authorized to contract with private schools where appropriate facilities were not available (N.Y. Educ. Law § 4402 [McKinney 1981]); the full cost of such contracting would be borne by the school district, subject to partial reimbursement by the state (N.Y. Educ. Law §§ 4405, 4407 [McKinney 1981]).

21. 1976 N.Y. Laws ch. 853, *repealing* former N.Y. Educ. Law Art. 89 (current version at N.Y. Educ. Law Art. 84 [McKinney 1981]). This legislative change clearly was induced by passage of the EHA by the federal Congress and in essence provided a specific framework for implementing the federal mandates within the particular New York State educational structure. *See, e.g.,* Governor's Memorandum Approving ch. 853, 1976 N.Y. Laws at 2448–49.

22. *Reid v. Board of Education, supra* note 19. In affirming the district court's abstention holding the Second Circuit Court of Appeals nevertheless held that the federal court should retain jurisdiction pending the determination of the state law claims by the New York courts. 453 F.2d at 240.

23. In the federal action, the *Reid* plaintiffs had purported to represent a class of the "brain-injured."

24. Matter of Riley Reid, Dec. of N.Y.S. Ed. Comm'r No. 8742, 13 Ed. Dept. Rep. 118 (1973); Interim Order of June 30, 1977; No. 9499; 17 Ed. Dept. Rep. 71 (1977); No. 9526; 17 Ed. Dept. Rep. 12 (1977). The initial 1973 order required that all children diagnosed as handicapped be placed "immediately" in appropriate public

or private school classes and that the Board submit "a plan to eliminate waiting lists for diagnosis and placement . . . by February 1, 1974." The June 1977 order found that the chronic evaluation and placement problem had worsened; waiting lists had increased from about 3,000 to over 6,000. The September 1977 decision ordered the Board to place all diagnosed handicapped students within 30 days or bear the expense of placement in an appropriate private school at the option of the parent. In addition, the Board was ordered to submit a new plan to eliminate waiting lists.

25. Letter from Harold Adler, attorney for petitioners to Commissioner Gordon M. Ambach (March 30, 1978).

26. The chancellor was also simultaneously negotiating with the federal authorities. In June 1978, the New York City Board of Education concluded an agreement with the U.S. Department of Health, Education and Welfare, Office for Civil Rights (OCR) which, among other things, committed the Board to place handicapped students in appropriate placements within 90 working days after referral until January 1, 1979, and within 60 working days after January 1, 1979. New York State Department of Education Assistant Commissioner Louis Grumet sent a letter to OCR dated June 22, 1978, in which he expressed "deep concern, dismay" over the agreement. He claimed it was inconsistent with New York state statutory and regulatory requirements that called for placement within 60, rather than 90, working days.

27. Letter from Louis Grumet to Dr. Charles Schonhaut, Acting Executive Director, Division of Special Education and Pupil Personnel Services (December 12, 1978). *See also* letter from Louis Grumet to Charles Schonhaut (November 28, 1978); letter from Chancellor Frank J. Macchiarola to Louis Grumet (December 15, 1978).

28. "The *Reid* [administrative] petition specifically reserved Federal constitutional and statutory claims. . . . [T]he strategy designed in *Reid* in 1973 envisioned the need for *Jose P.*, as it was brought in 1979. [The four Commissioner's Orders] in the absence of compliance [established] a basis for demonstration in Federal Court that every effort to obtain adequate relief from the State had failed, again laying the foundation for *Jose P.*" Letter from Carolyn M. Heft (original attorney for the *Reid* plaintiffs) to John Chipman Gray, Jr. (November 1, 1985).

29. Jose P. v. Ambach, No. 79 Civ. 270, Complaint ¶ 57.

30. Jose P. v. Ambach, Memorandum of Law in Opposition to Motion for Preliminary Judgment of defendant Board of Education, *et al.*, at 2–3. Defendant State Commissioner similarly alleged that he and his predecessors had "acted in every respect in an appropriate manner in exercising that office with respect to the contentions made by plaintiffs, and significant progress has been made, and is being made, in the effort to educate handicapped children in the New York City school district, and there is currently being implemented a fully adequate plan for further improving such performance in a timely manner, which plan should be allowed to be realized." *Jose P. v. Ambach*, Answer of defendant Ambach, Fifth Affirmative Defense.

31. Transcript of April 3, 1979, p. 47.

32. Jose P. v. Ambach, 3 Education of the Handicapped Law Reporter (EHLR) 551:245, 247 (E.D.N.Y. 1979). *Cf.* Hart v. Community School Board, 383 F. Supp. 699 (E.D. N.Y. 1974), *aff'd* 512 F.2d 37 (2d Cir. 1975) (court takes jurisdiction of desegregation case despite ongoing efforts of New York City chancellor to compel

community school boards to provide effective remedy). The court also rejected the state defendants' position on exhaustion of administrative remedies, noting that "at a hearing before this Court on March 6, 1979, counsel for the Commissioner conceded that he would be unable expeditiously to process the appeals of all the members of plaintiffs' class should they pursue administrative proceedings." *Id.* at 247.

33. Jose P. v. Ambach, 3 EHLR 551:245, 247 (E.D.N.Y. 1979).

34. Plaintiffs in this case (United Cerebral Palsy of New York City v. Board of Education, No. 79 Civ. 560 [E.D.N.Y. 1979]), were an organization that both operated educational programs for the physically handicapped and acted as an advocate for the rights of all the physically handicapped, as well as six physically handicapped children, suing individually and on behalf of a class of all physically handicapped students not receiving adequate services from the New York City Board of Education.

35. UCP v. Board of Education, No. 79 Civ. 560 (1979), Prayer for Relief, ¶ 7. For a discussion of the administrative problems presented by the traditional organization of special education activities in New York through "a structure of bureaus within the central administration that possessed unmitigated powers," and the extent to which this structure was in conflict with federal law, *see* Viteritti, *supra* note 15, at 163–66, and Office of the Deputy Chancellor, Educational Policy Analysis Unit, Board of Education of the City of New York, January 1977, p. 8. Many of the *UCP* claims were based on the findings of system-wide structural problems set forth in a "Report on New York City's Education of Handicapped Students: Problems, Issues and Programs" (January 1979) of Assistant State Commissioner Grumet to the Board of Regents.

36. ASPIRA v. Board of Education, No. 72 Civ. 4002 Slip Op. (S.D.N.Y. 1974) (unreported Memorandum and Order); *see also* 58 F.R.D. 62 (S.D.N.Y. 1973).

37. EHLR 551:245, 247 (E.D.N.Y. 1979). In addition to the specific powers of a Special Master set forth in Rule 53 of the Federal Rules of Civil Procedure, the Master was given wide-ranging authority to consult informally with the parties and outside experts, conduct informal working sessions with counsel and members of the public and concerned private agencies, have full access to reports and studies, have full technical assistance required to familiarize himself with the workings of the school system, and engage legal, administrative, and clerical aides as he deemed necessary, subject to the approval of the court.

38. The court issued a separate decision in the *UCP* case on August 13, 1979. That decision rejected defendants' motion to dismiss based on various procedural arguments (private right of action, administrative exhaustion, and standing), but deferred consideration of plaintiffs' motion for class certification. The court specifically noted the relationship between the issues in the *UCP* case and those in *Jose P.* and indicated that the Special Master's report in *Jose P.* would undoubtedly deal with many of the overlapping issues involved in the case. In the course of the working sessions and negotiations with the Special Master, the parties decided to consolidate the proceedings in *Jose P., UCP,* and a third case, Dyrcia S. v. Ambach, No. 79 Civ. 2562 (E.D.N.Y.), which had been brought on behalf of a class of Spanish-speaking handicapped students who claimed inadequate bilingual special educational services. Subsequently, the consolidated cases have been referred to by the caption of the first listed case, Jose P. v. Ambach, a practice that will also be followed in this chapter.

39. The *Dyrcia S.* complaint did allege intentional discrimination, but this was intentional discrimination based on plaintiffs' "national origin" and not their handicapping condition. (*Dyrcia S.* Complaint, ¶¶ 39, 42).

40. "[T]he Board of Education is under both a moral and legal obligation to provide an appropriate public school education for all handicapped children who choose to avail themselves of such services. We will, of course, fulfill this obligation." Affidavit of Irving Anker, Chancellor, October 3, 1977, p. 2, submitted to Commissioner of Education in *Matter of Reid, supra* note 24.

41. Aside from the attorneys for the parties in the three lawsuits, the official list of invitees to the working sessions with the Special Master included the Public Education Association, Advocates for Children, Association for the Help of Retarded Children, the Legal Aid Society Juvenile Rights Division, the United Federation of Teachers, the Handicapped Persons' Legal Support Unit, U.S. Department of Health, Education and Welfare, and two parents of handicapped children who had expressed interest in the proceedings. The notice forms also generally stated in addition, "[I]f anyone knows of others to whom notice should be given, please give such notice directly or advise the undersigned."

42. *See* Special Master's Report No. 1, September 17, 1979.

43. Letter from Harold Adler, attorney for *Jose P.* plaintiffs to Marvin E. Frankel (August 17, 1979).

44. Letter from Michael A. Rebell, Jane R. Stern, and Robert S. Peck to Marvin E. Frankel (August 30, 1979).

45. Special Master Report No. 1, September 17, 1979, p. 4.

46. For a detailed sketch of the contents of the Special Education in Transition Plan, *see* Viteritti, *supra* note 15, at 175–78.

47. The decree is reported at 3 EHLR 551:412 (1980). A parallel decree, containing identical substantive provisions, was separately entered in the *UCP* and *Dyrcia S.* cases on February 27, 1980.

48. Consolidated Judgments, ¶ 16. Interim timelines for conversion to the new system were also established. *Id.* at ¶ 19.

49. *Id.* at ¶ 13.

50. *Id.* at ¶ 12. The judgment also included specific structural innovations suggested by plaintiffs, such as the appointment of a special "placement officer" at each of the 32 local committees on the handicapped to expedite the process. *Id.* at ¶ 27.

51. *Id.* at ¶¶ 38–40. The idea of guaranteeing that at least one building in each district or region would be fully accessible had been suggested by the Board's Department of Buildings as the only feasible way to ensure access at reasonable cost. Plaintiffs accepted this approach as the core commitment, but insisted on a proviso that "all students have full access within a reasonable distance from their homes to all services from which they are capable of benefitting." (*Id.* at ¶ 39.) Additional commitments were obtained concerning relocation of headquarters of the committees on the handicapped, many of which, ironically, were located on the third or fourth floors of buildings without elevators. (*Id.* at ¶ 40.)

52. *Id.* at ¶¶ 41–47.

53. *Id.* at ¶¶ 52–60.

54. *Id.* at ¶¶ 63–69. In regard to both the January Plan and the April Plan, the

basic documents were to be formulated by the defendants, with the plaintiffs retaining a right to raise objections to any of the details of the plans with the Special Master.

55. The Board's uncertainty as to its ability to comply with this judgment was stated at the time of its signing. Although the Board's attorneys had actively participated in the negotiation of the decree, the Board decided after much strategic deliberation not to consent to its contents but instead to indicate to the court that the Board would accept the decree if entered by the court and "would not appeal it." Viteritti, *supra* note 15, at 178. (There was some question as to whether the Board had in fact instructed its attorneys to give even that commitment. *Id.* at 179.) Chancellor Macchiarola stated at the time, "Clearly we have a moral obligation to these children as well as a legal one. But we have a real concern about our capacity to help them according to their needs." *New School Aid for the Disabled Ordered in the City*, N.Y. Times at B12, col. 1 (December 21, 1979). The president of the Board of Education, Stephan R. Aiello, added that compliance with the order would require $350 million over the next three years, "an amount he said the Board could not afford." *Id.* Entry of the decree undoubtedly aided the Board in its negotiations to obtain additional funding from the city. This was probably a factor in the Board's ultimate acquiesence to its signing.

56. 3 EHLR 551:412 ¶ 52. Further specification of these requirements was set forth in paragraphs 53–59 of the judgment. Paragraph 60 also set forth a procedure for plaintiffs, state defendants, and *amici* to serve on other parties and file with the Special Master their comments on the basic January Plan. Any issues in dispute would be submitted to the Special Master and the Court for resolution by the end of February 1980.

57. *Id.* at ¶ 63. In addition, paragraphs 38–40 required that the April Plan also provide detailed assurances on appropriate facilities accessibility for physically handicapped students. Again, plaintiffs, state defendants, and *amici* were specifically accorded a right to file comments on the plan and to bring any issues in dispute before the Special Master and the court for resolution in May 1980 (¶ 69). The April Plan was also to provide timelines to ensure full implementation of the entire program throughout the city no later than April 1981 (¶ 63).

58. The detailed description of a "continuum of services" to be included in the January Plan under the terms of the original judgment was by agreement of the parties further deferred and included in the April Plan.

59. The May 1981 version of the April Plan, by agreement of the parties, contained only a temporary description of the continuum of services. Negotiation of a detailed new continuum of services was not completed until 1985, after the adoption of new state regulations emphasizing the functional grouping of children in special education programs. Important aspects of staffing, instructional supplies, and classroom space are still unresolved at the time of this writing.

60. On the plaintiffs' side, the lawyers included South Brooklyn Legal Services Corp. B, and Community Action for Legal Services, Inc. Handicapped Persons Legal Support Unit, attorneys for the original *Jose P.* plaintiffs, Rebell & Krieger, the private law firm representing the *UCP* plaintiffs, and the Puerto Rican Legal Defense and Education Fund, representing the original *Dyrcia S.* plaintiffs. In addition,

attorneys from two of the major education advocacy organizations in the city, Advocates for Children and Public Education Association, participated regularly as *amicus curiae*. (Advocates for Children later became co-counsel to the *Jose P.* plaintiffs, substituting for the Handicapped Persons Legal Support Unit.) On the defendants' side were the attorneys from the New York City Corporation Counsel's office (the official litigation counsel for the Board of Education), together with separate in-house counsel from the Chancellor's Law Office and the Board of Education and attorneys from the State Education Department.

61. Robert Bergen, Counsel for City Defendants, quoted in Viteritti, *supra* note 15, at 187. An analogous negotiating process undertaken under the direct auspices of Judge Becker, at one stage in the implementation of the *PARC* decree (*supra* note 16) was also reported to be on balance a success although apparently more in regard to procedural rather than "quality education" issues. *See* Rosenberg and Phillips, *The Institutionalization Conflict in the Reform of Schools: A Case Study of Court Implementation of the PARC Decree*, 57 IND. L.J. 425 (1982). *See also* M. REBELL AND A. BLOCK, EDUCATIONAL POLICY MAKING AND THE COURTS 69–70 (1982); Brazil, *Special Masters in Complex Cases: Extending the Judiciary or Reshaping Adjudication*, 53 CHI. L. REV. 394 (1986).

62. These issues were: (1) whether "preventive services" for children in general education should be considered a mandatory aspect of the continuum of services required under the judgment (Special Master Report No. 3, November 10, 1980); (2) whether the regular Board of Examiners' licensing procedures should be bypassed in order to improve the Board's ability to recruit new special education teachers (Special Master Reports Nos. 6, June 3, 1981, and 7, December 14, 1981); and (3) the grounds for excluding particular students from the Board's general obligation to provide mainstreaming opportunities (Special Master Report No. 6, June 3, 1981, discussed *supra*, at pp. 49–50). The Special Master recommended decisions favorable to the plaintiffs on all three issues. (On the licensing point, the Board of Education had joined with the plaintiffs over the objections of the State Education Department defendants.) The court upheld the Special Master's recommendation on the mainstreaming issue, but did not follow his recommendations on preventive services and licensing. *See* Memorandum and Order of January 9, 1981; Memorandum and Order of May 20, 1982. The Special Master's further recommendations, contained in nine other Special Master Reports, concerning a variety of compliance issues were fully approved by the court.

63. *See* Special Master Report No. 4, May 12, 1981. The Special Master was largely sympathetic to plaintiffs on this issue. Following further allegations of noncompliance, he recommended new procedures, based on a prior administrative remedy of the Commissioner of Education, which would permit parents of handicapped students who had not been evaluated and placed within 60 days of referral unilaterally to place their children in appropriate non-public facilities at the Board of Education's expense (Special Master Report No. 8, December 14, 1981; Special Master Report No. 10, March 10, 1982). These recommendations were fully accepted by the court and issued in the form of a formal order on July 2, 1982.

64. Special Master Reports Nos. 5, May 27, 1981, and 9, December 21, 1981. Although agreeing with plaintiffs on the facts of noncompliance on both these occa-

sions, the Special Master denied the relief sought, on the first occasion because the request was made too close to the summer to permit adequate planning, and on the second occasion because of the Special Master's "formidible doubts about the propriety of ordering the City Board to create a summer school program."

65. This plan was submitted in response to the court's order issued pursuant to Special Master Report No. 9. The "less heroic" remedy Judge Frankel had recommended in Special Master Report No. 9, *supra* note 64, and the court had adopted, was for the Board to submit "a particularized program of measures to be taken (and a projected schedule of results) for the elimination of the waiting lists." (*Id.* at 11.)

66. New York Board of Education's Plan to Eliminate Evaluation and Placement Lists, January 21, 1982. In a concluding section of the report entitled "Constraints on Timely Evaluation and Placement," the Board cited as "significant causes of evaluation delays" such factors as student mobility, absenteeism, and "the necessity of accommodating the convenience of students and parents in scheduling conferences and assessment sessions." *Id.* at 12. It also spoke of the difficulties of converting a huge system to the new SBST model.

67. "Objections of Plaintiffs and *Amici* to City Defendants' Plan to Eliminate Waiting Lists and Proposed Order" (February 22, 1982). Plaintiffs' motion for further relief was accompanied by a lengthy memorandum of law that provided documentation of alleged noncompliance in a wide variety of areas including evaluation procedures, mainstreaming, facilities accessibility, instructional supplies, and parental due process rights. Much of this evidence was taken from site visit reports issued the previous year by the State Education Department. The State Education Department issued an even stronger attack on the city's new waiting list plan and asked the court to undertake a detailed management study of the Board's operations and immediately to authorize the state to take over the training of all personnel in the city school district. "Position of the Commissioner of Education with Respect to the School District's Plan to Eliminate Waiting Lists" (February 1982). The state's response also included evidence compiled in an informal "undercover" project the State Education Department (SED) had organized to test the Board's seriousness of purpose in hiring new teachers. The evidence consisted of alleged misleading and evasive responses that SED staff members who had pretended to be applicants calling about teaching jobs had received from Board of Education staff.

68. Joseph Viteritti, a special assistant to Chancellor Macchiarola, indicated that Macchiarola retained strong confidence in Gross and had tried to dissuade him from resigning. However, Gross felt frustrated by the situation and the fact that "the Board was generally unhappy that we had a court case. . . . [T]hey felt they were losing control, that they were not making decisions." Viteritti, *supra* note 15, at 192. Viteritti concluded: "In the end, the question remained as to whether Gross had ever managed effectively to break through the old structure of the bureaucracy with which he had to contend. Gross had a fine reputation as a special educator, and a wealth of experience, but he had never dealt with an organization as large as the one at Livingston Street. The Special Education Division was the most entrenched and difficult part of that bureaucracy, and many believed that Gross and his staff were simply not prepared for it." *Id.* at 193.

69. Upon his resignation on May 11, 1983, Dr. Gartner issued a press release,

which stated, *inter alia*, at p. 3, "The regulations of the State Education Department and the consequences of actions of the plaintiffs in *Jose P. v. Ambach* are such that we are building an increasingly separate and racially segregated system, without need for justice and service, and contrary to sound educational practice."

70. Affidavit of Frank J. Macchiarola, sworn to on March 3, 1982, ¶ 4.

71. *Id.* at ¶ 11.

72. *Id.* at ¶ 12.

73. *Id.* at ¶ 13.

74. *Id.* at ¶¶ 25, 32. *See also* Viteritti, *supra* note 15, at 199.

75. Affidavit of Frank Macchiarola at ¶ 36.

76. *Disabled Pupils Termed Victims of Legal Action*, N.Y. Times, March 4, 1982, B3, col. 2. In ¶¶ 47–48 of his affidavit, Macchiarola also sharply attacked the State Education Department for its lack of cooperation and assistance and, *inter alia*, cited the state's opposition to plaintiffs' and city defendants' joint motion to add provisions to the judgment to create a contingency licensing plan (¶ 48). He also cited the court findings in Board of Education, Levittown Union Free School District v. Nyquist, 94 Misc.2d 466 (Sup. Ct. Nassau Co. 1978), *aff'd* 83 A.D.2d 21 (2d Dept. 1981), *rev'd* 57 N.Y.2d 27 (1982) to show the unfair burden state educational finance laws and practices had placed on the New York City school system (¶ 45).

77. Special Master Report No. 11, August 27, 1982. Plaintiffs' original request for 225 additional teams had been increased in the course of the hearings to 325, based largely on testimony of State Education Department officials that such a number was required. The Special Master's decision recommending 150 was expressed as follows: "The total of 325 that plaintiffs urge may well be excessive. Without a certain sense that the number is 'correct,' the recommendation is that defendants be ordered to employ, by not later than November 15, 1982, the personnel necessary for the creation of 150 more teams."

78. Special Master Report No. 12, September 7, 1982. Although finding that plaintiffs had proven that the defendants had organized their procedures "so that substantial numbers of children will, as a matter of sure prediction, remain unplaced beyond the time limits prescribed by the judgments" (*id.* at 5), Judge Frankel declined to adopt plaintiffs' call for an order setting forth specific mandatory standards and practices. He said instead, in language that partially seemed directed to Chancellor Macchiarola's affidavit (*see supra*, p. 39), "The time has come, it is now believed, for defendants either to comply with the judgments or to confront the familiar consequences of noncompliance. Unless or until a receiver comes to take over the Division of Special Education, defendants invoke sound principles when they argue that they, rather than the Court, should be determining the administrative techniques, estimates, and procedures for complying with their obligations. Demanding respect for their expertise, defendants ought to get it. Promising compliance, they ought to achieve it or face contempt charges. It will be recommended therefore, that the Court draw stark lines." *Id.* at 5–6.

79. Memorandum in Support of City Defendants' Motion to Vacate or Modify Judgment, October 5, 1982; Affidavit of Alan G. Gartner, October 1, 1982; Affidavit of Richard Halverson, Deputy Chancellor, September 29, 1982. The Board's legal position was based primarily on the Supreme Court decisions in Board of Education

v. Rowley, 458 U.S. 176 (1982) and Southeastern Community College v. Davis, 442 U.S. 397 (1979).

80. Plaintiffs' Memorandum of Law in Opposition to City Defendants' Motion to Vacate or Modify the Judgment, November 30, 1982; Affidavit of John C. Gray, Jr., November 29, 1982; Affidavit of Michael A. Rebell, December 9, 1982. Plaintiffs argued that *Rowley* did not speak to the broad issues of the role of the courts in institutional reform litigations, and also stressed that the Supreme Court's decision in *Davis* had been issued prior to issuance of the original liability decision and judgment in *Jose P.*

81. Jose P. v. Ambach, 557 F. Supp. 1230 (E.D.N.Y. 1983).

82. *Id.* at 1234. Judge Nickerson also noted, "[T]he Court does not agree with City Defendants that under the *Rowley* case, the Education for Handicapped Act creates substantive rights only to 'access' and not 'quality.' On the other hand, it is clear, and the *Rowley* case illustrates, that 'quality' or 'programmatic' issues are less yielding to judicial determination." *Id.* at 1243.

83. *Id.* at 1237.

84. *Id.* at 1240.

85. *Id.* at 1242.

86. *Id.* at 1243.

87. Magistrate Caden made it clear that he would proceed in accordance with traditional judicial processes. That meant that, in contrast to Judge Frankel's quick-moving negotiating process, hearings before the new Special Master would require lengthy evidentiary showings on each point in contention and extensive adversary briefing on all proposed remedies. The parties agreed that this cumbersome process should be avoided if at all possible.

88. Sermier had served for the previous two years as Budget Director of the Board of Education.

89. Stipulation of June 8, 1983, ¶¶ 11, 26. The 600 clinical professionals would staff approximately 200 SBST teams, 50 more than the number that had been recommended by Judge Frankel after the hotly contested hearings on this issue the previous year.

90. *Id.* at ¶¶ 15–22. Defendants also agreed to hire a data consultant of plaintiffs' choosing, at their expense. *Id.* at ¶ 19. Plaintiffs had requested appointment of such a data consultant from Judge Nickerson but the Court had specifically declined to provide this form of specific relief. *See* Jose P. v. Ambach, 557 F. Supp. at 1242, discussed in the preceding chapter.

91. *Id.* at ¶¶ 2–10.

92. *Id.* at ¶ 23.

93. *Id.* at ¶ 28.

94. *Id.* at ¶ 16.

95. *Id.* at ¶ 40. As part of the stipulation, the city defendants also agreed that plaintiffs might designate an educational policy consultant who would meet on a regular basis with Board of Education personnel on issues such as continuum development, specialized equipment, and mainstreaming. The consultant's salary and expenses would be paid by the city defendants.

96. The State Education Department (SED) did not participate in these ses-

sions. It adopted a hands-off attitude to the litigation at this stage and specifically declined invitations to participate in drafting the 1983–1984 stipulations or to participate in the negotiations at the Thursday sessions. The Board of Education did, however, keep SED representatives apprised of developments and obtained their approval for aspects of the agreements that impacted on state law or regulations.

97. Stipulation of June 14, 1984.

98. Order of August 24, 1987.

99. Report and Recommendation, March 4, 1988, p. 65.

100. Stipulation of July 28, 1988, entered as an Order of the Court on August 3, 1988.

101. New York City Public Schools, Division of Special Education "Report on Growth in the Division of Special Education: 1978–81."

102. COMMISSION ON SPECIAL EDUCATION, SPECIAL EDUCATION: A CALL FOR QUALITY, table 4 (1985) (hereinafter Mayor's Commission Report). The current figure represents about 12 percent of all New York City public school children, a proportion that is equivalent to the general national pattern. This rapid rise in the registers may, in fact, be too "successful." There is growing perception in New York City that many children who do not have true handicapping conditions but need some extra support services are being referred only because the regular education system has been stripped of support personnel since the 1976 budget crisis. Consistent with this view is the paucity of movement of children back to regular education: In 1982 and 1984, only 1.5 percent and 2 percent of the special education population were "decertified." (Id., appendix, table 15.) The "one-team per school model" set forth in the August 1988 stipulation is to provide "preventive," as well as evaluative and related services in response to this problem.

103. Office of Management and Budget of the City of New York, Special Education Budget, Fiscal Year 1978 to Fiscal Year 1985; Office of Management and Budget, Executive Budget, Fiscal Year 1986.

104. Figures cited are taken from the official "Jose P. Periodic Reports" filed monthly with the plaintiffs and the court. Waiting list information for specific related services was not included in the regular monthly reports prior to 1983. The 1982 related services figures are taken from an affidavit submitted by Dr. Alan Gartner, November 30, 1982, Exhibit B.

105. Applicable federal and state regulations (34 C.F.R. § 300.534[b] [1984], 8 NYCRR § 200.4[f] [1962 Supp. 1984]) require that students who are placed in special education programs undergo a comprehensive battery of evaluation tests at least every three years to determine whether they are still in need of such services, and the propriety of their present placement. The Board's failure to comply with this requirement was a major issue in the early years of the Jose P. case.

106. Triennial Management Report, 1983–1984, November 1, 1984.

107. As indicated above, plaintiffs returned to court asking for more evaluation staff and other remedies to rectify the growing evaluation waiting list problem.

108. April Plan, May 27, 1981, Supplement III, p. 61. "Teacher" for these purposes includes not only regular classroom teachers, but also those assigned for "crisis and coverage" purposes, teacher trainers, and attendance teachers (formerly known as truant officers).

109. *Id.*

110. *Id.* at 22.

111. Verification from official Board of Education records set forth in a letter from Stephen Hittman, Director, Office of Related and Contractual Services, to Michael A. Rebell (July 22, 1985).

112. The Board obtained an emergency class size variance from the State Education Department in the fall of 1980. It permitted increases in many class categories from ten to 15, or from 15 to 18 students; in some cases these increases were conditioned upon the hiring of an additional paraprofessional in the classroom. Waivers were also granted concerning certain teacher certification requirements. *See* letter from Robert R. Spillane, Deputy Commissioner, State Education Department, to Richard Halverson, Deputy Chancellor, New York City Board of Education (October 17, 1980). Plaintiffs objected to these variances and especially to the defendants' failure to notify them and the court of the fact that such variances had been requested. *See* April Plan, p. 23.

113. Under New York State law, teachers in the city of New York, in addition to being certified by the state, must be licensed on the basis of a thorough examination of their "merit and fitness" by a special testing agency, independent of the Board of Education, known as the Board of Examiners. N.Y. EDUC. LAW §§ 2573, 2569 (McKinney 1981). These special requirements do not apply to most other school districts in the state. The examination procedures are perceived to be cumbersome and dilatory and problems of adverse impact on minorities and the tests' validity under the Uniform Guidelines on Employee Selection Procedures (20 C.F.R. Part 1607 [1978]) have repeatedly been raised. Consequently, the Board of Examiners' procedures are generally considered to be a serious impediment to teacher recruitment. For a general discussion of the role of the Board of Examiners, *see* P. TRACTENBERG, TESTING THE TEACHER (1973); M. REBELL AND A. BLOCK, EDUCATIONAL POLICY MAKING AND THE COURTS, ch. 6 (1982).

114. Surprisingly, funding did not emerge as a major factor. The Board at all times represented that it had commitments from the relevant city authorities to provide sufficient funds to cover all necessary positions. Moreover, during the 1980–1981 school year, the Special Education Division actually ran a surplus of $5.6 million and in 1981–1982 it ran a surplus of approximately $7.6 million. (Memorandum from Noel Ferris, Assistant Corporation Counsel to Special Master, *et al.* [July 13, 1982]).

115. April Plan, pp. 23–30 and April Plan Appendix, pp. A.99–A.105.

116. Objections of Plaintiffs and *Amici* to City Defendants' Second Revised April Plan, p. 41 (January 13, 1981). The hiring halls were clearly anything but an individualized recruitment process. The total number of individuals invited to the hiring halls held between August 24, and 28, and September 2, and 9, 1981, was 5,671. (Memorandum from Noel Ferris, Assistant Corporation Counsel to Special Master, *et al.* [July 23, 1983]).

117. "After endless discussion, plaintiffs and *amici* know as well as city defendants the impediments to making firm job offers by the New York City Board of Education." Reply to Objections of Plaintiffs and *Amici* to City Defendants' April Plan (January 7, 1981), p. 24 (January 19, 1981).

118. *City Is Seeking More Teachers of Handicapped*, N.Y. Times, Sept. 1, 1983, at B3, col. 6.

119. Memorandum to Assistant Superintendents, *et al.* from Harold Coopchik (April 17, 1984).

120. "Official Vacancy Report," September 5, 1984. These figures did not include vacancies in high schools (the first official division of high school vacancy report for the 1984–1985 school year showed 39 high school vacancies as of October 4, 1984) nor vacancies for clinical staff (which included 12 psychologists, one social worker and 31 educational evaluators as of October 18, 1984). A disproportionate number of the remaining vacancies were in the Bronx in areas that were apparently considered unattractive by potential new teachers.

121. *See* Resolution of Board of Education on "Establishment of the 'Special Educator-in-Training' Program," June 5, 1985.

122. The program actually resulted in approximately 100 specially qualified teachers' being assigned to the hard-to-staff schools in the fall of 1985, although paper processing and testing problems with the Board of Examiners delayed the assignment data for many of these new teachers well past the critical school opening weeks. The program was continued in subsequent years with a shift in emphasis to bilingual teachers, for whom there continues to be an acute shortage. Plaintiffs also continued to press for substantial modification of the Board of Examiners licensing system. The delays and complexities involved in the licensing process mean that substantial numbers of special education teachers (approximately 25 percent of the staff in the 1983–1984 school year) are not fully licensed and teach on "temporary per diem certificates." This system had obvious deleterious implications, both in terms of the system's ability to recruit staff and in assuring high levels of competence. *See* letter from Michael A. Rebell to Sherrie Brown (February 9, 1984). For a discussion of the court's rejection of plaintiffs' and city defendants' joint attempt to modify the Board of Examiners procedures, *see supra* note 62.

123. Paragraph 13b of the original judgment had set forth a contracting out mechanism that would require the Board to enter into requirements contracts with independent agencies to conduct evaluations if waiting lists were not promptly eliminated. As the waiting lists continued to mount through 1980 and 1981, plaintiffs pressed the Board to implement the contracting out plan in regard to both the evaluations and the provision of related services. Although the Board conducted some limited contracting out experiments during this period, plaintiffs complained of inordinate delay and lack of seriousness of purpose in implementing the contracting out scheme. Plaintiffs' Statement of Objections to Defendants' April Plan (1st Part), pp. 20–23 (June 2, 1980).

124. Stipulation of June 8, 1983, ¶ 29.

125. Amended resolution of the Board of Education, entitled "Amendment of Resolutions Authorizing the Chancellor to Enter into Agreements with Certain Hospitals, Clinics and/or Educational Institutions for Assessments, Counseling and Related Services to Be Provided Children Suspected and/or Certified as Having a Handicapping Condition," adopted November 16, 1983.

126. Letter of Stephan Hittman to Michael Rebell, *supra* note 111.

127. *See* discussion *supra* at page 44. Remaining problems in this area related

to information gaps concerning which students needed the services and occasional instances of contractor inability to provide services promptly.

128. These procedures were an extension of the concept of unilateral parental enrollment in private school for students for whom no placements were made available by the Board of Education. *See* discussion *supra* note 63. *See also* Zvi D. v. Ambach, 694 F.2d 904 (2d Cir. 1982); School Commission of Burlington v. Massachusetts Department of Education, 105 S. Ct. 1996 (1985).

129. As of May 1987, six students were reported to be receiving occupational therapy services through RSA vouchers, 30 physical therapy, seven health therapy and 11 speech therapy. At various times, generally because of gaps in contractor services, several hundred letters of eligibility to obtain services through the RSA mechanisms have been sent to students in need of counseling or speech services, but few of these vouchers have actually been utilized.

130. Magistrate Report and Recommendation of March 4, 1988, p. 24.

131. Stipulation of July 28, 1988, ¶¶ 17–21. Magistrate Caden had suggested that the parties continue good faith negotiations on a loan forgiveness plan, but had not recommended an order for a specific allocation.

132. *See* 20 U.S.C. §§ 1412(5)(B), 1414(a)(1)(C)(iv) (1982); 34 CFR §§ 300.346(c), 300.55. *See also,* 34 CFR §§ 84.34, 84.37. For an analysis of the legislative history and policy considerations behind mainstreaming, *see* Turnbull *et al., A Policy Analysis of "Least Restrictive" Education of Handicapped Children,* 14 RUTGERS L.J. 489 (1983). For a comprehensive summary of the literature on mainstreaming, as well as the state of the art in a number of school systems around the country, *see* P. HEPNER AND P. CRULL, MAINSTREAMING IN NEW YORK: CHILDREN CAUGHT IN THE CURRENTS: A REPORT OF THE PUBLIC EDUCATION ASSOCIATION (1984). The authors of the latter document conclude, "The progress toward integration appears slow in part because the legal analysis has pushed the LRE mandate to its logical extent before educational programs to facilitate mainstreaming could be widely disseminated." *Id.* at 10.

133. According to the Sixth Annual Report to Congress on Implementation of P.L. 94–142, U.S. Department of Education, quoted in the Mayor's Commission Report, appendix, table 13, New York state had 57 percent of its disabled population in restrictive self-contained class and separate school programs and 43 percent in "mainstreamed resource room programs," as against a national average of 70 percent in the more mainstreamed environment. Prior to entry of the *Jose P.* decree in 1979, virtually all of New York City's special education population had been in self-contained classroom programs.

134. Specifically, ¶ 55(m) of the judgment required the Board of Education to develop, in the January Plan, procedures for implementing the new continuum of services in each particular school "including mainstreaming opportunities for students in self-contained programs"; paragraph 57(e), which sets forth the basic requirement for the development of a continuum of programs and services to provide the "least restrictive environment," also specified that every self-contained class program must include "appropriate interactions with non-handicapped students."

135. Plaintiffs' Statement of Objections to Defendants' April Plan (1st and 2nd Parts), pp. 16–17 (October 7, 1980).

136. City Defendants' April Plan, draft, March 9, 1981, p. 47.

137. "Objections of Plaintiffs and *Amici* to City Defendants' Second Revised April Plan," p. 30 (January 13, 1981).

138. Special Master Report No. 6, p. 3 (June 3, 1981).

139. *Id.* at 5.

140. Memorandum and Order of September, 1981, p. 3. Following the court's order, a formal regulation of the chancellor was issued informing all principals and other personnel of these new requirements. Regulation B-450, March 9, 1982. It was accompanied by a detailed "Handbook on Mainstreaming: Non-Academic Activities" (February 1982), which described factors promoting successful mainstreaming. It included specific examples on how to promote the integration of handicapped and non-handicapped children in a variety of special events, activities, and lunchroom settings.

141. SED High School Site Visit Report, 1980–1981, p. 15.

142. Memorandum to Alan Gartner from Edith B. Wolff re: Report on Mainstreaming, October 15, 1981, p. 6.

143. Judge Nickerson frankly acknowledged that mainstreaming was one of the issues in the case that did not appear capable of resolution through traditional judicial processes, and he omitted it from the list of eight specific issues set down for prompt contempt hearings. Instead, he specifically abjured the parties to find a negotiated solution to this problem. 557 F. Supp. at 1243.

144. The Board's seriousness of purpose in completing this document was also aided by the fact that a major change in applicable state regulations (8 N.Y.C.R.R. § 200.6 [1984]) required the Board to develop a revised continuum of services to meet new functional grouping mandates.

145. Plaintiffs' Response to Continuum Document of March 1, 1984, p. 3 (March 25, 1984).

146. "Some Recommendations Designed to Facilitate the Mainstreaming of Handicapped Pupils," prepared by Dr. Shirley Cohen, plaintiffs' educational consultant (January 23, 1984).

147. Special Circular No. 1, 1987–1988 (July 22, 1987). Mainstreaming in New York City is, as noted above, directly affected by the decentralized structure of the New York City school system. Prompt adoption of the Mastruzzi Committee's mainstreaming plan actually resulted from the settlement of a state court lawsuit concerning the decentralization of special education instruction services in which several of the *Jose P.* plaintiffs and their attorneys participated as petitioners. The lack of an effective mainstreaming plan in the Board's December 1986 decentralization resolution had been one of the precipitating causes of the state court litigation. *See* Coalition Against Immediate Decentralization of Special Education v. Board of Education (N.Y. Sup. Ct. Index No. 10168/87).

Under the stipulation of settlement signed by the parties on July 9, 1987, special education instructional services for elementary and junior high schools were placed under the operative jurisdiction of 32 community school boards, subject to an extensive central monitoring operation, of which Dr. Mastruzzi was appointed the head. Evaluation and placement activities are still run centrally, although pilot projects are in effect in nine of the community districts to explore the feasibility of extending decentralization to these areas). Some progress toward implementation of academic mainstreaming had already taken effect in September, 1985, when the new continuum of services was "phased in" to the city system. As part of the new continuum, many physically handicapped students with normal or above average intellectual functioning, who previously had been educated in self-contained programs, were now mainstreamed into regular classrooms with appropriate services.

148. In August 1988, plaintiffs in the state court case returned to court seeking an order mandating $15 million full funding for the mainstreaming plan. The Board responded by stating that its $4 million allocation was sufficient. In a decision issued in October, Justice Beatrice Shainswit held that since the school year had already commenced, the petition would be dismissed "without prejudice" to plaintiffs' right to seek a trial later in the year to put the Board "to the test as to whether its word [that the mainstreaming plan could be fully implemented for $4 million] is borne out by its actions." Decision of October 8, 1988, p. 4 (N.Y. Sup. Ct. Index No. 14832/88).

CHAPTER 3

Allen v. McDonough: Special Education Reform in Boston

MICHAEL A. REBELL

WHEN THE COMPLAINT in *Allen v. McDonough* was filed in 1976, the city of Boston was in the throes of the implementation phase of *Morgan v. Hennigan*,[1] one of the most confrontational school desegregation cases in modern American history. Two years before, U.S. District Judge W. Arthur Garrity had ruled that the Boston School Committee had intentionally carried out a systematic program of school segregation. Accordingly, beginning with the 1974–1975 school year, Boston's schools were subject to desegregation orders involving mandatory busing, which met open resistance from school committee members and parents and resulted in ongoing racial violence, arrests, and school suspensions.[2]

The fact that the *Allen* case was initiated at the height of Boston's desegregation battles clearly affected the nature of the special education litigation. Unlike New York, where from the time of its filing *Jose P.* was the main educational policy case before the courts, in Boston the federal desegregation case occupied center stage; consequently, the special education litigation had to be played out in the wings. Massive restructuring of the Boston education system took place in the late 1970s, but most of it was being shaped by the desegregation decree, rather than by special education mandates.

This basic reality had major implications for developments in *Allen.* On the negative side were problems created by the system's preoccupation with implementation of the desegregation decree: It consumed resources, energy, and attention that might otherwise have been devoted to the needs of handicapped children. The daily threat of violence in the schools was the overwhelming concern of school administrators.[3] Reassignment of special education teachers pursuant to the court-ordered desegregation mandates caused delays in the delivery of special education services.[4] The fiscal constraints placed upon the system by desegregation needs led, at times, to the lay-off or reassignment of experienced special education staff, and mandated minority hiring goals exacerbated difficulties in recruiting special education staff in shortage areas.

On the other hand, the school system's experiences with the desegregation order also had certain benefits for the special education case. For example, mainstreaming, one of the major areas of judicial concern in the New York City special education case, never became a significant issue in *Allen*. Judge Garrity, having been made aware of the newly promulgated mainstreaming requirements for special needs students, included specific mainstreaming guidelines in his final desegregation order.[5]

The desegregation litigation also affected the Boston School Committee's reaction to the filing of the *Allen* complaint. In contrast to its posture in vigorously contesting every step of the *Morgan* proceedings, the School Committee in *Allen* acknowledged its responsibilities to implement the law and quickly negotiated a consent agreement with the plaintiffs. The Committee's conciliatory stance in *Allen* was undoubtedly influenced by the continuing focus of its energy and resources on the desegregation problems and its desire to avoid providing another judge with an opportunity to impose an unpalatable remedy on them.[6]

In addition to desegregation factors, special education reform in Boston also was affected by the highly politicized school committee system, which had been described three decades earlier by a state watchdog committee in terms that remained germane:

> "Politics" has dealt a paralyzing blow to progress in Boston schools. Politics is given as the cause of relatively incompetent persons holding responsible positions, of decisions being made that are contrary to educators' best judgment. . . . The result is deadly to honest thinking, professional initiative, courageous leadership, and progress in all portions of the school system.[7]

This climate created numerous problems on the day-to-day operational level. For example, the student assignment process in the desegregation case and the student evaluation process in the special education case were both frustrated by the lack of accurate and up-to-date student records and reliable data management systems.[8] Moreover, administrative authority was seriously fragmented, as indicated by the fact that between 1972 and 1981, there were five superintendents and two acting superintendents,[9] and the majority of schools lacked permanent or full-time principals.[10]

THE LIABILITY PHASE

If Boston's dogged resistance to the desegregation decree can be said to reflect the parochial, conservative side of its municipal soul, its response to the needs of the handicapped might, on the other hand, be said to reflect its cosmopolitan, liberal dimension. Boston historically has been a prime world center for education, medicine, and the allied health professions. Schools, hospitals, and treatment centers for all types of handicapping conditions had their origins here. Consistent with this enlightened tradition, in July 1972, Massachusetts enacted the nation's first comprehensive special education statute, known as Chapter 766.[11] The Act predated the federal Education of All Handicapped Children's Act and was considered landmark legislation upon which both the federal statute and other state Acts came to be modeled.[12]

Chapter 766 mandated fundamental reform in the delivery of special education services. It was passed in response to a widespread concern about abuses, omissions and stigmatization under prior programs. Its goal is to "develop the educational potential of children with special needs."[13] It seeks to do this by defining special needs and designing special programs in a flexible manner that considers each child's individual needs and potential[14] while minimizing categorical labeling.[15]

Chapter 766 became effective on September 1, 1974, after a two-year preparation period. At that time, parents and professionals concerned about special education founded the Boston 766 Monitoring Project.[16] Their goal was to identify systemic areas of noncompliance with the law and to bring these areas to the attention of officials at all levels who were responsible for Chapter 766 implementation. In March 1975 the Project issued *The Mandate and the Reality*,[17] a report on special education in Boston, which concluded that the city's progress toward implementation had been slow and faltering at best.

The report described and documented numerous instances of noncompliance. Five general areas were of major significance:

1. Half of the "special needs children" in Boston were totally unidentified, and therefore unserved.
2. The administration of special education services was still structured categorically.
3. Boston had hired many unqualified personnel to fill special education positions created by the law.
4. The system had failed to take rudimentary administrative steps, such as providing in-service training and establishing role descriptions for special education personnel.
5. Special needs children were assigned to quarters considered unfit for ordinary students.

During the year following the publication of *The Mandate and the Reality*, the Boston 766 Monitoring Project increased its advocacy efforts. The group sought greater representation of parents of "special needs children" in the citizens' groups that were involved in implementing the desegregation order in *Morgan*. They also requested from Marion Fahey, then Superintendent of

Schools, information on the number of children awaiting legally mandated evaluations and services, as well as permission to observe the provision of Chapter 766 services in the Boston schools.[18]

The data gathered from this monitoring effort showed that little or no progress had been made during the first half of the 1975–1976 school year on the major issues cited in the Project's report. One of the attorneys from the Massachusetts Advocacy Center initiated a series of meetings with Boston's Associate Superintendent for Special Services in an attempt to press progress toward compliance. By this time, the Center was also considering litigation. In the spring of 1976, the Center determined that continued negotiations were unlikely to bring about substantial progress, and the decision was made to go to court.[19]

The strategy chosen by the Center was to litigate narrow issues on which it would be relatively easy to prevail, allowing the focus of the lawsuit to move quickly to the remedy stage. Even a narrow lawsuit, they reasoned, could be used as a means to bring about broader changes. This might be accomplished either directly by expanding the scope of the suit at a later stage or by establishing a favorable negotiating position that would give plaintiffs clout to press for broader relief, or indirectly by providing information that could be used in future publicity and advocacy efforts.[20]

Two narrowly focused "waiting list issues" were chosen as the immediate noncompliance matters to be litigated: A significant number of children were not being provided with educational plans within the statutorily mandated time period,[21] and large numbers of children already in special education programs were not being given the periodic reviews required by the law.[22] These violations of Chapter 766 were easy to define and easy to prove; the school district's own data showed that hundreds of children had failed to receive educational plans and reviews in a timely manner.

The choice of issues to be litigated also logically led to the choice of the forum in which to file the lawsuit. Since the plaintiffs' claims would be based entirely on state law (most of the provisions of the federal law had not yet become effective), the case would be filed in the state court and not in Judge Garrity's federal court.[23]

Accordingly, *Allen v. McDonough* was filed on June 10, 1976, in the Superior Court, Suffolk County. It was denominated a class action on behalf of two groups of school age children in Boston: those who had waited more than 30 days for completed educational plans and those who had waited over ten months for their periodic reviews.[24] The plaintiffs alleged that there were approximately 1,400 children in the first category and approximately 7,250 children in the second. They asked the court to issue a preliminary injunction requiring the defendants to provide the required educational plans and reviews to all members of the plaintiff class within 30 days and, after a full hearing, issue a permanent injunction requiring the defendants to continue to provide timely educational plans and reviews to all Boston special needs children.

THE REMEDIAL PHASE: CRAFTING THE INITIAL CONSENT DECREE

The period immediately following the filing of the complaint was one of optimism on the part of all concerned about Boston's ability and readiness to comply with the Chapter 766 provisions at issue. The School Committee responded positively to the plaintiffs' concerns, and immediately joined in intensive settlement negotiations. Their counsel stated that the filing of the suit had the salutory effect of moving the attention of the superintendent, the School Committee, and the mayor away from their institutional preoccupation with the desegregation case.[25] It was a necessary catalyst that raised the issue to a level higher than that of the assistant superintendent; that is, to a level where major policy decisions could be made. Although they expected less resistance than had been exhibited in the desegregation litigation, plaintiffs' attorneys nevertheless were amazed at the speed with which the defendants responded to their demands.[26] On June 23, 1976, only 13 days after the complaint was filed, the parties submitted a proposed consent decree to the court.

This consent decree provided plaintiffs immediate preliminary relief. The parties stipulated that there were approximately 750 children waiting more than 30 days for educational plans and approximately 963 children waiting for periodic reviews. The defendants agreed to provide educational plans and reviews for each of the named plaintiffs within ten days and for the rest of the identified children within 45 days. They also agreed to provide the plaintiffs with specific information on the status of these plans and reviews during the 45-day period. The defendants' financial obligation for enforcement of the decree was specifically limited to $600,000.[27]

Recognizing that only preliminary issues had been addressed, the decree provided that a supplemental consent decree would be filed by mid-August to ensure the full protection of the plaintiffs' statutory right to educational plans and reviews. The parties hoped to use the summer months to clear the backlog of overdue plans and reviews and to undertake the planning necessary to allow the system to be in a position to provide educational plans and reviews in a timely manner by the start of the school year in September.

The ease and rapidity of the first stage of the litigation was not, however, to be repeated in subsequent rounds. First, procedural complications arose. Two interested parties not named in the original complaint now sought permission to participate in the litigation. The Boston Teachers Union (BTU), concerned about the effect the court's judgments might have on their collective bargaining agreement, moved to intervene as a party defendant.[28] The state Department of Education (DOE) also sought official party status on the plaintiffs' side.

The DOE's primary interest was to ensure that sufficient consideration was given to the state's interpretations of Chapter 766 in any remedial mechanisms.[29] Plaintiffs, however, were not pleased with the prospect of having to share their legal initiatives with this would-be ally. Since the DOE is charged with ensuring compliance by school districts with Chapter 766 and its regulations, they considered the DOE partially responsible for Boston's failures and therefore logically more a defendant than a plaintiff.[30] However, since the plaintiffs here—unlike the plaintiffs in *Jose P.*— had failed to name the DOE in their list of defendants, the court accepted their advocacy claims and granted the motions of both the DOE and the BTU to become full parties.

As the summer wore on, the need to gather additional data also bogged down the negotiations. The School Committee employed a management analyst to determine the number of staff needed to complete Chapter 766 plans and reviews during the 1976–1977 school year. As his figures were being considered, the parties agreed to delay the filing of the supplemental consent decree for a month.

The document that was subsequently filed on September 14, 1976, essentially comprised an agreement by the defendants to comply with the law and the prior consent decree. The School Committee committed itself to provide educational plans and reviews within the time periods mandated by Chapter 766, and to adopt procedures to ensure compliance with other mandates of the law, and to process within a month the cases that had been backlogged on June 23. The defendants also committed themselves to file a detailed plan for compliance by September 30, 1976, and to report specific information to the plaintiffs on a weekly basis that would enable them to monitor the defendants' progress toward compliance.

THE REMEDIAL PHASE: BROADENING THE SCOPE OF REFORM

This Supplemental Consent decree clearly illustrated the limitations of plaintiffs' quick liability strategy. The document closely tracked the narrow issues that had been pleaded in the complaint: It required the defendants, on pain of contempt, to provide educational plans and reviews within mandated timelines. However, once the evaluations were done and the special services needed by each child were thereby identified, it was unlikely that the defendants would have available the teachers and other resources necessary to provide these services.[31] The critical issues of structural reform necessary to meet this obvious reality had not been explicitly addressed.

On the other hand, the supplemental decree could be said to have opened up a number of avenues beyond the confines of the initial pleadings, which would inevitably lead to broadened court involvement and ultimate structural reform. Most notable in this regard was the commitment to provide by September 30, 1976, "a description and timetable for the administrative reorganization of the Department of Special Services."[32] This commitment harkened back to one of the structural reform emphases of *The Mandate and the Reality*. Despite their failure to include specifically the issue in the *Allen* complaint, plaintiffs had pressed the school district during the summer negotiations to reform their categorical departmental structure. The inclusion of the timetable commitment in the supplemental decree gave plaintiffs a legal basis to complain to the court of defendants' delays in implementing their promised reorganization plan and thus to incorporate administrative reorganization within the ambit of the *Allen* court's jurisdiction.[33] Similarly, inclusion in the supplemental decree of requirements for descriptions and timetables concerning referral and evaluation procedures,[34] and in-service training of teachers,[35] as well as statements of "present and projected capabilities of the defendants to provide assessments, core evaluations, and 'reviews,'"[36] and "to provide 'educational plans' and 'reviews' to non-English speaking children,"[37] broadened the case well beyond the limited stated parameters of the complaint. The detailed reporting requirements of the supplemental decree also implied the need for a sophisticated data management system.[38]

Defendants realized that the supplemental decree constituted an expansion of the issues in the case. They nevertheless accepted the broadened new directions "because of their commitment to full implementation"[39]— and apparently because they did not anticipate that such implementation would be as long and hard in coming as actually proved to be the case.[40]

A Finding of Contempt, Notwithstanding Good Faith

The initial "honeymoon" period of the *Allen* litigation was short-lived. The defendants did not meet the September 30, 1976, deadline for filing their detailed administrative reorganization plans and timetables, and in mid-October the plaintiffs filed a motion to compel compliance. Superintendent Fahey had, in fact, nominated candidates for four positions, which comprised approximately half the reorganization, but the School Committee failed to vote on any of them.[41] Plaintiffs responded decisively to this foot-dragging. They quickly filed another motion to find the individual members of the School Committee and the superintendent in contempt.

Plaintiffs' request for relief asked for the immediate submission of the overdue plans and timetables. In addition, it asked for concrete steps such as the hiring of additional psychologists, the contracting out of core evaluation services, and the expansion of educational programming capacity "so that all children . . . shall, upon the approval of the 'educational plan' by their parent or guardian, be placed immediately in such programs and receive all special education services required for the implementation of their 'educational plans.' " [42] Thus, the general commitment in the supplemental consent decree to provide plans and timetables now became a basis for plaintiffs to seek extensive, court-ordered structural reforms.

The contempt motion was heard by Justice Thomas R. Morse, Jr. Justice Morse had been sitting in the motion part when the original Consent Decree was submitted the prior June. Although superior court cases generally are not assigned for all purposes to a single judge, he had kept the case as a special assignment. After Justice Morse approved the final form of the Consent Decree and the Supplemental Consent Decree, he had assumed the matter had been disposed of. He was somewhat surprised, however, to find the parties back before him so soon in a contempt mode.[43] Rather than rule immediately on plaintiffs' motion, Justice Morse decided to meet informally with the parties in an attempt to secure compliance. Accordingly, for the next few months the parties met with the judge on a weekly or bi-weekly basis.

Despite his active role in the negotiating process, Justice Morse was not successful at this point in securing compliance through negotiation. Although he got the parties to agree on further timelines in regard to the placement of children after completion of their education plans and reviews,[44] plaintiffs filed a further motion to find the defendants in contempt of court. A five-day trial on the contempt motion ensued.

In mid-April, Justice Morse issued his decision: "I am obliged to conclude that civil contempt on the part of the defendants has been established." [45] This conclusion was supported by 25 pages of detailed findings. The judge began by specifying the number of children awaiting educational plans and reviews.[46] Consistent with the expanded emphasis on the placement process contained in his Implementing Order, he also set forth figures on waiting lists for specific programs and for related services such as speech therapy, physical therapy, and counseling.[47] In addition, the decision criticized the planning and managerial operations of the school system and specifically its failure to hire personnel needed to carry out mandated functions.

At the same time that he listed dozens of specific findings of noncompliance, however, Justice Morse also took pains to describe the efforts that the defendants had made to comply with the consent decrees and court orders. Thus, for example, in determining that only 32 of 38 budgeted speech therapist slots had been filled, he noted that this shortfall was "notwithstanding good faith efforts." [48]

Plainly, the judge was somewhat reluctant to hold the defendants in contempt, but he concluded that the facts and the law compelled him to do so. In finding the defendants in contempt, however, Justice Morse's decision explicitly stated that there should be no implication of bad faith on their part despite the extensive degree of noncompliance. His reasoning was as follows:

> This case presents difficult problems. Chapter 766 demands that special educational services be furnished within fixed time limits, and the judgment of this Court tracks these requirements. Schools are run by humans and deal with humans. Chapter 766 does not allow for human frailty. An observer cannot help but wonder whether machine-like precision is necessarily consistent with sound educational, fiscal responsibility and the best interests of the children entitled to those services. Yet it is the duty of the Court to accept legislation as enacted. . . .
>
> A finding of civil contempt may imply defiance or obstructionism, notwithstanding good faith efforts on the part of the alleged contemnor. Such an implication is wholly unwarranted here. The administration of the Boston public schools has indeed made a good faith effort to comply with the requirements of Chapter 766, the pertinent regulations and the order of the Court. The Court has every reason to expect that these efforts will continue which is of greater importance than casting about to lay blame at any particular person or persons. The function of a civil contempt proceeding is remedial, not punitive. But good faith, absence of willful disobedience and lack of intent to violate a decree do not constitute a defense to civil contempt.[49]

The Compensatory Services: Remedy—An Ineffective Reform

Still to be decided was the content of the contempt judgment. Plaintiffs had proposed a broad variety of remedies, including additional administrative reorganization plans, expanded timetables for the delivery of services, mandatory staffing requirements, and the development and implementation of information management systems. Their most controversial proposal was to assess $15 daily fines against the defendants and pay these sums to the parents of children who were being denied their court-ordered entitlement to special education.[50] Both defendants and the state DOE strongly opposed monetary damages,[51] the latter arguing that adoption of this traditional contempt remedy here would serve only to reduce funds available to the school system to improve services.[52] Justice Morse concurred in this reasoning. He also anticipated that such an order would be appealed, and it would take a long time before any money would actually be paid. He believed that a form of sanctions that would take effect promptly was necessary if the order was to have any effect.[53]

The judge then suggested an alternative concept—a compensatory services remedy.[54] The plaintiffs formulated an outline for providing educational services, rather than monetary damages, to parents of children whose rights under the law had been violated. Their proposal served as a working document around which a consensus among the parties began to emerge.[55] The final compensatory services plan contained in the judgment entered on October 11, 1977, called for the defendants to offer compensatory special education services to all children who had waited more than 60 days to receive court-ordered Chapter 766 entitlements. The court did not specify the particular form such services need take, but the judgment suggested enrichment programs, after-school or weekend tutoring, increasing the intensity of special services already being provided, and offering comprehensive special services during the summer. Plaintiffs and defendants would jointly draft letters advising parents of their rights to obtain and select compensatory programs, and defendants would report to plaintiffs the names of those accepting programs. In addition, the parties were to recommend to the court candidates for a newly created position to monitor and evaluate the implementation of the compensatory program.

For the next two years, compensatory services were at the center of the *Allen* case. The defendants implemented the program, and during the first year provided some type of compensatory service to most of the eligible children whose parents requested participation.[56] Most successful were the summer programs, which enrolled approximately 150 children with a wide range of handicapping conditions.[57] The program's limitations soon became apparent, however. Cost factors, lack of parent involvement, and administrative problems quickly surfaced. The low participation rate was a major concern; approximately 75 percent of the students eligible for compensation did not ask for or receive services.[58]

In addition, the compensatory services remedy was not proving effective in bringing about compliance with the Chapter 766 statute and regulations. New violations continued to mount at an accelerating rate. Because students whose rights were violated could be compensated with an opportunity to obtain supplementary services, there was no real pressure to undertake systemic change that would assure that the basic violations did not occur.[59] In response to plaintiffs' concerns, Justice Morse included in his May 1979 Order reiterating the guidelines on compensatory services a requirement that the defendants furnish to the court by September 1 of that year a plan for achieving compliance with the court's orders.[60]

The plan that the school district submitted that September proposed new structural changes, such as the establishment of a Parents Advisory Council and the distribution of a parents' guide to special education services.[61] Yet it offered the plaintiffs no assurance of timely implementation.

Plaintiffs entered into direct negotiations with Superintendent Robert Wood on the continuing noncompliance problem. These negotiations resulted in an agreement that the monitoring function would be expanded to include oversight of all special education services and not just the compensatory programs.[62] The court was by this time well aware of the shortcomings of compensatory services and enthusiastically accepted the idea of a full-time monitor.[63] Thus, the Further Order of August 9, 1980, provided that an independent monitor, to be funded by the defendants, would be appointed by the court for a two-year term. This appointment was to change dramatically the direction of the *Allen* litigation.

Monitoring as an Impetus for Change: 1980–1983

In negotiating the monitoring concept with plaintiffs, Superintendent Wood had assumed that the monitor would function as a management consultant, reviewing operations and telling administrators how to operate more efficiently.[64] Justice Morse, however, had a broader function in mind. Having become disenchanted with the compensatory services remedy, he now was convinced that a full-time professional, answerable to the court, who could goad the defendants into meaningful compliance was the way to bring this case to a reasonable conclusion.[65]

Accordingly, the court's Order of August 19, 1980, established the office of a monitor who would "review and report to the Court and the parties on the progress towards implementation of the Orders of the Court."[66] Although the order explicitly stated that "the Monitor will have no direct or administrative responsibility for defendants' compliance with the Orders of this Court,"[67] it was clear that Justice Morse expected the monitor to operate with a broad swath. His scope of responsibility was defined in terms of determining "the most effective methods for the functioning of the special education program,"[68] and he was to be granted prompt access to all written information and personnel as required to discharge his duties.[69] The monitor was empowered to make formal recommendations with regard to implementation of any of the orders of the court. These would be binding on the defendants unless they filed an objection, in which event the court would convene a hearing.[70] The defendants were ordered to pay the monitor sufficient funds not only to cover his salary and expenses but also to hire a staff that would assist him in conducting a study of the reasons for noncompliance with the court's orders.[71]

By the time the order had been entered, Superintendent Wood had been replaced by Paul Kennedy, a new interim superintendent who was opposed to the idea of any type of monitor, even one with a limited role. The defendants therefore attempted to have the order establishing the monitor amended. Moreover, they declined to join the plaintiffs in proposing candidates for the position.

This strategy backfired on them. Not only did the court deny their motion, but it quickly appointed as monitor the plaintiffs' candidate, Alex Rodriguez, who had been the only name proposed. Rodriguez, an administrator with the Massachusetts Commission Against Discrimination, had been involved in the drafting of Chapter 766 and had served on the Board of the Massachusetts Advocacy Center, the plaintiffs' attorneys parent organization. To the defendants, Rodriguez, with his advocacy background, was the exact opposite of the technician that they had envisioned when they originally agreed to the idea of a monitor. They saw him as being zealous and political; in their eyes, he was "not a technician, but a bomb thrower."[72]

Rodriguez's appointment commenced a new, more activist stage of compliance oversight in *Allen v. McDonough*. The May 1979 Order provided a flexible mandate and sufficient resources, but as the defendants correctly surmised, much of the monitor's actual influence was to come from the power of Rodriguez's personality. He made the defendants feel that he and derivatively the court were omnipresent, which resulted in substantially increased compliance pressure on the defendants' special education operations.

Even before his appointment formally took effect, Rodriguez's active presence began to be felt. On December 10, 1980, he issued a Monitor's Plan to guide the functioning of his office. Three particular aspects of this planning document are worthy of comment. First, Rodriguez saw his authority as encompassing full implementation of the Chapter 766 statute and regulations, rather than being limited to the issues that had been specifically addressed in the court's orders.[73] Second, the Monitor's Plan stated that "Boston must develop a Management Information System (MIS) that provides valid and reliable information documenting the school system's ability to maintain the zero rejection level and an ongoing mechanism to determine when and how the law is being violated."[74] Finally, Rodriguez's monitoring methodology provided a design for comprehensive structural reform. Once the reasons for noncompliance were identified and a data tracking system developed, a plan for implementation of necessary changes involving close cooperation between the Monitor's Office and the school department would be made.[75]

While the monitoring design provided a framework for structural reform, Rodriguez did not see implementation of such reforms as his direct responsibility or that of the court. Influenced by his personal involvement in the Boston desegregation case, his view was that courts operate in a political vacuum when they become directly involved in attempts to restructure bureaucratic systems. Legislatures do not do much better, even when they enact detailed statutes like Chapter 766 because teachers in the field do not read the statute and the lack of documentation of compliance problems means that no one really knows what is going on.[76]

Rodriguez's emphasis on improving data systems was designed to overcome both these problems. The monitor's job was "to build a data base that would compel the system to restructure itself to comply with the law."[77] Rodriguez believed that "calling attention to the problem leads to its correction."[78] His office's role would be to document comprehensively both the extent of noncompliance and the structural shortcomings that were causing it. It would be left entirely to the defendants to design and implement the changes necessary to remedy these shortcomings.

The monitor's ability to accomplish the tasks set forth in his ambitious planning design were, however, substantially impeded during his first year of operation by the fiscal crisis that hit the Boston public school system during the 1980–1981 school year. The passage of Proposition 2-1/2, which became effective in November 1980, imposed a cap on the amount of money that could be raised by the municipal property tax. The school system was fiscally dependent on the city of Boston for its appropriations. When it requested an increase of $40 million in its appropriation for the 1980–1981 school year to cover increased costs for special education and other services, the city refused to fund the amount.

The matter was quickly brought before the state superior court in suits brought by the *Allen* plaintiffs against the School Committee and by the School Committee against the city.[79] While the litigations pursued their course, it became evident that whatever the final legal outcome, the school system's level of expenditures had to be reduced. The School Committee announced that approximately 700 teachers would be laid off on April 1, 1981. Special education would be particularly affected by these cuts because the union contract required reverse seniority layoffs, and special education staff tended to have low seniority.[80]

The monitor saw it as his responsibility to try to minimize the detrimental impact of the cuts. Rodriguez met with all the parties and affected parents to discuss the impact of the budget reductions on special education and issued a report that assessed the likely impact of the reductions on compliance possibilities.[81] He also attempted to negotiate compromises in individual cases where the effects of the cutbacks on particular special needs classes or students would be especially severe.[82]

The impact of budget reductions continued to be a major problem in the next school year. The provision of special education services was further affected by contractual requirements and administrative procedures that delayed the filling of even those special education positions that had been funded.[83] Not surprisingly the monitor's end-of-year statistics revealed an increase in Chapter 766 noncompliance for the 1981–1982 school year.[84]

Reflecting frustration at the continuing levels of noncompliance, the plaintiffs wrote to the monitor and asked that his office "devote less attention to quantification and verification of noncompliance and more attention to defendants' procedures and practices that may be responsible for their noncompliance."[85] The monitor apparently responded to this pressure. His March 1982 report focused more directly on structural reform issues. It charged that the Boston schools lacked the basic attributes to educate children in general and special needs children in particular. The monitor described the schools as a "nonsystem" lacking the requisite organization and stability to implement judicial and legislative mandates:

> Evidence that the Boston Public Schools are a non-system is overwhelming. Laws and regulations are not followed. Codes of discipline are established and then shelved. Superintendent's circulars are diligently written and then ignored. Orders of federal and state courts are not implemented. The main reason for Boston's inability to implement Chapter 766 is that its one hundred and twenty-three individual schools do not operate as a unified whole.[86]

In order to remedy this situation, Rodriguez recommended a series of specific organizational and structural changes. These included reorganizing the Department of Student Support Services, developing timelines for the implementation of a computerized data management system known as SEIMS, and calling for the immediate hiring of all staff necessary to comply with Chapter 766. In order to ensure effective delivery of services at the local level, the report also proposed setting aside all inconsistent school district regulations and budget controls that impeded the principal's ability to place needed staff promptly in school-based special education planning. Despite the acerbity of his rhetoric, however, the monitor did not suggest a more activist posture for the court.

In the ensuing negotiations, the defendants stipulated to those recommendations that they considered feasible and resisted the others.[87] Almost all of the stipulations that resulted from this process called for the defendants to prepare plans, undertake assessments, or establish task forces; the defendants would not stipulate to recommendations that specified concrete structural reforms, and the monitor did not press them to do so. The monitor's next report reflected obvious frustration with the limited progress that had been made in implementing these reforms. Of ten stipulations that had been agreed to, he considered two to have been sufficiently addressed, four minimally complied with, and four largely ignored.[88]

The continuing high levels of noncompliance and the failure of the Monitor's Office to achieve major systemic change led to growing dissatisfaction by the plaintiffs with Rodriguez's performance. By the summer of 1982, Rodriguez had served a year and a half of his original two-year term, and the plaintiffs began to consider whether they would support the renewal of his mandate.

The group of plaintiffs contemplating this issue was far different from the group that had supported Rodriguez's appointment in 1980. By 1982, the active plaintiffs included not only the children and parents named in the *Allen* complaint as class representatives but also—and perhaps primarily—a new group of vocal parents, who had emerged as advocates for the rights of special needs children in the Boston Public Schools.[89] These parents were originally brought together as the Parent Advisory Group to the Monitor. They were, however, dissatisfied from the beginning with the monitor.

The Parent Advisory Group wanted to take on a direct role in the monitoring process. The monitor, on the other hand, envisioned the group as an advisory panel and resisted its direct involvement. Rodriguez, despite the defendants' contrary perceptions, saw his role as a neutral agent of the court and not that of an advocate. Accordingly, he wanted to avoid close identification with any group.[90] The parents' dissatisfaction with this stance led them to meet with the plaintiffs' attorney, who explained that, aside from their participation as advisors to Rodriguez, they could continue to be involved in shaping the case as members of the plaintiff class. From that point forward the group exerted its prime influence not through its affiliation with the Monitor's Office but as an independent advocacy group and through the plaintiffs' attorney.[91]

The parents' group became increasingly critical of Rodriguez's approach to monitoring. They wanted to see visible progress in compliance, and they felt that the monitor should move more aggressively against the School Committee to force it to make needed changes. The rift caused by these conflicting conceptions of the monitor's role were aggravated by personality conflicts and led to a growing power struggle between the monitor and the parents. After the monitor's first six-month report was issued, the plaintiffs criticized the slow pace of progress and his emphasis on statistical quantification.[92] When the monitor's second report was issued, the Parent Advisory Group critiqued it directly and, after the monitor released a press statement summarizing the report, they issued their own press statement criticizing it.[93]

Not surprisingly, after the parents had urged the monitor to recommend in his 1982 proposals for future monitoring functions that the Advisory Group be given expanded status and support staff, Rodriguez's recommendation went in the opposite direction. He proposed that the group function as an advisory committee to the Department of Student Support Services and be totally detached from the monitor.[94] Plaintiffs' attorneys countered by recommending that if the Monitor's Office should continue past the expiration of the initial two-year term, the Parent Advisory Committee should nominate the monitor and that the staff should include non-professional parents of special needs children.[95]

Rodriguez's overall recommendation to the court was that his office be continued "until such time as there has been full compliance with the Orders of the Court," but that the School Department also implement an internal investigating presence responsible to the court as a step toward an ultimate reduction of the monitor's role.[96] The Parent Advisory Committee and the plaintiffs' attorney expressed in separate letters to the court their concern that a monitor or court consultant independent of the School Department continue to exist, but neither supported the continuation of Rodriguez in the office.[97]

The court granted an extension of Rodriguez's term for another six months as a transitional phase in which the monitor would assist the School Department in developing an internal monitoring capacity. Justice Morse stated his hopes for reducing judicial oversight as follows:

> Areas of noncompliance still exist, but significantly fewer children are now affected and the nature of the violations are less significant. The manner in which the violations are counted overstates the extent of remaining difficulties . . .
>
> I am persuaded and so find that it is probable that the present School Committee and Superintendent will continue to work toward reducing "violations" and "noncompliance." It is more likely that educational professionalism will be the force that will continue to improve compliance rather than the continuing presence of the Court. In the expectation that this is likely to be so, the court is prepared to reduce the monitoring presence.[98]

Modified Monitoring: 1983–1985   In early 1983 it was clear that the court was reconsidering its role in *Allen* and that both the plaintiffs and the defendants were attempting to shape the next phase of the lawsuit. The plaintiffs expressed their concern that the monitor had minimized the extent of the remaining noncompliance, and they made clear that they did not want the monitoring function to be entrusted to the School Department.[99] The defendants, on the other hand, sought to convince the court that they were willing and able to take the steps necessary to comply fully with Chapter 766; specifically, they declared that they were prepared to institute accurate and effective self-monitoring. Superintendent Spillane issued a "Compliance Assurance Circular" to all building administrators in which he emphasized the importance of accurate reporting and a commitment to full implementation of Chapter 766. In it he warned that individuals who failed to submit required reports or to achieve full compliance on matters within their control would be subject to appropriate discipline, including reassignment, demotion, and dismissal.[100]

In May 1983, the monitor issued what was to be his final report. In it Rodriguez stated that the overall rate of noncompliance for September through December of the 1982–1983 school year was higher than the overall rate for the prior year. Considering comparable individual months for each of those years, however, he found an improvement.[101] In the critical category of "IEPs not fully implemented," the figures showed a slight increase in the September through December periods, from 2,164 to 2,178.[102] The report also emphasized defendants' efforts to develop an internal monitoring system, which included a verification strategy to increase the validity and reliability of data gathered at the school level and the initial stage of implementation of the SEIMS computer system.[103]

The report concluded that the *Allen* case was now "ripe for the [c]ourt's disengagement," and noted that the monitor had initiated discussions among the parties regarding disengagement criteria.[104] The monitor formally recommended that his office continue until the end of 1983 and that it be given the responsibility to work out a plan to transfer all monitoring activities to the State Department of Education.[105]

It was, however, far from clear why the case was "ripe for disengagement" at this particular time. The monitor's analysis did not show any improvement in the noncompliance statistics; rather the monitor emphasized that there was "stability."[106] Moreover, there were 31 outstanding organizational and structural recommendations of the monitor, of which the School Committee had agreed to implement 27.[107] In certain other areas, such as transportation, data gathering was still at a primitive stage, which left "only a weak basis upon which to make statements about transportation problems and their contribution to unimplemented IEPs."[108]

Whatever the perceptions of the ripeness of moving toward disengagement at this point, it was clear that all concerned had come to agree that the monitor's office, or at least its present incumbent, should not be further extended. Accordingly, the court granted the monitor a final extension until August 15, 1983, stating that this time was to be used to effect a transition to a new monitoring system.[109] At the same time, the court formalized the role of the School Department's internal monitoring and created a new modified "Independent Monitor's" Office to operate in conjunction with the school system's internal operation. Two monitors would be appointed for terms extending at least until June 30, 1984,[110] and, at least until the defendants purged themselves of civil contempt, they would be accountable to the court. The monitors were to furnish the court with three written reports containing their findings on the defendants' compliance during the year, and they would have the authority to make formal recommendations.[111]

By the time the Court Monitor's Office closed in the summer of 1983, internal monitoring by the Boston school system[112] and external monitoring by the state DOE[113] had already been put into place. The monitoring system was based on a number of interrelated systems of information and verification, which included a monthly data management report listing violations reported by special education personnel at each school; the superintendent's assurance checklist, which requires building administrators to verify once a month that requisite services are actually being delivered to each child;[114] and regular comprehensive site visits involving folder reviews, staff interviews, and direct observations conducted by the Department of Student Support Services.[115] During the 1986–1987 school year, the School Department also finally achieved system-wide implementation of the computer-based SEIMS system, which has resulted in a more accurate and timely information flow.[116]

PROSPECTS FOR DISENGAGEMENT:
1986–1988

Prior to the opening of school for the September 1984 school term, Chief Justice Morse called upon "all persons that are responsible for compliance to make every effort to achieve the goal of substantial compliance by the end of the current school year. If that is achieved, the Court will entertain a motion to purge the defendants of contempt."[117] Justice Morse's hopes that substantial compliance would be achieved by the end of the 1984–1985 school year were, however, not to be realized. Large numbers of violations continued to be reported, and in some areas, such as "IEPs not fully implemented," the number of violations was actually higher than during the previous two years.[118]

A major part of the compliance problems stemmed from continued staffing difficulties. When school opened in September 1984, approximately 10 percent of the budget lines for special education remained vacant.[119] Shortages were especially acute in specialized areas like occupational and physical therapy,[120] and in bilingual teaching and evaluation, which represented almost one-third of the vacancies.[121] Transportation problems were also of increasing concern. The number of complaints and violations regarding late pick-up or failures to pick up increased dramatically from 1,654 in the first half of the 1983–1984 school year to 3,985 in the comparable period for 1984–1985.[122]

Despite these continuing compliance problems—or, perhaps because of them—Chief Justice Morse remained undaunted in his determination to bring the case to a conclusion. In June 1985 he issued an order providing for the appointment of a consultant to study "the delivery of reliable, timely and substantially uninterrupted transportation." Having dealt with the transportation problem in this way, the next year he also appointed a personnel consultant, who was charged with the responsibility of studying "the reasons for the school defendants' noncompliance with orders of this Court resulting from insufficient special education teachers and specialists."[123]

On January 8, 1986, Justice Morse took a further step to move the case toward a final resolution: He appointed a consultant on disengagement. The consultant's assignment was to organize monthly meetings of the parties to discuss the disengagement process, to promote a joint agreement on these issues to the extent possible, and to make recommendations to the court on disengagement.[124] After six months of intensive negotiation with the consultant, the parties agreed on a conceptual framework for a disengagement process, which was presented to the court for its approval.

The "Disengagement Order," signed by Justice Morse in July 1986, began with a "history and current status of the case," which stated:

> Since entry of the contempt citation in April 1977, defendants have succeeded in reducing measurably the level of non-compliance. For example, at the end of May 1986, the number of children awaiting an overdue education plan had been reduced to 186 (plus an additional 79 which defendants believed to be excusable); and the number of children waiting for a review had been reduced to 106 (plus an additional 23 which defendants believed to be excusable). These waiting list reductions occurred at a time when the special education population in the city increased to approximately 12,136 from approximately 7,900 at the time of entry of the contempt finding. Nevertheless, the parties agreed that defendants still are not in complete compliance with the requirements of Ch. 766 and outstanding Orders in this case.[125]

The order then set forth a two-phase disengagement process. During Phase I, the case would remain on the court's active docket. The independent monitor would continue to report on the School Department's compliance efforts and in addition a Disengagement Master would be appointed to "help resolve promptly any issues which may arise under this Disengagement Order or prior orders of the Court."[126]

The innovative core provision of the Disengagement Order was its specific definition of "substantial compliance" in each outstanding problem area. For example, in regard to original evaluations, the order defined "substantial compliance" as completion of 90 percent of the required team meetings within the requisite 30-school-day time frame; 95 percent within a period of an additional 15 school working days; and 97.5 percent within 60 school working days. Similarly, in the area of "IEPs not fully implemented," substantial compliance was deemed to occur when 97.5 percent of IEPs for each category of service were fully implemented in the applicable month and 99 percent within 15 days of their due date.[127]

The disengagement process would move to Phase II upon defendants' achievement of substantial compliance in each of the eight specified areas for a period of at least six of the ten school months and averaged for one school year. In Phase II, a permanent injunction would be issued requiring defendants to continue to comply with Chapter 766 and all prior court orders and the case would be removed from the court's active docket. For a period of at least five years the comprehensive internal monitoring system (described in detail in the order's appendix) would need to be maintained in place.[128]

At the end of the 1987–1988 school year, after almost two years of operations under the Disengagement Order, defendants still had not achieved the requisite levels of compliance.[129] Nevertheless, the parties agreed that the Disengagement Order had established a meaningful framework for organizing the various monitoring systems and provided clear compliance standards that would facilitate defendants' compliance efforts. When (and whether) the concrete substantial compliance goals set forth in the Disengagement Order will be achieved remains to be seen.[130]

THE ROLE OF THE COURTS: CONCLUDING PERSPECTIVES

The theory of structural discrimination discussed in Chapter 2 distinguished the disability rights context from race discrimination situations by suggesting that the discriminatory animus at issue is less invidious but that the structural obstacles that need to be overcome are more open-ended. Based on these differences, one would anticipate that litigations involving rights of the disabled would be less vituperative in their liability stages but more extensive in their remedial stages than desegregation or other civil rights cases. The New York and Boston case studies bore out these expectations.

The brevity of the liability phase in both cases was striking. In *Jose P.* there was no trial and almost no discovery process.[131] The determination of defendants' liability was based on a single, one-hour hearing at which the defendants admitted the existence of extensive waiting lists. In *Allen*, the defendants virtually conceded liability before any hearing had even been held, and the initial consent judgment was negotiated in less than two weeks. Those brief liability phases stand in sharp contrast to the lengthy, still unfolding remedial process in both cases.[132]

Later developments in both lawsuits were significantly influenced by the brevity of the liability phases. For one thing, the level of adversarial antagonism was clearly reduced. Compared with desegregation cases, where remedial reforms tend to be implemented only after protracted, bitter discovery disputes and trials, here both sides promptly agreed on plaintiffs' legal entitlements. Given this non-vituperative commencement, it is not surprising that the parties quickly entered into cooperative negotiations.

In addition, the brevity of the liability phases influenced judicial attitudes in the later stages of each case. Because the judges did not invest substantial time and energy in a lengthy trial, their knowledge of the problems tended to be relatively limited. Moreover, because they were not called upon to probe defendants' shortcomings at the beginning of the case, they tended to be more patient with excuses for noncompliance, at least at initial noncompliance hearings. Illustrative of this point was Judge Nickerson's refusal in the early *Jose P.* compliance skirmish to order specific structural reforms recommended by the Special Master, and Justice Morse's attribution of good faith to the Boston defendants in his first contempt findings.

The second significant aspect of the legal process revealed by the *Jose P.* and *Allen* case studies was that in both cases, it was the parties themselves, rather than the judges, who devised the structural solutions that were then written into the court orders. In *Jose P.*, the extensive institutional reforms set forth in the judgment, the January Plan and the April Plan, and the later stipulations, resulted from the weekly negotiating sessions of the parties and their consultants. Judge Nickerson's noncompliance orders implicitly recognized and endorsed this pattern. Most notable in this regard was the 1983 decision in which, despite strong findings of noncompliance, Judge Nickerson declined to order the particular remedies requested by plaintiffs, or even those endorsed by the Special Master. Instead, he raised the threshold for defendants to return to the negotiating table by ordering further hearings and threatening contempt citations.[133]

The pattern of prompt movement to a negotiating mode also surfaced early and definitively in *Allen*. The parties there put together both the consent judgment and the Supplemental Consent decree in their initial summer negotiations without any substantive input from the court. Creation of the various innovative monitoring structures that were the hallmark of the Boston case also emerged from negotiations among the parties and their joint dialogue with Justice Morse.[134]

The fact that both *Jose P.* and *Allen* exhibited analogous negotiating modes was not coincidental. Structural discrimination theory explains why such negotiating processes are likely to be prevalant in special education cases. In the absence of established definitions of what is an "appropriate education," a judge is unable on his or her own to mandate a series of appropriate educational standards, or even to call upon an expert to provide a set of standards that are prevalant in the field. Implementation of rights to "appropriate education" necessarily calls for extensive discussion and deliberation to formulate situationally defined goals and standards. In short, the articulation of a right to special education is inherently a process approach that requires ongoing negotiating mechanisms.

Given this strong orientation to negotiation, the court's role in each case was to serve as an agenda-setter and a catalyst for a negotiating process in which the parties themselves would formulate the appropriate structural changes. Judicial pressure encouraged the parties to devise acceptable solutions. At times, the negotiating process would break down, but even on these occasions, the orders issued by the court were largely exhortations to the parties to work out their differences more effectively, rather than judicial mandates to adopt a concrete course of action.

Despite the fundamental similarity of their remedial processes, the negotiating process took on different forms in the two cities. In *Jose P.*, the attorneys for the plaintiffs and their educational consultants, fortified by the court's periodic liability or contempt findings and by means of their weekly meetings, were able to apply almost continual pressure on the administration to recognize shortcomings and to work cooperatively to devise solutions. Despite plaintiffs' ongoing presence and their participation in the planning process, however, the prime responsibility for developing and implementing administrative solutions for the problems raised remained with the defendants. In short, the remedial process in *Jose P.* might be described as one of ongoing plaintiff participation, in an ombudsman-like mode.

Overall, this "structural ombudsman" pressure affected the functioning of the bureaucracy in two major ways. First, it significantly influenced attitudes of central administrators and field staff once compliance with the specifics of the judgment and the state and federal laws upon which it was based became a recognized criterion for performance evaluations. Second, the ongoing negotiating process provided opportunities for creative individuals in the system to devise solutions for long-standing problems and to have these solutions funded and put into practice.

In Boston, there was less direct plaintiff participation and more emphasis on independent monitoring. The ombudsman pressures in *Allen* tended to come more from the Monitor's Office in its various incarnations than from the ongoing presence of plaintiffs' attorneys and educational consultants. Monitoring began on a part-time basis as an aspect of the compensatory services contempt remedy. It quickly grew into an active, fully staffed Monitor's Office under Alex Rodriguez and was reconstituted in the later years of the case as an "independent adjunct" to the school system's own internal monitoring functions. Finally, the monitoring system became the core of the Disengagement Order, which articulated precise, numerical definitions of compliance and contemplated a gradual shift of all external monitoring responsibilities to the state Department of Education.

The manner in which the litigation process actually unfolded in each city was, of course, a product of local structures, events, and personalities. In New York, Judge Nickerson's ready acceptance of institutional reform responsibilities and his choice as Special Master—Marvin Frankel, an individual possessing rare talents for motivating the parties to work together to devise joint solutions to basic problems—clearly influenced the form that the negotiating process took. The readiness of Executive Director Jerry Gross and the various Corporation Counsel attorneys to work cooperatively with a group of plaintiffs' attorneys, who themselves were experienced in educational affairs, were additional factors that shaped the plaintiffs' participation approach to institutional reform in New York.

The emphasis on monitoring in *Allen* resulted primarily from Alex Rodriguez's personality and philosophy. His bombastic style gave the monitoring function its force and its initial influence. Even more significant, his conception that the proper monitoring/judicial role was to provide systematic data to define comprehensively problems whose solution would then be entrusted to the school authorities became the *modus operandi* of the case.

Rodriguez was not, of course, the only critical influence on the direction of events. Justice Morse's enthusiastic acceptance of monitoring—perhaps because it accorded well with his personal view of the need to goad the sleepy bureaucracy—also was of critical significance. Also of obvious relevance in Boston was the fact that the monitoring approach provided greater discretion in devising and implementing structural changes to the school officials, who were simultaneously under extensive pressure to carry out structural reforms under the desegregation order.

Has *Allen*'s monitoring model been more or less effective than *Jose P.*'s plaintiff participation approach? That intriguing question raises philosophical and methodological issues that go well beyond the purposes of the present chapter.[135] What can be said with reasonable confidence is that in both New York and Boston, significant improvement in the provision of educational services to handicapped children has been accomplished through judicial involvement. Moreover, the very differences in the two models illustrate the fundamental premise of structural discrimination theory that the particular form that institutional changes will take cannot be predicted in advance. The unfolding reform process has an inherent creativity, grounded in local conditions, that will lead to different structural outcomes in different settings, despite the commonality of the legal mandate to which all are responding.

Previous empirical studies of the early stages of implementation of the recently enacted special education statutes have generally concluded that there has been procedural compliance, and that "the letter of the law is being met, by and large. Yet this falls far short of meeting the spirit or intent of the law." [136] The present case studies of *Jose P.* and *Allen*, however, lead to a different conclusion. Over the past decade there has been not only improved procedural compliance in New York and Boston, but extensive structural changes reflecting the "spirit" of the laws have also taken hold. The number of students served in New York has more than doubled, an entirely new school-based support team administrative structure has been successfully implemented, and more than 50 school buildings have been renovated to provide accessibility to the physically handicapped.[137] In Boston, new hiring techniques and contracting-out mechanisms have been put into place and innovative structures for parental participation have been instituted.

Although the achievement of significant structural reform in both cities is beyond dispute, the extent of the courts' role in this process, and its legitimacy, remain controversial. Former New York Schools Chancellor Macchiarola, although acknowledging the value of the *Jose P.* suit in its early stages, believed that the court's continued involvement became an "unhealthy fetter." His position directly addresses two controversial questions:

First, what form should judicial oversight take in the implementation stage of a reform litigation, and second, when should the courts' jurisdiction terminate?

In regard to the first question, the empirical experiences revealed by both the New York and Boston case studies confirm the theoretical premise of structural discrimination theory that an active and ongoing involvement of the courts is an important—and perhaps a necessary—stimulus for meaningful structural reform when the rights of the disabled are at issue. Without the sustained judicial pressure that motivated the parties to devise innovative structural reforms to meet the needs of the handicapped, it is doubtful that the legislative reforms or administrative regulations regarding special education could have been effectively implemented.[138]

Jose P. clearly was a major change agent, if not *the* major change agent, for New York City's Special Education Division. Joseph Viteritti, Chancellor Macchiarola's special assistant, has noted in this regard that "it was the successful litigation that first established the educational rights of the handicapped." [139] The court's role in promoting special education reform in Boston was equally important. Given the city's preoccupation with school desegregation, effective implementation of Chapter 766 could not have occurred without the active stimulus provided by the *Allen* litigation.[140] In short, the answer to the first question posed by Chancellor Macchiarola is that the judicial role in cases involving the rights of the handicapped must be extensive if it is to be effective.

How long this judicially shaped structural reform process should continue, the second question posed, is less easily determined. To the extent that courts in new model institutional reform litigations, such as *Jose P.*, serve as "structural ombudsmen," their continuing presence arguably will be necessary for as long as countervailing pressure to affirm individual rights against large governmental bureaucracies is needed—that is, forever. On the other hand, as Justice Morse indicated by his insistence on pressing for a disengagement framework in *Allen*, a court that is perceived (or perceives itself) as a permanent part of the system is likely to become susceptible to many of the same bureaucratic rigidities that it purports to reform. At some point, then, a court must bow out.

What is that point? If the level of compliance used to define it is too high, unrealistic expectations may be raised as to what law reform can accomplish in an imperfect world. Such expectations would lead either to unending, ineffectual judicial oversight or to frustrated, premature judicial withdrawal.[141] On the other hand, if the court's definition of acceptable compliance is set too low, major social ills may never be rectified.

These difficult termination issues have begun to surface as major problems in the mature stages of long-pending desegregation cases where courts are called upon to determine whether a "unitary" school system has been achieved.[142] The conceptual difficulties here are perhaps exacerbated by questions of when, if ever, acts of intentional discrimination have ceased, and how to assess the lingering impact of vestiges of such intentional discrimination.

Disability rights cases may provide a clearer setting for conceptualizing the basic termination issue. Structural discrimination theory can be particularly useful in this regard. Since the theory calls for the delineation of priority areas and the establishment of workable parameters for structural change within those priorities, an acceptable stopping point might be said to be reached once these essential priorities and parameters have been established. The key question here is to determine when the priority areas and parameters have been sufficiently defined and when their reform has been sufficiently accomplished.

The process aspects of structural discrimination theory provide a useful framework in this regard. If, as we have concluded, the substance of meaningful reform in a structural discrimination context is defined through the workings of a dynamic adversarial process, the proper termination point can also be said to be defined by that same adversarial process. Accordingly, an appropriate termination point of a structural reform litigation can be said to be reached either when the court determines that the major substantive requirements negotiated by the parties have been met and the level of adversarial confrontation has subsided,[143] or when the system meets standards for substantial compliance that the parties themselves, as in both *Allen* and *Jose P.*, have formulated in their negotiations.

So long as core concerns like mainstreaming in New York or bilingual staffing in Boston have not been substantially resolved, the structural reform process obviously cannot be called complete. However, once the parties have defined these problems as priorities and mechanisms are put in place that are remedying these problems in a meaningful way, the court can determine (or the parties can stipulate) that full adherence to all the myriad requirements contained in the court decree or in underlying legal mandates may be left to the defendants' own internal monitoring and state regulatory mechanisms.

In sum, then, the precise point at which a court can be said to have outlived its usefulness is a question that only the judge and the parties, after considering all of the facts in the particular case, can appropriately determine. From the perspective of structural discrimination theory, the task for the court and for the parties participating in an ongoing adversary process is to understand the need for thorough structural reform, to establish mechanisms that can substantially accomplish it, and then to terminate jurisdiction when the court's role has become unnecessary or counterproductive—but not before.

NOTES

Acknowledgments: Initial field research for this chapter was undertaken by Carol Press while she was a student at the Yale Law School. Carol Press's initial drafts and analytic insights also constituted invaluable contributions to this project. The author would also like to thank, for their helpful comments on drafts of this chapter, John Blackmore, Nancy Mehlem, Thomas Mela, Rhoda Schneider, and Marya Yee. The participation of Chief Judge Thomas R. Morse, Michael Betcher, Thomas Mela, and Nancy Mehlem in a seminar discussion of the case at the Yale Law School in December 1985 is also gratefully acknowledged.

Note: Beginning in January 1986, the author participated in this litigation as a consultant on disengagement and as Disengagement Master.

1. 379 F. Supp. 410 (D.Mass. 1979), *aff'd sub nom.,* Morgan v. Kerrigan, 509 F.2d 580 (1st Cir. 1974), *cert. denied,* 421 U.S. 963 (1975). Comprehensive accounts of the *Morgan* litigation and its implementation are contained in R. SMITH, *Two Centuries and Twenty-four Months: A Chronicle of the Struggle to Desegregate the Boston Public Schools,* in LIMITS OF JUSTICE, 25 (H. Kalodner and J. Fishman eds. 1978); R. DENTLER AND M. SCOTT, SCHOOLS ON TRIAL (1981); J. ANTHONY LUKAS, COMMON GROUND: A TURBULENT DECADE IN THE LIVES OF THREE AMERICAN FAMILIES (1985).

2. There were recorded disturbances on 130 out of 174 school days in the 1974–1975 school year. SMITH, *supra* note 1, at 67. Over 8,000 students were suspended and 459 students were arrested. *Id.* at 69–70.

3. Interview with Michael Betcher, Counsel to the Boston School Committee, in Boston, Massachusetts (October 23, 1984). When advocates for the handicapped began to question the lack of progress in implementing recently enacted state special education laws, they were specifically told by the system's special services director that the desegregation orders were a major reason for the system's noncompliance with the statutory requirements. MASSACHUSETTS ADVOCACY CENTER AND THE COALITION FOR SPECIAL EDUCATION, SPECIAL EDUCATION IN BOSTON: THE MANDATE AND THE REALITY, REPORT OF THE BOSTON 766 MONITORING PROJECT 29–30 (1975).

4. THE MANDATE AND THE REALITY, *supra* note 3, at 30.

5. Morgan v. Kerrigan, 401 F. Supp. 216 (D. Mass. 1975). After Judge Garrity relieved the school system of its responsibility for these mainstreaming requirements in his October 1984 termination decision, there were indications that mainstreaming problems were developing. A report issued by the Massachusetts Advocacy Center found that "the number of students and the placement rate for segregated day problems increased steadily from 1974 to 1985." MASSACHUSETTS ADVOCACY CENTER, OUT OF THE MAINSTREAM 16 (1987).

6. Betcher Interview.

7. LUKAS, *supra* note 1, at 122–23. *See also* M. Zanger, *Book Review of Lukas: Common Ground,* THE NATION 316–19 (October 5, 1985). In the 1970s, the situation was, if anything, worse: "Only 14% of school committee votes concerned educational policy and curriculum, while 74% dealt with hiring, firing, promotion and assignment of individual school employees. . . . [T]he average member appointed 30 to

40 custodians, aides or night school teachers during his term on the committee; the chairman up to 200." LUKAS, *supra* note 1, at 122–23.

8. *See* DENTLER AND SCOTT, *supra* note 1, at 25–26, 63. ("All student records were in poor condition, but the record system in use for special needs children was primitive." *Id.* at 147.)

9. *See* DENTLER AND SCOTT, *supra* note 1, at 21 (description of the administrative structure and its effect on the school committee's ability to plan a desegregation remedy). In special education, a major problem in this regard has been the lack of consolidated authority to hire and deploy the staff needed to comply with Chapter 766. Interview with Rhoda Schneider, General Counsel, State Education Department in Quincy, Massachusetts (November 19, 1984). A. RODRIGUEZ, COURT MONITOR'S REPORT 58–60 (March 1982).

10. DENTLER AND SCOTT, *supra* note 1, at 16. The court's desegregation order specifically required each school to have a permanently assigned principal or headmaster. Morgan v. Kerrigan, 401 F. Supp. at 251.

11. 1972 Mass. Acts Ch. 766, § 1 (principally codified as amended at Mass. Gen. Laws Ann. Ch. 71B, §§ 1–14 (West 1982 and Supp. 1983).

12. R. WEATHERLEY, REFORMING SPECIAL EDUCATION: POLICY IMPLEMENTATION FROM STATE LEVEL TO STREET LEVEL 4 (1979); DENTLER AND SCOTT, *supra* note 1, at 144–45. To this day, the Massachusetts Act and its implementing regulations (Mass. Admin. Code tit. 603, 28.00 *et seq.*) are more comprehensive—and comprehensible—than the federal law and regulations, especially on instructional programming matters. *See, e.g.,* Mass. Admin. Code Tit. 603, § 322.1 (1982) (IEP statements must include number of days per year, opportunities for parent/child instruction, and types of specialized materials and equipment).

13. Ch. 71B § 1.

14. Ch. 71B, § 1 historical note (legislative findings).

15. Ch. 71B, § 2; Mass. Admin. Code Tit. 603, § 500.0 *et seq.* Massachusetts law and regulations place a greater emphasis on delabeling than does the federal EHA.

16. The Boston 766 Monitoring Project was sponsored by the Coalition for Special Education and the Massachusetts Advocacy Center.

17. THE MANDATE AND THE REALITY, *supra* note 3.

18. F. Garfunkel and M. Bloom, *Litigation as a Means of Enforcing Educational Reform: The Case of* Allen v. McDonough, 2 EDUC. UNLIMITED 34, 35 (1980).

19. Interview with Thomas Mela, Esq., Counsel for Plaintiffs, Boston, Massachusetts (November 16, 1984). (This interview and other interviews conducted on October 5, 1984, and December 13, 1984, will hereafter be jointly referred to as the Mela Interviews.)

20. This approach was criticized by Rhoda Schneider, General Counsel to the State Education Department, which later intervened as plaintiffs. Her position was that "if you are going to have a comprehensive case, at least as a matter of civil procedure, you should plead all the issues at the outset." Schneider Interview.

21. These educational plans are analogous to the "individualized education program," or IEP, of the federal EHA. Current Chapter 766 regulations use the term "IEP" rather than educational plan. The statute requires that a child's parents be notified within five days after the child's referral for a special education evaluation,

and that the educational plan be provided within 30 days after parental notification. Ch. 71B, § 3.

22. Reviews must occur within ten months of the original placement and annually thereafter. *Id.*

23. Mela Interview.

24. The complaint named as defendants the members of the Boston School Committee (commencing with John J. McDonough, Chairman of the Committee), the Superintendent of the Boston Public Schools, and the Associate Superintendent for Special Services.

25. Statements of Michael Betcher at Yale Law School Seminar (December 3, 1985). Betcher's general view was that the defendants remained favorably disposed toward plaintiffs' claims and that problems of noncompliance in later years were due primarily to fiscal constraints. Betcher Interview.

26. Mela Interview. Mela attributed at least part of the conciliatory atmosphere and the promptness of the defendants' response to the school committee's decision to permit its in-house legal staff to handle the case rather than retaining outside counsel, as had been done in *Morgan* and other major litigations.

27. Consent Decree at ¶ 13 (June 23, 1976).

28. *See* Boston Teachers Union's Motion to Intervene and Answer in Intervention (June 23, 1976).

29. *See* Department of Education's Motion to Intervene and Complaint in Intervention (July 8, 1976); Schneider Interview. In discussing the reasons for the city's noncompliance, Schneider emphasized administrative and managerial problems as being more significant than fiscal, and, in regard to the desegregation decree, opined, "It's easy for the City to blame desegregation for a lot of problems with the system, but [the fact is that] the system was disserving white as well as black kids."

30. Plaintiffs were also wary that if the state were allowed in as plaintiffs, given their more conservative bent, the court would listen more to them than to the plaintiffs. Mela Interviews.

31. *See* THE MANDATE AND THE REALITY, *supra* note 3, at 14 (providing services for identified special needs children is a greater problem than performing evaluations).

32. Supplemental Consent Decree ¶ 17(d) (September 14, 1976).

33. *See* Plaintiffs' Exhibit, Administrative Reorganization: A Chronology (November 12, 1976).

34. Supplemental Consent Decree at ¶ 17(a), (b).

35. *Id.* at ¶ 17(h).

36. *Id.* at ¶ 17(c).

37. *Id.* at ¶ 17(g).

38. The decree required the defendants to submit to the plaintiffs voluminous information about individual students (*e.g.*, a timetable for the completion of each child's educational plan for all children who as of June 23, 1976, had waited more than 30 days for a plan to be provided) and about aggregate characteristics of the special needs population (*e.g.*, the number of children by district, recommended placement, age, and race awaiting placement in a special education program). Supplemental Consent Decree at ¶ 18. This information could not accurately be furnished with-

out changes in the defendants' data management system. *See* Garfunkel and Bloom, *supra* note 18, at 37.

39. Betcher Interview.

40. When interviewed in 1984, Betcher expressed some regret at this initial stance since "now everyone assumes these are part of the case and disengagement becomes more difficult."

41. Plaintiffs' Exhibit, *supra* note 33.

42. Plaintiffs' Proposed Order for Purging of Civil Contempt at ¶ 6 (undated).

43. Interview with Hon. Thomas R. Morse, Chief Justice, Commonwealth of Massachusetts, Superior Court Department, Boston, Massachusetts (December 14, 1984). Justice Morse, who was appointed Chief Justice in 1982, retained jurisdiction of this case until his retirement in July 1988.

44. The Implementing Order required that placement occur within seven to fifteen days, depending upon the type of placement recommended. *See* Findings, Rulings and Order at ¶ 3 (April 13, 1977) (Bench order of November 24 included in findings made after the trial on plaintiffs' contempt motion and designated an Implementing Order). This order established a basis for a later expansion of the scope of the issues in the case. Justice Morse did not appear uncomfortable with this expansion because "here was a statute enacted by the legislature with no exceptions. It meant the School Committee had to do what the regulations required." Morse Interview.

45. Findings, Rulings and Order *supra* note 44, at 28.

46. *Id.* at ¶¶ 1–5. The court found that as of January 31, 1977, 239 children had been awaiting educational plans for more than 30 days, and 421 children had not received required reviews. Although these findings violated the terms of the consent decree, they also indicated that compliance had improved since its entry.

47. Compared with the totals in *Jose P. v. Ambach*, these placement waiting lists were quite small. Specifically, Justice Morse found a total of 68 children with signed educational plans awaiting speech therapy, 77 awaiting learning disability specialists, 20 awaiting counseling and 20 awaiting physical therapy, occupational therapy, and other services. Findings, Rulings and Order, *supra* note 44, at ¶ 52.

48. *Id.* at ¶ 59.

49. *Id.* at ¶¶ 26–27.

50. Plaintiffs' Proposed Contempt Judgment at ¶ 2 (May 2, 1977).

51. *See* Plaintiff–Intervenor's Proposal on Compensatory Services (July 1, 1977); Defendants' Proposed Form of Judgment (August 18, 1977).

52. Schneider Interview.

53. Morse Interview. In 1986, after finding the defendants in contempt for failing to provide transportation during the 12 days of a bus strike, Justice Morse did accept plaintiffs' proposal for compensatory fines to parents of $20 per day amounting to approximately $1 million in total fines. (order of March 5, 1986). This order was upheld by the Supreme Judicial Court on June 4, 1987.

54. Although the parties in their interviews could not recollect where this idea originated, Justice Morse stated at the Yale Seminar, "I made it all up on my own. I thought it was a splendid idea. Now I see it was all wrong."

55. Plaintiffs' Revised Proposed Contempt Judgment ¶ 1 (June 7, 1977). The

state had reservations about compensatory services because "when you build in a remedy that doesn't directly address the problem, you build in an 'out,'" but nevertheless, it did not actively oppose the proposals. Schneider Interview.

56. Garfunkel and Bloom, *supra* note 18, at 39.

57. *Id.* at 41.

58. N. Mehlem, *Special Education Legal Reform: Compensatory Services and Monitoring to Secure Compliance* 112 (1980) (doctoral dissertation, Boston University School of Education). Dr. Mehlem was the compensatory services monitor appointed in *Allen v. McDonough.*

59. *Id.* at 131, 137; Interview with Frank Garfunkel, Professor of Special Education, Boston University (December 6, 1984).

60. Further Order at ¶ 9 (May 25, 1979).

61. Defendants' Plan to Establish Full Compliance with the Orders of the Court in *Allen v. McDonough* (September 1979).

62. Betcher Interview.

63. Morse Interview. Justice Morse stated that he viewed the proposal for a monitor as a "relief" from the increasing weight of the compliance problems in the case. He had been pleased with the performance of the part-time monitor and expected a full-time monitor to do even better. Statement at Yale Seminar.

64. Betcher Interview.

65. Morse Interview. Justice Morse noted that federal judges have the advantage of permanent officers, secretarial staff, and other institutional supports that were not available to a Massachusetts Superior Court judge. A court-appointed monitor, funded by the defendants, was a necessity to provide continuity of management when the case reached a stage of compliance complexity.

66. Further Order at ¶ 11 (August 19, 1980).

67. *Id.*

68. *Id.* at ¶ 8.

69. *Id.* at ¶ 12. The order also provided that the monitor would meet periodically with representatives of the parties and monthly with an advisory group of parents (¶ 15).

70. *Id.* at ¶ 14. The monitor was authorized to make informal recommendations to the defendants at any time (¶ 13). Written reports, containing the monitor's formal recommendations and a review of the defendants' progress toward compliance were to be filed with the court every six months (¶ 15).

71. For all compensation and expenses, the monitor's office would be entitled to receive from the defendants up to $200,000 during the first year and up to $250,000 during the second year of operation. *Id.* at ¶¶ 9–10. With this appropriation, the monitor was able to hire a staff of nine by June 1982. *See* Final Report on Monitor's Office Survey of Evaluation Team Leaders (June 1982).

72. Betcher Interview. Plaintiffs had proposed an individual with an advocacy point of view because they saw his role as pressing compliance, not as serving as a Special Master. Statements of Tom Mela at Yale Seminar. Rodriguez characterizes himself as a politician and saw one of his strengths as being able to manipulate people. Interview with Alex Rodriguez, Boston, Massachusetts (October 23, 1984).

73. A. RODRIGUEZ, MONITOR'S PLAN (December 10, 1980). Rodriguez wrote

that, unlike a master in a desegregation case who is often invested with sanctioning authority, his role in *Allen* was "more narrowly defined . . . to serve as information gatherer and observer." *Id.* at 1. In undertaking this task, however, Rodriguez stated that his mission was to determine "the most effective method for the functioning of the special education program in Boston." Thus, although he recognized that he lacked direct sanctioning authority, Rodriguez's task definition (especially when combined with the power to recommend sanctions to the court) contemplated a comprehensive functional role.

74. *Id.* at 2. The defendants' data management system, which was the primary source of information on Chapter 766 compliance, relied on reporting by thousands of individuals at the school building level; the monitor considered such a system not only inefficient but bound to produce a great deal of error. Rodriguez Interview.

75. RODRIGUEZ, MONITOR'S PLAN, *supra* note 73, at 9–11.

76. Rodriguez Interview.

77. *Id.*

78. *Id.*

79. The School Committee claimed that the city, which had threatened to close the schools early if authorized appropriations were exhausted, was compelled by Chapter 766 to provide full funding for special education, and by other statutory provisions to fund a full 180-day school year. This complex web of funding litigations was assigned to Justice Morse. He ruled that the city was required to operate the schools for the full 180-day school term notwithstanding the School Committee's exhaustion of appropriations. On appeal, however, this order was modified to make clear that the mayor can require the school committee to expend its funds at a rate consistent with its budget appropriation and that, at least barring a showing that it would otherwise be impossible to operate the public schools, the state had no obligation to supply necessary funds if the city's coffers were empty. *See* School Committee of Boston v. City of Boston, 383 Mass. 693, 421 N.E.2d 1187 (1981) and Board of Education v. City of Boston, 386 Mass. 103, 434 N.E.2d 1224 (1982). *See also* Boston Teachers Union, Local 66 v. City of Boston, 382 Mass. 553, 416 N.E.2d 1363 (1981) (additional $15.1 million supplemental appropriation ordered to fund executed collective bargaining agreements).

80. The plaintiffs filed a motion for a temporary restraining order on March 31, 1981, the day before the cuts were scheduled to take effect. They argued that the cutbacks would make progress toward compliance impossible and that the disruption caused by midyear cutbacks would inevitably cause additional violations of the rights of special needs children. Justice Morse denied the motion because of his belief that even if the requisite facts and legal justifications could be established, a court order would do little good. Since the money wasn't there, entry of an order to hire teachers could have led only to further appeals, and the school year would have ended before anyone would have benefited by it. Morse Interview.

81. A. RODRIGUEZ, MONITOR'S SIX-MONTH REPORT 19–25 (July 31, 1981) (detailing meetings with the parties) and A. RODRIGUEZ, MONITOR'S REPORT ON SPECIAL NEEDS REDUCTIONS, CONSOLIDATIONS AND REORGANIZATION (March 30, 1981).

82. Rodriguez said that the union allowed him some flexibility from contrac-

tual requirements, especially in avoiding layoffs of teachers in ".4" (self-contained class) programs in order to avoid embarrassing publicity. Rodriguez Interview. The head of the teacher's union indicated that the union stuck to its contractual arrangements but the layoffs ceased and the issue died. Interview with Tom Gosnell, Boston, Massachusetts (December 13, 1984).

83. *See* RODRIGUEZ, COURT MONITOR'S REPORT 51–52 (March 1982); Garfunkel Interview; Betcher Interview.

84. There were 5,601 reported violations in 1981–1982, compared with 4,848 reported violations in 1980–1981. *See* RODRIGUEZ, COURT MONITOR'S REPORT 35–40 (October 1982). There had been some hope of improvement at the beginning of the year when Dr. Robert Spillane, the newly appointed superintendent, who replaced the deceased Paul Kennedy, had pledged in a letter to Rodriguez that he was "prepared to recommend to the School Committee that the School Department provide *whatever services are necessary* to remain in compliance with Chapter 766 regulations." Despite Spillane's positive intentions, the promise of improvement obviously was not realized.

85. Letter from Tom Mela to Alex Rodriguez (September 3, 1981). Mela also criticized the monitor's planning and activities for the prior year for emphasizing "discrete activities to be accomplished by [his] office, rather than an overall 'change strategy' to be applied to the school department."

86. RODRIGUEZ, COURT MONITOR'S REPORT, *supra* note 83, at 5.

87. Defendants' main motivation for entering into these stipulations appeared to be the potential embarrassment stemming from the monitor's dramatic examples. Since they regarded Rodriguez as "a bomb thrower," they were motivated to do as much as they could to satisfy his concerns and have his role terminated. Betcher Interview.

88. RODRIGUEZ, COURT MONITOR'S REPORT, *supra* note 83, at 7–32.

89. These parents all had special needs children in the schools; however, they saw their role as protecting the rights not only of their own children but of all special needs children and parents. Interview with Diane Molle, Vice Chairperson of the Parents' Advisory Council, Boston, Massachusetts (December 6, 1984). These parents were, of course, part of the plaintiff class before 1982; the change was not one of legal composition, but of the increased organization and activism of a group of parents within the class.

90. Rodriguez Interview; Garfunkel Interview.

91. Molle Interview.

92. *See* Letter from Thomas Mela to Alex Rodriguez, *supra* note 85.

93. Letter from Stephanie Parrott, Chairperson, Parent Advisory Group, to Alex Rodriguez (March 12, 1982); Press Release of Parent Advisory Group (March 18, 1982).

94. RODRIGUEZ, COURT MONITOR'S REPORT, *supra* note 83 at 58. The parents saw this recommendation as "a kick in the teeth." They believed that an advisory role to the School Department without the power of the court behind them was fruitless. Molle Interview.

95. Letter from Thomas Mela to Alex Rodriguez (July 22, 1982).

96. RODRIGUEZ, COURT MONITOR'S REPORT, *supra* note 83, at 53–54.

97. Letter from Thomas Mela to Judge Thomas Morse (November 12, 1982); Letter from Parent Advisory Committee to Judge Thomas Morse (November 18, 1982).

98. Memorandum at 2 (January 6, 1983). As an example of "overstatement" of noncompliance, Justice Morse noted that if an aide arrives late to a special education class with an enrollment of eight, eight violations will be recorded. The basis for the court's conclusion that "significantly fewer children are now affected" by noncompliance is, however, less clear since the previous official Monitor's Report had shown an increase in the number of children affected. *See supra* note 84.

99. Letter from Thomas Mela to Judge Thomas Morse (March 18, 1983). Plaintiffs felt that toward the end Rodriguez tended to "whitewash" the situation to emphasize the progress that had been made during his tenure. Mela Interview.

100. Superintendent's Circular (April 12, 1983).

101. RODRIGUEZ, COURT MONITOR'S REPORT 40–47 (May 1983). In 1981–1982 5,601 violations were reported; 3,441 in September through December, and 2,160 in January through June. There were 2,822 reported violations from September through December 1982. Stated in another way, the rate of violations dropped from 48.5 per school day for September through December 1981–1982 to 19.8 per day for January through June of that year, but rose again to 39.7 for September through December 1982–1983.

102. *Id.* at 48–49. The figures for 1982 may not have been fully comparable because of a change in reporting procedures.

103. *Id.* at 58–62.

104. *Id.* at 71. These discussions did not produce an agreement among the parties on disengagement criteria. *See* N. MEHLEM AND E. KEARSE, INDEPENDENT MONITOR'S REPORT OF THE SCHOOL DEFENDANTS' COMPLIANCE WITH THE ORDERS OF THIS COURT 11–13 (July 6, 1984).

105. RODRIGUEZ, COURT MONITOR'S REPORT 78 (May 1983).

106. *Id.* at 71–72.

107. *Id.* at 56.

108. *Id.* at 66.

109. Memorandum and Further Order (July 18, 1983). In the Memorandum, Justice Morse noted the accomplishments of the monitor in reducing noncompliance and stressed that the development of the defendants' internal monitoring capacity and the DOE's willingness to take a more active monitoring role had influenced his decision to discontinue the Monitor's Office. Justice Morse also stated, "[E]ven though there is disagreement about the level or levels of noncompliance, fair-minded persons would agree that the means of identifying noncompliance had improved significantly as well as the means of eliminating it."

110. Nancy Mehlem, who had been the part-time monitor for compensatory services and then became a member of Rodriguez's staff, had already been selected and employed by the School Department for one of these positions. Justice Morse's high opinion of her ability to "find out what's going on," as well as his faith in Superintendent Spillane, who had impressed the judge with his professional commitment to compliance and his initiative in "communicating it to those in the system," were clearly major factors in this decision. Morse Interview.

111. Memorandum and Further Order, *supra* note 109, at 4. The independent monitors were to be housed on the school system's premises and, in contrast to Rodriguez, would not have independent staffing resources.

112. *See* BOSTON PUBLIC SCHOOLS: COMPREHENSIVE INTERNAL PROGRAM RE-VIEW PROCESS: A PLAN TO MONITOR AND EVALUATE SPECIAL EDUCATION PRO-GRAMS IN BOSTON PUBLIC SCHOOLS (January 1983); N. MEHLEM AND E. KEARSE, INDEPENDENT MONITOR'S REPORT OF THE SCHOOL DEFENDANTS' COMPLIANCE WITH THE ORDERS OF THIS COURT (December 9, 1983).

113. *See* DEPARTMENT OF EDUCATION: PLAN TO MONITOR BOSTON PUBLIC SCHOOLS SPECIAL EDUCATION 1983–84, RELATIVE TO ALLEN V. MCDONOUGH (July 26, 1983); DEPARTMENT OF EDUCATION. MONITORING REPORT ON BOSTON PUBLIC SCHOOLS' SPECIAL EDUCATION 1983–1984, RELATIVE TO ALLEN V. MC-DONOUGH 2 (February 1984). The DOE's plan to review the Boston School Com-mittee's Chapter 766 compliance was in addition to the general oversight and moni-toring functions that it performs in all Massachusetts school districts pursuant to federal and state special education laws. Boston agreed to pay the DOE consul-tants who would be hired to work directly on the *Allen* monitoring. Interview with Arlene Dale, DOE Monitor, and Marie Lindahl, DOE Boston Liaison, Boston, Massachusetts (November 29, 1984).

114. The monitors have also used site visits to check the validity of information being submitted, and they have generally found a high level of consistency between the information reported by building administrators and their observations made during the site visits. *See* N. MEHLEM AND E. KEARSE, INDEPENDENT MONITOR'S REPORT OF THE SCHOOL DEFENDANTS' COMPLIANCE WITH THE ORDERS OF THIS COURT 1–5 (April 5, 1984); MEHLEM AND KEARSE, *supra* note 112, at 1–5.

115. This program is known as the Comprehensive Internal Program Review Process, or CIPRP. The independent monitor and a parent generally accompany School Department personnel on these visits. The program uses as a basis a moni-toring process developed by the DOE. Dale and Lindahl Interview.

116. See letter from Nancy I. Mehlem, Independent Monitor to Chief Justice Morse (March 5, 1986) (SEIMS Status Report). The SEIMS system has two major goals: to provide a tracking system following all students through the entire Chapter 766 process and to generate computerized IEP and progress reports.

117. Letter from Chief Justice Thomas R. Morse to Michael Betcher (August 20, 1984).

118. For example, the number of IEPs not fully implemented for the first three months of the 1984–1985 school year was 3,563 compared with 2,363 for the 1983–1984 school year and 1,866 for 1982–1983. A. DALE, N. MEHLEM, ET AL., JOINT MONITORING REPORT ON BOSTON PUBLIC SCHOOLS SPECIAL EDUCATION 1984–1985, RELATIVE TO ALLEN V. MCDONOUGH 60 (April 1985).

119. *Id.* at 59.

120. DEPARTMENT OF EDUCATION, MONITORING REPORT, *supra* note 113, at 6.

121. JOINT MONITORING REPORT, *supra* note 118 at 60. The qualifications of those who filled bilingual vacancies also was an issue. Of 64 bilingual special educa-tion teachers hired for the 1984–1985 school year, only 38 were appropriately certi-fied. *Id.* at 63. The system was also experiencing substantial difficulties in its ability

to translate IEPs into Spanish; the number of IEPs awaiting translation increased to 941 as of January 1985. *Id.* at 70.

122. *Id.* at 67.

123. Order of June 5, 1986 at ¶ 3.

124. Further Order Concerning Independent Monitor (January 8, 1986). Michael A. Rebell, the author of this article, was the consultant appointed.

125. Order Concerning Disengagement at ¶ 6 (July 30, 1986).

126. *Id.* at ¶ 12. Michael A. Rebell, the disengagement consultant, was appointed Disengagement Master.

127. *Id.* at ¶ 15. A series of "exceptions," such as parental requests for delays or a need for special additional assessments, which were defined in detail in the appendix to the order, would not be included in these calculations.

128. Shortly after the conclusion of the 1986–1987 school year, Chief Justice Morse signed an Amended Order Concerning Disengagement (July 28, 1987). This document made certain technical modifications in the definitions of substantial compliance in response to technical difficulties experienced in the first year of the order's operation. In addition, the order enhanced the role of the PAC by granting it staff support and funding at the School District's expense (¶ 18). (Issues concerning school system funding of PAC activities had been the single matter brought for formal resolution before the Disengagement Master during the 1986–1987 school year.)

129. The monthly data report for June 1988 indicated a cumulative compliance rate as of March 1988 with regard to original evaluations of 60 percent within 30 school working days and 90 percent within 60 school working days, instead of the 90 percent and 99 percent rates required under the Amended Disengagement Order. In some categories of "IEPs not implemented," such as psychological counseling, resource rooms, and physical therapy, the 97.5 percent compliance requirement was achieved.

130. At the end of the 1987–1988 school year, Chief Justice Morse signed a Supplemental Disengagement Order, which, in furtherance of the Disengagement Plan, replaced the independent monitor with an "*Allen* Monitor" operating under the auspices of the state DOE (but with defined, independent responsibilities). The order also required the School Department to submit a "Compliance Action Plan," which would identify each area of current noncompliance, explain the noncompliance, and describe specific remedial actions that would be taken to remedy each such area. By the end of the summer, the defendants had submitted their plan and, despite the mayor's earlier imposition of a ceiling on increases in education expenditures, he had agreed to provide supplemental funding necessary to carry out the designated remedial measures.

131. In the initially separate *UCP* case, a set of interrogatories was submitted and answered, but no depositions or other forms of discovery were undertaken.

132. A hallmark of all "new model" institutional reform litigations is the length of their remedial stages. (*See, e.g.,* Chayes, *The Role of the Judge in Public Law Litigation,* 89 HARV. L. REV. 1281, 1298–1302 (1976). In other types of new model cases, such as desegregation, however, the lengthy remedial phase is generally preceded by an extensive liability stage, as discovery processes and a hotly contested trial can take years to complete.

133. Ironically, but not surprisingly from the viewpoint stated in the text, the three specific remedial devices that Judge Nickerson mentioned in his 1983 order but specifically declined to mandate, that is, appointment of a data consultant, appointment of an educational policy consultant, and the mandatory hiring of 75 additional SBST teams, were each incorporated in the stipulation signed by the parties the following summer. This seeming irony merely illustrates the fundamental point being made: The court, on its own initiative, was not inclined to mandate specific structural reforms, levels of resource commitment, or even particular negotiating techniques. Its pressure did, however, induce the defendants to reconsider—and this time to accept—remedial devices that plaintiffs and the Special Master had previously proposed.

134. In contrast to Judge Nickerson's consistent reliance on the parties for reform proposals in *Jose P.*, Justice Morse did at one stage initiate an important compliance mechanism, namely the compensatory services program. The general dissatisfaction with the workings of this remedy makes it the exception that proves the rule: This judicial initiative based on traditional compensatory principles did not provide structural reforms geared to the unique needs of the disabled in this case.

135. Comparative assessments between systems with different underlying structures require extensive analysis and methodological sensitivity. For example, *Jose P.*'s active plaintiff participation mode would appear to represent a more intrusive form of judicial involvement. It could be argued, however, that the ongoing presence of the bombastic Rodriguez and his eight-person staff, which conducted visits to a substantial proportion of Boston schools, constituted a more significant interference with daily school operations than did the weekly meetings of plaintiffs' and defendants' counsels in *Jose P.* Even in its later reduced forms, the permanent presence of external monitors arguably imposed more formidable, judicial pressure than *Jose P.*'s extensive, yet intermittent, plaintiff presence. For an overview of the variety of forms that judicial intervention has taken in a number of analogous institutional reform litigations, *see* Reynolds, Dooley, and Parry, *Court Monitors and Special Masters in Mental Disability Litigation*, 12 MENTAL AND PHYS. DIS. L. REP. 322 (1988).

136. DAVID AND GREENE, *Organizational Barriers to Full Implementation of P.L. 94–142*, in SPECIAL EDUCATION POLITICS 115, 127 (J. Chambers and W. Hartman eds. 1983). *See also* Kirp, Buss, and Kuriloff, *Legal Reform of Special Education: Empirical Studies and Procedural Proposals*, 62 CAL. L. REV. 40 (1975); Lipsky and Weatherly, *Street Level Bureaucrats and Institutional Innovation: Implementing Special Education Reform*, 47 HARV. L. REV. 171 (1977); R. WEATHERLY, REFORMING SPECIAL EDUCATION: POLICY IMPLEMENTATION FROM STATE LEVEL TO STREET LEVEL (1979); KIRST AND BERTHEN, *Due Process Hearings in Special Education: Some Early Findings from California*, SPECIAL EDUCATION POLITICS, *supra* at 136; M. REBELL, IMPLEMENTATION OF COURT MANDATES CONCERNING SPECIAL EDUCATION: THE PROBLEMS AND THE POTENTIAL (1981); Rosenburg and Philips, *The Institutionalization of Conflict in the Reform of Schools: A Case Study of Court Implementation of the PARC Decree*, 57 IND. L.J. 425 (1982); Neal and Kirp, *The Allure of Legalization Reconsidered: The Case of Special Education*, 48 LAW AND CONT. PROB. 63 (1985).

137. "The *Jose P.* litigation has had a major impact on the delivery of special services in the school system. The school-based structure for conducting evaluations, the renovation of buildings to provide accessibility, and the detailed procedures for

parent participation are examples of the substantial systemic changes that have occurred. In many ways, the litigation has been instrumental in clarifying the legal rights of handicapped students to educators and administrators at every level of the school system." Fafard, Hanlon, and Bryson, *Jose P. v. Ambach: Progress Toward Compliance*, 52 EXCEPTIONAL CHILD. 313, 321 (1986). (It is relevant to note that one of the authors of the aforementioned article is an official of the defendant's Division of Special Education, one is its Chief Compliance Officer, and one is the lead counsel for defendants in *Jose P.*) *See also* COMMISSION ON SPECIAL EDUCATION, SPECIAL EDUCATION: A CALL FOR QUALITY 6 (1985).

138. Chicago presents an interesting case for comparison. No major class action litigation concerning implementation of P.L. 94–142 had been filed there, although the Office of Civil Rights of the U.S. Department of Education had monitored compliance since at least 1979. On August 12, 1988, an OCR administrative law judge issued an extensive ruling, which concluded:

> [T]he Board has been woefully neglectful during the recent past in fulfilling its obligations to afford handicapped children their federally-mandated "meaningful access" to an education. Thousands of children have plainly been denied evaluations and reevaluations for many months; a significant number of those found to need special education have been required to wait manifestly unacceptable periods of time to be afforded such assistance.

In the Matter of Chicago Board of Education, Compliance Proceeding, Dkt. No. 87–504–2, p. 47 (August 12, 1988). The administrative law judge recommended that federal funding for the special education programs be terminated. *Id.* at 48.

139. J. VITERITTI, ACROSS THE RIVER: POLITICS AND EDUCATION IN THE CITY 206 (1983). COMMISSION REPORT, *supra* note 137, at 3, similarly concluded: "The *Jose P. v. Ambach* lawsuit, brought in 1979, spawned federal court judgments, stipulations and implementation plans that now govern (in over 200 separate detailed provisions) virtually every facet of the New York City special education system."

140. "Without the case, special ed would have had less priority, especially when there was a budget cut in 1980. . . . [S]pecial ed was never cut like other programs. . . . [T]he class action was very significant in this respect." Betcher Interview.

Note also that, consistent with structural discrimination theory, despite the narrow framing of the original complaint in desegregation-conscious Boston, the judicial process in the *Allen* case soon evolved into an active institutional reform process.

141. *See, e.g.*, Steven, Wyatt v. Stickney *Concludes with a Whimper*, 11 MENTAL AND PHYS. DIS. L. REP. 139 (1987) (landmark institutional reform case is terminated at a time when "600 institutionalized residents remain housed in the sub-standard Bryce Hospital building, which sparked the original litigation").

142. *Compare, e.g.*, Penick v. Columbus Board of Education (S.D. Ohio 1985, unreported) (court injunction dissolved in light of "substantial accomplishment" of desegregation goals) and Morgan v. McDonough, 554 F. Supp. 169 (D. Mass. 1982), *aff'd on other grounds*, 726 F.2d 11 (1st Cir. 1983) (plan for court disengagement with continued monitoring responsibility to be vested in state education department), *with* Keyes v. School District No. 1, Denver, Colo., 609 F. Supp. 1491 (D. Colo. 1985) (termination of jurisdiction denied since all students do not yet have "equal access

to the opportunity for education") and Vaughns v. Board of Education of Prince George's County, 758 F.2d 983 (4th Cir. 1985) (previously terminated desegregation case reopened). *See generally,* Gewirtz, *Choice in the Transition: School Desegregation and the Corrective Ideal*, 86 COLUM. L. REV. 728, 789–798 (1986).

143. *See, e.g.*, Ricci v. Callahan, 646 F. Supp. 378 (D. Mass. 1986) (court disengages from class action concerning rights of the mentally retarded, based on findings of substantial compliance); *cf.* B. ACKERMAN, RECONSTRUCTING AMERICAN LAW 35 (1984) ("A final judgment no longer suggests that everything worth saying has been said, only that it is best, all things considered, to say no more for a time").

PART III

Equal Educational Opportunities
for Women

CHAPTER 4

Judicial Oversight of Agency Enforcement: The *Adams* and *WEAL* Litigation

ROSEMARY SALOMONE

THE BROAD DEBATE over the court's role in education litigation conjures up bold images of federal judges taking over the management of large urban school systems through seemingly endless decrees. Using the mechanism of injunctive relief, judges have defined local instructional methods, education goals, and budgetary priorities in order to achieve social reform through structural reform. That is the way the American public views the judicial activism of recent years, for the drama of institutional takeovers is newsworthy, politically provocative, and intellectually debatable.

We find no such broadscale litigation aimed at reforming local education institutions to promote the rights of women. In fact, with regard to women's rights, judicial activism has operated, in a direct way, more at the macro level of national civil rights policy than at the micro level of local practice. Obviously, federal policy determinations eventually filter down and influence school practice, but that type of constitutional interpretation and statutory fine-tuning does not necessarily involve the courts in the daily management of school systems.

Nevertheless, while the courts have not promoted sex equity through local school implementation decrees, one longstanding court case has used the structural reform model of litigation to shape social policy on a national scale through judicial oversight of federal agency enforcement. In the debate over the court's role in education litigation, *Women's Educational Action League (WEAL) v. Cavazos*[1] and its companion case, *Adams v. Cavazos*,[2] provide a uniquely interesting perspective on the place of the judiciary in the administrative state. This ongoing litigation, dating back to 1970, addresses the court's role in overseeing the enforcement activities of executive level agencies, in this case the Office for Civil Rights (OCR) within the Department of Education.[3]

The *Adams* case was initially brought as a race discrimination case, challenging the failure of the former Department of Health, Education and Welfare (HEW) to enforce Title VI of the Civil Rights Act of 1964.[4] The litigation eventually expanded to include the agency's enforcement activities on behalf of linguistic minorities under Title VI, women under Title IX of the Education Amendments of 1972,[5] and the handicapped under § 504 of the Rehabilitation Act of 1973.[6] The *WEAL* case, brought in 1974, challenged the federal government's failure to enforce certain sex discrimination laws, including OCR's unimpressive record of Title IX enforcement.[7]

Adams and *WEAL* taken together represent a coordinated and concentrated struggle on the part of civil rights groups to force the federal government to investigate and resolve speedily and fairly allegations of discrimination in educational institutions across the country. These are essentially procedural cases. The outcome sought in the litigation is fair process to overcome a systemic and pervasive disregard for the educational rights of women students and faculty.

As compared with other forms of discrimination, such as race and handicap, sex discrimination derives a certain validity from two factors, both of which heighten the importance of fair process in decision making. First of all, while most Americans agree that black children should be afforded educational opportunities equal to those of white children (albeit with considerable disagreement over the precise remedy to achieve that end), there does not exist the same consensus as to the education of women. Many in our society still blatantly support traditional sex role stereotypes. Similarly, while few people would absolutely deny educational access in some degree to handicapped children, denial of educational access is widely and overtly practiced against women—sometimes justified under the guise of protectionism; other times more boldly promoted for administrative convenience, financial economy, or just plain social attitudes.

Second, many of the underlying complaints brought by women lack at first blush the immediacy of race or handicap bias claims. In comparison, some claims may appear poorly substantiated, such as the denial of an application for promotion to administrative ranks. Others appear even trivial, such as the failure of a school to establish an intercollegiate basketball program for girls where one exists for boys or the refusal by a university to permit women to play on a student–faculty graduate school team. Yet on closer examination, these are serious denials to educational access—to enjoy all the social as well as educational advantages that come with full participation in the academic community. On an equally significant symbolic level, the foreclosure of women from any aspect of the educational enterprise conveys the message to all involved that women are less than equal to men. The reality of limited opportunities and frustrated dreams eventually manifests itself in lower aspirations on the part of women themselves—a vicious cycle indeed.

Over the years, the failure of OCR to enforce civil rights laws has taken many forms in response to a mixture of changing politics and the ongoing intervention of the court. The *Adams* and *WEAL* litigation was initially spurred by an express refusal on the part of the OCR to use its administrative machinery to enforce Title VI. When pushed by court order to do so, the agency refused to address Title IX violations. In later years, although obligated to utilize adequate procedures in the processing of all civil rights complaints, civil rights groups charged the agency with widespread delays in conducting investigations and processing complaints, lack of complainant input into conciliation agreements made with educational institutions, and failure to monitor the implementation of negotiated settlements. Despite this dismal picture, the agency in recent years has aggressively pursued release from any judicial oversight of its enforcement mechanism.

At the heart of the controversy is the remedy imposed by the district court in the mid 1970s—a system of timeframes within which the agency must carry out its enforcement duties of complaint resolution and compliance reviews. The plaintiffs continue to charge OCR officials with abrogation of their statutorily defined duties to enforce civil rights laws in the educational arena. The defendants now charge the court with having violated separation of powers doctrine by acting as the managerial overseer of an executive agency. They also claim that the plaintiffs lack standing to sue. For the plaintiffs this has always been and still is a clear civil rights action. For the defendants it strikes at the core of managerial prerogative and governmental structure. In between sits the district court judge who, until seemingly pushed to dismiss the case under the weight of Supreme Court developments, doggedly maintained jurisdiction over the case while carving out a limited role in overseeing the agency's procedure and not the substance of its decisions.

As a case study on law, politics, and policy in the context of structural reform, the following analysis attempts to view litigation of this nature as a critical component of the political bargaining process through which public policy is shaped over time. The facts as they have unfolded over more than a decade and a half lead us through four presidential administrations, either resigned, sympathetic, or hostile to civil rights concerns; through a dramatically changed political climate; and through crucial developments in Supreme Court doctrine that bear on the outcomes of this dispute in particular and on the future of public law litigation in general. Specifically, the case illustrates both the political potential and the institutional limitations of achieving social reform through litigation. It also underscores the degree to which successful implementation of the court decree, especially over time, depends on the surrounding political environment and the stability of political consensus. Law, in a sense, emerges as much as a function of politics as of legal principle.

The legal issues raised in the *WEAL* and *Adams* litigation focus directly on judicial legitimacy while the facts and political events shed light on judicial capacity. The discussion that follows addresses both the normative questions on the proper role of the courts *vis à vis* the other branches of government, and the descriptive questions concerning the district court's ability to shape and implement public policy effectively in a political and legal climate over which it has no control. In examining OCR's Title IX enforcement activities before and since the *WEAL* and *Adams* court-ordered timeframes, the study concludes that the federal court has served as an effective and a necessary voice in the enforcement of educational rights for minorities in general and for women in particular. But before turning to the particular events of the case as they continue to unfold, we must establish the theoretical framework for the discussion and draw the political and social landscape against which the case has taken shape.

THEORETICAL FRAMEWORK

Courts as Policymakers

Since the early 1960s, the mobilization of interest groups has become an increasingly popular phenomenon on the American political scene. Spurred on by "rising expectations" and attitudes of "entitlement," the phenomenon of group mobilization has inundated the policy-making arena.[8] As the courts became caught up in that process, initially through race desegregation cases in the 1960s, group activity expanded beyond legislative lobbying and into the realm of litigation. As the federal courts relaxed procedural requirements for class action suits during those early years, litigants were able to pursue court action with a potentially broad social impact. The field of public interest law evolved and proved successful in protecting and expanding minority rights. Out of these developments grew a new model of *public law litigation* requiring revised approaches to party configuration and to the relationship between the substantive violation and the relief sought.[9] That model has carried the courts beyond their traditional dispute resolution mode and into the realms of legislative policy making and executive and administrative enforcement activities.

Taking their lead from the model developed by the NAACP that had led up to the Supreme Court's decision in *Brown v. Board of Education*,[10] other advocacy organizations adopted *planned litigation* as a vehicle for incremental social reform.[11] As the Supreme Court developed constitutional doctrine that expanded the protection afforded racial minorities, other groups attempted to piggyback onto those rights. Interest groups historically underrepresented in the majoritarian political process—women, linguistic minorities, the handicapped—began to make an end-run around the legislative branch and carry their claims before the federal courts. This increasingly popular strategy served to legitimize certain concerns and to pull together the requisite interest groups to press for a political solution.[12]

During the 1970s in particular, this interplay between the courts and

Congress in fact became established as a distinct pattern of educational policy making. First, the courts determined constitutional guarantees; then Congress gave substance to those definitions and established remedies and procedures for the enforcement of rights defined; and then the courts in the next cycle clarified legislative ambiguities or cast the issues back into the political arena for further congressional fine-tuning. The executive branch, with its regulatory and enforcement powers expanded by Congress, weaved in and out of this interplay.

The court's role as an actor in the policy-making process has captured the attention of lawyers, political scientists, and policy analysts. One approach views the policy-making process as one of "mutual adjustment" with one side making tacit but important concessions to the other.[13] Law and politics reshape each other. The political process, increasingly pluralist in nature, must take constitutional values into account, while the judicial process tends to avoid authoritative order in favor of a search for agreement.[14] On the broad scale, the judge is just one voice among many in the public inquiry that gives meaning to the ambiguous and often conflicting values contained in the Constitution.[15] Political scientists in particular view the court as a political institution. However, the judicial proceeding is only one step leading toward the ultimate resolution of conflicts with other solutions subsequently pursued through the legislative and administrative machinery.[16] Litigation serves a useful preliminary function in redistributing power and influence in the political arena. As already noted, it may provide the initial catalyst for change by politicizing individual discontents and mobilizing a constituency for action.[17] Court action may also serve as an agenda-setter: defining the issues, exploring policy options, testing public opinion for subsequent legislative or administrative action.[18]

Other commentators have been more skeptical, and even critical, of the court's role in the policy-making process. The interplay between courts and legislatures has been described as a "tug of war." The more effectively each institution "plays its role," the more remote a decided victory for either side becomes.[19] One set of arguments against judicial activism focuses on the issue of *legitimacy*—maintaining the proper balance in separation of powers, protecting majoritarian government, and assuring the representativeness of the parties litigating for those ultimately affected by the court's decision. Another line of attack concerns judicial *capacity*. Here the arguments focus on the inability of courts to obtain adequate social science data in the fact-finding process, the lack of judicial expertise in certain policy areas, and the institutional limitations of the courts in implementing and monitoring public policy.[20]

The opponents of this role argue that courts, in "trying to create a better society, have increasingly lost the respect and trust of the people"[21] and that judicial review may "dwarf the political capacity of the people" and "deaden its sense of moral responsibility."[22] Where courts usurp power from the legislative branch in order to remedy an evil that the people choose not to remedy, this "smacks of the discarded doctrine that 'the end justifies the means.'"[23] And where the legislature has already taken a position on an issue, the court should not "thwart it except where the legislature imposes on individuals or minorities in so fundamental a fashion as to necessitate invoking the safeguards of the Constitution."[24]

Courts as Administrators

The discussion so far has focused on the quasi-legislative aspect of judicial activism; namely, the role of the courts in shaping public policy and reforming society through constitutional and statutory interpretation. The courts in recent years have also become engaged in defining and overseeing enforcement activities of administrative agencies. This body of case law covering *structural* or *institutional* reform is a subset of *public law litigation.* However, here the specific aim is not only to reshape social policy in a broad sense, but to reform more directly specific public institutions charged with carrying out legislative policy and constitutional values. Unlike the conventional dispute resolution model of litigation, the focus in structural reform is not on the actual "wrongdoing," but rather on a "social condition" and the "bureaucratic dynamics" that have produced it. The organization must bear the costs and managerial burdens of reformation not necessarily because it has engaged in any wrongdoing, but because the organizational *status quo* threatens "constitutional values."[25]

In litigation of this nature, the remedy is shaped and reshaped over time through a continuous relationship developed between the judge and the parties. The implementation of the decree is both "incremental" and "cyclical," each step followed by "assessment, reaction, and further adjustment."[26] By actively orchestrating this gradual and cyclical process, the judge becomes a policy planner, manager, and political powerbroker.

Judicial activism in structural reform has generated considerable scholarly debate. Some see this role as not only legitimate but necessary. Courts need not have the only word, or even the last word, but they must be allowed to speak and to speak with some authority.[27] In the more narrow context of the individual case, the court can "facilitate the processes of mutual understanding, communication, and consensus building."[28] Litigation can open up both the political and the administrative processes to new groups and interests and, in so doing, prompt administrative agencies to take their claims seriously.[29] In this scenario, the court becomes a "partner" in the broader political struggle "to make the bureaucracy behave" and is, therefore, a necessary actor in the "modern administrative state."[30] If the other branches want to avoid court intervention then their officials should diligently exercise their responsibility for overseeing constitutional values.[31]

On the other side of the issue, the opponents of court-managed institutional reform have assailed the federal courts for expanding the use of discretionary equitable relief beyond its intended limitations. They maintain that courts have distorted the concept of remedy from compensation for individual wrongs to assuaging the effects of past wrongs.[32] According to this argument, an activist federal judiciary has destroyed the nexus between wrong and remedy. An individual wrong now demands a group remedy.[33] And down from the scholarly dialectics on judicial legitimacy and capacity, court intervention in "social policy administration," it is argued, reduces, in effect, administrative "responsibility," "range of discretion," and "authority"; "gives greater weight to theoretical than practical or clinical considerations" and to the "speculations" of social scientists; and increases the "power of the legal and the more theoretical professions" over that of the practitioners.[34]

The debate concerning the court's appropriate role in the legislative and enforcement processes, however, refocuses somewhat when the decree implementation stage engages the federal court not in managing the affairs of local and state agencies but in overseeing the managerial discretion of a coordinate branch of the federal government. In cases of this nature, federalism concerns do not apply and criticism centers on constitutional legitimacy. For those who advocate judicial restraint, the involvement of the court as a third party enforcer of executive agency responsibilities not only undermines the doctrine of separation of powers but raises the connection between wrong and remedy to an even higher degree of remoteness than commonly found in public law litigation. Judicial activists, on the other hand, hail such litigation for its broader potential impact on national policy as compared with action taken against individual school systems or institutions. With civil rights requirements often tied to conditional grants of federal funds, judicial intervention in agency activities can enhance the power of the federal purse in effectively and efficiently achieving legislative goals.

Viewed in either micro or macro perspective, the underlying question remains. Just how far may the courts go in protecting minority rights where political institutions have arguably abrogated their moral and legal responsibility to do so? The answer to that question becomes more problematic, and the efficacy of a court decree more uncertain, where the institution charged is not a direct provider of services such as a school system or institution of higher education, but a governmental enforcer of legal rights such as the U.S. Department of Education.

THE SETTING

Historical Perspective on Women's Rights

Historically, the unequal treatment of women has stemmed from both economic motives and social misconceptions. These two factors have significantly constrained the opportunities open to women and have limited their life chances. Social attitudes are difficult to change. More than a century after the first wave of feminist activity, women have yet to achieve full equality of consideration with men. Nevertheless, in the past two decades, broad scale government intervention has permitted women to make great strides in achieving social and economic equality. In forging this new national agenda to promote women's rights, the federal courts have given life and momentum to a movement that could progress just so far in the ambivalence and caution of the legislative and executive branches. In the field of education, judicial activity has been vigorous and steady. This is of particular significance, as sex biases are so deeply entrenched in social attitudes, and education serves as a primary vehicle in molding those attitudes for the future.

The push for educational equity for women began in the early nineteenth century. At that time, women of the privileged class began to promote the education of women. Catharine Beecher, outraged by the increasing numbers of women working in the mills, suggested that all women be afforded "a well-rounded education." However, her work in establishing normal schools for training teachers was equally motivated by a belief that it was more important "that women be educated to the virtuous, useful, and pious, than that they become learned or accomplished."[35] Emma Willard had a somewhat different perspective on intellectual development. In 1821, she opened the Troy Female Seminary. At a time when high school education was closed to women, she offered courses in advanced algebra and geometry and thereby began to dispel the traditional notion that women were intellectually inferior to men.[36] Oberlin College pioneered coeducation and racially integrated higher education in 1833 but, in reality, fostered the belief that women were to be "helpmates" to assist men in carrying out their missionary calling on the frontier.[37]

With the industrialization that followed the Civil War, women's education picked up momentum and high schools were opened for girls. The elite sister schools had opened their doors to upper-class women and had affiliated with their male counterparts in the Ivy League. Yet equality had its price. The intellectual and domestic aspects of womanhood could not coexist. Most female college graduates in the late nineteenth century never married, and the careers they chose were typically "nurturing" ones—social worker, librarian, nurse, and teacher.[38] This ghettoization of women into a narrow band of career choices has perpetuated those professions as low-status and low-paying to the present day.[39]

These early efforts to bring women into the educational sphere as students and teachers were directed at an elite group of the socially and economically privileged. The impact of these reforms on broader social policy and attitudes was negligible. It would take almost a century and a complete social upheaval before women would begin to enjoy the full advantages of equal educational access. In fact, it was not until the early 1970s that sex bias in American society finally emerged as a major policy issue. The previous decade had witnessed a broad expansion in college education for the "baby boom" generation. As those women entered the work force in record numbers, they were confronted with a world of limited employment opportunities, barriers to professional advancement, and a persistent earnings gap between the sexes.

The successes of racial minorities in achieving social policy reform through legislative and judicial action encouraged women. The tone of the country was supportive of individual rights, and the prospects of piggybacking onto the gains of the civil rights movement were promising. Involvement in the civil rights and anti-war efforts of the 1960s had trained a cadre of female activists in the art of organizing group pressure to promote political and social causes. Disillusioned by the male dominance of these earlier rights-oriented groups, women gradually formed their own political associations, such as the National Organization for Women (NOW) and the Women's Equity Action League (WEAL).[40]

In the 1960s, early efforts to promote sex equity focused on employment discrimination. During those years, Congress enacted the Equal Pay Act of 1963,[41] which requires equal salaries and wages for equal work, and Title VII of the Civil Rights Act of 1964,[42] forbidding discrimination in employment on the grounds of race, color, religion, sex, or national origin. In 1967, President Johnson amended Executive Order 11246 to include sex discrimination.[43] That order requires federal contractors with at least $50,000 worth of contracts and 50 or more employees to develop a written affirmative action plan in order to remedy the effects of past discrimination and prevent current discrimination.

With the establishment of advocacy groups such as NOW and WEAL in the late 1960s, women continued to seek court enforcement of employment rights through litigation. At the same time, the movement intensified its efforts to break down the legal and social barriers that were impeding women's educational development. Initial research on the issue unmasked a deeply entrenched system of traditional sex roles and pervasive differential treatment of the sexes. Inequities were found throughout, from kindergarten to higher education, in admissions, instructional offerings, guidance and career counseling, vocational education opportunities, athletics, and employment.

In 1971–1972, women received 44 percent of the bachelor's degrees nationwide but only 16 percent of the doctorates and 6 percent of first professional degrees.[44] In 1972–1973, 79 percent of all girls enrolled in vocational education classes were in home economics or an office/business program.[45] In contrast, during that same period, boys accounted for 73 percent of all students enrolled in high school physics and 66 percent enrolled in trigonometry.[46] More than 80 percent of students participating in inter-scholastic high school sports were male.[47] The proportions were similar for intercollegiate sports at four-year colleges.[48]

The employment figures were equally grim. While women represented approximately 63 percent of the total number of educational professionals in 1972–1973, more than 99 percent of the superintendents were men and the percentages of male high school principals were 98 percent, 97 percent in the junior high schools, and 80 percent in the elementary schools.[49] In 1975–1976, of all the instructional faculty in institutions of higher educa-tion, only 24 percent were women. Among the highest rank of professor, women accounted for only 10 percent.[50]

As already noted, efforts to achieve equality for women have assumed a congruence between civil rights and women's rights. Relying on the race analogy, women's groups have pushed litigation and legislation in the di-rection of equal access to jobs, schools, athletics programs, and other social institutions. Similar to the development of federal policy on race discrimi-nation, early litigation focused on the definition of constitutional norms through the Fourteenth Amendment equal protection clause.[51] With the enactment of Title IX and its 1975 implementing regulations,[52] that law emerged as the primary tool for defining equal educational opportunity for women. And the federal courts took to the task of breathing life into what appeared to be a vaguely and ambiguously articulated statement of legislative reform.

Title IX: The Legal and Political Environment

From the school desegregation experience, women learned both the potential and the limitations of constitutional litigation as a vehicle for social reform. In fact, it was not until the Civil Rights Act of 1964 and its implementing regulations put teeth into the constitutional values embodied in the Fourteenth Amendment that the courts were able to achieve signifi-cant school desegregation throughout the South in the late 1960s. During those years the three branches worked hand-in-hand to realize the promise of *Brown v. Board of Education.*

But when the women's movement took hold in the early 1970s, the politi-cal tide had begun to turn. The executive branch had become less sympa-thetic to equality issues and a backlash had begun to develop in Congress. With the passage of Title IX in 1972,[53] it became clear that the only hope for effective and substantial change was a strong regulatory scheme and en-forcement mechanism. Women's groups undertook an organized lobbying effort, despite opposition from some segments within the feminist ranks who feared that the "hierarchical," non-participatory nature of lobbying would merely legitimize Washington, D.C.'s "sexist political order."[54] Groups such as NOW and WEAL channeled their energies into two outcomes: passage of the Federal Equal Rights Amendment (ERA) and the administrative enforcement of statutory protection in employment and education.

The ERA, which had languished in Washington since 1923, gained popularity in the early 1970s only to meet narrow defeat in the state ratification process.[55] With the promise of a comprehensive constitutional amendment left behind, the piecemeal legislation enacted by Congress over the previous two decades gained renewed importance in the struggle to develop sex equity as national policy. As for educational rights, Title IX took center stage.

Congress enacted Title IX of the Education Amendments of 1972 as part of a larger legislative package that included amendments to Title VII of the Civil Rights Act of 1964[56] (repealing the exemption of educational institutions), Title IV of the Act[57] (authorizing the Attorney General to bring suit in sex discrimination cases regarding admissions and allowing Title IV funds to be allocated to end sex discrimination), and the Equal Pay Act of 1963[58] (repealing the exemption of managerial and executive positions). The Act's legislative history provides little evidence of any strong political support for the measure.[59] The year was 1972 and congressional battles over court-ordered busing to achieve racial balance in the schools eclipsed any implications Title IX might have had for reforming American education. In fact, Title IX was largely the product of skilled drafting and bargaining on the part of Rep. Edith Green (D.-Ore.) and Sen. Birch Bayh (D.-Ind.). Contrary to popular belief, Title IX did not grow out of a lobbying effort from the women's groups, which were not as tightly organized as they later came to be and which, at that time, were focusing their lobbying efforts on ratification of the ERA.

The battles over Title IX began after the law was enacted and the Department of Health, Education and Welfare (HEW) set about the task of carrying out its statutory duty to promulgate implementing regulations. A series of post-enactment amendments to the law[60] made HEW both uncertain of the law's coverage and mindful of a persistent movement within Congress to limit the law's scope. One such proposed amendment, introduced by Senator John Tower (R.-Tex.), which would have exempted revenue-producing sports from Title IX prohibitions, in fact prodded HEW into issuing proposed Title IX regulations in June 1974. At this point a coalition of women's groups, which later became known as the Education Task Force, was formed to persuade Congress to approve the final regulations.[61] The small size but large presence of this group was aptly described by one of its members:

> It was far more effective than it ever should have been. It was a dog and pony show that we walked around Washington. It was a small group that represented American voters. It was a very political process. It angered the "old boy network"—calling [HEW Secretary] Weinberger from Harvard and Yale to lay hands off [i.e., yield to their demands]. [anonymity requested]

HEW did not submit its final Title IX regulations to Congress until June 1975, one year after it had issued its proposed regulations and three years after Congress had enacted the law. Drawing on Title IX's exhaustive legislative history, the agency interpreted the law's mandates and prohibitions to include employment, athletics, admission and financial aid policies,[62] testing,[63] recruitment efforts,[64] counseling,[65] and criteria for selection of sports programs[66] that have a disproportionate effect on students of one sex.[67]

The HEW regulations included various mechanisms for determining violations. School districts and educational institutions were required to submit with each application for federal assistance, regardless of funding source, an assurance that they would operate the proposed program in compliance with the law.[68] In addition, the Title IX regulations incorporated by reference a detailed set of procedures applicable to race and national origin discrimination under Title VI of the Civil Rights Act of 1964.[69] Those procedures granted OCR the authority to demand compliance reports of federal aid recipients[70] and access to the recipients' books, accounts, and records.[71]

The Title VI procedures, as applied to Title IX, granted federal officials (in this case OCR officials) the authority and express responsibility for investigating cases of possible noncompliance and to take affirmative steps where voluntary compliance could not be achieved. More specifically, those procedures required OCR to conduct periodic compliance reviews of educational institutions receiving federal aid,[72] to process complaints filed with the agency by individuals and groups,[73] and to conduct a prompt investigation whenever a review, report, or complaint revealed a "possible failure to comply" with Title IX.[74] Where the agency could not resolve the matter informally, it was required to achieve compliance by terminating or refusing to grant federal funds to the institution or by "any other means authorized by law," including reference to the Justice Department.[75]

With the publication of the final Title IX regulations in 1975, Congress and the executive branch, acting through HEW, seemed to take a pro-active stance toward establishing sex equity in education as national policy. History would prove otherwise. The ambiguities in statutory language necessary to achieve political consensus and the subsequent dilatory enforcement practices within HEW soon threatened to eviscerate Title IX and turn its original promise on its head. The federal courts were again called upon to wrest Title IX from the opposing forces; namely, school systems and institutions that blatantly defied the law and legally challenged its scope, as well as the federal bureaucracy that more subtly dragged its feet in enforcement activities.

Despite the detailed procedures set forth in the federal regulations, OCR's efforts to enforce Title IX were slow and ineffective. According to a 1978 study conducted by the Project on Equal Education Rights, OCR resolved only 20 percent of the Title IX complaints filed against elementary and secondary schools between June 1972, when the law became effective, and October 1976.[76] During that period, the number of complaints rose steadily from 129 in 1973 to 424 in 1976.[77] Ninety-six percent of the complaints filed in 1973 were still pending in 1976 without either findings or negotiated remedies.[78] The cases OCR did resolve during those years waited an average of 14 months for final action.[79] As time wore on, the gap between complaints resolved and those originally filed widened from three out of 127 in 1973 (a gap of 124) to 75 out of 317 in 1976 (a gap of 242).[80] During the period from 1972 to 1976, 564 of the total Title IX complaints filed related to employment, 351 to athletics, 289 to access to courses, 187 to procedural requirements, 130 to student rules, and 64 to miscellaneous violations.[81] Subsequent data were equally disheartening. In fiscal year 1979, there was an average time lag of one year and five months between receipt and closure of a Title IX complaint. At the beginning of fiscal year 1980, of those cases still unresolved, 60 percent had been pending before the agency for more than one year.[82]

If OCR's initial three-year lag in publishing the Title IX regulations signaled a rough road ahead for Title IX implementation, the inefficiencies and ineffectiveness of the complaint review process were even clearer signs of administrative apathy. Faced with limited enforcement activities and processing backlogs, women began to seek direct redress in the federal courts. That body of litigation, together with the complaint resolution and compliance review process within OCR, engaged the federal courts for the next decade in the task of determining the specific contours of Title IX coverage. During those years, the Supreme Court upheld a private right to sue under Title IX (removing women's rights from under OCR's foot-dragging in processing complaints),[83] and determined that Title IX prohibits sex discrimination against educational employees and not just students.[84]

Despite these early victories, Title IX enforcement efforts experienced a serious setback in 1984 in *Grove City College v. Bell*.[85] On the one hand, the Court held that only the specific educational program receiving federal aid, including indirect financial aid that goes directly to students and not the institution, is sufficient to set Title IX in motion. On the other hand, the Court held that only the specific educational program receiving federal aid and not the educational program as a whole would be covered by the Title IX mandates. In other words, most athletics programs, which typically do not receive federal financial support, would no longer come under Title IX. The exception would be athletic scholarships awarded through the institutions' financial aid programs that are federally funded through government guaranteed loans and grants to students.[86]

These threshold legal skirmishes over preliminary scope and coverage significantly slowed the pace of sex equity in education. By limiting themselves to technical legal issues, these cases failed to resolve at the national level whether doing X, Y, or Z was in fact sex discrimination. In a more fundamental sense, the litigation created a climate of uncertainty with OCR, which in turn all but brought the enforcement process to a grinding halt on certain key issues. As these lawsuits worked their way up to the Supreme Court, conflicting lower court decisions created inconsistencies in the law's enforcement across regional OCR offices and caused the central office to set aside certain types of complaints until final determination by the Court. Employment and athletics complaints became the primary casualties under this unofficial policy.

ORIGINS OF THE LAWSUIT

Early History of the Office for Civil Rights

To understand the political climate in which the *WEAL* and *Adams* litigation was born, we must first back up to the 1960s and examine the origin of OCR itself. Only then can we understand the external stresses and strains that weighed upon the agency during those early years, defined and redefined its mission, and ultimately pushed the advocacy groups into court.

When the Civil Rights Act of 1964 was initially enacted, Congress placed the enforcement of Title VI, as to educational matters, within the Office of Education. This marked a radical change in that office's mission and scope of authority. The aggressive enforcement stance demanded by that Act, together with the programmatic authority given to the Office of Education the following year under the Elementary and Secondary Education Act (ESEA), clearly ran counter to the office's long-standing policy to respect local autonomy. Historically, the federal government had shown great deference to the decentralized structure of American politics and to the strong political culture of local control over education. ESEA, however, represented the first massive infusion of federal dollars into education. At the same time, Title VI enforcement efforts engaged the Office of Education in establishing regulations and guidelines to move the nation's schools swiftly and effectively toward racial integration.

During the first two years of Title VI, the power of the federal purse served as a strong incentive toward school integration. However, national reaction to what was perceived as creeping federal intrusion soon began to mount. In order to stave off a movement within Congress to eviscerate federal control by consolidating categorical programs into a block grant, HEW Secretary John Gardner removed civil rights enforcement power from the Office of Education and placed it in a newly created Office for Civil Rights within HEW. By wresting civil rights compliance from Commissioner of Education Harold Howe, whose aggressive enforcement policy particularly had angered southern congressional members, Gardner was able to achieve two critical objectives. He realized that he had to defuse congressional opposition to the Office of Education and maintain federal poverty programs. At the same time, he had to maintain the enforcement program's morale which would have been destroyed had he dismissed the commissioner.[87]

The newly created Office for Civil Rights (OCR) decentralized many of its activities to HEW regional offices, while working closely with the Civil Rights division of the Justice Department to desegregate southern schools and put northern school systems on notice to desegregate. In March 1968, OCR issued a firm set of guidelines directing school officials to submit desegregation plans by the fall of 1969 for those districts where freedom-of-choice programs had failed to bring about racial integration.[88] Those guidelines were reinforced by the Supreme Court that same year.[89]

As OCR carried out its enforcement mission with increasing vigor, a conservative tide began to swell. That tide brought Richard Nixon to the presidency. Soon after coming to power, the Nixon administration was faced with a dilemma: either maintain the President's campaign support for freedom-of-choice and local discretion or begin the process of terminating funds from southern school districts that failed to meet the 1969 compliance deadlines.[90]

The route chosen was determined as much by political constraints as by conscious policy choice. Despite mounting congressional opposition to HEW's enforcement policies during the late Johnson years, there still existed a slim majority supporting the effort. As long as that majority continued to cast a pro-desegregation vote, the Nixon administration was foreclosed from disengaging the HEW machinery through radical legislative change. Added to congressional resistance were a federal court system that was beginning to apply the Title VI law, regulations, and guidelines in a spirited way, and the HEW bureaucracy itself, which was staffed by a core of zealous civil rights activists who specialized in Title VI compliance and were protected from removal by civil service laws.

Political and practical constraints forced the administration to seek more indirect avenues for policy change. It did so by using the "thin layer of political appointees" at the top of HEW to redefine gradually the agency's goals and narrow the scope of compliance remedies. For all appearances, nothing seemed to change much since the previous administration. The Title VI law and regulations remained. Lower-level bureaucrats in the regional offices continued to investigate pending cases and recommend compliance steps to the Washington office, but in Washington the enforcement process encountered a stone wall at the top. Without approval from high-level Nixon appointees, all the energy and commitment from below would never trigger enforcement proceedings, and without the signature of the Secretary of HEW, funds could not be terminated.[91]

HEW's fund termination powers became an early target for the administration. In July 1969, HEW Secretary Robert Finch and Attorney General John Mitchell announced a new policy whereby HEW, rather than engaging the agency's fund-termination powers, would henceforth refer cases to the Justice Department for enforcement through litigation.[92] That policy statement touched off a heated controversy within the Nixon administration that soon forced the resignation of the Director of the Office for Civil Rights, Leon Panetta. The response from the ranks of HEW career employees to the Panetta resignation was dramatic and "unprecedented." Close to 1,800 employees petitioned the Secretary of HEW for clarification of the agency's civil rights policies.[93]

With the last HEW proponent of fund termination no longer in command and high-level Nixon administration officials expressly threatening to reassign or even dismiss federal officials who continued to promote busing,[94] OCR became an "agency without a mission."[95] From an office that originally had been given the task, just a few short years prior, to eradicate dual school systems, OCR had been turned into a paper mill, churning out endless compliance reports while school desegregation efforts nearly came to a grinding halt.

The immediate impact of the Finch–Mitchell policy shift was striking. Between 1964, when the Civil Rights Act was passed, and March 1970, HEW terminated funds from an average of 60 noncomplying school systems per year.[96] In contrast, in 1969 HEW conducted only 16 compliance reviews. That figure declined steadily over the next five years; by 1974, no reviews were being conducted.[97] Between March 1970 following the Panetta dismissal and February 1971, HEW brought no enforcement proceedings but continued to advance federal funds to schools found in violation of Title VI.[98] As the agency's indifference "filtered down" to the local level, school systems began to withdraw desegregation plans, submit new ones, or completely ignore the law.[99] Against this backdrop of enforcement breakdown, civil rights groups went to court in 1970 in an attempt to reactivate HEW's fund termination mechanism.

Expanding the Agency's Mission

Through the early 1970s, as the Nixon administration repeatedly took the teeth out of OCR's enforcement powers under Title VI, Congress heaped more responsibility on the agency to enforce the provisions of Title IX (sex discrimination), 504 of the Rehabilitation Act (handicap discrimination), and the national origin provisions of Title VI (linguistic minority discrimination).[100] In one sense, this expansion of groups under the civil rights umbrella strengthened the movement by providing civil rights advocates with a comprehensive arsenal of legal weapons. Yet, in another sense, it threatened to weaken the movement by pitting interest against interest in the competition for federal enforcement resources and attention. HEW itself became increasingly immobilized by confusion within its ranks and by the increasingly complex and diverse mound of paperwork.

OCR had been established in the 1960s with one goal—school desegregation. That was the way even the pro–civil rights holdovers continued to see the agency's mission. When sex discrimination reared its head and finally became OCR's legal responsibility, some staff resisted. Faced with the ambivalence of top officials and the subtle but effective policy changes instituted by the Nixon administration, OCR staff feared that the agency's expanded workload would only dilute their efforts to desegregate the nation's schools.

But it was not only philosophical differences that created the climate for a broadened litigation effort. OCR's very mission forced it to address controversial social and political issues such as busing to achieve school integration, bilingual education for linguistic minorities, and sex equity in intercollegiate sports, among others. As a result, the agency became crisis-oriented, moving "from one crisis to another without any long-range planning or clear policy direction."[101] With a change in administration and a change in policy less than two years into its life, OCR failed to establish a structured management system in its early years. Through the 1970s, as its mission moved beyond race and into sex, handicap, and national origin discrimination, the agency was ill-prepared to handle the volume and complexity of its workload. In 1969, OCR received fewer than 300 complaints. By 1975, that figure had increased by seven or eight fold. At the end of 1969, OCR had only 58 unresolved complaints. Six years later, there were 1,800.[102] By the time the Carter administration took over in 1977, "people found boxes of letters and complaints that no one had answered."[103] The perils of poor management finally surfaced in the court-ordered timeframes that subsequently became the central focus of contention.

THE MANY FACES OF THE LITIGATION

By 1970, it became clear to civil rights activists in Washington that nothing short of a federal court order could revive OCR's enforcement efforts. In October of that year, the NAACP Legal Defense and Educational Fund (LDF) joined with Joseph Rauh, Jr., and John Silard, two Washington attorneys long active in the civil rights movement, to bring action against then HEW Secretary Elliot Richardson individually and as head of the agency. In the ensuing decade and a half, that initial effort developed into a web of collateral actions brought by women's groups (*WEAL v. Cavazos*); intervention on behalf of women, the handicapped, and linguistic minorities; and a series of court orders mandating succeeding presidential administrations to enforce legal mandates.

ADAMS V. RICHARDSON:
MAPPING THE STRATEGY

In litigation of any nature strategy is all-important. In public law litigation, in particular, the complexity of the issues, the diversity of interests at stake, and the potential for protracted and close judicial involvement in the implementation stage all demand the most carefully designed strategy from the onset. Attorneys are mindful that they are seeking a type of relief and a degree of judicial intervention that courts grant reluctantly and only in the most extreme circumstances. Thus attorneys must respond to judicial concerns by defining the issues in the context of judicially manageable standards, by supporting their arguments with defensible statistics, and by framing the court's role in the narrowest terms possible.

The architects of the initial litigation were master strategists. They realized the political implications of engaging the federal judiciary in the enforcement activities of the executive branch. They also realized the setback that the civil rights movement would suffer if their strategy failed. Early on it was agreed that Rauh and Silard (later joined by their partner, Elliott Lichtman) would be responsible for the legal work, while the LDF staff would gather supporting data on compliance with the court's order.[104] They chose the June 1969 Finch–Mitchell policy statement as the symbolic act against which to vent their outrage. They used data drawn from OCR files to give substance to the lawsuit. The focus was HEW's failure to bring enforcement proceedings against southern and border states with regard to elementary, secondary, higher, and vocational education.

The attorneys were keenly aware of certain threshold hurdles they would have to overcome. Chief among these was the question of "standing," that is, whether the plaintiffs had suffered or were in immediate danger of suffering some direct injury stemming from HEW's failure to enforce Title VI. To meet that requirement, they selected as plaintiffs individual students attending segregated schools under desegregation plans that HEW had failed to enforce. Many of these were children of community activists and known to cooperating attorneys or community organizers. Kenneth Adams, a high school student in Brandon, Mississippi, and the son of local community activist, John Quincy Adams, was one of these. Yet despite the care with which the attorneys selected the plaintiffs back in 1970, the standing issue would potentially become the litigation's nemesis in later years as the initial parties were graduated from school and were replaced in 1982 and 1984 by students attending schools where OCR had current complaints, compliance reviews, and investigations pending.

The attorneys further recognized that, in asking the federal court to grant injunctive relief (an extreme remedy in any case) against a co-equal branch of government, they were challenging the much revered doctrine of "separation of powers." This was indeed a bold effort, particularly in the historical context of 1970 prior to the expansion of the public law litigation model during the ensuing decade. With these political and institutional constraints in mind, the attorneys were cautious and conservative in what they sought from the court. As Elliott Lichtman notes, from the beginning they established a pattern of "framing the issues as procedural issues—using OCR's own data —careful not to give information on particular cases." [105] In other words, the attorneys did not ask the court to examine or overturn substantive decisions made by OCR in specific cases, but rather focused their arguments and the relief sought on the procedures established by the agency for enforcing legal compliance. This approach permitted the court to devise an order that could be enforced against judicially manageable procedural criteria and, at the same time, be imposed with the least intrusion on agency discretion.

THE EARLY ORDERS: PASSIVE RESISTANCE

Agency discretion was in fact at the core of HEW's defense in the first round of the litigation and has continued as a major point of argument. HEW officials maintained that it was within their agency's "absolute" discretion to secure compliance by voluntary means. In *Adams v. Richardson*, [106] the district court ruled otherwise. In an opinion that laid the foundation in approach, judicial philosophy, and party roles for the numerous court orders that were to follow, Judge John H. Pratt of the federal district court in Washington, D.C., granted summary judgment to the plaintiffs.

Typical of the *Adams* opinions, the court's 1972 decision was long on "findings of fact," but somewhat short on "conclusions of law." In an apparent effort to undergird the court's order against the agency, the opinion presented detailed data on HEW's failure to enforce Title VI under the Finch–Mitchell policy, in contrast to the agency's earlier aggressive enforcement activities. The court concluded that HEW had only "limited" discretion in seeking voluntary compliance. "Where a substantial period of time has elapsed," during which the agency has sought compliance through negotiation, its "discretion is ended." Agency officials then have a duty either to initiate enforcement proceedings through fund termination or use any other means authorized by law, such as referring the case to the Justice Department.[107] As for the exact wording and substance of the order, the court requested that the plaintiffs consult with the defendants and report back within 30 days.

In an affirmation of the federal court's power and duty to render such an order, the final order drew on the Supreme Court's decision the previous year in *Swann v. Charlotte–Mecklenburg Board of Education*, [108] where the Court had upheld the broad powers of federal district courts to fashion appropriate remedies in race desegregation cases. Judge Pratt's reliance in *Adams* on the urgency and social significance of the race issue, undergirded by Supreme Court doctrine, would become more apparent in later years as other victims of discrimination, most notably women, attempted to piggy-back on to the *Adams* orders. The judge directed the agency to submit periodic reports to plaintiffs' counsel on progress made toward compliance with the order.[109] This was the first in a series of increasingly detailed, process-oriented deadlines that would engage the court in an agency-oversight role for more than a decade.

At the time of the ruling, Congress had just enacted the Title IX prohibitions against sex discrimination. The enactment of a similar law against handicap discrimination during that session looked promising (Congress enacted § 503 of the Rehabilitation Act of 1973 later that year). Agency officials feared that new statutes would add to their enforcement workload, a workload the court would now closely scrutinize. Anxious to overturn what they hoped was an aberrant judicial nod to the civil rights groups, HEW appealed. In June of that year the appeals court, sitting *en banc*, unanimously sustained the basic elements of Judge Pratt's order (with minor exceptions pertaining to higher education, which are not noteworthy here).[110] The court rejected as untenable HEW's contention that the means of enforcement was a matter of absolute agency discretion. In language more caustic than that used by the district court, the appeals panel zeroed in on the plaintiffs' challenge that HEW had "consciously and expressly adopted a general policy which is in effect an abdication of its statutory duty."[111] This reference to HEW's abandonment of all enforcement activities resulting from the 1969 Finch–Mitchell policy statement would be used by the government a decade later to justify its release from the court's continued oversight. The court further underscored the narrowness of the district court's involvement. "Far from dictating the final *result* with regard to any of these districts, the order merely requires *initiation* of a *process* which, excepting contemptuous conduct, will then pass beyond the District Court's continuing control and supervision" (emphasis added).[112] The district court, more than a decade later, would rely on this limiting language to disengage itself from the case.

The strong language used by the appeals court and the unanimity of its decision dissuaded HEW officials from appealing to the U.S. Supreme Court.[113] Instead they complied, swiftly initiating enforcement proceedings, accelerating site reviews, issuing letters of noncompliance, and settling some cases. The agency's apparent resignation to the court order, however, produced a lot of shaking but very little movement toward bringing recipients of federal funds into legal compliance.[114] The situation, in fact, was a harbinger of things to come. The court had framed the order in "procedural" terms, and the agency was offering a "procedural response." By addressing the processing failures identified by the court, the agency was left free to make the fewest "substantive changes" possible.[115]

In 1974, the plaintiffs were back in court moving for further relief and timeframes to force HEW enforcement efforts. In its first supplemental order, in March 1975,[116] the district court reprimanded HEW for its continued foot-dragging. With regard to the 17 southern and border states covered in the 1973 order, the court imposed what was to become the first in a series of timeframes for each stage of the administrative enforcement process. In a 90-90-30 day framework, the court mandated that HEW determine whether a district is in Title VI compliance within 90 days of receiving a complaint or other information of racial discrimination. Where noncompliance was found, HEW had an additional 90 days to seek voluntary compliance through negotiation and 30 days beyond the total 180 to initiate enforcement proceedings. The court again ordered HEW officials to submit periodic verified reports to plaintiffs' attorneys including a summary of steps taken to comply with the timelines. Those deadlines henceforth would not only apply to pending cases, but would also bind future government officials on prospective complaints and compliance reviews.[117]

NEW RIGHTS, NEW ISSUES, AND NEW PARTIES

Structural reform litigation has several unique characteristics that distinguish it from the traditional adversarial process. Two of these are of particular relevance here. First of all, litigation of this nature is multidimensional. As the court tries to achieve justice both in the particular case and in the larger context of righting a social wrong, the court's decision may draw into the litigation other individuals or groups whose interests have been affected. After the first few court orders in protracted litigation of this type, it is not uncommon for new plaintiffs to intervene in the case, thereby assuring that the court will weigh their interests in subsequent deliberations. Second, one must consider the larger political environment in which the court operates. The issues before the court are essentially social issues. As such, they are broader than what they initially appear to be in the context of the lawsuit. The court is not the only arena in which they may be addressed. The effectiveness of the court's decision depends on policy choices that continue to be made in the legislative arena. However, the court is constrained to balance only those interests before it. The judge may be well aware of concurrent legislative action that could undercut its order at the implementation stage by creating new competing interests and place additional strain on the agency. The court must ignore these concerns until presented by the affected parties. Nevertheless, this collateral activity may continuously define and redefine the legal claims and recharge the litigation for years.

The *Adams* litigation clearly fits this model. As it reached a critical juncture in 1974, the district court's order, with a powerful affirmance by a unanimous appeals court, had placed HEW under the gun—at the very least—to reactivate its Title VI enforcement machinery. With few results achieved, the *Adams* plaintiffs were back in court in 1974 seeking supplemental relief. In the meantime, Congress had enacted Title IX in 1972. By 1974, not only had HEW failed to publish Title IX regulations, but the agency was channeling its resources into Title VI enforcement at the expense of other categories of discrimination. Congress had also enacted the § 504 handicap discrimination provisions in 1973, but HEW had not made any significant movement toward establishing a regulatory scheme or enforcing the law by 1974. This expansion of statutory rights in the early 1970s and HEW's unwillingness or inability to enforce those rights would soon turn the district court judge into the primary guardian of civil rights policy in the educational arena. The first sign of this came in 1974, when the Women's Equity Action League (WEAL) initiated a sex discrimination suit similar to the *Adams* litigation.

ENTER WEAL

The Women's Equity Action League (WEAL), a small Washington-based civil rights organization of approximately 2,000 voting members, was founded in 1968 by dissidents from the National Organization for Women (NOW). At that time, several disagreements erupted within the NOW ranks and the organization "fissioned off" several new groups. The radicals, particularly the younger members of the movement from New York, sought to replace what they perceived as NOW's "elitist structure" with a system whereby decision-making positions would be "chosen by lot and frequently rotated." From this splinter group grew the "October 17 Movement," which eventually came to be known as "The Feminists." For the conservatives within NOW, the break came over what some considered militant tactics employed by the NOW mainstream at the organization's second annual conference the previous year in Pittsburgh. More specifically, this group opposed NOW's early support of abortion law repeal, a position that many of them eventually embraced. WEAL emerged from this end of NOW's political spectrum.[118]

WEAL's founder was Elizabeth Boyer, an Ohio lawyer, university professor, and organizer of that state's NOW chapter. Boyer established a conservative image for the organization not only to provide a structured forum for those who perceived NOW as too radical, but also to recruit more politically moderate women who already held professional positions of power. In those early days, WEAL called itself the "right wing of the movement" and even required sponsorship for membership in the organization.[119] As described by Bernice Sandler, an early WEAL board member and one of the chief architects of the WEAL political strategy: "Many of the early members were women like myself who would not, at least in those days, march in the streets. WEAL attracted activist middle-class women and placed on its Board several congresswomen and judges. . . . It still maintains a good deal of credibility on the Hill." [120]

WEAL's early attempts to establish a separate litigation arm similar to NOW and the LDF ended in a further "schism" over strategy. The splinter group, led by Jane Pinker, founded the Women's Law Fund under Ford Foundation support, thereby causing a temporary setback to the fund-raising efforts of the newly established WEAL Fund.

In lieu of maintaining its own staff of attorneys, WEAL relied on the volunteer services of attorney members of the organization, primarily on the commitment and skills of feminist attorney Marcia Greenberger. When first approached by WEAL in 1972, Greenberger was a staff lawyer at the Center for Law and Social Policy. At that time, the Center functioned as a public interest law firm based at Catholic University in Washington with substantial funding in its early days from the Ford Foundation. The Center subsequently formed the Women's Rights Project under Greenberger's direction.[121] The Project disengaged from the university in 1981, and presently has an independent existence as the National Women's Law Center, still based in Washington, D.C. The Center serves as in-house counsel to WEAL, which moved its headquarters to Washington in 1972.

As a lobbying and litigation group, WEAL has focused its efforts on discrimination against students and faculty, particularly in higher education. It has been a leader in academic discrimination litigation, an area of law from which most women's organizations have shied away. WEAL's interest in higher education in particular dates back to the organization's beginnings.[122] A number of WEAL board members were faculty members at universities across the country and thereby served as conduits for complaints on academic discrimination issues.[123]

In the late 1960s, Bernice Sandler contacted Mary Boyer concerning the untapped potential of Executive Order 11246[124] as a means to root out sex discrimination in academe. In 1970, WEAL filed its first complaint challenging sex discrimination in higher education institutions covered under the order. WEAL subsequently encouraged its members to file complaints with HEW. In the years that followed, WEAL itself filed, represented, or assisted women in filing more than 300 sex discrimination complaints against educational employers.[125] Sandler joined the effort by disseminating information through the Association of American Colleges. When the numerous complaints filed under WEAL supervision or encouragement went unresolved at HEW, it became clear that the agency was not enforcing the order. The situation rose to critical proportions as WEAL began to receive the fallout from campus action. Carol Polowy, former WEAL general counsel, describes the events leading to the *WEAL* litigation as follows: "People would file and generate a little campus action, but they were then alienated, ostracized, and retaliated against. All this was coming through the pipeline to WEAL. . . . People expected WEAL to do something. . . . All these women had put themselves on the line."[126]

Polowy enlisted the aid of Marcia Greenberger, and together they mapped out a litigation strategy similar to that used in *Adams*. However, unlike *Adams*, which had been brought on behalf of numerous individual students, the *WEAL* suit hinged on both organizational and individual plaintiffs. The WEAL attorneys were keenly aware of the long history of retaliation against women, and therefore had foremost in their minds protecting their members from further adverse action on campus. From the numerous complaints WEAL had on file, they searched for individuals who were relatively invulnerable to retaliation. They were particularly careful to include no untenured professors.

They finally identified five suitable and willing candidates. Two of these, Dorothy Raffel and Elizabeth Farians, who continue to have a live controversy with OCR, remain as named plaintiffs in the case.[127] Raffel, was a 13-year-old junior high school student from Pennsylvania. She charged her school with Title IX violations in providing an interscholastic basketball team for boys and not for girls and by unduly restricting her access to the school gymnasium after school hours. As a minor, she became a plaintiff in the case through her mother, Norma Raffel, whose own standing in the community, it was believed, would serve as a bulwark against any adverse community response to her daughter. The complaint charged that because of HEW's failure to issue Title IX regulations defining the scope of the law and providing complaint procedures, Raffel had been unable to "benefit from a school athletic program which is free from inhibited sex discrimination."[128] She subsequently went on to become a high school All-State basketball player in the state of Pennsylvania and attend Indiana University on an athletic scholarship. In February 1985, 11 years after her first OCR complaint, Raffel, then a graduate student at Pennsylvania State University, filed a complaint with OCR alleging that the university had discriminated against her on the basis of sex by refusing her participation on the all-male graduate student–faculty basketball team. According to her complaint, the situation denied her "social opportunities that could prove helpful in advancing (her) career and success in school."[129] OCR representatives subsequently tried to convince her to withdraw the complaint or to accept a resolution that would still fail to guarantee women graduate students "equal access" to intramural basketball. In May 1985, Raffel filed a similar complaint against the university with regard to its intramural soccer program.[130]

The second individual plaintiff who has remained in the case is Elizabeth Farians. In 1970, Farians filed a sex discrimination complaint with the Department of Labor (DOL) under Executive Order 11246 when she was denied renewal of her two-year contract as an Assistant Professor of Theology by Loyola University of Chicago. Under threat that the agency would otherwise close her file, she reluctantly accepted a settlement offer negotiated through HEW in December 1972. The Office of Federal Contract Compliance (OFCCP) within DOL subsequently intervened and found that there were sufficient grounds for questioning HEW's role in the negotiations and the terms of the settlement reached. Following a hearing, her case was closed. Farians maintains that while the agency has technically complied with Judge Pratt's order in ultimately processing her complaint, she questions the substance of that decision.[131]

In addition to the five individual plaintiffs, the WEAL complaint listed a number of organizational plaintiffs who sued in their organizational capacity, including WEAL itself, the National Organization for Women (NOW), the National Education Association (NEA), the Federation of Professional Women (FOPW), the Association for Women in Science (AWIS), and the U.S. Student Association (USSA). Neither the original complaint of November 1974 nor the amended complaint filed in January 1975 cited any specific injury to either the organizations or their members stemming from the government's failure to enforce the laws. They merely stated in general terms the interests that each organization sought to promote on behalf of women's educational equity. This deficiency was probably more a reflection of the broad permissible scope of standing doctrine during that period than the result of any tactical error in drafting the litigation documents. Nevertheless, this failure to address more fully the standing issue would come back to haunt the attorneys a decade later.

Aside from the legal status quo of the day, another probable explanation for the attorneys' having addressed standing requirements minimally was their reliance on the class action device to protect them from dismissal on the grounds of mootness or lack of standing.[132] The attorneys looked to the long haul. In view of the "amorphous and transitory" composition of the plaintiff class and the protracted nature of such litigation, it is not uncommon, in school cases for example, for the students named as representatives of the class to have graduated during the pendency of the lawsuit.[133] When this occurs, the court may permit the plaintiffs to add additional named parties to the class.[134] On the other hand, courts are more reluctant to add new party plaintiffs where the litigation seeks to redress not the rights of a broad class but of several individuals. There further exists a certain political advantage to the class action device. Neither the government agency under attack nor the court can dismiss a legal grievance defined in group terms as easily as an individual or an organizational claim.[135]

Armed with this conventional wisdom, the WEAL attorneys brought the action on behalf of "organizations devoted to the elimination of sex discrimination in all aspects of education; women who are, have been, or seek to be employees of educational institutions; students and parents of students in educational institutions; and taxpayers." They believed that the organizational plaintiffs would provide the *numerosity* of aggrieved individuals and the individual plaintiffs the *typicality* of claims to support their motion for certification as a class action suit.[136] The district court denied that request two years later and set the plaintiffs on an eventual uphill battle to defend their presence in court and the legal worthiness of their claims.

The litigation itself built on the *Adams* strategy of procedural safeguards. The action focused on fair process and the failure of the federal government to establish adequate and fair procedures to carry out its duties, particularly under Executive Order 11246 (as amended by Executive Order 11375), under Title IX, and under the procedural requirements and equal protection provisions of the due process clause of the Fifth Amendment.[137] The complaint did not reach the substance of agency decisions, but rather clearly spoke in the language of fair process as a means of promoting educational access. In addition to inadequate management and recordkeeping at HEW, the complaint attacked "the agency's procedures for enforcing the executive orders, particularly the failure to accord complainants the right of notice and participation in all stages of complaint investigation, negotiation, and resolution."[138]

The complaint specifically charged HEW with having abrogated its statutory duty by failing to issue final regulations establishing a formalized scheme to enforce Title IX.[139] As Marcia Greenberger notes: "We believed that if the process were carried out fairly, then the substance of decisions would be improved. . . . In fact, when the *WEAL* action was brought in 1974, there was no 'substance' to Title IX because there were no regs."[140]

WEAL AS INTERVENOR IN *ADAMS*

Initially, the women's groups involved in the WEAL action had no interest in joining the *Adams* litigation. They were content to have framed their own legal arguments, which they supported with compelling data on HEW's failure to carry out its enforcement responsibilities under Title IX and Executive Order 11246. However, Judge Pratt's March 1975 Supplemental Order in *Adams*, with its stringent timeframes for Title VI enforcement, changed the political picture. Enforcement of Title IX in the 17 southern and border states covered by the *Adams* order had come to a virtual halt. The following October, the HEW regional office in Dallas, which encompasses most of the 17 states, announced a policy whereby it would no longer enforce Title IX. HEW began sending letters to individuals filing Title IX as well as Title VI national origin complaints informing them that, for the indefinite future, their grievances would not be addressed. That December, representatives of women's groups met with HEW Secretary David

Mathews but were unsuccessful in their attempt to move him toward Title IX enforcement.

Realizing that Mathews' refusal closed off administrative channels of relief, the plaintiffs had little choice but to turn to the courts. They drew upon the complaint filed in the *WEAL* case the previous year and filed a motion for a preliminary injunction enjoining HEW from refusing to process Title IX complaints in the Dallas region. That action, taken in January 1976, prompted HEW to move in *Adams* for modification of the March 1975 order. HEW requested that the agency's proposed 1976 Annual Enforcement Plan, which would have included Title IX enforcement, be adopted by the district court in the *Adams* litigation, but the proposal would have required that HEW process only one-quarter each of the Title VI and Title IX complaints received. The women's groups demanded that HEW be required to investigate all Title IX complaints.[141]

With HEW attempting to bargain away Title IX enforcement under the aegis of *Adams*, WEAL decided to intervene in the case and have its voice heard. The women's coalition, represented by Marcia Greenberger and WEAL attorney Carol Polowy, went back to identifying appropriate plaintiffs, this time as intervenors. They selected two individual plaintiffs: a faculty member, Kay Paul Whyburn, and a student, Cynthia Buxton.

In October 1975, Whyburn had filed a complaint with the HEW regional office in Dallas alleging that she had been denied promotion to administrative positions in the North Forest Independent School District in Houston, Texas. She claimed that she had been discriminated against on the basis of sex; that is, that males with lesser qualifications had been granted such promotions. The following month, the Dallas office informed her by letter that the "priorities" established by the *Adams* court order made it "impossible to schedule Title IX complaint investigations at this time."[142] In October 1974, she had also filed a complaint, along with two other women, against the Houston Independent School District, alleging sex discrimination in areas including counseling, curriculum, employment, textbooks, and sports. As of March 1975, the HEW Dallas office had failed to process that complaint. Whyburn has continued as a named plaintiff throughout the litigation. In 1982, eight years after the Houston complaint was filed, the Dallas office of OCR sent her a letter asking if she still wanted OCR to investigate the complaint. Despite her affirmative reply, OCR failed to notify her further on the matter.

The second individual plaintiff intervenor was a student, Cynthia L. Buxton, who had filed a complaint with the Dallas OCR office alleging sex discrimination in her junior high school's athletics program. Buxton charged that the school district offered only volleyball and swimming as competitive sports for girls, while boys were offered more competitive athletic activities, including football and basketball. The complaint was filed in November

1975. While it remained unresolved as of the date of WEAL's motion to intervene in *Adams*, it was resolved at a later date, and Buxton subsequently was dropped as a named plaintiff. The suit also included organizational plaintiffs—WEAL, NOW, NEA, and FOPW.

Later in November, in what has been interpreted by some as a sign of disapproval as to the WEAL claims in *Adams*, Judge Pratt denied WEAL's motion to intervene, while granting that of the Mexican-American intervenors. According to the judge, the Title IX issues were best left to the *WEAL* suit.[143] WEAL found itself in a "Catch-22" situation. The same day, Judge Waddy, to whom the *WEAL* case had been assigned, denied the motion for preliminary injunction in that suit on the ground that the motion had been mooted by the WEAL plaintiffs' application for intervention in the *Adams* litigation. WEAL apprised Judge Pratt of the incorrect assumptions of both orders in an unopposed motion for reconsideration. When he denied that motion, WEAL moved for summary reversal in the Court of Appeals for the District of Columbia. The appellate court reversed, noting that HEW's motion for modification of the 1975 *Adams* order had "put squarely at issue the question of what amount of HEW resources should be devoted to the enforcement of Title IX" and that the interests of the WEAL plaintiffs were not represented by any of the parties to those proceedings.[144]

THE 1976 ORDER:
CONCILIATION AND RESIGNATION

The year 1976 marked a turning point in the litigation. The *Adams* suit now covered three areas of discrimination: race, national origin, and sex. The Title IX regulations had been set in place and could soon bury HEW in an avalanche of long overdue complaints. The handicap advocacy groups were clamoring for HEW to develop regulations pursuant to § 504. Once published, these could swiftly exhaust HEW's resources in complaint resolutions and compliance reviews. HEW officials realized the limitations of those resources and the agency's inability, given the best of intentions, to manage its current workload, much less what loomed on the horizon. Therefore they first unsuccessfully sought relief from the 1975 timeframes. They then agreed, at Judge Pratt's request, to negotiate with the plaintiffs.

Negotiations extended throughout the Spring of 1976, culminating in a settlement agreement entered by the district court as an order that June. HEW initially opposed incorporating the settlement into a court order, contending that the plaintiffs could seek judicial enforcement of any violations of the agreement itself. But Judge Pratt concluded otherwise, no doubt in response to the agency's poor record of compliance with the 1975 order.

For the first time since the commencement of the litigation, OCR's top staff, now headed by Martin Gerry, and attorneys for plaintiffs and intervenors were able to devise a mutually agreeable set of procedures that promised to both achieve civil rights enforcement and allow HEW some flexibility. The parties agreed to maintain the 90-90-30 day timeframe of the 1975 order. HEW agreed to expand the applicability of the timeframes beyond individual complaints to compliance reviews and to all cases covering national origin discrimination under Title VI and sex discrimination under Title IX. The agreement required HEW to publish an annual operating plan for OCR, to survey school districts in order to determine problem areas that necessitated compliance reviews, and to establish extensive reporting procedures for the agency to apprise the court and the plaintiffs of its enforcement activities.

In return, the plaintiffs agreed that OCR could suspend the timeframes for as many as 20 percent of the complaints where an excessive complaint workload had developed, that OCR could except from the timeframes up to 10 percent of the compliance reviews where the timeframes could not reasonably be met, and that the agency could extend the time rules for witness unavailability and could delay the start of the complaint timeframes until a complaint was complete.[145] The 1976 order contained no provisions covering Executive Order 11246. It also remained applicable only to the 17 southern and border states identified in the original 1970 complaint.

IMPLEMENTATION UNDER THE FORD ADMINISTRATION

Through 1977, the *Adams* and *WEAL* litigation had developed against the backdrop of the Nixon and Ford administrations. While Richard Nixon had taken a strong anti-busing position, neither he nor his successor had been openly hostile to civil rights concerns. The attorneys for the plaintiffs seem to agree that neither administration was as aggressive as plaintiffs would have liked, but "when forced to do things, they did so with a sense of the spirit of the law instead of trying to undercut it."[146] In fact, under the Ford administration, OCR had agreed to the first set of timeframes in 1975, published the Title IX regulations, and issued a set of guidelines for enforcing the rights of linguistic minority children, better known as the "*Lau* Remedies.*"

Gerry, who had been on OCR's staff since 1969, was thoroughly familiar with the agency's history of noncompliance and with its managerial problems. As he recalls the 1976 *Adams* order, "It was a pretty amicable set of negotiations. There were no serious differences on the basic timeframes or on principles. I had more problems selling them to my staff than with negotiating them."[147]

From a legal perspective, Gerry had serious concerns about the separation of powers issue raised by the court's involvement in the day-to-day management of the agency, but from a political standpoint he found the timeframes to be a useful management tool and used them to carry out his own agenda for operating the agency. The timeframes in fact provided him with leverage to decentralize the agency's workload and delegate decision making to OCR's regional offices. By shifting primary responsibility for complaint processing and compliance reviews to the regions, he believed he could not only speed up the enforcement process but hold the directors accountable for their decisions and thereby maintain quality control. The Washington office would not review cases unless specifically asked to do so by the regions.

Gerry admits that decentralization created a certain risk—particularly that regional staff would skimp on the process to move cases and meet deadlines. His office never succeeded in solving the problem of quality control. More rigorous accountability might have done the job.

> We were pretty good on the question, "Are we doing what we say we're doing?" But, "Are we doing it right?"—well that was more problematic. Some regions were closing cases just to get rid of the workload. . . . Maybe we should have held line managers more accountable—fire them if the case they worked on didn't hold up.[148]

Gerry saw OCR's role essentially as a prosecutorial one. The agency's job was to enforce the law and not to serve as a mediator in disputes between complainants and school systems. Federal law tied his hands on the integration issue. A 1974 congressional enactment of complex anti-busing legislation prohibited executive agencies from ordering the transportation of students farther than the school closest or next closest to their homes.[149] With student transportation eliminated as an available remedy, OCR turned to investigating "second generation" desegregation problems, such as patterns of discipline and expulsion, testing and tracking of minority students, segregation of faculty, and the broader issues surrounding educational access for women, linguistic minorities, and the handicapped. As a result of the investigations begun during the Nixon years, OCR initiated enforcement proceedings against the Chicago schools in the spring of 1976 and issued letters of findings to the New York City school system later that year.[150] These activities were collateral to the *Adams* order of 1976. Nevertheless, they place the enforcement of the *Adams* timeframes in the broader context of how the agency perceived its role, defined the problems to be addressed, and established its resource priorities during the Ford years.

THE CARTER ADMINISTRATION AND THE 1977 ORDER

Despite OCR's efforts to address systemic discrimination in the large urban school systems of the North, within a year of the 1976 settlement agreement it became apparent to the plaintiffs that HEW was again defaulting. OCR had permitted "hundreds of unresolved complaints" to accumulate and had committed "wide-ranging violations of the timeframes."[151] By 1977 this enormous complaint backlog had again brought enforcement to a virtual standstill. Title IX, § 504, and Title VI national origin complaints, especially from Hispanics filing with HEW's regional office in Dallas, were presenting OCR with a workload beyond its capabilities.[152] The problem the agency faced was "that the commitment Gerry had made to these groups to process complaints added up to more resources than OCR had."[153]

In fact, OCR began fiscal year 1978 with a backlog of approximately 3,025 complaints. The situation was such despite the commitment of what was apparently a friendly administration. In early 1977, President Carter announced to HEW employees:

> I'm committed . . . to complete equality of opportunity in our nation, to the elimination of discrimination in our schools, and to the rigid enforcement of all Federal laws. There will never be any attempt made while I'm President to weaken the basic provisions or the detailed provisions of the great civil rights acts that have been passed in years gone by.[154]

During his first week in office, HEW Secretary Joseph Califano announced a review of OCR policies, stating that there had been "too much data collection and too little enforcement."[155] The following month, he announced measures aimed at "rekindling the commitment of the Department . . . to forceful and fair enforcement of the civil rights laws." The Secretary clearly stated that "lengthy delays can undermine the purpose of the civil rights laws and destroy confidence in the Government's will to enforce them." He warned educational institutions, "[T]o insure compliance . . . we will order fund cutoffs if we must."[156]

Despite these early pronouncements, the Carter administration's civil rights record on enforcement fell far short of its rhetoric.[157] In a letter sent by Elmer B. Staats, Comptroller General of the United States, to Senator Birch Bayh, a number of contributing factors were cited, including "lack of a comprehensive and reliable management information system" and "lack of uniform policy guidelines and compliance standards."[158] Added to this were the agency's failure to fill vacancies, a mounting complaint backlog, and a growing number of lawsuits that required additional staff attention.

In June of that year, plaintiffs and intervenors in *Adams* again sought supplemental relief from Judge Pratt. Despite the administration's supportive position on civil rights, the new Carter appointees in HEW initially resisted further court intervention. The following September, HEW moved the court to adopt OCR's "Annual Operating Plan for Fiscal Year 1978." The plan called for a major reorganization including internally developed timeframes and enforcement objectives in place of those established by the 1976 court order.[159] Judge Pratt denied the motion and ordered the plaintiffs and HEW officials back to the bargaining table to negotiate a new order. After two months of negotiations over the workability of the timeframes and the need for flexibility, the parties entered into a carefully designed agreement, which became incorporated into a consent decree. That agreement, contained in 54 pages of 88 separately numbered paragraphs, reflected compromises on both sides. All the parties agreed that the consent decree would also apply to the separate *WEAL* litigation.

OCR agreed to maintain the 90-90-30 day timeframe of the previous orders and to apply them comprehensively to the agency's compliance activities nationwide with regard to race, national origin, sex, and handicap discrimination.[160] OCR further agreed to use its "best administrative efforts" to increase efficiency in the compliance process and "to apply for additional OCR personnel if necessary." In return for this expanded coverage and stepped-up enforcement efforts, the plaintiffs and intervenors agreed to a suspension of the timeframes for almost two years, until September 30, 1979. This would allow the agencies (the order brought the Office of Federal Contract Compliance's enforcement of Executive Order 11246 under the court's supervision) sufficient time to hire and train additional staff and develop a management system to eliminate the backlog.

One aspect of major significance in the 1977 order that often goes unnoticed is the due process principles promoted by the additional procedural safeguards. Henceforth, the agency would have to notify the school district or institution of the nature of any complaint filed, notify the complainant of the applicable timeframes, and notify all the parties of the investigation's preliminary findings. In other words, complainants would not only know the rules of the enforcement game, but would have information on initial agency findings in order to map out a strategy for bringing the issue to a fair and speedy resolution.[161]

Rather than resist compliance with the timeframes, HEW officials used the court order as leverage to get additional funds from Congress to increase the agency's staff and institute a broad range of management reforms. David Tatel, then OCR director and a longtime civil rights advocate, found both the court order and the timeframes useful in carrying out his administrative agenda:

> I went back to Congress with the help of the court order and got 900 more positions, increasing the staff from 1,000 to 1,900. . . . It was not just more money and staff. The consent decree helped in negotiating settlements with school districts and universities. An investigator would tell fund recipients, "Look, I have 90 days to complete this. If you don't cooperate, other steps will have to be taken." It gave some backbone to the whole enforcement process.[162]

When Tatel took over the agency, there was no structured management system. In addition to the enormous backlog of complaints, the agency was not conducting compliance reviews. Tatel subsequently negotiated the 1977 agreement to allow specifically for compliance reviews as well as complaint processing. He believed that by focusing on both, the agency would be able to address larger problems of discrimination while maintaining its responsiveness to individuals. In order to achieve those dual goals, he saw the need to initiate good management practices and to improve the training level of the staff. Under his direction, OCR developed a training center, a quality control system, and a management system. In other words, Tatel capitalized on the court order and converted it into management standards. By the time he left the agency in 1979, he "left behind a good training program and a significantly decreased complaint backlog."[163]

Tatel not only recognized the utility of the timeframes as a managerial tool, but he also knew how to translate them into a political medium that was effective and understandable in Congress. Rather than report the agency's progress to Congress in terms of the number of complaints processed or the number of investigations completed, he would report, "We helped 25,000 students in black schools go to integrated schools" or "50,000 young girls now have access to athletic programs."[164] By reporting in terms of the number of individuals whose rights had been protected, he was able to closely link management data to the agency's mission and thereby maintain congressional support.

Between 1977 and 1979, OCR moved the complaint resolution process forward with unprecedented speed. By November 1979, the complaint backlog from December 1977 had decreased from more than 3,100 complaints to approximately 360[165] "despite a heavy flow of new complaints and the simultaneous conduct of over 600 compliance reviews."[166] Plaintiffs' attorneys admit that credit for that progress goes largely to David Tatel himself, who "made a real good effort to comply with the court order. . . . A lot was lost when Tatel left."[167]

Nevertheless, compliance problems remained, especially in the area of Title IX. The 1977 order required HEW to resolve all "carryover" complaints by March 1979 and all "backlog" complaints by September 30, 1979.[168] As of June 30, 1979, OCR had not resolved 485 of the carryover complaints, 368 of which had been filed under Title IX. There were also a substantial number of unresolved backlog complaints, particularly concerning intercollegiate athletics and appearance codes.[169] The 1977 order further required the agency to process complaints within a given timeframe. However, as of August 1979, "OCR was meeting the timeframes of issuing letters of findings and for referral to Washington headquarters in only 60 percent of the Title IX complaints. And while its performance on compliance reviews was the most successful to date, as of August 1979, OCR was meeting only 29 percent of the timelines established in the court order."[170]

A substantial portion of these indications on noncompliance reflected OCR's failure to establish policies in two areas: intercollegiate athletics and appearance or dress codes. Added to this was the failure of the lower federal courts to concur on the issue of whether Title IX covered employment discrimination or was limited to students as the beneficiaries of federally funded educational services. In December 1978, one full year after the last court order, OCR published proposed policy interpretations on intercollegiate athletics[171] and proposed amendments to the Title IX regulations covering appearance codes.[172] By June 1979, a year and a half later, the agency had still not published final guidelines on either of these issues. At that time, HEW notified the WEAL attorneys that the agency was suspending any further enforcement of intercollegiate athletics under Title IX for an indefinite period.[173] In its report to the WEAL plaintiffs that same month, HEW admitted that it was delaying indefinitely consideration of 157 Title IX complaints pending "policy resolutions." The following month, the plaintiffs in *WEAL* and *Adams* returned to court seeking a contempt citation against HEW. Judge Pratt denied that request in November of that year.[174]

And so the Carter years ended with the *Adams* and *WEAL* plaintiffs back in court, despite the apparent progress made toward civil rights enforcement and the obvious goodwill existing between the plaintiffs and the agency, especially under Tatel's leadership. Satisfied with the agreement reached in the 1977 court order, plaintiffs were no longer seeking supplemental relief as they had in pre-1977 motions. They asked the court to hold the government in contempt of court for its "cavalier attitude" toward the 1977 order, but the contempt route was apparently too radical a departure from Judge Pratt's role as mediator and conciliator. The plaintiffs would more vigorously push him toward contempt as the Carter years turned into the Reagan years, and he would continue to push them to the bargaining table.

THE SHIFTING TIDES OF POLITICAL IDEOLOGY

Ronald Reagan's ascendency to the presidency in 1980 marked the beginning of a new ideological perspective on government. His campaign platform promised to "restore common sense and quality to education . . . [and] support deregulation by the federal government of public education." [175] Upon taking office, he characterized the governmental legacy left to him as intrusive, unmanageable, ineffective, costly, and not accountable. His minimalist approach to the federal role in education had broad implications for civil rights enforcement efforts.

Early on in his administration, high-ranking officials within the newly created Department of Education and the Justice Department began to translate this shift in political ideology into specific policy changes. Theirs was a broadscale attack on existing laws, regulations, and policies. Education Department officials proposed amendments to the handicap law and regulations and modifications that would weaken the bilingual education mandate for linguistic minority students. The Justice Department settled cases with minimal remedies, refused to support busing in school desegregation cases, shifted policy in pending litigation, refused to appeal lower court rulings limiting the government's enforcement power, and supported proposed legislation that would limit the power of federal courts to order busing remedies.

The Reagan administration's philosophy on government and civil rights quickly affected the scope and direction of OCR's enforcement efforts. In April 1981, Secretary of Education Terrel Bell clearly summarized his position in a letter to Senator Paul Laxalt (R.-Nev.): "Your support for my efforts to decrease the undue harassment of schools and colleges would be appreciated. It seems that we have some laws that we should not have, and my obligation to enforce them is against my own philosophy."[176]

That letter specifically addressed the issues of intercollegiate athletics and dress codes. On the first, Secretary Bell maintained that he had streamlined the size of investigations and investigative teams as a result of OCR having underestimated the staff needed to enforce the new Title IX regulations on intercollegiate athletics. On the second, he noted that he had taken action to withdraw the Title IX regulations governing appearance and dress. In a subsequent letter that year to Attorney General William French Smith, Bell denounced the Title IX regulations governing employment and revealed his plans to propose an amendment to those regulations that would significantly narrow their scope.[177] In response to protests from women's groups, the Department of Education pulled back the notice of proposed rule making. Nevertheless, the employment issue was decided by the Supreme Court the following year in *North Haven Board of Education v. Bell*,[178] where the Court ruled that Title IX does cover faculty as well as students.

These radical departures from longstanding civil rights policies set administration officials in direct confrontation with civil rights groups. Critics assailed the Reagan administration for failing "to develop—and implement —cohesive and consistent civil rights policies"[179] and for having "inadequately enforced and otherwise undermined, if not violated outright, settled law in the field of civil rights."[180] For the first time since the civil rights movement had begun two decades previously, civil rights activists were put on the defensive. The debate had shifted from one concerning the evils of government neglect to the evils of government intrusion.

As the issues became redefined, so did the specific arguments advanced on both sides. The public debate over civil rights took a new direction, and administration officials were eager to take on a social activist federal judiciary. Against this political backdrop, the *Adams* and *WEAL* litigation reached a critical juncture in the early 1980s. At that point, OCR and Justice Department officials advanced new defenses to get out from under the court-ordered timeframes, forcing the plaintiffs to modify their strategy and to pursue the case more vigorously than ever.

THE CONSENSUS BREAKS DOWN

From the very beginning of the litigation in 1970, plaintiffs had consistently used OCR's own data when framing their arguments before the court. The 1976 court order had formalized this strategy by requiring OCR officials to submit periodic reports to the court and to the plaintiffs on the agency's progress toward compliance.

The report OCR submitted in May 1981 indicated that the agency's compliance record was deteriorating rather than improving as time wore on. OCR had failed to complete the investigative stage of compliance reviews as mandated under the 1977 court order in every case throughout January, February, March, and April of that year. During the first quarter of that fiscal year, 79 to 88 percent of the compliance reviews were behind schedule. Data on complaint processing was similarly unimpressive. Between October 1980 and May 1981, OCR had failed to meet the timeframes for closing the investigation or referring for enforcement in approximately 60 percent of the cases in each of those two categories. In fact, the agency had met these timeframes in only 34 percent of the cases due between January and April 1981, a sharp decline from the 76 percent compliance rate in August 1979.[181] The report revealed several ongoing factors that continued to impede the agency's Title IX enforcement work. Included among these were "adverse court decisions" (Title IX's coverage of employment discrimination), "collateral federal court litigation" (the private right to sue under Title IX), and "the lack of policy in particular areas" (intercollegiate athletics and appearance codes).[182]

In June 1981, the *Adams* and *WEAL* plaintiffs once again moved for an order to show cause against the Department of Education and the Department of Labor's Office of Federal Contract Compliance (*WEAL* plaintiffs only) alleging that the agencies were in contempt of court for failure to comply with the 1977 timeframes. At a three-day hearing held before Judge Pratt in March 1982, the government made three arguments: First, the 1977 order required OCR to channel resources into complaint investigations, which provided fewer direct benefits and were less cost effective than compliance reviews; second, the time demands of more comprehensive reviews encouraged staff to undertake more single-issue reviews in order to increase the volume of deadlines met; and third, between 1977 and 1982, the increased number of § 504 complaints (eight to 36 percent) as compared with Title IX (36 to 12 percent) and Title VI (36 to 24 percent) complaints increased the need for additional resources to analyze the issues and train staff in the medical technology and data incident to claims relating to handicap discrimination.[183]

Judge Pratt found the agencies in violation of the 1977 court order, and affirming his continued jurisdiction over the case, expressed doubt that these violations would be "eventually eliminated without the coercive power of the court." However, ever mindful of the limited role he had carved out for the court from the inception of the litigation, he stopped short of finding current administration officials in contempt because they had "arrived on the scene relatively late."[184] Instead, he sent the parties back to the bargaining table, giving them until August 15, 1982 to arrive at a mutually agreeable consent order. In framing that order, he gave the parties two alternatives: Either they could reinstitute the 1977 guidelines, or they could modify them in view of the "changed circumstances" argued by the defendants; namely, the change in the "mix of cases" and the increased "complexity and difficulty" of the cases handled by the agencies since the court had imposed the timeframes.

What the judge failed to perceive, or did perceive but hoped to overcome, was that the parties were no longer operating under the same set of legal principles or under a political ideology that would permit a meeting of the minds through bargaining and compromise. Over the course of that summer, Judge Pratt conferred with the attorneys for both sides in his chambers and urged that the 1977 order be the starting point of any discussions: "[T]aking the structure of, say, our last order, which sets out these specific frame works of compliance in the various categories, that might very well be used as the format for your input with respect to the change of cases and the change of mix."[185]

As the August 15 deadline drew closer, it became clear to the plaintiffs and intervenors that the government would accept nothing short of radical departures from, and preferably the vacatur of, the 1977 court order. Having failed to reach an agreement by the court-designated date, each side submitted proposed revisions of the 1977 order. The government urged the court to vacate the five-year-old mandate, or in the alternative to allow the deadlines to be phased out or considerably relaxed. The draft orders submitted by OCR and OFCCP each contained a sunset clause whereby the jurisdiction of the district court over these matters would terminate after January 20, 1985.[186] The plaintiffs and intervenors, on the other hand, suggested that the original timeframes be maintained while permitting the Departments of Education and Labor to place 20 percent of their complaints on an extended schedule of no more than 30 days for resolution.[187]

In a March 1983 order, which included no fact findings, Judge Pratt entered a new injunction. This detailed 37-page order generally adopted the plaintiffs' proposals with some procedural changes from the 1977 order and with expanded recordkeeping requirements.[188] In those cases where investigations had been completed, the agencies had either to settle the case or take enforcement action within 90 days of the March 11 order. In those cases where investigations had not been completed, the agencies had 180 days to settle the case. In a major strengthening of the 1977 order, the court closed a loophole under which the agencies could delay resolving up to 20 percent of the cases indefinitely. However, it ordered the agencies to resolve even the exempt 20 percent within 345 days of receiving a complaint or within 330 days of initiating a compliance review. To provide civil rights groups with a regular data flow for compliance monitoring, the court ordered the agencies to submit to the district court, twice annually, comprehensive reports on their enforcement activities.

THE LITIGATION CHANGES FOCUS ON APPEAL

Reagan administration officials did not resign themselves to the court's mandate as previous administrations had done. Unlike their predecessors, they were not inclined to weave in and out of compliance reports and contempt motions or to follow the ground rules laid down by others. They aggressively pursued completely vacating the 1977 order. They viewed the timeframes not only as administratively burdensome, but as representing a political perspective on government that was contrary to their own. It was this more fundamental objection to the court's involvement in agency affairs that shaped the arguments on appeal. Taking the offensive, Justice Department attorneys went into court with both guns blazing, relying on recent developments in Supreme Court doctrine to support their legal arguments.

Key arguments advanced by both sides in their briefs and oral arguments before the court of appeals in March 1984 were as follows. The agencies challenged the constitutionality of the timeframes, questioned whether they reflected the intent of Congress in civil rights enforcement, and charged that the district court's oversight of their activities violated the constitutional principle of separation of powers. On this last count, the government maintained that the timeframes had established the district court as the "perpetual supervisor" of the two agencies, thereby placing them in an "endless judicial receivership." Specifically, the agencies argued that the timeframes had no support in the relevant statutes, that is, Title VI, Title IX, and § 504, nor in Executive Order 11246. They argued that the court had established an extra-statutory procedural framework and had intruded on the agency's resource allocation and budget process. By maintaining the force of the consent decree from one administration to the next, the court had permitted officials to "mortgage their responsibilities" and tie "their successor's hands in the overall management of the agency."

The government also argued that circumstances had changed since the original litigation had been brought. HEW's conscious policy of non-enforcement, which had triggered the litigation in the first instance, no longer existed. The Finch–Mitchell policy had long been withdrawn and OCR was now enforcing the law. Finally, they asserted that, since the Supreme Court had upheld a private right of action to enforce the provisions of Title IX (and impliedly Title VI and § 504) in *Cannon v. University of Chicago*[189] in 1979, OCR's primary role should be shifted to more systemic and not individual cases of discrimination.[190]

The government's arguments forced the civil rights groups to address thorny legal issues that had been hovering over the litigation since its inception. In response to the "separation of powers" argument advanced by the agencies, the plaintiffs argued that the district court had entered the 1977 consent decree at the "joint request of the plaintiffs and the executive agencies themselves." The executive branch, they maintained, may not hide behind separation of powers doctrine in violation of "important constitutional and legal rights." The plaintiffs maintained that the "changed circumstances" advanced by the agencies were indeed "picayune," and that the "private right of action (under Title VI) had been repeatedly recognized by the courts as far back as 1967," long before either the 1977 court order or the Supreme Court's 1979 decision in *Cannon*.[191]

By the following September when the court rendered its opinion, developments in Supreme Court doctrine had pushed the court in an unforeseen direction. The appeals court, in fact, did not reach the merits of the arguments. Instead, considering the government's fundamental argument that the district court had "lost sight of the specific goals of the initial suit," the court found itself obliged to address on its own motion "threshold Article III impediments to the initiation and maintenance of the action."[192] Relying primarily on the Supreme Court's opinion in *Allen v. Wright*,[193] decided during the pendency of the appeal, the court raised questions related to two specific Article III barriers: first, whether plaintiffs had standing to seek "broad and continued judicial superintendence of Executive Branch activity," and second, whether the case was moot; that is, whether the claimants continued to experience harm or were likely to experience future harm. The appeals panel felt constrained by the Supreme Court's pointed admonition to that very court in *Allen* to pay close attention to the standing doctrine as the Court had now clarified it in "suits challenging not specifically identifiable Government violations of the law, but the particular programs agencies establish to carry out their legal obligations." The court then noted the limitations placed on the federal courts not only by the standing doctrine, but by the doctrine of separation of powers, which according to the court, "counsels against recognizing standing in a case brought, not to enforce specific

legal obligations whose violation works a direct harm, but to seek a restructuring of the apparatus established by the Executive Branch to fulfill its legal
duties."[194]

In framing their arguments before the appeals court, the agencies had
merely raised the standing and mootness issues in a footnote to the brief
submitted to the court.[195] Nevertheless, these were the issues upon which the
appeals court refocused the case on remand. The court's specific directive to
the district court was "to determine the existence of at least one plaintiff asserting each claim, who was able to 'allege personal injury fairly traceable to
the defendant's allegedly unlawful conduct and likely to be redressed by the
requested relief.' "[196] In January 1985, Judge Pratt allowed the defendants to
take discovery on the standing and mootness questions.

Through the following months, the agencies proceeded to take very extensive discovery, serving interrogatories on each of the plaintiffs and intervenors in both *Adams* and *WEAL*. In July 1985, they moved to dismiss,
arguing that none of the parties in either case met essential standing requirements. Relying on the elements of standing laid down by the Supreme
Court in *Allen*, the defendants maintained that plaintiffs' injury, if any, was
not traceable to any unlawful conduct of the government. The agencies were
not responsible for the action or inaction of schools and colleges whose discriminatory practices may have caused plaintiffs' injury. Defendants further
argued that, given their lack of control over the practices of educational institutions, the relief sought, that is, stepped-up agency enforcement, was not
likely to redress the injury claimed. On the issue of mootness, the agencies
maintained that *Adams* intervenors and *WEAL* plaintiffs had failed to meet
the Article III *case or controversy* requirement of the U.S. Constitution mandating that the "controversy be extant at all stages of review and not merely
at the outset."[197]

While the appeals court had remanded the case specifically for a *case
or controversy* ruling, the defendants, in their brief submitted to the district
court, asked the court to consider their separation of powers arguments as
an alternative ground for dismissal. Picking up the *Allen dicta* cited by the
appeals court to undergird their argument, the agencies again attacked the
1977 timeframes, which allowed agency officials no leeway, but rather "imposed on them an all-encompassing prospective, regulatory scheme, establishing '*de facto* enforcement policies, which may or may not represent the
current views of the agencies' directors.' "[198] Despite the narrowness of the
appeals court's directive, the government attorneys were eager to reintro-
duce this broader argument on remand. Given Judge Pratt's proclivity to add
new plaintiffs each year, the standing argument was a bit uncertain, whereas
the assertion of "judicial receivership" stemming from separation of powers
doctrine was clearly the stronger of the two arguments.[199] In other words,

executive agency officials ought not to be bound by agreements voluntarily entered into by their predecessors.

The following month, the *Adams* and *WEAL* plaintiffs filed papers in the district court to support their standing. The *Adams* plaintiffs specifically relied on that court's May 1984 order permitting the original plaintiffs to add new members (although not the intervenors such as the women's groups) and certifying the case as a class action. At that point, the named plaintiffs in *Adams* were 40 individuals and eight plaintiff-intervenors. The *Adams* attorneys also responded to the defendants' separation of powers argument. Rather than "restructuring executive programs and managing OCR's investigations and evaluations," as the agencies contended, they maintained that the timeframes "merely set deadlines (with generous allowance for exceptions) for substantive outcomes that are determined by the agency itself." Again the plaintiffs urged the court not to dismiss the action "[p]articularly in view of the defendants' reiterated consent and this court's openness to reasonable modifications." [200]

Unlike *Adams*, the *WEAL* case had never been certified as a class action. Although the *WEAL* attorneys had never relied on individual plaintiffs alone but primarily on organizations asserting their standing in both a representational and organizational capacity,[201] they believed that these named groups (including, among others, the National Organization for Women and the National Education Association) were sufficient to maintain standing in their organizational capacity even if their representational standing should become problematic.[202]

In response to the standing challenge raised on remand, the *WEAL* plaintiffs maintained that while the identities of the organizational members had changed over the course of the litigation, the actions and policies of the defendant agencies and their broad impact on victims of sex discrimination had not. The agencies' failure to enforce Title IX and Executive Order 11246 had redirected the mission and reordered the priorities of the plaintiff organizations. Not only were they forced to devote additional resources to this litigation, but the demand for informational, counseling, and referral services had significantly increased, thereby diluting the effectiveness of the services they generally offered.

The plaintiffs' brief further noted that the original named plaintiffs, Dorothy Raffel and Kay Paul Whyburn, whose claims were still alive, continued to suffer from unremedied discrimination. Plaintiffs argued that they met the three-part standing test of *Allen* because they had suffered specific "injury in fact" by the agencies' failure to enforce the law; those injuries were "directly traceable" to such agency action or inaction (that is, but for the agencies' failure to adhere to the court mandated timeframes, the injuries to plaintiffs' procedural rights would have been remedied); and their injury in suffering sex discrimination was "likely to get redressed" by a favorable court ruling. The *WEAL* plaintiffs pointedly addressed the separation of powers question. They reiterated their previous argument that the defendants back in 1977 had conceded their liability in failing to enforce the respective statutes and noted that the timeframes were "minimal methods designed to secure enforcement" of legal entitlements.[203]

In oral arguments before Judge Pratt the following December, Elliott Lichtman, representing the *Adams* plaintiffs, urged the court to confine the hearing to the specific remand questions concerning standing, mootness, and separation of powers. Lichtman took exception to the government's attempt to "relitigate" the merits of the timeframes that the district court had decided in its 1983 order.[204] In keeping with the pattern that had developed over the course of this litigation, he asked the court to consider the plaintiffs' and intervenors' proposed order, which consisted of six pages of findings and conclusions on the narrow remand issues:

> We submitted it because it's our understanding that if the government loses, it is prepared to take this one all the way up, all the way to the Supreme Court, and should that occur, we believe that the higher courts, the Court of Appeals as well as the Supreme Court, would be interested in a detailed explanation as to whatever conclusion your honor should reach.[205]

Judge Pratt's order, which did not come for another two years, appeared to signal the end of nearly two decades of judicial oversight of OCR. His December 1987 ruling granted the government's motion to vacate the 1977 consent decree and to dismiss the *Adams* and *WEAL* cases. According to the judge, "all of the plaintiffs and intervenors in *Adams*, as well as all of the plaintiffs in *WEAL*, lack standing to continue the litigation." [206]

Both the framework of analysis and the general tone of the opinion make clear that the judge took seriously the appeals court's directive on remand to consider the threshhold issues of standing and separation of powers in the context of the Supreme Court's 1984 decision in *Allen v. Wright*. The order is replete with references to *Allen* as well as to previous appeals court decisions limiting the scope of the initial *Adams* order to "the initiation of the enforcement process, and not the perpetual supervision of the details of any enforcement program." [207] Applying the three-part standing test of *Allen*, the judge concluded that while the *Adams* plaintiffs in particular continued to suffer *injury* in the failure of state institutions to provide them with a racially integrated education, neither they nor the *Adams* intervenors or *WEAL* plaintiffs could adequately prove that their injuries were directly *caused* by OCR's failure to process complaints and compliance review promptly nor could they prove that court action could *redress* their grievances. In the judge's view, the injury that plaintiffs alleged was the result not of federal inaction but of state and local practices, and so he concluded that the plaintiffs lacked standing and that his previous order intruded on the functions of the Executive branch.

Judge Pratt's opinion, in fact, "mystified" the attorneys representing the women intervenors in *Adams* and the *WEAL* plaintiffs.[208] Not only did he not address organizational standing on which the women's groups had strongly relied, but he never even mentioned the individual female plaintiffs or Title IX and Executive Order 11246 in his discussion of injury.[209] The female plaintiffs thought that perhaps this gap in the court's rationale could prove a blessing in disguise. It could move the appeals court to remand the case again for further determination on the standing issue.

The civil rights groups did not accept this ruling as the final judicial exit but rather appealed Judge Pratt's decision to the Circuit Court of Appeals. Strategically, they were well aware of a decided split among the members of the D.C. Circuit on standing in general and organizational standing in particular.[210] That split could work in their favor, depending on the particular panel members deciding the case on appeal.

In July 1989, a panel of the D.C. Circuit, in an opinion written by Judge Ruth Bader Ginsburg who had joined in the court's 1984 opinion in this case, concluded that the *Adams* and *WEAL* plaintiffs did in fact have standing.[211] Distinguishing the case from *Allen v. Wright*, the appeals panel held that the plaintiffs or those they represented differed significantly from those in *Allen*. Unlike the *Allen* plaintiffs, who alleged a mere stigmatizing effect of discrimination by schools they had never even sought to attend, here the plaintiffs suffered actual harm as a result of the government's actions, being "personally subject to the challenged discrimination."[212] In that sense, the appeals court agreed with Judge Pratt's finding of *injury*. However, the panel went even further to find that the plaintiffs also met the *Allen* elements of *causation* and *redressability*. Not only is continued federal funding of institutions that engage in discrimination "in part causative of such discrimination"[213] but fund termination proceedings are particularly effective in achieving compliance with federal civil rights laws.

The appeals panel further criticized the district court for having "obscured" the separation of powers issue under the rubric of standing.[214] For them, separation of powers revolves around executive discretion, which can only be addressed in the context of legislative intent. In other words, in enacting the civil rights laws in question, did Congress intend greater agency action than the government has been willing to put forth? If so, judicial intervention would appropriately serve to promote, rather than impair, the separation of powers by pushing the executive branch to carry out the legislature's will.[215]

With the standing issue and the applicability of *Allen* laid to rest, the appeals court refocused the case back on the substantive merits of the government's arguments that the court had set aside in its 1984 remand to the

district court. This shifted the analysis to another body of legal developments. The question now to be addressed was whether "recent Supreme
Court decisions limit judicial supervision of agency law enforcement processes at the behest of statutory beneficiaries."[216] To that end, the court
requested that the parties address the following three questions in briefs to
be submitted to the appeals court and argued during the 1989–1990 term:

1. Do the civil rights laws in question authorize court action directly
   against the agencies?
2. Do the laws authorize the district court to impose additional procedural or enforcement requirements (e.g., timeframes) beyond those
   established in the laws themselves?
3. Is the current administration bound by a consent decree agreed upon
   by prior administrations? If so, what must current agency officials
   show in order to be removed from or modify that decree?

The court's willingness to distinguish this case from *Allen v. Wright* could
signal a trend in appellate court thinking on the Supreme Court's apparent
narrowing of the standing doctrine over the past decade. Such a loosening
of the standing ties could help free the hands of the federal judiciary in
reviewing the merits of similar claims brought to achieve social and structural reform. But the *Adams* and *WEAL* plaintiffs still face an uphill battle as
the D.C. Circuit finally reaches the very core of the litigation as it has now
evolved. What are the limits of executive discretion in carrying out legislative policy? To what extent may the federal judiciary review the exercise of
that discretion? The ultimate outcome could bear significantly on the delicate balance of power among the three branches of government in governing
and shaping the administrative state.

Even if the plaintiffs do prevail on the standing issue, they still face appellate review of the case on the merits. Considering the vigor with which
the government has pursued the separation of powers argument in recent
years, this litigation could wind up in the Supreme Court. A substantive
ruling on the timeframes themselves would have broad implications for judicial review of executive agency action in general and for the status of civil
rights in particular. If in fact the jurisdiction of the federal courts over executive agency actions were significantly curtailed, such a situation would
shift the burden to the legislative branch to monitor more aggressively the
implementation and enforcement of federal laws. This appears to be exactly
what the Supreme Court had in mind when it stated in *Allen*, "Carried to its
logical end, [respondents'] approach would have the federal courts as virtually continuing monitors of the wisdom and soundness of Executive action;
such a role is appropriate for Congress, acting through its committees and
the 'power of the purse.'"[217]

JUDICIAL STRATEGY AND ATTITUDE

In protracted litigation such as *Adams* and *WEAL*, one might envision the judge as the embodiment of all the criticism cast at judicial activism—dictating the daily affairs of governmental agencies, seizing all discretionary decision making from government officials—truly a member of the "imperial judiciary."[218] Yet the role played by Judge Pratt throughout this litigation is a portrait of a judge mindful of the legal and institutional limitations of his office while outraged and frustrated by the government's failure to carry out the law. His anti-government posture in this case is seemingly inconsistent with his general reputation in Washington. As one former OCR official noted:

> I've gotten the sense from Justice Department lawyers who've been pretty successful with Pratt in TRO and preliminary injunction hearings that he's usually pro-government. But here the situation was a blatant disregard for OCR's responsibilities. Cases would drag on four or five years, especially in higher education—just a miserable record.[219]

From the onset of the lawsuit in 1970, Judge Pratt has carved out a narrow role for the court. His management of the case over more than a decade and a half is a study in judicial supervision through judicial restraint. Civil rights activists, in general, consider him "a good judge—no qualms about second-guessing himself on the constitutionality of what he's done."[220] According to David Tatel, they view him as having "done a good job of balancing the need for federal court intervention and federal agency discretion."[221]

In a sense, the plaintiffs have helped him in that task. From the beginning, they have framed the issues as procedural ones, using the agencies' own data to prove noncompliance. They have also avoided giving the court information on the government's ultimate disposition of particular cases. In this way, they have enabled him to frame his orders in procedural terms without questioning the substance of agency decisions.

Over the years, Judge Pratt has shifted back and forth between his traditional role as judge and a more unconventional role as conciliator and mediator between the parties. He has remained in the background, repeatedly bringing the parties together to shape and reshape a resolution by consensus. Rather than impose his own views of an appropriate remedy, he has relied on the lawyers representing both sides to draft proposed orders for the court to consider.

What has held Judge Pratt's interest in the case, say those involved in the litigation, is the race discrimination issue. Those familiar with the case note that he has given the WEAL intervenors and plaintiffs "a bad time," has in fact been "hostile" to them, and has permitted WEAL to win only when piggy-backed on *Adams*. The record indicates that he does not regard sex discrimination as rising to the level of constitutional prohibition that race discrimination does. In 1976, he denied WEAL's motion for intervention in the *Adams* litigation while, at the same time, granting intervention to Mexican Americans and the following year, to the handicapped. In the December 1985 hearings on the standing issue, he even trivialized the sex discrimination claims advanced by the *WEAL* plaintiffs. In questioning the WEAL attorney, he noted, tongue-in-cheek:

> In terms of the volume of your complaints, they are minimal compared with the complaints filed by the people represented in *Adams*. . . . I looked over some of them. They had to do with such things as girls not being able to wear the same uniforms in the high school band . . . or having a father–son club and the girls shouldn't belong to that.[222]

In fact, these were not the type of unresolved complaints that the WEAL plaintiffs had identified for the court. But by overlooking the systemic cases such as discrimination in employment, athletics, and the award of academic honors, the judge in a quick brush stroke negated the significance of WEAL's claims and questioned the presence of their attorney before the court. Again, in his December 1977 order, he failed even to discuss the organizational standing on which the women's attorneys had so heavily relied in their 1985 arguments before him. For the women's groups, this conspicuous "oversight" is just another indication of his disagreement or even hostility toward their claims.[223]

Going back to the December 1985 hearing, the tone and substance of Judge Pratt's questioning revealed more than his view of the sex discrimination claims. Here was a judge caught between directives from higher up the judicial ranks and his own uneasiness about the future of civil rights enforcement. On the one hand, he was deeply concerned about the standing and separation of powers issues raised by the court of appeals. How relevant to the facts of this case was the Supreme Court's decision in *Allen v. Wright?* Looking beyond to the merits of the case, what remedies could possibly be effected, especially in higher education? How much did the court's imposition of the 1977 timeframes depend on the government's acquiescence? On the other hand, despite these questions, one cannot but remember the concern he expressed in his 1983 order as to what would happen if the order were lifted. There he stated that if OCR were left to its own devices, "the manpower that would normally be devoted to [compliance] . . . might be shunted off into other directions, will fade away, and the substance of compliance will eventually go out the window."[224]

His hesitation to pull out was again revealed in his August 1988 order denying the plaintiffs a stay pending appeal. Here he denied the motion "without prejudice" and left open the opportunity for a future stay (which would effectively put the 1977 timeframes back in place while the case awaited a decision by the appeals court) if the government should alter its "current position of voluntarily adhering to the timeframes and procedures previously imposed by the district court." [225]

Nevertheless, the court of appeals remand and recent Supreme Court doctrine obviously caused the judge some discomfort. Judging from his 1987 dismissal, the legal concerns surrounding the case together with apparent efforts by OCR officials to comply voluntarily with the "letter" of the law overrode his longstanding suspicion of OCR when left to its own devices. To continue enforcing the 1977 timeframes would have set him swimming against the political tide. But more significantly, it would have set him against the tide of developing legal trends. The membership of the Supreme Court had shifted further toward the conservative pole since 1984, thereby strengthening the bare majority vote in *Allen*. To have ignored *Allen*'s admonitions to the lower courts might have cost the judge more political capital than all but the most maverick of district court judges would be willing to expend. Or perhaps, as one of the plaintiffs' attorneys put it, "He just got tired. He may have thought the Court of Appeals was giving him an out . . . or was actually telling him to get rid of the case on the basis of standing." [226] As observers of structural reform litigation know, this phenomenon of "judicial burnout" is not uncommon. From that perspective, the appeals court's 1988 reversal on standing may have come as an unwelcome surprise to the judge. His continued involvement in the case now hangs in the balance of the next round of appellate review, this time on the very merits of his oversight role.

THE LETTER AND THE SPIRIT OF THE LAW

Civil rights groups have maintained all along that if Judge Pratt withdrew from the case, OCR "would be in more of a shambles. What's kept the place together is the constant threat of judicial intervention." [227] Opponents of the court's continued jurisdiction disagree. According to Clarence Thomas, DOE's former Assistant Secretary for Civil Rights, a court pullout would "restore agency discretion to run the agency as it ought to be run." [228] Partisan speculation aside, policy changes within OCR in recent years have provided strong indication of the direction in which the agency is choosing to move when unfettered by the court timeframes.

Back in 1970 when civil rights activists initiated the *Adams* litigation, OCR was clearly not carrying out its legal responsibility to enforce the law. The timeframes that eventually formed the substance of the court's order aimed specifically at forcing the agency to do its job and do it efficiently. By placing emphasis on the number of complaints resolved and compliance investigations conducted, the order left open a large discretionary area where the agency could, given the will, comply with the letter of the decree and of the law itself while engaging in practices that violate the spirit of both. According to the plaintiffs in *Adams* and *WEAL*, this is exactly the current situation within OCR. They maintain that the Reagan administration's attempt to reformulate civil rights policy into specific programmatic changes has seriously undercut the quality of the agency's enforcement work.

This distinction between the letter and spirit of compliance has surfaced in two congressional investigations. In the summer and fall of 1985, the Intergovernmental Relations and Human Resources Subcommittee of the House Committee on Government Operations conducted oversight hearings directed at OCR's apparent failure to enforce civil rights laws.[229] From January through March 1988, staff of the House Committee on Education and Labor further investigated enforcement policies and practices at six of the ten OCR regional offices (San Francisco, Seattle, Atlanta, Philadelphia, Dallas, and Chicago).[230] The reports published by those committees paint a grim portrait of bureaucratic mismanagement, intra-agency conflict, and indecisive leadership.

During the 1985 House hearings, testimony of then current and former OCR officials and civil rights activists portrayed an agency that made greater strides toward complying with the court-ordered procedural deadlines under the Reagan administration than under any of its predecessors while at the same time ignoring the quality or "correctness" of its substantive decisions. According to Harry Singleton, former Assistant Secretary for Civil Rights, between 1982 and 1984, OCR reduced the average number of days for complaint processing from 1,297 to 229 and the average age of pending compliance reviews from 1,036 days to 271 days.[231] These impressive figures, however, must be viewed in the broader context of overall agency policies, many of which were brought into question in a subsequent congressional report issued in December 1985.[232] That report draws an indicting conclusion from information gathered in the course of the 1985 House hearings.

Title VI, Title IX, and § 504 provide OCR with two enforcement options. The agency can either initiate fund termination proceedings or refer the case to the Justice Department. According to the congressional report, the majority of administrative enforcement cases and Justice Department referrals were initiated only after the court's 1983 *Adams* order. As Julius Chambers, Director–Counsel of the NAACP Legal Defense and Educational Fund notes, "After the 1983 *Adams* order set deadlines for securing compliance in pending cases, OCR took 23 cases to administrative law judges and referred 18 cases to the Department of Justice. That order generated more enforcement proceedings than had occurred in all of the previous decade."[233]

The report charged that OCR used the "referral of cases to Justice as an effective method of circumventing the *Adams* order and escaping the court's jurisdiction."[234] Once a case is referred, it no longer falls under the court's jurisdiction. Between 1981 and 1985, OCR referred 24 cases to the Justice Department. As of July 1985, 16 of these still remained "idle," five had been returned to OCR, one was the subject of pending litigation, and two had been resolved by consent decrees.[235] As for the 27 administrative enforcement actions initiated between 1981 and 1985, 22 had been initiated in response to the *Adams* order and 13 had been settled or closed. Upon examining the substance of these settlements, the House subcommittee found that "many of them did not adequately address the issues raised by OCR investigations," and that Singleton had interceded in some cases to weaken settlements that had been proposed by the institutions themselves.[236]

In June 1985, OCR disbanded its Washington-based Quality Assurance Staff (QAS) whose function it was to review investigations and policies. Singleton testified that he considered QAS "more of a nuisance than it was a help."[237] In May 1984, in its last major report completed, QAS discovered an "error and defect rate of 28 percent for 116 cases closed by OCR's regional offices during May and June 1983." The congressional report noted that "Singleton denied any familiarity with the QAS report," which also included "11 recommendations for improving the OCR operation."[238] The House subcommittee concluded that Singleton's "main reaction to the findings was to disband QAS, without replacing it with an organized system to monitor the internal workings of OCR."[239] The QAS issue surfaced again in the 1988 congressional investigations of regional offices. Staff interviewed maintained that the national office had failed to provide adequate training staff in their quality assessment. In fact, according to those interviewed, QAS was found to be low on the regional offices' priority of responsibilities.[240]

Between January 1981 and 1985, OCR settled more than 300 cases using a technique called Early Complaint Resolution (ECR). In cases where a complaint concerned an individual rather than a class issue, OCR attempted to settle the complaint through mediation before initiating an investigation.[241] In fiscal year 1985, the agency offered ECR in 238 complaints of which 138, or 58 percent, were accepted. Of that 138, OCR used mediation to resolve 101 cases.[242] Civil rights groups have assailed OCR's use of ECR, claiming that deals have been struck to settle cases.[243] A November 1981 memorandum from the Justice Department to OCR indicates that not only may the agency's use of ECR have been illegal, but it failed to protect the rights of complainants and jeopardized future enforcement and litigation in cases based on similar fact situations.[244]

The 1988 congressional investigation of OCR regional offices yields similar findings of the agency's failure to enforce civil rights laws aggressively. According to the report detailing those findings, the QAS situation was not unique. OCR failed to establish adequate policies in general to guide regional office staff while those policies established, in fact, impeded civil rights enforcement. Regional staff noted that the central office interpreted the *Adams* timeframes in such a way as to place additional pressure on staff to close cases without adequately investigating them or to narrow the scope of investigations. Instead of the 195 days required by the court order, the Reagan administration forced OCR staff to establish jurisdiction, investigate a case, and seek a voluntary settlement within 105 days.[245]

Between fiscal year 1983 and fiscal year 1988, 58 percent of complaint investigations led to a finding of "no violation."[246] During that same period, OCR closed 40 percent of all investigated complaints and 72 percent of all compliance reviews with a "violations corrected" Letter of Findings even where the school district had merely promised that it would take corrective action.[247] During that time, 99 percent of compliance reviews were closed with either a finding of no violation at all or by settlement prior to issuing a Letter of Findings.[248]

Regional office staff seemed to agree that the national office would rarely disseminate nationwide policy statements. Those policies handed down generally came in a fragmented way through responses to draft Letters of Findings, "marginal notes," or telephone calls from the national to regional offices.[249] This ad hoc policy making, which at times was driven by other than legal considerations, could not be challenged as there was rarely any written evidence of the policy.[250] The national office, according to regional office staff, further made it almost impossible to find a civil rights violation, requiring that there be proof of "intent" to discriminate. Many regional staff interviewed questioned this stringent standard, which the agency had adopted informally through various intra-agency memoranda and which has never been firmly articulated by the courts.[251] There was also a general understanding among regional staff that certain types of cases, including Title IX athletics cases, were off limits to complaint processing or compliance reviews. Accordingly, the national office would refuse to approve a finding of discrimination in such cases unless there were "horror stories."[252]

Aside from specific policy changes and despite its ever-burgeoning workload, OCR's budget requests have significantly declined since the early 1980s and the agency has underutilized funds appropriated by Congress. Between fiscal year 1982 and fiscal year 1989, OCR's budget recommendations decreased from $51 million to $41 million.[253] Between 1980 and 1985, OCR failed to use more than $20 million of the $272 million appropriated by Congress.[254] Of that amount, $8 million was returned to the Treasury, $7 million was used to defray mail penalty expenses for the entire Education Department, and $5 million was allocated to Howard University.[255] The percent of OCR's overall appropriation that was allowed to lapse ranged from an estimated 0.4 percent in 1988 to 6.1 percent in 1984.[256] In fact, staff shortages were cited both by the court in 1977[257] and in a 1981 study within OCR itself[258] as a major factor contributing to OCR's failure to meet the court-ordered timeframes. The number of OCR employees decreased from

1,099 in fiscal year 1981 to an estimated 820 in fiscal year 1988, a loss of 25 percent.[259]

These policy changes all relate to management decisions made within OCR concerning the process of achieving civil rights compliance. Other policy directives have struck at the scope of civil rights coverage itself. In March 1984, the Supreme Court ruled in *Grove City College v. Bell*[260] that Title IX covers only those educational programs that directly receive federal funds. Within three months, "OCR had relied on that decision to close 23 civil rights investigations, to narrow the scope of 18 investigations, and to review 31 other cases. While most of these concerned sex discrimination, 9 of the 18 modified investigations and 8 of the 31 under review concerned either Title VI or § 504."[261] Within a year after *Grove City*, OCR had moved to close, limit, or suspend at least 63 discrimination cases. Forty-four of these had been brought under Title IX, five under Title VI, and 14 under § 504.[262] Most of these concerned higher education claims. OCR's July 1984 memorandum to regional directors[263] provided some civil rights protections in elementary and secondary school. That policy guideline instructed the regions to apply Title IX, Title VI, and § 504 on an institutionwide basis at schools receiving funds under the Chapter 2 program.[264] However, in a December 1985 internal memorandum, just prior to the effective date of his resignation, Singleton directed OCR regional offices to apply the three laws only to specific programs within a school that received direct Chapter 2 funding.[265] Civil rights groups quickly attacked the directive, particularly for its inevitable impact on achieving sex equity in athletics, since most sports and physical education activities do not receive Chapter 2 or any direct federal funds. That memorandum was negated subsequently by congressional action in the Civil Rights Restoration Act of 1987.

OCR clearly has exercised the broad managerial discretion left to it even when operating under the 1977 timeframes to chart a new course in civil rights enforcement. Agency officials have argued that change has been necessary to meet the new and broadened demands placed upon the office. Civil rights groups have maintained that these new policies are symptomatic of a more pervasive hostility toward civil rights concerns among OCR top officials and within the Reagan administration in general. In recent years, congressional hearings and investigations and two highly critical reports together with possibly related staff resignations have focused public attention on the agency. Whether the Bush administration will follow its predecessor's lead remains to be seen, especially if the appeals court releases the agency from the 1977 timeframes. Nevertheless, the internal maneuverings within OCR during the Reagan years and the apparent inability of the agency to handle its increasingly complex workload lead one to question whether it is time to reassess and redefine OCR's mission.

LAW, POLICY, AND POLITICS

The ongoing saga of these lawsuits reveals both the potential and limitations of developing social policy through institutional reform. It also demonstrates how the success of such efforts can be enhanced or constrained by changes in legal developments and organizational and political climate over the course of prolonged litigation.

The inferences and conclusions drawn from this case have broad applicability to the study of court intervention. The case provides a unique insight into judicial supervision not over a provider of public services such as a school system, or hospital, or prison, but over a governmental agency with powers both to define and enforce legal rights. On the one hand, this narrows the scope of judicial intrusion by allowing the court to focus on the enforcement process without addressing the substance of the agency's decisions or the adequacy or appropriateness of the services ultimately provided. On the other hand, it raises serious questions as to the effectiveness of court involvement in ultimately redressing legal rights from such a remote vantage point. This summary analysis of the *Adams* and *WEAL* cases must be considered in the context of both their typical and atypical aspects.

The *Adams* and *WEAL* litigation has covered a span of years marked by the most rapid expansion in legal rights in America's history. *Adams* originally was brought as a race discrimination case in response to HEW's stated policy not to enforce the law. It was essentially a political decision on the part of the Nixon administration. Fund termination sanctions were then, and continue to be, politically unpopular from Congress on down to the local level. Those were the circumstances under which Judge Pratt initially took jurisdiction over this case—the administration's blatant failure to remedy race discrimination in educational institutions in the southern and border states.

Thereafter, the litigation expanded to include other groups whose rights, in the court's view, may be of lesser constitutional significance and may demand less extreme remedies. Early on it became clear that there is little progress in promoting civil rights when enforcement efforts are insufficiently funded. As civil rights law itself rapidly expanded through congressional, administrative, and judicial action, the bureaucracy became caught up in shaping the very rights the plaintiffs sought to enforce. The more diligently OCR defined legal rights through the regulatory process, the more it fueled the legal claims of the parties. As Congress broadened the national civil rights agenda to include Title IX and § 504, OCR had to develop new criteria and techniques for assessing violations and new remedial strategies. Title IX enforcement posed particular problems as lower courts struggled over specific coverage issues. While the advocacy groups successfully pushed HEW to carve out detailed protections and entitlements through the regulatory process, the agency was unable to follow through on enforcement. The additional civil rights enforcement duties effectively immobilized an agency that already suffered from lack of any structured management.

By focusing on procedure, the remedy ultimately imposed by the court struck at the core of OCR's management problems. As long as OCR's failure to enforce the law was due to poor management rather than ideological differences, then the court's order held some promise of achieving its goal. While both Ford and Carter administration officials initially resisted the timeframes as an impermissible judicial intrusion, they eventually used them to carry out their own agenda for improving agency management. The timeframes permitted Martin Gerry to decentralize the agency and force accountability onto regional directors. David Tatel used them as leverage to obtain more resources from Congress and as a stick to wield when confronting resistant school districts. In that way, the court order forced certain organizational changes, which in turn permitted the agency to move toward legal compliance. While civil rights enforcement was the immediate goal of the timeframes, sound management was necessary as a prerequisite. OCR subsequently computerized its recordkeeping and instituted a management information system to assist in decree compliance.

Recent history has demonstrated that while efficient management alone may support the letter of a court order, the mere processing of volume is not enough to support the spirit of the decree. This again illustrates the limitations of judicial intervention in achieving social reform. The *Adams* and *WEAL* litigation underscores the institutional limitations of the court and the constraints placed upon it: in an institutional sense by the remedies available to it, and in a political sense by the capital expended when parties refuse to comply with its decrees. In these cases, the judge defined both a narrow role for himself and a narrow remedy. His willingness to serve as a catalyst at each step of the litigation, from developing the remedy through implementation, kept pressure on the government to maintain the initial momentum and prevent backsliding. However, it eventually became clear that the success of this minimalist method depends in large part on the willingness of both sides to reach consensus. So long as the administration in power viewed the court order as a support to its own civil rights agenda, compromise and agreement were possible.

The link between administrative perspective and the success of institutional reform came into sharper focus under the Reagan administration. Here the government's resistance to the court's remedy was not merely political as it had been under Nixon or organizational as under Ford and Carter, but more fundamentally ideologically based. Simply stated, the Reagan administration's agenda for civil rights enforcement and the federal role in education ran counter to the underlying claims in general and the court decree in particular. In the broader civil rights arena, the administration reversed federal policy established over the previous decade under both Republican and Democratic leadership. Education officials maintained that they should not be bound by the decisions of their predecessors and that the federal court, in effect, was managing the daily operation of OCR's enforcement program. No longer willing to operate in Judge Pratt's conciliatory mode, the government sought complete release from the court's supervision.

Despite the government's threats to push the issue to the Supreme Court, OCR still prides itself on having achieved greater compliance with the timeframes than under previous administrations. This assertion, viewed in the larger context of agency policy directives, merely affirms the limitations of court intervention. The court-ordered timeframes focused specifically on procedure as a quantitative measure. Compliance was reported in terms of the number of complaints processed and the number of compliance reviews initiated. The 1977 court order and subsequent modifications dictated no substantive result in any specific complaint investigation or compliance review. In other words, there was no quality measure built into the court's remedy. The narrowness of the order itself permitted the agency wide discretion not only on its final decisions, but on broader policy changes that had a direct bearing on the status of civil rights.

That being the case, it appears that the *Adams* and *WEAL* litigation achieved their immediate purpose during the Reagan years in getting OCR to enforce the law, if we measure enforcement in terms of the expeditious processing of claims. However, if the litigation's ultimate goal is to improve educational access and provide appropriate educational services to racial and linguistic minorities, women, and the handicapped, then its success apparently has run into ideological roadblocks. When the court of appeals forced the district court to examine the members of plaintiff and intervenor groups in order to address standing and mootness concerns, it made a significant statement about litigation of this nature. In choosing form over substance, the court defined these cases as seeking vindication of individual rights rather than recognizing the more generalized social injury stemming from OCR's failure to enforce the law effectively. Depending on one's point of view, standards of "traceability," "redressability," and "ongoing controversy" in litigation that aims at redressing pervasive social injustices are either easy to meet or of little relevance to the ultimate goals that the parties seek to achieve.

Given that the aims of structural reform litigation are indeed broad and perhaps overambitious, the success of any given case of judicial involvement is difficult to judge. Whether constrained by federalism concerns and the strong political culture of local control over education or by the separation of powers doctrine built into our constitutional structure, courts can only skirt the edges of administrative discretion without ever reaching its core.

As a result, compliance with court decrees is typically measured in quantitative and not qualitative terms. What percentage of minority children now attend majority schools? How many children have been referred and placed in special education? How many Title IX complaints have been processed? The most a court can do is impose a remedy where compliance can be measured in judicially manageable numbers in the hope that judicial oversight in general and expeditious processing in particular will promote fairness in government decision making. The remedy, therefore, aims at the immediate administrative wrong with an attenuated link to the ultimate social injury suffered or the legal claim asserted. However, for the court to scrutinize the substance of administrative decisions not only extends its legitimacy and capacity beyond permissible bounds, but diverts and exhausts the court's energies from its traditional task of interpreting the law.

Perhaps a more valid and useful measure of the significance of judicial intervention and its success in a given case is the political value of the court decree and the extent to which the litigation sets in motion collateral forces that move the institution and society toward the desired goals. Viewed from that perspective, it is not just the substance of the court's remedy that is important but also the very fact that the judiciary has spoken authoritatively, made a preliminary determination of rights, and provided the forum for the parties to negotiate the substance of a resolution.

Applying that approach to *Adams* and *WEAL*, the district court's ongoing oversight succeeded in protecting the rights of minorities from adverse majoritarian politics, stabilizing rights and insulating them from the vagaries of ideological and political flux, and serving as a bulwark against further agency regression. The court itself provided the arena for defining the issues, testing public opinion, and galvanizing public support. This, in turn, triggered action by a collateral branch of government, in this case the legislative oversight powers of congressional committees and the subsequent resignation of the agency's director. The court established the agenda and opened the public debate for a possible political solution. While the litigation itself received meager media attention, the congressional hearings and investigations that it provoked placed OCR and its civil rights enforcement efforts under public scrutiny and laid bare the agency's mission and underlying philosophy.

Nevertheless, this case also illustrates the limitations of legislative oversight as a means of effectively controlling agency discretion. In its 1984 decision, the appeals court pointedly suggested that monitoring the "wisdom and soundness" of executive agencies is more appropriate for Congress through its committees and appropriations powers. Yet here we see an agency whose mismanagement, counterproductive policies, and underutilization of resources appear unaffected despite congressional oversight. Many of the problems identified in the 1985 congressional hearings surfaced again three years later in the 1988 regional office investigations. This leads one to wonder why OCR has been so resistant to political pressure. Perhaps part of OCR's problem lies in its ambiguity of mission. This is not surprising, as Congress itself and society in general, for that matter, have failed to achieve consensus over the purposes and importance of civil rights enforcement.

Has the *Adams* and *WEAL* litigation changed the broad landscape of civil rights? No, but it was never intended to do so. Has it made modest gains toward protecting educational rights for women? Yes. The question remains as to whether and how long the judge should continue to oversee the agency's enforcement efforts, particularly in light of the agency's recent adverse climate. That remains the irresolvable question underlying structural reform litigation. Nevertheless, common sense and experience dictate that a court must not pull out precipitously by vacating its order, but should gradually disengage its oversight and, in so doing, institutionalize certain safeguards that build in organizational accountability and prevent backsliding. This has been done effectively in cases on the local level. Whether this is legally permissible or politically possible at the federal agency level in view of developments in the law remains to be seen. Nevertheless, given the fundamental ideological differences between the parties, together with the government's efforts not only to circumvent the law but to change it, the continued presence of the district court as the objective guardian of governmental "good faith" perhaps has become a necessity. And yet, the district court in 1987 withdrew its supervision under what it perceived as external legal pressure.

As this case clearly proves, managerial safeguards alone cannot ensure an effective court disengagement. The key to a successful court pullout is a serious commitment by the Executive, clearly articulated to agency officials, to continue working toward the immediate institutional objectives and the broad social goals that the court order attempted to achieve in the first instance. The Reagan administration, by its own accounts, did not share that commitment and vision with the court. Yet if managerial safeguards plus institutional commitment are the essential prerequisites to an effective judicial withdrawal, then the future of OCR's civil rights enforcement efforts hinge on the ability and political will of the Bush administration to guide the seemingly ungovernable bureaucracy toward compliance with the spirit and not merely the letter of the law.

NOTES

1. The most recent decision in this ongoing litigation is WEAL v. Cavazos, No. 88-5065 (D.C. Cir., July 7, 1989).

2. This case was decided together with *WEAL* by the district court in 1987 as *Adams v. Cavazos* and is also pending appellate review on the merits.

3. Under the Department of Education Organization Act, P.L. 96-88, 93 Stat. 671, the Department of Health, Education and Welfare (HEW) was dismantled as of October 1, 1979, 20 U.S.C. § 3411 (Supp. 1987). Most of the former HEW's education rule making and enforcement functions subsequently were transferred to the Office for Civil Rights within the newly formed Department of Education as of May 9, 1980.

4. 42 U.S.C. § 2000d *et seq.* (Supp. 1987).

5. 20 U.S.C. § 1681 *et seq.* (Supp. 1987).

6. 29 U.S.C. § 794 (Supp. 1987).

7. The *WEAL* litigation was brought not only under Title IX, but under Exec. Order No. 11246 as amended by Exec. Order 11375, 3 C.F.R. 169 (1987); Titles VII and VIII of the Public Health Service Act, 42 U.S.C. §§ 295h-9, 298b-z; the Administrative Procedure Act, 5 U.S.C. § 551 *et seq.*; and the equal protection and due process requirements applicable to federal action through the due process clause of the Fifth Amendment to the U.S. Constitution. Since this discussion focuses on the court's oversight of OCR enforcement activities, the analysis will center on Title IX.

8. *See* A. CIGLER AND B. LOOMIS, Introduction to INTEREST GROUP POLITICS 21 (A. Cigler and B. Loomis eds. 1983).

9. *See* Chayes, *The Role of the Judge in Public Law Litigation*, 89 HARV. L. REV. 1281 (1976). In a more recent analysis, Chayes has shifted focus from the decree as "the centerpiece of the emerging public law model." On further reflection, he concludes that "the nature of the controversy, the sources of the governing law, and the consequent extended impact of the decision—rather than the form of relief—are what really differentiate public law from private litigation." Chayes, *The Supreme Court 1981 Term, Forward: Public Law Litigation and the Burger Court*, 96 HARV. L. REV. 4, 58 (1982). His updated analysis views judicial activism "as part of a gathering effort" not merely to review legislative pronouncements but "to control the bureaucracies of the modern administrative state." *Id.* at 60.

10. 347 U.S. 483 (1954).

11. *See* HAHN, *The NAACP Legal Defense and Educational Fund: Its Judicial Strategy and Tactics*, in AMERICAN GOVERNMENT AND POLITICS (S. Wasby ed. 1973). *See also* K. O'CONNOR, WOMEN'S ORGANIZATIONS' USE OF THE COURTS (1980).

12. *E.g.*, the procedural protections built into the Education for All Handicapped Children Act, 20 U.S.C. § 1401 *et seq.* (Supp. 1987) and the concept of *appropriate* educational services grew out of two lower court decisions, Mills v. Board of Education, 348 F. Supp. 866 (D.D.C. 1972) and Pennsylvania Association for Retarded Children v. Pennsylvania, 343 F. Supp. 279 (E.D. Pa. 1972) (consent decree). The Equal Educational Opportunities Act of 1974, 20 U.S.C. § 1703(f) (Supp. 1987) similarly codified into statutory law a standard of *effective participation* for linguistic minority students adopted by the Supreme Court earlier that same year in Lau v. Nichols, 414 U.S. 563 (1974).

13. C. LINDLOM, THE INTELLIGENCE OF DEMOCRACY (1965).

14. Kirp, *Law, Politics and Equal Educational Opportunity: The Limits of Judicial Involvement*, 47 HARV. EDUC. REV. 117, 137 (1977).

15. Fiss, *The Supreme Court 1978 Term, Forward: The Forms of Justices*, 93 HARV. L. REV. 1, 2 (1979).

16. H. JACOB, JUSTICE IN AMERICA: COURTS, LAWYERS AND THE JUDICIAL PROCESS 12 (4th ed. 1984).

17. S. Wasby, *Is Planned Litigation Planned?* (unpublished paper presented at the 1983 Annual Meeting of the American Political Science Association).

18. For a discussion of courts as agenda-setters in the context of school finance reform, *see* R. LEHNE, THE QUEST FOR JUSTICE (1978). For a similar analysis of the court's role in church–state relations, particularly with regard to state regulation of religiously affiliated schools, *see* R. Salomone, *Church, State, and Education: A Preliminary Analysis of Legislative and Judicial Policymaking* (report submitted to the National Institute of Education, Law and Government Program, January 1985).

19. R. ELMORE AND M. MCLAUGHLIN, RETRENCHMENT AND REFORM 21 (1983).

20. For an analysis of the limits of judicial capacity as examined through five cases litigated in the federal courts, *see* D. HOROWITZ, THE COURTS AND SOCIAL POLICY (1977). Horowitz maintains that both the personnel of the adjudicative process (judges) and the nature of the process itself constrain courts in their ability to resolve disputes over social policy. For an empirical comparison of judicial and legislative capacity in policy making, *see* M. REBELL AND A. BLOCK, EDUCATIONAL POLICY MAKING AND THE COURTS: AN EMPIRICAL STUDY OF JUDICIAL ACTIVISM (1982). The authors conclude that when measured on indices of interest representation, fact-finding, and remedial capabilities, courts fare just as well as, if not better than, legislatures. For an argument in defense of judicial policy making as a legitimate exercise in preserving rights despite the court's limited capacities, *see* Youngblood and Folse, *Can Courts Govern? An Inquiry into Capacity and Purpose*, in GOVERNING THROUGH COURTS 23 (R. Gambitta, M. May, and J. Foster eds. 1981).

21. Glazer, *Towards an Imperial Judiciary?* 41 PUB. INTEREST 104, 122 (1975).

22. A. BICKEL, THE LEAST DANGEROUS BRANCH 22 (1962), *citing* THAYER, JOHN MARSHALL 57, 84 (1901).

23. R. BERGER, GOVERNMENT BY JUDICIARY 409 (1977).

24. P. KURLAND, POLITICS, THE CONSTITUTION, AND THE WARREN COURT 174 (1970).

25. Fiss, *supra* note 15, at 22–23, 28.

26. Diver, *The Judge as Political Powerbroker: Superintending Structural Change in Public Institutions*, 65 VAL. L. REV. 43, 63 (1979).

27. Fiss, *supra* note 15, at 2.

28. Yudof, *Implementation Theories and Desegregation Realities*, 32 ALA. L. REV. 441, 463 (1981).

29. Grossman and Sarat, *Access to Justice and the Limits of Law*, in GOVERNING THROUGH COURTS 77, *supra* note 20, at 78, 85.

30. Chayes (1982), *supra* note 9, at 60. *See also* Sunstein, *Reviewing Agency Action After* Heckler v. Chaney, 52 U. CHI. L. REV. 653, 670 (1985).

31. Johnson, *The Role of the Federal Courts in Institutional Litigation*, 32 ALA. L. REV. 271, 279 (1981).

32. G. MCDOWELL, EQUITY AND THE CONSTITUTION 10 (1982).

33. N. GLAZER, *Individual Rights Against Group Rights*, in ETHNIC DILEMMAS 254 (N. Glazer ed. 1983).

34. Glazer, *Should Judges Administer Social Services?* 50 PUB. INTEREST 64, 80 (Winter 1978).

35. M. GREENE, LANDSCAPES OF LEARNING 231 (1978), *citing* Beecher, *The Education of Female Teachers*, in THE EDUCATED WOMAN IN AMERICA 68–69 (B. Cross ed. 1972).

36. GREENE, *id.* at 231–32.

37. *Id.* at 234.

38. *Id.* at 235.

39. By 1870, approximately 60 percent of the national teaching force were women. By the turn of the century, that figure had risen to 70 percent and peaked at 86 percent by 1920. *See* TYACK AND STROBER, *Jobs and Gender: A History of the Structuring of Educational Employment by Sex*, in EDUCATIONAL POLICY AND MANAGEMENT 131, 133 (P. Schmuck, W. Charteris, and R. Carlson eds. 1981). For a more general history of the struggle for women's rights, *see* A. SACHS AND J. H. WILSON, SEXISM AND THE LAW 67–132 (1978).

40. NOW was organized in 1966, while WEAL was formed two years later. *See* A. FISHEL AND J. POTTKER, NATIONAL POLITICS AND SEX DISCRIMINATION IN EDUCATION 4–5 (1977).

41. 29 U.S.C. § 206 (d)(1) (Supp. 1987).

42. 42 U.S.C. § 2000(e) *et seq.* (Supp. 1987). Title VII is enforced by the Equal Employment Opportunity Commission. In 1972, Congress amended the Equal Pay Act and Title VII to extend coverage to employees of state and local governments and educational institutions exempted under the original legislation.

43. Exec. Order No. 11246 as amended by Exec. Order No. 11375, 3 C.F.R. § 169 (1987) is enforced by the Office of Federal Contract Compliance within the Department of Labor and covers the same protected groups as those under Title VII.

44. NATIONAL ADVISORY COUNCIL ON WOMEN'S EDUCATIONAL PROGRAMS, TITLE IX: THE HALF FULL, HALF EMPTY GLASS 28 (1981).

45. N. OSSO, CHARACTERISTICS OF STUDENTS AND STAFF IN VOCATIONAL EDUCATION 1972 (1974), cited in SEX BIAS IN THE SCHOOLS: THE RESEARCH EVIDENCE 104 (J. Pottker and A. Fishel eds. 1977).

46. U.S. OFFICE OF EDUCATION, DIGEST OF EDUCATIONAL STATISTICS 1973 (1974), cited in SEX BIAS IN THE SCHOOLS; *supra* note 45 at 104.

47. *Supra* note 44, at 41. For a general discussion of sex discrimination in elementary and secondary schools, *see* SEX BIAS IN THE SCHOOLS, *supra* note 45.

48. U.S. COMMISSION ON CIVIL RIGHTS, MORE HURDLES TO CLEAR: WOMEN AND GIRLS IN COMPETITIVE ATHLETICS 22 (July 1980).

49. NATIONAL EDUCATION ASSOCIATION RESEARCH DIVISION, 26TH BIENNIAL SALARY AND STAFF SURVEY OF PUBLIC SCHOOL PROFESSIONAL PERSONNEL, 1972–73, 9–10 (1973).

50. U.S. OFFICE OF EDUCATION, DIGEST OF EDUCATION STATISTICS, 1976 (1977).

51. The Fourteenth Amendment to the U.S. Constitution provides in part that no state shall "deny to any person within its jurisdiction the equal protection of the laws."

52. 34 C.F.R. Part 106 (1988).

53. 20 U.S.C. § 1681 (Supp. 1988) states: "(a) No person in the United States

shall, on the basis of sex, be excluded from participation in, be denied the benefits of, or be subjected to discrimination under any education program or activity receiving Federal financial assistance."

54. *See*, A. COSTAIN AND D. COSTAIN, *The Women's Lobby: The Impact of a Movement on Congress*, in INTEREST GROUP POLITICS, *supra* note 8, at 194–95.

55. The Equal Rights Amendment provided that "Equality of rights under the law shall not be denied or abridged by the United States or by any state on account of sex." By the fall of 1977, 35 of the necessary 38 states had voted for ratification. Within the next year, in response to a powerfully orchestrated STOP-ERA movement, three of those states voted to rescind. By June 30, 1982, the extended deadline for final ratification, only 34 states had approved the ERA.

56. 42 U.S.C. § 2000(e) *et seq.* (Supp. 1988).

57. In 1972, P.L. 92-318 inserted "sex" following "religion" (codified as amended as 42 U.S.C. § 2000[c]-6[a][2] [Supp. 1988]). The Justice Department has no independent authority with respect to sex discrimination apart from admissions. The Department of Education may refer such cases to the Justice Department if the Department of Education has been unsuccessful in negotiating voluntary compliance and seeks to resolve the matter through litigation.

58. 29 U.S.C. § 206(a) (Supp. 1988).

59. A. COSTAIN, *Eliminating Sex Discrimination in Education: Lobbying for Implementation of Title IX*, in RACE, SEX AND POLICY PROBLEMS 5 (M. Palley and M. Preston eds. 1979).

60. Two years following the law's enactment, after HEW had issued its proposed regulations, Congress amended the law to exclude social fraternities and sororities, Boy Scouts, Girl Scouts, YMCA, YWCA, Camp Fire Girls, and other voluntary youth service organizations. 20 U.S.C. § 1681(a)(6) (Supp. 1988). In 1976, Congress again amended the law to exclude boy or girl conferences, 20 U.S.C. § 1681 (a)(7); father–son and mother–daughter activities, 20 U.S.C. § 1681 (a)(8); and scholarships awarded as prizes for beauty pageants, 20 U.S.C. § 1681(a)(9).

61. The Education Task Force combined educational organizations such as the American Association of University Women, lobbying groups such as the Women's Lobby, research organizations such as the Project on Equal Education Rights (PEER), and mass-membership groups such as the League of Women Voters. This broad span of interests allowed the Task Force to exercise influence through a variety of channels. For a complete listing of Task Force member organizations, see A. COSTAIN, *supra* note 59, at 11, n. 11.

62. 34 C.F.R. Part 106 (1988).

63. 34 C.F.R. § 106.21(b)(2) (1988).

64. 34 C.F.R. § 106.23 (1988).

65. 34 C.F.R. § 106.36 (1988).

66. 34 C.F.R. § 106.41 (1988).

67. Title IX forms part of a comprehensive federal scheme to promote civil rights through financial inducements. The Act, however, differs from its companion statutes covering race, handicap, and age discrimination in that it is expressly limited to the educational arena. This limitation targets responsibility for enforcing and monitoring compliance with the law and regulations within the Office for

Civil Rights (OCR) of the Department of Education (formerly the Department of Health, Education and Welfare). As of May 9, 1980, with the dismantling of the Department of Health, Education and Welfare, rule making and enforcement powers under Title IX were transferred to the newly created Department of Education. The Title IX regulations as originally promulgated by HEW in 1975 were printed in 45 C.F.R. Part 86. Simultaneous with the transfer of HEW jurisdiction over Title IX to the Department of Education, these regulations were issued in identical form in 34 C.F.R. Part 106, 45 Fed. Reg. 30802 (May 9, 1980).

68. 34 C.F.R. § 106.3(c) (1988). The regulations as published in 1975 futher required that, within one year of their effective date, each recipient conduct a Title IX self-evaluation to be maintained on file for three years. 34 C.F.R. § 106.3(c) (1988).

69. 42 U.S.C. § 2000d *et seq.* (Supp. 1988). The Title VI procedural regulations are contained in 34 C.F.R. § 100.6–100.11 and 34 C.F.R. Part 101 (1988) and are incorporated by reference into Title IX in 34 C.F.R. § 106.71 (1988).

70. 34 C.F.R. § 100.6(b) (1988).

71. 34 C.F.R. § 100.6(c) (1988).

72. 34 C.F.R. § 100.7(a) (1988).

73. 34 C.F.R. § 100.7(b) (1988).

74. 34 C.F.R. § 100.7(c) (1988).

75. 34 C.F.R. § 100.8(a) (1988).

76. PROJECT ON EQUAL EDUCATION RIGHTS, NOW LEGAL DEFENSE AND EDUCATION FUND, STALLED AT THE START: GOVERNMENT ACTION ON SEX BIAS IN THE SCHOOLS 7 (1978).

77. *Id.* at 58.

78. *Id.* at 61.

79. *Id.* at 7.

80. *Id.* at 59.

81. *Id.* at 19.

82. Prepared response to Question 20, supplied in HEW response to a self-administered questionnaire sent by the U.S. Commission on Civil Rights in December 1979 to assist in preparation of the report entitled ENFORCING TITLE IX (October 1980). *Id.* at 19 (prepared response to Question 18, supplied in HEW response). These data primarily reflect the fact that HEW had suspended complaint processing in three major policy areas pending policy determination by regulation or court order. The areas in question covered intercollegiate athletics (policy interpretation published in 44 Fed. Reg. 71,413 [1979]), rules of appearance (regulation published in 34 C.F.R. § 106.31[b][5] prohibiting discrimination in the application of codes of personal appearance revoked, 47 Fed. Reg. 32,526), and employment (resolved by Supreme Court decision in North Haven Board of Education v. Bell, 456 U.S. 512 [1982]).

83. Cannon v. University of Chicago, 441 U.S. 677 (1979). In a later ruling in this case, the Court refused to review a Seventh Circuit Court of Appeals decision that proof of discriminatory effect alone is not sufficient to establish a Title IX violation. The claimant must prove discriminatory intent on the part of the educational institution. Cannon v. University of Chicago, 648 F.2d 1104 (7th Cir.), *cert. denied,* 454 U.S. 1128 (1981).

84. *North Haven Board of Education v. Bell, supra* note 82.

85. 465 U.S. 555 (1984). The *Grove City* case set the Supreme Court as arbiter between the Justice Department on the one hand and civil rights groups supported by a bipartisan coalition within Congress on the other. For the first time in its short history, Title IX was left before the Court without either side defending the law's broad scope of coverage. The Justice Department reversed long-standing federal policy on Title IX enforcement and argued before the Court that Grove City need comply only with respect to financial aid, as that was the only program receiving federal funds. Women's groups requested to participate in oral arguments, but the Court refused. More than two dozen civil rights and women's organizations joined a bipartisan group of 47 representatives and three senators in an *amicus curiae* brief in which they maintained that the Reagan administration had seriously misinterpreted the law. Their position was reasserted in a November 1983 "sense of the House" resolution approved by the House by a 414 to eight vote. H.R. Res. 190, 98th Cong. 1st Sess. (1983).

86. Within days of the *Grove City* ruling, the Assistant Attorney General for Civil Rights told reporters that the administration would apply not only Title IX but Title IV and § 504 to federally funded programs only. *See* Educ. Week, March 2, 1984, at 1. The Department of Education soon took a similar position. In a July 1984 memorandum, the Assistant Secretary for Civil Rights issued to OCR regional directors a statement of policy guidelines stating that he entertained "no doubt that the Court's decision is applicable to OCR's other statutory authorities which include the phrase 'program or activity receiving Federal financial assistance.'" Memorandum from Assistant Secretary for Civil Rights Harry M. Singleton to Regional Civil Rights Directors, Analysis of the Decision in *Grove City College v. Bell* and Initial Guidance on Its Application to OCR Enforcement Activities, July 31, 1984, at 6. Several measures were introduced in the 98th, 99th, and 100th Congresses to overturn effectively the *Grove City* decision. Finally in 1987, after three years of political wrangling, Congress enacted the Civil Rights Restoration Act, S.557, which affords Title IX, as well as Title VI, § 504, and the Age Discrimination Act, an institution-wide coverage.

87. G. ORFIELD, THE RECONSTRUCTION OF SOUTHERN EDUCATION 320 (1969).

88. Office for Civil Rights, Policies on Elementary and Secondary School Compliance with Title VI of the Civil Rights Act of 1964 (March 1968).

89. Green v. County School Board of New Kent County, 391 U.S. 430 (1968).

90. G. ORFIELD, MUST WE BUS? SEGREGATED SCHOOLS AND NATIONAL POLICY 285–86 (1978).

91. *Id.* at 280.

92. Departments of Justice and Health, Education and Welfare, joint press release (July 3, 1969), cited in ORFIELD, *supra* note 90, at 286–87.

93. *Id.* at 287–88.

94. Cong. Quarterly, August 28, 1971, at 1829. As stated by White House Press Secretary Ronald L. Ziegler in reference to the Nixon administration's busing directives: "Those who are not responsive will find themselves involved in other assignments or quite possibly in assignments other than the federal government."

95. ORFIELD, *supra* note 90, at 291.

96. See EDELMAN, *Southern School Desegregation from 1954–1973: A Judicial–Political Overview*, in BLACKS AND THE LAW, ANNALS OF THE AMERICAN ACADEMY OF POLITICAL SCIENCE 40, n. 30 (May 1973).

97. R. KLUGER, SIMPLE JUSTICE 764 (1977).

98. A. J. JONES, LAW, BUREAUCRACY AND POLITICS: THE IMPLEMENTATION OF TITLE VI OF THE CIVIL RIGHTS ACT OF 1964, 115 (1982).

99. ORFIELD, *supra* note 90, at 291.

100. In 1970, HEW issued a policy guideline requiring school districts to take "affirmative steps" to rectify language deficiency where inability to speak or understand English excluded students from "effective participation in the education program." Identification of Discrimination and Denial of Services on the Basis of National Origin, 35 Fed. Reg. 11,595 (1970). In 1974, the Supreme Court ruled in Lau v. Nichols, 414 U.S. 563 (1974), that merely providing linguistic minority students with the same facilities, textbooks, teachers, and curriculum effectively forecloses them from "any meaningful education" as required under Title VI. *Id.* at 563. The following year, HEW translated that ruling into a requirement of bilingual education in what has come to be known as the "*Lau* Remedies." *See* U.S. Department of Education, Office for Civil Rights, Task Force Findings Specifying Remedies for Eliminating Past Educational Practices Ruled Unlawful Under *Lau v. Nichols* (1975).

101. FISHEL AND POTTKER, *supra* note 40, at 143–44.

102. *Id.* at 145.

103. Telephone interview with Bernice Sandler, Executive Director, Project on the Status and Education of Women of the Association of American Colleges (February 13, 1986).

104. Telephone interview with Phyllis McClure, NAACP Legal Defense and Educational Fund (December 20, 1985).

105. Interview with Elliott Lichtman, partner, Rauh, Silard and Lichtman, Washington, D.C. (September 18, 1985).

106. 351 F. Supp. 636 (D.D.C. 1972).

107. *Id.* at 641.

108. 402 U.S. 1 (1971). In *Swann*, the Court sanctioned the use of racial quotas as a starting point in shaping a desegregation remedy and the use of systemwide transportation as one tool of desegregation.

109. Adams v. Richardson, 356 F. Supp. 92 (D.D.C. 1973).

110. Adams v. Richardson, 480 F.2d 1159 (D.C. Cir. 1973).

111. *Id.* at 1162.

112. *Id.* at 1163, n. 5.

113. ORFIELD, *supra* note 90, at 294.

114. U.S. COMM. ON CIVIL RIGHTS, THE FEDERAL CIVIL RIGHTS ENFORCEMENT EFFORT—1974, VOL. 3: TO ENSURE EQUAL EDUCATIONAL OPPORTUNITY 102–9 (1975), cited in ORFIELD, *supra* note 90, at 294.

115. ORFIELD, *supra* note 90, at 294.

116. Adams v. Weinberger, 391 F. Supp. 269 (D.D.C. 1975).

117. As a brief aside, in 1976 Judge John Sirica of the federal district court in Washington imposed a similar system of timeframes against HEW in a collateral action, Brown v. Weinberger, 417 F. Supp. 1215 (D.D.C. 1976), on behalf of 18

public school students attending schools that received federal aid from HEW. The litigation was again led by the trio of Rauh, Silard, and Lichtman in collaboration with the LDF. Here the focus was on HEW's failure to enforce Title VI in the public schools of 33 northern and western states.

118. *See* J. FREEMAN, THE POLITICS OF WOMEN'S LIBERATION 80–81 (1975); O'CONNOR, *supra* note 11, at 105.

119. FREEMAN, *supra* note 118, at 152.

120. Sandler Interview, *supra* note 103.

121. O'CONNOR, *supra* note 11, at 106.

122. *Id.* at 107.

123. Sandler Interview, *supra* note 103.

124. 3 C.F.R. 339 (1965), as amended by Exec. Order No. 11375, 3 C.F.R. 684 (1966–1970 compilation), *reprinted in* 42 U.S.C. § 2000e at 1232–1236. Until 1978, HEW had actual responsibility for enforcing Exec. Order 11246 under the oversight of the Office of Federal Contract Compliance (OFCCP) within the Department of Labor. As of that date, OFCCP assumed responsibility for enforcing the executive order, including investigating sex-based claims of discrimination in employment in higher education institutions with substantial government contracts and conducting compliance reviews of such institutions. Exec. Order No. 12086, 43 Fed. Reg. 46,501 (1978). Until 1972 when Title IX was enacted and Title VII of the Civil Rights Act of 1964 was amended to include educational institutions, Exec. Order 11246 was the only legal course available to victims of sex discrimination in employment in higher education. *See* SANDLER, *Sex Discrimination, Educational Institutions, and the Law: A New Issue on Campus*, in WOMEN IN ACADEMIA: TOWARD EQUAL OPPORTUNITIES 20 (E. Wasserman, A. Lewin, and L. Bleisweis eds. 1975).

125. Amended Complaint for Declaratory and Other Relief at 4, WEAL v. Weinberger, C.A. No. 74-1720, filed January 16, 1975, at 3.

126. Telephone interview with Carol Polowy, former general counsel of WEAL (December 20, 1985).

127. The other three plaintiffs were Verna Wittrock, Carol Weiss, and Marna Tucker. Wittrock had filed an employment discrimination complaint with HEW under Exec. Order 11246 in July 1971. According to plaintiff Wittrock's complaint, not only did an HEW investigator schedule an investigation when he was aware that she would be out of town, but he failed to contact all her witnesses. As of January 1975, HEW had still taken no corrective action. Weiss had filed a similar complaint alleging sex discrimination in August 1971. Despite a December 1972 letter of findings from OCR stating that she had been discriminated against, no corrective action had been taken by January 1975. Tucker sued as a citizen and taxpayer and also as a part-time university professor on the grounds that her future employment potential was limited by HEW's failure to enforce the law throughout higher education institutions. *See* Amended Complaint *supra* note 125, at 7–9.

128. *Id.* at 7.

129. Affirmation of Dorothy Raffel at 2, WEAL v. Bennett, C.A. No. 74-1720 (D.D.C. August 6, 1985).

130. Amended Complaint, *supra* note 125 at 9.

131. *Id.* at 9.

132. *Special Project: The Remedial Process in Institutional Reform Litigation*, 78 COLUM. L. REV. 784, 876 (1978).

133. *Id.* at 874.

134. *Id.* at 877.

135. Diver, *supra* note 26, at 68.

136. *See also* Plaintiffs' Motion for Certification as Class Action Under Fed. R. Civ. P. 23, WEAL v. Mathews, C.A., No. 74-1720 (D.D.C. February 21, 1975). According to Rule 23:

> One or more members of a class may sue or be sued as representative parties on behalf of all only if (1) the class is so *numerous* that joinder of all members is impracticable, (2) there are questions of law or fact common to the class, (3) the claims or defenses of the representative parties are *typical* of the claims or defenses of the class, and (4) the representative parties will fairly and adequately protect the interests of the class (emphasis added).

137. The Fifth Amendment to the U.S. Constitution states in part, "No person shall be . . . deprived of life, liberty, or property without due process of law." In Bolling v. Sharpe, 347 U.S. 497 (1954) and subsequent cases, the Supreme Court has read the concept of "equal protection of the laws" into this clause, similar to the equal protection provision contained within the Fourteenth Amendment.

138. Amended Complaint, *supra* note 125, at 32.

139. *Id.* at 36.

140. Interview with Marcia Greenberger, managing attorney, National Women's Law Center, Washington, D.C. (December 12, 1985).

141. FISHEL AND POTTKER, *supra* note 40, at 129–30.

142. Letter from John A. Bell, Chief, Elementary and Secondary Education Branch Region VI, Office for Civil Rights, Department of Health, Education and Welfare to Kay Paul Whyburn, November 20, 1975.

143. Order Granting Intervenors Martinez *et al.* Motion to Intervene, Adams v. Mathews, C.A. 70-3095 (D.D.C. March 30, 1976); Order Denying Intervenors Buxton *et al.* Motion to Intervene, Adams v. Mathews, C.A. 70-3095 (D.D.C. March 31, 1976). Intervenors Martinez *et al.* have since been represented in this action by the Mexican American Legal Defense and Educational Fund together with the Washington, D.C., law firm of Arnold and Porter.

144. Adams v. Mathews, 536 F.2d 417, 418 (D.C.Cir. 1976).

145. Adams v. Mathews, C.A. 70-3095 (D.D.C. June 14, 1976).

146. Greenberger Interview, *supra* note 140.

147. Telephone Interview with Martin Gerry, Former Director, Office for Civil Rights, Department of Health, Education and Welfare (February 20, 1986).

148. *Id.*

149. 20 U.S.C. § 1714(a) (Supp. 1987).

150. G. ORFIELD, *supra* note 90, at 298–301.

151. Plaintiffs' Memorandum on Pending Matters, filed June 27, 1977, at 2–4; Plaintiff–Intervenors Buxton *et al.* Motion for Further Relief, filed June 27, 1977, at 2, cited in Brief for Appellees at 14, Adams v. Bell, C.A. 83-1590 and WEAL v. Bell, C.A. 83-1516, 743 F.2d 42 (D.C. Cir. 1984).

152. McClure Interview, *supra* note 104.

153. Telephone interview with David Tatel, Former Director, Office for Civil Rights, Department of Health, Education and Welfare (December 20, 1985).

154. *Weekly Compilation of Presidential Documents*, address and remarks, Vol. 13, No. 8 (February 21, 1977) at 203, cited in THE STATE OF CIVIL RIGHTS: U.S. COMMISSION ON CIVIL RIGHTS at 12, n. 55 (February 1978).

155. Wash. Post, January 27, 1977, at A4.

156. Statement of Joseph A. Califano, Jr., Secretary of Health, Education and Welfare, HEW News Release, February 17, 1977, cited in THE STATE OF CIVIL RIGHTS, *supra* note 154, at 12, n. 56.

157. Statement by Joseph A. Califano, HEW News Release, February 17, 1977, at 1, cited in THE STATE OF CIVIL RIGHTS, *supra* note 154, at 13, n. 68.

158. Letter from Elmer B. Staats, Comptroller General of the United States to Senator Birch Bayh, March 30, 1977, at 4–11, cited in THE STATE OF CIVIL RIGHTS, *supra* note 154, at 13, n. 69.

159. 42 Fed. Reg. 39, 824 (August 5, 1977), cited in THE STATE OF CIVIL RIGHTS, *supra* note 154, at 13, n. 73.

160. Earlier that year, the district court had granted the National Federation of the Blind's Motion to Intervene on behalf of § 504 claimants, Order Granting Intervenors' National Federation of the Blind Motion to Intervene, Adams v. Califano, C.A. 70-3095 (D.D.C. October 7, 1977). They were later represented in the litigation by the Washington, D.C., firm of Covington and Burling. The consent order covered three actions pending before the district court: *Adams v. Califano* (brought by representatives of racial minorities in 17 southern and border states and including representatives of national origin minorities, women, and the handicapped as intervenors); *WEAL v. Califano* (brought by representatives of women); and *Brown v. Califano* (brought by representatives of racial minorities in the 33 other states).

161. Adams v. Califano, C.A. 70-3095 and WEAL v. Califano, C.A. 74-1720 (D.D.C. December 29, 1977).

162. Tatel Interview, *supra* note 153.

163. *Id.*

164. *Id.*

165. Affidavit of Cynthia Brown, Exhibit I at 1–2, cited in Brief for Appellees at 18, Adams v. Bell, C.A. 83-1590 and WEAL v. Bell, C.A. 83-1516, 743 F.2d 42 (D.D.C. 1984).

166. Testimony of David Tatel, March 12, 1982, tr. 12–15, cited in Brief for Appellees at 18, Adams v. Bell, C.A. 70-3095 and WEAL v. Bell, C.A. 74-1720 (D.D.C.), 48 Fed. Reg. 15,509 (1983).

167. Interview with Elliott Lichtman, partner, Rauh, Silard, and Lichtman, Washington, D.C. (December 20, 1985).

168. Carryover complaints represented complaints on which HEW had done some work but which had not been completed as of the December 1977 order. Backlog complaints were those on which HEW had done no work as of the December 1977 order.

169. Reply to Defendants' Opposition to Plaintiffs' Motion for Execution of Judgment or in the Alternative Requiring Defendants to Show Cause Why They

Should Not Be Held in Contempt (hereinafter Reply) at 2, Adams v. Harris, C.A. 70-3095 and WEAL v. Harris, C.A. 74-1720 (D.D.C. October 19, 1979).

170. *Id.* at 3.

171. 43 Fed. Reg. 58,070 (1978).

172. Reply, *supra* note 169, at 8. These were not published officially as proposed regulations until April 1981, 46 Fed. Reg. 23,081 (1981).

173. Letter from Albert T. Hamlin, Assistant General Counsel of HEW, to Marcia Greenberger (June 22, 1979).

174. Order Denying Plaintiffs' Motion, Adams v. Califano, C.A. 70-3095 and WEAL v. Califano, C.A. 74-1720 (D.D.C. November 9, 1979).

175. Republican National Convention, Republican Party Platform, July 14, 1980, Detroit, Michigan.

176. Letter from Terrel H. Bell, Secretary, Department of Education, to Senator Paul Laxalt (April 14, 1981).

177. Letter from Secretary Bell to Attorney General William French Smith (July 22, 1981). According to the proposal, Title IX would have covered employment discrimination only where the complainant showed a clear nexus between the alleged employment discrimination and discrimination against students, or where the complainant was a beneficiary of a federally funded program whose primary objective was to provide employment.

178. 456 U.S. 512 (1982).

179. Washington Council of Lawyers, *Reagan Civil Rights: The First Twenty Months, A Report by the Washington Council of Lawyers* 2 (1982).

180. Days, *Turning Back the Clock: The Reagan Administration and Civil Rights*, 19 HARV. C.R.–C.L.L. REV. 309 (1984).

181. Plaintiffs' Women's Equity Action League *et al.*'s Motion for Order to Show Cause at 3–5 WEAL v. Bell, C.A. 74-1720 (D.D.C. June 24, 1981).

182. Report to the Court and Plaintiffs on OCR's Efforts to Comply with the Consent Order, dated December 29, 1977, at 34, in Adams *et al.* v. Califano, C.A. 70-3095 (D.D.C. May 27, 1981).

183. Brief for the Appellants at 15–25, Adams v. Bell, C.A. 83-1590 and WEAL v. Bell, C.A. 83-1516 (D.C. Cir. 1983); 48 Fed. Reg. 15,509 (1983).

184. Transcript of Hearing, Adams v. Bell, C.A. 70-3095 and WEAL v. Bell, C.A. 74-1720 (D.D.C. March 15, 1982).

185. Transcript of meeting between Judge Pratt and attorneys at 10 (July 13, 1982) cited in letter from Elliott Lichtman to Richard A. Levie, attorney, Department of Justice (July 22, 1982).

186. Defendants' Proposed Changes in 1977 Order, Adams v. Bell, C.A. 70-3095 and WEAL v. Bell, C.A. 74-1720 (D.D.C. August 16, 1982).

187. Plaintiffs' and Intervenors' Memorandum in Opposition to Defendants' Proposed Major Changes in this Court's 1977 Order and in Support of Proposed Limited Changes, Adams v. Bell, C.A. 70-3095 and WEAL v. Bell, C.A. 74-1720 (D.D.C. August 16, 1982).

188. Order, Adams v. Bell, C.A. 70-3095 and WEAL v. Bell, C.A. 74-1720 (D.D.C. March 11, 1983); 48 Fed. Reg. 15,509 (1983).

189. Brief for Appellants at 29–64, Adams v. Bell, C.A. 83-1590, and WEAL v.

Bell, C.A. 83-1516, 743 F.2d 42 (D.C. Cir. 1984), citing Adams v. Bell, 711 F.2d 161, 166 (D.C. Cir. 1983).

190. 441 U.S. 677 (1970).

191. Brief for Appellees, Adams v. Bell, C.A. 83-1590 and WEAL v. Bell, C.A. 83-1516 at 24–55, 743 F.2d 42 (D.C. Cir. 1984).

192. 743 F.2d at 43. Article III of the U.S. Constitution limits the jurisdiction of the federal courts to "cases" and "controversies." These words have come to limit the scope of federal court power to issues that are presented in an adversary context that are particularly appropriate for judicial resolution.

193. 468 U.S. 737 (1984). This nationwide class action was initiated by parents of black children who attended public schools that were in the process of desegregating. Plaintiffs alleged that the Internal Revenue Service had not developed adequate standards and procedures to fulfill its legal obligation to deny tax-exempt status to schools that practice racial discrimination. Such failure on the part of the IRS, they claimed, had encouraged the expansion of racially segregated private schools and had thereby interfered with the ability of black children to receive a racially integrated education. In a 5–3 opinion written by Justice O'Connor, the majority ruled that the plaintiffs failed to meet the essential *standing* requirement that the alleged injury must be fairly "traceable" to the challenged governmental conduct and "likely to be redressed" by the requested relief. The Court maintained that standing is "grounded in the idea of separation of powers," which in turn "counsels against recognizing standing in a case brought not to enforce specific legal obligations . . . but to seek a restructuring of the apparatus established by the Executive Branch to fulfill its legal duties." *Id.* at 761.

194. 743 F.2d at 44, *citing Allen v. Wright* at 761. The appeals court subsequently vacated the district court's March 1983 order and reimposed the 1977 order, modified by the timeframe exception, tolling, and reporting requirements of 1983.

195. Brief for Appellants at 58, n. 57, Adams v. Bell, C.A. 83-1590 and WEAL v. Bell, C.A. 83-1516, 743 F.2d 42 (D.C. Cir. 1984).

196. 743 F.2d at 44, *citing Allen v. Wright* at 751.

197. Points and Authorities in Support of Defendants' Motion to Dismiss and in Opposition to *Adams* Plaintiffs' Motion for Ruling Establishing Standing at 14–27, Adams v. Bennett, C.A. 70-3095 and WEAL v. Bennett, C.A. 74-1720 (D.D.C. July 1, 1985).

198. *Id.* at 34–36.

199. Interview with David Anderson, Director, Federal Programs Branch, Department of Justice, Washington, D.C. (September 18, 1985).

200. Plaintiffs' Opposition to Defendants' Motion to Dismiss and Reply in support of Motion for Ruling Establishing Their Standing at 3–4, Adams v. Bennett, C.A. 70-3095 (D.D.C. August 14, 1985).

201. The WEAL plaintiffs, in fact, had moved for class certification back in January 1975. Two years later, in February 1977, Judge Pratt granted the defendants' motion to deny class action certification. At the same time, the judge denied defendants' motion to dismiss for lack of standing.

202. Interview with Ellen Vargyas, attorney, National Women's Law Center, Washington, D.C. (February 28, 1986).

203. WEAL Plaintiffs' and Buxton Intervenors' Opposition to Defendants' Mo-

tion to Dismiss at 6–27 (D.D.C. August 19, 1985).

204. Transcript of hearing at 23, Adams v. Bennett, C.A. 70-3095 and WEAL v. Bennett, C.A. 74-1720 (D.D.C. December 12, 1985).

205. *Id.* at 53.

206. 675 F. Supp. 668 at 681 (D.D.C. 1987).

207. *Id.* at 674, *citing Adams I,* 480 F.2d 1159 at 1163 n. 5 (D.C. Cir. 1973) and *Adams II,* 711 F.2d 161 at 165 (D.C. Cir. 1983).

208. Telephone interview with Brenda Smith, attorney, National Women's Law Center, Washington, D.C. (December 6, 1988).

209. The opinion does mention the *WEAL* plaintiffs and the *Adams* plaintiff-intervenors in the context of the government's arguments that their claims are now moot. The opinion upholds these arguments obliquely but sidesteps any decision on the issue in view of the court's conclusion on standing.

210. In two recent *en banc* decisions, the D.C. Circuit Court of Appeals was evenly divided on the standing issue (Hotel and Restaurant Employees Union, Local 25 v. Smith, 846 F.2d 1499 [D.C. Cir. 1988], and Center for Auto Safety v. Thomas, 847 F.2d 843 [D.C. Cir. 1988], *vacated,* 856 F.2d 1557 [D.C. Cir. 1988]).

211. WEAL v. Cavazos, No. 88-5065 (D.C. Cir. April 11, 1989).

212. *Id.* at 11 *citing Allen v. Wright* at 755.

213. *Id.* at 12.

214. *Id.* at 14.

215. *Id.* at 13, *citing* Sunstein, *Reviewing Agency Inaction After* Heckler v. Chaney, 52 U. CHI. L. REV. 653, 670 (1985).

216. *Id.* at 14.

217. 468 U.S. 737 at 760, *cited* in Adams v. Bennett, 675 F. Supp. 668 at 680.

218. Glazer, *supra* note 21.

219. Telephone interview with Antonio Califa, former Director of Policy and Enforcement Service, Office for Civil Rights, Department of Education (November 19, 1985). It should be noted, however, that some of Judge Pratt's decisions that appear to be pro-government were, in fact, rulings upholding either federal agencies' regulations per se or their enforcement of regulations rather than the failure to enforce as in the *Adams* and *WEAL* litigation. *See e.g.,* National Conference of Catholic Bishops v. Bell, 490 F. Supp. 734 (D.D.C. 1984) (upholding abortion provision of the Pregnancy Discrimination Act of 1968); Caymun Turtle Farm, Ltd. v. Andrus, 478 F. Supp. 125 (D.D.C. 1979) (upholding regulations protecting turtles in navigable waters; the Environmental Defense Fund had intervened for the defendant–government); P.F.Z. Properties, Inc. v. Train, 393 F. Supp. 1370 (D.D.C. 1975) (upholding permit requirements of the Federal Water Pollution Control Act).

220. Califa Interview, *supra* note 219.

221. Tatel Interview, *supra* note 153.

222. Transcript, *supra* note 204, at 62–63.

223. Smith Interview, *supra* note 208.

224. Adams v. Bell, C.A. 70-3095 and WEAL v. Bell, C.A. 74-1720, 48 Fed. Reg. 15, 509 (1983).

225. Order Denying Motion for Stay Pending Appeal, WEAL v. Bennett, C.A. 88-5065 (D.D.C. August 8, 1988).

226. Smith Interview, *supra* note 208.

227. Second Lichtman Interview, *supra* note 167.

228. Telephone interview with Clarence Thomas, Former Assistant Secretary for Civil Rights, Department of Education (January 16, 1986).

229. *Civil Rights Enforcement by the Department of Education, 1985: Hearings Before the Subcommittee on Intergovernmental Relations and Human Resources of the House Committee on Government Operations* (hereinafter *Hearings*), 99th Congress, 1st Session (1985).

230. House Committee on Education and Labor, *A Report on the Investigation of the Civil Rights Enforcement Activities of the Office for Civil Rights, U.S. Department of Education* (hereinafter *1988 Investigation*), H.R. Rep. No. 100-FF, 100th Cong., 2d Sess. (1988).

231. *Hearings, supra* note 229 (statement of Harry M. Singleton, Assistant Secretary of Civil Rights, Department of Education, transcript at 125).

232. House Subcommittee on Intergovernmental Relations and Human Resources of the House Committee on Government Operations, *Investigation of Civil Rights Enforcement by the Office for Civil Rights at the Department of Education*, (hereinafter *1985 Investigation*) H.R. Rep. No. 99-458, 99th Cong., 1st Sess. (1985).

233. *Hearings, supra* note 229 (statement of Julius Chambers, Director–Counsel, NAACP Legal Defense and Educational Fund, Inc., transcript at 6).

234. *1985 Investigation, supra* note 232, at 11.

235. *Id.* at 6.

236. *Id.* at 13–14.

237. *Id.* at 22.

238. *Id.* at 19.

239. *Id.* at 22.

240. *1988 Investigation, supra* note 230, at 58.

241. *1985 Investigation, supra* note 232, at 22.

242. Final Annual Operating Plan for the Office for Civil Rights, 50 Fed. Reg. 48,624, 48,625 (1985).

243. Evans, *Civil Rights Office Settles Many Cases Using Method Challenged by Justice Department, House Unit Told*, Chronicle of Higher Educ., July 31, 1985, at 15, col. 4.

244. Letter from Stuart B. Oneglia, Chief, Coordination and Review Section, Civil Rights Division, Department of Justice to Kristine M. Marcy, Director, Planning and Compliance Operations Service, Office for Civil Rights, Department of Education (November 13, 1981).

245. *1988 Investigation, supra* note 230, at 4.

246. *Id.* at 2.

247. *Id.* at 2.

248. *Id.* at 2.

249. *Id.* at 33.

250. *Id.* at 34.

251. *See* Guardians Association *et al.* v. Civil Service Commission of the City of New York *et al.*, 463 U.S. 582 (1983) (Title VI). *See also Cannon v. University of Chicago, supra* note 83 (Title IX).

252. *1988 Investigation, supra* note 230, at 35.

253. *Id.* at 3.

254. *1985 Investigation, supra* note 232, at 30.

255. Tugend, *Rights Agency: Lost Consensus, Uncertain Goals,* Educ. Week, March 5, 1986, 14, col. 5.

256. *1988 Investigation, supra* note 230, at 19.

257. Office for Civil Rights, Department of Education, *Fourth Annual Report, Fiscal Year 1984,* at 13; information provided in writing by Thomas E. Esterley, Congressional Liaison, Office for Civil Rights (March 3, 1986).

258. Office for Civil Rights, Department of Education, *A Narrative History of the Adams Litigation from October 9, 1970, to December 29, 1977,* cited in *1985 Investigation, supra* note 232 at 31, n. 86.

259. *1988 Investigation, supra* note 230, at 3.

260. 465 U.S. 555 (1984).

261. N.Y. Times, June 3, 1984, at 36.

262. PROJECT ON EQUAL EDUCATION RIGHTS, NOW LEGAL DEFENSE AND EDUCATION FUND, INJUSTICE UNDER THE LAW: THE IMPACT OF THE GROVE CITY COLLEGE DECISION ON CIVIL RIGHTS (February 1985).

263. *See supra* note 86.

264. 20 U.S.C. 3811 (Supp. 1987). In 1981, Congress enacted Chapter 2 as part of the Education Consolidation and Improvement Act. Popularly known as the "education block grant," the law consolidated 29 former categorical programs into one block grant to be allocated through the states to local school districts. Districts can spend the funds with complete discretion within any combination of three broad categories, including basic skills development, educational improvement and support services, and special projects.

265. Tugend, *E.D. Policy Shift Will Sharply Limit Rights Coverage,* Educ. Week, February 26, 1986, at 1.

PART IV

Equal Access and Educational
Opportunities for Racial and
Linguistic Minority Students

CHAPTER 5

Endless Journey: Integration and the Provision of Equal Educational Opportunity in Denver's Public Schools: A Study of *Keyes v. School District No. 1*

JAMES J. FISHMAN
AND LAWRENCE STRAUSS

DENVER WAS THE FIRST non-southern city to undergo extensive litigation over the desegregation of its schools. In this context it has become a mirror for the way America deals with its most pressing social problem: the integration of minorities into the educational, political, and economic mainstream through equal educational opportunity. This study examines the difficulties of creating a unitary public school system and developing a plan that would provide an equal educational opportunity to the large Hispanic minority.

THE SETTING: A PORTRAIT OF THE CITY

Since Denver was founded in 1858 by William Larimer as a stopping point for victims of "gold fever" after the discovery of the mineral at Pike's Peak, it has served as the gateway to Colorado and the Rockies. Today, Denver is a major metropolitan area. Its problems and prospects reflect more of urban America than of the West.

Between 1940 and 1970, the population and economy of Denver expanded greatly. Colorado became a sophisticated service economy. The Denver metropolitan area enjoyed substantial growth during the 1970s, spurred in part by the energy boom and by a national demographic shift to the Sun Belt.[1] The population of eight counties in the Denver metropolitan area increased from 1,237,529 in 1970 to 1,691,921 in 1980. The city of Denver's population declined, however, dropping 4.5 percent from 514,678 in 1970 to 491,396 a decade later. Its population had increased in the 1960 to 1970 decade from 493,889 to 514,678.[2]

Minority Patterns

Blacks have lived in Denver from its earliest years. They clung to their rights and, at least initially, had some political influence. From a population of 1,000 in the 1880s, Denver's black population grew to 6,000 in the 1910s, concentrated in the Five Points area east of the business district. World War II created job openings in skilled factory jobs in the local defense industry. Governmental offices and military facilities established in the 1940s also provided employment. Since World War II, a major aspiration of the black community has been progress toward middle-class status.[3]

The first Mexican immigrants were brought into the state in the earliest years of the twentieth century by sugar beet companies and by the Colorado Fuel and Iron Corporation to work in its steel mills. By 1930, 13,000 Coloradoans were born in Mexico and another 28,000 were Hispanics from New Mexico. Most settled in rural areas and small towns where they faced segregation, prejudice, and harassment.[4]

Today Hispanics are the largest minority group in Denver and by 1980, Hispanics comprised 19 percent of the city's population.[5] In 1964, Hispanics made up 17 percent of the school population; 19.1 percent by 1975; and 32 percent by 1981.

The Hispanic population has always been a highly disadvantaged group. The percentage of Hispanics classified as "professional" and their median income and education are the lowest of any ethnic group in Denver.[6] Twice as many Hispanics as other racial groups occupied Denver's urban poverty area in the northern half of the city. Yet, when Hispanics reached middle-class economic status and moved into white neighborhoods, they did not receive the hostility directed at blacks.

One of the most significant developments of the present decade is the emergence of the Hispanic community as a political force. The constitutional demands of desegregation do not always correlate with the needs and aspirations of the Hispanic community. Many Hispanics opposed the school integration suit as a form of cultural hegemony and favored better education rather than more integration. The tri-ethnic mix has complicated desegregation in Denver.

Housing Patterns

In 1970, blacks were concentrated in inner-city neighborhoods, particularly Five Points, which extended east from the central business district. Since the end of World War II, however, blacks have slowly moved east from the Five Points area into the Park Hill area, a trend that formed the underpinnings of the *Keyes* case. When blacks moved in, whites moved out. These inner-city areas were all 50 percent or more black.

Residential segregation against Hispanics has always been less complete than for blacks. The Hispanic concentrations are west of the business district. Few neighborhoods in Denver have large concentrations of both blacks and Hispanics. Also, Hispanics tend to be more dispersed throughout the city, in part because they outnumber blacks.[7]

Minorities and the Denver Public School System

Racially segregated schooling has been a continuing phenomenon in Denver. In the 1925–1926 school year, 60 percent of the 789 black children enrolled in Denver's elementary schools attended either the Gilpin or Whittier Schools. One junior high school enrolled 85 percent of the black students, and Manual High School had 75 percent of the blacks. Eighty percent of the 1,004 Spanish-speaking children attended five elementary schools. Only seven Spanish-speaking children were enrolled in junior high school and but two in day time high school.[8]

Over the years the Denver Board of Education engaged in a variety of techniques that assured the continuance of racially unbalanced schools, such as situating schools in a way that guaranteed their racial imbalance and purposefully failing to adjust school boundary lines to relieve overcrowding at predominately white or black schools in a way that would have promoted integration. The Board adjusted boundaries to perpetuate racial isolation, used mobile classrooms to continue racial imbalance at certain schools, and assigned minority faculty principally to minority schools.[9] The Court in *Keyes* concluded that the Board had conscious knowledge of the racial consequences of its acts.[10]

In 1962, the Vorhees Special Study Committee on Equality in Educational Opportunity in the Denver Public Schools recommended that the school Board consider racial, ethnic, and socio-economic factors in establishing school boundaries and selecting school sites. It also suggested that boundaries be set to establish heterogeneous schools and communities. The Board adopted a resolution to implement the Vorhees Committee's recommendations.

A second study group, the Berge Committee, established in 1966 to examine the policies of the Board with respect to the location of new schools in northeast Denver, suggested changes that would further school integration. In 1968 the Board resolved to direct the Superintendent of Schools to submit to the Board a comprehensive plan for the integration of Denver's schools. Thereafter, the Board spent from January to April 1969 studying 14 alternative plans and then passed, by a five to two vote, Resolutions 1520, 1524, and 1531, which were designed to eliminate segregation in the black schools in Park Hill, while stabilizing the composition of schools in racial transition. The resolutions offered a concrete plan of affirmative action, including busing, to lessen racial imbalance. Their impact on the Denver community was electric.

A school Board election in May 1969 became the focal point of the busing issue. An incumbent, Edward Benton, and a newcomer, Monte Pascoe, both backers of the plan, were defeated two and a half to one by opponents of the resolution. For the next decade busing defined Denver's politics.

On June 9, 1969, Resolutions 1520, 1524, and 1531 were rescinded and superseded by Resolution 1533, which sought to achieve desegregation on a voluntary basis. The Board's justification was a response to the community sentiment expressed in the school board election. Ten days later, eight parents of Denver public school students sought to enjoin the implementation of Resolution 1533 and the rescission of Resolutions 1520, 1524, and 1531. Twenty-one years later, *Keyes v. School District No. 1* remains an active lawsuit.

A LEGAL CHRONOLOGY

The Liability Phase to the Final Order (1969–1974)

The complaint stated two claims for relief: first, that the rescision of the resolutions be temporarily and permanently enjoined; second, that a declaratory judgment be issued that the rescission of the resolutions by the school board constituted a violation of the equal protection clause.

In hearing the injunction claim, District Court Judge William E. Doyle found that during the ten-year period preceding the passage of Resolutions 1520, 1524, and 1531, the Board had carried out a policy of racial segregation, and the rescission of the school integration plan would perpetuate school segregation and chill the plaintiffs' rights of equal educational opportunity. The court issued a preliminary injunction. The Board appealed successfully to the Tenth Circuit Court of Appeals.

After a trial on the merits, the district court found that the Board had acted in violation of the plaintiffs' Fourteenth Amendment rights. The Board's segregative acts were taken with knowledge of their effect on attempts to desegregate the school system. The court concluded that the only feasible and constitutionally acceptable program would be a system of desegregation and integration that provided compensatory education in an integrated environment. The court delayed the implementation of such a plan for one year and adopted an interim plan, which applied to 15 core-city schools.[11]

The court of appeals affirmed the trial court's conclusion that the Board's actions in one neighborhood, the Park Hill section of Denver, during the 1960s constituted *de jure* segregation; affirmed the trial court's conclusions that plaintiffs had failed to make a *prima facie* showing concerning the core-city schools; but reversed the district court conclusion that maintenance of *de facto* segregated schools in the core of the city violated the Fourteenth Amendment.[12]

The U.S. Supreme Court reversed the circuit court's opinion relating to the existence of actionable segregation in the core-city schools. *Keyes* was the first non-southern desegregation case to be decided by the Supreme Court. The majority found that where school authorities had "carried out a systematic program of segregation affecting a substantial portion of the students, schools, teachers, and facilities within the school system, it [was] only common sense to conclude that there exist[ed] a predicate for a finding of the existence of a dual school system." The purposeful concentration of minority students in certain schools had the reciprocal effect of keeping other schools Anglo.[13]

The high court established the presumption that the Board's segregative acts in a substantial portion of the school district rendered the entire district a dual system and directed the district court on remand to offer the Board the opportunity to prove that the Park Hill area was a separate, identifiable, and unrelated section of the district. In the event the Board should fail in this proof, the district court was to determine whether the Board's conduct in deliberately segregating Park Hill schools made the entire school system a dual school system.[14] If so determined, the Board had the affirmative duty to desegregate the entire system root and branch.

Judge Doyle, on remand, concluded that the segregative acts of the Board in Park Hill did constitute the rest of the district as a dual school system, and the Board's intentional segregation in Park Hill substantially affected schools outside the area.[15] On December 13, 1973, the court ordered the parties to submit plans for desegregation of the entire school district. After finding unacceptable the desegregation plans submitted by both the plaintiffs and the defendants, the court appointed its own expert, Dr. John N. Finger, and thereafter approved his desegregation plan, known as the Finger Plan.

The Initial Remedy (1974–1976)

The plan adopted by the district court desegregated Denver's schools by re-zoning attendance areas across all grade levels, ordering busing, and reassigning elementary school minority students. Approximately 37 schools were to be organized in pairs or clusters for purposes of part-time reassignment of students on a classroom basis.

Junior and senior high schools were desegregated by new attendance zones and satellites. The court set a 40 percent minimum percentage and a 70 percent maximum percentage of Anglo students in every elementary school.[16] In the secondary schools the minimum was set at 50 to 60 percent Anglos. There were deviations permitted from those percentages for particular areas and schools.

Eight elementary schools were to have Anglo enrollments below 40 percent because of the school's inaccessibility and the desire to continue or to institute bilingual–bicultural programs at predominately Hispanic schools. These five elementary schools were to have been left with minority enrollments ranging between 77 percent and 88 percent.

On appeal, the tenth circuit affirmed most of the desegregation plan, but rejected the part-time pairing plan and ordered implementation of a full-time desegregated school environment.[17] It reversed an order to consolidate two of the high schools. The circuit court also faulted the plan for leaving five elementary schools as segregated Hispanic schools.[18]

The court found that the five schools were substantially disproportionate in their racial composition, and therefore, under *Swann v. Charlotte–Mecklenburg Board of Education*,[19] a presumption existed against the school district's compliance with its constitutional responsibility. It held that continued segregation at these schools could be justified only on the basis that practical or other legitimate considerations rendered desegregation unwise, or on the basis of proof that the racial composition of these schools was not the result of past discriminatory action on the part of the school Board.

The circuit court ruled that bilingual education was not a substitute for desegregation, and such instruction had to be subordinate to a plan of school desegregation. Whether the five predominately Hispanic schools could be justified was remanded to Judge Doyle. The stipulated plan for desegregation agreed to by the parties after the remand, approved by Judge Doyle in an order entered on March 26, 1976, contained nothing related to issues of limited English language proficiency (LEP). The five predominately Hispanic elementary schools were now included in the overall desegregation plan. The circuit court's opinion resulted in an increase in the number of elementary school students bused. According to Willis Hawley, later a court appointed expert: "After a full implementation of the desegregation plan in 1975 Denver achieved approximately eighty-five percent of possible districtwide racial balance."[20] An order dated March 26, 1976, approved the issuance of an agreed plan in response to the court of appeal's decision.

After the entry of the 1976 order, the case was assigned to a worthy successor to Judge Doyle, Judge Richard Matsch. He had been appointed to the district court bench by President Nixon. The son of German Lutheran parents, who came to Denver from Burlington, Iowa, Judge Matsch began his legal career with a Denver law firm, Holme Roberts & Owen, worked in the offices of the U.S. Attorney and Denver City Attorney, and was a bankruptcy judge before nomination to the federal bench in March 1974 at the age of 43. A private, austere, and closely disciplined person, Judge Matsch is a well respected jurist. His forcefulness in the Denver case surprised many.

From the Moratorium on Changing School Assignments
to the Court Selected Plan (1976–1979)

Upon entry of the 1976 order by Judge Doyle, the Board requested a moratorium on student reassignment. Judge Matsch granted the request from 1976 to 1979. It was hoped this moratorium would provide stability and continuity and would stem the exodus of Anglo students from the system. Nonetheless, a decline in student population occurred. After the Community Education Council (CEC), a court-appointed monitoring group, expressed concerns that imbalances in racial composition and crowded conditions had developed in some schools, court hearings were held in January 1979 to consider the status of those schools.[21]

The CEC had requested the hearing to obtain a status report from the school Board and the Denver Public Schools (DPS) administration on the comprehensive, city-wide plan for the schools, which would be implemented after the three-year moratorium on altering student assignments expired. The Board developed a new plan, Resolution No. 2060, dealing with school closings and pupil assignments for the 1979–1980 school year. The proposal was designed to increase the number of students who attended their neighborhood schools and to decrease busing. The burdens of the plan were not equally shared. Some children would be bused; others would attend neighborhood schools. The Board never considered upon whom the burdens would fall. After the CEC and plaintiffs objected to the plan of Resolution 2060, the Board never met in legislative session nor considered alternatives. The administrative staff's reaction to the CEC was hostile, petulant, and decisive. Clearly, it took its cue from the Board. The staff developed several delaying proposals for further study. A decision had to be made. The Board left Judge Matsch to make the necessary changes in student assignments. Matsch later said that the Board's dereliction of duty enabled its members to avoid criticism from the community and permitted them to continue their politically popular protest against judicial intervention in local self-governance.[22] This time Matsch ordered the student assignment changes.

*Four School Board Members in Search of a
Non-busing Plan: From the Ad Hoc Plan to Total
Access to the Consensus Plan (1979–1982)*

The Board procrastinated in the development of a plan for a permanent unitary school district once the court relinquished control.[23] From July 1979 until the spring of 1982, the Board split along philosophical and political lines, with the anti-busers holding a four-to-three majority.

The July 30, 1979, memorandum issued by Judge Matsch ordered the Board to develop a plan for a permanent unitary school district. Matsch essentially said it was time to close out the ten-year-old suit.[24] On March 15, 1982, nearly 32 months after the memorandum, Judge Matsch rejected the Total Access Plan, a proposal whose major tenets were open enrollments and magnet schools, not busing.[25] The Board had approved the plan by a four to three vote, over the objections of the three liberals and after the Board had spent considerable time working out a completely different desegregation proposal that called for continued busing, although on a more limited basis. Throughout this period there was ongoing conflict among the Board members. By May 1982 the Board still had the lawsuit to resist.

The Ad Hoc Plan

In 1980, an Ad Hoc Committee was formed by Board resolution to formulate a plan acceptable to the court. The committee included representatives of the black and Hispanic communities, as well as teachers, the League of Women Voters, and the Denver Parent–Teacher–Student Association and held public hearings for additional input from the community.[26]

The Ad Hoc Committee's report, released on June 5, 1981, called for maintaining 26 walk-in, or neighborhood, elementary schools, creating five new walk-in junior high schools, and eliminating 27 satellite attendance areas. The plan also proposed establishing two magnet schools at the elementary school level. In all, the plan proposed blanketing two-thirds of the city with walk-in schools.[27]

The Ad Hoc Committee's plan was resisted by the Community Education Council as an attempt to return to segregation. On October 11, 1981, the Board adopted a plan under which 2,600 fewer children would ride the bus, and eight additional neighborhood schools would be created.[28]

At that same meeting, Board member William Schroeder presented his own plan, the key feature of which was to eliminate forced busing. He wanted students assigned to schools nearest their homes, unless they preferred a different school.

Schroeder's proposal did not sit well with many Denver residents, particularly minorities, who saw the plan as an attempt to resegregate the schools.[29] At its next meeting, the Board resolved to send two desegregation plans to the judge. One was Schroeder's, the other was a successor to the Ad Hoc Committee's plan.[30] This second plan called for restoration of up to 19 walk-in schools, all of them in neighborhoods considered residentially integrated, and the continuation of busing, although to a lesser degree.

The submission of the two plans was an attempt by the bitterly divided Board to shirk its elected responsibility to set the policy of the Denver public schools (DPS). The judge refused to select either of the plans. After receiving the two proposals, he bluntly ordered the Board to submit one "definite plan." Matsch did not want to assume a receivership position over the Denver schools as had occurred in Boston, nor did he want to give board members a way out of their elected responsibilities. Throughout this case, the court pushed and urged the Board toward the goal of a unified system.

The Total Access Plan

Rebuffed by the court, on November 30, 1981, the Board voted four to two to formulate another plan by December 10th. The Board's anti-busing majority directed DPS staff to come up with a plan that would halt mandatory busing. Called the Total Access Plan (TAP), the plan's foundations were open enrollments and magnet schools, both of which, a majority of the Board felt, could create and sustain a unitary school system.[31]

TAP was presented on December 10, 1981, by then-superintendent Dr. Joseph Brzeinski. The Board approved the plan four to three, the usual tally during that period, with the three liberals opposing it.[32] In addition to allowing students to attend schools close to their homes, the Total Access Plan proposed creating 35 magnet schools throughout the city, many of them at the elementary school level. There would be no mandatory busing. Total Access also stipulated that students who wished to remain at their current schools would be given priority.[33]

The DPS staff had less than two weeks to design the proposal to meet Matsch's deadline for a unitary plan. By contrast, an alternative consensus plan, which the Board voted not to send to the judge, went through a much longer planning process and had the benefit of input from the public, not just from DPS staff.

In January 1982, the school Board, once again by a four to three vote, approved hiring a public relations firm to publicize TAP and a law firm to defend the plan at an upcoming hearing before Judge Matsch. TAP incited resistance very quickly. In early February 1982, approximately 20 teachers sent letters to Judge Matsch expressing their objections to the proposal. Enrollment figures began to surface that didn't bode well for the plan's future success with Judge Matsch. DPS staff projections indicated that under the plan, preponderately one-race schools, most of which had disappeared under the 1974 consent decree, would reappear in certain parts of the city. The same patterns recurred at the junior high and high school levels, according to the projections.

The four-member majority of the school Board held its ground, however, determined to rid DPS of mandatory busing.[34] The hearing began on March 1, 1982. Despite some favorable testimony, Judge Matsch rejected the plan on March 15, saying it would fail to remove "the vestiges of racial discrimination in pupil assignment." The judge called the plan incomplete, saying, "I'm not certain that [sic] would happen, what central administration and staff would be doing." He added the school Board was asking him to accept the plan "as an act of faith."[35] Last, Judge Matsch noted "the abrupt switch to what a witness has described accurately as a radical plan." In this the judge was referring to the Board's decision in late 1981 to send him the Total Access Plan, instead of what had grown out of the Ad Hoc Committee's plan. "In summary, the total access plan was lacking in concern, commitment and capacity." He ordered the Board to come up with another plan in 30 days.

The Consensus Plan

After Judge Matsch's March 15 ruling the Board began anew. On March 18, it reviewed and approved the Consensus Plan, most of which grew out of the alternative plan the Board had approved the previous fall before it submitted the Total Access Plan to the judge. Under the new proposal, the number of students bused for integration, approximately 14,500, would be reduced by about 2,600. Seventeen new walk-in schools, 11 at the elementary school level and six junior high schools, would be created. There would also be two magnet elementary schools, one stressing fundamentals and the other having an extended day program.

On May 12, 1982, nearly three years after he ordered the Board to come up with a suitable proposal for a unitary district in an effort to end the lawsuit, Judge Matsch approved the Consensus Plan. Matsch wasn't particularly happy with the plan. It did not end the suit and applied only to the 1982–1983 school year. The judge said he would remain active in the case to make sure future reforms were enacted: "I am not convinced the incumbent school board had shown a commitment to the creation of a unitary school system which will have adequate capacity for the delivery of educational services without racial advantages."[36]

The Board, split by philosophical and political differences and its majority opposed to busing as a desegregation remedy, was still a long way from settling the then 13-year-old suit. Although Judge Matsch viewed the Consensus Plan implemented in the fall of 1982 as an interim measure, with a few minor changes, it was in effect for six years. Moreover, Matsch wrote in his June 3, 1985, opinion, "[t]he proposal was premised on a hope that there would be a discernible movement toward natural integration of these attendance zones by changes in housing patterns."[37]

Although Denver has become residentially more integrated over the past ten years, residential segregation persists and has had an impact upon school enrollment. In 1982, the plaintiffs objected to the Consensus Plan on several grounds, one of which was that it would lead to racially identifiable schools. They were right.

The Consensus Plan, originally an interim compromise measure that came at the end of a long, acrimonious period during which the Board tried to convince the judge to rely on magnet and neighborhood schools (not busing), did not have much chance of becoming a future blueprint. It was a political compromise, patched together by a school Board whose majority abhorred busing. Not surprisingly, it provided little in the way of guidelines toward establishment of a unitary system.

IMPLEMENTING THE REMEDY:
HINDRANCES TO COURT WITHDRAWAL

White Flight

In the mid 1970s the demographic changes evident throughout the city and its school system inevitably made the original desegregation plan obsolete. As with many other big-city school districts undergoing court-ordered busing, Denver experienced an exodus of Anglo students. There are differences of opinion as to how much of the exodus was actually spurred by the court order and how much could be attributed, at least in part, to factors such as the declining birth rate among Anglos. For example, in 1974, the year court-ordered desegregation first took effect, there were 43,576 Anglo students in the Denver public schools. By the fall of 1983, that number had dropped to 20,000. The most severe declines in the enrollment of Anglos, though, occurred during the first three years after Judge Doyle issued the busing order.

At the same time as Anglo students were leaving the system, the black enrollment in the Denver public schools declined, though not as precipitously as the Anglo student population. The black population, which stood at 14,831 in 1974, decreased to 13,598 in 1983. Hispanic enrollment increased slightly, rising from 21,832 students in 1975 to 23,199 in 1983.[38]

Some argue that white flight would have occurred without court-ordered busing in Denver. The number of whites leaving the city returned to "a normal demographic trend" in 1978, four years after the order took effect.[39] The Poundstone Amendment, passed in 1974, prevented the city and county of Denver from annexing any counties unless a majority of residents approved and was a key barrier to increasing Anglo school enrollment. In recent years, a few rehabilitated inner-city neighborhoods in Denver have begun to attract whites, some of them with school-age children. Despite these gains, however, most of the minority students in the Denver metropolitan area sit in DPS classrooms.

Busing and Politics: The Politicalization of the School Board

In the course of the litigation, the Denver school Board, like many of its big-city counterparts, became an extremely political governing body and a lauching pad for political careers. This trend had an adverse effect on the desegregation remedy.

Since the late 1960s, few elected offices in Denver have offered so much visibility. Busing continued to be an issue for the Board throughout the 1970s and into the 1980s, ebbing and flowing, sharpening in intensity and then softening—but always there. The issue remains, years after the court's initial busing order took effect, although much of the Board's anti-busing rhetoric has softened.

The Board was given the politically difficult task of implementing an unpopular court order and resisted—a phenomenon that has had a wide range of effects on the school system as well as the court-ordered remedy. Not all Denver school Board members have opposed busing as a way to integrate public schools. Some fought for busing, arguing it was the best alternative for the school system. The conflict between the pro- and anti-busers often was played out in the local media. The lack of a consensus among the Board members impeded the remedy's implementation.[40]

Until *Keyes*, those who served on the Board were members of the Denver establishment. Board membership was not a highly visible position politically. The 1969 school Board election was a watershed. From then on, elections became ideological battlegrounds centered on busing. Increasingly sophisticated political tactics were used for a position that paid nothing. A brief look at the Board elections from 1975, the year after the original remedy was implemented, until the election in May 1985 reveals the tenacious grip the busing issue has had on the Board's politics and how much the Board has evolved as a political animal—most notably when it came to getting elected and, more important, to staking out a political constituency.

In 1977, Kay Schomp, one of the Board's liberals and a firm supporter of busing, was re-elected to a second six-year term. Also re-elected that year was Robert Crider, the staunch anti-busing proponent who later was elected to the Denver City Council. Crider ran on a slate sponsored by the School Board Committee, an anti-busing group. Only 18 percent of the electorate voted in that election, however. Despite the media attention the campaigns receive, light turnouts have been the rule in school Board elections. In 1979 another anti-busing candidate, William Schroeder, was elected.

Two years later, Franklin Mullen, spent approximately $100,000 on his successful anti-busing campaign, the first person to spend so much, using television to increase his name recognition.[41] Anti-busing proponent Naomi Bradford was also reelected that year and later became president of the Board. In the 1980s, candidates discussed issues other than busing, although the issue had not disappeared. It was more subtle.

High visibility has made election to the school Board a political stepping stone to higher office. Robert Crider and Ted Hackworth, whose name recognition originated with their school Board membership, both became city councilmen. Naomi Bradford ran unsuccessfully for Congress on the Republican ticket. Former school Board member Frank Southworth ran for Congress in 1970 while still on the Board.

The politicalization of the school Board has meant that certain Board candidates have run for office with the understanding they would oppose the court order, particularly busing—or not support it publicly. There has been a stable constituency in Denver that supports that stance. As a result, the Board, in varying degrees, has been recalcitrant, and in some cases openly defiant toward court-ordered busing, creating definite obstacles to the decree's implementation.

Specific Problems Hindering Implementation of the Decree: DPS Bureaucratic Inertia

Observers of the *Keyes* case contend the Board's reluctance to approach the remedy in a positive light filtered down in the school system in a variety of ways such as a lack of support by the DPS bureaucracy for Denver public school staff who attempted to integrate students.[42] This is difficult to quantify.

The DPS bureaucracy resisted input on implementation from a panel appointed by Judge Matsch after the Consensus Plan was adopted. The three-member panel—M. Beatriz Arias, Assistant Professor of Education, Stanford University; Willis Hawley, Dean of the George Peabody College for Teachers at Vanderbilt University; and Charles Willie, Professor of Education at Harvard—was charged "[t]o meet with the Board of Education, any committee or administrative staff designated by the Board, and with counsel for the parties herein, for the purpose of preparing appropriate guidelines for pupil assignment plans for subsequent years, including long-range plans." The DPS administrative staff treated the Community Education Council with contempt.[43]

The Board actively discouraged participation by DPS staff in assisting the Compliance Assistance Panel established by the court. When the panel visited Denver to discuss proposals to recruit minority teachers, they were unable to speak with school administrators: "Our meeting was interrupted by a school Board member [Naomi Bradford] who insisted on arguing about whether desegregation was a good idea."[44]

In-Service Training

A lack of in-service training was one of several barriers impeding implementation of the court order. Many teachers and administrators lacked a commitment to desegregation or to making the plan succeed. An administrator's passive or negative attitude to the plan would be easily conveyed to teachers and subordinate staff. Often, teachers had no experience with members of other cultural and racial groups or social classes and thus had little empathy for the stress to which the children were subjected. Former Board member Bernard Valdez offered a different view of the teaching situation: "We should have bused the teachers."[45]

Racial Imbalance in Student Suspensions

Racially disproportionate discipline has been an ongoing problem. In the fall semester of 1980, 86 percent of the elementary students suspended were black or Hispanic. The minority enrollment at that grade level was 57.6 percent. In 1982, 39 percent of the students suspended were black, whereas whites, who outnumbered blacks, accounted for 25 percent of the suspensions.[46]

In 1986, a study of DPS records indicated that 74 percent of the students suspended in the spring of 1985 were black or Hispanic, though the groups made up only 55 percent of the student population. Anglos, who represented 39 percent of the student population, accounted for only 24 percent of the students suspended.[47]

The Denver results correlate with national findings. The district claimed that pupils were suspended because of an infraction of the rules rather than ethnicity. However, in April 1987, as part of the guidelines that redefine integration for the Denver public schools, the Board monitors suspensions and expulsions to "ensure that discipline is administered without racial discrimination or bias." The issue may be more complex than just racially suspect numbers. There have been complaints that a disproportionate number of minority administrators have been placed into disciplinary as opposed to decision-making positions.[48]

"Hardship" Transfers

Hardship transfer abuses have continued to be a problem. In his June 3, 1985, decision, Judge Matsch pointed at the abuses in the hardship transfer program as an indicator that Denver did not have a unitary system.[49] Such abuses have occurred because of the benign attitude if not active connivance of the Board.

As a result of the June 1985 decision, the Board tightened its policy for granting transfers initiated by parents for work-related reasons. In February 1986, the Board approved a majority–minority transfer plan that allowed students to transfer voluntarily only if the transfer improved integration. A student may transfer out of any school where his or her ethnic or racial group is more than 50 percent of the enrollment to a school where the ethnic or racial group is less than 50 percent.[50]

Faculty Integration

Integration of faculty throughout the school system has been an ongoing problem. In a brief filed in early 1985 in opposition to the Board's motion to end the lawsuit, the Congress of Hispanic Educators summarized many of its concerns with the remedy: predominantly one-race classrooms, the shortage of minority teachers, the uneven racial mix of teachers and the drop in the hiring rate for Hispanic teachers, even in years when the overall hiring rate increased. In addition, the program for the gifted and talented was "staffed by a teaching force more than 80 percent white and serves a student population more than 67 percent white."[51]

The low percentage of minority teachers continues to be a concern. The goals DPS set for itself in 1974—16 percent black teaching staff and 14 percent Hispanic—were designed to reflect the percentage of minority students in the district at the time. Since then, minority enrollment has increased, while Anglo students have left the system. In 1984, the teaching staff was 13.9 percent black and 9.7 percent Hispanic, far below the student percentages. With few exceptions, the percentage of minority faculty members at individual schools fell well below the percentage of minority students in DPS. One-third of the administrative staff in 1984 was minority.[52] In the June 1985 decision, the court found that one of the reasons the DPS had not complied with the 1974 desegregation order was that minority teachers were not evenly distributed throughout the district.[53]

One-Race Classrooms: Resegregation?

Another barrier to successful implementation of the court order has been the continued existence of predominantly one-race classrooms, which is largely the result of academic grouping. Although statistics on this sensitive issue are difficult to find, according to reports from parents, attorneys, and administrators, one-race classrooms exist even after schools have been integrated. DPS statistics reveal that during 1985–1986 Anglos were four times more likely than blacks or Hispanics to be admitted into accelerated or advanced placement classes, which give intensive preparation for college. Forty percent of Anglos were in such programs, whereas only 11.5 percent of all blacks and 9.7 percent of Hispanics were.[54] The "Challenge" programs for gifted and talented children tell the same story.

The figures for special education programs are particularly distressing because the consequences are usually final: Once a student is placed in special education, he rarely returns to the regular track.[55] In this area DPS conducted business as usual, out of the glare of the lawsuit. The results have been especially harmful to minorities.

According to studies released in March 1986, blacks were enrolled at a higher rate than other ethnic groups in programs for students with emotional and learning disabilities. Hispanics, on the other hand, were enrolled at a lower rate than their student population.

In January 1987 the outside auditors suggested that DPS should reevaluate 3,000 black and Hispanic students to determine whether they were improperly assigned to special education programs. They also reported that the Denver schools relied excessively on a culturally biased IQ test,[56] which resulted in minorities' significant overrepresentation in special education programs. Some students had been mislabeled and assigned to classes improperly. The auditors urged Denver school officials to cease use of the test. They also pointed out that children were not tested in their native languages and may have been assigned to programs because of language difficulties and that once labeled and placed in special education programs, the children never returned to main track because the school system lacked sufficient guidelines to determine when students were ready to return to the regular program.[57]

As a result of the report, DPS agreed to review 5,000 student files to make certain that children were correctly placed. In addition, the Board agreed to revise testing procedures, relying less on IQ tests, to retest students who needed or whose parents requested testing, to better inform and involve parents of children who are considered for the special programs, to attempt to keep children in the regular classroom as much as possible, and to set up a system of support so that students can leave the special education programs and return to regular instruction.

Housing and School Desegregation

The placement and racial composition of publicly subsidized housing has a direct effect on school desegregation. In the Denver metropolitan area, whites living in subsidized housing tend to be in the suburbs and blacks within the city limits. The housing projects themselves tend to be overwhelmingly of one race.

The fragile relationship between housing and school desegregation can be seen in the attempts to integrate the Barrett, Mitchell, and Harrington elementary schools, which have proven a road block to ending the lawsuit. In 1985–1986 only ten more Anglo children were needed to integrate Barrett and Harrington elementary schools to comply with court integration guidelines. Mitchell required 26 more Anglo children.[58] However, segregated public housing was a key factor in contributing to continuing school segregation. For instance, at Mitchell, where 86 percent of the student body is minority, 55 percent of neighborhood housing is public housing, and 99 percent of public housing residents are minority.

Not all public housing is of the large project variety. Denver public housing programs include dispersed housing, scattered throughout an area, and rent subsidy programs. Even in these programs, 77 to 90 percent of the participants are minority.[59]

Urban demographic patterns change over time. In many cities, including Denver, younger professional people are moving into the city and renovating older houses. If they send their children to public schools, the Denver school system, which is a good system in comparison with other large cities, may be able to reverse the decrease in Anglo enrollment. Until such time, however, the success of a permanently integrated school system is problematic.

TOWARD A UNITARY SCHOOL SYSTEM (1983 TO THE PRESENT)

Four elusive and intractable questions have bedeviled the court and the parties to this lawsuit. The first two—How did the policy of containment of blacks in northeast Denver affect the DPS as a whole? and What was required to remove these effects?—flowed throughout the lawsuit.[60] In the late 1970s, as the demographics of the city changed and earlier racial balancing in the schools became more difficult to maintain, a third question arose: What must be done to protect against future resegregation and a return to a dual system of white and minority schools? Then, as the lawsuit reached its fifteenth year, the Board raised a fourth question: How and when would the court conclude that the DPS was a unitary system?

Legal Criteria for a Unitary System

In 1982 Judge Matsch defined a unitary system:

A unitary school system is one in which all of the students have equal access to the opportunity for education, with the publicly provided educational resources distributed equitably, and with the expectation that all students can acquire a community defined level of knowledge and skills consistent with their individual efforts and abilities. It provides a chance to develop fully each individual's potentials, without being restricted by an identification with any racial or ethnic groups.[61]

In concluding whether a school system is unitary, district courts must keep in mind the uniqueness of each district, the efforts of public school officials, and whether the end of the lawsuit will lead to future resegregation and a return to a dual system.

The Supreme Court has not provided specific guidance as to when a racially unbalanced school system should be considered unitary, when a district court should return control to school authorities, or the manner in which a school desegregation case should be closed. The court made clear in *Brown II*[62] that its function was to offer general guidance on broad principles of constitutional law, but it was the responsibility of district courts to apply those principles to the case at hand. Unfortunately, the cases at hand usually arrived back at the Supreme Court. Instead of specific guidelines, the Court has offered a number of maxims, which like most generalities, are subject to exception and ad hoc construction. Of course, this is an old tradition of equity jurisprudence.[63]

In school desegregation cases, the Supreme Court has told us that the scope of the remedy is to be determined by the nature and scope of the constitutional violation, that the decree must be remedial in nature, and that courts must consider the interests of local authorities in managing their own affairs so long as such management is consistent with the Constitution.[64] District courts must make "every effort to achieve the greatest possible degree of actual desegregation, taking into account the practicables of the situation."[65] School authorities are clearly charged with the "affirmative duty to take whatever steps might be necessary to convert to a unitary system in which racial discrimination would be eliminated root and branch."[66] If school authorities fail in their affirmative obligations under these holdings, judicial authority may be invoked, and that equitable power is broad. "[Not] every school in every community must always reflect the racial composition of the school system as a whole."[67] "The adequacy of any desegregation plan is measured not by its intentions but by its effectiveness."[68] The Constitution does not compel the constant application of racial ratios for every school in the district.[69]

District courts have grappled with these aphorisms and attempted to concretize what boards should do and when courts can dismiss these proceedings. *Green v. County School Board* offered several criteria to measure whether a district had become a racially non-discriminatory school system: the composition of the student body, faculty, staff; the school transportation system; the physical condition of the school system; and extracurricular activities.[70]

Determining whether such a system has become unitary involves more than counting black, Anglo, and Hispanic faces in the classroom. In 1982 Judge Matsch, admitting the difficulty of the task and the inappropriateness of the adversary system for such evaluation, appointed a panel of experts to assist in such judgments.[71]

A Change in Strategy

In December 1983 the school Board changed its strategy. Instead of delaying and then grudgingly complying with the court's orders, the Board voted unanimously to seek a court declaration that the school system was unitary and desegregated and that it be released from court control. The origins of the Board's action, and its surprising unanimity, lay in litigation weariness—the suit was nearly 15 years old—and in a belief that the times, or at least the legal context of desegregation remedies, had changed. The request for a return of DPS to local control was also a reflection of Reagan administration policies toward forced busing and integration. The settlement of a prolonged desegregation lawsuit in Pasadena, California,[72] and a desegregation agreement between the Bakersfield, California, school system and the U.S. Department of Justice lifted the Board's expectations.[73]

The Board filed a formal motion on January 19, 1984, for entry of a declaration that the DPS was a unitary system, a modification and dissolution of the injunction relating to the assignment of students to schools, and an end to supervision.

The Board claimed that the school district was firmly committed to the maintenance of a non-discriminatory educational program. Plaintiff's counsel, Gordon Greiner introduced evidence showing that the 15 schools were more racially unbalanced in 1982 than previously projected and that they were still more unbalanced in 1983. The court summarily denied the Board's motion to separate the bilingual issues from the desegregation ones.

Federal Intervention

On February 8, 1984, the Board received a boost when the Department of Justice moved to intervene as *amicus curiae*. This was the first
time that the Justice Department had intervened in a private, that is, citizen-
filed, desegregation case. The Department said it would intervene in cases
in which court-ordered busing was in effect only upon the school Board's request. However, the Denver Board never formally requested the Department
to intervene, nor voted to do so. The Board president, Naomi Bradford, on
her own initiative, requested Justice Department intervention.[74] The Justice
Department decided to intervene after the Board unanimously resolved to
ask Matsch to declare the system unitary. The court permitted intervention.

The Defendant's Position

The prime thesis of the Board's and the Department of Justice's
position was that the 1974 Final Judgment and Decree as modified in 1976
was a complete remedy for all constitutional violations and adequate to desegregate the school district. If the Board had implemented this plan and
refrained from unconstitutional segregative acts, "pupil assignment unitariness will have been demonstrated and the District Court must end its supervision of pupil assignments." As each of the criteria for a unitary system was
fulfilled, the defendants theorized, that aspect could be removed from court
supervision. One major issue, bilingual–bicultural education, stood clearly
in the way of the defendant's theory.

SIDESHOW: THE BILINGUAL–
BICULTURAL ISSUE

The U.S. Supreme Court decision involving *Keyes* formally recognized that Hispanics suffered many of the same economic and cultural
deprivations as blacks and that petitioners were entitled to have schools with
a combined predominance of blacks and Hispanics included in the category
of segregated schools.[75]

Upon remand to the district court, the Congress of Hispanic Educators (CHE) and 13 Mexican-American parents, represented by the Mexican
American Legal Defense and Education Fund (MALDEF), moved to intervene. The intervenors wanted (1) equitable treatment in any desegregation
plan; (2) the remedy of historical patterns of employment discrimination
remedied; and (3) the desegregation order to protect and enhance bilingual
programs.

The Cardenas Plan

The special interests and needs of Hispanic children had been addressed in 1974 in part of the Finger Plan, developed by Dr. Jose Cardenas,

an expert witness of the plaintiffs. The Cardenas proposal was "premised on the theory that the poor performance of minority children in public schools resulted from 'incompatibilities' between the cultural and developmental characteristics of minority children on the one hand, and the methods and expectations of the school system on the other." Because most school systems were operated to meet the needs of middle-class Anglo children, schools inevitably failed to meet the differing needs of poor minority children.[76]

The Cardenas Plan, therefore, required an overhaul of the school system's entire approach to educating minorities. Its proposals extended to matters of educational philosophy, governance, instructional scope and sequence, curriculum, student evaluation staffing, non-instructional service, and community involvement. It also included a mechanism for comprehensive monitoring of the program's progress.

The circuit court felt that the lower court's adoption of the Cardenas Plan overstepped the limits of its remedial powers.[77] The district court had made no finding on remand from the Supreme Court that either the school district's curricular offerings or its method of educating minority students constituted illegal segregative conduct but did conclude that since "many elementary school Chicano children are expected . . . to acquire normal basic learning skills which are taught through the medium of an unfamiliar language," a meaningful desegregation plan must provide for the transition of Spanish-speaking children to the English language.[78]

Offering a lesson in judicial restraint, the circuit court vacated the lower court's acceptance of the Cardenas Plan because it went beyond merely removing obstacles to effective desegregation and helping Hispanic children to reach the proficiency in English necessary to learn other basic subjects.

The court concluded that the district court's adoption of the Cardenas Plan would "unjustifiably interfere" with state and local attempts to deal with the problem of educating minority children. The implication of plaintiffs' arguments was that minority students were entitled under the Fourteenth Amendment to an educational experience tailored to their unique cultural and developmental needs. "Although enlightened theory may well demand as much, the Constitution does not,"[79] and the court remanded the bilingual issue for a determination of the relief, if any, necessary to insure that Hispanics and other minority children would have the opportunity to acquire proficiency in the English language.

The circuit court decision meant that if a Hispanic community wished to piggyback a language order into a desegregation ruling, it had to establish that English language deficiencies were a product of unlawful segregative acts. Also, entire schools could not be maintained as segregated in the name of bilingual education while the school system is under court order to desegregate. The decision did allow some degree of clustering to maintain administratively viable language programs.[80]

For nearly four years efforts to negotiate a resolution of the English language proficiency issues were unsuccessful. The intervenors had little leverage and the school district little interest in reaching a settlement. On November 3, 1980, the plaintiff intervenors filed a supplemental complaint in intervention adding a claim under a provision of the Equal Educational Opportunities Act of 1974 (EEOA) and the Colorado English Language Proficiency Act (CELPA).[81]

The Statutory Framework: The Equal Educational Opportunities Act of 1974

Section 1703(f) of the Equal Educational Opportunities Act of 1974 makes it unlawful for a state to deny equal educational opportunity to an individual on account of his or her race, color, sex, or national origin by failing to overcome language barriers that impede equal participation in school.[82]

This was the gravamen of the plaintiff intervenor's claim. EEOA and the Bilingual Education Act were enacted as 1974 amendments to the Elementary and Secondary Education Act, yet Congress in describing the remedial obligation it sought to impose on the states did not specify that a state had to provide a program of "bilingual education" to all limited English-speaking students. Congress's use of the less specific term, "appropriate action" rather than "bilingual education" has been interpreted to indicate "that Congress intended to leave state and local educational authorities a substantial amount of latitude in choosing the programs and techniques they would use to meet their obligations under EEOA."[83]

In determining whether a school system is using appropriate and good faith remediation efforts, courts have utilized a three-part analysis: (1) Is the school district pursuing a program based upon an educational theory recognized as sound or at least as a legitimate experimental strategy by some of the experts in the field; (2) Is the program reasonably calculated to implement that theory; and (3) After being used for sufficient time to be a legitimate trial, has the program produced satisfactory results?[84]

The Colorado English Language Proficiency Act is essentially a funding statute, but it does establish an affirmative duty, among other things (1) to identify students whose dominant language may not be English; and (2) to administer and provide programs for such students.[85] Colorado has not directed the use of any particular type of language program.

The statute's classification system is based upon that developed by the then Department of Health, Education and Welfare (HEW) as part of its *Lau* guidelines, which HEW drafted as administrative recommendations following the U.S. Supreme Court decision in *Lau v. Nichols*.[86] The Denver school district uses these classifications.[87]

The Bilingual Program in School District No. 1

At the time of trial in April 1982, the Denver school district had identified 3,322 children as limited-English-speaking. Although 42 languages were represented among the district's limited-English proficiency children in 1981–1982, the majority fell into two language groups, Spanish and one of four Indochinese languages.

School District No. 1's Theory of Bilingual Education

The Denver school system elected to use what is called a "transitional bilingual approach":

> The intent of bilingual education is to facilitate the integration of the child into the regular school curriculum. English is not sacrificed, in fact it is emphasized; the native language is used as a medium of instruction to ensure academic success in content areas such as math, social studies, etc., while the child at the same time is acquiring proficiency of the English language.[88]

A bilingual program is what the name implies. Students placed in bilingual classrooms participate with the rest of the student body for classes in art, music, and physical education and for lunch and recess. The pupils then lose no learning time when compared with their English-speaking schoolmates.

Ideally, every child would be taught by teachers fluent in the student's native language. However, the number of foreign languages spoken in the school district, 42 at the time of trial and 52 in 1984, made it impossible to find a sufficient number of fluent teachers. As a result, most non-English-speaking children were enrolled in English as a Second Language programs (ESL). In elementary schools these programs were run by part-time or "travel" teachers who visited several schools one or two days each week. The certified bilingual teachers were aided by native language tutors or interpreters. The theory was to start non-English-speaking children in small groups of four to eight. As they learn to speak, write, and read English, they are moved to larger classes with certified teachers. When they are able to function in regular class, they are placed there.[89]

The Denver Bilingual Program in 1982

At the time of trial a transitional bilingual program existed at 12 elementary schools. Most of these schools had one designated bilingual classroom for each grade level in the program. Because of the dearth of certified teachers, no non-Spanish, non-English-speaking children or any Spanish-speaking "Lau C level" children received instruction in designated bilingual classrooms.

There were differences in the teaching staff in the desegregated bilingual schools. Each bilingual classroom was taught by a certified teacher, but many of those teachers spoke only English. Most teachers, including all of the monolingual English teachers, had a bilingual aide to assist in communication. In several designated bilingual classrooms, there were full or part-time English as a Second Language tutors who assisted in English language instruction. In other classrooms, ESL was taught by teachers and aides.[90]

At the secondary level, there was no program comparable to that found in the designated bilingual elementary schools. The principal program for secondary-level limited-English-proficiency students was ESL taught by teachers and tutors for about 45 minutes each day. At four of the district's 30 secondary schools, ESL instruction was not available.

One of the central aspects of the bilingual suit was the status of the *Lau* C level children with home language backgrounds other than English, who comprehended and spoke English, but did very poorly on reading and writing tests. The school district's position was that these students were simply low achievers, therefore DPS's only responsibility was to provide the same programs offered to other low achievers.[91] The intervenors offered expert testimony to show that a student could have minimally acceptable oral proficiency while suffering an impediment in writing and reading skills owing to his non-English home language background. The intervenors argued, and the court agreed, that the failure to address the reading and writing deficiencies was a denial of equal educational opportunity and a violation of section 1703(f).

The identification of limited-English-speaking children, and the placement of those children in *Lau* categories A, B, and C, did not occur through a formal testing process, but through a questionnaire that was filled out by each child's parents and reviewed by a teacher. If the parents and teacher concurred that the child was not limited-English-speaking, the district determined the child to be ineligible for the bilingual/ESL program.[92]

Parents commonly overstated the language abilities of their children. While the teacher's involvement was intended to safeguard against that, most of the district's teachers were not trained in linguistics, bilingual education, other languages, or in detecting language problems. Testimony was introduced of the subtle pressures that existed within the school system to overstate a child's English language skills, which served to minimize the district's obligations to address bilingual needs, particularly when they were difficult and expensive to meet. Many teachers were philosophically opposed to bilingual programs.[93]

The school district used standardized tests to measure the progress of elementary school children receiving bilingual and ESL instruction. If the student scored well on the test, he or she would graduate from the ESL Program unless the tutor or teacher determined that it would be inappropriate to mainstream the student at that point. No records were kept of the progress of children who had left either the bilingual or ESL programs. Nor was continuing support provided to students who exited from either program.

Judge Matsch's 1983 Opinion on the Language Issues

On December 30, 1983, Judge Matsch issued an opinion on the bilingual issue. The court specified that while the opinion was directed toward the bicultural issue, the analysis was made in the context of a desegregation case, which had been in the court for more than a decade.[94] Joining the desegregation to the bilingual issues facilitated the resolution of the latter.

The judge applied the tripartite analysis to the § 1703(f) claims. He held that Denver's "transitional bilingual approach" was a recognized and satisfactory educational theory. However, the court found the school district in violation of § 1703(f) when it applied the second prong of the analysis: whether Denver pursued its bilingual program with adequate resources, personnel, and practices. Teachers assigned to bilingual classes often lacked the necessary skills and were not given training to develop them. Assignments often were based on seniority. Another criticism by the court was that bilingual classes were available at only 11 elementary schools and that only students who spoke Spanish and lived near one of those schools were assigned to the bilingual program.[95]

The third prong of the *Castenada* analysis—whether the Denver transitional bilingual program achieved satisfactory results—is the most difficult because it raises qualitative issues of measurement. Again, Judge Matsch sounded the clarion of judicial restraint:

> It is beyond the competence of the courts to determine appropriate measurements of academic achievement and there is damage to the fabric of federalism when national courts dictate the use of any component of the educational process in schools governed by elected officers of local government.
>
> Fortunately, it is not now necessary to discuss this question because of the findings of the district's failure to take reasonable action to implement the bilingual education policy which it adopted.[96]

In ordering a remedy, Judge Matsch brought the language issues into the mainstream of the desegregation litigation. He did not order a discrete remedy for the language issues but linked their resolution to the creation of a unitary school system. The failure to remove the language barriers was a failure to establish a unitary system.[97] Only a changed attitude by the Board and greater institutional commitment to equal educational opportunities would suffice. The Board said the court had to have a broader focus than forced busing. The language issues were related to the other aspects that made up the requirement of a unitary school system. As Matsch attempted to draw the Board away from its fixation with busing, he squarely placed the responsibilities for remedying the bilingual program on elected officials.

Opposition to the Board's Motion

Judge Matsch's December 1983 decision on the bilingual issue militated against the Board's January 1984 motion for a declaration that DPS was a unitary system and that previously ordered remedies ended the need for continued court supervision. Opposition to the Board's motion soon surfaced. On February 15, 1984, lawyers for the bilingual intervenors filed a brief stating that until all vestiges of segregation, including differences in achievement between minority and white students, were eliminated, the court should deny the district's motion that the schools be declared integrated.[98]

On April 10, 1984, the Board unanimously approved Resolution 2233, a declaration of policy that was intended to follow the termination of court supervision. The Resolution stated that the Denver schools should be operated in conformity with all federal laws, that "there shall be no sudden alteration of the court ordered busing plan then in effect," that no practices would be taken for the purposes of discriminating against any person, that the Board would attempt to achieve the beneficial effects of integration, that the beneficial effects of integration are most fully realized in stabilizing integrated neighborhood schools, and that the Board "shall preserve contiguous attendance zones for schools that are integrated and shall establish contiguous attendance zones wherever it appears that stable integration can be maintained in the schools serving such areas."[99]

The April 1984 Hearing

In addition to its new counsel, Chicago attorney Phillip Neal, the Board retained John Michael Ross, a Washington statistician who had prepared evidence for the hearings leading to the Pasadena settlement. Ross, who was paid nearly $200,000 for his efforts, offered complex testimony that served only to confuse and annoy Matsch.[100]

Ross's statistics attempted to show that extensive movement of population within Denver and a steady and large decline in enrollment, almost all of which represented a loss of Anglo students, were the prime causes of racial imbalance in certain schools.[101] Matsch criticized the Ross presentation for failing to give a complete picture of the demographic movements of Denver residents, particularly those who lived in Denver in 1975 but moved away before 1980.[102]

In his opening statement Greiner said that there had been substantial problems for the last two years with the Board's compliance with court decrees in such fields as affirmative hiring, pupil assignments, and disproportionate disciplining of minority students. He termed the "consensus" desegregation plan "a disastrous step backward for minority students." He also offered a new school assignment proposal, requiring additional busing for eleven elementary schools.[103] This would desegregate the four elementary schools with the fewest Anglo students of any in the city. On May 23, the last day of the hearings, Matsch denied the plaintiff's new busing plan on the ground that the racial imbalances at the four schools were "chronic, not acute." He felt that the desegregation efforts at the four elementary schools should await resolution of the larger issues in the case.[104]

As the hearing developed, the chances of the Board's succeeding on its motion lessened. Board members' testimony did not help their own case. Omar Blair, the only black member of the Board, admitted under cross-examination he did not sufficiently trust his colleagues on the Board to seek or maintain desegregation. He believed that racist practices still occurred in schools and that the three new members of the Board had nearly destroyed the credibility of the district by wresting authority from the superintendent.[105]

Two other members of the Board testified that they voted to seek relief from court-ordered busing without knowing or having asked whether the segregative violations had been corrected. When Board Vice-President Franklin Mullen was questioned by Norma Cantu, attorney for bilingual intervenors, whether the Board had ever requested standardized achievement scores to be broken down by ethnicity, Mullen responded that he didn't put much stock in standardized test scores.[106]

The court-appointed desegregation experts testified that the Board had been unresponsive to their efforts to help develop and implement a plan to end court control of the system. Willis Hawley testified that he wrote several letters to Michael Jackson, school Board attorney, offering to collaborate on the court-appointed tasks and proposing plans and programs for discussion. Seven months went by before he even received any response to his letters.[107] Another court-appointed expert, Charles V. Willie, a professor of education and urban studies at the Harvard Graduate School of Education, citing data showing that faculty in 48 of the district's 108 schools were grossly unbalanced racially, testified: "Denver schools have never achieved a unitary affirmative action [employment] system." Willie called Denver's record "abominable." [108]

By the beginning of February 1985, the settlement talks had broken down. There had been no substantive discussions for nearly three months. The sticking point, as it had been in the past, was the racial imbalance of four elementary schools—Mitchell, Barrett, Harrington and Gilpin—the most segregated in the district. A lack of communication and consensus over Board strategy emerged. The vice-president, Franklin Mullen, said the school district's failure to negotiate was "inexcusable." [109]

In the middle of February 1985, the Board switched gears and publicly announced that it had instructed its counsel to move more aggressively toward

an out-of-court settlement of the lawsuit.[110] At the same time, a new superintendent, James Scamman, who had overseen desegregation in South Bend,
Indiana, had been selected. The Board's negotiating posture was much more
conciliatory than its final brief had indicated. It presented a compromise plan
for integration of the elementary schools. "It's the same thing we rejected
five months ago." responded Greiner.[111] The two sides did not meet until
the end of March.

Changes in the Litigation Environment

The middle of May 1985 brought several changes in the environment of the lawsuit. First, the new superintendent of schools became more
actively involved. Second, public criticism had arisen over the costs of the
litigation and the fees spent for court experts.[112] An indicator of this change
was the May 21 school Board election for two school Board seats, which
resulted in anti-busing advocate William Schroeder's defeat and a change
in the political balance of the Board. In addition, two liberals were elected:
Edward Garner, a marketing specialist, who became the only black member of the Board, and Carol McCotter, a former teacher. Of those elected
during the 1970s, when busing was the major issue, only Naomi Bradford
remained. Another indicator that the political climate of school Board elections had changed was that only 7 percent of the voters turned out, less than
half of the usual 15 to 18 percent turnout for an off-year Denver school
Board election.[113]

Realizing they would lose on their motion to declare the district unitary, the Board began to negotiate seriously a settlement that would end the
suit and make certain the district would be subject to no additional busing
after the resolution of the bilingual issues. On the other hand, the plaintiffs
wanted to ensure that a settlement would not decrease any of the desegregation programs in place, particularly busing and—a most difficult problem
—desegregation of a few racially unbalanced elementary schools.[114]

Reaction to the Bilingual Decision

Unlike the posturing that followed other court opinions involving
pupil assignments, the Board's reaction to the December 1983 decision on
bilingual education issues was muted and responsive. One reason for the
change was the Board's mid-December 1983 application to the court for the
system to be declared unitary.

By January 5, 1984, at the time the Board was prosecuting its motion to
end the desegregation aspects of the lawsuit, the school district's staff members unveiled a series of proposals to improve the bilingual program. The
proposals included: (1) the creation of clusters of elementary schools from
which LEP pupils would be bused to a central location and given instruction

in English as a second language, (2) expansion of the English tutoring program at individual high schools, and (3) a commitment of the Board to seek ways to keep the seniority provisions of the union contract from preventing the assignment of bilingual teachers to bilingual schools.[115] The suggestion of busing elementary students out of their neighborhoods to a central school split the Board's anti-busing majority.

Resolution of the Bilingual Issues

Board President Bradford had commented that the bilingual decision was not completely negative. This was read by the plaintiff intervenors as an opening. As Board president, she was considered crucial to any resolution of the dispute. Immediately after the decision, the plaintiff intervenors, led by Peter Roos, an attorney with the Mexican-American Legal Defense and Education Fund, met with the Board and advised Judge Matsch that the parties would like to attempt to negotiate a settlement and work things out themselves rather than presenting alternative plans in formal judicial proceedings.

At the outset, Roos made a determination to insist that the school district's representatives include members of the Board and its president: "I had been through too many negotiations with school officials and found them blown apart at the board level."[116]

The Board established a committee on students with limited English proficiency, composed of Bradford, the Board's president; Judy Morton, chairman of the Board's education committee; Paul Sandoval, Board member; James B. Bailey, deputy superintendent of schools; Michael Jackson, counsel for the school board; and Terry Marshall and Dale Vigil, consultants. The committee met with the plaintiffs every two weeks, sometimes without counsel present, sometimes more frequently, through the spring of 1984 until June, when a report to the board of education, "A Program for Limited English Proficient Students," was published and became the basis for the August 1984 out-of-court settlement.

According to Roos, the negotiations were non-adversarial and the parties worked hard toward reaching a settlement. In presenting plans, the plaintiffs argued for good educational programs and accountability—items that also mattered greatly to the Board members. They attempted to assuage the Board's concerns. Both parties shared the belief that many bilingual programs were "mostly fluff." Thus, the final settlement had extensive testing and accountability provisions. The plaintiffs saw the settlement plan as an opportunity for Denver to achieve a model program that would be on the cutting edge of bilingual–bicultural education.

Judge Matsch remained in the background. The parties met several times with him. When establishing the negotiations, the parties agreed that a report to Matsch would be submitted every month. However, Matsch had an important backup role, which gave leverage to the plaintiffs. If the negotiations fell through, the plaintiffs could always return to court to hold more formal hearings. This approach was later used successfully by the plaintiffs in the desegregation portion of the lawsuit. Agreement was reached in the spring and the bilingual issues were settled in August 1984.

Matsch's Decision: June 3, 1985

On June 3, 1985, nearly 18 months after the Board filed its motion to dismiss the lawsuit, Judge Matsch denied it. Reviewing the history of the lawsuit, the court highlighted the years of the Board's intractability and lack of commitment to remedying the constitutional violations; the acceptance by the court of the consensus plan in 1982; the well-founded reservations because of the Board's lack of commitment to a unitary system; the Board's lack of compliance with the Tenth Circuit's requirement that the district assign personnel so that in each school the ratio of minority-to-Anglo staff be not less than 50 percent of the ratio of minority teachers to staff of the entire system; the failure to develop a policy to distribute neutrally the number of minority teachers throughout the district; a hardship transfer program, which functioned as the equivalent to a "voluntary transfer program" for neighborhood schools and had a resegregative effect;[117] and a failure by the Board to keep records as to the effects of the transfer program on transferor or transferee schools.

The Future of the Court's Jurisdiction

The court also indicated it would retain jurisdiction until it was convinced there was no reasonable expectation that constitutional violations would remain whether or not the school system should be found unitary.[118] Even accepting the defendant's argument that the modified 1974 final judgment and decree constituted a complete and adequate remedy, the court's jurisdiction would continue because it was compelled to conclude that resegregation was inevitable if the school Board followed the Colorado constitution provision prohibiting busing.[119]

The court placed little reliance on Resolution 2228 or on any other resolution binding future boards. Thus, with the uncertainty of the legal requirements as to when a school district is unitary, and the anti-busing provision of the Colorado constitution, the court would not dismiss the case. Whenever *Keyes* ended, the court would issue a final injunctive order.[120]

What the court would require was the development of a decision-making structure for local government authorities and assurance that those who make such decisions have adequate information and provide for minority participation to act in concert with the principles of equal educational opportunity.[121] The court explicitly cited the Ad Hoc Committee's guidelines as a useful working framework within which such a structure could be developed. It requested the parties to negotiate a settlement of the lawsuit and to develop a consensual final order.

Stumbling Toward Settlement

On June 7, 1985, four days after the decision was issued, lawyers for both sides conferred with Superintendent of Schools James Scamman. On the weekend of June 9, Scamman and the Board met at a retreat to develop goals and a negotiating strategy to settle the lawsuit.

The Board and Scamman, hoping to reach a mutually agreeable settlement, which would be presented jointly to the court at the end of June,[122] drafted new educational goals to resolve the case. Once again, strategy changed as the Board focused upon educational rather than legal issues. The goals, which were aimed at assuring equal educational opportunity for all students, included transferring teachers to reduce the number of schools dominated by minority faculty and students; reviewing "hardship transfers"; creating magnet programs; improving teacher training and sensitivity; establishing an independent committee of community representatives for various ethnic groups to monitor desegregation; and using computers to track the individual progress of students.[123]

On June 21, 1985, eight days before counsel were to meet again with Judge Matsch to discuss the development of a process to achieve settlement, Scamman announced he would reassign 40 teachers and review 1,000 hardship student transfers. In the fall of 1985, as a first step toward meeting the objections raised by the court, 13 schools with the most obvious racial imbalance would have teachers reassigned. The Board also announced that it was developing a comprehensive data bank, which included information on faculty and student racial balances in all schools and on programs within schools, to monitor integration.[124]

Despite visible efforts and verbal commitments to come to terms with the June decision, the Board was silent on the most difficult issue: the integration of three still substantially segregated elementary schools—Barrett, Mitchell, and Hampton.[125]

In early July 1985, the Board offered plaintiffs a settlement proposal. It did not, however, include a plan to end the racial isolation of the three elementary schools. The Board earlier had offered to shift students to balance the three schools racially but retreated from that position. Matsch told the attorneys to report to him on a monthly basis regarding their efforts to end the litigation.

The desegregation of the three elementary schools was returned to Judge Matsch on October 15, 1985, when plaintiffs moved the court to direct the defendants to file plans that would lead to a unitary school system. On October 29, 1985, Matsch ordered the Board to integrate the three schools and to issue guidelines to ensure even distribution of minority faculty and to monitor hardship transfers. At the end of November, the Board introduced its plan to integrate the three schools by establishing them as magnets to offer Montessori classes for kindergarteners and first graders. New computer centers, reduced class sizes, and pilot programs of various educational methods would be introduced along with drama, music, dance, and art after-school programs and the opportunity to study Spanish as a second language. The cost of the programs was estimated at $1 million. Concurrently, the Board appealed Matsch's decision to the Tenth Circuit.[126]

On Sunday, December 15, 1985 the case was almost settled during a four-hour negotiating session between Greiner, lawyers for the school Board, and the Board members. Plaintiffs would not have called for additional busing or boundary changes. The school district would have been able to remove itself from active court supervision as soon as the three largely minority schools were at least 30 percent Anglo. The Board would drop its appeal of Matsch's June 1985 opinion and would agree to a permanent court order that would require DPS to maintain bilingual schools, not to create racially identifiable schools or to resegregate the district, and to continue faculty integration.[127]

There were two troublesome points. One was the language of the requirement forbidding the Board to create one-race or racially identifiable schools. The other was that the Board wanted assurance that it could be declared a unitary district and be released from the court order. Despite the inability to reach agreement on a settlement, the sides seemed to move closer together and be more conciliatory.

On Saturday, March 15, 1986, Judge Matsch ruled DPS could implement its plan to integrate the Mitchell, Barrett, and Harrington elementary schools. He noted that the district had not come up with guidelines for determining when integration had been achieved but felt that the district had complied with his October order to submit plans to desegregate the three elementary schools, to deal with transfer policies that increased one-race schools, and to set guidelines to distribute minority faculty better.[128]

The jostling between the plaintiffs and defendants continued. The district wanted the judge to give up his supervision of DPS and declare that the school system had fully complied with previously issued integration orders. Plaintiffs requested court supervision for at least three more years, in part because Judge Matsch had not issued a final ruling and the efforts of the school Board were inadequate to make the system unitary. Plaintiffs requested additional relief through more specific directions to implement the decree and the entry of additional orders for detailed monitoring and reporting requirements.[129]

On February 25, 1987, Judge Matsch issued a ruling relaxing court control over the Denver public schools. However, since the district had chosen not to increase the amount of busing to integrate the school system for fear that it would have a destabilizing effect but utilized more subtle methods to achieve a unitary system, the court would retain jurisdiction to ensure that the methods were effective. The court rejected the plaintiff's request for detailed monitoring and reporting requirements because the district probably would conduct such data collection and monitoring by itself to convince the court that the system was unitary and that court supervision should end. Judge Matsch stated that a permanent injunction was the logical conclusion to the lawsuit because the court had the responsibility to define the duty owed to the plaintiffs by the defendants. A final injunctive order also was necessary because of the proscription against student transportation to achieve racial balance in the Colorado constitution, and it would protect those who might be adversely affected by Board action. The court turned aside the defendant's argument that a final permanent injunctive order would be inappropriate because the Board cannot bind future boards. The court agreed and stated that was exactly why there had to be a permanent injunctive order.[130]

In April 1987 the Board adopted new guidelines to redefine integration for the schools. The guidelines deal with more than racial balance between schools but within schools and within special programs as well. The guidelines were a response to Judge Matsch's criticism that previous guidelines were neither specific enough nor a guide to future action.

Proposals were submitted and hearings held for an interim decree to replace existing orders on June 24, 1987. The interim decree enabled the defendants to operate the school system under general remedial standards rather than specific judicial directives. To a great extent it placed the responsibility and oversight of creating a unitary school system on the school Board. The decree relinquished reporting requirements to the court and eliminated the need for prior court approval before DPS made changes in student assignments, programs, pairings, and attendance zones. The Board's operation of its schools and efforts to eradicate the past racial discrimination will determine whether to enter a final permanent injunction to the Board.[131]

The Settlement of the Bilingual Issues

The bilingual settlement, which was accepted by the court in August 1984, focused on student identification, assessment and reclassification, selection and qualification of personnel, elementary and secondary curricular programming, and special attention to non-Spanish-speaking minorities.

A result of improved identification and assessment techniques, put into effect even prior to the settlement of the dispute, was to raise the number of students classified as LEP from 4,000 to 8,300.[132] The school system was required to publish an accurate census of LEP students by October 15 of each school year. The classification process was improved so that if a child was reclassified as English proficient and the parents disagreed with such classifications, due process procedures were introduced.

Unlike the situation at the time of trial, where seniority under the school district's contract with the teacher's union was the sole criterion for selection as a bilingual teacher, the settlement required that bilingual teachers be certified by passing the New Mexico Test of Spanish Language Skills, and it required the district to train bilingual and ESL teachers.

The elementary school program required bilingual programming for Spanish-proficient students when a sufficient number were present in a particular school. For speakers of the 51 other languages, where the number of students at an individual school does not justify a bilingual program or qualified teachers are unavailable, a meaningful English language development program such as ESL is required. A unique aspect of the Denver settlement is that the number of Spanish-speaking children in a *school* rather than in a class justifies a program.[133]

In addition to schools identified as bilingual schools, at least one school in each zone is designated as bilingual whenever at least three grade levels in the zone have ten or more LEP students of the same language. The settlement also contained detailed provisions on curriculum development and implementation, requiring the same skill level and curriculum content as required of non-bilingual students. Regular assessment of student progress also was to be required.

LEP students who are not in a bilingual classroom were to be given intensive English as a second language assistance for a minimum of 30 percent of the school day or two hours, whichever is greater. *Lau* C students were to be provided with ESL for a minimum of 10 percent of the school day or one hour, whichever is greater. The student–teacher ratio in ESL programs was set at no greater than 15 to one.[134] A district-wide advisory committee was established with one parent representative from each designated bilingual school and one representative from each additional school with 20 or more LEP students.

Trial testimony had indicated that secondary-school-level bilingual programming may be more important than at the elementary school level because the curriculum is so much more advanced that it cannot possibly be negotiated in a language that is not easily comprehended.[135] The settlement provided that all LEP Spanish-speaking students could be clustered at three middle schools. In any school where 30 or more students were Spanish-speaking, such students were to be instructed by a qualified bilingual teacher in the core curriculum of mathematics, science, social studies, and English. Non-Spanish-speaking LEP students in middle schools were to be instructed in the core curriculum by a qualified ESL teacher. The pupil–teacher ratio was to be 15 to one.

At any high school with 40 or more *Lau* A and B Spanish-speaking students, qualified bilingual teachers were to be designated in each of the core area departments.[136] Other students were to be taught by ESL teachers.

Three approaches were adopted for addressing the needs of non-Spanish-speaking LEP students. Students were entitled to intensive ESL instruction —at least two hours each day of small-group instruction by trained teachers for students who failed the oral proficiency assessment. One day of ESL instruction was to be given for those who were designated LEP because of low written test scores. Paraprofessional aid was to be provided on a ratio of one to 15.[137]

As a result of the settlement, 20 additional elementary schools became designated as bilingual, for a total of 31 schools out of 81 elementary schools in the system.[138] Some of the new bilingual schools are "zone" schools to which LEP students are bused. The Board initiated a campaign to recruit more than 100 additional bilingual teachers.[139]

CONCLUSIONS: THE IMPACT OF 16 YEARS OF LITIGATION ON DENVER'S SCHOOLS

How one perceives the impact of the 16 years of litigation on Denver and its school system depends upon one's attitude toward the busing remedy. Opponents feel it ruined the district and caused white flight. Proponents of desegregation feel the lawsuit and resulting decree have had a positive impact on both the school system and the community. They cite the increasing equality and quality within the school system, saying that the lawsuit affected the whole school system by making people aware for the first time of the differences in the quality of education provided in different schools, by teaching people from different backgrounds and cultures to live with one another with less fear, and by promoting a better understanding between the races.

There is general agreement that schools throughout the system have improved, and the quality of education in Denver is much higher than before.

There has been more public examination of equipment, assignment of teachers, and utilization of school facilities. The school district is more responsive to minorities. The disparity in assignment of teachers has been cleaned up. Equalization of facilities has been cleaned up. *Keyes* has helped minorities. It's given minorities a chance to enter the mainstream. Better opportunities have opened up for minority teachers and administrators.[140]

Of particular importance is that the lawsuit has brought the Hispanic population into the political and educational process. Former school Board member Bernard Valdez claimed the suit has had a positive impact beyond the classroom, especially in the city's Hispanic community.

I think the emotional dynamics that the court order has created—the shock of their kids going off to another school—mixing blacks and Hispanics and other minorities created a more democratic society. I think the whole community is better as a result. That's why we have a Hispanic Mayor [Tony Pena, elected in 1983]. The dynamics played a role in that.[141]

Integration Within DPS

Denver public schools appear to be more integrated than they were when the lawsuit commenced. However, heavy concentrations of minorities and Anglos remain in some schools. In 1969, Denver's high schools, with the exception of Manual, were predominately Anglo. Fourteen years later in 1983, at least statistically, things had changed. Throughout the school district, Anglo enrollment was 38.8 percent but any particular school, according to the court order, could swing from 53.8 percent to 23.8 percent—within 15 percentage points of the district-wide Anglo enrollment. Only three high schools—South, Jefferson, and West—did not meet this criterion.

At the elementary school level in 1969, many of the schools tended to be predominately one-race institutions. Of the district's 93 elementary schools that year, 42 of them were at least, and usually well in excess of, 60 percent Anglo. In 1983, the number of racially isolated institutions had diminished considerably, but there were still exceptions. Barrett Elementary School, for instance, was 77 percent black and only 14.8 percent Anglo—far below the minimum level ordered by the court. Whittier Elementary School's black enrollment stood at 63.7 percent that year, also above the court-ordered level, and Stedman's black population was 67.8 percent.[142] The district-wide black enrollment that year was 22.7 percent, meaning the highest black enrollment in any particular school should have been 37.2 percent. Also, while the schools were more integrated numerically in the mid-1980s than they were before the *Keyes* case commenced, within schools, ability grouping has tended to make classrooms predominately one race. This issue is just being addressed.

An Analysis of the Bilingual Settlement

Denver's bilingual program is ambitious and expensive. It offers for the first time the hope of equal educational opportunity for students with limited English proficiency. From the beginning, the bilingual litigation was a lawsuit within a suit, subordinate to the larger desegregation issues. The plaintiff intervenors' counsel tended to focus on *Milliken II* remedies[143] dealing with remediation, whereas the larger lawsuit was concerned with racial balances, ostensibly *Milliken I* aspects.[144] In one sense, independent resolution of the bilingual question, because it was tied to the larger issues, was more difficult. However, distinctions from the desegregation issues enabled the creation of a consensus for resolution.

First, there was broader moral agreement to provide for educational needs of Hispanic students than for upgrading educational opportunities for black students. Indeed, many whites questioned whether education for blacks was inferior. Most whites and some blacks doubted that integration through forced busing was the best way to remedy past discrimination. Bilingual issues did not foster the same political divisiveness as did desegregation. There was little dispute that students who could not understand English were at a severe disadvantage in an English-speaking classroom. Even conservative Board members could understand the need to teach Spanish children English.

Another distinguishing factor was that the burden and benefit of the bilingual remedy largely influenced one identifiable group: limited-English-proficiency students. In contrast, busing and racial integration affected the lives of all students and parents in the school system. Bilingual–bicultural education issues could be addressed without reassigning or otherwise dislocating majority students. In addition, the bilingual deficiencies might be cured by additional money, much of which would come from federal and state sources rather than from the school district. Moreover, the Board did not bear the full brunt of blame for the deficiencies in bilingual–bicultural education that were pointed out in Matsch's 1983 decision. The placement of unqualified bilingual and ESL teachers in classrooms was blamed on the teachers' union contract.[145]

Nonetheless, negotiations to reach an out-of-court settlement dragged on for ten years before agreement. Resolution became possible only when the bilingual–bicultural settlement became part of a larger strategy adopted by the school Board to end the desegregation suit. If the bilingual issues could be solved, the Board reasoned, settlement would demonstrate the Board's good faith and lead to the return of the school system to the Board without judicial oversight. Ironically, although the political problems were less intractable than those relating to the desegregation issue, the attainment of improved educational outcomes resulting from settlement was perhaps more problematic. By appealing to conservative Board members' desires for effective programs, the plaintiffs succeeded in instituting a bilingual–bicultural program containing provisions for accountability and assessment.

Since many of the provisions of the settlement have been introduced only recently, it may be too early to evaluate the impact of the bilingual lawsuit upon the community. However, as Bernard Valdez has suggested:

> A court order has helped the Hispanic community politically in terms of changing the value systems of the whole community. In other words, parents whose kids get mixed up with other minorities are not so scared any more. After meeting parents in the school setting . . . they are not that different. We can work with them—that kind of thing.[146]

For all bilingual communities, the lawsuit connected parents to the educational process, many for the first time. Within the school system, there is now evident a much greater sensitivity to language issues and a higher level of visibility. Previously, the administration of the bilingual program had been located far away from the central Board of Education. Now its office is on the same floor as the deputy superintendent in the main building.

However, the ultimate success of the bilingual settlement will not be in bringing individuals into the political process, but in achieving educational success. Will the dropout rate of minorities decline? Will children be able to be channeled back into English language educational programs?

New Goals and Realities

Times change. School districts do too. The primary focus of minority parents now is on the quality of education their children receive rather than where or with whom they go to school. Resource allocation is a very real concern. As Denver's demographics have changed, the northwest part of the city, largely Hispanic, has suffered severe overcrowding. New pockets of racially unbalanced schools have emerged. From a legal perspective, the racial imbalance in the Northwest is different from that of the schools that led to the *Keyes* suit, for it has resulted from shifting demographic patterns. As it has not been caused by either DPS or state action, this racial imbalance has not become part of the lawsuit. Nor is there a constitutional infraction.

Hispanic parents are more concerned with the overcrowding and perceived lack of quality in these northwest schools than the racial imbalance. The Mexican American Legal Defense and Education Fund, which filed suit in Los Angeles protesting against similar overcrowding and lack of resources for Hispanic schools, has stated it will wait to see how DPS will reduce the overcrowding in that part of the city.[147]

For blacks, too, quality education within schools, no matter where children attend, has become the prime concern. The NAACP, the Denver Urban League, and other civic groups have formed Citizens Concerned About Quality Education.[148] Test results have shown that Anglos and Asians have done as well or better on statewide or national standardized tests, but blacks and Hispanics score below state and national norms.[149] The concern over quality education, imbalance of resources, and the tracking of minorities into special education are second-generation problems that will concern the DPS long after this lawsuit is settled.

The Lawsuit and the School System

There can be little dispute that the protracted litigation has increased the school district's sensitivity and responsiveness to the educational needs of its constituents. Accompanying this has been an increase in the educational system's fairness. Throughout the system, in terms of the allocation of resources for facilities, distribution of teachers, and efforts toward those with special educational needs, the quality of education and the quantity of resources has measurably improved. There is now a sincere effort to promote equal educational opportunity. Such gains are likely to be maintained because the lawsuit has also increased DPS's accountability.

The politicalization of the Board was a prime factor in the prolongation of the lawsuit, because educational issues became political ones. Nevertheless, public awareness of educational issues—particularly the usually silent public: minorities and parents of children with special needs—has forced the school system to respond and to be held accountable. The lawsuit has led to an ongoing monitoring process.

The political process itself has forced Board members to change their positions. The lawsuit has brought into the educational process minorities, such as the Indo-Chinese and Hispanic communities, that had been completely ignored heretofore.

The Role of the Court

The *Keyes* case is a classic example of multi-polar public law litigation so common in efforts at institutional reform: the sprawling and amorphous party structure; a diffused adversarial relationship intermixed with negotiating and mediating processes; the judge as a dominant figure in guiding the case; the wide range of outside experts drawn upon for support and oversight assistance; and the court as a manager of ongoing relief.[150] However, we disagree with participants in the judicial activism debate that the *Keyes* judge adopted a new activist role.[151] In the context of this litigation, the judge exercised remarkable judicial restraint. The actions of Judge Matsch in pushing the school system toward a unitary system reflect Professor Diver's view of the judge as a political power broker, alternately threatening, extolling, and pushing the educational system toward reform.[152]

As in all extended litigation, the political, legal, and, in this case, the educational environment, changed during the course of the lawsuit. These changes, ranging from varying U.S. Supreme Court standards relating to the finding of a constitutional fault to changing attitudes by the lower courts of their remedial capacity, served to lengthen the litigation and decrease the court's flexibility in reacting to changes.

Courts have surprisingly little leeway and flexibility in multi-polar public law litigation unless the trial judge wants to supersede the parties and either run the institution him- or herself or through a surrogate, such as a Master. Certainly, Judge Matsch did not desire to adopt this role.

When Judge Matsch took over the *Keyes* case, he told the Community Education Council, which had been monitoring the desegregation of the school system, "I'm looking forward to having a very minor role in the desegregation of the schools."[153] While he was wrong on his evaluation of his role, the judge has been consistent in attempting to withdraw the court from oversight of the school system so long as it can be achieved by constitutional means. This case is not an example of aggressive judicial activism. Rather, it demonstrates courts' reluctance to control school systems, combined with a readiness to exercise their remedial powers in the face of a recalcitrant Board of Education.

Once the plan goes into effect, a court is particularly limited in its ability to alter it, even if demographics change. People—particularly the children —affected by a desegregation plan make changes in that plan difficult. When the consensus plan in *Keyes* was adopted, even though with reservation, it developed a momentum of its own. In a sense, the real measure of a board's commitment to develop a unitary system and to get the court to withdraw from a desegregation lawsuit comes at the point where the student reassignment plan must be changed. The demographics of urban school systems are such that change is constant. Typically, immediately following the implementation of a desegregation remedy, an erosion of white students increases racial imbalance in some schools. Bureaucracies tend to favor inertia. School systems facing politically hostile reactions to increased busing are reluctant to alter an implemented plan. At some point, school boundaries must be shifted and new groups of students bused. Whether the board affirmatively attempts to implement these changes, or as in Denver, places the burden on the court and seeks to hinder and delay, change is the benchmark for ending the lawsuit. Over time, the court's flexibility seemed to decrease. The court forced the school Board to make decisions that maximized integration within the constraints of the situation.

The judicial process itself operates as a facilitator of change. In *Keyes*, it freed the Board to make decisions, while allowing it to escape the political consequences. The court creates a framework for the parties to come together. Through its decisions, the court educates the Board and the public.

In the latter stages of litigation, Judge Matsch was passive, serving as a boundary. Only when the parties were unable to resolve an issue would he make substantive choices. For instance, during the hearings on the Board's motion to dismiss, the plaintiffs demanded that the three racially unbalanced elementary schools be integrated. Judge Matsch demurred from ordering such a step because he wanted it to be part of the final negotiated settlement. When the issue could not be resolved by the parties themselves, Matsch ordered the solution.

The ongoing supervision by Judge Matsch is similar to that of courts in other areas of the law, such as trusts, probate, bankruptcy, and antitrust.[154] The difference is primarily in the number of people directly affected and the extent of public scrutiny of the results. Still, we suggest that the role of the judge in *Keyes* was traditional and passive. Rather than adopt a policy-making role, Judge Matsch assumed a boundary-setting responsibility. The leeway and scope of the remedy were determined within limits set by the parties. In *Keyes*, the court never did control the Denver public school system. The court forced the schools to create an information system that would enable plaintiffs and the public to monitor the desegregation process. This case is not an example of the substitution of government by the federal judiciary. The court used its remedial powers to force the appropriate bodies to exercise their responsibilities, but it did not supersede them unless absolutely necessary.

This is not to suggest that the judicial process does not distort the functioning of our system of separation of powers. It does force reallocation of limited funds within the school system and external allocation of money to the educational system. The distortion is that normally the legislative branch has the responsibility to allocate monies.[155] The judicial process in this case served as a means of getting other branches of government and administrative agencies involved.

The lawsuit has led to the legalization of educational change in Denver. Issues that are traditionally considered issues of educational policy have legal overtures that may subsume the former. Educational decisionmakers now focus upon the legal implications of a course of action, often at the expense of educational implications. We suggest that the courts will remain as the prime arena to work through (i.e., test, evaluate, refine, and approve) educational policy. When additional grievances arise, they will be less likely to be resolved through the educational system. Courts will become policy mediators for future disputes. The educational system's constituents have learned that access to a court is more likely to vindicate constitutional rights and to force the educational system to change. The increasing use of the courts to settle public policy disputes is the way our political system now works in many areas, not only in education.

NOTES

1. C. Abbott, S. Leonard, and D. McComb, Colorado: A History of the Centennial State 52–53, 233, 315–17 (rev. ed. 1982).

2. Denver Regional Council of Governments, Profiles of 1970–1980, Socio-Economic Change by County and Census Tract 1 (April 1983).

3. Colorado, *supra* note 1, at 205–09, 302–04.

4. *Id.* at 295–98.

5. Branscombe, *New Desegregation Plan Unveiled*, Denver Post, March 12, 1983, at 1B.

6. Pearson & Pearson, *The Denver Case: Keyes v. School District No. 1*, in H. Kalodner and J. Fishman, Limits of Justice: The Courts' Roles in School Desegregation 167, 169 (1978).

7. F. James, B. McCummings, and E. Tynan, Discrimination, Segregation and Minority Housing Conditions in Sunbelt Cities: A Study of Denver, Houston and Phoenix 46, 49 (1982).

8. Colorado, *supra* note 1, at 295.

9. Keyes v. School District No. 1, 303 F. Supp. 289, 290–95 (D. Colo. 1969).

10. *Id.*, 303 F. Supp. 289, 290 (D. Colo. 1969); 313 F. Supp. 61, 65 (D. Colo. 1970).

11. *Id.*, 313 F. Supp. 61, 90 (D. Colo. 1970).

12. *Id.*, 445 F.2d 990 (10th Cir. 1971).

13. *Id.*, 413 U.S. 189, 201, 208 (1973).

14. *Id.* at 213.

15. *Id.*, 368 F. Supp. 207 (D. Colo. 1973).

16. *Id.*, 521 F.2d 465, 476 (10th Cir. 1975).

17. *Id.* at 479 (10th Cir. 1975).

18. This is with minority enrollments varying between 77 and 88 percent. It was remanded for a determination whether the continued segregation of schools could be justified on grounds other than the institution of bilingual programs. *Id.* at 480. Bilingual education was not a substitute for desegregation.

19. 402 U.S. 1, 26 (1971).

20. Hawley *et al.*, Strategies for Effective Desegregation 36 (1983).

21. This period is detailed in Keyes v. School District No. 1, 474 F. Supp. 1265 (D. Colo. 1979) and summarized in *id.* 609 F. Supp. 1491, 1500–01 (D. Colo. 1985).

22. *Id.*, 609 F. Supp. at 1501.

23. *Id.*, 474 F. Supp. 1265, 1271–72 (D. Colo. 1979). Interview with Gordon Greiner, lead counsel for plaintiffs, in Denver (September 12, 1984).

24. "The ultimate objective is to define and create a unitary system so that jurisdiction of the Court over Denver schools may be relinquished," Matsch wrote. He added, "It is important that the burden of busing be shared and that there be no disproportionate impact on a racial or ethnic balance." Keyes v. School District No. 1, 474 F. Supp. 1265, 1270 (D. Colo. 1979).

25. *Id.*, 540 F. Supp. 399 (D. Colo. 1982).

26. Telephone interview with Kay Schomp, former member, Denver School Board (November 8, 1985).

27. Keyes v. School District No. 1, 609 F. Supp. 1491, 1502 (D. Colo. 1985). Branscombe, *Questions Arise in "Unitary" School Desegregation Plan*, Denver Post, June 14, 1981, at 1F.

28. Branscombe, *Bold School Plan Being Readied*, Denver Post, October 12, 1981, at 1B.

29. Branscombe, *School Board Proposal Termed Resegregation*, Denver Post, October 21, 1981, at 1B.

30. Branscombe, *Schools Ordered to Choose One Integration Plan*, Denver Post, November 13, 1981, at 1B.

31. Branscombe, *School Board Moves to End Forced Busing*, Denver Post, December 1, 1981, at 1A.

32. Branscombe, *Denver's Plan for No Busing for Schools Sent to U.S. Judge*, Denver Post, December 11, 1981, at 1A. Said Board member Rev. Marion Hammond, "I

think this is educationally one of the worst things I've ever seen." Also at the meeting, Mullen accused Blair of not speaking for the majority of the black community: "They're embarrassed and tired of having Blair represent them."

33. Branscombe, *"Magnet" Desegregation Plan Ready*, Denver Post, December 10, 1981, at 1A.

34. One of the Board members, Robert Crider, said in an interview that the remedy "took a growing school district and killed it." "Educationally, things haven't changed," he added. "The kids who were learning before still learn; the kids who weren't learning still aren't learning. Using transportation to remedy the situation is a mistake. People leave." Interview with Robert Crider, former member, Denver Public School Board, in Denver (September 13, 1984).

35. Branscombe, *Judge Rejects Denver School Board Plan on Busing*, Denver Post, March 16, 1982, at 1A.

36. Keyes v. School District No. 1, 540 F. Supp. at 402.

37. *Id.*, 609 F. Supp. at 1507.

38. S. Hostetter, Colorado Department of Educ. Statistics, August 1, 1984.

39. Weaver, *Busing Triggered White Flight? Truism Debunked by Experts*, Denver Post, April 14, 1985, at 6.

40. Former Denver Board member Kay Schomp offered an example of this phenomenon:

> Now, for the first three years that I was on the board of education, I was part of a board of education that was not committed to the court order. They did everything that they possibly could to disrupt it—they dragged their feet wherever possible. They did not try to get sufficient funds, which they should have. . . . Instead, they kept appealing the case and did not approach the thing in a positive manner.

Interview with Kay Schomp, member Denver Board of Education, 1971–1973 in Denver (September 12, 1984).

41. Branscombe, *Denver School Board Gets Anti-busing Majority*, Denver Post, May 20, 1981, at 1.

42. Interview with James Ward, former principal, Manual High School, Denver (September 11, 1984).

43. Gordon Greiner described the residence to the panel:

> Two years ago, he [Judge Matsch] appointed this Compliance Assistance Panel. And he did that to help the district answer his concerns in eighteen different areas. You have these people that were appointed to the panel, were experts, that had a lot of good ideas and basically just got stonewalled.

Greiner Interview, *supra* note 23.

44. Branscombe, *Denver Schools Not Desegregated, Court's Expert Says*, Denver Post, May 10, 1984, at 7A.

45. Interview with Bernard Valdez, in Denver (September 12, 1984). Asked if he thought the suit had resulted in a more equitable distribution of quality teachers throughout the system, Valdez responded:

You see, initially, using seniority as a right to get transferred, the best teachers moved to the schools where children were moved to. The worst teachers remained in the ghetto schools. . . . So as a consequence there was no question in my mind that education was inferior in the lower socio-economic schools. Then . . . children were moved all over—for the first time to mix, to see some teachers who really were interested in education—but I think as the years went on, the transfers began to . . . result in the same inequalities." *Id.*

46. Branscombe, *Minority-Student Suspension Rate in Denver School System Criticized*, Denver Post, December 16, 1981, at 16A. DENVER PUBLIC SCHOOLS, ELEMENTARY AND SECONDARY SCHOOLS CIVIL RIGHTS SURVEY 159 (1982).

47. Bingham, *Black, Hispanic Students Lead Suspensions*, Denver Post, March 6, 1986, at 1A.

48. Bingham, *Schools Set Rules to Curb Racism*, Denver Post, April 8, 1987, at B1, col. 5.

49. Keyes v. School District No. 1, 609 F. Supp. 1491, 1512–14 (D. Colo. 1985).

50. Bingham, *Pupils Can Switch Schools if Move Aids Integration*, Denver Post, February 21, 1986, at 1B. Keyes v. School District No. 1, 653 F. Supp. 1536, 1537 (D. Colo. 1987).

51. Bingham, *Brief Opposes Desegregation Plan Update*, Denver Post, February 20, 1985, at 2A.

52. Bingham, *DPS Short of Minority Hiring Goals*, Denver Post, November 23, 1984, at 1. Minority teachers are especially scarce at the middle- and senior-high school levels, according to DPS faculty statistics from the 1982–1983 school year.

53. Keyes v. School District No. 1, 609 F. Supp. 1491, 1508–12.

54. Bingham, *Anglos Dominate College Prep*, Denver Post, March 15, 1986, at 1B.

55. Gallagher, *The Special Education Contract for Mildly Handicapped Children*, 38 J. EXCEPTIONAL CHILDREN 527, 529 (1972).

56. The test used was the Wechsler Intelligence Scale for Children—Revised. Bingham, *IQ Test Laced with Cultural Bias, Educators Say*, Denver Post, January 22, 1987, at 8A. IQ tests have been successfully judicially challenged. *See* Larry P. v. Riles, 495 F. Supp. 926 (N.D. Cal. 1979) *modified* 793 F.2d 969 (9th Cir. 1984).

57. Bingham, *School Auditors: Retest Minorities in Special Ed*, Denver Post, January 22, 1987, at 1A.

58. Bingham, *Just 26 More Anglos Would Meet Court's Desegregation Guidelines*, Denver Post, November 27, 1985.

59. Bingham, *Public Housing a Key Factor in School Segregation*, Denver Post, January 19, 1986, at 3B.

60. Keyes v. School District No. 1, 609 F. Supp. 1491, 1499 (D.C. Colo. 1985).

61. *Id.*, 504 F. Supp. 399, 403–04 (D.C. Colo. 1982).

62. Brown v. Board of Education, 349 U.S. 294 (1955).

63. *See* 4 Pomeroy, Equity, Jurisprudence § 363 (5th ed. 1941); Pound, *The Maxims of Equity*, 34 HARV. L. REV. 809 (1921).

64. Milliken v. Bradley, 433 U.S. 267, 280–81 (1977).

65. Davis v. Board of School Commissioners of Mobile County, 402 U.S. 33, 37 (1971).

66. Green v. County School Board, 391 U.S. 430, 437–38 (1968).

67. Swann v. Charlotte–Mecklenburg Board of Education, 402 U.S. 1, 24 (1971).

68. Dayton Board of Education v. Brinkman, 443 U.S. 526, 539 (1979).

69. Pasadena City Board of Education v. Spangler, 427 U.S. 424 (1976).

70. Green v. County School Board, 391 U.S. 430, 435–37 (1968).

71. Keyes v. School District No. 1, 540 F. Supp. 399 at 404 (D.C. Colo. 1982).

72. Spangler v. Pasadena City Board of Education, 611 F.2d 1239 (9th Cir. 1979).

73. *Dispute over Bakersfield, California, to Complete Its Desegregation Efforts by Offer-ing Special Programs to Attract White Students*, N.Y. Times, February 12, 1984, at I, 28, col. 1; *Reagan Admin. Proposes Blueprint for Desegregation*, N.Y. Times, January 26, 1984, at I, 1, col. 1. The Bakersfield program used magnet schools. The Pasadena school system also ended court oversight despite continued difficulty in reaching racial guidelines. At this time, the Denver Board added out-of-town counsel who had been successful in settling the Pasadena litigation.

74. Branscombe, *Matsch Allows Intervention*, Denver Post, February 10, 1984, at 1A.

75. Keyes v. School District No. 1, 413 U.S. 189, 197–98 (1973).

76. *Id.*, 521 F.2d 465, 480 (10th Cir. 1975).

77. *Id.*, 521 F.2d at 483.

78. *Id.*, 380 F. Supp. at 695.

79. *Id.*, 521 F.2d at 482–83.

80. Roos, *Implementation of the Federal Bilingual Education Mandate: The Keyes Case as a Paradigm*, 6–7 (unpublished paper on file, the Institute of Judicial Administra-tion).

81. Equal Education Opportunities Act of 1974, § 202, 20 U.S.C. §§ 1701 *et seq.* (1974).

82. *Id.*, 20 U.S.C.A. 1703 (1974).

83. Castenada v. Pickard, 648 F.2d 989, 1009 (5th Cir. 1981). The Fifth Circuit in *Castenada* concluded that by granting limited English speaking students a private right of action to enforce the obligations to address the problems of language bar-riers in the EEOA, Congress must have intended that schools make a genuine effort, consistent with local circumstances and resources to remedy the language difficulties.

84. United States v. State of Texas, 680 F.2d 356, 371 (5th Cir. 1982).

85. Colo. Rev. Stat. § 22–24–105 (1982 Cum. Supp.).

86. Keyes v. School District No. 1, 576 F. Supp. at 1511.

87. Colo. Rev. Stat. § 22–24–103(4) (1982 Cum. Supp.).

88. Intervenors Exhibit 26 *cited in* Keyes v. School District No. 1, 576 F. Supp. at 1516.

89. Branscombe, *Bilingual Program Evolving: English Taught the "Hard Way,"* Den-ver Post, January 16, 1984, at 5A.

90. Keyes v. School District No. 1, 576 F. Supp. at 1512.

91. *Roos, supra* note 80, at 11.

92. *Id.* at 10.

93. Keyes v. School District No. 1, 576 F. Supp. at 1513–14.

94. *Id.*, 576 F. Supp. 1503 (D. Colo. 1983). The judge said the delay stemmed from the difficulties involved in using the adversary process to assess the efforts made by a public school district to achieve a unitary school system.

95. Other concerns were the reliance on oral skills, the disregard of any special curricular needs of the *Lau* C children, and the lack of adequate tests to measure the district's results. Most students with limited English proficiency were not in those classes and attended schools without a bilingual program. *"Lau* A" and *"Lau* B" children were receiving no content instruction in a language that they understood. Keyes v. School District No. 1, 576 F. Supp. at 1516.

96. *Id.*, 576 F. Supp. at 1518.

97. *Id.* at 1521–22.

98. Burling, *Continued Supervision Urged for Denver Schools*, Rocky Mountain News, February 16, 1984, at 8.

99. Branscombe, *School Board Will "Promote Integration,"* Denver Post, April 11, 1984, at 4A.

100. Branscombe, *School Board Claims Data Proves Its Full Compliance*, Denver Post, April 17, 1984, at 4A; Enda, *Judge Puzzled by Consultant for DPS Plan*, Rocky Mountain News, May 12, 1985, at 19. Ross was paid $119,825 on a per diem arrangement that claimed from $400 per day to $500 by May 1985. He also received $37,078 for travel and clerical expenses and spent $37,462 for computer time. These expenses, along with the legal fees, when made public became an embarrassment to the Board.

101. Keyes v. School District No. 1, 609 F. Supp. 1491, 1508 (D.C. Colo. 1985); Weaver, *Busing Triggered White Flight? Truism Being Debunked by Experts*, Denver Post, April 14, 1985, at 6E.

102. Keyes v. School District No. 1, 609 F. Supp. 1491, 1508 (D.C. Colo. 1985).

103. Branscombe, *Plaintiffs Offer Enlarged Busing Plan*, Denver Post, April 26, 1984, at 1A.

104. Branscombe, *More City School Busing Is Denied*, Denver Post, May 24, 1984, at 1A.

105. Branscombe, *DPS Release from Court Control Urged*, Denver Post, April 20, 1984, at 4A.

106. Cantu then asked whether Mullen recalled that one of the original complaints in the case was that some minority schools had low standardized test scores. "That's something everybody is concerned about," he responded. Mullen admitted he had never received a list of low achieving schools before voting on the resolution. Branscombe, *Board Member Didn't Know if Bias Violations Ended*, Denver Post, April 26, 1984, at 3A.

107. Branscombe, *School Board Shunned Offers Expert Says*, Denver Post, May 9, 1984, at 9. Hawley said beginning March 4, 1983, he and Charles Willie sent a series of letters to Michael Jackson, Board attorney, offering cooperation and suggesting DPS staffers be appointed to work with the panel. He received no answer at all until October 11 and no answer in any way responsive until November 2, 1983.

108. Branscombe, *Denver Schools Not Desegregated, Court's Expert Says*, Denver Post, May 10, 1984, at 7A. Willie also testified about the Board's lack of response to compliance assistance panel initiatives. *See id.* at 16.

109. Enda, *Talks to End DPS Suit Breakdown*, Rocky Mountain News, February 3, 1985, at 6.

110. *School Board Seeking Speedy Suit Settlement*, Denver Post, February 15, 1985, at 8B.

111. Bingham, *Board to Offer Integration Plans for 3 Schools*, Denver Post, February 21, 1985, § 5, at 3.

112. Enda, *Judge Puzzled by Consultant for DPS Plan*, Rocky Mountain News, May 12, 1985, at 19.

113. In suburban school elections where desegregation has not been an issue, only 1 to 2 percent of the electorate usually votes. Bingham, *Garner, McCotter Win Denver School Election*, Denver Post, May 22, 1985, at 1A.

114. Branscombe, *School Plaintiff Talks Aim at Busing Freeze*, Denver Post, October 2, 1984, at 1A. Negotiations continued through the fall of 1984 but then stalled. Greiner refused to negotiate and prepare a final brief at the same time. After receiving two extensions on November 28, 1984, an impatient Matsch refused to give him additional time to file his brief. Bingham, *Desegregation Suit Negotiations Stalled*, Denver Post, November 17, 1984, at 7A. Matsch wanted to render his decision during the then current school year to permit the district time to implement changes in pupil assignments before the start of the next school year. Greiner was ordered to file his final brief by December 18, 1984. Bingham, *Extension Denied in DPS Busing Case*, Denver Post, November 29, 1984, at 8A.

115. Branscombe, *Bilingual Program Changes Proposal*, Denver Post, January 6, 1984, at 1B.

116. Telephone Interview with Peter Roos, Counsel for plaintiff intervenors (September 18, 1985).

117. Keyes v. School District No. 1, 609 F. Supp. 1491, 1507, 1512 (D. Colo. 1985).

118. *Id.* at 1514.

119. The constitution of the state of Colorado expressly prohibits the use of such busing in the following language of the "anti-busing" amendment, adopted in 1974: "No sectarian tenets or doctrines shall ever be taught in the public school, nor shall any distinction or classification of pupils be made on account of race or color, nor shall any pupil be assigned or transported to any public educational institution for the purpose of achieving racial balance."
Colo. Const. Art. IX, § 8. The Supremacy Clause of the U.S. Constitution, Art. IV § 2, permitted the operation of the Denver schools under the existing busing plan, which otherwise was a clear violation of the Colorado constitution.

120. The Fifth Circuit, which has probably had the greatest experience in school desegregation cases, requires a court to retain jurisdiction for three years following judicial determination that a school district is unitary. This assures that determination of unitary status is not premature. In that period, the district files semi-annual reports with the court. At the end of the three years a hearing is held at which plaintiffs may show cause why the case should not be dismissed. The district court then makes a final determination as to whether the district has achieved unitary status and at that time may dismiss the case. *See* Ross v. Houston Independent School District, 699 F.2d 218 (5th Cir. 1983); United States v. Texas Education Agency, 509 F.2d 192 (5th Cir. 1975).

121. Keyes v. School District No. 1, 609 F. Supp. at 1521.

122. Bingham, *DPS Drafts Bold Goals to End Integration Suit*, Denver Post, June 13, 1985, at 1A.

123. Enda, *School Board Plan Misses on Key Issues*, Rocky Mountain News, July 11, 1985, at 7. Other goals included curriculum reviews for more personalized learning plans for elementary students, reduction of class sizes, and the dropout rate. Bingham, *DPS Drafts Bold Goals to End Integration Suit*, Denver Post, June 13, 1985, at 1A.

124. Bingham, *Data Bank Will Monitor City School Integration*, Denver Post, June 22, 1985, at 1A.

125. Barrett was the focus of the original lawsuit in 1969. Bingham, *Board Hopes for New Integration Guidance*, Denver Post, June 27, 1985, at 5A.

126. Bingham, *3 Schools Unveil Integration Plan*, Denver Post, December 3, 1985, at 1B.

127. Bingham, *Desegregation Deadlock Broken?*, Denver Post, December 15, 1985, at 1A. Bingham, *Desegregation Issue Still Plagues Schools*, Denver Post, December 16, 1985, at 1A.

128. Bingham, *Judge Gives Board OK on Integrating 3 Denver Schools*, Denver Post, March 16, 1986, at 1B.

129. Keyes v. School District No. 1, 653 F. Supp. 1536, 1538–40 (D. Colo. 1987); Corcoran, *DPS Wants Ruling from Higher Court*, Denver Post, April 8, 1986, at 1B. The plaintiffs argued that the district should have only two years to meet its goals of tightening transfers and for integrating the three elementary schools and if integration did not improve by the Fall of 1987 to develop alternative plans. They wanted the district to make specific orders for detailing monitoring and reporting. Bingham, *Brief Urges Judge to Keep School Role*, Denver Post, April 22, 1986, at 1B. Keyes v. School District No. 1, 653 F. Supp. at 1539.

130. Keyes v. School District No. 1, 653 F. Supp. 1536, 1540–02 (D. Colo. 1987).

131. *Id.*, 670 F. Supp. 1513 (D. Colo. 1987).

132. Bingham, *20 Schools Are Going Bilingual*, Denver Post, October 13, 1984, at 1A.

133. Roos, *supra* note 80, at 25.

134. The settlement is detailed in DENVER PUBLIC SCHOOLS SYSTEM, REPORT ON BILINGUAL EDUCATION (1985) [hereinafter REPORT].

135. Roos, *supra* note 80, at 27.

136. REPORT, *supra* note 134, at 19, D23.

137. *Id.*, at 12–13.

138. Bingham, *20 Schools Are Going Bilingual*, Denver Post, October 13, 1984, at 1A.

139. Bingham, *4300 More Denver Pupils Need Bilingual Aid*, Denver Post, October 19, 1984, at 2A.

140. Interview with George Bardwell, researcher for plaintiffs, in Denver (September 16, 1984).

141. Valdez Interview, *supra* note 45.

142. Denver Public Schools, Enrollment Figures (1983). A copy is on file at the Institute of Judicial Administration.

143. Milliken v. Bradley, 433 U.S. 267 (1977), Milliken II. After Milliken I, 418 U.S. 717 (1974), where the Supreme Court refused to order a metropolitan integra-

tion plan, the district court ordered a Detroit-only busing plan and ordered the local board to provide a broad range of compensatory educational programs half-financed by the state of Michigan. The state defendants appealed on the grounds that the order exceeded the scope of the constitutional violation. The Supreme Court upheld the district court's order of the compensatory programs.

144. Milliken v. Bradley, 418 U.S. 717 (1974).

145. *Cf.* Keyes v. School District No. 1, 576 F. Supp. at 1517. Branscombe, *Bilingual Program Changes Proposed*, Denver Post, January 6, 1984, at 5B.

146. Valdez Interview, *supra* note 45.

147. Bingham, *Hispanics Protect Crowded Denver Schools*, Denver Post, December 8, 1985, at 1C.

148. Bingham, *Schooling, Not Busing, the Issue*, Denver Post, March 10, 1986, at 1B.

149. Bingham, *Denver Anglos, Asians Did Well in School Tests*, Denver Post, August 6, 1986, at 1A. The same results occurred on achievement tests administered by DPS as part of an academic excellence plan and more rigorous graduation standards. Bingham, *Minorities Weaker on DPS Tests*, Denver Post, January 14, 1986, at 1A.

150. *See* Chayes, *The Role of the Judge in Public Law Litigation*, 89 HARV. L. REV. 1281, 1282–84 (1976).

151. *See* REBELL and BLOCK, EDUCATIONAL POLICY MAKING AND THE COURTS (1982); Horowitz, *Decreeing Organizational Change: Judicial Supervision of Public Institutions* 1983 DUKE L. J. 1265 (1983).

152. Diver, *The Judge as Political Powerbroker: Superintending Structural Change in Public Institutions*, 64 VA. L. REV. 43 (1979).

153. Parsons, *The Busing Judge*, Denver Post, February 5, 1984, at 1A.

154. *See* Eisenberg and Yeazell, *The Ordinary and the Extraordinary in Institutional Litigation*, 93 HARV. L. REV. 465, 481–91 (1980).

155. *See* Nagel, *Separation of Powers and the Scope of Federal Equitable Remedies*, 30 STAN. L. REV. 661 (1978); Frug, *The Judicial Power of the Purse*, 126 U. OF PA. L. REV. 715 (1978).

CHAPTER 6

Voluntary Interdistrict School
Desegregation in St. Louis:
The Special Master's Tale

D. BRUCE LA PIERRE

INTERDISTRICT SCHOOL DESEGREGATION is rare. Three cities have implemented interdistrict student transfer plans under court orders, and a few other cities have voluntarily instituted very limited interdistrict student transfer programs.[1] Interdistrict school desegregation in St. Louis is a unique example of this rare phenomenon. St. Louis adopted and implemented a substantial, voluntary interdistrict student transfer program as a settlement of an interdistrict school desegregation case. It is the only city in the United States that has resolved interdistrict school desegregation issues through a process of compromise and consent.

In the 1987–1988 school year, 10,971 black students from the city of St. Louis attended predominately white suburban schools in St. Louis County, and 581 white students from the county attended school in the predominately black city school system.[2] In the 1988–1989 school year, 11,901 black city students are attending county schools, and 724 white students are transferring to the city schools.[3] These interdistrict transfers are part of a Settlement Agreement that was approved by the courts to resolve the metropolitan St. Louis school desegregation case. This Settlement Agreement was adopted by 23 suburban school districts in St. Louis County, by the NAACP and the Liddell plaintiffs (who are the two representatives of the plaintiff class), and by the Board of Education of the city of St. Louis. The Settlement Agreement is the crucial component of the St. Louis case that distinguishes it from all other school desegregation cases.

The Settlement Agreement, which was adopted in 1983, is the product of long but sporadic efforts to desegregate the St. Louis city school system. Although the original complaint was filed in 1972, the case did not go to trial

Source: The Institute of Judicial Administration, Inc., under a grant from the Ford Foundation, commissioned the research for this chapter. A previous report appeared under the same title in 1987 WISC. L. REV. 971.

until 1978, and the district court did not order an intradistrict remedy until 1980. Because the intradistrict order left two-thirds of the black students in the city schools in all-black schools and because the court had deferred consideration of interdistrict desegregation, attention turned to metropolitan school desegregation issues. Interdistrict desegregation efforts proceeded down three paths from 1980 through 1983. First, the district court ordered the formulation of a mandatory interdistrict plan and suggested that it had the power to impose such a plan without first conducting a trial to determine an interdistrict constitutional violation. Second, the NAACP and the Board of Education initiated an interdistrict action against the St. Louis County suburban school districts. Third, many suburban school districts agreed to participate in a limited interdistrict program of voluntary student transfers, and the interdistrict litigation against these districts was stayed. Under my supervision as a Special Master, these three paths merged in five months of negotiations that led to an agreement in the spring of 1983 to settle the interdistrict aspects of the St. Louis school desegregation case.

As subsequently approved and modified by the courts, the Settlement Agreement was first implemented in the 1983–1984 school year. More than five years later, in the middle of the 1988–1989 school year and the sixth year of implementation, the Settlement Agreement offers some constructive lessons. The principal lesson is that successful negotiation of an agreement by more than 25 parties with sharply divergent interests is possible. Difficult issues of interdistrict school desegregation and, perhaps, other complex social and legal issues can be resolved through a process of compromise, consent, and innovative thinking. The terms of the Settlement Agreement provide a second lesson, which is both more practical and more limited. Given the distinct legal and factual setting of the St. Louis case, the particular terms of the St. Louis Settlement Agreement are not susceptible to direct replication in other metropolitan areas. Nevertheless, the particular provisions do provide an instructive model for other communities.[4]

Notwithstanding these constructive lessons, during the first five years there were substantial reasons to doubt the ultimate success of the Settlement Agreement. Although the Settlement Agreement program for the interdistrict transfer of black students from the city of St. Louis to predominately white suburban schools was very successful, other major components of the Settlement Agreement were not successfully implemented. Five years after its adoption, the Settlement Agreement's provisions for the establishment of magnet schools in the city to attract white suburban students and the provisions for special quality education programs in all-black city schools had not been fully implemented; no capital improvements in city school facilities had been made. In short, significant promises of the Settlement Agreement had been broken. The result was that at the end of the 1987–1988 school year approximately 19,000 black children, 45 percent of all the black students in the city school system, remained in all-black city schools,[5] and these children had been denied the remedy contemplated by the Settlement Agreement. Moreover, there were threats to dismantle both the intradistrict desegregation order and the interdistrict settlement. In 1987 and 1988, there was political pressure in the city of St. Louis to abandon intradistrict deseg-- regation efforts, and the state of Missouri attempted to reduce or to escape its substantial financial responsibilities under the Settlement Agreement at the completion of the fifth year of implementation.

In the late summer of 1987 and in 1988, the courts took several im- portant steps to resolve the problems of implementation and to address challenges to continued desegregation. The courts approved comprehen- sive magnet school and capital improvements programs and established the means to finance these expensive components of the Settlement Agreement.[6] They spurred implementation of a crucial Settlement Agreement provision to improve the quality of education in all-black city schools by reducing pupil–teacher ratios.[7] The courts forcefully repudiated the state of Missouri's efforts to abandon its duty to fund the voluntary interdistrict student trans- fer program and ensured that interdistrict transfers to suburban schools will continue for the foreseeable future to be the major means of desegregating the city school system.[8]

The courts' intervention to enforce the provisions of the Settlement Agreement, albeit long-delayed, now strongly suggests that the broken prom- ises of the Settlement Agreement will be mended. If the court's funding mechanisms are successful, black children in the schools of the city of St. Louis will have a remedy for the violation of their constitutional rights. These children will now have an opportunity, created by the Settlement Agreement, to obtain the benefits of substantial improvements in the quality of education either in an integrated setting in suburban schools or in the predominately black city school system.

PROLOGUE: INTRADISTRICT SCHOOL
DESEGREGATION AND INTERDISTRICT
ALTERNATIVES

School Desegregation in St. Louis, 1972–1982

In 1972, Minnie Liddell, her son Craton, and several other black students and parents initiated the St. Louis school desegregation case by filing suit against the Board of Education of the city of St. Louis. The case was subsequently expanded by the intervention of additional plaintiffs including the U.S. Department of Justice and a group of black students represented by the NAACP, and by the joinder of the state of Missouri as a defendant. The district court refused, however, to add an interdistrict component to the intradistrict city school desegregation case and denied a motion to join suburban school districts in St. Louis County as defendants. After eight years of litigation, on May 21, 1980, the district court held that both the Board and the state were liable for *de jure* segregation of the public schools of the city of St. Louis. The court approved a desegregation plan drafted by the Board of Education[9] and ordered the Board to implement this plan beginning with the 1980–1981 school year. It also ordered the state and the Board to share equally the costs of the intradistrict desegregation plan.[10]

Recognizing that some 30,000 black students, approximately two-thirds of the black students in the city school system, would remain in all-black schools after implementation of the intradistrict plan, the district court ordered the state, the Board of Education, and the United States to explore interdistrict remedies to relieve segregation in the city schools.[11] In paragraph 12(a), the district court ordered these three parties to develop a "voluntary, cooperative plan of pupil exchanges" between the city schools and the suburban school districts in St. Louis County.[12] The court also ordered them in paragraph 12(c) "[t]o develop and submit . . . a suggested plan of inter-district school desegregation necessary to eradicate the remaining vestiges of government-imposed school segregation in the City of St. Louis and St. Louis County."[13] These two court-ordered plans, which were quickly dubbed the 12(a) voluntary plan and the 12(c) mandatory plan, created two paths toward interdistrict desegregation. The January 1981 motions of the NAACP and the Board to join the 23 suburban school districts in St. Louis County as defendants[14] suggested a third path: the initiation of interdistrict litigation.

In the 1980–1981 school year, the first year after approval of the intradistrict plan, most efforts to achieve interdistrict desegregation focused on the 12(a) voluntary plan.[15] Although the state and the suburban school districts objected to this planning requirement, District Court Judge William L. Hungate[16] broke the impasse by ordering Edward T. Foote, the chairman of a court-appointed desegregation monitoring committee, to draft a 12(a) plan.[17] After three weeks of hectic negotiations, Foote submitted a plan in March 1981 entitled *An Educational Plan for Voluntary, Cooperative Desegregation*,[18] which he hoped would be the basis for a settlement of the interdistrict case. Although this first effort to settle the interdistrict case failed,[19] the district court adopted most of Foote's proposals when it approved a 12(a) plan in July 1981. Foote's plan laid the groundwork for a final settlement of the case two years later in March 1983.

Under the district court's 12(a) plan,[20] suburban school districts that accepted it (called participating districts) had a very limited obligation to enroll black students who voluntarily transferred from the city school district. In the first year of the plan, each suburban district with an enrollment of less than 8,000 students had to accept 50 permissive interdistrict transfer students, and districts with an enrollment greater than 8,000 students had to accept 100 permissive interdistrict transfer students.[21] Each succeeding year, a participating district had to make available spaces for additional transfer students equivalent to 1 percent of its resident enrollment until it achieved its plan ratio, which was either a 15 percent increase in minority enrollment or a 25 percent minority enrollment.[22]

Although the district court's 12(a) plan made some changes in Foote's proposal for voluntary student exchanges between the city school system and suburban school districts,[23] it basically tracked his proposals for the creation of magnet schools in the city to attract white county transfer students, for state payment of fiscal incentives to participating districts to cover the incremental costs of educating transfer students, and for state payment of the costs of interdistrict transportation.[24] The major difference between the district court's plan and Foote's *Educational Plan* was that the district court's plan did not include provisions for a final settlement through a phased disengagement from litigation.[25] Instead, the district court's plan provided that participation by a suburban school district "shall not be deemed an admission of liability nor an element of proof of liability in any inter-district school desegregation case" and promised that participation "would be a factor in weighing the necessity of a compulsory inter-district plan." [26]

For many suburban school districts, these assurances simply did not provide an adequate incentive to participate in a voluntary desegregation plan.[27] To the extent that the suburban school districts had been interested in Foote's plan, their interest had hinged on obtaining a final settlement and being freed from the threat of litigation. These suburban school districts viewed the provisions in the *Educational Plan* for a phased disengagement from litigation leading to a final settlement as the *quid pro quo* for participating in a voluntary plan and for waiving their opportunity to litigate the question of their liability for constitutional violations. The district court's 12(a) plan failed to provide this incentive.[28]

When the district court's August 6, 1981, deadline for participation in its 12(a) voluntary plan passed, only four suburban school districts had submitted conditional acceptances.[29] The court's response, on August 24, was to order these four districts (and a fifth district that agreed to participate two days later), the Board of Education, and the state to implement the 12(a) plan as a "pilot project" and to stay the pending interdistrict action against each of the five districts "for so long as it is participating in good faith to achieve a level of integration satisfactory to the Court." [30]

With respect to the suburban school districts in St. Louis County that declined to participate, the court immediately took two preliminary steps to begin consideration of a mandatory interdistrict remedy. First, the court resumed the previously suspended consideration of mandatory interdistrict relief under paragraph 12(c) by ordering the state, the United States, and the Board of Education to file 12(c) plans. The court set a hearing on these plans for March 1, 1982. Second, the district court approved the initiation of the interdistrict school desegregation case by granting in part the January 1981 motions of the NAACP and the Board of Education to join non-participating St. Louis County school districts and by ordering discovery to be completed within 90 days.[31]

After entry of these orders in August 1981, questions about the nature and extent of an interdistrict remedy and about the court's power to impose a mandatory interdistrict desegregation plan occupied center stage during the fall of 1981 and the early winter of 1982. The public's attention was riveted on two proposed 12(c) plans drafted by court-appointed education experts and on a 12(c) plan drafted by the Board of Education. All three plans provided for consolidating the suburban St. Louis County school districts and the city school system into a single metropolitan school district, or into five large, unified districts. Two of the proposed 12(c) plans also required mandatory reassignment of students between the city school system and the suburban school districts.[32]

At the same time, the parties were appealing both the district court's management of the interdistrict case and its power to impose a mandatory interdistrict desegregation plan under paragraph 12(c). Most of the suburban school districts appealed the district court's August 24 order joining them as defendants in the existing intradistrict case and initiating the interdistrict action on the ground that the new interdistrict issues should be tried in a separate, distinct lawsuit.[33] The interdistrict plaintiffs (the NAACP and the Board of Education) also appealed the joinder order because the district court had limited the scope of the interdistrict case by staying their motions to join suburban school districts in all of the counties surrounding the city of St. Louis.[34]

With the interdistrict litigation in limbo after Judge Hungate's decision to recuse himself from this portion of the case in September 1981[35] and the hearings on the 12(c) plans scheduled for March 1, 1982, the focus of the appeals was on the implementation of paragraph 12(c). The issues were the district court's power under paragraph 12(c) to impose a mandatory interdistrict desegregation plan and the relation of a 12(c) plan to any remedy that the district court might order if the litigation led to a finding of interdistrict constitutional violations by the state and the suburban school districts.[36]

The court-appointed experts' 12(c) plans for school district consolidation and mandatory interdistrict student transfers were as far-reaching as any desegregation plan that might have been imposed had the interdistrict litigation led to a finding of liability. The suburban school districts feared that the district court would order a mandatory desegregation plan without any hearing for them and without any determination of their liability for constitutional violations. Although a mandatory desegregation plan under paragraph

12(c) would in effect have made moot the interdistrict litigation, the district court apparently believed that it had the authority under paragraph 12(c) to order interdistrict student transfers and school district consolidation solely on the basis of the state's previously established intradistrict violation and the state's control over the suburban school districts as its "instrumentalities."[37] In its appeal, the state renewed its objections to this interpretation of paragraph 12(c). The state argued that it was unfair to order interdistrict student transfers and to reorganize the suburban school districts without affording them a hearing. The state also argued that its intradistrict violation did not justify such broad relief and that it lacked sufficient authority over the suburban school districts as its "instrumentalities" to warrant the proposed relief absent a determination that the suburban school districts were liable for segregation of the city schools.[38]

On January 11, 1982, when the Eighth Circuit heard arguments on these appeals, just seven weeks before the scheduled March 1 hearing on the 12(c) plans and the deadline for suburban school districts' decisions whether to participate in the district court's voluntary 12(a) plan,[39] the future course of metropolitan desegregation was uncertain. The district court had clearly signaled its intention to order a mandatory interdistrict desegregation plan because most of the suburban school districts had refused to participate in the court's voluntary 12(a) plan. The appeals, however, raised a substantial question whether a mandatory plan would be imposed promptly under paragraph 12(c) or whether any mandatory plan would be long delayed until the interdistrict litigation was completed and the district court determined if there was an interdistrict constitutional violation. Although implementation of the district court's voluntary 12(a) plan had enjoyed a modest success,[40] its future was also in doubt. The state had appealed orders that it pay the costs of implementing the 12(a) plan.[41] The interdistrict plaintiffs' appeals from the district court's orders staying their motions to join all of the suburban districts as defendants raised the question of the court's power to stay interdistrict litigation against the participating districts.[42]

Liddell V: Framework for an Interdistrict Settlement

The court of appeals' February 25, 1982, decision, now commonly called *Liddell V,* resolved most of the confusion about the future course of the metropolitan school desegregation case.[43] This decision, with the benefit of hindsight, proved to be the most important opinion on St. Louis interdistrict desegregation. It determined the appropriate scope of 12(c) plans and their relation to the interdistrict litigation. It upheld the district court's voluntary 12(a) plan. Most important, this opinion set the stage for a final settlement.

The clarification of the relationship between paragraph 12(c) and the interdistrict case was one important aspect of the decision. In a significant victory for the suburban school districts, the court of appeals defined the permissible scope of interdistrict relief under paragraph 12(c) in very narrow terms.[44] The court confined any 12(c) plan, which would have been based on the state's established intradistrict violation, to measures that either would have no direct effect on the suburban school districts or that would involve only voluntary action by the suburban school districts. As examples of permissible provisions of a 12(c) plan, the appeals court suggested that the district court could order the state (1) to improve the quality of education in all-black city schools; (2) to establish additional magnet schools either in the city or in the county if the suburban school districts agreed; (3) to provide additional part-time integrative programs for students in all-black city schools with students in suburban schools if these districts agreed to cooperate; and (4) to provide additional incentives for voluntary interdistrict transfers. The court of appeals specifically disapproved such measures as mandatory interdistrict student transfers and school district reorganization on the ground that they would "materially affect" the suburban school districts that were not parties to the intradistrict case. The appeals court held that the proposed broad 12(c) plans of the experts and the Board of Education "cannot be implemented in the context of the present 12(c) proceedings."[45]

A mandatory desegregation plan involving interdistrict student transfers and consolidation of school districts could be ordered only after the suburban school districts had been afforded an opportunity to be heard. Moreover, such a plan could be imposed only on findings either that the suburban school districts had contributed to segregation in the city schools or that the state, through its control over the suburban districts, had contributed to segregation in the city school system.[46] The court of appeals suggested that the issue of the state's and the suburban school districts' interdistrict liability should be tried promptly after the district court entered an order under paragraph 12(c).[47] It also permitted the interdistrict litigation to proceed on a limited basis solely against the suburban school districts in St. Louis County by declining to interfere with the district court's order granting only in part the interdistrict plaintiffs' January 1981 motions to join additional defendants.[48]

With respect to the voluntary 12(a) plan, the court of appeals upheld the district court's orders[49] that the state must pay the costs of voluntary student transfers between the city school system and the suburban school districts.[50] The appeals court also declined to interfere with the district court's order staying the interdistrict litigation against the five participating districts.[51]

It was generally recognized that *Liddell V* established a framework for consideration of a mandatory interdistrict desegregation plan. It was not generally recognized, however, that *Liddell V* also set the stage for a settlement of the metropolitan desegregation case. The stage for a final settlement was set in part by the determination of the court of appeals that student reassignments and school district consolidation could be ordered only after litigation and a finding that the state or the suburban school districts were liable for interdistrict violations. The interdistrict plaintiffs and the suburban school districts could now make a rational calculation about the probability that the interdistrict litigation would lead to a mandatory desegregation remedy apart from any question whether the same relief might be imposed under a 12(c) plan. The key to a settlement was not, however, the establishment of a procedural framework for consideration of a mandatory desegregation plan. The key was the court of appeals' determination that the state was liable for the full costs of any voluntary interdistrict desegregation plan solely on the basis of its previously established intradistrict constitutional violation.

It is true, of course, that the court of appeals did not expressly hold that the state was liable for the full costs of a voluntary desegregation plan, but I argued at the time[52] that this conclusion followed inescapably from a close, fair reading of the *Liddell V* opinion. The Eighth Circuit upheld the district court's orders requiring the state to pay fiscal incentives and transportation costs for permissive interdistrict transfer students under the 12(a) voluntary plan and requiring the state to pay the budget of the Coordinating Committee charged with supervision of the voluntary plan.[53] The appeals court rested these holdings on the ground that the state, on the basis of its responsibility for segregation of the city schools, "can be required to take those actions which will further the desegregation of the city schools even if the actions required will occur outside the boundaries of the city school district."[54] Moreover, in the context of its discussion of interdistrict relief under 12(c), the court of appeals held that the district court could require the state to establish magnet schools and to provide additional incentives for voluntary interdistrict transfers.[55] On the basis of this evidence, I concluded that the court of appeals was firmly committed to the proposition that the costs of voluntary interdistrict desegregation remedies for segregation in the city schools were chargeable to the state.

The major unresolved issues in the settlement negotiations over the terms of the *Educational Plan* in March 1981 were financial issues.[56] The major stumbling blocks to a final settlement of the metropolitan school desegregation case were funding for magnet schools, fiscal incentives to be paid to both the home and host districts for each permissive interdistrict transfer student, and funding for quality education programs for students who would remain in all-black city schools after implementation of a voluntary interdistrict plan. In March 1981, the Board of Education, many suburban school districts, the Department of Justice, and representatives of the plaintiff class of black city school students had come close to an agreement on almost all of the non-financial issues of the voluntary desegregation plan proposed by Foote.[57] I argued that they should now be able to reach an agreement because *Liddell V* eliminated these funding issues.[58]

I also predicted that the suburban school districts and the interdistrict plaintiffs would be interested in a settlement after *Liddell V*. After the court of appeals' opinion, the suburban school districts could be confident that neither mandatory interdistrict transfers nor school district consolidation would be imposed under paragraph 12(c) and, in addition, that any mandatory desegregation plan would be delayed until after the interdistrict case was tried. Nevertheless, they faced the risk that the district court would order a mandatory desegregation remedy either on the basis of the state's established intradistrict violation and its authority over the suburban school districts as its "instrumentalities" or on the basis of findings that the state or the suburban districts had committed interdistrict constitutional violations.[59] The interdistrict plaintiffs faced the risks that they would not be able to prove liability and that even if they did, the findings of interdistrict constitutional violations might not support a comprehensive remedy including school district consolidation and substantial interdistrict student transfers. Given the uncertain outcome of the interdistrict litigation and the state's obligation to pay the costs of a voluntary interdistrict desegregation plan, I argued that the interdistrict plaintiffs and the suburban school districts had strong incentives to strike a mutually acceptable compromise.

Although I believed that it would be desirable to include the state in any new round of settlement negotiations,[60] I noted that the state's agreement to a settlement was no longer necessary. I suggested that the district court could approve a settlement between the interdistrict plaintiffs and the suburban school districts. Assuming such a settlement did not require the state to take any action that the district court could not otherwise order, there was no logical barrier to approval of a settlement notwithstanding the state's possible objections. In light of the court of appeals' determination that the state must bear the costs of voluntary interdistrict desegregation plans in order to remedy its intradistrict violation, it seemed unlikely that the terms of any reasonable settlement between the interdistrict plaintiffs and the suburban school districts would exceed the obligations that the district court could impose on the state independently under *Liddell V*.

On October 15, 1982, Judge Hungate appointed me Special Master "for the purpose of exploring possibilities of settlement" among the original Liddell plaintiffs, the NAACP, the Board of Education, 23 suburban school districts, the state of Missouri, the Department of Justice, the city of St. Louis, and St. Louis County.[61]

THE INTERDISTRICT SETTLEMENT

After the February 25, 1982, *Liddell V* judgment, the number of suburban school districts participating in the 12(a) voluntary plan grew from five to 14 under the nurturing of the district court and the pressure of the pending interdistrict litigation against non-participating districts. Until I was appointed Special Master on October 15, 1982, no consideration was given to the possibility that *Liddell V* provided the framework for a settlement. For the next four months until the eve of the interdistrict liability trial set for Valentine's Day, February 14, 1983, it was not clear whether the settlement negotiations would succeed. On February 14, 1983, I reported to the district court that settlement was a strong possibility, and the district court granted the first of many trial postponements to permit the parties to complete their settlement negotiations.[62] We submitted the Settlement Agreement on March 30, 1983,[63] and the district court approved it on July 5, 1983.[64] The interdistrict school desegregation plan of the Settlement Agreement was first implemented in the 1983–1984 school year. The court of appeals subsequently upheld the Settlement Agreement with a few modifications on February 8, 1984, and the Supreme Court declined to review the case.[65]

The Setting: Political Geography and Participants

The interdistrict school desegregation settlement involves both the city of St. Louis and St. Louis County. The boundaries of the city of St. Louis form a flat oval nestled against the Mississippi River on the east, and St. Louis County surrounds the city on the north, west, and south (see Figure 6-1). At the beginning of the 1982–1983 school year, the combined enrollment of the public schools in the city of St. Louis and in St. Louis County was 190,074.[66] The combined white enrollment was 115,641, or 60.84 percent, and the combined black enrollment was 74,433, or 39.16 percent. St. Louis County is in turn bordered on the south and west by Jefferson County and on the north and west by St. Charles County. Portions of both of these two counties are closer to the city of St. Louis than some of the suburban school districts in St. Louis County.

The city of St. Louis, an area of approximately 62 square miles, constitutes the city school system.[67] At the beginning of the 1982–1983 school year, the total enrollment in the city schools was 59,117. The white enrollment was 12,207, or 20.65 percent, and the black enrollment was 46,910, or 79.35 percent. The northern half of the city is predominately black, and the south side is predominately white. The central corridor is integrated. Even after implementation of the intradistrict plan, the schools reflected this racial division of the city. Some 30,000 black students were isolated in all-black schools on the predominately black north side,[68] and some 7,032 white and 7,168 black students attended integrated schools located in the central corridor and on the south side.[69]

St. Louis County is an area of 510 square miles, and it contains 23 suburban school districts and a Special School District, which is responsible for educating mentally and physically disabled children on a county-wide basis.[70] At the beginning of the 1982–1983 school year, the total enrollment

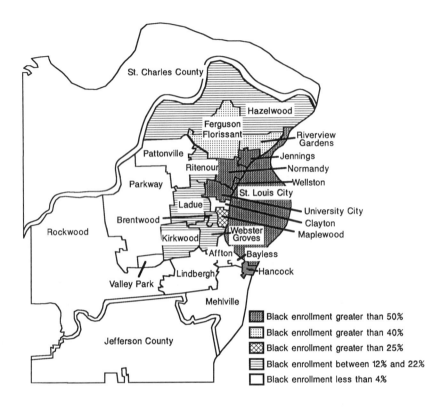

FIGURE 6-1. School Districts in St. Louis County and Percentage of Black Enrollment as of September 30, 1982

in St. Louis County schools, apart from the Special School District, was 130,957. The white enrollment was 103,434, or 78.98 percent, and the black enrollment was 27,523, or 21.02 percent. There were substantial differences between the 23 suburban school districts in terms of size, distance from the city, and percentage of black enrollment (see Table 6-1). The smallest district (Valley Park) had only 629 students, and the largest district (Parkway) had more than 20,000 students. Although some schools in the first ring of suburban districts were closer to the predominately black schools in north St. Louis city than city schools in south St. Louis, schools in outlying suburban districts like Rockwood were more than 35 miles from the city.

Black students attending county public schools were concentrated in six suburban school districts immediately adjacent or very close to the predominately black north side schools in the city of St. Louis. Four St. Louis County suburban school districts (Jennings, Normandy, University City, and Wellston) had black enrollments greater than 50 percent and a total of

TABLE 6-1. School District Enrollment for St. Louis County and the
city of St. Louis as of September 30, 1982

District	Total Enrollment	White	Black	Percent Black
Affton	2,067	2,064	3	.15
Bayless	1,336	1,334	2	.15
Brentwood	834	652	182	21.82
Clayton	1,573	1,553	20	1.27
Ferguson-Florissant	12,669	7,532	5,137	40.55
Hancock Place	1,447	1,442	5	.34
Hazelwood	17,129	14,148	2,981	17.40
Jennings	2,332	1,047	1,285	55.10
Kirkwood	4,496	3,682	764	17.18
Ladue	3,060	2,669	391	12.78
Lindbergh	5,546	5,502	44	.79
Maplewood	1,436	1,020	416	28.97
Mehlville	9,675	9,644	31	.32
Normandy	7,127	932	6,195	86.92
Parkway	20,693	20,283	410	1.98
Pattonville	6,535	6,292	243	3.72
Ritenour	6,456	5,617	839	13.00
Riverview Gardens	5,060	2,904	2,156	42.60
Rockwood	10,354	10,256	98	.95
University City	5,627	1,286	4,341	77.15
Valley Park	629	626	3	.48
Webster Groves	3,640	2,917	723	19.86
Wellston	1,261	7	1,254	99.45
Total St. Louis County	130,957	103,434	27,523	21.02
St. Louis City	59,117	12,207	46,910	79.35
Grand City/County Total	190,074	115,641	74,433	39.16

13,075 black students. Two other districts (Ferguson-Florissant and Riverview Gardens) had black enrollments of more than 40 percent and a total
of 7,293 black students. The combined black enrollment of these six districts was 20,368, or more than 74 percent of all the black students enrolled
in suburban St. Louis County public schools. Ten other suburban school
districts presented the opposite picture. These ten districts enrolled more
than 45 percent of all the public school students in St. Louis County, but

each district had a black enrollment under 4 percent. Between these two extremes, there were six suburban school districts with black enrollments between 12 and 22 percent, and one district with a black enrollment of almost 29 percent.

Consistent with the size and complexity of this metropolitan school desegregation case, there were more than 30 principal participants or parties represented by over 20 different lawyers and law firms. These participants or parties and their lawyers may be divided into three groups. The first group was the interdistrict plaintiffs, which included the Board of Education, the NAACP, and the original Liddell plaintiffs. The Board of Education of the city of St. Louis was a defendant in the intradistrict case and was held liable for violating the constitutional rights of black students in the city school system. The Board became an interdistrict plaintiff when the district court granted its motion to add the suburban school districts in St. Louis County as defendants.[71] Although the NAACP and the Liddell group were both certified as class representatives of all students, black and white, in the city of St. Louis and St. Louis County, these two groups more directly represented a class of black students. The focus of the Liddell group was black students in the city schools, especially the all-black schools that remained on the north side after implementation of the intradistrict plan. The NAACP focused on this group in addition to the black students who were concentrated in the six suburban St. Louis County school districts with black enrollments in excess of 40 percent. The NAACP and the Board of Education were represented by both local and national counsel. The Board, the NAACP, and the Liddell group worked closely together throughout the interdistrict component of the case, but they occasionally took different positions in light of the special demands and needs of their different constituencies.

The second group of participants was the defendants or potential defendants in the interdistrict case, and it included the 23 suburban school districts in St. Louis County and the state of Missouri. The major concerns of most of the suburban school districts were to avoid consolidation with the city school system and to avoid interdistrict transfer of white students to the city schools. Nevertheless, given important differences in size, location, level of black enrollment, and constituencies, the interests of these school districts were not monolithic. Moreover, 15 of these districts decided to participate in a voluntary interdistrict student transfer plan to avoid or postpone interdistrict litigation, and seven chose to proceed as defendants in the interdistrict case.[72] The 23 suburban school districts were represented by 14 different lawyers. Although the state of Missouri shared the major concerns of the suburban school districts, it had a separate, distinct interest in avoiding the imposition of the costs of an interdistrict desegregation plan.

The third group of participants included the city of St. Louis, St. Louis County, the Special School District of St. Louis County, and the Depart-

ment of Justice. The primary concern of the city of St. Louis was the effect any desegregation plan would have on its tax revenues. The city of St.
Louis feared that the demands of the Board of Education for revenue to
satisfy its desegregation obligations under any interdistrict plan might reduce the revenues needed for other public purposes. The chief concern
of St. Louis County was the possible effect of an interdistrict desegregation plan on housing. The Special School District of St. Louis County was
primarily interested in the question whether an interdistrict desegregation
plan for regular elementary and secondary schools would require any consolidation with the special education programs of the city school system.
It also was concerned about provisions for special services for handicapped
interdistrict transfer students. The Department of Justice could be grouped
with the interdistrict plaintiffs because it initially supported their efforts to
obtain some measure of interdistrict relief; however, its efforts were primarily directed to ensuring that any interdistrict desegregation plan would
be consistent with its policies for school desegregation.

*Preparations for Trial and Growth
of the 12(a) Voluntary Plan*

Shortly after *Liddell V* was decided, the district court held the
scheduled hearings on the proposed 12(c) plans[73] beginning on March 1,
1982. After the hearings were completed in late March and while the 12(c)
plans were under submission, the district court immediately proceeded with
preparations for trial.[74] Discovery, pretrial motions, and other trial preparations continued under the district court's direction and encouragement
throughout 1982.[75] On August 6, 1982, the district court issued an interim
order on the 12(c) plans.[76] This order strongly indicated that if liability were
found, the remedy would include the abolition of existing school districts
and consolidation into a single metropolitan school district, a uniform tax
rate, and reassignment of a substantial number of white county students to
the predominately black schools in the city of St. Louis.[77] Trial was set for
February 14, 1983.

While the case was proceeding down a path toward litigation of the issue
of interdistrict constitutional violations, the district court encouraged participation in the 12(a) voluntary plan.[78] The court denied the NAACP's motion to lift the stay of the interdistrict litigation,[79] and it also denied the Board
of Education's motion to condition the stay on the participating districts'
compliance with specific, enforceable yearly goals for accepting permissive
interdistrict transfer students.[80] Between April and September 1982, nine
additional suburban school districts joined the original five participants.[81]
Although the number of suburban school districts participating in the 12(a)
voluntary plan almost tripled, the interdistrict transfer program was still
quite limited in scope. At the start of the second semester of the 1982–83

school year, with 14 suburban school districts participating in the 12(a) voluntary plan, there were only 856 black city students attending school in a predominately white suburban school district and only 350 white county students attending school in the city of St. Louis.[82] Given some 30,000 black students attending all-black schools in the city, the 12(a) permissive interdistrict student transfer program did little to relieve segregated conditions in the city schools.

The growth of the voluntary plan was a direct response to the threat of the interdistrict litigation and to an assessment of the costs and benefits of participation in the 12(a) voluntary plan. Under the district court's 12(a) voluntary plan, the state paid transportation costs and a fiscal incentive to cover the costs of educating interdistrict transfer students, and the only "cost" to a suburban school district was that it had to accept a limited number of black students from the city school system. The number of permissive interdistrict transfer students that a participating district had to accept was quite small.[83] For example, Parkway, the largest suburban school district, with more than 20,000 students (see Table 6-1), was required to make spaces available for only 100 transfer students in the first year and 200 more transfer students in each succeeding year.

The principal benefit of participation was the stay of the interdistrict litigation. The stay permitted participating districts to avoid for an indefinite period the financial costs of interdistrict litigation.[84] It also permitted them to avoid, at least temporarily, the risk of a finding of liability and the imposition of a mandatory interdistrict desegregation plan.[85] A mandatory interdistrict desegregation plan seemed particularly threatening because the district court had already stated in tentatively approving a 12(c) plan that it would order consolidation of the suburban school districts with the city school district in a metropolitan school district and reassignment of white county students to the predominately black city schools.[86] For many suburban school districts, the benefits of a stay apparently outweighed the minor cost of accepting a limited number of black permissive interdistrict transfer students.

At the beginning of the 1982–1983 school year, 14 of the 23 suburban school districts in St. Louis County had agreed to participate in the district court's 12(a) voluntary plan, and a fifteenth district subsequently joined.[87] The interdistrict litigation against these participating districts had been stayed. Trial of the interdistrict case against the state and seven non-participating districts was set for February 14, 1983. The district court had tentatively approved a 12(c) mandatory plan, and it appeared that school district consolidation and interdistrict busing of white students into the black city schools would be the remedy if liability was established.

The Settlement Negotiations

Shuttle Diplomacy. During the first four months of my tenure as Special Master, my work could best be described as shuttle diplomacy. I met with the attorneys involved in the case only individually or in groups with common interests. I moved back and forth between the parties carrying pro-posals, counter-proposals and suggestions. I advanced the argument, which I had made in my then recently published article,[88] that *Liddell V* created a new framework for a settlement. I also used these initial meetings to gather information, to solicit and to discuss suggestions about the design of a pos-sible settlement, and to determine bargaining positions. There was broad agreement that three crucial provisions of the 12(a) voluntary plan should be incorporated in any settlement and should not be subject to negotiation. These three provisions were (1) no mandatory interdistrict student trans-fers; (2) no school district consolidation; and (3) the costs of the settlement, like the costs of the 12(a) plan, would be borne primarily by the state.

By early December 1982, I had identified "five principal elements" of a possible settlement that were to become the "five basic elements" of an Agreement in Principle that, in turn, would be the basis of the Settlement Agreement. The five principal elements included three that, at least when worded at a sufficiently high level of generality, were relatively uncontro-versial. The first "principal element" was the agreement of suburban school districts to accept black interdistrict transfer students from the city schools up to their plan ratio within a specific number of years. It was derived di-rectly from Foote's *Educational Plan* and the district court's 12(a) voluntary plan with one very significant qualification: There would be no "space avail-able" condition.[89] All student transfers would be voluntary, and I projected that it might be possible to provide an opportunity for up to 15,000 black students to transfer to suburban schools. The second "principal element" was the establishment of magnet schools to attract white county students to the city school system. It also was derived from the *Educational Plan* and the 12(a) plan and was relatively uncontroversial. The third "principal ele-ment" was new: improvement of the quality of education in the city schools. It included a proposal to make special provisions for all-black schools on the theory that even if there were a large number of interdistrict transfers, a substantial number of black students would remain in one-race schools in the city. Although it was new, the general notion of improving the quality of education was easy to support.

The fourth and fifth elements together presented the crucial issue in the settlement negotiations. The fourth element combined provisions to ensure that the first three elements, especially the interdistrict transfer provisions of element one, would be carried out fully and fairly with provisions to ensure that they would have a substantial effect in reducing segregation in the city schools. The fifth element was a mechanism to ensure that the settlement would be a final resolution of the case and that no obligations beyond those assumed under the first three elements would subsequently be imposed on the defendants.

The interdistrict plaintiffs were reluctant to agree to element five, a final settlement, because it could not be known in advance how effective the first three elements would be in reducing segregation. They preferred a "stay" pending implementation of the first three elements with an opportunity to renew litigation if the provisions of a settlement plan were not effective. A "stay," however, was not acceptable to many of the suburban school districts because the nature and extent of their obligations would not be settled. Only a final settlement would provide the certainty that their obligations were limited to the terms of any settlement plan and that no additional obligations could be imposed. Thus, the crucial issue was to provide the interdistrict plaintiffs with a guarantee that a settlement plan would have a significant effect in relieving segregation of the city schools (the fourth element) consistent with the interdistrict defendants' demands for a final settlement (the fifth element). The failure to resolve this same issue was one of the reasons why Chairman Foote's earlier efforts to settle the interdistrict case had fallen short.[90]

In December 1982, I conducted a second round of meetings with all of the attorneys, either individually or in appropriate groups with common interests, and explained the "five principal elements." The focus of these meetings, and of all my subsequent efforts, was to devise a means of resolving the conflict between the fourth and fifth elements. The parties worked hard to devise an appropriate compromise of these two elements and produced several innovative and thoughtful suggestions. In January and the first week of February, I discussed proposals and counter-proposals with the parties. On February 10, on the basis of both desperation and a nascent sense that a solution to the conflicting demands for a stay and a final settlement could be designed, I decided, for the first time, to reduce the five elements to a formal written proposal and to draft several potential compromises on the fourth and fifth elements. I circulated this formal proposal to all of the attorneys, and we discussed them at great length over the weekend of February 12–13. On the eve of the interdistrict trial, I decided that a satisfactory solution was at hand: a stay of the litigation coupled with both (1) the possibility of obtaining a final judgment during the period of the stay and (2) limitations on any further relief that could be imposed after the stay expired. With the assent of all the parties, I asked the court to postpone the interdistrict litigation for one day and to order the parties to attempt to hammer out an agreement in principle.

The Agreement in Principle.   Monday, February 14, 1983, was the date set both for my report on the progress of the settlement negotiations[91] and for the beginning of the interdistrict trial. I reported that, after some 250 hours of preliminary negotiations through the Special Master, direct negotiations between the parties might be fruitful in light of some promising developments in the last 48 hours. The court granted a series of short trial postponements to continue the settlement negotiations. During the 60-hour period from Monday morning through Wednesday afternoon, the lawyers negotiated for more than 40 hours before reaching an agreement in principle to settle the interdistrict case.[92] Late on the afternoon of Wednesday, February 16, I reported to the court that the attorneys for the Liddell plaintiffs, the NAACP, the Board of Education, and 20 of the 23 suburban school districts had reached an Agreement in Principle (AIP) to settle the interdistrict case and would recommend it to their clients. Following this report, the court granted my request that the attorneys be given until Tuesday, February 22, 1983 to report whether their clients had accepted the AIP.[93]

The AIP that the attorneys presented to their clients marked in broad outline the terms of a final settlement, and it admittedly left "many significant subsidiary issues and details" to be resolved.[94] The AIP tracked closely the form of my February 10 proposal and many of the basic points were unchanged. The negotiations, however, did produce some substantial modifications and additions. Instead of "three crucial provisions,"[95] the AIP now stated that there were "four critical propositions" to be incorporated explicitly in the final settlement. The first two propositions, like their predecessors, forbade mandatory interdistrict student transfers and school district consolidation. The third critical proposition was that the costs of the settlement would be paid "by such combination of State funding and a tax rate increase in the City of St. Louis as shall be ordered by the Court."[96] The reference to a tax rate increase was new. The fourth proposition was also new. The AIP now provided that "black students in suburban school districts that have a minority enrollment of 50% or greater would enjoy the [interdistrict] transfer rights."[97] This last critical proposition marked a significant expansion of the settlement. Under this proposition, black students in the four suburban school districts with a black enrollment in excess of 50 percent,[98] as well as black students in the city schools, could transfer to the 16 predominately white suburban school districts.

Although the five "principal" elements of my formal February 10 proposal were renamed the five "basic" elements in the AIP, the first three elements emerged from the negotiations with few changes. Like its predecessor,[99] the first element still provided that the suburban school districts would accept black transfer students from the city, but it now specified that the plan ratio would be achieved in five years.[100] The second and third elements providing for magnet schools and quality education improvements in the city schools were essentially the same.[101] The major accomplishment of the negotiations leading to the AIP was the resolution in principle of the crucial issue of providing the interdistrict plaintiffs with an adequate guarantee that a settlement plan would relieve effectively segregation of the city schools (the fourth element) consistent with the interdistrict defendants' demands for a final settlement (the fifth element).

The AIP resolved this problem in part by specifying in element four "[p]rovisions to ensure that the proposed settlement will be carried out fully and fairly and that it will have a substantial impact."[102] Element five, however, was the key. In this fifth element, the parties designed an innovative stay provision.[103] Litigation would be stayed for five years to permit full implementation of the provisions for interdistrict transfers, magnet schools, and quality education improvements in the city schools. This five-year stay was designed to answer the interdistrict plaintiffs' concern that the effectiveness of any desegregation plan could be judged only after the fact of implementation. This stay was then coupled with two significant provisions designed to answer the demands of the suburban school districts for both certainty and a limitation on the obligations that could be imposed on them beyond the terms of any settlement plan. The fifth element of the AIP coupled the five-year stay with an opportunity for the suburban school districts to obtain a final judgment during the stay if they achieved their specific obligations to accept interdistrict transfer students. It also coupled the five-year stay with limitations on the obligations, if any, that could be imposed on the suburban school districts after the stay expired. The AIP provided that if a suburban school district failed to fulfill its obligations to accept black interdistrict transfer students within five years, the plaintiffs would first pursue negotiation. If these negotiations failed, the interdistrict plaintiffs could impose further obligations on the suburban school districts that had failed to meet their obligations only if they established liability after trial. Moreover, the remedy that could be ordered by the courts was limited. The interdistrict plaintiffs agreed not to seek either school district consolidation or minority enrollment in excess of 25 percent.

After the lawyers had submitted the AIP to their clients, I reported on February 22, 1983, that the Board of Education, the NAACP, the Liddell plaintiffs, and 22 of the 23 suburban school districts accepted the Agreement in Principle "subject to the drafting of a detailed implementation plan consistent with the agreement in principle and satisfactory to the parties."[104] Only one suburban school district, Riverview Gardens, did not approve the AIP. Although I requested 60 days for the parties to draft the detailed implementation plan, Judge Hungate ordered that this plan be submitted within 30 days, on March 24, 1983, and he set trial against Riverview Gardens for April 11, 1983.[105]

Drafting the Settlement Agreement. In the short period of 30 days set by Judge Hungate's order, the parties faced the difficult task of converting the broad principles of the Agreement in Principle into the precise, detailed terms of a Settlement Agreement. The dimensions of this task are suggested by the fact that the ten-page, double-spaced AIP was converted into a 75-page, single-spaced Settlement Agreement with a 270-page appendix describing quality education programs for the city schools. Although the negotiations over the terms of the settlement must remain confidential, the attorneys for the interdistrict plaintiffs and the suburban school districts that had adopted the AIP ultimately reached an agreement after many volatile meetings and after the court granted a six-day extension.

On March 30, we filed the Settlement Agreement. In my report, I noted that the attorneys for the interdistrict plaintiffs and the suburban school districts had not yet had an opportunity to submit this detailed plan for implementing the AIP to their clients, and I asked that the parties be granted until April 4, 1983, to report whether they would adopt the detailed plan as a settlement agreement.[106] I also noted that the state, the city of St. Louis, St. Louis County, and the Department of Justice had not participated in the drafting of the Settlement Agreement and suggested that they be ordered to report on the same date whether they would adopt it. At this time, we also filed a memorandum outlining the procedures and standards for approval of a class action settlement.[107] By an order issued the next day, the district court adopted the April 4, 1983, reporting date and kept in force the April 11, 1983, trial date.[108]

The Terms of the Settlement Agreement

The parties adopted the Settlement Agreement to settle both the 12(c) proceedings and the interdistrict litigation initiated by the January 1981 motions of the NAACP and the Board of Education to add the suburban school districts in St. Louis County as defendants.[109] The settlement, which incorporates the Agreement in Principle,[110] is a complex document. The principal components of the Settlement Agreement are (1) provisions for voluntary interdistrict transfers and related provisions for a stay of the 12(c) proceedings and the interdistrict litigation; (2) provisions for the establishment of magnet schools; and (3) provisions to improve the quality of education in the city schools and to make capital improvements in the facilities. In addition to these components, the Settlement Agreement includes significant provisions that establish hiring goals for black teachers and administrators and that create a program of voluntary teacher exchanges between the city and county schools.[111] It also establishes a Voluntary Interdistrict Coordinating Council (VICC) to administer the interdistrict student transfer and faculty exchange programs.[112] Finally, the Settlement Agreement makes explicit provisions for financing.

Voluntary Interdistrict Transfers.   A key aspect of the Settlement Agreement is that all interdistrict student transfers are voluntary.[113] The

TABLE 6-2. Suburban School Districts with Minority Enrollment Under 25 Percent in Fall 1982

Participating District	Plan Ratio (Percent Black)	Plan Goal (Percent Black)
Affton	15.15	25
Bayless	15.15	25
Brentwood	25.00	25
Clayton	16.27	25
Hancock Place	15.34	25
Hazelwood	25.00	25
Kirkwood	25.00	25
Ladue	25.00	25
Lindbergh	15.79	25
Mehlville	15.32	25
Parkway	16.98	25
Pattonville	18.72	25
Ritenour	25.00	25
Rockwood	15.95	25
Valley Park	15.48	25
Webster Groves	25.00	25

settlement establishes a ratio of 25 percent black students and 75 percent white students as the "plan goal," and the "plan ratio" is "an increase of black student enrollment of 15 percentage points or achievement of the plan goal, whichever is less."[114] On the basis of each suburban school district's minority enrollment in the fall of 1982, the Settlement Agreement creates three groups of school districts with distinct obligations. The first group includes the 16 suburban school districts with a minority enrollment of less than 25 percent,[115] shown in Table 6-2. The second group includes four suburban school districts (Jennings, Normandy, University City, and Wellston) with a minority enrollment in excess of 50 percent and the St. Louis city schools.[116] The third group includes three suburban school districts (Ferguson-Florissant, Riverview Gardens, and Maplewood-Richmond Heights) with a black resident student enrollment between 25 percent and 50 percent.[117]

The 16 suburban school districts with a minority enrollment of less than 25 percent in the fall of 1982 have an obligation under the settlement to accept black transfer students and either to increase minority enrollment by 15 percent or to achieve a minority enrollment of 25 percent, whichever is less.[118] The interdistrict litigation against these 16 school districts is stayed for five years.[119] Each one of these districts that achieves its plan ratio within five years "is entitled to a final judgment declaring that it has satisfied its interdistrict pupil desegregation obligations."[120] After obtaining a final judgment, a suburban school district's "only continuing interdistrict obligations" are to participate in the promotion and recruitment of interdistrict transfer students and to accept such students in order to reach and maintain the plan goal of a 25 percent minority enrollment.[121]

If any one of the 16 districts with an original minority enrollment of less than 25 percent does not meet its plan ratio within five years, the settlement contemplates further negotiations and an extension of the stay if the interdistrict plaintiffs and the particular suburban school district can reach an agreement.[122] If the parties to these negotiations do not reach an agreement, then any one of the interdistrict plaintiffs has a two-year period in which to renew the litigation against a school district that fails to achieve its plan ratio within the five-year period of the original stay.[123] In such litigation, the interdistrict plaintiffs must prove liability, and the plaintiffs agreed in the settlement that they would not seek school district consolidation or minority enrollment in excess of 25 percent as remedies.[124]

In contrast to the detailed obligations of the 16 suburban school districts with minority enrollments of less than 25 percent, the other seven school districts in St. Louis County with a minority enrollment in excess of 25 percent have no substantial interdistrict transfer obligations. The settlement entitles these seven districts to an immediate final judgment that they have satisfied their pupil desegregation obligations.[125] Prior to judicial modification,[126] the settlement provided that the four suburban school districts with a minority enrollment in excess of 50 percent had only two obligations. These obligations, which were in fact rights or opportunities to reduce racial imbalance, were to establish magnet schools to increase white enrollment and to cooperate in the interdistrict transfer of their black students to the 16 predominately white suburban school districts.[127] The three suburban school districts with a minority enrollment between 25 percent and 50 percent have an obligation only to facilitate the transfer of their white students who chose to enroll in St. Louis city schools.[128]

As drafted and prior to judicial modification,[129] the settlement provided that black students in the four suburban school districts with a minority enrollment in excess of 50 percent and students in the city school system could transfer to the 16 predominately white suburban school districts,[130] and it established a complex formula for allocating the transfer rights between black students in the four suburban school districts and black students in the city school system.[131] It also authorizes white students in the 19 suburban school districts with a white enrollment in excess of 50 percent to transfer to the city schools.[132] In addition to these eligibility criteria for interdistrict transfers, the settlement also grants interdistrict transfer students a broad right to choose the particular school district and school in which they will become students.[133] It sets standards to ensure that transfer students are treated equitably under the same standards that apply to students of the host district.[134] The Settlement Agreement assigns to the state the responsibility of providing transportation.[135]

Magnet Schools. Provisions for the establishment of magnet schools are the second principal component of the Settlement Agreement.[136] Although the court of appeals has modified these provisions substantially,[137] the settlement sets an ambitious, and at least with the benefit of hindsight, unrealistic goal of up to 20,000 students in magnet schools. It provides that a minimum of 12,000 students would be served by magnet schools in the city and a maximum of 8,000 would be served by magnets in the suburban school districts.[138] The settlement establishes a student enrollment goal in magnet schools of 50 percent black and 50 percent white with a 10 percent variance,[139] and it also establishes eligibility criteria and standards for allocating magnet school seats between black students in the predominately black suburban school districts and black students in the city schools.[140] Planning, approval, and evaluation of magnet schools are assigned to a Magnet Review Committee composed of two representatives of the Board of Education, two representatives of the suburban school districts, one representative selected by the NAACP and the Liddell plaintiffs, and one representative of the state.[141]

Quality Education and Capital Improvements in City School Facilities. The drafters of the Settlement Agreement recognized that, even after full implementation of both the voluntary interdistrict transfer and magnet school programs, approximately 10,000 to 15,000 black students would remain in all-black city schools.[142] For these students, the provisions for improvements in the quality of education and for capital improvements in school facilities are the key components of the settlement.[143] Although all of the parties to the Settlement Agreement stated that they "recognize the importance of the concept of the improvement of the quality of education in schools in the City of St. Louis and their responsibility to submit specific provisions concerning same to the Court,"[144] they did not reach an agreement on specific programs. Instead, they reported that the Board of Education had developed a quality education program "of the kind and scope to satisfy" the quality education requirements of the Agreement in Principle.[145] This quality education program was attached as an appendix and was summarized in section IV of the Settlement Agreement. The suburban school districts, however, did not endorse any specific quality education programs.[146]

The quality education component of the settlement provides for both district-wide improvements and for improvements in the all-black schools. The district-wide programs include the restoration and maintenance of art, music, and physical education programs to state AAA standards,[147] the establishment of pre-school centers and all-day kindergarten classes, staff expansion, and programs to improve planning and curriculum development. The special provisions for the all-black schools include a broad array of compensatory and remedial programs. The most visible, and perhaps the most important, part of the quality education package are the provisions for reduction of the pupil–teacher ratios. In the 1982–1983 school year, the pupil–teacher ratio in the city schools was at best 35 to 1, and in many schools it was probably higher. The Settlement Agreement calls for a district-wide reduction of the pupil–teacher ratio to 25 to 1, which was believed to be the average pupil–teacher ratio in St. Louis County.[148] It also calls for a further reduction in the pupil–teacher ratio in the all-black schools to 20 to 1.[149]

In addition to these programs to improve the quality of education, the Board of Education described the general condition of the city schools as "one of rapid deterioration, extreme deferred maintenance, and general old age." [150] Given these conditions, the quality education package calls for "a major deferred maintenance program [and] a general improvement, renovation and modernization program." [151]

Financial Provisions. The Settlement Agreement assigns all costs either to the state or to the Board of Education, the two entities that had been held liable for operating a dual, segregated school system in the city of St. Louis. Under a complex formula, the state must make payments to both the home and host school districts for each interdistrict transfer student.[152] These payments, which were called "fiscal incentives" in earlier voluntary plans,[153] are, on average, approximately two times what the state would otherwise have paid per pupil if the student had not made an interdistrict transfer from the city school system to a suburban school district.[154] The payment to a host district is designed to cover that district's incremental costs, and the payment to home districts is designed to assist districts that experience a net loss of students through interdistrict transfers to maintain educational quality for students remaining in the district.[155] The Settlement Agreement also requires the state to pay the attorneys' fees of the interdistrict plaintiffs.[156]

All other costs under the settlement are to be paid by "such combination of additional State funding [under *Liddell V*] and a tax rate increase in the City of St. Louis as shall be ordered by the Court." [157] These "other costs" specifically include

[t]he cost of the incentives for . . . voluntary teacher exchanges, . . . the cost of student recruitment, start-up costs and building modification costs of

new magnet schools and expanded magnet costs to schools programs, one-time extraordinary costs . . . such as the costs associated with reopening a closed school, the costs of community involvment [sic] centers and part-time educational programs, transportation of transferring pupils, the operating expense of the VICC, . . . [and] the costs relating to the improvements in educational programs offered by the City Board.[158]

Although the settlement gives the court broad discretion to allocate these "other costs" of the settlement between the state and the Board of Education, *Liddell V* had assigned the state responsibility for the costs of a very broad range of voluntary interdistrict desegregation measures.[159] Thus, it was reasonable to assume that most of these "other costs" would be assigned to the state and not to the Board of Education.

Adoption, Approval, and Modification of the Settlement Agreement

Adoption by the Interdistrict Plaintiffs and Suburban School Districts. Between March 30 and April 4, the NAACP,[160] the Liddell plaintiffs,[161] the Board of Education,[162] and 22 of the 23 suburban school districts[163] in St. Louis County reported to the court that they had accepted the detailed implementation plan as a settlement agreement. Two suburban school districts, Rockwood and Mehlville, however, adopted the implementation plan only on the condition, inconsistent with the terms of the settlement, that the court could terminate their obligations on a showing of "good cause."[164] The University City school district, which was an original member of the 12(a) voluntary plan and a signatory to the AIP,[165] was the only suburban school district that declined to adopt the implementation plan as a settlement.[166] University City, one of the four predominately black (77.15 percent) suburban school districts, explained its decision on the grounds that its participation would not relieve segregation of the city schools and that the settlement's provisions for funds to improve the quality of education in the city schools and not in the University City school system were inequitable because both school systems were approximately 75 percent black.[167]

Four other parties, who had not participated in the settlement negotiations, also filed reports. St. Louis County reported that, to the extent that the settlement was acceptable to the suburban school districts, it had "no objection that the Settlement Agreement as drafted be implemented according to its terms."[168] The city of St. Louis declined to adopt the settlement because of the financing provisions.[169] The city complained that the allocation of costs to city residents rather than residents of suburban school districts was inequitable and that a court-ordered tax increase would make it harder for the municipality, which has a finite tax base, to raise funds for other public needs. Finally, the city argued that a court-ordered tax increase would be unconstitutional. The Department of Justice declined to endorse the settlement fully because its concerns about the Agreement in Principle [170] had not been addressed by the detailed implementation plan.[171]

The state of Missouri submitted "comments on the settlement agreement," responded that it could not "in good conscience accept portions of the settlement agreement," and requested "a full and complete hearing on all the issues" raised in its comments.[172] Although the state generally applauded the efforts to reach a voluntary settlement,[173] it objected strongly to the financing provisions of the settlement. The state recognized the Special Master's theory that it could be ordered to fund the settlement agreement without its assent,[174] but it complained about the total cost of the settlement, which it estimated at $100 million annually. In particular, the state objected that the costs of the "fiscal incentives" for interdistrict student transfers were "excessive" and that the quality education component was "a blank check [issued to the Board of Education] to rebuild its entire school system." [175]

Two days after receipt of the reports of the parties on acceptance of the settlement, the court met with counsel to discuss the next steps in the proceedings.[176] At the court's direction, on April 7, 1983, I submitted a proposed order setting a hearing on the settlement and a proposed notice of a class action settlement.[177] On April 8, 1983, the court set the stage for approval of the Settlement Agreement. It scheduled a fairness hearing on the settlement and funding issues for April 28, 1983,[178] approved a notice of a class action settlement,[179] and reset the interdistrict liability trial for two weeks after its ruling on the proposed settlement "unless rendered moot by the Court's approval of the proposed settlement after the fairness hearing." [180]

The Fairness Hearing.   Both the city of St. Louis and the state objected to the adequacy of the class notice and the timing of the fairness hearing,[181] but the court rejected their arguments.[182] The fairness hearing began as scheduled on April 28, 1983, and continued over five days through mid-May. The principal issues at this hearing were whether the Settlement Agreement should be approved as a "fair, reasonable and adequate" settlement of the class action and how the programs established by the Settlement Agreement should be funded. Given the statement in the Settlement Agreement that the suburban school districts neither agreed nor disagreed with the specific quality education programs in the appendix,[183] the court also had some concern about the quality education component of the settlement.[184] At the beginning of the hearings, the court directed the submission of specific programs and cost estimates so that interested parties could comment on the quality education provisions.[185]

At the fairness hearing the court considered first the arguments of the signatories in support of the agreement. The interdistrict plaintiffs and the suburban school districts that had adopted the settlement agreement without conditions submitted a joint memorandum in support of the settlement,[186] and they also coordinated their testimony. During the course of these presentations, the Board of Education presented a refined version of the quality education component of the settlement (Exhibit 2) and a proposed first year budget (Exhibit 3) of $87 million. After the conclusion of the fairness hearing, the signatories responded to the court's concern about the status of their agreement on the quality education component of the Settlement Agreement. They reported agreement "concerning Section IV of the Settlement Agreement [quality education summary] and that Exhibit 2, along with [Section] III.1 of the Agreement on magnet schools and related material, provide a basis for implementing the quality education and magnet portions of the Settlement Agreement."[187]

In addition to the arguments of the proponents of the settlement, the court considered the status of the two suburban school districts (Rockwood and Mehlville) that had adopted the settlement conditionally,[188] the position of the Department of Justice,[189] a wide range of public comments,[190] and the objections of the state and the city of St. Louis. The state argued that the costs of the settlement made it unfair and unreasonable and that the court lacked the power to impose these costs on a party that had rejected the settlement.[191] The state strongly objected to (1) the costs of the quality education component of the settlement, which it estimated as between $87 million annually and $125 million annually for five years; (2) the costs of capital improvements, which it estimated at $30 million annually for eight years; and (3) the costs of additional staff, which it estimated at $57 million. The state also objected to the fiscal incentives, which it characterized as a windfall to participating school districts, and to transportation costs that it estimated at $1,100 per student. The city of St. Louis argued vehemently that any court-ordered tax increase would be unconstitutional and that the imposition of a tax increase only on city residents, and not on county residents, would be inequitable.[192]

After the conclusion of the fairness hearing on May 17, 1983, two significant events occurred prior to the court's approval of the Settlement Agreement on July 5, 1983. First, University City, the only suburban school district that had declined to adopt the Settlement Agreement, decided to adopt it on June 1, 1983.[193] The second major event before the approval of the Settlement Agreement was the court's decision to appoint a financial advisor, Dr. Warren M. Brown, and to order him to submit a report on the financial aspects of the proposed settlement.[194] On June 13, 1983, Dr. Brown submitted his report,[195] and this report subsequently had a very significant effect on the approval and implementation of the Settlement Agreement.

Dr. Brown recommended that the quality education component should be implemented in phases, and his estimate of $37 million for the first year was substantially lower than both the Board of Education's estimate of $87 million and the state's projection of up to $125 million annually. He also recommended a budget approval process for resolving disputes about quality education programs. He proposed that the Board of Education should revise its quality education proposals and provide more detailed justifications for each of its programs. Then, under the supervision of the court, the Board and the state would meet to resolve any disputes about particular programs or levels of funding for programs to be implemented in the following years. Dr. Brown also recommended a variety of methods to reduce the costs of fiscal incentives, interdistrict transportation, and capital improvements. He canvassed all possible sources of funding, made suggestions about the allocation of settlement costs among the state, the Board of Education, and the suburban school districts, and recommended a local tax rate increase in the city of St. Louis.

District Court Approval. On July 5, 1983, the district court approved the Settlement Agreement including the Appendix and Exhibit 2 as "fair, reasonable, adequate, and constitutionally permissible" and ordered implementation in the upcoming 1983–1984 school year.[196] The district court devised a creative solution to the conditional acceptances of Rockwood and Mehlville,[197] and it approved ten of the 12 sections of the Settlement Agreement "without substantive change." Although the court described its rulings on the other two sections, Section IV (Quality Education) and Section X (Financing), as "non-substantive," [198] they were in fact quite significant. The district court's rulings resolved the ambiguities of the quality education component and established a framework for financing the settlement. In the short run, the rulings on quality education and funding were sufficient to permit implementation to begin, but in the long run, they set the stage for continuing litigation over the implementation of the Settlement Agreement.

With regard to the quality education component, the district court concluded that, notwithstanding some "apparent lack of agreement on the programs listed in the Appendix and its companion Exhibit 2," the signatories (the interdistrict plaintiffs and the suburban school districts) had agreed to a limited set of programs that were referenced in portions of the settlement other than Section IV on quality education.[199] These programs, which were not identified precisely, should be "among the earliest implemented." [200] Apart from this indefinite, limited set of quality education programs, the district court did not determine the extent to which the programs in the Appendix and Exhibit 2 were approved. The specific approval of the settlement, the Appendix, and Exhibit as "fair, reasonable, adequate, and constitutionally permissible" suggested full approval of the quality education component. Nevertheless, the district court's statement that it "is not expressing either endorsement or disapproval of all the programs mentioned in the Appendix or Exhibit 2, nor is the Court intending to limit or preclude consideration of additional quality education programs" suggested less than complete approval of the quality education program as submitted.[201]

The actual resolution was to create a budget review process[202] to determine over time the precise contours of the quality education component of the settlement. The court adopted the financial advisor's recommendation that for each year of implementation the Board of Education should refine its quality education programs and present them to the state for its consideration. Then the state and the Board of Education should meet, with the possible assistance of the financial advisor, to identify their areas of agreement and disagreement. Any disagreements over the budget would then be resolved by the court. The parties to the settlement, however, had failed to agree completely on the quality education component,[203] and the court did not fill this gap. By deferring approval of specific quality education programs to a budget review process requiring the two principal antagonists, the state and the Board of Education, to negotiate and to compromise, the district court ensured continuing conflict and litigation over the implementation of the quality education component of the Settlement Agreement.[204]

The district court's decision on magnet schools had a similar result. The court adopted the financial advisor's recommendation that new magnet schools should be instituted "only after a rigorous needs assessment."[205] The Settlement Agreement provides that a set of magnet schools and programs listed in the agreement are "authorized but not mandated" for implementation in the first two years of the plan.[206] Any other magnet schools subsequently created are subject to review and evaluation by a Magnet Review Committee.[207] In the absence of a mandate in the settlement that the first and second year magnets be established, the district court directed the "plan participants to analyze and review the need of each expanded and new magnet proposed for 1983–1984 and 1984–1985 prior to the program's implementation."[208] This order effectively postponed full implementation of the magnet school component of the settlement and encouraged the state to resist through litigation the establishment of magnet schools.

Although its rulings on quality education and magnet schools reduced the initial costs of the settlement and made the imposition of any funding order easier, the district court did not determine a precise first-year settlement plan budget. Instead, it merely noted the wide range of estimates.[209] Even though the first year budget was not settled, the district court still had the responsibility under the settlement to allocate the costs between the state and the Board of Education and to ensure adequate financing for the settlement's programs.[210] The district court did allocate the costs and devise a financing plan to ensure that the budgets would be funded, but the financing issues, which the signatories had left to the court, were resolved only in the short run. These issues, as well as the court's determinations about magnets and quality education, would become the subject of litigation during implementation of the settlement.

The court initially approved the assignment of the costs of the settlement to the state and the Board of Education. The court found that "primary responsibility for funding the Settlement Plan rests with those parties who have been adjudicated as liable under the Constitution for segregated conditions with the City's public schools—the State of Missouri and the Board of Education of the City of St. Louis."[211] The court determined that it had the authority under *Liddell V*[212] to order the state to fund the settlement.[213] It also held that it had the authority to order the Board of Education to increase its tax rate.[214] Although the court declined to order a general tax rate increase to fund the Board of Education's share of settlement costs, it did prohibit a scheduled tax decrease.[215] Under a state law adopted by the voters in the fall of 1982 (Proposition C), school officials were required to reduce their property taxes by an amount equal to 50 percent of the revenues that school districts would receive under a new increase of the state sales tax. The district court enjoined the scheduled property tax rollback and ordered the Board of Education to use the approximately $9 million produced to fund, in part, its share of the first year settlement plan costs.

In addition to approving the assignment of settlement costs to the state and the Board of Education, the court also allocated these costs and established a plan for the Board of Education to fund its share. The court allocated most of the costs of the Settlement Agreement to the state. It adopted a general formula that allocated to the state and the Board 50 percent of the reasonable, actual costs of programs implemented within the city of St. Louis and that allocated to the state 100 percent of the reasonable, actual costs of programs implemented outside of the city.[216] The principal consequence of this formula was to allocate on a 50–50 basis the costs of quality education programs. Apart from this formula, the court specifically allocated to the state the actual, reasonable costs of magnet programs and schools, part-time educational programs, interdistrict transportation and other provisions of the settlement related to interdistrict student transportation, and attorneys' fees for the interdistrict plaintiffs. Moreover, the court specifically approved the provisions of the Settlement Agreement making the state responsible for the "fiscal incentives" for interdistrict student transfers.[217] The court assigned principal responsibility for capital improvements to the Board of Education, but it also provided that "[a]ny amount raised for capital expenditures through a voter-approved bond issue at any time during 1983–1984 shall be matched equally by the State of Missouri."[218]

Although the court gave the state the discretion to determine the source of funds to pay its share,[219] it entered a detailed order governing how the Board should fund its share of settlement costs.[220] The court ordered the Board to certify the amount needed to finance its share and the tax rate necessary to fund these costs. It directed the Board to submit a bond issue to finance capital improvements in school facilities to the voters before February 8, 1984. If the bond issue failed, the court indicated that it would consider an appropriate order. If the funds generated by enjoining the scheduled tax rollback were not sufficient, the court stated that it would consider an appropriate order to increase the property tax rate.

After the district court upheld the Settlement Agreement, the plan was first implemented at the beginning of the 1983–1984 school year. Although the city of St. Louis filed a petition for a writ of prohibition and the state sought a stay pending appeal, the court of appeals denied these applications in September 1983.[221] Halfway through the first year of implementation, the court of appeals sustained the Settlement Agreement with some significant modifications and additions.

Liddell VII—*The Court of Appeals' Approval and Modification of the Settlement Agreement.* The state of Missouri, the city of St. Louis, the North St. Louis Parents and Citizens for Quality Education, and the St. Louis teachers union appealed from the district court's order approving the settlement.[222] The court of appeals upheld the Settlement Agreement with some significant modifications of its voluntary interdistrict transfer, magnet schools, and quality education components. These changes, in the aggregate, substantially reduced the state's financial obligations.[223] The court of appeals also ordered the establishment of a Budget Review Committee, which was a major addition to the district court's funding provisions. In light of these changes, the court of appeals offered the signatories the option of accepting the changes or proceeding to trial.[224] All of the signatories chose to accept the Settlement Agreement as modified.[225]

Most of the changes made by the court of appeals in the voluntary interdistrict transfer and magnet schools components of the Settlement Agreement were completely warranted. *Liddell V* had held that the state was liable for the costs of interdistrict measures designed to remedy its established intradistrict constitutional violation.[226] The Settlement Agreement contained provisions that were not designed to remedy segregation in the city schools and that instead were designed to relieve racial imbalance in the four predominately black suburban school districts. These provisions, which were not part of the original settlement proposal, were added during the course of negotiations over the AIP and the Settlement Agreement.[227] Recognizing that the state's liability was limited to measures related to desegregation of the city schools, the court of appeals disapproved the settlement provisions requiring state funding for relief of racial imbalance in the suburban school districts in St. Louis County. Although these changes were correct, they substantially disrupted the expectations of some of the signatories.

The court of appeals made two major changes in the voluntary inter-district transfer component of the Settlement Agreement. First, it placed a limit of 15,000 on interdistrict transfers from the city to the suburban school districts.[228] The Settlement Agreement did not contain any such limit,[229] and the court of appeals apparently imposed this limit as a means of reducing the state's costs. The 15,000 cap on interdistrict transfers is a potential concern for all of the signatories. Assuming that more than 15,000 black city students eventually may be interested in interdistrict transfers, this ruling limits the capacity of interdistrict transfers to desegregate city schools. Again assuming demand in excess of 15,000, the cap on interdistrict transfers may at some point interfere with the ability of suburban school districts either initially to reach their plan ratios or plan goals or subsequently to reach and maintain their plan goal of a 25 percent minority enrollment.

The second change that the court of appeals made in the interdistrict transfer program was based on the limits of the state's liability for its intradistrict violation. The court disapproved state funding for student transfers between suburban school districts in St. Louis County because these county-to-county transfers were not designed to remedy the intradistrict violation in the city of St. Louis.[230] This change has a major impact on the four predominately black school districts in St. Louis County. It eliminates the possibility of reducing the concentration of black students either by black student transfers to one of the 16 predominately white suburban districts or by transfers of white students into one of these four districts. The disapproval of county-to-county transfers also has a potentially negative impact on the 16 predominately white suburban school districts. It reduces the number of black students who can transfer to these districts to satisfy their plan ratio and plan goal obligations. Because some of the four predominately black districts are geographically closer to some of the predominately white suburban districts, county-to-county transfers were viewed by some, at the time of the settlement, as a particularly important means of meeting their pupil desegregation obligations under the settlement.

Notwithstanding these two major changes, the court of appeals approved the rest of the voluntary interdistrict transfer component of the Settlement Agreement governing city-to-county interdistrict transfers. It reaffirmed the state's liability for the costs of interdistrict transfers between the city and suburban schools.[231] It upheld the district court's order approving the settlement provisions requiring the state to pay fiscal incentives to both home and host districts and directing the state to pay interdistrict transportation costs.[232] The court of appeals also specifically approved the Settlement

Agreement provisions for a final judgment for suburban school districts that satisfy their pupil desegregation obligations.[233] Because the 15,000 cap may never come into play and county-to-county transfers were not the major focus of the settlement, the court of appeals properly concluded that these changes "do not alter the essential character of the plan."[234]

The court of appeals made one major change in the magnet schools component of the Settlement Agreement. Although panels of the court of appeals had approved twice previously the placement of magnet schools in the suburban school districts, the court *en banc* disapproved the provision in the Settlement Agreement for state funding of magnet schools located in St. Louis County.[235] The disapproval of state funding for county magnets was a major blow for many of the predominately black suburban school districts that had viewed state funding of magnet schools as a major reason to join the settlement.[236] Nevertheless, it was, on the whole, a relatively minor change because it did not undermine substantially the capacity of the settlement to desegregate the city schools. Magnet schools with an enrollment of up to 14,000 students[237] could still be located in the city, and the state would pay "the full capital and operating cost."[238] Subsequently, the court of appeals reduced further the size of the interdistrict magnet component of the Settlement Agreement. It allocated 8,000 of the 14,000 magnet slots to the intradistrict desegregation plan, which is funded equally by the state and the Board, and the remaining 6,000 slots to the interdistrict plan, which is funded exclusively by the state.[239]

The court of appeals' comments on the magnet school program, however, proved to have a more significant effect than its disapproval of county magnets. The court noted and approved the state's arguments that magnet schools funded under the settlement should be the subject of careful planning and review by the Magnet Review Committee and the district court.[240] This planning process should ensure that magnet schools "present a reasonable probability of attracting suburban white students" and "only those schools which demonstrate such a probability should be approved."[241] This requirement is intended to guarantee that magnets funded by the state under the settlement will in fact relieve segregation in the city schools and not simply provide new funding for city schools and programs unrelated to desegregation. This goal is, of course, entirely consistent with the magnet provisions of the Settlement Agreement. Unfortunately, satisfaction of the court's planning requirements has proved difficult, and the planning process has worked in practice to frustrate implementation of the magnet schools component of the Settlement Agreement.[242]

In addition to these changes in the voluntary interdistrict transfer and magnet components of the Settlement Agreement, the court of appeals also modified the quality education component. The state's principal argument

on appeal was that the district court had approved quality education programs for general educational improvements that were unrelated to desegregation.[243] In response to this argument, the court of appeals attempted to
draw a thin line between remedial programs and general educational improvements not directly related to integration.[244] Applying this distinction
to the quality education programs approved by the district court, the court
of appeals upheld, with a few minor qualifications, the programs intended
for implementation in the all-black schools.[245] It did not, however, agree
completely with the district court that all of the quality education programs
intended for district-wide application were related to integration.[246] The
court of appeals then both approved and disapproved some of the programs
intended for implementation in the city's integrated schools that the district
court had previously approved.[247]

The distinction between remedial programs and general educational programs, introduced and applied by the court of appeals, added a new complexity to determining the already imprecise bounds of the quality education
component of the Settlement Agreement. By eliminating quality education
programs unrelated to desegregation, the court of appeals substantially reduced the state's financial burdens. Given its approval of the district court's
order that the state pay half of the cost of quality education programs in
the city,[248] the court of appeals' opinion gave the state a strong incentive to
characterize as much of the Appendix and Exhibit 2 as possible as general
educational improvements unrelated to desegregation. Identification of the
quality education programs included in the Appendix and Exhibit 2 as either
remedial or general improvements became a major bone of contention that
contributed to delay in improving the quality of education in city schools.[249]

Apart from the modifications of the three principal components of the
Settlement Agreement, the court of appeals made one other major change.
It ordered the creation of a Budget Review Committee (BRC)[250] because it
believed that the budgeting procedures established by the district court[251]
were inadequate. The BRC is composed of two representatives of the state,
one representative of the Board of Education, one representative chosen
jointly by the Caldwell (NAACP) and Liddell plaintiffs, and a school finance
expert selected by the district court to serve as chairman.[252] The BRC has a
major role in the implementation of the Settlement Agreement. It must prepare an annual budget for each element of the desegregation plan. Each year
the participating school districts and the state must submit budgets to the
BRC and identify areas of agreement and disagreement.[253] The BRC must
resolve these differences "in accordance with the principles set forth in the
settlement agreement, the district court's order and [the court of appeals']
opinion."[254] Any differences that the BRC cannot resolve must be resolved
by the district court.

Finally, the court of appeals attempted to ensure that the Settlement Agreement as approved and tailored would be adequately funded. In particular, the court outlined

> the steps that the district court must take before it can require an increase in real estate taxes to fund the City Board's share of the quality education component of the plan without a vote of the people, and the steps that the court must take before it can require that bonds be issued to fund the City Board's share of capital improvements without a similar vote.[255]

With respect to the Board's duty to pay its share of the quality education component, the court of appeals held that "the district court's broad equitable powers to remedy the evils of segregation include a narrowly defined power to order increases in local tax levies on real estate."[256] Although it disapproved the district court's order prohibiting a rollback of a property tax because "it was not accompanied by a factual finding . . . that all other fiscal alternatives were unavailable or insufficient,"[257] the court of appeals outlined a process by which a similar order could be entered in the future.[258]

With regard to financing capital improvements, the court of appeals approved the district court's order allocating equal financial responsibility to the state and to the Board of Education for improvements of city school facilities.[259] It noted that the Board of Education had submitted a $63.5 million bond issue to the voters in November 1983 and that the issue had failed to obtain the requisite two-thirds approval.[260] The court of appeals' solution was to order the submission of another bond issue to the voters and to threaten court issuance of bonds without voter approval under the same procedure outlined for real estate tax increases without voter approval.[261]

Notwithstanding the changes that the court of appeals made in the Settlement Agreement, its conclusion that these modifications "do not alter the essential character of the plan" is correct. After the U.S. Supreme Court refused to review the court of appeals' judgment upholding the Settlement Agreement,[262] the framework for implementation was set. Nevertheless, the framework was now set by four documents—the Agreement in Principle, the Settlement Agreement (including the Appendix and Exhibit 2), the district court's opinion, and the court of appeals' opinion. Under this framework, the court of appeals asserted that "no party found to have violated the Constitution [the state and the Board of Education] will be permitted to escape its obligation to provide equal educational opportunity to the black children of St. Louis."[263] In the first five years of implementation, there would be substantial accomplishments. Unfortunately, some of the most important promises of the Settlement Agreement to provide "equal educational opportunity to the black children of St. Louis" would be broken.

IMPLEMENTATION OF THE SETTLEMENT
AGREEMENT: 1983–1988

The Settlement Agreement was first implemented in the 1983–1984 school year. After five and one-half years of implementation through the middle of the 1988–1989 school year, it is clear that the voluntary interdistrict transfer program is the most successful component. In the sixth year of the plan, more than 11,900 black students from the city transferred to suburban school districts in St. Louis County. Unfortunately, the components of the settlement designed to provide a remedy for black students who remain in the city school system were not as successful. The magnet school component, which is intended to draw white county students to the city and to expand the opportunity for education in integrated city schools, was paralyzed, for the most part, after the second year of the plan. Although there were substantial achievements in the district-wide programs of the quality education component, the special compensatory and remedial programs for the all-black schools were not implemented completely. No capital improvements in city school facilities were made under the settlement. Successful implementation of these components of the Settlement Agreement was held hostage by litigation between the two proven constitutional violators, the state and the Board of Education, and by the failure of these parties and the courts to resolve funding problems.

When the Settlement Agreement was negotiated, there were approximately 30,000 black children in all-black schools in the city of St. Louis. Five years later, thanks primarily to the success of the voluntary interdistrict transfer program, this number had been reduced to 19,178.[264] Notwithstanding this accomplishment, many black children remain in all-black city schools. Given the incomplete implementation of quality education programs in the all-black schools, delays in establishing interdistrict magnets, and the total failure to make any capital improvements, these children—after five years of implementation—were still being denied a full remedy for the violation of their constitutional rights to equal educational opportunity. Significant promises of the Settlement Agreement had been broken.

Voluntary Interdistrict Transfers

Viewed from all perspectives and judged by almost any criteria, the voluntary interdistrict transfer program of city students to suburban schools is remarkably successful. Judged by the number of interdistrict student transfers and by the level of integration achieved, the program is successful. During the six years of the settlement plan, the number of black city students enrolled in suburban schools has grown from 2,496 in the first year[265] to over 11,900 in the 1988–1989 school year.[266] Before the Settlement Agreement, minority enrollment in the 16 participating districts with

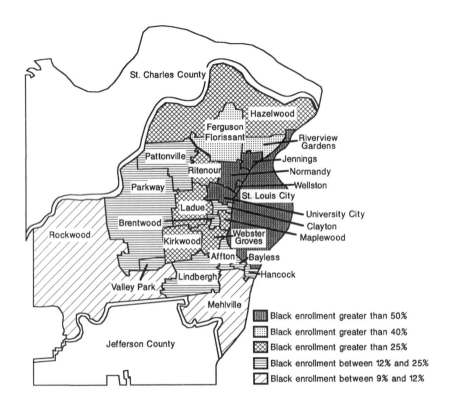

FIGURE 6-2. School Districts in St. Louis County and Percentage of Black Enrollment as of June 30, 1988

obligations to accept black transfer students ranged from 0.1 percent to 23.9 percent. At the end of the fifth year of implementation, the range of minority enrollment was from 9.4 percent to 26.98 percent.[267] Most of the 117 schools in these 16 suburban school districts now have a minority enrollment between 10 percent and 25 percent, and only seven schools have a minority enrollment under 7 percent. The dramatic increase of minority enrollment in suburban St. Louis County school districts is illustrated by Figure 6-2.

In terms of the suburban school districts' satisfaction of their pupil desegregation obligations, the voluntary interdistrict transfer program is also successful. After the end of the fifth year of implementation, 14 of the 16 suburban school districts that had a minority enrollment of less than 25 percent when the settlement was negotiated have received final judgments that they have satisfied their pupil desegregation obligations.[268] Rockwood and Mehlville are the only two school districts that failed to achieve their plan ratio within the five-year period in which the interdistrict litigation was stayed under the Settlement Agreement.[269] Nonetheless, pursuant to the provisions of the Settlement Agreement for an extension of the stay,[270] the interdistrict plaintiffs and both Rockwood and Mehlville agreed to extend the deadline to achieve their plan ratios.[271]

Most important, in terms of the treatment of transfer students, the interdistrict transfer program appears to be a success.[272] Although most of the evidence is impressionistic and anecdotal,[273] black students who have transferred to suburban schools appear to be well-received and fairly treated.[274] Most of the suburban districts appear to have made a firm commitment to treat transfer students on the same basis as all other students. Nevertheless, there is some reason for concern about both high withdrawal rates[275] and high suspension rates of black interdistrict transfer students in some county school districts for disciplinary problems.[276] Transportation is one other problem area. After several years of substantial difficulties,[277] there now seems to be agreement that the state is doing a good job of providing transportation both to regular school sessions and to "late" activities and weekend performances. Unfortunately, in the 1987–1988 school year, 28 percent of the black transfer students still rode one hour or more to and from school each day.[278]

The principal problem with the voluntary interdistrict student transfer program is that it is effectively a one-way system. In contrast to the 11,901 black students who were enrolled in county schools at the beginning of the 1988–1989 school year, there were only 724 white county students enrolled in city schools.[279] In short, in the sixth year of implementation, approximately 5.8 percent of the interdistrict transfer students were white and 94.2 percent were black. This disparity in the burdens of desegregation is in large part a consequence of the incomplete implementation of the magnet school component of the Settlement Agreement.

Magnet Schools

The Settlement Agreement has failed to attract white voluntary transfer students from the county to the city schools. At the end of the 1986–1987 school year, there were only seven interdistrict magnet schools in operation, and four of them had been created under the old 12(a) plan. The three interdistrict magnets established under the settlement were started in the first two years, and no new magnets were added in the third and fourth years of implementation. In the 1986–1987 school year, these seven magnets had a total enrollment of only 2,129 students, a total far short of the 6,000 interdistrict magnet seats provided by the settlement as modified by the court of appeals.[280] Approximately 536 of the 577 white county transfer students were enrolled in city magnet schools in the fall of 1986.[281] Four hundred were in intradistrict magnets established under the intradistrict desegregation plan, and 136 were in the seven interdistrict magnets. The intradistrict and interdistrict magnets had the same low rate of white county enrollment. In both types of magnets, white county students were only 14 percent of the student body. Although one additional interdistrict magnet was added in the 1987–1988 school year, there is no dispute that at the end of the fifth year of implementation the magnet school component had not been fully implemented.[282]

There is no shortage of explanations—some of them self-serving—for the failure of the magnet school component of the Settlement Agreement. Bitter and protracted fighting between the state and the Board of Education over the planning, operation, and funding of magnet schools has been a major cause of the delay in creating interdistrict magnets under the settlement.[283] The state is frequently accused of resisting the creation of additional interdistrict magnets by all possible means.[284] Because the state must bear the full capital and operating costs of these schools, which may each cost $6–7 million, foot-dragging by the state is certainly understandable, even if unacceptable. The Board of Education is often accused of being greedy. Although both intradistrict and interdistrict magnets attract white county students at the same low 14 percent rate, the state pays 100 percent of the costs of interdistrict magnets and shares equally with the Board of Education the costs of intradistrict magnets. Given these facts, some believe that the Board is attempting to transfer its financial obligations to educate city students to the state by seeking the creation of interdistrict magnets.[285]

In the face of this intransigence, the magnet school planning and evaluation procedures of the settlement[286] are apparently not equal to the task. Many say the Magnet Review Committee is ineffective.[287] The courts' financial advisor is said by some to be unduly sympathetic to the state's financial concerns and insufficiently sympathetic with the intent of the settling parties to establish magnet schools.[288] The district court is, at least in the eyes of some people, too tolerant of the constant, and often intemperate, bickering of the state and Board of Education. Other informed observers argue, in defense of the Magnet Review Committee, the financial advisor, and the court, that the delay in establishing interdistrict magnets is simply a consequence of the failure of the existing magnet schools to provide the high-quality programs that they advertise. The very high withdrawal rate (27.2 percent) of white county students who transfer to city schools[289] supports this argument. Given their lack of success in attracting and retaining county white students, it is argued that magnet schools are not cost effective desegregation tools.

In its *Liddell IX* opinion in the fall of 1986, the court of appeals attempted to break this logjam.[290] The court ordered an increase of 2,000 in interdistrict magnet enrollment by the beginning of the 1987–1988 school year and an increase to the 6,000 authorized total by 1989–1990.[291] The court also set a 40 percent white county student enrollment standard to be met by existing interdistrict magnets within two years and by new interdistrict magnets by the beginning of the school's third year of operation.[292] Given the rather dismal record of interdistrict magnets in the first four years of the settlement, these were tall orders: an increase from 536 to 2,400 white county magnet students and an increase from 2,129 to 6,000 in total interdistrict magnet enrollment in just three years. The court of appeals ordered the MRC to act on pending magnet proposals promptly so that the 1987–1988 magnet school goal could be obtained,[293] but the district court subsequently disapproved all six magnets that the MRC approved.[294] Instead, the district court ordered the MRC to submit a master plan for magnet schools by September 14, 1987.[295] Although these orders effectively precluded compliance with the *Liddell IX* mandate to establish new magnet schools for the 1987–1988 school year, the court of appeals upheld the district court's order requiring the development of a magnet schools master plan.[296] Given the delay in establishing new interdistrict magnet schools and in expanding magnet school enrollment, the Eighth Circuit ordered that the master plan be completed "with dispatch" and that "[n]o delay in providing the necessary facilities . . . be countenanced."[297]

The master plan was completed in September 1987.[298] If this plan had been approved and implemented promptly, there would have been an opportunity to start in the 1988–1989 school year on *Liddell IX*'s three-year goal of increasing interdistrict magnet school enrollment by 4,000 students. Unfortunately, the district court did not approve a comprehensive magnet school plan until August 1988, shortly before the beginning of the 1988–1989 school year and the sixth year of implementation.[299] Nonetheless, the district court's order is a thoughtful effort to resolve the problems that have plagued the magnet school component of the Settlement Agreement. The new magnet plan eliminates the distinction between intradistrict and interdistrict magnets, and it allocates to the state and the Board of Education specific financial responsibilities for the capital, regular operating, and special program costs of the unified system of magnet schools.[300] The approval and authorization of 27 magnet schools with specific educational programs, enrollments, and staffs[301] should eliminate most of the disputes between the state and the Board. The district court's magnet plan also establishes a capital budget of $51,472,626 and a funding formula.[302] The state must pay $36,802,928 (71.5 percent) in three installments over three years.[303] The Board must pay $14,669,698 (28.5 percent) in nine installments over a period of nine years.[304] Complete implementation of the district court's magnet school plan is not scheduled until the 1992–1993 school year,[305] nine years after the approval of the Settlement Agreement.

Although the new magnet school plan is a major, albeit long-delayed, step, two substantial questions about the ultimate success of the magnet school component of the Settlement Agreement remain. First, given the Board of Education's difficulty in financing the capital improvements of city school facilities required by the settlement,[306] there is a substantial question whether the Board will be able to meet its $14,669,698 obligation for magnet school capital costs and its share of regular operating and special costs of magnet schools in addition to its $57,358,970.50 share of general capital improvements ordered by the district court in September 1987.[307] The Board, which has consistently complained about its lack of funds, must satisfy these orders without jeopardizing its general educational program. Second, even if the magnet school plan is completely funded and implemented, it remains to be seen whether a substantial number of white county students will transfer to the predominately black city school system. The district court's magnet school plan appears to satisfy a concern of the court of appeals: "The plain fact is that recruitment of suburban students will be difficult, if not impossible, unless the physical facilities are reasonably comparable with those of the suburban districts from which the students are transferring and are well located from the point of view of both City and county students."[308] Nonetheless, if magnet schools are going to create an opportunity for a substantial number of black city students to attend integrated city schools, they must be established in the overall context of a city school system that, by virtue of the quality education and capital improvement component of the settlement, is attractive to county students and their parents.

Quality Education and Capital Improvements

Most persons involved with the implementation of the quality education component of the settlement agree that there have been substantial improvements in the city schools, but it is very hard to determine precisely how much of the quality education component of the settlement has in fact been implemented. Even after the orders of the district court and the court of appeals[309] reducing and modifying the original settlement quality education Appendix and Exhibit 2 and after five years of implementation, there is still no generally accepted comprehensive description of the approved quality education component.[310] Nonetheless, one person close to the process estimates that some 65 percent to 75 percent of the quality education package as refined by the courts was implemented over the first four years. The accomplishments so far, however, appear to be concentrated in the district-wide programs, and most of the implementation problems are in the settlement programs designed for the all-black schools.

For example, it appears that the Board of Education has been very successful in reducing the pupil–teacher ratio on a district-wide basis to levels at or below the state AAA standards of 35 to one for high schools and 30 to one for lower schools.[311] However, there was little or no effort initially to lower the pupil–teacher ratio in the all-black schools below the district-wide average.[312] An examination of the second- and third-year budgets shows no funds approved or spent for this purpose. In September 1986, the court of appeals in *Liddell IX* ordered a reduction to a 24 to one ratio for the 1986–1987 school year and a further reduction in the 1987–1988 school year to the 20 to one ratio established by the Settlement Agreement.[313] After the Board reported that it could not achieve the 20 to one ratio in the 1987–1988 school year "because of space and fiscal difficulties," the court ordered the Board to comply by the beginning of the next school year.[314] Notwithstanding this mandate, the Board of Education did not achieve the 20 to one pupil–teacher ratio for the all-black schools at the beginning of the 1988–1989 school year,[315] and five years after the approval of the Settlement Agreement, the district court finally turned to the threat of a contempt citation to force the Board to implement this key quality education program for the all-black schools.[316]

Consistent with the Board's success in reducing the pupil–teacher ratio on a district-wide basis, one finds that other district-wide settlement programs, like all-day kindergarten classes and the restoration of art, music, and physical education programs to AAA standards, have been successful. Nevertheless, the record with respect to settlement programs for the all-black schools is not satisfactory.[317] To date, no one has prepared a complete, comparative analysis measuring the all-black schools' programs that have been implemented against the indefinite standard of the settlement as modified by the courts, but one analyst has described the situation as "severe under-implementation." Another, more charitable analyst acknowledges that some individual programs have not been implemented and that only portions of others have been implemented. One indication of the problems is underspending by the Board of the funds approved for implementation of the special programs for the all-black schools. In the second year, the court approved $3,472,592, but the Board spent only 53 percent, or $1,831,892. In the third year, the court approved $5,249,200, but the Board spent only 61 percent of these funds.

The problems of implementing the quality education programs are frequently ascribed to the following process.[318] First, the state and the Board of Education dispute whether a particular program should be implemented. The state is said to engage in "guerilla warfare" tactics. The Board is described as attempting to shift its responsibility for basic educational costs to state-funded quality education programs. The district court approves less than the Board requests, perhaps as a function of the Board's record of underspending. Although the state pays the sums ordered by the court, year-end audits reveal incomplete implementation and underspending by the Board. The underspending is then explained, depending on the source, as a function of court orders approving budgets that come so late in the school year that it is difficult for the Board to plan and implement or as a function of Board mismanagement. Other explanations include the Board's lack of funds to meet its 50 percent share of the costs of quality education programs and the Board's refusal to allocate limited funds needed in its judgment for district-wide educational programs to the special settlement programs for the all-black schools. This process is then repeated each year. In addition to these problems, some commentators attribute, in part, the incomplete implementation of the special quality education programs for the all-black schools to insufficient monitoring by the *Liddell* plaintiffs and the NAACP, who both lack the necessary financial resources for this task.

Although the quality education programs of the settlement, especially the district-wide provisions, have improved city schools, no capital improvements in the city school facilities were made under the Settlement Agreement in the first five years of the plan. Under court orders, capital improvements are funded equally by the state and the Board of Education. The state's obligation to pay for capital improvements is to match funds raised by the Board of Education through bond issues.[319] Notwithstanding strong efforts, the Board has failed on three occasions after approval of the settlement to obtain the requisite two-thirds voter approval of a bond issue[320] necessary to fund its share of capital improvements.[321] Although these bond issues have been supported by the predominately black north side, they have failed to garner adequate support on the predominately white south side.[322] Consequently, no capital improvements have been made.

In the spring of 1987, at the end of the fourth year of implementation, the prospects for the capital improvements in school facilities required by the Settlement Agreement were quite dim. No school bond issue had passed in the city of St. Louis since 1962.[323] Three bond issues to fund capital improvements under the settlement had failed to obtain the requisite two-thirds super-majority. The Board and the state remained deeply divided over the extent of capital improvements to school facilities required by the settlement. In the spring of 1986, the state proposed about $40 million in capital improvements, and the Board had asked the court to approve a $420,600,000 plan.[324] The courts were content to order resubmission of bond issues to the voters and to hold in abeyance the threat of a court-ordered bond issue financed by a court-ordered tax levy.[325]

Notwithstanding these dim prospects, at the beginning of the 1987–1988 school year in September 1987, the district court approved a detailed, comprehensive $114,717,941 capital improvements program designed to correct the "deplorable" physical conditions of the city schools.[326] The court ordered the state and the Board of Education to share equally the costs of the program.[327] It ordered the state to pay its share of $57,358,970.50 over three years in three equal annual installments of $19,119,656.83 and to make its first payment within 31 days of the order.[328] The court ordered the Board to pay the same amount over nine years in eight annual installments of $7 million (and a ninth payment of $1,358,970.50) and to make its first payment within 31 days after the order.[329]

This order is a major accomplishment because it solves the two basic problems that have prevented implementation of the capital improvements component of the Settlement Agreement. The district court's first major achievement is the resolution of the long-standing dispute between the state and the Board about the nature and extent of capital improvements required by the settlement. The court ordered some school closings and consolidation, and it identified specific categories of construction work and rehabilitation (such as site work, building envelope and interior, mechanical, electrical, and new gymnasiums) with precise budgets for each of the remaining 104 city schools.[330] The court directed the Board "to begin immediately to prepare specifications for major improvement projects" in all-black elementary and middle schools and in intradistrict magnets,[331] and it also established a goal of completing construction work in six years.[332]

The court's second significant achievement is the provision for financing capital improvements independent of a bond issue.[333] Judge Hungate's original judgment approving the settlement limited the state's obligation to pay for capital improvements to matching the proceeds of a bond issue approved by the voters of St. Louis,[334] but Judge Limbaugh abandoned this approach to financing.[335] Instead of permitting the state to postpone its payment for capital improvements until after approval of a city school bond issue, the court simply ordered the state to pay its 50 percent of capital improvements. Although the district court permitted the Board to finance its share of capital improvements by a bond issue,[336] it concluded that the Board had "other means to provide the required funding immediately."[337] On the basis of a report by its financial advisor, the court concluded that, without damage to its instructional programs, the Board could fund its share of capital improvements over nine years out of its existing reserves and by cutting costs.[338]

One week after entry of the order, the Board of Education voted unanimously to comply with the district court's capital improvements program.[339] The Board reported that it had adequate funds for its first annual payment of $7 million and that it would seek additional revenues to meet its capital improvements obligations in the future.[340] The president of the Board stated that planning would begin immediately and that renovation would begin in the spring or summer of 1988.[341] It now appears that at least some of the Settlement Agreement's long-delayed capital improvements of city schools will be made. Although there are still reasons to doubt the Board of Education's ability to fund completely its share of the capital improvements program,[342] the district court has ordered the Board to reduce its expenses and to reallocate funds to desegregation programs.[343] More important, a consultant has devised a plan to circumvent the two-thirds super-majority requirement for voter approval of bond issues, which has frustrated the Board's efforts to finance capital improvements.[344] Under the consultant's proposal, the Board will issue "leasehold revenue bonds" that do not require voter approval and that are secured by deeds to school buildings.[345] If the proposed issue in March 1989 of approximately $50 million of these bonds is successful,[346] then the Board should have adequate resources to fund its share of capital improvements.

THE FUTURE OF THE
SETTLEMENT AGREEMENT

The future of the Settlement Agreement in the middle of the 1988–1989 school year, the sixth year of the plan, is much brighter than it was the year before. After five years, substantial promises of the settlement had been broken.[347] Successful implementation of the magnet schools, quality education, and capital improvements provisions had been held hostage by litigation between the two primary constitutional violators, the state and the Board of Education, and by the courts' failure to resolve funding problems. There were also threats to dismantle both the intradistrict plan and the settlement. In the city of St. Louis, there was strong political pressure to abandon the intradistrict plan,[348] and the state of Missouri attempted to escape its substantial financial responsibilities under the settlement after the fifth year.[349]

Fortunately, beginning in the summer of 1987, the courts issued orders that will go a long way toward mending the broken promises of the Settlement Agreement. In July 1987 in *Liddell XII*,[350] the court of appeals surveyed the problems that had developed in the first four years and ordered complete compliance with the terms of the settlement.[351] In particular, the court ordered prompt completion of the magnet school master plan and prompt implementation.[352] Although the district court did not approve a magnet master plan until one year later in August 1988, this new plan is designed to ensure complete implementation of the magnet school component of the Settlement Agreement by the beginning of the 1992–1993 school year.[353] The appeals court also ordered the Board of Education to achieve a 20 to one pupil–teacher ratio in the all-black city schools by the beginning of the 1988–1989 school year.[354] The Board did not comply with this order, but the district court acted firmly to ensure compliance with this key quality education provision.[355] Although the court of appeals continued to rely on a bond issue to finance capital improvements,[356] the district court, in September 1987, approved a capital improvements program and budget, and it created a financing mechanism independent of voter approval of a bond issue.[357]

In *Liddell XII* the court of appeals also ensured the continued success of the voluntary interdistrict student transfer program. In light of the clear provisions in the settlement to continue this program for more than five years,[358] the court of appeals clearly, if indirectly, held that the voluntary interdistrict transfer program would continue for the foreseeable future. The court held that the goal of 15,000 interdistrict transfer students must be achieved by the 1990–1991 school year,[359] which will be the eighth year of the settlement. Following this lead, the district court in May 1988 firmly rejected the state's attempt to reduce its financial responsibilities for interdistrict student transfers.[360] The district court held that both the suburban school districts' obligations to reach and maintain the plan goal of 25 percent minority enrollment and the state's duty to fund these interdistrict transfers are not limited either by the five-year stay of the Settlement Agreement or by a cap of 15,000 interdistrict student transfers.[361] The state's duty to pay fiscal incentives and transportation costs for the voluntary interdistrict transfer program and the suburban school districts' responsibility to educate black city interdistrict transfer students will continue until "the vestiges of segregation have been eliminated."[362] In short, the voluntary interdistrict transfer program is to continue for the foreseeable future until there is a finding of a unitary school system.[363]

Although the continued and final success of all three major components of the Settlement Agreement—voluntary interdistrict transfers, magnet schools, and quality education and capital improvements—is now more certain after *Liddell XII* and the district court's responses, much remains to be done to ensure full implementation. The district court must enforce the provisions of the new magnet school master plan in order to guarantee the prompt establishment of magnet schools that are a fair test of the city's ability to attract white county students. Complete implementation of the Settlement Agreement will also require both renewed judicial attention to the special programs for the all-black city schools and careful monitoring and enforcement of the state's and the Board's obligations. Although the court of appeals in *Liddell XII* noted that many of the compensatory and remedial programs for the all-black schools had not been implemented fully,[364] it did not order implementation. The court ordered only compliance with the 20 to one pupil–teacher ratio. The courts must now turn their attention to the other settlement provisions for the all-black city schools.

Finally, after five years of delay and *Liddell XII*'s promise of complete implementation of the Settlement Agreement, additional delays cannot be tolerated. The courts must monitor carefully and enforce all of the state's and the Board's obligations. If the state fails to meet its financial responsibilities for capital improvements, new magnet schools under the master plan, and quality education programs for the all-black schools, then the courts will be forced to consider strong measures.[365] If the Board's funds are not adequate to finance its share of the capital improvements program, the magnet school plan, and quality education programs for the all-black schools, then the courts will have to reconsider ordering a tax increase or invalidating the two-thirds super-majority requirement for bond approval.[366] The courts cannot permit the voters to frustrate the duty of their agent, the Board of Education, to remedy its constitutional violation. If the Board continues to delay providing a 20 to one pupil–teacher ratio in the all-black schools or fails to implement other quality education programs for these schools, the courts have the tools—contempt and direct supervision—to ensure compliance. Such strong measures, however, should not be necessary if the lessons learned in negotiating the Settlement Agreement are applied to solving the problems of implementation: A community that voluntarily fulfills its constitutional responsibilities through a process of compromise and consent can avoid harsh judicially imposed solutions.

The Settlement Agreement has been expensive in the first five years,[367] and complete implementation will substantially increase costs. The costs of the voluntary interdistrict transfer program will increase as the number of students rises from 11,900 after six years to 15,000 in the 1990–1991 school year. The capital costs for new magnets under the magnet master plan is $51,472,626. Implementation of special programs for the all-black schools will be expensive. The district court's capital improvements program will cost almost $115 million. Given these substantial financial burdens, it is important to remember both that the Settlement Agreement is a remarkable achievement and that it is worth saving by ensuring full implementation.

It is a remarkable achievement because St. Louis is the only major city in the country with a voluntary, interdistrict desegregation plan. More important, St. Louis achieved this goal through a process of compromise and consent while other cities had to resolve their differences through litigation and court orders. The Settlement Agreement is worth saving because it has already worked and because if fully implemented it can provide a complete and effective remedy. The voluntary interdistrict transfer program already provides desegregated education in suburban schools for some 11,900 black city students, and it may ultimately provide this opportunity for more than 15,000 children. If the district court's new magnet plan is implemented consistent with *Liddell IX*, an additional 2,400 black students could be educated in desegregated city schools, and the burdens of desegregating city schools will be distributed more equitably between blacks and whites.[368] Black children in the city schools have been the beneficiaries of substantial improvements in the quality of education under the district-wide programs of the settlement and, to an uncertain extent, under the special provisions for the all-black schools. If these special remedial and compensatory programs are promptly and fully implemented and if sorely needed capital improvements are made, then the approximately 15,000 black children who remain in the all-black schools in the 1990–1991 school year[369] will have a complete remedy.

When the Settlement Agreement was approved, I expressed the hope that in a few short years it would become such an established, successful

component of public education in metropolitan St. Louis that it would be
ignored for the most part by the press and forgotten by the lawyers. One
component of the Settlement Agreement, voluntary interdistrict transfers
from the city to the county, has come a long way toward that goal. I hope that
in the next few years we can say the same thing about the magnet school,
quality education, and capital improvements components of the Settlement
Agreement.

NOTES

Note: I was appointed by the U.S. District Court for the Eastern District of
Missouri on October 15, 1982, as Special Master "for the purpose of exploring
possibilities of settlement" of the interdistrict aspects of the St. Louis school desegregation case, and I served in this capacity through June 16, 1983. By the terms
of this appointment, I agreed "to abide by traditional legal principles of confidentiality" with respect to the settlement negotiations and conferences. Although the
story of the negotiation process would be interesting and would cast honor on the
participants, the pledge of confidentiality ensured open, creative, and fair negotiations. Accordingly, I have honored this pledge by omitting any discussion of either
the bargaining positions of the parties or the specific compromises that led to the
agreement.

One other disclaimer is necessary. The discussion of the principal provisions of
the Settlement Agreement is not intended to be a post-adoption extrinsic aid to interpretation, and it should not be read as a "legislative history." *See, e.g.*, State
Wholesale Grocers v. Great Atlantic and Pacific Tea Co., 154 F. Supp. 471, 484–85
(N.D. Ill. 1957), *modified on other grounds*, 258 F.2d 831 (7th Cir. 1958), *cert. denied*,
358 U.S. 947 (1959) (publication by congressman is not an authoritative source of
interpretation of a statute that he helped draft).

1. Indianapolis, Wilmington, and Louisville have court-ordered interdistrict desegregation plans. *See* United States v. Board of School Commissioners, 677 F.2d
1185 (7th Cir.), *cert. denied*, 459 U.S. 1086 (1982) (Indianapolis); Evans v. Buchanan,
416 F. Supp. 328 (D. Del. 1976) (Wilmington); Newburg Area Council v. Board of
Education, 510 F.2d 1358 (6th Cir. 1974), *cert. denied*, 421 U.S. 931 (1975) (Louisville). The Eighth Circuit has recently ordered an interdistrict remedy in Little Rock.
Little Rock School District v. Pulaski County Special School District, 778 F.2d 404
(8th Cir. 1985), *cert. denied*, 476 U.S. 1186 (1986). *See generally*, Chermerinsky, *Ending
the Dual System of American Public Education: The Urgent Need for Legislative Action*,
32 DE PAUL L. REV. 77 (1983); Note, *Interdistrict Remedies for Segregated Schools*, 79
COLUM. L. REV. 1168 (1979). Hartford, Boston, Rochester, and a few other cities
have small, voluntary interdistrict student exchange programs. Interview with Susan
Uchitelle, Executive Director of the Interdistrict Student Exchange Program in St.
Louis (January 1987).

2. Voluntary Interdistrict Coordinating Council, *Fifth Report to the United States
District Court*, L(2100)88, at i, 22 (table 1), 24 (table 3) (August 15, 1988).

3. Bell, *Overall Enrollment Up in Area Public Schools*, St. Louis Post-Dispatch, November 17, 1988, at W1, col. 4–6.

4. Wells, *St. Louis Evaluates Its Pioneer Integration Plan*, N.Y. Times, June 8, 1988, at 23, col. 1 (nat'l ed.) (interdistrict student transfer plan a model for Milwaukee and for proposed Connecticut legislation).

5. Gross, *Report: Demographics Thwart Desegregation*, St. Louis Post-Dispatch, September 8, 1988, at A1, col. 4, A8, col. 2.

6. *See infra* text accompanying notes 298–308, 326–38.

7. *See infra* text accompanying notes 313–16.

8. *See infra* text accompanying notes 358–63.

9. Liddell v. Board of Education, 491 F. Supp. 351 (E.D. Mo. 1980), *aff'd*, 667 F.2d 643 (8th Cir.), *cert. denied*, 454 U.S. 1091 (1981). The procedural history of the intradistrict case is traced in detail in the district court's initial opinion holding that neither the state of Missouri nor the Board of Education had unconstitutionally segregated the St. Louis city public schools and in the court of appeals' opinion reversing this judgment. Liddell v. Board of Education, 469 F. Supp. 1304, 1309–12 (E.D. Mo. 1979), *rev'd and remanded sub nom.*, Adams v. United States, 620 F.2d 1277, 1281–84 (8th Cir.) (*en banc*), *cert. denied*, 449 U.S. 826 (1980).

10. Liddell v. Board of Education, 491 F. Supp. at 353, 357.

11. *Id.* at 353. The court of appeals previously had urged the district court to consider a program for student exchanges between the city schools and the suburban school districts. Liddell v. Board of Education, 546 F.2d 768, 774 (8th Cir.) (*Liddell I*), *cert. denied*, 433 U.S. 914 (1977); Adams v. United States, 620 F.2d 1277, 1296 (8th Cir.) (*en banc*), *cert. denied*, 449 U.S. 826 (1980).

12. In paragraph 12(a), the district court ordered the three parties

[t]o make every feasible effort to work out with the appropriate school districts in the St. Louis County and develop, for 1980–81 implementation, a voluntary, cooperative plan of pupil exchanges which will assist in alleviating the school segregation in the City of St. Louis, and which also insures that inter-district pupil transfers will not impair the desegregation of the St. Louis school district ordered herein, and submit such plan to the Court for approval by July 1, 1980.

Liddell v. Board of Education, 491 F. Supp. at 353.

13. *Id.* Paragraph 12 also imposed three other planning requirements. Subparagraphs (d) and (e) of paragraph 12 required plans for ensuring that the operation of federally assisted housing programs in the metropolitan area would facilitate school desegregation and for ensuring that all city schools would be eligible for certain federal grants. *Id.* at 354.

Subparagraph 12(b) required "a plan for the consolidation or merger and full desegregation of the separate vocational educational programs operated by the Special School District of St. Louis County and the school district of the City of St. Louis, for implementation in the 1981–82 school year." *Id.* at 353. The Special School District was joined as a defendant on September 12, 1980. *See* Special School District v. Mallory, 506 F. Supp. 183 (E.D. Mo. 1980). The district court held that the state had committed an interdistrict constitutional violation by operating segregated vocational education programs in the city and in St. Louis County. Pursuant to 12(b), the parties proposed a plan for desegregating the vocational schools, and the district court entered a consent decree adopting this plan on June 11, 1981. The court of appeals subsequently approved this desegregation plan and upheld the consent decree. Liddell v. Board of Education, 677 F.2d 626, 632–38 (8th Cir.) (*Liddell V*), *cert. denied*, 459 U.S. 877 (1982).

Vocational education was the first success for the district court's plan for interdistrict desegregation, but the potential effect of desegregation of vocational schools was quite limited because there were only four vocational schools, three in St. Louis County and one in the city of St. Louis. Moreover, a plan for interdistrict desegregation of vocational schools did not set any precedent for other aspects of interdistrict desegregation because the district court found that the state had maintained a dual vocational system and that the state had the power to merge the city and county vocational educational programs. Liddell v. Board of Education, 491 F. Supp. at 358. Such findings had not been made about the general education programs of the public schools in the city and county.

In June 1987, at the end of the sixth year of implementation of the 12(b) vocational school plan, the Eighth Circuit found that "desegregation ha[d] not been achieved, and total enrollment . . . ha[d] plunged." Liddell v. Board of Education, 822 F.2d 1446, 1452 (8th Cir. 1987) (*Liddell XI*). The court ordered the parties to take steps to make the 12(b) plan effective and threatened "to order the complete merger of the vocational programs with a unified government and taxing structure." *Id.* at 1460.

14. Motion of the Board of Education of St. Louis for Leave to Amend Its Answer to Add a Cross-Claim (January 9, 1981); Caldwell Plaintiffs-Intervenors' Motion for Leave to Add Additional Parties Defendant and to File [An] Amended, Supplemental and Cross Complaint (January 16, 1981).

15. For a discussion of the implementation of the 12(a) and 12(c) plans between 1980 and 1982 and of an effort to convert a 12(a) plan into a settlement of the interdistrict case, *see* La Pierre, *Voluntary Metropolitan School Desegregation in St. Louis— An Opportunity Lost or a Second Chance?* 2 PUB. L.F. 69 (1982).

16. Judge James H. Meredith presided over the St. Louis school desegregation case from its inception in 1972 through December 21, 1980. Judge William L. Hungate, who succeeded Judge Meredith, subsequently was responsible for implementation of the intradistrict plan and for the interdistrict aspects of the case through January 31, 1985, when he was replaced by Judge Stephen N. Limbaugh. Most of the district court's orders in the St. Louis school desegregation case are not reported. These unreported orders are cited by number and date as they appear on the docket sheet for Liddell v. Board of Education of St. Louis, No. 72–100 C(4)(E.D. Mo.). These orders and all other documents in the record bear the designation "H" through January 31, 1985, when Judge Hungate presided. After Judge Limbaugh was assigned to the case on February 1, 1985, court documents bear the designation "L."

17. La Pierre, *supra* note 15.

18. The Educational Plan is reprinted in *An Educational Plan for Voluntary, Cooperative Desegregation*, 2 PUB. L.F. 35–68 (1982). It is discussed in detail in La Pierre, *supra* note 15, at 79–87.

19. La Pierre, *supra* note 15, at 88–96.

20. An Educational Plan for Voluntary, Cooperative Desegregation of Schools in the St. Louis, Missouri Metropolitan Area, H(226)81 (July 2, 1981).

21. *Id.* at 14.

22. *Id.* at 13–14.

23. Under Foote's *Educational Plan*, black city students could not transfer unless the host suburban school district had "space available" to accommodate them, and his plan did not require participating districts to achieve their plan ratios or to make available a set number of spaces after the first year. *See* La Pierre, *supra* note 15, at 80–81. The district court's 12(a) plan required the participating districts to make a minimum additional amount of space available each year until its plan ratio for minority enrollment was achieved. *See supra* text accompanying note 22.

24. *Compare Educational Plan, supra* note 18, *with* Order H(226)81 (July 2, 1981), *supra* note 20, at 7–27.

25. Foote's *Educational Plan* proposed that the voluntary desegregation plan would be implemented in two three-year phases after judicial review and approval. During the first phase, the participating districts would gradually take actions to fulfill the substantive requirements of the *Educational Plan*. The interdistrict plaintiffs would gradually abandon the threat of interdistrict litigation against the participating districts by withdrawing their January 1981 motions to add the suburban districts as defendants, then by agreeing that any litigation would be only by way of a new action, and, finally, by refraining in the third year from any legal activity connected to an interdistrict lawsuit.

At the end of either of the first two years of phase one, each participating district would have the right to withdraw, and the interdistrict plaintiffs would have the right to resume litigation if they were dissatisfied with the implementation of the plan. At the end of the third year, the interdistrict plaintiffs and each participating district could either abandon all further voluntary efforts or prepare and submit to the court a proposal for a second three-year phase to complete implementation of the *Educational Plan*. They could also seek judicial approval of the second phase as a final settlement of the metropolitan school desegregation case. *Educational Plan, supra* note 18, at 59–64.

26. Order H(226)81, *supra* note 20, at 29, 31.

27. *See, e.g.,* Lerner and Defty, *Big Rejection of Voluntary Proposal Disappoints Many in Schools Effort*, St. Louis Post-Dispatch, August 7, 1981, at A1, A4, col. 5 ("[I]n St. Louis, most agree that the major stumbling block for many districts was the fact that no protection was offered against further litigation even if they chose to participate."); Vespereny, *6 More Districts Reject School Plan*, St. Louis Post-Dispatch, July 15, 1981, at A1, col. 6 (attorney reported as saying that "schools wanted assurances that there would be no litigation imposing a mandatory desegregation plan before they would agree to a voluntary plan").

28. Moreover, many of the suburban school districts read the district court's plan as suggesting that litigation would continue regardless of their participation. The district court had warned that "if the goal of constitutional compliance cannot be met through this voluntary plan, the Court must give serious consideration to the validity of the imposition of a compulsory interdistrict remedy." Order H(226)81, *supra* note 20, at 31. Although the district court subsequently stayed interdistrict liti-

gation against suburban school districts that agreed to participate in the voluntary plan (*see infra* text accompanying note 30), this stay had little value as a guarantee because it was not entered as part of a binding class action settlement and could not bar future litigation. Thus, even after entry of the order staying litigation against participating districts, no additional suburban school districts agreed to participate before the expiration of the court's second deadline (March 1, 1982) for joining the voluntary plan. However, before the beginning of the 1982–1983 school year, nine more suburban school districts agreed to participate in the 12(a) plan. *See infra* note 81 and accompanying text.

29. The four suburban school districts that initially agreed to participate in the district court's voluntary plan were Clayton, Kirkwood, Ritenour, and University City. *See* Order H(337)81 (August 24, 1981). Pattonville was the fifth suburban school district to decide to participate. *See* Order H(494)81, at 1 note 1 (September 24, 1981).

30. H(336)81 (August 24, 1981). The court stayed the interdistrict litigation against participating districts by staying the January 1981 motions of the Board of Education and the NAACP to add these suburban districts as defendants and by staying any related discovery. H(337)81 (August 24, 1981).

31. H(337)81 (August 24, 1981). The court limited the scope of the interdistrict case by staying motions to add as defendants suburban school districts in Jefferson and St. Charles counties, officials of these two counties, and various housing authorities.

32. *See* Liddell v. Board of Education, 677 F.2d 626, 640–41 (8th Cir.) (*Liddell V*), *cert. denied*, 459 U.S. 877 (1982).

33. *Liddell V*, 677 F.2d at 639.

34. *Id.*

35. H(494)81 (September 24, 1981). *See Liddell V*, 677 F.2d at 642–44.

36. *Liddell V*, 677 F.2d at 639–42.

37. *See id.* at 640 n. 38.

38. *Id.* at 640.

39. The district court, in its July 2, 1981, order adopting a 12(a) voluntary plan, set August 6, 1981, as the deadline for suburban school districts' decisions about participation in the plan for the 1981–1982 school year and January 31, 1982, as the deadline for decisions about participation in the 1982–1983 school year. H(226)81, *supra* note 20, at 28. The January 31 deadline was later extended to March 1, 1982. Order H(761)82 (January 25, 1982).

40. As of March 31, 1982, four participating districts (Clayton, Kirkwood, Pattonville, and Ritenour) had accepted 191 black permissive interdistrict transfer students from the city school system. The fifth participating district, University City, was precluded from accepting such students because its percentage of black students exceeded the plan ratio. Forty-three students from participating districts and 257 students from non-participating districts in St. Louis, Jefferson, and St. Charles counties were attending city schools. *See School Transfers on Rise*, St. Louis Post-Dispatch, April 8, 1982, at 1–W, col. 1 (table).

41. *Liddell V*, 677 F.2d at 629–30.

42. *Id.* at 628, 638–39.

43. Liddell v. Board of Education, 677 F.2d 626 (8th Cir.) (*Liddell V*), *cert. denied,* 459 U.S. 877 (1982).

44. *Id.* at 639–42.

45. *Id.* at 641.

46. The determination of the court of appeals that the district court could not order mandatory interdistrict student transfers or reorganization of the suburban school districts under paragraph 12(c) on the basis of the state's established intradistrict violation rested on two grounds. First, it would be unfair to impose remedies that would have a direct, material effect on the suburban school districts without affording them a hearing. Second, the court had previously assured the suburban school districts that such relief would not be ordered without a hearing. *Id.* at 640 and 640 n. 38.

The court of appeals did not hold that mandatory interdistrict student transfers could not be imposed unless the suburban school districts were held liable for contributing to segregation of the city schools. The court expressly stated that the district court could consider, in the interdistrict liability hearing, the arguments that the suburban school districts were "instrumentalities" of the state. It implicitly approved consideration of the argument that mandatory, interdistrict student transfers and school district reorganization could be ordered on the basis of the state's proven intradistrict constitutional violation and its authority over the suburban school districts. *Id.* See generally Benson, *The Liability of Missouri Suburban School Districts for the Unconstitutional Segregation of Neighboring Urban School Districts,* 53 U.M.K.C. L. Rev. 349 (1985).

47. *Liddell V,* 677 F.2d at 642.

48. The court of appeals held that it lacked jurisdiction to review Judge Hungate's orders granting in part and denying in part the interdistrict plaintiffs' January 1981 motions to add additional defendants because interlocutory appeals on matters of case management are not permitted. *Id.* at 638–39. Although the court of appeals also held that it lacked jurisdiction to review Judge Hungate's order recusing himself from the interdistrict liability aspects of the case (*see supra* text accompanying note 35), it urged him to reassume control over the entire case. *Id.* at 642–44. Judge Hungate then resumed control of the interdistrict liability component of the case. H(818)82 (February 25, 1982).

49. H(464)81 (September 21, 1981); H(499)81 (September 25, 1981).

50. *Liddell V,* 677 F.2d at 629–30.

51. *Id.* at 638–39.

52. La Pierre, *supra* note 15.

53. *See supra* text accompanying notes 48–49.

54. *Liddell V,* 677 F.2d at 630.

55. *Id.* at 642.

56. La Pierre, *supra* note 15, at 82–84.

57. Dr. Gary Orfield, the court-appointed desegregation expert, concluded in his review of Foote's proposal on April 5, 1981 that "[t]here is a genuine interest in a voluntary plan on both sides and a sincere desire to explore a possible settlement for the metropolitan case" and that "there is a significant possibility of an agreement, although very difficult issues remain." G. ORFIELD, THE VOLUNTARY METROPOLI-

TAN PLAN: AN ANALYSIS OF EDWARD T. FOOTE'S PROPOSAL 7, 8 (A Report to Judge William Hungate, U.S. District Court, St. Louis) (dated April 5, 1981, and filed on April 6, 1981).

58. In the March 1981 initial efforts to settle the interdistrict case (*see supra* text accompanying notes 16–18), the question of "fiscal incentives" was one important financial issue that was imperfectly resolved. The interdistrict plaintiffs believed that the best "fiscal incentive" for school districts to participate in the permissive inter-district transfer program would be full payment of state educational funds for each transfer student to both the home and host districts. For each permissive interdistrict transfer student, the state would pay the host district the funds normally allotted to that particular district for each pupil enrolled in the district. The state would also pay the home district the funds that it would have received if the student had not transferred. The state was concerned that this approach would increase substantially its costs for each transfer student. The Board of Education was concerned that the "fiscal incentives" for permissive interdistrict transfers would not be adequate to ensure that if it experienced a net loss of students through interdistrict transfers, it would still receive sufficient state aid to provide a high-quality education for students who chose not to transfer. Given the holding of the court of appeals that the district court could order the state to provide incentives for voluntary interdistrict transfers in addition to the "fiscal incentives" ordered under 12(a) (*see Liddell V*, 677 F.2d at 642), I predicted that it would be easier to design a voluntary desegregation plan that would satisfy the Board of Education.

When the *Educational Plan* was under discussion, some representatives of the plaintiff class wanted a voluntary plan to provide assurances that the quality of educa-tion for students who remained in all-black city schools after the implementation of a voluntary interdistrict plan would be improved. I predicted that this concern would now be easier to meet because the court of appeals had held that the district court could order the state to take additional steps to improve the quality of education in these schools. *Liddell V*, 677 F.2d 641–42.

59. *See supra* note 46.

60. When the *Educational Plan* was advanced as a proposed settlement in March 1981, Chairman Foote sought an agreement between the Board of Education, the Department of Justice, and representatives of black city school students on one side and the state and suburban school districts on the other side.

61. H(1485)82 (October 15, 1982).

62. H(2119)83 (February 14, 1983).

63. H(2217)83 (March 30, 1983).

64. Liddell v. Board of Education, 567 F. Supp. 1037 (E.D. Mo. 1983).

65. Liddell v. Board of Education, 731 F.2d 1294 (8th Cir.) (*en banc*) (*Liddell VII*), *cert. denied*, 469 U.S. 816 (1984).

66. This figure is drawn from reports filed by school districts with the Missouri Department of Elementary and Secondary Education. The enrollment data dis-cussed below are all drawn from these reports, which are on file with the author. The enrollment data for the city school system and for the 23 suburban school districts in St. Louis County are collated in Table 6-1.

67. MISSOURI ADVISORY COMMISSION TO THE UNITED STATES COMMISSION

ON CIVIL RIGHTS, SCHOOL DESEGREGATION IN THE ST. LOUIS AND KANSAS CITY AREAS: METROPOLITAN INTERDISTRICT OPTIONS 2–3.

68. *See* Liddell v. Board of Education, 677 F.2d 626, 628 (8th Cir.) (*Liddell V*), *cert. denied,* 459 U.S. 877 (1982).

69. DESEGREGATION MONITORING AND ADVISORY COMMITTEE, ANALYSIS OF BOARD OF EDUCATION ENROLLMENT REPORTS (November 10, 1982) (on file with the author). These figures include only students in regular schools and in first to twelfth grades. They do not include students in kindergarten classes, in magnet schools, in technical schools, or in schools that were exempted from the intradistrict desegregation plan. Approximately 3,700 black and 3,100 white students attended integrated magnet schools in the 1982–1983 school year.

70. METROPOLITAN INTERDISTRICT OPTIONS, *supra* note 67 at 2–3.

71. *See supra* text accompanying note 14.

72. One district, Ferguson-Florissant, had been created by a previous school desegregation order consolidating three county school districts. *See* United States v. Missouri, 515 F.2d 1365 (8th Cir.), *cert. denied,* 423 U.S. 951 (1975). Its status in the interdistrict case was never entirely clear.

73. *See supra* text following note 30.

74. In a direct response to the court of appeals' mandate that he "proceed promptly" with trial of the interdistrict liability issues, Judge Hungate, on April 7, 1982, entered the first of many pretrial orders setting procedures for discovery and for management of the case. H(881)82 (April 7, 1982).

75. *See, e.g.,* H(1196)82 (August 13, 1982) (order that discovery be completed by November 1, 1982).

76. Interim Order for Mandatory Interdistrict Desegregation, H(1183)82 (August 6, 1982). The district court issued the order "to provide guidance for any mandatory interdistrict remedial plan that it may be necessary to implement following the Court's ruling on the issues of liability and constitutional violation." *Id.* at 3–4. The policies for designing a mandatory interdistrict plan included "abolition of the presently-existing school districts and their consolidation into one unified metropolitan-wide school district"; "[a] uniform tax rate . . . to support the unified district-wide educational system"; and student reassignments by race. *Id.* at 4, 8, 9.

77. *Id.*

78. *See, e.g.,* H(1249)82 and H(1248)82 (September 1, 1982) (two orders limiting the duties of the participating districts to proceedings under paragraph 12(a)); H(1196)82 (August 13, 1982) (order exempting school districts participating in the voluntary 12(a) plan from discovery in the interdistrict liability case); H(932)82 (April 30, 1982) (order approving a budget for the 12(a) voluntary plan).

79. *See* H(998)82 (May 25, 1982); H(1167)82 (July 30, 1982); H(1179)82 (August 4, 1982); H(1340)82 (September 14, 1982).

80. *See* H(989)82 (May 20, 1982); H(1417)82 (September 29, 1982).

81. The five original participating districts were Clayton, Kirkwood, Ritenour, University City, and Pattonville. *See supra* note 29. The nine additional participants listed in the order in which the district court accepted their applications were Brentwood, Ladue, Parkway, Lindbergh, Normandy, Affton, Wellston, Hancock Place, and Jennings. H(901)82 (April 20, 1982); H(979a)82 (May 17, 1982); H(1003)82

(May 28, 1982); H(1102)82 (June 28, 1982); H(1156)82 (July 23, 1982); H(1233)82 (August 30, 1982); H(1234)82 (August 30, 1982); H(1365)82 (September 17, 1982); H(1367)82 (September 17, 1982).

82. 1982–83 Interdistrict Transfer Count (January 20, 1983) (on file with the author). For a comprehensive overview of the interdistrict student transfer program under the 12(a) plan, *see* COORDINATING COMMITTEE FOR AN EDUCATIONAL PLAN FOR VOLUNTARY, COOPERATIVE DESEGREGATION, Report No. 4, H(2489)83 (June 29, 1983).

83. *See supra* text at notes 21–22.

84. *See* Defty, *Desegregation Fight Costly for Districts*, St. Louis Post-Dispatch, May 2, 1982, at 1F, col. 1 (comparison of legal fees of participating districts and districts involved in the interdistrict liability litigation).

85. School board members of suburban school districts who voted to participate in the 12(a) voluntary plan reported that they chose participation in order to avoid the risk of a mandatory desegregation plan. *See* Hannon and Singer, *Parkway Board Votes for Area School Plan*, St. Louis Post-Dispatch, May 17, 1982, at 1, col. 1; Vespereny, *Ladue Becomes 7th County School District to Enter Desegregation Plan*, St. Louis Post-Dispatch, April 30, 1982, at 1, col. 1.

86. *See supra* notes 76–77 and accompanying text.

87. Maplewood-Richmond Heights was the fifteenth suburban school district to join the 12(a) voluntary plan. Its application was approved on January 20, 1983. H(1978)83 (January 20, 1983).

88. *See supra* notes 15, 52–60, and accompanying text.

89. *See supra* text accompanying notes 20–22 and note 23.

90. *See supra* notes 25–28 and accompanying text.

91. Order H(1788)82 (December 14, 1982).

92. Shortly after the court granted the first postponement on Monday morning, I met with all of the attorneys and presented, as the basis for the negotiations, a revised draft of the formal February 10 settlement proposal that had been under consideration during the preceding weekend. In an effort to promote serious and efficient negotiations among a very large number of lawyers, I asked the attorneys for the interdistrict plaintiffs and the suburban school districts to designate negotiating teams. I also limited participation to the parties most directly involved and excused representatives from the Department of Justice, the city of St. Louis, St. Louis County, and the Special School District. The state of Missouri participated in these negotiations on a limited, but very helpful, basis. Shulamith Simon, an *amicus curiae* appointed by the district court to represent the public interest, helped to supervise the negotiations. Although the negotiations were confidential, a remarkably accurate account of these tense, often heated, and dramatic transactions subsequently appeared in a local newspaper. Rogers and Futterman, *Tense Moments in School Talks*, St. Louis Post-Dispatch, March 1, 1983, at 11A, col. 3–6.

93. Order H(2133)83 (February 16, 1983). Judge Hungate warned the lawyers that "[t]hose unable to agree shall have their day in court beginning at 10:00 a.m. on February 22nd." *Id.*

94. H(2217)83, *supra* note 63, at I–2 [hereinafter S.A.]. The text of the AIP is included in my February 22, 1983, report to the court. REPORT OF THE SPECIAL

Master, H(2141)83 (February 22, 1983). The Settlement Agreement also includes the AIP as § I A. Report of the Special Master, H(2217)83 (March 30, 1983). Citations here are to the text of the AIP as it is reproduced in the Settlement Agreement.

95. *See supra* text following note 88.

96. AIP, *supra* note 94, at I–2.

97. *Id.*

98. *See supra* Table 6-1 and text following note 70.

99. *See supra* text accompanying note 89.

100. AIP, *supra* note 94, at I–2 to I–3.

101. *Id.* at I–3 to I–4.

102. *Id.* at I–5 to I–6.

103. AIP at I–6 to I–7.

104. Report of the Special Master, H(2141)83 (February 22, 1983). The report included four statements of positions on the AIP. The Department of Justice reported general approval subject to the drafting of a detailed plan and noted its disapproval of several provisions related to housing, faculty hiring ratios, and a tax increase in the city. *Id.* (letter dated February 18, 1983, to the Special Master from William Bradford Reynolds, Assistant Attorney General, Civil Rights Division). Although St. Louis County expressed doubt that it had any role in these proceedings, it stated a desire to exclude housing issues from the settlement. *Id.* (St. Louis County Government Defendants and the 12(c) proceeding). The state noted that the AIP had "been negotiated by the local school districts with little involvement by the State defendants," but it agreed to participate in the drafting of a detailed implementation plan with respect to "finances." *Id.* (State Defendants' Response to Special Master's Report). The city of St. Louis strongly objected to the AIP, which it read as authorizing federal courts to levy a tax on city residents in order to finance a settlement. Statement of Plaintiff Intervenor city of St. Louis Concerning 12(C) "Agreement in Principle," H(2143)83 (February 22, 1983).

105. H(2142)83 (February 22, 1983).

106. Report of the Special Master, H(2217)83 (March 30, 1983).

107. Suggestions for Rule 23(e) Compliance, H(2218)83 (March 30, 1983).

108. H(2224)83 (March 31, 1983).

109. S.A., *supra* note 94, § IA., at I–1. *See supra* text accompanying notes 14, 30–48.

110. S.A., *supra* note 94, § IA. (Purpose), at I–2 to I–8.

111. *Id.*, § VI. (Faculty), at VI–1 to VI–7. In the 1987–1988 school year, there were only three county teachers who transferred to city schools and four city teachers who transferred to county schools. Fifth Report, *supra* note 2, at 50.

112. S.A., *supra* note 94, § IX (Administration). There are also provisions creating part-time education programs designed to enhance the opportunity for integrated learning experiences. *Id.*, § V, at V–1 to V–2. Most of the remaining provisions of the Settlement Agreement are discussed herein in relation to its three principal components.

113. *Id.*, § IA. (Purpose–AIP), at I–3.

114. *Id.*, § IIA., at II–1.

115. *Id.*, § IIA.2.b., at II–1 to II–2.

116. *Id.*, § IIA.2.c.i., at II–2.

117. *Id.*, § IIA.2.c.ii., at II–3.

118. *Id.*, § IIA.3., A.4., at II–3 to II–6.

119. *Id.*, § XIIA., at XII–1.

120. *Id.*, § XIID., at XII–1. The Settlement Agreement also creates a complex formula granting a final judgment to a school district that has achieved within five years 90 percent of its plan ratio if the other suburban school districts have in fact exceeded their plan ratios and the total number of interdistrict transfer students in the 16 suburban school districts equals or exceeds the number of interdistrict transfer students that would have existed if all 16 districts had met their plan ratios. *Id.* at XII–1 and n. 1.

121. *Id.*, § XII, at XII–3. The settlement provides that the court will relinquish active supervision of these continuing obligations two years after the end of the five-year stay. *Id.*

122. *Id.*, § XIIE.1., F., G., at XII–2 to XII–4. If necessary, these negotiations were to commence at the start of the fifth year of implementation in October 1987. Only two of the 16 suburban school districts failed to achieve their plan ratios within the five-year period of the stay, and both districts successfully negotiated extensions under the provisions of the Settlement Agreement. *See infra* notes 269–71 and accompanying text.

123. *Id.*, § XIIF.5., 6., at XII–4.

124. *Id.*, § XIIE.2., at XII–3.

125. *Id.*, § IIA.2.c., at II–2 to II–3.

126. *See infra* note 230 and accompanying text.

127. S.A., *supra* note 94, § IIA.2.c.i., at II–2 to II–3.

128. *Id.*, § IIA.2.c.ii., at II–3. This obligation is stated in terms of facilitating transfers to any school district with a minority enrollment in excess of 50 percent; however, after a judicial modification eliminated intra-county transfers (*see infra* note 230 and accompanying text), the transfer obligation exists only with regard to the city schools.

These four school districts had an additional obligation to permit black students in individual schools with a black student population of more than 50 percent to make interdistrict transfers to predominately white suburban school districts. *Id.*, § XIF.1., at XI–1 to XI–2. The court of appeals subsequently eliminated the right of black county students to make interdistrict transfers. *See infra* note 230 and accompanying text.

129. *See infra* note 230 and accompanying text.

130. S.A., *supra* note 94, § IIB.1., 2.a., at II–7.

131. *Id.*, § IIB.3., at II–8.

132. *Id.*, § IIB.2.b., at II–7. As drafted, the Settlement Agreement provided that white students in the 19 county school districts could also transfer to any one of the four predominately black suburban school districts. A subsequent judicial decision limiting the state's duty to pay for intra-county transfers (*see infra* note 230 and accompanying text) substantially reduced the potential effect of this provision.

133. Each voluntary interdistrict transfer student may request assignment to

"up to three . . . school districts and two school[s] . . . within each district." *Id.*, § IIC.2.b.ii., at II–9. Every effort is made to honor the students' choices. *Id.*, § IIC.3., at II–10.

134. *Id.*, § IIC.–F., at II–9 to II–13.

135. *Id.*, § VIII, at VIII–1.

136. *Id.*, § III, at III–1 to III–9.

137. *See infra* notes 235–39 and accompanying text.

138. S.A., *supra* note 94, § IIIA.3.c., at III–1.

139. *Id.*, § III A.3.d., at III–1.

140. *Id.*, § IIIJ.–L., at III–8.

141. *Id.*, § IIIC.–E., at III–5 to III–7.

142. *See id.*, § IA.3.b. (AIP), at I–4.

143. *Id.*, § IV, at IV–1 to IV–15, Appendix.

144. *Id.*, § IV, at IV–1.

145. *Id.*

146. *Id.* ("[T]he St. Louis County School districts do not have the necessary information about the city schools to form an opinion on the details of the Appendix and, therefore, they do not agree or disagree with all of the specifics in this basic design").

147. *See generally* MISSOURI DEPARTMENT OF ELEMENTARY AND SECONDARY EDUCATION, HANDBOOK FOR CLASSIFICATION AND ACCREDITATION OF PUBLIC SCHOOL DISTRICTS IN MISSOURI (1980).

148. *Id.*, § IV, at IV–2. *See id.*, § I (AIP), at I–4.

149. *Id.*, § IV, at IV–2.

150. *Id.*, § IV, at IV–9.

151. *Id.* at IV–11.

152. *Id.*, § XB.1., 2., at X–1 to X–2.

153. *See supra* text accompanying note 24 and note 58.

154. This figure is for the 1985–1986 school year, and it is based on data provided to the author by the Voluntary Interdistrict Coordinating Council. For an example of a calculation of the effect of the payment of state per pupil financial aid to both home and host districts, *see* La Pierre, *supra* note 15, at 83 n. 31.

155. *See* S.A., *supra* note 94, § XB.1., 2, at X–1 to X–2.

156. *Id.*, § XIE., at XI–1.

157. *Id.*, § XB.3., at X–2.

158. *Id.*

159. *See supra* text accompanying notes 53–55.

160. Caldwell Plaintiffs' Report to the Court, H(2220)83 (March 30, 1983).

161. Response of Plaintiffs Craton Liddell, *et al.*, to Report of the Special Master on the Settlement Agreement, H(2249)83 (April 4, 1983).

162. City Board Acceptance of Detailed Implementation Plan, H(2252)83 (April 4, 1983).

163. The acceptances are listed in the order in which they were filed. H(2221)83 (March 30, 1983) (Maplewood-Richmond Heights); H(2222)83 (March 30, 1983) (Valley Park); H(2223)83 (March 31, 1983) (Riverview Gardens); H(2226)83 (March 31, 1983) (Hazelwood); H(2232)83 (April 1, 1983) (Normandy); H(2233)83 (April 1, 1983) (Ferguson-Florissant); H(2235)83 (April 1, 1983) (Ritenour); H(2236)83 (April

4, 1983) (Affton); H(2237)83 (April 4, 1983) (Lindbergh); H(2238)83 (April 4, 1983) (Wellston); H(2240)83 (April 4, 1983) (Ladue); H(2243)83 (April 4, 1983) (Mehlville); H(2244)83 (April 4, 1983) (Bayless); H(2245)83 (April 4, 1983) (Brentwood); H(2246)83 (April 4, 1983) (Clayton); H(2247)83 (April 4, 1983) (Hancock Place); H(2248)83 (April 4, 1983) (Jennings); H(2250)83 (April 4, 1983) (Rockwood); H(2251)83 (April 4, 1983) (Webster Groves); H(2255)83 (April 4, 1983) (Kirkwood); H(2260)83 (April 4, 1983) (Parkway); H(2262)83 (April 4, 1983) (Pattonville).

164. *See* Rockwood School District's Acceptance of Detailed Implementation Plan, H(2250)83 (April 4, 1983); Mehlville School District's Report to the Court, H(2243)83 (April 4, 1983). The "good cause" condition was an attempt by these two school districts to limit the duration of the settlement plan and to create an opportunity to end their obligations. It was inconsistent with the Settlement Agreement, which specifically stated the obligations of the 16 suburban school districts, including Rockwood and Mehlville (*see supra* Table 6-2), with minority enrollments of less than 25 percent. *See supra* text at notes 118–24.

165. *See supra* notes 29, 93, and accompanying text.

166. Declination by School District of University City to Agree to Detailed Implementation Plan, H(2257)83 (April 4, 1983).

167. *Id.*

168. Position of St. Louis County Government Defendants Regarding Settlement Agreement at 2, H(2239)83 (April 4, 1983).

169. Comments of City of St. Louis on H(2217)83, H(2234)83 (April 1, 1983).

170. *See supra* note 104.

171. Response to Order H(2224)83, H(2261)83 (April 4, 1983).

172. State Defendants' Response to Settlement Agreement at 1, 11, H(2259)83 (April 4, 1983).

173. *Id.* ("Although we may disagree with certain approaches taken by Professor La Pierre and the agreement reached by the parties thereto, we nonetheless applaud all efforts to reach a voluntary settlement"). The state, however, had attempted to scuttle the settlement just three days before this report was filed. On April 1, 1983, the Attorney General of the state of Missouri sent a letter to all of the attorneys for the suburban school districts. The letter, which outlined alleged defects in the settlement, was clearly intended to persuade the suburban school districts to reject the settlement. *See Ashcroft's Message to Schools*, St. Louis Globe-Democrat, April 2–3, 1983, at 6D, col. 1.

174. *See supra* notes 52–60 and accompanying text.

175. State Defendants' Response to Settlement Agreement, *supra* note 172 at 3.

176. *See* Order H(2263)83 (April 4, 1983).

177. REPORT OF THE SPECIAL MASTER, H(2273)83 (April 7, 1983).

178. Order H(2278)83 (April 8, 1983); Order H(2276)83 (April 8, 1983).

179. Notice to Class Members of a Proposed Settlement in the St. Louis School Desegregation Case, H(2277)83 (April 8, 1983).

180. Order H(2279)83 (April 8, 1983).

181. The city of St. Louis argued that the notice "gravely misle[d] the classes about the funding provisions of the proposed settlement" because it did not state clearly that the plan allows the court to order state funding and a tax rate increase in the city of St. Louis. Memorandum in Support of Motion to Set Aside Order

[H(2276)83] Approving Notice to Class Members and to Order Supplementation of Such Notice, and to Reset Fairness Hearing at 1, H(2290)83 (April 18, 1983). The state joined the city's motion. State Defendants' Response to the Motion of the City of St. Louis to Set Aside Order H(2276)83, H(2304)83 (April 21, 1983). *See* Plaintiffs Liddell, Caldwell and City Board's Memorandum in Opposition to Motion of City of St. Louis to Set Aside Order [H(2276)83] Approving Notice to Class Members, to Order Supplementation of Such Notice, and to Reset Fairness Hearing, H(2326)83 (April 25, 1983); Response of Defendants St. Louis County School Districts to Motion of the City of St. Louis to Set Aside Order H(2276)83 and to Reset Fairness Hearing, H(2316)83 (April 25, 1983).

182. Order and Memorandum H(2343)83 (April 28, 1983). The court also denied the motions of two groups to intervene as parties.

The North St. Louis Parents and Citizens for Quality Education sought to intervene for the purpose of arguing that the settlement was not designed adequately to achieve quality education in the north side all-black schools and that instead it was designed to achieve integration, a goal that many did not desire. *See* Memorandum and Motion to Object to Proposed Settlement and to Intervene as Plaintiff, H(2161)83 (March 2, 1983). This motion was supported by the City of St. Louis. Memorandum in Support, H(2199)83 (March 18, 1983). It was opposed by most of the county school districts and the interdistrict plaintiffs. Reply to "Objectors," H(2230)83 (March 31, 1983); Joint Response to Motion, H(2227)83 (March 31, 1983); Response to Motion, H(2185)83 (March 9, 1983). The court denied the motion to intervene, but it permitted this group to present its objections at the fairness hearing. Order and Memorandum, H(2270)83 (April 6, 1983). *See* Notice of Intent to Appear, H(2315)83 (April 25, 1983) (North St. Louis Parents and Citizens for Quality Education's Notice of intent to appear at the fairness hearing).

The union representing the teachers in the city schools also sought to intervene. Motion of St. Louis Teachers Union Local 420, American Federation of Teachers to Intervene as to Remedy and Objections to Approval of Portions of the Proposed Settlement Agreement, H(2293)83 (April 18, 1983); Motion for Leave to File Motion of St. Louis Teachers Union Local 420 to Intervene as to Remedy, H(2292)83 (April 18, 1983). This motion to intervene was opposed by the interdistrict plaintiffs and the suburban school districts. Joint Memorandum of City Board, Liddell and Caldwell, H(2328)83 (April 25, 1983); Defendant St. Louis County School Districts' Memorandum in Opposition, H(2317)83 (April 25, 1983). The court deferred action on this motion to intervene until after the conclusion of the fairness hearing. Order H(2341)83 (April 28, 1983). The teachers union did participate in the fairness hearing. *See* Statement of St. Louis Teachers Union in Regard to Proposed Settlement, H(2305)83 (April 22, 1983). The court subsequently denied the motion to intervene. Liddell v. Board of Education, 98 F.R.D. 548 (E.D. Mo. 1983).

183. *See supra* note 146.

184. Memorandum of Concerns 2–3, H(2339)83 (April 28, 1983).

185. *Id.* at 3.

186. Signatories' Pre-Hearing Memorandum, H(2325)83 (April 25, 1983).

187. Joint Signatories' Response to Memorandum of Concerns [H(2339)83] and Suggestions for Further Proceedings, H(2455)83 (June 1, 1983).

188. Although the interdistrict plaintiffs objected to the participation of Rockwood and Mehlville in the fairness hearing on the ground that the conditions of their acceptances of the settlement were inconsistent with the Agreement in Principle (*see supra* note 164 and accompanying text), the court permitted these two school districts to make separate presentations. Order H(2422)83 (May 13, 1983). Rockwood argued that its obligations under the settlement should be subject to termination two years after the five-year stay period on a showing of good cause. Rockwood School District's Notice of Intent to Appear, H(2331)83 (April 25, 1983). In particular, Rockwood argued that, notwithstanding good faith implementation, it might not be able to achieve its plan ratio and plan goal because black city students might choose not to travel the long distance (up to 35 miles) to Rockwood. Such a failure to comply with the settlement would be due to circumstances beyond Rockwood's control and should constitute good cause to terminate its obligations. Mehlville joined this argument that the settlement agreement should include a provision for termination or modification after the five-year stay period. Mehlville School District R–9 Witness List, Exhibit List, and Brief in Support of its Position on the Proposed Settlement Agreement at 8–9, H(2320)83 (April 25, 1983). Although both districts' arguments were directly contrary to the specific terms of the Settlement Agreement, these two suburban school districts claimed that their conditional acceptances were consistent with the terms of the settlement and the Agreement in Principle. *See* Rockwood School District's Brief in Support of Its Right to Participate in Fairness Hearing at 3, H(2375)83 (May 6, 1983); Memorandum of Defendant Mehlville School District at 4, H(2374)83 (May 6, 1983).

189. The U.S. Department of Justice (DOJ) limited its participation in the fairness hearing to cross-examination, but it submitted a brief recommending that the court should not approve the settlement in its present form. Brief of the United States on Proposed Settlement at 3, H(2336)83 (April 27, 1983); Pretrial Materials of the United States on Proposed Settlement Agreement, H(2322)83 (April 25, 1983). The DOJ noted three objections. First, it objected to the provisions of the settlement that measured a suburban school district's compliance with the interdistrict student transfer requirements solely in numerical terms, and it urged the addition of a provision recognizing good faith compliance where failure to reach the plan ratio was due to circumstances beyond the control of a suburban school district. Second, it objected to the provisions of the settlement that it read to require faculty hiring solely on the basis of race. Finally, the DOJ objected to the provision for a tax increase and to the imposition of substantial costs on the state. Brief of the United States on Proposed Settlement at 4, H(2336)83 (April 27, 1983).

190. The court heard testimony from 11 non-party opponents of the settlement and reviewed 42 written comments. Liddell v. Board of Education, 567 F. Supp. 1037, 1044 (E.D. Mo. 1983).

191. State Defendants Pre-Trial Brief For Settlement Agreement Hearing at 5, 11, H(2334)83 (April 25, 1983).

192. Pre-Fairness Hearing Brief of City of St. Louis, H(2323)83 (April 25, 1983).

193. Acceptance by School District of University City of Detailed Implementation Plan, H(2459)83 (June 1, 1983). University City had declined to adopt the

settlement because it believed that the settlement did not do enough for the predominately black suburban school districts. *See supra* text accompanying notes 165–67. Although it, like the city, had a black enrollment of more than 75 percent, the settlement did not provide any funds to improve the quality of education in University City. Statement of University City School Board Pursuant to H(2276)83 at 3, H(2408)83 (May 10, 1983). Moreover, white students in University City could not make interdistrict transfers to other school districts because such transfers would increase racial isolation in University City and, as University City read the settlement, its white students could not attend magnet schools established under the settlement in University City. *Id.*

In response to these concerns and after negotiations that I conducted between University City and the signatories, the signatories submitted an amendment to the Settlement Agreement on June 1, 1983. This amendment listed three additional magnet schools to be established in University City, and it corrected a "drafting error" in the settlement that would have restricted the eligibility of students to attend magnet schools in their home districts. Proponents' Memorandum Attaching Addenda to the Settlement Agreement, H(2458)83 (June 1, 1983). Although University City then adopted the Settlement Agreement, it adhered to the view that the settlement "does not fully address the concerns of students in black-majority County districts." Statement Supplementing Memorandum of Acceptance of Settlement Agreement, H(2459)83, H(2464)83 (June 2, 1983).

194. Order H(2431) (May 19, 1983); Order H(2410)83 (May 10, 1983).

195. Financial Analysis of the Proposed Settlement Agreement, H(2474)83 (June 13, 1983).

196. Liddell v. Board of Education, 567 F. Supp. 1037, 1047, 1055 (E.D. Mo. 1983), *aff'd as modified,* 731 F.2d 1294 (8th Cir.) (*en banc*) (*Liddell VII*), *cert. denied,* 469 U.S. 816 (1984).

197. The court approved the two school districts' conditions to the extent that they were not inconsistent with the Settlement Agreement and held that they were "members in good standing of the Settlement Plan." Liddell v. Board of Education, 567 F. Supp. at 1041. The court then placed the burden on these two school districts by ruling that if, instead of participating in the settlement, they wished to litigate, they should notify the court, and the interdistrict liability trial against them would begin on July 25. *Id.* at 1041, 1055. Neither Rockwood nor Mehlville accepted the court's invitation to be the sole defendants in an interdistrict trial.

198. *Id.* at 1047.

199. *Id.* at 1049.

200. *Id.* at 1049–50.

201. *Id.* at 1051.

202. *Id.* at 1057.

203. *See supra* notes 183–87 and accompanying text.

204. *See infra* text accompanying notes 309–18.

205. Liddell v. Board of Education, 567 F. Supp. at 1048. The district court also accepted the financial advisor's recommendation that the "City Board complete a long-range study of its plant facilities." *Id.* at 1051.

206. S.A., *supra* note 94, § IIIB., at III-2.

207. *See supra* text accompanying note 141.

208. Liddell v. Board of Education, 567 F. Supp. at 1048.

209. The estimates of the first year settlement costs ranged from $37 million (financial advisor) to $87 million (Board of Education) to more than $100 million (state). *Id.* at 1051.

210. *See supra* text accompanying notes 157–59. Under the Settlement Agreement, "[t]he fulfillment of the obligations of the parties is contingent upon an Order by the Court which establishes adequate funding for the obligations of the parties. . . ." S.A., *supra* note 94, § XA., at X–1.

211. Liddell v. Board of Education, 567 F. Supp. at 1051.

212. The state's responsibility for funding voluntary interdistrict desegregation measures under this case is discussed *supra* in the text accompanying notes 53–55.

213. Liddell v. Board of Education, 567 F. Supp. at 1052.

214. *Id.*

215. *Id.* at 1054.

216. *Id.* at 1055.

217. *Id.* at 1048. The court did urge the signatories to consider the financial advisor's recommendations to reduce the costs of fiscal incentives paid to both the home and host districts.

218. *Id.* at 1055.

219. *Id.* at 1056.

220. *Id.* at 1055–56.

221. Liddell v. Board of Education, 717 F.2d 1180 (8th Cir. 1983) (*en banc*) (*Liddell VI*).

222. *Liddell VII*, 731 F.2d at 1301. Most of the appellants' arguments are considered below in the discussion of the court of appeals' opinion. In separate sections of its opinion, the court of appeals upheld the district court's order denying the teachers union the right of intervention and rejected the North St. Louis Parents' argument that the settlement "sacrifices the interests of black students who will remain in the all-black schools for the interests of the black students who will transfer to county schools." *Id.* at 1325.

The United States did not appeal, but it filed a brief and was allowed to argue that the case should be remanded to the district court for detailed findings that the remedial measures funded by the state were necessary to eliminate remaining segregation in the city schools and for a determination whether the order prohibiting the tax rollback was necessary for the Board of Education to finance its share of settlement costs. *See id.* at 1301 n. 6.

223. *Id.* at 1298 ("the cost of the plan, particularly to the State, will be significantly reduced").

224. *Id.*

225. The district court subsequently gave the signatories until March 2, 1984, to decide whether they would withdraw from the Settlement Agreement in light of the changes made by the court of appeals. No one withdrew. *See County Districts Accept Desegregation Rules*, St. Louis Post-Dispatch, March 3, 1984, at 4A, col. 1.

226. *See supra* text accompanying notes 53–55.

227. *Compare supra* text accompanying notes 89–90 *with supra* text accompanying notes 97–98.

228. *Liddell VII*, 731 F.2d at 1309.

229. The AIP did estimate that there would be an opportunity for approximately 15,000 interdistrict transfers from the city schools to the suburban school districts under its plan ratio provisions. S.A., *supra* note 94, § IA.1.c., at I–3. The district court subsequently concluded that the court of appeals did not intend to impose a 15,000 cap on interdistrict transfers. *See infra* text accompanying note 361.

230. *Liddell VII*, 731 F.2d at 1309. Although the court disapproved state funding, it noted that county-to-county voluntary transfers could nonetheless proceed without such funding. *Id.*

231. *Id.* at 1302–08.

232. *Id.* at 1302.

233. *Id.* at 1297.

234. *Id.* at 1298.

235. *Id.* at 1312. The court's rationale for imposing this change, apart from an implicit effort to reduce the state's costs, is not clear. With regard to magnet schools to be located in predominately black suburban school districts and designed to attract white students from the 16 predominately white suburban school districts, the disapproval is consistent with the court's determination that the state's intradistrict violation in the city schools is not a basis for imposing responsibility to reduce racial isolation in black county school districts. The disapproval of magnets to be located in the 16 predominately white county school districts and designed to attract black students from the city schools cannot be explained on the same theory. The court, however, offered no explanation for its change of heart other than the oblique statement that the "Court *en banc* does not believe that the record sufficiently supports" state funding of county magnet schools. *Id.*

236. *See supra* note 193.

237. The Settlement Agreement provided for up to 20,000 magnet seats and allocated 12,000 to 14,000 to the city and 6,000 to 8,000 to the county. *See supra* text accompanying notes 137–39. Consistent with its disapproval of state funding for county magnet schools and with the terms of the settlement, the court of appeals then placed a cap of 14,000 students on city magnet school enrollment. *Liddell VII*, 731 F.2d at 1312.

238. *Liddell VII*, 731 F.2d at 1311.

239. Liddell v. Board of Education, 758 F.2d 290, 303–04 (8th Cir. 1985) (*Liddell VIII*). In 1988, the district court made major changes in the magnet component of the Settlement Agreement. *See infra* notes 299–308 and accompanying text.

240. *Liddell VII*, 731 F.2d at 1310, 1311.

241. *Id.* at 1312.

242. *See infra* notes 283–97 and accompanying text.

243. *Liddell VII*, 731 F.2d at 1315.

244. *Id.* at 1316.

245. *Id.* at 1316–17.

246. *Id.* at 1317.

247. *Id.* at 1317–18.

248. *Id.* at 1297.

249. *See infra* text accompanying note 318.

250. *Liddell VII*, 731 F.2d at 1323–25.

251. *See supra* text accompanying notes 202–4.

252. *Liddell VII*, 731 F.2d at 1324.

253. *Id.* at 1324–25.

254. *Id.* at 1325.

255. *Id.* at 1297.

256. *Id.* at 1320.

257. *Id.* at 1323.

258. *Id.* The district court's first step is to identify the amount of money required to fund the Board of Education's share of the desegregation budget. The second step is to determine whether existing resources are adequate. If the Board's resources are not adequate, then the district court, as a third step, must explore alternative sources of revenue. Fourth, if the court determines that alternatives are either insufficient or unavailable, then it may enter "a judgment sufficient to cure the constitutional violations." *Id.* The district court has not been forced to follow these procedures. In the next five years, through July 1988, the voters of St. Louis have agreed to delay the scheduled rollback in property taxes. Gayle, Gillerman, and O'Neil, *School, City Payroll Taxes Pass*, St. Louis Post-Dispatch, June 8, 1988, at 1A.

259. *Liddell VII*, 731 F.2d at 1319.

260. *Id.* at 1319. Fifty-five percent of the voters had approved the bond issue. Although 84 percent of the voters in the predominately black voting districts supported the bond issue, 65 percent of the voters in the predominately white areas voted against it. *Id.*

261. *Id. See supra* note 258.

262. Leggett v. Liddell, 469 U.S. 816 (1984); Missouri v. Liddell, 469 U.S. 816 (1984); North St. Louis Parents and Citizens for Quality Education v. Liddell, 469 U.S. 816 (1984).

263. *Liddell VII*, 731 F.2d at 1297.

264. Gross, *supra* note 5, at 1, col. 2. The analysis of the implementation of the Settlement Agreement is based on the author's discussions with educators and attorneys involved in the school desegregation case. Some of the information that they provided is not available in any public document, but it is on file with the author. In order to obtain frank and candid assessments of the implementation of the settlement, the author promised his sources that they would remain anonymous.

265. Fifth Report, *supra* note 2, at i.

266. *See supra* text accompanying note 3.

267. Fifth Report, *supra* note 2, at ii.

268. The 14 suburban school districts that have reached their plan ratio and obtained final judgments are Affton, Bayless, Brentwood, Clayton, Hancock Place, Hazelwood, Kirkwood, Ladue, Lindbergh, Parkway, Pattonville, Ritenour, Valley Park, and Webster Groves. Fifth Report, *supra* note 2, at vi, 2–3, 25 (table 4); *see, e.g.*, Final Judgment of Satisfaction for Bayless, L(1155)86 (November 6, 1986).

269. Fifth Report, *supra* note 2, at 2–3, 25 (table 4).

270. *See supra* text accompanying notes 122–24.

271. *See* Liddell v. Board of Education, 696 F. Supp. 442 (E.D. Mo. 1988) (Rockwood); Liddell v. Board of Education, 687 F. Supp. 1368 (E.D. Mo. 1988) (Mehlville). Although the parties agreed to a three-year extension of the stay for

Mehlville, the district court ordered this school district to achieve its plan ratio in two years allocated to Rockwood. *Id. See* Gross and Bell, *Judge Extends Minority Enrollment Deadline,* St. Louis Post-Dispatch, June 2, 1988, at 7W, col. 1; Earley and Todd, *Distance Is an Enemy in Meeting Desegregation Goals,* St. Louis Post-Dispatch, February 24, 1988, at 3W, col. 1.

272. *See generally* Fifth Report, *supra* note 2. A study completed after the first year of implementation of the settlement concluded, "There is general agreement among Saint Louis educators and community leaders that the Voluntary Interdistrict Transfer Program is working well for participating students." M. GRADY AND C. WILLIE, METROPOLITAN SCHOOL DESEGREGATION: A CASE STUDY OF THE SAINT LOUIS AREA VOLUNTARY TRANSFER PROGRAM 84 (1986).

273. In April 1987, the Board of Education and the NAACP asked the district court to order the Voluntary Interdistrict Coordinating Council to collect additional information and data about the interdistrict student transfer program. These two parties argued that the information reported by the VICC in its annual reports was not adequate to permit a comprehensive evaluation of the interdistrict desegregation plan. Joint Motion of the Board and the Caldwell Plaintiffs to Require Reporting of Information for Monitoring Settlement Agreement, L(1398)87 (April 20, 1987); Joint Memorandum of St. Louis County School Districts In Opposition to the Joint Motion of the Board of Education and the Caldwell Plaintiffs to Require Reporting of Information for Monitoring of Settlement Agreement [L(1398)87], L(1445)87 (May 15, 1987). *See* Uhlenbrock, *School Board, NAACP Seek Data from Council About Transfers,* St. Louis Post-Dispatch, April 22, 1987, at 6A, col. 4. The courts granted the interdistrict plaintiffs' requests for additional information about black interdistrict transfer students, but they denied the request for information about resident students, which would have permitted a statistical comparison of black interdistrict transfer students with resident students. Liddell v. Board of Education, 851 F.2d 1104 (8th Cir. 1988) *(Liddell XIV). See* Gross, *Appeals Court Rules That Records of Transfer Students Be Opened,* St. Louis Post-Dispatch, July 15, 1988, at 6A, col. 2.

274. *See generally Desegregation: Fifth Year Report,* St. Louis Post-Dispatch, February 22, 1988, at 1A, col. 1. (an eight-part investigative report published over eight days from February 22 through February 28). A newsletter published by Voluntary Interdistrict Coordinating Council reports that many interdistrict transfer students have earned substantial honors including election to class offices and academic societies. Voluntary Interdistrict Coordinating Council, The Volunteer—Highlights of the St. Louis Voluntary Transfer Plan (Spring 1987). For a story of one interdistrict transfer student's experiences, *see* Freivogel, *Student Experiences 14th Amendment at Work,* St. Louis Post-Dispatch, May 24, 1987, at 4B, col. 1.

275. Fifth Report, *supra* note 2, at iv–v, 123–25; *see* Voluntary Interdistrict Coordinating Council, Progress Report at 6 (table 3), L(1141)86 (October 31, 1986).

276. *See* Fifth Report, *supra* note 2, at 107–14; Rogers, *Officials: Discipline Unbiased,* St. Louis Post-Dispatch, August 23, 1987, at 4C, col. 6.

277. *See, e.g.* Eardley, *Transport of Transfer Students Called "a Disaster,"* St. Louis Post-Dispatch, September 26, 1985, at 1.

278. Fifth Report, *supra* note 2, at 129.

279. *See supra* text accompanying note 2.

280. *See supra* text accompanying note 239.

281. Progress Report, *supra* note 275, at 6 (table 2).

282. Fifth Report, *supra* note 2, at 94.

283. *See* Liddell v. Board of Education, 801 F.2d 278, 282 (8th Cir. 1986) (*Liddell IX*) ("serious differences" between the state and the Board); Order L(1336)87 at 3 (March 17, 1987) ("Today, the City Board and the State do not have 'serious differences,' they apparently have irreconcilable differences. When the City Board and State meet to address the issue of magnets, they do not meet to discuss, but rather meet to do battle").

284. *Liddell IX*, 801 F.2d at 282 ("The City Board . . . contends that its efforts to implement effective interdistrict magnets are continuously frustrated by the State's objections to its proposals and the State's refusal to pay for adequate facilities and programs").

285. *Id.* ("The State argues that the Board is using the interdistrict magnets as a method of requiring the State to pay 100 percent of the cost of educating City students"). Order L(1336)87 at 10 (March 17, 1987) ("This Court fears that magnet schools are becoming favored replacements for city schools, thus relieving the City Board not only of fiscal responsibility, but academic responsibility for educating its students").

286. *See supra* text accompanying note 141.

287. Order L(1336)87 at 10 (March 17, 1987) ("It is apparent that the chaotic nature of the magnet process will continue as long as the City Board believes that it has carte blanche to create magnet proposals and the MRC's participation is not to analyze, but generally rubberstamp approval on all City Board magnet creations").

288. *See* Motion of Plaintiffs Liddell and the Board of Education of the City of St. Louis to Remove Dr. Warren Brown as Financial Advisor and as BRC Chairperson or, in the Alternative, to Remove Dr. Brown as BRC Chairperson, L(742)86 (February 2, 1986).

289. Fifth Report, *supra* note 2, at v.

290. Liddell v. Board of Education, 801 F.2d 278, 282–84 (8th Cir.) (*Liddell IX*), *reh'g denied*, 804 F.2d 500 (8th Cir. 1986) (*Liddell X*).

291. *Liddell IX*, 801 F.2d at 282.

292. *Id.* The court of appeals also held that if a particular magnet school does not make its goal, the state may move to have the school converted to an intradistrict magnet (which is funded equally by the state and the Board) or terminated. The court added that the state's cooperation with the Board would be an important factor in ruling on such motions. *Id.* at 282–83.

293. *Id.* at 283.

294. Order L(1336)87 (March 17, 1987).

295. *Id.*

296. Liddell v. Board of Education, 823 F.2d 1252, 1255 (8th Cir. 1987) (*Liddell XII*).

297. *Id.* at 1253, 1256.

298. Long-Range Comprehensive Plan for the Magnet Schools of St. Louis, Missouri, L(1585)87 (September 14, 1987); *see* Rogers, *Plan Would Revamp Magnet Schools*, St. Louis Post-Dispatch, September 1, 1987, at 1, col. 1.

299. Liddell v. Board of Education, 696 F. Supp. 442 (E.D. Mo. 1988).

300. *Id.* at 452–54.

301. *Id.* at 460–62, 465–68, 470 (table 3).

302. *Id.* at 463.

303. *Id.* at 463–64.

304. *Id.*

305. *Id.* at 468.

306. *See infra* notes 320–25 and accompanying text.

307. *See infra* note 329 and accompanying text.

308. *Liddell IX*, 801 F.2d at 283. *See Liddell XII*, 823 F.2d at 1256 (magnet "programs must be attractive to county parents and students, and the facilities must be well located and comparable to facilities in the county schools").

309. *See supra* text accompanying notes 199–204, 243–49.

310. *See* Liddell v. Board of Education, 758 F.2d 290, 293–98 (8th Cir. 1985) (*Liddell VIII*) (continuing dispute over determination of approved quality education programs).

311. *Liddell XII*, 823 F.2d at 1253 ("Pupil/teacher ratios in the high schools and in the integrated elementary and middle schools have been reduced to AAA standards").

312. A court-appointed committee reported in 1987 that the Board of Education had employed a "policy of lowering district-wide ratios beyond AAA levels *before* making further reductions in non-integrated schools" and that these reductions had been financed with funds that "could and should have been spent on reducing pupil–teacher ratios in the district's non-integrated schools." Response of the Committee on Quality Education to the Board's Report to Lower Pupil–Teacher Ratios in Non-Integrated Schools at 2–3, L(1338)87 (March 19, 1987) (emphasis in original).

313. *Liddell IX*, 801 F.2d at 280–81.

314. *Liddell XII*, 823 F.2d at 1253, 1254. The court also prohibited any further reduction of the pupil–teacher ratio in integrated schools until the 20 to one ratio is achieved in the all-black schools. *Id.* at 1255.

315. In October 1988, the Committee on Quality Education reported that "the Board continues to disregard the actions required to implement" the 20-to-one pupil–teacher ratio for all-black schools, and that "[o]ver the course of the past one and one-half years, the Court has been extremely patient with the Board's inaction and ill-prepared plans." Report of the Committee on Quality Education in Reply to Board Response to Order L(2109)88 at 1,4, L(2156)88 (October 12, 1988).

316. *See* Browning, *Judge Asked to Stop City Pupil Transfers*, St. Louis Post-Dispatch, October 13, 1988, at 12A, col. 5.

317. *Liddell XII*, 823 F.2d at 1253 ("Remedial and compensatory programs, along with part-time integrative programs, were to be offered in non-integrated schools. Some of the required programs are now being offered and are adequately funded; others have yet to be offered; and still others are underfunded." [citation omitted]).

In June 1987, the Committee on Quality Education released two reports strongly criticizing the Board's failure to implement completely Settlement Agreement programs for all-black schools. Assessment of Remedial Services in Non-Integrated Schools, L(1469)87 (June 3, 1987); A Report on the School of Emphasis Program, L(1468)87 (June 3, 1987). *See* Rogers, *Remedial Courses Criticized*, St. Louis Post-Dispatch, June 4, 1987, at 1A, col. 1. One year later, after five full years of the settlement, the Committee again issued two reports harshly condemning the Board's failure to implement quality education programs for the all-black schools. In one report, the Committee found that the Board had failed to solve the problems identified in one of its previous 1987 reports. Report to the Court on the Status of the Schools of Emphasis Program, L(1943)88 (May 6, 1988). The second report concluded that one particular quality education program (After-School and Saturday Programs) suffers from the same difficulties as other programs for the all-black schools: "lack of district commitment, insufficient resources, understaffing, and a reluctance to comply with the spirit of the Settlement Agreement which requires that students in non-integrated schools be provided compensatory educational opportunities." Status Report on the After-School and Saturday Programs at 3, L(1987)88 (June 8, 1988).

318. See Liddell VIII, 758 F.2d at 293–98, 300–02.

319. See supra text at note 218.

320. Mo. Const. art. X, 11(c); Mo. Rev. Stat. §§ 164.141, 164.151 (1987).

321. The voters rejected a $63.5 million bond issue for capital improvement in November 1983. Shirk, City Voters Reject Bonds for Schools, St. Louis Post-Dispatch, November 9, 1983, at 1A, col. 5. A second bond issue for the same amount was rejected in June 1984. Kohn and Singer, Hungate Says Bond Sale Not His to Order, St. Louis Post-Dispatch, June 7, 1984, at 1A, col. 6. In November 1985, the voters turned down a $155.3 million bond issue. Eardley and O'Neil, South Siders Doom School Bonds, St. Louis Post-Dispatch, November 6, 1985, at 1A, col. 1.

322. Liddell v. Board of Education, 674 F. Supp. 687, 690–91 (E.D. Mo. 1987). In the November 1985 election, voters in black wards supported the bond issue by an 87–13 margin, but the voter turnout was a low 26 percent. In the white wards, the voters opposed the bond issue by a 69–31 margin and 41 percent of the electorate voted. Eardley and O'Neil, supra note 321, at 5A, col. 2.

323. Liddell VII, 731 F.2d at 1318.

324. Eardley, City School Board Asks for $420.6 Million Plan, St. Louis Post-Dispatch, May 11, 1986, at 3A, col. 4.

325. Liddell XII, 823 F.2d at 1255; Liddell IX, 801 F.2d at 284–85; Liddell VIII, 758 F.2d at 302; Liddell v. Board of Education, 674 F. Supp. at 690–97 (summary of the efforts of the court of appeals and the district court over four years to implement the capital improvements component of the Settlement Agreement).

326. Liddell v. Board of Education, 674 F. Supp. at 689.

The schools have not received major repairs in the memory of most of the staffs. Roofs leak in over half the schools. The leaks receive only temporary attention. In classroom after classroom, in gymnasiums, in libraries and study halls and in cafeterias, water is everywhere. It drips from the ceiling, down the walls and even from light fixtures.

Cans, buckets and other receptacles are all over. A sixth grader in a reading class leans over in her chair to avoid the steady drip of water going into a bucket at her feet.

Some of the plumbing is intolerable. On one occasion in a school when the water was flushed from a urinal, portions came down a wall in the room below, while a devoted teacher was attempting to teach her students in that room.

Ceiling tile in many rooms no longer exists or is so permeated with water that it hangs perilously. Plaster falls to the floor sometimes placing the student or teacher in some danger.

Paint peels from many walls and exposes the plaster or wall board and sometimes the studs.

Many buildings are old and dilapidated and were designed for education seventy-five years ago. Some have no gymnasiums. Others have gymnasiums, but the ceilings are only seven or eight feet high. In many schools, a student must bend or duck going from some rooms to others to avoid hitting exposed pipes or mechanical supports.

See Rogers, *16 Schools Ordered Closed*, St. Louis Post-Dispatch, September 4, 1987, at 1, col. 1; Rogers, *Judge's Homework Pays Off in School Plan*, St. Louis Post-Dispatch, September 6, 1987, at 1C, col. 2–4.

327. Liddell v. Board of Education, 674 F. Supp. at 726, 729.

328. *Id.* at 727.

329. *Id.* The court also ordered the Board to set aside $5 million annually "for continued maintenance and additional capital improvements" after the ninth payment "until further notice of the Court." *Id.*

330. *Id.* at 707–15.

331. *Id.* at 728.

332. *Id.* at 727.

333. *Id.* at 722. ("The Eighth Circuit has often referred to a bond issue as a means of financing a capital improvements program. However, a bond issue is not the only means available to fund the capital improvements program. This Court is empowered to order a property tax increase or any other fiscal alternative it deems necessary and reasonable to remedy the situation.")

334. *See supra* text accompanying note 218.

335. Judge Stephen N. Limbaugh was assigned to the case and replaced Judge William L. Hungate on February 1, 1985. *See supra* note 16.

336. *Liddell*, 674 F. Supp. at 722. The court specifically declined to invalidate the two-thirds majority vote requirement for approval of bond issues (*see supra* note 320 and accompanying text), and it also declined to order a property tax increase. *Id.* at 722–23.

337. *Id.* at 723.

338. *Id.* at 723, 726.

339. Hick, *Board Backs Judge on School Closings*, St. Louis Post-Dispatch, September 10, 1987, at 1A, col. 5–6.

340. *Id.* at 5A, col. 1.

341. *Id.* at 1A, col. 2.

342. *See* Memorandum and Order at 3, L(2041)88 (July 7, 1988) ("The City Board's ability to fund desegregation programs still remains unstable"). *See* Gross, *U.S. Judge Orders St. Louis Schools to Cut Expenses*, St. Louis Post-Dispatch, July 7, 1988, at 1A, col. 5.

343. *Id.*

344. *See supra* text accompanying notes 319–25.

345. Hicks, *Adviser Suggests Firm for School Bonds*, St. Louis Post-Dispatch, November 16, 1988, at 4A, col. 3.

346. Bryant, *Bond Money May Be Released to Repair St. Louis Schools*, St. Louis Post-Dispatch, February 18, 1989, at 10A, col. 1.

347. *See* La Pierre, *Voluntary Metropolitan School Desegregation in St. Louis—Substantial Achievements and Broken Promises* 34 ST. LOUIS B. J. 34 (Summer 1987) (after four years of delay, strong judicial action necessary to fulfill the broken promises of the settlement).

348. In the spring of 1987, three individuals, who campaigned on a promise to end desegregation programs, were elected to the Board of Education of the city of St. Louis, and they have voted subsequently to oppose both intradistrict and interdistrict school desegregation. Schuster and Bishop, *Here Comes the Judge—Unless St. Louis School Plan Makes the Grade*, Riverfront Times, August 19–25, 1987, at 6A, col. 4, 12A, cols. 3–4. Shortly before this election, in February 1987, the Board of Education narrowly defeated by a 6–5 vote a motion to eliminate student assignments by race. Eardley and Rogers, *School Board to Seek Change in Bond Law*, St. Louis Post-Dispatch, February 25, 1987, at 6A, col. 5.

In addition to opposition to desegregation within the Board of Education, the city of St. Louis and the Department of Justice have both filed motions in the district court seeking an end to intradistrict busing. *City Seeks End to Busing Plan*, St. Louis Post-Dispatch, May 18, 1986, at 4C, col. 1.

349. In 1987 and 1988, the state filed motions to limit its obligations to fund voluntary interdistrict student transfers at the end of the fifth year of the Settlement Agreement. *See* Liddell v. Board of Education, 686 F. Supp. 235 (E.D. Mo. 1988). For example, in August 1987, the state took a position that suggests an attempt to limit its financial responsibilities under the Settlement Agreement after the fifth year. Affton, a suburban school district in St. Louis County that has achieved its plan ratio of 15.15 percent black students, requested state funds for the capital costs of construction of new classrooms to accommodate more voluntary interdistrict transfer students. Budget Review Committee Report on Affton's Capitol Budget Request, L(1538)87 (August 6, 1987). The state responded that it has no obligation to fund capital improvements to increase the number of transfer students beyond the plan ratio. *Id.* at Appendix 2 (State Position on Affton School District's Request for Capital Improvements Funding).

350. Liddell v. Board of Education, 823 F.2d 1252 (8th Cir. 1987).

351. *Id.* at 1253 ("We emphasize today that . . . [the] requirements [of the Settlement Agreement as approved and modified in *Liddell VII*] must be fulfilled even though this order may allow their fulfillment to be delayed in certain specific instances"). *See* Liddell v. Board of Education, 839 F.2d 400 (8th Cir. 1988) (*Liddell XIII*) (holding the state responsible for suburban school districts' capital costs of accommodating interdistrict transfer students).

352. *Liddell XII*, 823 F.2d at 1256.

353. *See supra* text accompanying notes 299–308.

354. *Liddell XII*, 823 F.2d at 1254.

355. *See supra* text accompanying notes 313–16.

356. *Liddell XII*, 823 F.2d at 1255.

357. *See supra* text accompanying notes 326–38.

358. *See supra* text accompanying note 121.

359. *Liddell XII*, 823 F.2d at 1254.

360. Liddell v. Board of Education, 686 F. Supp. 235 (E.D. Mo. 1988).

361. *Id.* at 237–39.

362. *Id.* at 239.

363. Two recent cases renewed interest in the never-settled question when a school system is unitary and the duty to desegregate ends, but the Supreme Court declined to provide an answer. *Compare* Dowell v. Board of Education, 795 F.2d 1516 (10th Cir.), *cert. denied,* 479 U.S. 938 (1986) (district court must reconsider permitting school board to alter desegregation plan after finding that school system was unitary) *with* Riddick v. School Board, 784 F.2d 521 (4th Cir.), *cert. denied,* 479 U.S. 938 (1986) (finding that formerly segregated school system had become unitary).

364. 823 F.2d at 1253.

365. *See, e.g.,* Halderman v. Pennhurst State School and Hospital, 673 F.2d 628 (3d Cir. 1982) (*en banc*), *cert. denied,* 465 U.S. 1038 (1984); (holding state official in civil contempt for failure to pay Special Master's costs in civil rights case); Gary W. v. Louisiana, 622 F.2d 804 (5th Cir. 1980), *cert. denied,* 450 U.S. 994 (1981) (order compelling state treasurer to satisfy civil rights attorneys' fee judgment against the state).

366. In the Kansas City, Missouri, school desegregation case, the district court, on September 16, 1987, ordered a property tax increase and a state income tax surcharge to finance the local Board of Education's share of desegregation costs. Jenkins v. Missouri, 672 F. Supp. 40 (W.D. Mo. 1987). Although the court of appeals reversed the income tax surcharge order, it upheld the property tax increase. Jenkins v. Missouri, 855 F.2d 1295 (8th Cir. 1988).

367. The combined cost of the intradistrict desegregation plan and the interdistrict settlement plan for the eight years from the 1980–1981 school year through the 1987–1988 school year has been estimated at $512,831,988. *See* Rogers, *Desegregation's Cost: 3-1/2 Domed Stadiums,* St. Louis Post-Dispatch, February 21, 1988, at 9A, col. 6 (table).

368. *See supra* text accompanying notes 290–92.

369. In July 1987, the court of appeals estimated that if the voluntary interdistrict transfer and magnet components of the Settlement Agreement are implemented completely, "fewer than 15,000 black students will be attending nonintegrated schools in the City." *Liddell XII,* 823 F.2d at 1254.

CHAPTER 7

Desegregation in Chicago: Settlement without a Trial

ALLEN E. SHOENBERGER

THE STORY OF Chicago's desegregation settlement is one that must be told for its singularity in employing the judicial process exclusively at the remedial stage of a litigation. Chicago's tale is not the usual one of competing arguments regarding the existence of discrimination; there were no student plaintiffs telling tales of woe, no witnesses testifying to the school Board's segregationist policies, no experts expounding on the damaging effects of discrimination, and no court-appointed Masters to supervise the integration effort. Why? Because in Chicago there was no trial.

EXECUTIVE SUMMARY

On the same day that the U.S. Justice Department filed suit against the Chicago Board of Education, the parties entered into a consent decree agreeing to make mutual best efforts to desegregate the schools and remedy the effects of past discrimination. The ensuing years of litigation have focused on the following:

1. What constitutes sufficient "best efforts" in a school system with a predominately minority population and continuously declining white enrollment?
2. Who must pay the price for remediation efforts?

The answer to the first question creates the burdens for the latter.

All of Chicago politics is deeply affected by sharp divisions on racial lines. The school desegregation that did develop occurred in a highly charged political climate in which black and Hispanic populations approached a majority of Chicago's population, while at the same time overwhelmingly dominating the public school population. Many decades of residential segregation in Chicago had strongly shaped the city.

Undoing decades of racism is an immense undertaking. The Chicago Board of Education chose to integrate as little as possible, however. Fearing further loss of white students from the city's few remaining white majority schools, the Board set a limit of 30 percent black enrollment at such schools and discouraged the redistribution of students beyond that goal. It thus continued to maintain a large complement of racially isolated schools, which, under Chicago's plan, then became entitled to remediation programs to end the effects of past discrimination.

In short, continued racial isolation could come only at great financial expense, and the U.S. government, by entering into the consent decree, was forced to become a limited partner in this investment. Political reasoning brought on this state of affairs, and the judiciary, when faced with its inflexibility, almost forced the dissolution of the partnership. To date, it is not clear whether the investment has paid off.

THE CHICAGO SCHOOL DESEGREGATION CASE: 1980–1989

Chicago has been called the most segregated city in the country.[1] Certainly the demographics of the city involve a considerable degree of residential segregation by race as well as by economic class.[2] The public school system, the third largest in the United States, has long reflected this segregated housing pattern. Such residential segregation, along with the neighborhood school policy, has produced a segregated school system. Despite the promise of *Shelly v. Kramer*,[3] banning racially restrictive real estate covenants, and *Brown v. Board of Education*,[4] segregated schooling has continued to be the norm in Chicago.

Chicago's first system-wide desegregation suit to result in any remedial efforts was brought by the Department of Justice in 1980 to address the *de facto* segregation problem.[5] By the summer of 1984, despite this suit and the consent decree that resulted from it, the enrollment at more than half of the Chicago schools remained more than 99 percent black or Hispanic; 70 percent of the black or Hispanic children in the school system continued to attend schools with more than 70 percent black or Hispanic students.[6] Chicago's background of racial segregation in its public schools, coupled with the city's drop in white population, seemed to pose insurmountable obstacles to full integration.

A desegregation suit typically states two related claims: first, that a system is hostile to minority students and segregates schools on racial grounds; and second, that the result of segregation is poorer educational services for minority students. Immediate entry of a consent decree in this case obviated the need for proof of discriminatory intent. As a result, the Board of Education simply focused on the elimination of the *results* of segregation. This narrowed focus poses a series of policy questions, which can be addressed only by a historical review of the Chicago case.

As a remedy for past segregative effects, Chicago's Board chose to provide remediation and enrichment programs to predominantly minority schools. Is education remediation a legitimate substitute for integration? If not, is it at least arguably valid when demographic patterns significantly eliminate the possibility of full integration? Remediation is expensive. Who should bear financial responsibility for these programs? If a defendant Board of Education has never been found at fault for its segregative conduct, how long should it be obliged to remedy its non-culpable conduct and at what cost? Chicago's court was faced with these questions. Its answers provide insight into the role of the judiciary in managing a litigation where there has never been a trial in which the court could consider the underlying facts.

Prior Lawsuits

Prior desegregation suits against the Chicago Board of Education have not succeeded; however, it is instructive to examine the history of those few abortive suits. In each case, adept political maneuvering by Chicago school authorities made moot the individual case and thus avoided judicial intervention.

Webb v. Board of Education[7] was a federal class action suit brought by a group of parents challenging the neighborhood school policy of the Chicago school Board. The plaintiffs alleged that the Board had violated the equal protection clause of the Fourteenth Amendment by deliberately creating and fostering a segregated school system. The allegations included gerrymandering school district boundary lines, adopting a permissive transfer plan for white students, and constructing additional schools in black areas while simultaneously failing to utilize vacant seats in white classrooms. Plaintiffs requested a preliminary injunction.

The Board's defense maintained that all such allegations were false. Superintendent of Schools Benjamin C. Willis explained that the use of branch schools and mobile classrooms, and the new building activity in black residential areas rather than in racially mixed or white areas, reflected "the large influx of Negroes into areas containing low cost public housing," and stressed that this fact affected the Board's construction policy.[8]

The request for a preliminary injunction in *Webb* posed the issue of whether a neighborhood school policy was, on its face, unconstitutional. Judge Abraham Lincoln Marovitz[9] ruled that the decision of the U.S. Court of Appeals for the Seventh Circuit in *Bell v. School Board of Gary, Indiana*,[10] upholding the constitutionality of a neighborhood school policy, was dispositive of the question. He denied the motion for a preliminary injunction.

Willis continued to insist that the system was integrated, but Board President Roddewig wanted to settle the litigation.[11] Pressure upon Mayor Daley, the state legislature, and the school Board all came to naught. Before trial on the permanent injunction, the *Webb* case was settled out of court. The settlement included an agreement that a study panel would be created to suggest recommendations on desegregating the school districts. A report emerged from this study by 1964. Its findings were adopted in principle, but few of the specific recommendations were enacted by the school Board. The Board specifically rejected any programs involving the busing of students to promote integration.

While the *Webb* case never went to trial on the merits, the opinion by Judge Marovitz on the preliminary injunction added gloss to both the *Bell* opinion and the infamous Parker doctrine.[12] It made clear to the plaintiffs that they had a very significant burden to carry in court, for it held that "[t]he Constitution only forbids States from actively pursuing a course of enforced segregation."[13] Plaintiffs were put on notice that, in order to prevail, they had to prove not only that the system had become segregated, but also that the Board of Education had fostered such a result actively. It was obvious that any victories were going to be hard-fought ones.

A decade passed before the next serious attempt was made to address school segregation problems through court action. In 1971, *Brown v. Board of Education* was filed on behalf of a class of all non-Caucasian students and a class of all students from families of low or moderate income or dependent economic status.[14] Plaintiffs claimed that the city's educational funds were allocated in a fashion that systematically discriminated against non-Caucasian and poor children. This suit went to trial before District Court Judge Richard McLaren.[15] The court found that Chicago had a racially segregated residential housing pattern and that an overwhelming majority of the public elementary schools in the city of Chicago had student body memberships of more than 90 percent of one racial group.[16] Although there was no evidence that any act by the Board of Education caused the segregated housing pattern,[17] the court ruled that "the Board must recognize that a racially-neutral policy may result in an invidious discrimination because of the established racial attendance patterns in the school system."[18] The court further found that many neighborhoods in Chicago were exclusive precincts of low- or moderate-income families or families of dependent economic status, while other neighborhoods were exclusive enclaves of middle- or upper-income families.[19] The neighborhood school policy followed by the Board meant that children of low-income families generally attended schools in poorer neighborhoods, while children of wealthier families attended schools in wealthier neighborhoods.

The testimony regarding disparate expenditures for the 1969–1970 and 1970–1971 school years established that the mean per-pupil expenditure for staffing costs at white schools exceeded those in predominantly non-Caucasian schools by more than eight percent.[20] The ratio, however, was improving.[21] The differences in per pupil costs were directly related to two major factors: the educational preparation and experience of teachers as reflected by salary, and the level of staffing in the classroom and in auxiliary areas.[22]

Such differences were explained, in part, by the historic use of a teacher transfer policy that permitted senior teachers, who also tended to be higher paid under the union contract, to transfer to more desirable schools in neighborhoods with higher socio-economic status.[23] As a result, teachers with less experience and education tended to cluster in schools in non-Caucasian neighborhoods.[24]

Applying the holding of the U.S. Supreme Court in *San Antonio Independent School District v. Rodriguez*,[25] the court found that there was sufficient proof regarding the plaintiff group neither to establish a suspect economic class nor to establish the absolute deprivation of a right. The court found variations in expenditure constitutionally permissible. Since the Board had undertaken corrective action and pledged to continue its efforts, the court held that no injunctive relief should be granted. "[S]ince the Board has adequately demonstrated its sincere desire to comply with the law, this Court will not interfere."[26] The case was dismissed granting no relief to the plaintiffs.[27]

In part, the dismissal reflected the lack of evidence to support any intentional segregative activity on the part of the Board. *Brown*, in this regard, was a precursor of the 1980 Justice Department suit, where no evidence of intentional segregative activity was offered because the case never went to trial. The plaintiffs' case in *Brown* was entirely a statistical one; when the Board made some minor shifts in assignments of senior teachers with high salaries, the statistical disparities, and the case, disappeared. Thus, while the *Brown* case resulted in a holding that the Board of Education had discriminated, the holding was limited to expenditures for two school years and resulted in no remedy for any class members. It was, in short, no more effective than the *Webb* settlement.

Before the filing of *United States v. Chicago Board of Education* in 1980, several suits were brought challenging the impact of the Board's policies on individual schools. One rather novel case, *Lawler v. Board of Education*, challenged the Board's policies by alleging that the Board "forced" white residents to move out of the O'Toole Elementary School area by failing to establish a ceiling on the number of black students permitted to attend the school.[28] The plaintiffs sought limited, or controlled, integration by and for the benefit of the remaining whites.[29] The complaint was dismissed by the district court and the Seventh Circuit on a finding that the plaintiffs had failed to state a cause of action. There is no constitutional right to a particular degree of racial mix or balance.[30] The court action did not resolve the dispute on the merits, and the problem of white flight continued throughout the 1970s.

A different challenge to alleged segregative practices was brought in 1976 in *Johnson v. Board of Education*,[31] which challenged a Board-originated desegregation plan developed to address the problem identified in the *Lawler* case. The Board plan, commonly known as the Racial Stabilization Quota Plan, established a ceiling on enrollments and imposed racial quotas at two southside high schools, Morgan Park and Gage Park. The case was brought in the name of black children and their parents who resided in the respective high school areas. The plans restricted the admission of minority students to these high schools solely on the basis of race. At both schools, the Board implemented a lottery system associated with target quotas. All white applicants were admitted but hundreds of black and Hispanic students were denied admission each year under the plan.[32] The legal challenge to the quota plans was two-fold:

1. Quotas violated the Illinois school code.[33]
2. They denied equal protection of the laws under the Fourteenth Amendment.

The case was to go to trial before Judge Herbert Will. At the last minute, however, the Board of Education stipulated to the facts and no trial took place.[34] The Board modified the plans, and the district court ordered merely that the amended plan be implemented.[35] The major alteration in the amended plan was the provision of bus transportation for students denied admission to Gage Park and Morgan Park to Chicago public high schools that were integrated.

On appeal, the Seventh Circuit affirmed the district court's decision that the amended plan was constitutional.[36] It stated that "Federal and State Courts have uniformly rejected the contention of a constitutional right to attend a particular school."[37] Thus, the challenged state action of adopting racial quotas with a benign purpose did not involve a fundamental right.[38] Applying *Bakke*,[39] the Seventh Circuit found the plans necessary to accomplish a permissible state objective in preventing overcrowding at Gage Park and Morgan Park.[40]

The Board's effort to deal voluntarily with the reality of white flight by a method designed to promote integration at these schools was commended, and the court stated:

> [I]n the limited circumstances of voluntary affirmative action, and in the absence of an invidious or pernicious intent attributable to the Board, we conclude that the Board was entitled to consider the probability of white flight in formulating a remedial plan to prevent *de facto* segregation in the public schools.[41]

Just as in the earlier court cases against the Chicago Board of Education, a modest change in the Board's method of conduct—here through minor alteration of plan details—eliminated any significant use of remedial judicial power. The Board continued to manage its own affairs without substantial outside intervention. It is also significant that neither by trial nor by stipulation of evidence was discriminatory intent on the part of the Board demonstrated.

United States v. Chicago Board of Education

Political events were central to the events leading up to the filing of the U.S. suit against the Chicago Board of Education. One significant event was the death of Mayor Daley on December 20, 1976, which had both local and national impact. Nationally, Chicago no longer had the clout to avoid detailed federal investigations and possible sanctions against its school system.[42] Within Chicago, Mayor Daley's death left the city with a caretaker mayor. The rate of political change accelerated as the Democratic machine lost its cohesiveness, and new political elements began to assert local political power.

The relationship between the suits that had been filed against the Board of Education in the 1960s and the investigation by the U.S. Department of Health, Education and Welfare (HEW) that led to the Justice Department suit also warrants examination. Although none of the earlier suits produced any direct relief from the practices of the Board of Education, they prompted the Board to begin collecting statistics on racial enrollment patterns within the school system. The statistics were the impetus for the HEW investigation, largely conducted by HEW lawyer James Goser.

Through Goser's efforts, detailed research was conducted under HEW's Big Cities compliance review.[43] The research was published as an Appendix to HEW's letter notifying Chicago's Board of Education that it was ineligible for Emergency School Aid Act (ESAA) funding.[44] The findings noted in the Appendix included the following:

1. Chicago's schools had long been and remained largely identifiable by race.
2. Chicago school officials had, on innumerable occasions, acted, or failed to act, in ways that naturally, probably, and foreseeably created or maintained racial segregation.
3. Apart from the foreseeable segregative effects of their decisions, the circumstances and alternatives surrounding these decisions demonstrated that school officials had acted, or had failed to act, for the purpose and with the effect of segregating students by race.
4. These actions and omissions were spread broadly through time and across virtually the entire geographic face of the system, indicating that they were a substantial cause in the creation and maintenance of unlawfully segregated schools system-wide.[45]

Previously, in 1977, an HEW administrative law judge had found that the Board had discriminated with respect to the assignment of professional staff and teachers.[46] That decision led to a settlement accord between HEW and the Board, which provided for faculty desegregation.[47] HEW's discontent with the level of compliance with this 1977 accord, along with its failure to reach any kind of agreement with the Board regarding pupil desegregation, led to its finding that the Board was ineligible for ESAA funds.

On April 9, 1979, HEW notified the Board of Education that it was ineligible to receive federal ESAA funds because its racially segregative practices violated Title VI.[48] On September 17, 1979, HEW notified the Board that if HEW's findings were not rebutted or explained, or if a plan was not developed to remedy the Board's unlawful discrimination, it would refer the case to the Department of Justice.[49]

On October 17, 1979, HEW received a letter from Superintendent Joseph P. Hannon, on behalf of the Board, denying that there were any violations of the Fourteenth Amendment or the Civil Rights Act.[50] The following day, HEW notified the Board that unless a plan was submitted within ten days, it would refer the matter to the Department of Justice. HEW sent the case to the Department of Justice on October 28, 1979.[51]

Negotiations between the Board and the Department of Justice failed to produce any breakthroughs during the remainder of 1979 or the beginning months of 1980.[52] These negotiations occurred under the stewardship of Michael A. Bilandic, who was first appointed and subsequently elected as mayor for the remainder of Daley's term. Bilandic lost his re-election bid to Jane Byrne in the 1980 Democratic primary, and Byrne went on to win the general election. Byrne was able to appoint new members to the school Board, and the impasse in negotiations disappeared.

Progress on settlement negotiations was reported during the summer of 1980. Newspaper accounts indicated that the Board negotiators recognized the need for some adherence to federal law and that, in return, federal officers agreed to stop assuming that "any desegregation proposal designed in Chicago must be phony."[53] Apparently, progress occurred because, according to Joyce Hughes, a black Northwestern University Law Professor and Chairperson of the School Board Desegregation Committee, the Board realized that "litigation would not be in [its] best interests."[54]

At the same time, however, the Department of Education notified the Board that it had failed to live up to its 1977 promises to resolve faculty desegregation issues. Under the October 1977 agreement, the composition of school faculty was to include 35 to 60 percent minority faculty. By the summer of 1980, 172 of 590 schools were not complying with the agreement.[55] The Board claimed that the noncompliance resulted from the necessity of trimming $60.1 million from the school budget.[56] However, even before these budget cuts were turned into staff reductions, 106 schools had already failed to comply with the agreement.[57]

Student desegregation was, however, the major item on the agenda. In April 1980, Drew Days III, director of the Justice Department's civil rights division, had written the Board that its responses to date had failed to move the Department of Justice from its conclusion that "[t]he Chicago Board had intentionally segregated students throughout a substantial portion of the school system."[58]

The problem was racial balance of the schools and the possible ways of addressing the issue. Busing was not the choice of many Chicagoans. The public reaction to the 1979 feasibility study done by HEW, which documented the need for long bus rides to achieve desegregation, was uniformly negative. Public opinion studies indicated that all three racial groups —whites, blacks and Hispanics—accepted the idea of bringing children of other races into their neighborhood schools, but only blacks accepted the idea of requiring their children to leave their neighborhood schools.[59] These public opinion polls indicated to the *Chicago Tribune* editors that massive, involuntary busing entailed the potential loss of the remaining white student body and "also many of the children of the black elite who have not already abandoned the public schools."[60]

Central to the busing issue were the target figures that inevitably emerge from any desegregation plan. The previous Board, under Superintendent Hannon, was willing to accept a target figure of no more than 70 percent white enrollment in any school to denominate the school racially stable.[61] However, during early 1980, HEW produced a feasibility study setting the target figure at no more than 50 percent white enrollment.[62] Negotiations continued, however, and within a matter of weeks, the Board and the Department of Justice reached a draft agreement.

It is clear that Jane Byrne's election and her restructuring of the Board of Education were the prime reasons a settlement and consent decree were achieved in such a brief time. It is also clear that the consent decree eliminated any forum in which there would be further dispute about the propriety of past Board activities.

The United States officially filed its lawsuit against the Chicago Board of Education on September 24, 1980, and, on the same date, the consent decree was approved.[63] It was assigned "off the wheel"[64] to Judge Milton Shadur.[65] The Justice Department's complaint alleged eight specific practices that promoted racial and ethnic (Hispanic) discrimination:

(a) The drawing and alteration of school attendance area boundaries in such a way as to create, maintain or increase racial or ethnic segregation of students;

(b) The adjustment of grade structures among schools so as to create or maintain racial or ethnic segregation;

(c) The maintenance of racially and ethnically segregated branches of schools;

(d) The placement of permanent and temporary facilities[66] to relieve student overcrowding and the failure of alternative, educationally-sound measures so that, by action and omission, racial and ethnic segregation of students was created and maintained;

(e) The maintenance of a racially-disproportionate number of severely overcrowded and thereby educationally inferior schools in such a way as to identify, in conjunction with the practices described . . . (in paragraphs f and g), those schools as intended for Black students and less crowded schools as intended for White students;

(f) The assignment of teachers and staff to schools in such a way as to match the race of the faculties with the race of the students attending the schools;

(g) The employment of a permissive transfer policy which allowed White students to avoid attending their schools of assignment when their race was in the minority in favor of attendance at other schools where their race constituted the majority of student enrollment; and

(h) The association of segregated schools with segregated housing projects.[67]

The complaint alleged that these practices occurred over a substantial period of time and in a substantial portion of the Chicago public schools, and constituted system-wide violation of the Constitution and the laws of the United States.[68] Injunctive relief was requested.[69]

The Consent Decree

Because the 20-page consent decree was entered the same day that the complaint was filed, no proof was offered in court concerning any of the allegations in the complaint. In the consent decree, the Board neither denied nor admitted the allegations; the extent of the violations alleged was never submitted to judicial scrutiny.[70] The Board agreed, however, that the Chicago public school system was characterized by substantial racial isolation of students,[71] and that such racial isolation was educationally disadvantageous to all students.[72] The Board avoided a finding of invidious discrimination and racist intent. It was thereby allowed to present remedies only for minimal desegregation and the educational effects of future continued segregation. Neither side foresaw the protracted litigation concerning remedies that was to follow.

Notwithstanding the complexity and size of the Chicago public school system, the consent decree can best be described as a brief statement of agreed principles. It promised no more than system-wide efforts to minimize the present and future effects of segregation on black and Hispanic students.[73] It established the basic structure for the plan that was yet to be developed.

Because fewer than 30 percent of the public school students were white, it was clear that system-wide desegregation was impossible unless suburban students were included. Thus, the decree promised only "the establishment of the greatest practicable number of stably desegregated schools, considering all the circumstances in Chicago."[74] The Board promised compensatory programs for black and Hispanic schools that remained segregated.[75] Relief was to be designed "to the greatest extent practicable" to provide for desegregation at all grade levels, but the "burdens of desegregation" were not to be "imposed arbitrarily on any racial or ethnic group."[76] The consent decree gave the school Board substantial discretion in implementing a desegregation plan. It recognized the school Board's familiarity with and sensitivity to the "unique situation presented in Chicago" and placed with the Board the responsibility of selecting a "plan that best meets the needs of the Chicago School District" from a broad range of constitutionally acceptable plans.

Moreover, the decree expressly stated that attaining racial and ethnic balance throughout Chicago was not practicable. Thus, the remedies included several voluntary techniques, such as permissive transfer,[77] and a separate list of mandatory techniques, other than mandatory transportation of students to effect integration.[78] Transportation or reassignment was required only to the extent that the other techniques proved insufficient.[79] The parties recognized that many schools would remain identifiable as black or Hispanic schools. The Board's responsibility was limited to providing specific justification for such situations.[80]

The novelty of the consent decree was its focus upon the use of compensatory programs for schools that were to remain segregated.[81] Such compensation was to be accomplished through, for example, the development of specific programs of remedial and compensatory education, improved curricula and pre-service and in-service instruction for school personnel.[82] Although the Board was encouraged to eliminate overcrowded schools, it was not required to do so.[83]

The consent decree was front page news in Chicago. Drew Days III, director of the Justice Department's Civil Rights Division, was prominently quoted: "Chicago has become the first major school district to see that the way to resolve this matter is not by protracted litigation."[84] Before the final negotiations preceding the settlement and drafting of the consent decree in April 1980, Days was reported to have held out a carrot to the Chicago System by stating, without mentioning a specific figure, that "Chicago could get a windfall" of federal aid.[85]

From a political perspective, the consent decree contained the threat of cross-district busing.[86] Thus, although the decree was viewed as having ended decades of disputes, it was clear from the first newspaper reports that the disputes were by no means over. Experts cautioned that the consent decree itself did not mean that a lengthy trial had been completely eliminated.[87] The key issue, and the issue reported to be the potential stumbling block during negotiations, was student desegregation. In 1979, reports indicated that negotiations under the former superintendent, Joseph Hannon, stuck on this point. "If Hannon could have gotten decent numerical standards, he would have run with it." Hannon reportedly would have accepted a standard that no school be more than 70 percent white.[88]

The consent decree, while "better than a bitter lawsuit,"[89] was not happily received by the NAACP. Thomas Atkins, General Counsel for the National NAACP, saw the agreement as another opportunity "for delay in obeying the law." Within a week, on October 3, 1980, the NAACP moved to intervene as a party plaintiff.[90] But this initial, highly negative reaction by the NAACP failed to generate any massive public reaction in the black community.

The court's view of its role in the litigation was first revealed in the context of the motions to intervene. An "activist court" would have become very deeply involved with the details of the desegregation plan. To impose "tight control" over the desegregation planning process, the court needed substantial and detailed assistance.[91]

Judge Shadur's "liberal" background may have portended judicial activism. Before taking the bench, upon appointment by President Carter, Judge Shadur had been one of the lead attorneys in the complicated *Hills v. Gautreaux*[92] litigation, which involved a challenge to the siting practices for low-income public housing of the Chicago Housing Authority and the U.S. Department of Housing and Urban Development (HUD). In that case, both the Chicago Housing Authority and HUD were found to have violated the constitutional and statutory rights of minorities.

Judge Shadur was the author of the Supreme Court brief in *Gautreaux*[93] that addressed the propriety of metropolitan area relief as opposed to relief limited to the city boundaries. The Supreme Court held metropolitan-based relief appropriate.[94] Since the problems of segregation in the Chicago public schools were accentuated by unconstitutional housing policies and practices, Judge Shadur's involvement in such litigation had direct relevance to desegregation of the city schools. However, by the time the Chicago desegregation suit was assigned to Judge Shadur, the decades of work on the *Gautreaux* litigation had suggested to him that "courts and litigation [in them] are not well suited to deal with social problems."[95] Since the desegregation plan was the outcome of consent, not litigation, Judge Shadur saw its development as primarily the responsibility of the Board, not the court.[96]

Though admitting a desire for "input from interested parties,"[97] Judge Shadur denied the NAACP and other groups leave to intervene as party plaintiffs.[98] He found that early intervention "would deflect the litigation from its essential goal of producing, at the earliest feasible date, a desegregated school system from the Chicago public schools, and more importantly, for the very classes whose rights the intervenors seek to protect."[99] The court understood that intervention might reopen the issue of the Board's liability, which "[t]he current Board—in office for less than a year—would contest vigorously."[100] Introducing such issues would simply "dilute the allocation of limited resources by requiring the Board, the United States, and the court to address issues that were not a substantive purpose of the litigation."[101]

The consent decree had obviated the need for a finding of liability.[102] It required that the Board submit a plan to the court by March 11, 1981.[103] The plan was not forthcoming until January of 1982[104] and not approved in final form until January 6, 1983, two and a half years after entry of the original consent decree.[105] Judge Shadur was firmly committed to the proposition that any plan that would be applied to Chicago had to be workable. Thus, once he had made the determination that the plan was not obviously unconstitutional, "further testing in the crucible of reality . . . would be an important plus for the constitutional evaluation that is the Court's responsibility."[106] Thus, it was not until January 6, 1983, when the Board was well into the second year of the plan's implementation, that Judge Shadur had reviewed its efficacy sufficiently to rule on it finally.[107]

As indicated by the appointment of Robert Green, Chief Desegregation Consultant for the Board of Education as of October 8, 1980, the Board began its part of the planning process with appropriate speed. Green was seen as a very credible appointment because of his extensive experience in desegregation planning as well as his credibility in the black community. Operation PUSH, a Chicago black organization headed by the Reverend Jesse Jackson, issued a press release calling Green, "one of the most competent and able educators in the nation [who] possesses consummate skill in the area of negotiating the intricate and difficult issues necessary to the implementation of meaningful urban desegregation programs."[108]

Green was convinced that there was a serious Board commitment to the consent decree.[109] He vowed to seek "total community input,"[110] recommending that public hearings be held throughout the city on proposals submitted by community organizations.[111] The series of public hearings served as sounding boards for the fears of Chicagoans.[112] Forced busing and mandatory relocation were particular targets of criticism.[113] Green, however, stated that he was impressed that citizens of all races were demanding quality education as their first goal.

While conducting these hearings, the Board also considered formation of a 35-member citizens' advisory panel on pupil desegregation[114] and recruitment of a new school superintendent. For the latter, they selected Dr. Ruth Love, the black superintendent of the Oakland, California, school system.[115]

Dr. Love's appointment as the first black superintendent over the Chicago schools was a significant symbol of commitment to the black community. That community reacted favorably. On her first day in office, she was greeted by a dozen red roses from the National Council of Negro Women and repeated standing ovations. She ended the official day at a reception in her honor hosted by black organizations with some 1,000 guests.[116]

In late March 1981, the Board revealed the initial framework of the plan. The plan set a 60 percent white cap on individual schools [117] and called for the reassignment of a quarter of the white students in the system, leaving only some 38,000 white students without reassignment. The plan also indicated that some 40,000 students might have to be bused at a cost of about $930 per student,[118] despite earlier statements by Green indicating that busing was a "last resort." [119]

On March 25, 1981, Dr. Love's first day as superintendent, Green described the plan as "defensible, modest, and somewhat conservative." [120] Reactions to the plan, however, were unfavorable.

Thomas Atkins of the NAACP found the 60 percent cap unacceptable. William Gordon, the Board's reassignment expert, thought the judge would accept no figure higher than 50 percent, as the 60 percent proposal would leave 250 schools entirely black.[121]

Only hours after the first public disclosure of the plan's details,[122] Mayor Byrne attacked the plan on fiscal grounds, saying that the school Board simply could not afford all the plan's components.[123] The cost for mandatory busing and reassignment was simply too much,[124] she said.

The Justice Department refused to comment publicly on the plan throughout the entire period of litigation. None of the persons interviewed would go on the record.

As a practical matter, the simple problem with the plan was that there were too few white students to make any serious dent in racial isolation. Thus, the difference in target percentages of 5 or 10 percent was, at best, symbolic. At the same time, although some details about the target numbers and schools to be affected were divulged, the plan lacked specificity in many areas,[125] most noticeably in the compensatory education areas for the hundreds of black and Hispanic schools that were to remain segregated.

Given widespread negative reaction from all political groups in the city —from blacks because it didn't go far enough, from whites because it involved excessive busing, and from Mayor Byrne because it cost so much— the Board immediately set out revising the draft plan. The Board was particularly concerned with the sensitive topic of student reassignment.[126] At a special Board meeting on April 15, 1981, the Board voted along racial lines to discard the mandatory busing and other reassignment portions of the desegregation plan.[127] Criticism from parents was a major factor in the vote.[128] Dr. Love described the Board's action as "passing an educational plan, not a school desegregation plan." [129] Green, in reaction to the Board's action, saw the planners as starting from scratch.

During the next several weeks, the Board, behind closed doors, hammered out a new plan relating to student reassignments. This new proposal, once again approved on racial lines, raised the cap on white students to 70 percent at any school[130] and pledged $100 million over the next three years to mount educational enrichment programs at schools that were to remain racially isolated.[131] The Board members agreed to postpone the start of any compulsory busing until the fall of the 1983 school year, giving the schools a full school year to recruit students on a voluntary basis.[132] This decision came after much public and political pressure, including a well-publicized letter urging postponement sent to the Board by twenty white aldermen.[133]

If the earlier plan had been "conservative and modest," as Green had described it, the revised plan was even more so. The 70 percent white cap figure was itself misleading because the plan required only that a school recruit enough students in the first year to bridge one-third of the gap toward the 70 percent goal. Each school had three years in which to reach the target. Few minority students would have to shift as a result of the plan. The most segregated white elementary school in the city, Grimes Elementary School on the southwest side, would have to recruit only 13 non-whites.[134] The high school counterpart to Grimes, the 95 percent white Bogan High School, would have to recruit 152 non-white students at the most, and indeed, probably fewer students would suffice.[135] The court ordered the parties to prepare briefs on the constitutionality of the proposal and indicated that it would decide whether the plan was constitutional no earlier than mid-summer.[136]

The brief from the Department of Justice not only found the plan "incomplete" but also asserted that the plan did not have much promise of accomplishing system-wide desegregation. According to the brief, there was too great a reliance on voluntary components and too little on mandatory backup techniques.[137] "Practicability" was a central theme. While recognizing that population patterns prevented elimination of all minority-only schools, the brief suggested that "all steps *practicable*" toward achieving that goal should be explored. Unfortunately, the brief failed to define what "practicable" meant.

The Justice Department's "slap" at the plan received mixed reactions. Officials of Operation PUSH, viewing it as a call for a complete redraft of the plan, endorsed the brief, but the NAACP called it "further footdragging and procrastination." School Board President Raul Villalobos, however, contended that the plan was "plainly constitutional" and that when the Board released its comprehensive student assignment plan in December 1981, people would see it as effective and likely to obtain the greatest desegregation practicable.[138] Former Board member Patricia O'Hern attacked the government brief's criticism of the 70 percent figure, since the limits for Atlanta, Milwaukee, Detroit, and St. Louis were either 70 or 75 percent.[139]

Even the Reagan administration reacted unfavorably to the draft plan. This reaction was attributed to the political policy of the administration to "assure Black Americans that it would continue to enforce civil rights laws." [140] This gesture toward civil rights enforcement, if it was one, was a short-lived moment.

At the end of August 1981, joint statements were presented to the court. Discussions between the Board of Education and the Department of Justice had convinced federal officials that the Board was serious in its commitment to desegregation. The Board's call for mandatory adjustments in school boundary lines and its representations that the 70 percent figure was only a starting point, helped the Justice Department officials reach this conclusion. The Justice Department urged the court to delay any final decision on the constitutionality of the plan until the final student desegregation plan was drawn and submitted in December of 1981. Assistant Attorney General William Bradford Reynolds signed the joint statement to the court and represented that the government's concerns in July had been based on "inferences" and faulty interpretation of Board proposals, which had since been "allayed or resolved." [141] The court acceded to this request, and the school year commenced without major incident. [142]

The pace of desegregation was not as rapid as hoped, but there was progress. Early reports indicated that 17,000 students system-wide enrolled in various volunteer desegregation programs, an increase of approximately 5,000 students from the preceding year. [143] The success in attracting whites to magnet schools was seen as particularly significant.

The unwillingness of the Board to press the compulsory busing issue was matched by the public position of the Department of Justice on the matter. In September 1981, Reynolds, speaking in Chicago, proclaimed that "forced busing had failed." This was taken as indicative of the Reagan administration's position on the matter. [144] Reynolds's statement advocated the use of voluntary techniques, such as magnet schools, and emphasized equal educational opportunity rather than mandatory busing. In mid-November, the Board described busing as an unlikely feature of the final plan.

The plan, which was ready on December 31, 1981, had more than 1,200 pages, including detailed school-by-school analyses. With the filing of this plan, the Board's submission to the court was complete. The desegregation plan was now to be applied to a school system in which white pupils were, for the first time, outnumbered by Hispanic pupils. [145] With so few whites, how could significant desegregation occur?

The Desegregation Plan

With the exception of comments by the Chicago Urban League indicating the critical need for funding of the educational components, the court received few comments from *amici* regarding the proposal for enrichment programs in schools that remained racially segregated. [146] The Department of Justice endorsed the educational components of the plan.[147] Indeed, despite the invitation of the court, neither *amici* nor the United States ever responded to the 416-page Annual Desegregation Review, (1983) Part II, Educational Components.[148] This detailed document was typical of Board submissions, including student assignment submissions, made to the court on an annual basis. This lack of response indicated that a key element of the Chicago desegregation plan, providing for separate but equal status for segregated schools, would be evaluated by the court primarily on the basis of Board of Education submissions.

In 1984, there were 407 schools with enrollments of more than 70 percent black or Hispanic students.[149] In the entire school system, more than 63 percent of the students attended schools having 90 percent or more minority enrollment.[150] Thus, the educational components were critical for large numbers of minority students. Nevertheless, the detailed planning with respect to student relocation garnered far more public input and scrutiny.[151] Indeed, the January 1983 decision validating the plan concentrated almost totally on the relocation issue.[152]

The student assignment aspect of the plan was easily described; the greatest possible number of stably desegregated schools was to be created. The educational aspect of the plan was not easily encapsulated. The goal was "to provide educational and related programs for schools that remained racially isolated." [153]

The Board developed an Effective Schools Program (ESP) to target the 45 most educationally deprived and minority-identified schools. In 1981–1982 and subsequent school years, these schools were to be given additional educational services. For the 1983–1984 school year, the 62 next lowest-ranked schools were selected for participation in the ESP program.[154] In that year, the full ESP program was to be implemented in all 107 targeted schools.[155] In reality, by 1983–1984, it was impossible to fund the ESP program fully at all 107 schools. Consequently, the Board provided a reduced level of programming.[156] During the 1984–1985 school year, the Board was again unable to implement its plan to expand the program to cover the 207 racially isolated schools.[157] In its October 1985 opinion, the court found that the 1985–1986 school year was the first full year in which the plan could be fully implemented.[158]

The Effective Schools Program (ESP) was based on educational research suggesting that the creation of proper learning conditions can enable all children, regardless of race, to learn.[159] Some of these learning conditions included extended day and extended year instruction and full-day kindergarten instruction.[160] The key elements in the Effective Schools Program were programmatic educational components addressing six major areas: instructional emphasis, including increased time on tasks; leadership; use of assessment data; parental support and involvement; general school climate; and staff development and training.[161] The program components of the plan included

1. the creation of a Trainers' Institute within the public schools in order to provide in-service training;
2. the establishment of a Management Information System to collect, analyze, review, and disseminate data related to desegregation activities;
3. the creation of a system-wide Staff Development Program for all racially identifiable schools;
4. the establishment of a Within-School Program to monitor assignment of pupils to classrooms within particular schools;
5. the creation of new magnet schools of various types;
6. the creation of a Special Education/Testing Program designed to ensure non-discriminatory assessment and placement of students in educable mentally handicapped classes;
7. the expansion and publicity of the Vocational and Technical Education Programs provided by the Board;
8. the attention to curriculum development through a Curriculum and Instruction Program;
9. the development of a Student Discipline Program that eliminated or alleviated unequal disciplinary treatment of minority pupils; and
10. the development of a Bilingual Educational Program to achieve national origin desegregation.[162]

In each case, the court found that ESP components would materially assist the Board in implementing its desegregation plan and that the projected costs by the Board were reasonable under the circumstances. There was no dispute that the cost of fully implementing these program components exceeded the funds available to the Board and that the Board had exercised every good faith effort to maximize the funds available for such purposes.[163]

The final student assignment plan the Board submitted was similar to that submitted at the end of April 1981. The plan relied upon voluntary student reassignment. Despite complaints from many parties, neither the 70 percent white student cap[164] nor the basic approach of the plan to avoid mandatory busing was altered.

At public hearings, some blacks criticized the plan for the inclusion of voluntary busing; they believed the plan placed the burden upon blacks to change schools and considered it unfair to force the black students to leave their home districts.[165] Public opinion polls, taken shortly after the final plan was submitted, indicated that while whites strongly opposed busing (81 percent), so did small majorities of blacks (51 percent) and Hispanics (55 per-

TABLE 7-1. Schools That Failed to Meet the 70 Percent Target in 1982

School	Percent White		Number of Black Transfers	Number of Hispanic Transfers
	1982	1983		
Byrne	76.4	69.1	33	3
Carroll	80.2	65.9	1	0
Cassell	71.9	62.8	44	0
Clissold	71.3	63.1	44	2
Dore	78.6	63.8	55	0
Pasteur	72.4	60.9	117	9
Taft H.S.	74.6	68.8	129	10

cent).[166] The poll also indicated that a large percentage of minority parents knew little about the plan. For example, 55 percent of the Hispanic parents and 77 percent of the black parents had not heard of magnet schools.[167]

It came as no surprise when the Justice Department, in early February 1982, approved the Board plan.[168] Despite objections that the burdens of voluntary transfer fell primarily upon black students, the report encouraged still more voluntary movement by blacks to integrate the system. Most white students could attend an integrated school simply by attending their neighborhood school.[169] The brief suggested that blacks had been more responsive to the technique of voluntary transfers than had other minority students. Therefore, the Board would be justified in "concentrating on the recruitment of Black students for voluntary transfers." [170]

The government's brief was perceived as an effort to harmonize the department's response to the school Board's final plan with its highly skeptical analysis of the plan as it was developing the previous July. From Assistant Attorney General William Bradford Reynolds's statement that "forced busing has failed," [171] to his proclamation in the spring of 1982 that the plan was the "best conceivable hope in the Chicago area," [172] the Chicago approach, a potpourri of innovative educational programs designed to lure students of all races and ethnic groups into mixed settings, was perceived by local observers as exemplifying the approach the Reagan administration favored.[173] "[T]here's no way you're going to come out without some schools being all one race," [174] said Reynolds, who described the plan as a potential national model "for how desegregation can be accomplished through education, not through transportation." [175]

By the time the court received the Justice Department's brief, the Board had had several years' experience with voluntary student relocation. By January 1983, only seven of nearly 600 schools in the Chicago public system still exceeded the 70 percent white target figure (see Table 7-1).[176] By October

TABLE 7-2. Schools That Met the 70 Percent Target in 1982 but Did
Not Improve in 1983

School	Percent White 1982	1983	Number of Black Transfers	Number of Hispanic Transfers
Twain	69.4	65.7	40	4
Shields	67.1	66.2	1	9
Eberhart	69.3	69.3	95	1

1983, every school met the target, although a few schools only barely did so
(see Table 7-2).[177]

Of all the major events in the case, the court's brief opinion granting final
approval of the plan was probably the most anticlimactic. Judge Shadur's
opinion, though clearly indicating that all objections had been considered,[178]
was almost entirely devoted to the validity of the Comprehensive Student Assignment Component.[179] Judge Shadur identified three constitutional considerations:

1. Did the plan's percentage definitions of "integration" and "desegregation" satisfy the Constitution?
2. Did the plan's collective treatment of all minorities (blacks, Hispanics, and others) comply with the Constitution?
3. Did the plan impose unconstitutional burdens on the minority student populations?

The plan defined three kinds of "integrated schools": (1) stably integrated schools, having no more than 70 percent white enrollment; (2) schools
now stably integrated, but with projected racial changes that threatened the
status; and (3) stably mixed schools, having 15 to 30 percent white enrollment.[180] Most of the public and courtroom debate about the plan centered
on the 70 percent cap on white enrollments; the court found that the 70
percent solution unquestionably complied with the Constitution.

The Board's plan anticipated a 65 percent figure by October 1983 in all
but two of the schools.[181] By the Fall of 1982, only seven schools failed to
meet the 70 percent figure.[182] Increases in enrollment at the few schools that
had not already met the 70 percent target in 1981 slightly exceeded the projections in the plan.[183] The court found that this progress had been achieved
without any significant white flight. Indeed, demographic analysis indicated
a slowing of the rate of white outflow from the system.[184]

The Board's plan made few distinctions between integration of Hispanics
and whites and integration of blacks and whites. The Board cited case law
indicating that "courts that have dealt with desegregation issues in multi-

TABLE 7-3. Students in Desegregated Schools, 1981–1982

	White	Black	Hispanic	Other	Total
Total in System Non-residential Children in Desegregation Programs	70,961	245,423	77,103	10,181	403,660
	4,710	14,776	3,620	933	24,037
Percent of totals	6.6	6	4.7	9.2	6
Percent of Non-residential Children	19.6	61.5	15.1	3.9	100

Source: Annual School Desegregation Review, 1983–1984, Part 1, Student Assignment at 6 (May 1984).

ethnic school districts have consistently approved plans with an inclusive definition of minorities like that adopted by the Plan."[185] Once again, from the court's perspective, the policy choice was the Board's, so long as it was within the ambit of permissible plans. The court accepted the Board's claim that it took deliberate steps to increase the movement of black children into integrated situations.[186] The Board's rejection of a mandatory minimum percentage of black children in all schools was also found appropriate and within the range of its constitutionally permissible actions. "To the extent the Board has chosen along the spectrum of constitutionally permissible alternatives, this Court cannot—and will not—interfere with that good faith choice."[187]

Critics of the plan alleged that it placed the burden primarily upon black students, particularly through the number and proportion of black students who had to leave their home school districts. The Board, however, deliberately chose not to focus on the number of students by race that would have to attend non-neighborhood schools to achieve desegregation targets.[188] The court found precedent for the Board's position that the Constitution did not mandate racial balance at all schools. According to the Seventh Circuit (see Tables 7-3 and 7-4),[189] continued existence of one-race schools was not clear evidence of unconstitutionality.[190] Instead, one-race schools had to be dealt with on a case-by-case basis.[191] "Thus the non-attainment of racial balance, or the presence of one-race schools, does not represent the imposition of an invalid disproportionate burden."[192]

Busing was not a major part of the plan. The Board adopted mandatory measures short of busing in combination with voluntary techniques.[193] In rejecting busing, the Board considered the potential for an accelerated exodus

TABLE 7-4. Racial/Ethnic Composition of Voluntary Transfer
Students: 1983

Percent	Total	Percent White	Percent Black	Percent Hispanic	Percent Other
Desegregated Schools	8,567	4.1	78.5	13.9	8.6
Transfer to Magnet Type Schools/ Programs	34,846	27.3	50.3	19.4	3.0
Total	43,414	22.7	55.8	18.3	3.2

Source: Annual School Desegregation Review, 1983–1984, Part I, Student Assignment at 6 (May 1984).

of whites. The commissioned public opinion poll indicated that mandatory busing would accelerate a decline in white enrollment.[194] Based on the experience of other cities, such as Los Angeles, Boston, and Detroit, where 40 to 45 percent of reassigned white students left the system, the Board chose not to adopt mandatory busing.[195] The decision whether to adopt mandatory busing was for the Board to make, so long as the Board was within the range of constitutionally permissible desegregation plans.[196]

Suggestions for appointment of an independent monitoring commission to oversee the Board's implementation of the plan were also rejected.[197] The Board had established a very extensive internal system to monitor the operation of the plan, and none of the organizations, notably the NAACP and MALDEF–PRLDEF, were critical of the operation of this internal reporting system after some initial problems were solved.[198] But in the view of some civil rights activists, the decision "closed the door to hopes of substantial school desegregation in Chicago."[199]

At least in the short run, the data indicate that the Board achieved a degree of desegregation in the schools while maintaining a relatively high level of white enrollment in the system. The total number of students attending integrated/desegregated magnet, scholastic, and metropolitan high schools continued to increase under the plan (see Table 7-5). Nevertheless, the school system continued to lose white students. By the spring of 1985, whites in the city system had dropped below 15 percent.[200]

Other measures indicated modest improvements attributable to the plan. The use of mobile classrooms, while not eliminated, was curtailed.[201] Over-

TABLE 7-5. Attendance at Integrated/Desegregated Magnet, Scholastic, and Metropolitan High Schools

Year	Number of Students
1981	90,889
1982	104,134
1983	112,481

Source: Annual School Desegregation Review, 1983–1984, Part 1, Student Assignment, at 77 (May 1984).

crowding was eliminated.[202] Progress was made toward eliminating within-school segregation, and monitoring was maintained by an annual, exhaustive, school-by-school analysis to determine whether the objectives of the plan were being met.[203] Nevertheless, most of the public schools in Chicago are now racially isolated and will remain so in the future. Short of cross-district busing, there is no remedy that could begin to address that situation.[204] However, from Judge Shadur's position, "what the Board did was impressive."[205]

The Independent Monitoring Commission and the Johnson Suit

At the close of summer 1983, various citizen groups revived the issue of whether an independent Monitoring Commission should be established to oversee the Board's implementation of the plan.[206] In the fall of 1981, Dr. Love had established an internal Monitoring Commission, chaired by Leon Finney, Jr., a prominent black activist, and with the assistance of consultant Dr. Mary Davidson. In February 1983, this Monitoring Commission issued an interim report.[207]

According to the report, the Commission's auditing teams encountered difficulties when visiting schools.[208] Often they were presented with overly general, and therefore inconclusive, data, despite earlier requests for specific, pertinent information. Further, the Board's personnel maintenance structure and computer programming system "thwarted review."[209]

The report highlighted the "fragility" of desegregation results already achieved. For example, it pointed out that, with the 70 percent cap on white students, a shift of only 246 students would tip all 21 schools that had come into compliance in 1982 back into noncompliance. At five of these schools, shifts of as few as two or three children would push the school back into noncompliance.[210] Dr. Davidson set forth a new monitoring strategy, with an extensive set of detailed questions that merited examination.

Those who renewed the request for an independent Monitoring Commission did so in large part because the Monitoring Commission's own reports reflected shortcomings in implementing the plan. The request was no longer that the composition of the Monitoring Commission be changed: "We are now of the view that the 'continuity' point made by the Urban League and the Monitoring Commission dictates retention of the present Commission and changes only in what the Urban League calls its 'auspices.'"[211] The essence of the request was, therefore, that a direct link be established between the court and the Monitoring Commission.[212]

On November 21, 1983, the court, in a ruling from the bench, denied the request.[213] As a preface to its ruling, the court ordered that, excepting emergencies, any subsequent challenges seeking modifications of the desegregation plan must first be submitted to the target of the prospective motion in order to work out or limit areas of dispute.[214]

The court was not convinced that it should be involved in the filling of existing vacancies on the Monitoring Commission. Most important, the court thought it wrong

> to take any action in the course of this proceeding that would make it appear, inaccurately, first, that this Court and not the Board have [sic], or is taking primary responsibility for accomplishing the goals of desegregation; or, second, that the Board is failing in the discharge of that responsibility.[215]

Under the consent decree, power, as well as responsibility, rested with the Board. The court did not want to be seen as disturbing that equilibrium. The court viewed the Board's decision to base its monitoring upon school-by-school analyses as basically "correct and useful,"[216] for only when power and responsibility are coincident can blame be assessed.

Board of Education v. United States: The Funding Case

In the spring of 1983, the focus of the case shifted to the funding issue. At that time, the Chicago Board of Education authorized its attorneys to begin litigation against the United States in order to secure significant financial assistance to meet the needs of the plan. The Department of Justice's case against the Board was based primarily upon statistical proof demonstrating that the Board had violated the civil rights of students in the school system. In fact, Justice Department attorneys had thought the evidence so strong that they planned to seek an early trial to speed up the generation of remedies. That prospect was short-circuited by entry of the consent decree. Then, after the Board spent several years developing a desegregation plan, the entire thrust of the case turned around and became a suit against the United States for failing to live up to its obligations under ¶ 15.1 of the consent decree. That section provided: "Each party is obligated to make every good faith effort to find and provide every available form of financial resources adequate for implementation of the desegregation plan."[217]

In June 1983, Judge Shadur conducted five days of hearings on the petition filed by the Board of Education that alleged that the United States had not lived up to its obligations under ¶ 15.1. He found that the Board had exercised good faith efforts to find and provide every available form of financial resource adequate to pay the cost of the plan,[218] but that the U.S. government had failed to do so.[219] "Since January 21, 1981, the Executive Branch of the United States and the Department of Education have been engaged in a continuous effort to strip away all means by which they could fulfill the United States' obligations under ¶ 15.1."[220]

The court found the obligation to act under ¶ 15.1, "unambiguous . . . clearly expressed and . . . not requir[ing] extrinsic evidence to be construed."[221] The obligation that the United States had incurred by the entry of the consent decree was binding upon all of the United States, including its officers, agents, servants, employees, and attorneys. This obligation was not only one to comply with the judgment of the court but also one in the nature of a contractual relationship.[222] The court ordered the United States to contribute at least $14.6 million as its share of the 1983–1984 plan costs, froze various federal accounts, and ordered the Executive Branch to take actions necessary to assure full implementation of the plan.

The government immediately appealed Judge Shadur's decision to the Seventh Circuit. The court of appeals focused on the district court's finding that funds were available and that the United States had not provided them to the Board. This finding was sufficient to validate the general thrust of the district court's order. On September 9, 1983, the court of appeals decision affirmed Judge Shadur's basic determination that "the United States, by failing to provide available funds to the Board, had violated the consent decree."[223] The circuit court ordered the district court to allow the Executive Branch to attempt voluntarily to comply with the consent order before imposing specific remedial measures.[224] Except for affirming the injunction restraining the expenditure of certain federal funds, the Seventh Circuit vacated all of Judge Shadur's remedial orders.[225] It remanded the case for further review of specific remedies.

Judge Shadur issued a lengthy opinion in June 1984 essentially reaffirming his previous conclusion. If anything, Judge Shadur found the situation to have worsened.[226] The language of the second opinion was less than temperate. The court cited the obligation of the United States to the Board as "freely-undertaken (and then freely-broken)."[227] It found a "false conflict" created by the establishment by the United States of an artificial limitation on funds otherwise available to satisfy the needs of the plan. This artificial limitation created the impression that by making claims against the federal fisc, the district court, and the Board of Education were "choking off deserving educational programs" in other states.[228] This was simply untrue.

> Because the United States had deliberately violated its original agreement to fund the Chicago desegregation plan, this Court has reluctantly found it necessary to prevent the distribution to other possible grantees of United States educational funds in order to reserve access to all the dollars that would be potentially available to fund (the obligation). . . . But as this Court has said during the course of hearings on this issue, the United States "has the key to its cell in its own pocket." On the sorry record reflected by the matters detailed in this long opinion, a private litigant that did what the United States has done would unquestionably be held in contempt—with the potential for being subjected to a fine or imprisonment as well as to an order for civil compliance.[229]

On August 13, 1984, this order was supplemented by a remedial opinion that ordered the United States to make every good faith effort to make available $103 million to the Chicago Board of Education for implementation of the plan.[230] The court was exasperated with what it saw as the government's systematic failures to comply with any basic requirements of the consent decree.

Instead of complying with its responsibility under the consent decree, the United States stonewalled, arguing that the consent decree was either worthless, without authority because it was not within the power of the U.S. Attorney General who negotiated it in 1980, or, alternatively, binding only upon President Carter, because no president can bind his successor, such action being "a concept that is the epitome of the personalized, imperial presidency."[231] The Department of Justice's response was described as "anarchic" or as a "state paper" evidencing bankruptcy, or perhaps something that totalitarian governments would recognize since *that* kind of United States would be one of their own![232] The court quoted *United States v. Lee*.[233]

> No man in this country is so high that he is above the law. No officer of the law may set that law at defiance with impunity. All the officers of the government, from the highest to the lowest, are creatures of the law, and are bound to obey it.[234]

Since there had been no change in the position of the United States[235] since the court's June opinion, the court entered an order, effective immediately, that required the United States to take detailed steps to secure funding for the Board programs. It ordered the government to take every step necessary to provide to the Board, on or before August 22, 1984, $17 million from the Secretary of Education's 1984 Discretionary Fund, and $11.75 million from the $24 million allocated to the Title IV subaccount for fiscal year 1984.[236] For the future, the United States was ordered to develop an affirmative plan for fiscal action in consultation with the Board on or before October 1 of the year preceding each upcoming school year.[237]

Judge Shadur's decision was once again appealed to the Seventh Circuit.[238] On September 26, 1984, the Seventh Circuit vacated both the opinion and the remedial order. The Seventh Circuit specifically rejected the district court's finding that legislative activity by the executive branch, such as lobbying, was mandated by ¶ 15.1.[239] The court found an open question for remand regarding receipt of the maximum level of funding that was available under the criteria of programs that could support desegregation efforts.[240] The case was reassigned to a new district court judge for determination of the maximum level of funding that the Board was entitled to receive.

The appellate court placed further affirmative duties upon the federal government. It noted that the U.S. government had agreed to its "duty to search among funds that Congress had indeed made . . . available.[241] The best proof that the government is fulfilling this duty would be the assignment of personnel to the task of periodically reviewing federal funding programs in various agencies."[242] In sum, the Seventh Circuit opinion discussed the bad faith issue in terms of the administration's legislative efforts, but did not determine whether the actual obligation of the government had been properly fulfilled.

Once again, the case returned to the district court, and the next major opinion, more than a year later, restored the case to its 1984 posture.[243] Judge Aspen began his October 1985 opinion where the Seventh Circuit had left off: "[T]he conduct of the United States had been less than honorable. . . . [T]he United States has violated the letter, as well as the spirit, of the Decree."[244] The movement of the United States was described as "begrudging"[245] and "glacial."[246] The federal government was accused of "Orwellian doublespeak."[247] According to Judge Aspen, the government had not met its obligations under the plan. "The United States' financial commitment under § 15.1 was the principal *quid pro quo* for the Board's willingness to forego litigation and develop its plan."[248] Despite the commitment to the Seventh Circuit about giving the Board top priority for various excess funds that would otherwise remain unspent, the Secretary of Education remained unresponsive, apparently "hell-bent on denying extra funds to the Board unless ordered to do so by statute or court order."[249]

The district court's opinion attempted to test the actions of the executive branch by direct reference to the Seventh Circuit's second opinion, which indicated that efforts by the executive officer to find funds for the Board would be a relevant factor in determining good faith. In fiscal year 1984, the district court concluded that "the Secretary did not 'make every good faith effort to find and provide' available Title IV funds."[250] The court found that search activity to help the Board find available federal funds was limited or non-existent. "From the time of the Court of Appeals' September 1983 decision, through at least February 22, 1985, no efforts were made to locate and identify funds available for the Board's Plan."[251]

On February 22, 1985, Dr. Thomas Fagan, at the Department of Education, was asked to coordinate an "effort to provide technical assistance to Chicago in identifying and applying for" assistance from Department of Education grant programs.[252] The search was confined to the Department of Education.[253] The search itself was a "one-time *ad hoc* event, by a person not holding top rank within the Department of Education and with limited knowledge about funding criteria."[254] This search was "too little, too late," and did not constitute a good faith effort to find and provide.[255]

Judge Shadur's original findings of bad faith on the part of the United States were more than amply substantiated by Judge Aspen's October 1985 opinion. However, Judge Aspen, while finding various government actions improper, stopped short of an explicit finding of bad faith. For example, Judge Aspen was careful to exclude most legislative activity from possible bad faith considerations, although he specifically included, as a possible basis, failure to comply with congressional requests for "reprogramming" of monies that otherwise would not be spent.[256] Significantly, Judge Aspen's opinion ordered the United States to pay a substantially reduced sum to the Board. While the monies were broken down into various categories, the immediate order to pay involved only $17.6 million, far less than the $103 million ordered by Judge Shadur for 1984.[257] Most of the order was stayed pending an appeal.

The Seventh Circuit reversed Judge Aspen's decision with instructions to assign the case on remand to yet another district judge.[258] Not only did the court vacate all of the extensive findings that had been made by both district courts,[259] but it also suggested that if the dispute could not be worked out, the entire consent decree would be vacated and the case set down for trial on the merits.[260] The circuit court held that the district court was not supposed to be an arbitrator, "alleviating the parties of the primary responsibility of conciliation,"[261] but instead was meant to exercise the "utmost restraint to avoid assuming complete control of the relationship."[262] The consent decree required cooperation; that is, cooperation of a consensual nature between federal officials and the Chicago school Board.

Although the circuit court found that the district court's resolution of the funding dispute was a plausible compromise, neither the ambiguous language of ¶ 15.1 nor the extrinsic evidence surrounding the negotiation supplied specific answers to these particular fund disputes. "The only thing clearly contemplated by both the parties and the court in November 1980 [*sic*] was that a cooperative Department of Education would make a good faith effort to provide the Board with a substantial amount of funding."[263]

Resolution of the dispute was primarily a matter for the parties, with the court retaining coercive powers to assist that resolution. In order to describe the district court's role more fully, the opinion attempted to set out the "general guidelines" for resolving the disputes under the decree.[264] Good faith was one of the central concerns of the court. The obligations of the decree did not fall solely upon the Department of Education. Thus, the government's obligation entailed searching beyond the Department of Education's budget for potential funds for Board programs,[265] and an additional obligation to consider the Board's needs when setting guidelines and choosing between priorities in the budget allocation process. Direct evidence of an intent to avoid ¶ 15.1 obligations could be construed legally from the use of a funding method that by its very nature reflected an absence of serious consideration of the needs of the Board.[266]

The court emphasized that the government had joined in a Board plan designed to alleviate the problems of racial segregation in one of the nation's largest public school systems. Such an effort was, and continues to be, beyond the means of the Board alone. Federal cooperation was a partial solution but not one that made the government a "conscripted supplier of dollars." The government was an integral part of the plan, and the plan required that both parties attempt to establish, at a minimum, a federal–municipal dialogue concerning the Board's needs and resources. The Board's needs were not merely more acute than those of other grantees; the government, upon entering into a consent decree, had assumed a substantial obligation to fund Board needs, a greater obligation than owed other potential Title IV grantees.[267] On the other hand, the Board could not design a plan assuming that the government was obliged to fund all educational programs that the Board included under the label of desegregation.[268]

> Neither this court nor the district court will further tolerate the parties' position that one of them must emerge the victor. Paragraph 15.1 imposes a continuing relationship between the parties, the responsibility for which cannot be avoided through litigation over the precise obligation imposed by the funding provision. This type of rigidity is itself a violation of the good faith/best efforts required by ¶ 15.1.[269]

The court gave the parties another chance to cooperate and set forth the role the court would play should cooperation not work. If the court found that any party had acted in bad faith, the court "must take necessary remedial steps to protect the integrity of its order."[270]

To enforce the order, the court had two options. The first, and most drastic remedy, is contempt.[271] Contempt is appropriate when "an unequivocal judicial command is callously ignored" or "where steps are taken to subvert the decree."[272] Not all bad faith was deemed to constitute contemptuous bad faith, however. Given the nebulous nature of the ¶ 15.1 obligation, an attempt to comply could amount to bad faith while not constituting direct defiance of the orders of the court. If conduct is not so egregious, the court could order "best efforts." [273] In the case of bad faith efforts by the federal government, the amount of the penalty would be the maximum amount the government could pay out under the parameters set out earlier in the opinion.[274]

Alternatively, the court had the option of finding that the entire decree included problems "too intractable for judicially-supervised resolution," [275] which could come about even in the absence of bad faith. The court stated that hindsight indicated that entry of a decree contemplating wide-reaching and expensive changes in a large, financially strapped school system, without explicit commitments for outside funding, may have been ill-advised.[276] In such a situation, the court could modify the decree to align costs with available funds, while maintaining the goals of the original decree, or vacate the decree, releasing both parties from their obligations and taking immediate steps to set the case for trial on the merits.[277] "If this decree is not capable of assuring the school children of Chicago the rights they allegedly are being deprived of . . . the public school children of Chicago may deserve more than this decree may be able to provide." [278]

Only in this last discussion did the Seventh Circuit focus on the underlying merits of the case—the impact of the desegregation plan on the school children of Chicago. The suggestion of vacatur may have been included merely for its shock value. The opinion indicated that the decree was only an instrument for achieving certain results and that if, for whatever reasons, acceptable results could not be achieved, the decree should not continue to constrain the court or the parties.

By the summer of 1987, the funding dispute was resolved with the passage of the second Yates Bill, which provided for $83 million of federal funding over the next five years.[279] Further, the Board reserved the right to apply for any other available federal educational funds on the same basis as any other school district. This consent decree was amended by replacing paragraph 15.1 with a settlement agreement submitted to the district court in October 1987 and adopted on December 1, 1987.[280] Thus, all the pieces of the plan were finally in place. Yet to date, the results of the desegregation dispute are mixed.

Cross-District Remedies—An Abortive Exploration

An option available since the entry of the decree was the addition of new parties, for the purpose of either adding potential fund sources, primarily the state of Illinois, or generating potential cross-district remedies involving various suburbs in the plan. Only by involving the suburbs could a desegregation plan be produced that would be substantially different from the current one, at least in racial mix, and then only by requiring substantial busing.[281]

Some exploratory investigation of these options had been done. The consent decree required the federal government to conduct two investigations, one of interdistrict school violations and another of the potential liability of third parties.

The Department of Education had reported the results of its interdistrict school violation investigation in a five-page report filed in the spring of 1983.[282] The report indicated that there was no evidence of student exchange between the Chicago public schools and any suburban schools that would warrant interdistrict relief.[283] There was evidence of minorities transferring from segregated Chicago schools to integrated high schools in the suburbs, but such transfers were not believed to be extensive, and the Chicago public schools did not know about them.[284] No evidence was found that whites were permitted to transfer from integrated schools within Chicago to all-white schools outside Chicago, although evidence was found of such transfers within Chicago.[285] Further, no evidence of boundary changes was found, partly because the boundaries of the Chicago school districts have been contiguous with those of the city of Chicago boundaries since the nineteenth century.[286] Last, the investigation did not find any evidence that state or local public officials influenced the siting of school buildings or the distribution of students between Chicago and the suburbs.[287]

Because of the current demographics of the Chicago area, it is difficult to understand how cross-district remedies could apply to the Chicago school situation. For example, two of the most integrated suburban school systems in the Chicago area—Oak Park, which directly adjoins Chicago on the west, and Evanston, which adjoins the city on the north—are relatively close to areas in Chicago from which minority pupils could be bused. The possibility of destabilizing these school systems would then be a serious concern. However, if one examines the demographics and location of suburban municipalities, such as those on the far southwest of Chicago, which would be "better" candidates presenting fewer concerns regarding racial destabilization, it is obvious that extended bus routes would be necessary to integrate the schools significantly through cross-district busing.[288] The suburban schools, with minority student populations that were studied by the Justice Department, were found to be substantially more integrated than Chicago schools.[289]

The state liability investigation had been conducted under the theory that the state of Illinois could be liable for its actions or inactions in permitting the Board of Education to continue segregationist policies.[290] This investigation, however, uncovered even less material than did the interdistrict investigation. To date, a final report has yet to be filed. The interim reports reflect great difficulty in conducting this investigation, especially because of the state Board of Education's lack of cooperation. The second interim report, though including some relevant data, indicates that much still requires exploration and suggests that potential state liability might indeed exist. According to the third interim report, whatever level of cooperation the state of Illinois had until then been rendering, ceased almost immediately upon the submission of the second interim report.[291]

Although the lack of cooperation hampered the investigation, the Board may have benefited politically from it. Under the consent decree, the Board of Education explicitly reserved the right to sue the state of Illinois for financial contribution.[292] To date, that right has not been exercised. Nevertheless, each budget year, the state of Illinois and the Board of Education negotiate the amount of aid the state will pay the Chicago school system. The Board has been relatively successful in obtaining state aid in the last several years.[293] It is possible that the threat of a financial contribution suit will be more effective in gaining state support than an actual law suit.

A suit against the state of Illinois by the Department of Justice raises political concerns. Illinois is one of the few populous states with a Republican governor and, therefore, not a likely target of a Republican administration political initiative. It is also both cheaper and politically preferable for the Justice Department to defend an affirmative suit against the United States than to undertake difficult and extensive explorations into thousands of archival documents that a suit against the state would entail.

CONCLUSION

The problems in the Chicago school system have been and remain massive. In times of chronic financial difficulties, legal costs themselves have become a problem. The city has spent $3.3 million on legal expenses since 1979.[294] The prospects for Chicago are not particularly bright. According to recently released census data, Chicago lost 201,568 middle-class families of all races between 1960 and 1980.[295] The percentage of middle-class families decreased from 63.6 percent of the population in 1960 to 52.9 percent in 1980. Estimates of the yearly impact of the loss of sales and property tax related to the flight of the middle class amount to $55 million.[296]

On the other hand, the litigation has eliminated policies that encouraged pupil segregation, such as voluntary transfers without regard to segregative impact. Moreover, the official policy of the Chicago Board of Education is now squarely opposed to segregation. This policy is not simply a symbolic result of the litigation. For example, the Board considers the efforts to remedy the impact of segregation as significant educational programs. The Board has resisted the Teachers Union's efforts to sacrifice funds allocated toward desegregation for purposes of raising teachers' salaries. While there has not been much time to determine the impact of these direct, programmatic, educational expenditures, the funds allocated are at least significant measures of the Board's efforts to remedy the impact of segregation and its companion substandard educational programs for minorities.[297] Without the lawsuit, these monies would not have been so allocated.

Despite the continued decline in white student enrollment in the Chicago public schools,[298] student desegregation targets have been met. The number of minority students attending integrated schools today has increased only marginally from the number attending integrated schools in 1980. In 1985–1986, only 5,660 more minority students attended high schools that were more than 30 percent white than did so in 1980–1981. The comparable figure for elementary schools is 6,202 additional minority students. Nonetheless, plan targets for "desegregating" the schools have been met at all grade levels.

From 1980 to 1986, most enrollment changes were small. Minority attendance increases at "desegregated" high schools (with more than 30 percent white enrollment) represented a shift of only 5.8 percent of all minority high school students. The comparable figure for elementary schools was a shift of only 2.3 percent. Indeed, by some measures, racial isolation worsened during this period. For example, in 1980–1981, 47 percent of black high school students were in all-minority schools; that figure increased to 55.9 percent in 1985–1986.[299] Similarly, 8,018 more Hispanic students attended elementary schools that were less than 15 percent white in 1985–1986. Therefore, the net impact of the program, measured by the numbers of students attending integrated schools, is modest at every level.

Realizing the promise of remedying problems of segregation through educational enrichment has been difficult during years of financial shortage. Further, Chicago schools once again began fall classes in 1987 with another strike, primarily over salary increases for teachers,[300] although another two-year union contract resulted.

For racially identifiable schools, (with less than 30 percent white enrollment) lack of funding has meant that their "special" education programs have not been fully funded. This is not the case for the most racially isolated schools (with no white enrollment), which have been fully funded in the "Effective Schools Project." These schools display gains, indeed, above the average for the system as a whole.[301] These gains suggest that supplemental educational programs can address some of the negative aspects of racial isolation.

One must question, therefore, the continued viability of a partially funded plan as a desegregation effort. The *de facto, underfunded* plan has never been determined by the district court to be within the boundaries of a constitutionally acceptable plan. Indeed, the district court has not been asked to answer that question.

The entire federal contribution of $83 million is now earmarked for expenditure as "Project CANAL" over the 1988–1993 school years.[302] That project targets the worst racially identifiable schools in the system with a focus on improved student achievement through enhancing staff professionalism and parental involvement.[303] The goal is that by August 1993 at least 50 percent of the participating students will perform at or above grade level in reading and mathematics.[304] Perhaps at that time it will be possible to make some clear assessment about the true promise of educational enrichment as an alternative to racial integration in a massive, metropolitan school system.

Large numbers of students continue to drop out of the system. The dropout rate for the 1982 class was 43 percent, while that for the 1985 class was 45 percent. In 1986, there was, however, a slight improvement to 41.4 percent.[305] Since a strong correlation exists between low reading scores and high dropout rates, the recent improvement in reading scores is encouraging. However, despite the improvements, the school system's projected dropout rate for the class of 1990 is still a very high 38 percent.

The investigation of cross-district busing remedies has uncovered no fruitful legal basis for creating a cross-district remedy. Indeed, a *Chicago Tribune* study published in the summer of 1987 reveals the futility of such a remedy. The study indicated the black *suburban* high school students are more likely to attend predominantly black schools than they were ten years ago.[306] The percentage of black enrollment has increased the most in suburbs closest in proximity to inner-city black populations; these changes can be attributed more to decline of white student enrollment than to increases of black student enrollment.[307] White enrollment in all non-city Cook County high schools dropped from 88 percent in 1977 to 78 percent in 1987.[308]

If it were possible to integrate all Cook County high school students, white high school students would constitute about 45 percent, blacks 38 percent, Hispanics 12 percent, and Asians 3.5 percent. Even without further white flight from such a system, white students would remain in the minority of the Cook County School System.[309] A busing plan with Cook County could accomplish only insignificant desegregation, which could not be justified given the outrageous expense and extraordinary commutation times required to accomplish such a plan.

The Illinois school system is ranked as the most segregated in the country. It also ranks *last* in percentage of black students attending schools with white students in a majority.[310] This phenomenon relates directly to racial segregation by residence in Illinois, most of which occurs in Cook County and Chicago. Therefore, it seems inconceivable that a markedly different pattern of school "integration" could have emerged in Chicago, even if the district court had ordered cross-district busing. The tragedy remains, however, that the plan has never been *fully* implemented, and is unlikely to be fully implemented in the future.

The most disturbing aspect of the current suit is its political overtones. The dispute regarding the funding obligation of the United States directly relates to the unwillingness of the Reagan administration to fulfill an agreement entered into by the Carter administration. To the late Mayor Richard Daley, there was nothing clearer than the relationship between money and principles.[311] Government could do little without funds. You do not build airports or skyscrapers without money. A commitment without the ability to carry it out was worse than useless; it was a fraud on the people. From that perspective, the Reagan administration's support for the Chicago Board of Education desegregation plan is just such a fraud. Scant funding must be seen as scant support for the new approach to desegregation, which moves away from "failed busing programs"[312] toward alternative devices involving enhanced educational programs.

The long-term impact of the suit can be measured only some time in the future, after the legal efforts shift from raising funds back to the basic issue of providing educational services in a desegregated system. Until that time, the Chicago public school system is about as desegregated as current political and practical constraints and circumstances will allow. For those students who are able to attend integrated schools, the effect of the suit is not just symbolic. For all the other students, those who attend the 200 schools where integration is not possible, the funding suit is the main hope for providing a remedy for the negative educational effects of segregated school systems.

Project CANAL will reach only 40 such schools, however. Not until 1993 will it be known whether its educational targets have been reached. If the Reagan administration was correct that busing has "failed" as a solution, it is fair in reply to state that the Reagan solution of educational supplementation has not proved a viable alternative. At best, the 1993 evaluation of Project CANAL may validate the theory for some students in a small number of schools. Meanwhile, for an entire generation of Chicago public school students who started school in 1980, 60 percent or fewer will have already graduated, and 40 percent or more will have dropped out of the system. For such students, the symbol of titular school desegregation is probably less significant than the symbol of the election of the first black mayor of Chicago, Harold Washington. Neither the school desegregation suit nor the Reagan administration had anything to do with that.

NOTES

Note: On September 24, 1980, the U.S. Department of Justice filed a civil complaint, Docket No. 80 C 5124, on behalf of the United States of America against the Chicago Board of Education. On that same day, the parties submitted a consent decree, which the court accepted. As a result, there has been no litigation regarding the issue of liability. All of the complicated litigation that followed concerned the appropriate remedy.

1. Chicago Tribune, September 17, 1985, at 10, col. 4. "[I]n Chicago and its suburbs, Blacks and Whites have very little contact. Studies have found Chicago to be the most segregated major city in the United States. In the course of a day, there is only a 1 in 25 chance that a Black in Chicago will see a White in his neighborhood or that a White will see a Black in his community, according to a 1983 study cited by the Illinois Criminal Justice Information Authority." *Id. A report of the United States Commission on Civil Rights, Twenty Years After Brown*, 1975, at 151, table 4.5. indicates that this has been so for a long time. The report ranks Chicago first nationwide in proportion of black population living in a census tract 90 percent or more black (77.7 percent) (based upon a special census tabulation prepared for the Office of Equal Opportunity, Department of Housing and Urban Environment by the Census Data Corp.) "By all measures, Chicago has a high degree of segregation, while San Francisco, Los Angeles, and New York show a relatively high degree of dispersion." *Id.* at 147.

2. Chicago has a history of bad race relations that dates back at least to the race riots of the summer of 1919. *See* Beauharnais v. Illinois, 343 U.S. 250, 258. (1952); *see also* M. ROYKO, BOSS 30–31 (1971).

3. 334 U.S. 1 (1948).

4. 347 U.S. 483 (1954).

5. United States v. Board of Education, 588 F. Supp. 132 (N.D. Ill. 1984). The litigation has generated 13 published decisions of the U.S. District Court and three opinions of the U.S. Court of Appeals for the Seventh Circuit. The most significant published opinions are cited in United States v. Board of Education, 799 F.2d 281 (7th Cir. 1986).

6. *Id.* at 157. In the fall of 1983, the Chicago Board of Education operated 580 schools, down from 634 schools in 1980–1981 because of school closures. *Id.* at 140. The city school population dropped from 577,679 pupils in 1970 to 434,042 pupils in 1983, a nearly 25 percent decline in public school enrollment. *Id.* at 153.

7. 223 F. Supp. 466 (N.D. Ill. 1963).

8. *Id.* at 467. Superintendent Willis was a national leader of educators who sought increased financial aid for education of the culturally disadvantaged. He was the first big-city school administrator to take the initiative in this regard. W. Vrame, *A History of School Desegregation in Chicago Since 1954* at 37 (1970) (unpublished dissertation available from University Microfilms, Ann Arbor, Michigan). Chicago's black community had come to view Willis as the city's most outspoken champion of minority rights. Prior to 1961, criticism for his failure to address desegregation issues was minimal. Later, he bore the brunt of attacks from civil rights groups regarding busing. Vrame at 37–41.

9. Judge Marovitz has been described as owing his appointment to the federal bench to Mayor Daly and as being one of the charmed inner circle permitted to spend time with Daley at party headquarters as election returns came in. *See*, ROYKO, *supra* note 2, at 49–50.

10. 324 F.2d 209 (7th Cir. 1963). The brief opinion in *Bell* is worth reading. Seventy percent of the black student population in Gary attended schools over 99 percent black. The *Bell* court cited with approval the infamous statement in Briggs v. Elliott, 132 F. Supp. 776, 777 (E.D.S.C. 1955): "The Constitution, in other words, does not require integration. It merely forbids discrimination." This state-

ment became known as the "Parker doctrine" in honor of its author Judge John Parker. It served to justify obstruction to integration of public schools for decades. *See* KLUGER, SIMPLE JUSTICE 751 *et seq.* (1976). Kluger also recounts the defeat of Parker's nomination to the U.S. Supreme Court in 1930. The nomination was vigorously resisted by both labor unions, on the grounds of Judge Parker's rulings on "yellow dog contracts," and the NAACP. The *Christian Science Monitor* attributed Parker's narrow defeat to "[t]he first national demonstration of the Negro's power since Reconstruction days." KLUGER at 144. Unfortunately, Judge Parker remained on the lower federal court bench, and his doctrine continued to cause trouble.

11. Hess, *Renegotiating a Multicultural Society: Participation in Desegregation Planning in Chicago*, 53 JOURNAL OF NEGRO EDUCATION 132, 135 n. 6 (1984). *See also* Vrame, *supra* note 8, at 39–45. Superintendent Willis remained adamantly opposed to busing even though implementation of the neighborhood school concept required the purchase of hundreds of mobile classrooms. By 1963, the expanding enrollment was under control though the mobile classrooms were bitterly resented by the black community. *Id.* at 74–75. Vrame concludes that "[b]y the time of Superintendent Willis's departure (in August 1966), civil rights leaders, for all their activity, found themselves no better off than they had been in 1961 when they first attempted to force school officials to desegregate the schools." *Id.* at 76.

12. *See* supra note 10.

13. 223 F. Supp. at 468. (emphasis in original). This language does not appear in *Bell*.

14. 386 F. Supp. 110 (N.D. Ill. 1974).

15. Judge McLaren had developed a reputation for commitment to principle and impartiality through his involvement in the Watergate affair. At that time, he was Assistant U.S. Attorney General and head of the Antitrust Division of the Department of Justice. One of the suits he brought while Assistant U.S. Attorney General was against ITT, a firm that was subsequently accused of paying $400,000 to the Republican national convention in exchange for dropping the case. *See* DEAN, BLIND AMBITION 51 *et seq.* (1976).

16. 386 F. Supp. at 115.

17. *Id.* at 116.

18. *Id.*

19. *Id.*

20. Richard A. Berk, plaintiff's expert witness, testified that during the 1969–1970 school year, the mean per pupil expenditure for predominantly black schools was $391, for white schools $423, and for mixed schools $406. For the 1970–1971 school year, a similar pattern existed, constituting an 8.2 and 8.3 percent difference for the two school years. This was not a new condition. Data from the 1960s indicated that such conclusions were reflective of a long-term historical pattern. 386 F. Supp. at 117.

21. Petitioners introduced no evidence on the two later years. *Id.* at 118.

22. *Id.*

23. *Id.* at 119.

24. *Id.*

25. 411 U.S. 1 (1973).

26. 386 F. Supp. at 126.

27. Costs were assessed against the defendant. *Id.*

28. Lawler v. Board of Education, 458 F.2d 660 (7th Cir. 1972). O'Toole is on the southside with its district bounded by 59th and 69th streets and Western and Ashland avenues.

29. Plaintiffs lacked standing to challenge the Board's policies on the grounds of the departure of other whites from the school area.

30. 458 F. Supp. at 662.

31. Complainant was the mother of the named plaintiff, a hard-working single parent who wanted to keep her children out of the ghetto. She had moved to the area in order to secure a better life for her children. Interview with Shalom L. Kohn, Esq., in Chicago (February 4, 1985). Kohn was, and still is, affiliated with the law firm of Sidley & Austin and had accepted the case on reference from the Lawyers' Committee for Civil Rights.

The case has a convoluted procedural history. It first went to the Seventh Circuit, 604 F.2d 504 (7th Cir. 1979) (rehearing *en banc* denied), which affirmed District Judge Herbert Will's decision, but the Seventh Circuit's decision was itself vacated and remanded by the U.S. Supreme Court, 449 U.S. 915 (1980). On remand, Judge Will found the case justiciable (unpublished opinion), and the Seventh Circuit affirmed the decision, 664 F.2d 1069 (7th Cir. 1981). However, the Supreme Court, in a *per curiam* decision, once again vacated and remanded to the Seventh Circuit with direction to consolidate the case with the Department of Justice suit, 457 U.S. 52 (1982). Justices Rehnquist and Marshall dissented.

32. 604 F.2d at 511–12.

33. Ill. Rev. Stat. ch. 122, ¶ 7 (1975). Paragraph 7 stated in part: "[N]o pupil shall be excluded from or segregated in any such school on account of his color, race, sex, or nationality. The board shall, as soon as practicable, and from time to time thereafter, change or revise existing sub-districts or create new sub-districts in a manner which will take into consideration the prevention of segregation and the elimination of separation of children in public schools because of color, race, sex, or nationality." The quoted first sentence, an affirmative statutory prohibition of discrimination based upon race, dates back to 1917. Laws of 1917, 50th General Assembly, at 730, § 136. This provision applied only to the Chicago school Board. An earlier statute of 1909 spoke only generally of the Chicago Board's power "to apportion the pupils to the several schools." Laws of 1909, at 380, § 133. The second quoted sentence traces its origin to the laws of 1963, 73 General Assembly, ¶ 1108. The Johnson court ignored the impact, if any, of a provision in the statute enacted in 1973: "Nothing herein shall be construed to permit or empower the State Board of Education to order, mandate, or require busing or other transportation of pupils for the purpose of achieving racial balance in any school." P.A. 78–881, 1973 Session, 78th General Assembly, effective October 1, 1973. This provision immunized the Chicago Board of Education from direct control by the state Board of Education regarding busing. The provisions of Chapter 34 continue to apply only to Chicago as the single city with a population of over 500,000 in Illinois.

34. Kohn Interview, *supra* note 31.

35. 604 F.2d at 509. The plaintiffs were granted costs but denied any attorneys' fees.

36. *Id.* at 507.
37. *Id.* at 515.
38. *Id.*
39. University of California Regents v. Bakke, 438 U.S. 265 (1978).
40. 604 F.2d at 515 n. 5.
41. *Id.* at 517. The court also considered and rejected the argument that a less discriminatory alternative could have been used to achieve the objective of preventing *de facto* segregation. *Id.* at 518–19.
42. Vrame describes Daley's ability to block federal pressure, including congressional hearings in Chicago held by Adam Clayton Powell on *de facto* segregation, which turned into a one-day hearing in praise of Superintendent Willis's efforts on behalf of minority groups. Vrame, *supra* note 8, at 75–76.
43. Telephone interview with John Frey, Attorney, Office of Civil Rights, U.S. Department of Education, in Chicago (January 10, 1986). This investigation was conducted by the Office of Civil Rights within HEW. The primary focus of this investigation was on the last two decades (1960s and 1970s). Appendix to Letter of Ineligibility to the Chicago Public School District Under the Emergency School Aid Act, at 2.
44. This ineligibility determination related to the 1980–1981 school year application.
45. Decision of February 15, 1977. Appendix, *supra* note 43, at 97.
46. Agreement dated October 12, 1977. Appendix, *supra* note 43, at 98. While the Board had not fully complied with this accord, significant faculty desegregation resulted. HEW saw faculty and professional segregation as indicative of the likelihood of unlawful segregative policies regarding students.
47. Frey Interview, *supra* note 43.
48. Complaint at 3, ¶ 7. Application for ESAA funds for the 1980–1981 school year also produced an HEW determination that the Board was ineligible because of unlawful racial segregation. The Board of Education defended itself in administrative proceedings, but the Department of Education reaffirmed the HEW determinations. Frey Interview, *supra* note 43.
49. Complaint at 3, ¶ 8.
50. *Id.* at 3, ¶ 9.
51. *Id.* at 3–4, ¶¶ 10–12.
52. Chicago Tribune, April 25, 1980, at 8, col. 1.
53. Chicago Sun Times, August 3, 1980, at 28, col. 1.
54. *Id.* at 28, col. 2. She cited four reasons in favor of settlement. They were (1) school officials could design their own desegregation plan; (2) the school Board could save enormous legal fees; (3) the school Board could minimize the bad feelings in the community; and (4) the school Board could receive federal money. Hughes, one of Mayor Byrne's nominees to the school Board, had earlier stated that she "would try to solve [the desegregation issue] as rapidly and as equitably as possible." Chicago Tribune, April 30, 1980, § 5, at 1, col. 7. The policy of the Byrne administration was clear even at that early date, well before the beginning of the months of "secret negotiation." In essence, the consent decree was presaged by the first reports of Mayor Byrne's Board of Education nominees.

55. Chicago Tribune, June 14, 1980, at 1, col 1 and at 5, col. 1.

56. *Id.* at 1, col. 2. The faculty desegregation plan had been approved October 12, 1977.

57. Chicago Tribune, June 14, 1980, at 5, col. 2.

58. *Id.* The April "ultimatum" letter had a stated Justice Department goal of settlement early in the summer. Chicago Sun Times, April 22, 1980, at 3, col. 3. The criteria were that any settlement would have to be system-wide; be approved in the form of a consent decree; and assure that all school closings, program changes, new construction, and other actions that shift children would not occur before a written analysis of its effects upon school segregation was conducted. *Id.* at 3 and 30.

59. Chicago Tribune, April 26, 1980, § 1, at 8, col. 2, editorial, *How Parents View the Schools*. Blacks accepted the idea of leaving the neighborhood school by 56 percent to 29 percent.

60. *Id.* A *Chicago Tribune* telephone poll indicated great differences based upon race in responses regarding busing. A majority of black respondents (56 percent) supported mandatory busing. Only 9 percent of the whites and 36 percent of Hispanics found busing acceptable. Sixty percent of white parents polled said they would pull their children out of the schools if there was compulsory busing. "That would mean that overnight the school system would plummet from 20 percent to 8 percent white." Chicago Tribune, April 20, 1980, § 1, at 10, col. 3. Casey Banas, education editor for the *Chicago Tribune*, wrote shortly after the entry of the consent decree, "I talked to some of these whites in our survey, and the depth of their feeling against mandatory reassignment out of their local schools runs very, very deep." Chicago Tribune, October 1, 1980, § 6, at 2, col. 6. Banas expressed initial pessimism about the success of the plan. "For years, the Whites controlled the school board. They could have worked out a reasonable and rational desegregation plan. But they chose to duck the issue. Now the resolution, such as it may be, is about to come, and one question is whether the school system will be even 10 percent white the day the plan begins." Chicago Tribune, October 1, 1980, § 6, at 2, col. 6. Both suburban and city residents expressed willingness to move or transfer their children if compulsory busing was adopted. Chicago Sun Times, January 4, 1980, at 3, col. 1–2.

61. *See infra* note 88 and accompanying text.

62. Discussed in Chicago Sun Times, April 22, 1980, at 30, col. 2.

63. Civil Action No. 80 C 5124. From the beginning, the case was staffed from Washington, as well as the local U.S. Attorney's Office.

64. "Off the wheel" refers to a random system of assigning new cases to federal judges.

65. Interview with U.S. District Judge Milton I. Shadur, in Chicago (February 18, 1985). By the time of this interview, upon remand from its decision of September 24, 1984, United States v. Board of Education, 744 F.2d 1300, *cert. denied*, 471 U.S. 1116 (1985), the U.S. Court of Appeals for the Seventh Circuit had indicated that the case would be reassigned pursuant to Circuit Rule 18. It was perhaps somewhat unusual for the case to be reassigned upon this second remand, but Circuit Rule 18 clearly provided the court of appeals with power to order reassignment.

66. Mobile classrooms, which had become known as Willis Wagons, after the former school superintendent, were still in use at some schools in Chicago.

67. Complaint at 5–6, ¶ 15 (e)–(h).

68. *Id.* at 6, ¶ 16.

69. *Id.* at 6–7.

70. Consent Decree at 2, ¶¶ 3, 5–6, accepted and entered by Judge Shadur (September 24, 1980). It was signed on behalf of the United States by Drew Days III, Assistant Attorney General, and Thomas P. Sullivan, U.S. Attorney, and on behalf of the Board by Robert C. Howard, of Pressman and Hartunian, Chtd.

71. *See supra* note 6 and accompanying text.

72. Consent Decree at 2, ¶¶ III–IV.

73. *Id.* at 4, ¶ I, 1.

74. *Id.* at 4, ¶ I, 2.1.

75. *Id.* at 4, ¶ I, 2.2.

76. *Id.* at 4, 5, ¶ I, 2.3, 2.4.

77. *Id.* at 6, ¶ I, 4.1. They included, in addition to permissive transfers, magnet schools and pairing and clustering of schools (with racial or ethnic quotas).

78. *Id.* at 6, ¶ I, 4.2. These techniques include redrawing attendance areas, adjusting feeder patterns, reorganizing grade structures, pairing and clustering schools, selecting sites for new schools, and closing some schools to enhance desegregation.

79. *Id.* at 6, ¶ I, 4.3.

80. *Id.* at 7, ¶ I, 5.1.

81. *Id.* at 9, ¶ I, 7. Indeed, as will be discussed below, *see infra* notes 153–58 and accompanying text, these schools were to be the bulk of the system.

82. *Id.* at 9, ¶ I, 7.1–7.3.

83. *Id.* at 9, ¶ I, 8.

84. Chicago Tribune, September 25, 1980, at 1, col. 1.

85. Chicago Tribune, April 27, 1980, § 3, at 9, col. 1.

86. A *Sun-Times* article carried the banner, "Pact's city–suburb busing clause could trigger new court hassles." September 25, 1980, at 4, col. 2. The headline was also printed on page one.

87. *See* Chicago Sun Times, September 26, 1980, at 12, col. 1. "[S]everal prominent civil rights attorneys warned that disagreements could have serious legal consequences." The possibility of a lengthy trial depended, in part, on "how the judge reads the consent decree itself." On the other hand, many prominent local political figures were cautiously optimistic. These included Chicago Urban League President James W. Compton and Citizens' Schools Committee Executive Director Hank Rubin.

88. Chicago Sun Times, September 25, 1980, at 4, col. 2.

89. Editorial, Chicago Tribune, September 26, 1980, § 3, at 2.

90. A subsequently filed motion on behalf of the NAACP added another NAACP branch and a young black student as a proposed class representative. United States v. Board of Education, 88 F.R.D. 679, 680 n. 1 (N.D. Ill. 1981). Various other entities, including MALDEF (Mexican American Legal Defense and Educational Fund) and PRLDEF (Puerto Rican Legal Defense and Educational Fund), also moved for permission to intervene in November 1980. There was a long series of attempts by various parties to intervene during the course of the case. All such attempts were denied by the court in the sense that party status was denied. These included attempts

by Chicago ward aldermen (members of the city council) (October 1981), renewed attempts by the NAACP (December 1981), and students and parents from Harrison High School (June 1983).

91. *See supra* notes 1–4 and accompanying text.

92. Hills v. Gautreaux, 425 U.S. 284 (1976).

93. *See* 47 L.Ed.2d 1008, 1009 (1976) for part of the brief filed in *Gautreaux* over Milton I. Shadur's signature.

94. 425 U.S. at 288–306.

95. Shadur Interview, *supra* note 65.

96. *Id.* "As long as the plan was within the range of constitutionally permissible ones—I know that the plan would not be a court determined plan. The responsibility was on the Board, and the Court would decide if the plan so developed fit the Constitution's requirements."

97. *See* 88 F.R.D. at 683 n. 6.

98. *Id.* at 679. The court eventually granted *amicus* status to many groups, including the NAACP and MALDEF–PRLDEF. From this position, these other voices brought in "thoughtful, observant perspectives and a more rounded picture of the controversy."

99. *Id.* at 682.

100. *Id.* In footnote 4, the court pointed to the responses of the intervenors to a directive from the court to address the impact of the class action allegations of their complaint in intervention on the issues now before the court. The NAACP response stated in part, "However, in the interest of judicial economy, we instead have sought to intervene in the within action and postpone any determination on the question of the liability of the defendant Board until it has an opportunity to prepare and submit its proposed desegregation plan." Thus, the risk of opening liability issues was a real possibility.

101. *Id.* at 683.

102. Shadur Interview, *supra* note 65.

103. Consent Decree at 29, Appendix A.

104. *See infra* notes 178–96 and accompanying text.

105. United States v. Board of Education, 554 F. Supp. 912 (N.D. Ill. 1983).

106. *Id.* at 915. "Because any effective plan must exist and work in the real world and not just on paper, this Court encouraged implementation of the first year of planned desegregation at the same time the full planning process was reaching fruition." *Id.* at 914: "Had the plan been obviously unconstitutional in any respect, this Court would have acted swiftly to reject it. But no such obvious flaw was involved. And because any interim statement by this Court to explain the reasons for deferral would have carried the serious possibility of being misunderstood as final approval at *that* time, the Court has perforce bided its time in silence." *Id.* at 915. (emphasis in original).

107. Shadur Interview, *supra* note 65.

108. Chicago Tribune, October 9, 1980, § 1, at 1, col. 1. The *Chicago Tribune* described Green as a person who "knows and cares about the educational aspects of desegregation plans." His background included work on the staff of the Southern Christian Leadership Conference and work directing an adult education and jobs

program in the blighted Lawndale neighborhood of Chicago. October 10, 1980, § 3, at 13, col. 1, editorial.

109. Chicago Tribune, October 10, 1980, § 1, at 1, col. 3. Green had written the educational aspects of desegregation plans in Indianapolis; Kalamazoo, Michigan; and Detroit, and had been involved in desegregation movements in 22 cities.

110. *Id.*

111. Chicago Tribune, October 10, 1980, § 1, at 22, col. 1.

112. Chicago Sun Times, December 4, 1980, at 18, col. 1; December 6, 1980, at 22, col. 1. The hearings were to run through January 8, 1981. The *Sun Times* editorialized that these hearings were inadequate, for they allowed no real "public participation." The Milwaukee committee of 119 citizens, and the St. Louis committee of 20 citizens were suggested as appropriate models. Chicago Sun Times December 9, 1980, at 41, col. 1.

113. Chicago Sun Times, December 16, 1980, at 36, col. 1. "Most of the 25 speakers said they would be reluctant even to send their children to better schools than those available close to home. Instead, they recommended that the Board concentrate its efforts on improving neighborhood schools." By the end, over 300 persons spoke at these hearings, but many of the speakers asked for further input opportunities. Chicago Tribune, January 16, 1981, § 3, at 5, col. 5.

114. Chicago Tribune, December 19, 1980, § 3, at 1, col. 5. Green advocated the panel's creation and expressed hope that a draft plan would be submitted to the panel by mid-February.

115. Chicago Tribune, January 15, 1981, § 1, at 3, col. 2. Her contract began on March 25, 1981, for a four-year period at the extraordinary annual salary of $120,000. This was and still is the highest salary an Illinois public official has ever been paid. Her replacement in 1985, Manfred Byrd, was not paid as much.

116. Chicago Sun Times, March 26, 1981, at 3, col. 2.

117. Chicago Sun Times, March 24, 1981, at 3, col. 1; Chicago Tribune, March 25, 1981, § 6, at 1, col. 1. The current head of the Board desegregation committee, Michael Scott, said that educational components of the plan have been completed, but, "[t]he numbers haven't been decided yet." Scott declined to state whether mandatory busing was involved. In absolute numbers, 122 *more* schools and programs were out of compliance *after* entry of the consent decree than were out of compliance in January of 1980. Chicago Tribune, February 18, 1981, § 6, at 1, col. 1. *See supra* notes 78–80 and accompanying text.

118. Chicago Sun Times, March 24, 1981, at 3, col. 1.

119. Chicago Sun Times, February 20, 1981, at 4, col. 1.

120. Chicago Tribune, April 4, 1981, § 1, at 4, col. 4.

121. Chicago Sun Times, March 4, 1981, at 3, col. 1 and at 58, col. 1.

122. *Byrne Rips Busing. Plan Draws Fire from Both Sides*, Chicago Sun Times, April 4, 1981, at 1, col. 2. *Desegregation Plan, Busing Hit by Byrne. School Bd. Can't Afford It, She Says*, Chicago Tribune, April 4, 1981, § 1, at 1, col. 2.

123. The school system was $700 million in the red only the year before. Mayor Byrne said, "I received the plan, saw the price tag, and thought, 'That's too bad.'" Estimates for the busing costs were approximately $24.5 million per year. Chicago Tribune, April 14, 1981, § 1, at 1, col. 4. Within days, U.S. Senator Charles H. Percy

visited Mayor Byrne and indicated that the city was unlikely to get any federal financial assistance. In a letter to the editor, Percy stated that federal law prohibited the use of federal funds for transportation of students or teachers in order to overcome racial imbalance in any school or school system though money might be available for educational components. Chicago Sun Times, April 15, 1981, at 44, col. 1. Mayor Byrne wrote the school Board president, Kenneth B. Smith, that "any desegregation plan that would further erode our tax base must be judged irresponsible, and ultimately unacceptable."

124. *Shouts, Howls Greet New School Proposal*, Chicago Tribune, April 4, 1981, § 1, at 1, col. 4.

125. The newspapers published lists of schools and reassignment numbers that covered full pages. These lists included schools slated for closings and some of the pairings, clusterings, and area reassignments involved. The Board of Education set up a desegregation hotline to address questions. Chicago Tribune, April 4, 1981, § 1, at 14, col. 1; April 5, 1981, § 1, at 14, col. 1.

126. Chicago Sun Times, April 9, 1981, at 3, col. 3.

127. On April 15, 1981, the white and Hispanic Board members voted in favor of scrapping the plan; the blacks voted in favor of keeping it. Michael Scott (the black head of the desegregation committee of the Board) estimated another six months would be needed to develop an alternative pupil reassignment proposal. Chicago Tribune, April 16, 1981, § 1, at 1, col. 1. *School Vote Blocks Busing*, Chicago Sun Times, April 15, 1981, at 3, col. 3.

128. *Id.*

129. Chicago Sun Times, April 16, 1981, at 3, col. 3.

130. Chicago Sun Times, April 30, 1981, at 4, col. 1. Leon Davis, one of two outgoing black Board members, charged that Mayor Byrne had developed the plan. That charge was denied by John D. Foster, another Board member. Davis claimed that Byrne had made clear that she was against busing, although she did not dictate specific terms. Former School Superintendent Hannon had proposed this same 70 percent figure in 1979 and had not been able to reach any agreement with the federal government. *See supra* notes 61, 88, and accompanying text. During April, the proposal under consideration by the Board first increased to 65 percent (Chicago Tribune, April 1, 1981, § 1, at 1, col. 1, banner headline reading, *School Plan, Mandatory Busing, 65% Lid on Whites*; and April 9, 1981, *School Aid Rips School Plan*, § 1, at 1, col. 1, and at 18, col. 1), but Board members pressed for higher increase to 70 percent (Chicago Sun Times, April 28, 1981, at 12, col. 3) and the Board decided on April 28 to seek a 70 percent limit (Chicago Sun Times, April 29, 1981, at 3, col. 1).

131. Chicago Sun Times, April 30, 1981, at 4, col. 1. Forty million dollars was pledged for the first two years, and $20 million for the third year. However, a pledge was just that and nothing more. There were serious practical problems the Board had to confront in attempting actually to raise that money. Not the least of these was that state law, as a result of past financial problems, required a balanced budget for the Chicago Board of Education. The Board first faced this requirement for the 1981–1982 school year. The Board was further required to submit its budget to the School Finance Authority for approval and could not open its doors in September

without such approval. Ill. Rev. Stat. Ch. 122, ¶¶ 34A–101 *et seq.* The plan contained a provision that reserved the Board's right to seek a waiver from the court on this pledge in case of extreme hardship. As it turned out, the Board was able to keep this particular commitment, and has not had to use the waiver provision. However, it later became clear that far more money was needed to finance the full costs of the compensatory educational programs.

132. Chicago Sun Times, April 21, 1981, at 3, col. 1.

133. Chicago Tribune, April 15, 1981, § 1, at 3, col. 4; April 16, 1981, § 1, at 1, col. 1. The banner headline on April 16 read, *School Vote Blocks Busing.* There are 50 aldermen in Chicago.

134. Chicago Sun Times, April 30, 1981, at 8, col. 1. These recruits could, of course, be non-black.

135. Bogan was also on the southwest side. If white enrollment dropped by 10 percent through attrition, only 128 non-white students would be needed. Since recent white enrollment drops had been 10 percent per year, the lower figure was more likely to apply. If Grimes followed the same pattern, only eight students would have to be recruited. *Id.*

136. Chicago Sun Times, April 30, 1981, at 4, col. 1. Docket item 33.

137. Chicago Tribune, July 23, 1981, § 1, at 11, col. 4, editorial, *City Bias Plan "Slap" Gets Mixed Reaction.*

138. Chicago Tribune, July 23, 1981, § 1, at 11, col. 2. *City, U.S. Play Game on Bias: NAACP,* Chicago Sun Times, July 23, 1981, at 3, col. 4.

139. Letter to Editor, Chicago Tribune, August 6, 1981, § 2, at 6, col. 4.

140. *Bias Plan Too Weak for Reagan,* Chicago Tribune, July 26, 1981, § 1, at 14, col. 1.

141. Chicago Sun Times, August 29, 1981, at 3, col. 1.

142. The routine start of schools was particularly surprising since the state's balanced budget requirement was being applied to the Chicago schools for the first time. Indications in late August were that the start of school was in doubt. Chicago Sun Times, August 25, 1981, at 3, col. 1.

143. Chicago Tribune, September 16, 1981, § 1, at 15, col. 3. "Magnets made desegregation work."

144. Chicago Tribune, September 28, 1981, at 1, col. 1. This speech, although of more immediate local impact, was very similar to the speech delivered earlier in the summer by U.S. Attorney General William French Smith, quoted in part in United States v. Board of Education, 588 F. Supp. 132, 146 (N.D. Ill. 1984).

145. Chicago Tribune, December 30, 1981, at 1, col. 1. Blacks were 60.7 percent of the enrollment, whites 17.2 percent, and Hispanics 19.6 percent. There was some comfort that the rate of decline in white students had not accelerated. Although sharp declines were noted in some northwest area white schools, the overall rate did not change.

146. United States v. Board of Education, 621 F. Supp. 1296, 1332–33 (N.D. Ill. 1985). The Urban League's fear was that the Board had committed itself only to the extent that funds were available.

147. *Id.* at 1331 (response of the United States filed July 1981). The response further indicated:

We expect that when these new educational programs are developed in detail and implemented, they will complement the student assignment principles by enhancing the workability of voluntary desegregation techniques and they will contribute to bringing about equality of educational opportunity in the one-race schools which remain under the final plan.

Later in the Joint Statement of August 28, 1981, the matter was mentioned again: "The United States fully endorses the Educational Components from a legal perspective, although it views the particular educational policy choices as within the Board's discretion." *Id.* at 1331–32.

148. *Id.* at 1334. The document includes extensive analysis and recommendations. Among other items, the report indicated improved attendance at schools targeted under the Effective Schools Project (36 out of 45 schools improved in the first year, with 33 of these improving the second year and seven additional schools improving). "Children cannot learn if they are not in school." Annual Desegregation Review (1983) Part II, at 67. Preliminary analysis of the results of the Iowa Test of Basic Skills indicated that 28 (62 percent) of 45 schools showed more grade medians increasing than decreasing. On one comparison, for schools that reported seven grade results, 81 percent improved, 11 percent declined and the remainder held steady. Annual Desegregation Review (1983) Part II, at 66. Since the Effective Schools Project was a key educational aspect of the attempt of the Chicago Plan to strike out in novel directions, this failure to comment is particularly surprising.

149. United States v. Board of Education, 621 F. Supp. at 1342. These figures exclude magnet schools and cover 69.8 percent of the system-wide enrollment.

150. *Id.* The percentage (69.4) reported in the opinion appears to be a typographical error, taken from the earlier opinion by Judge Shadur, 588 F. Supp. at 157. System-wide enrollment was 434,042, with 303,159 students attending schools 70 percent or more minority, and 275,091 students attending schools 90 percent or more minority. 588 F. Supp. at 157.

151. *See supra* notes 112–13 and accompanying text.

152. United States v. Board of Education, 554 F. Supp. 912, 915–926 (N.D. Ill. 1983). The court refers to the thousands of pages generated by the case up until now and declines to respond to all concerns for fear of losing sight of the forest for the trees. *Id.* at 926.

153. 621 F. Supp. at 1334–35.

154. Using the same formulas as above. *Id.* at 1346–47.

155. That was possible only because of the special congressional appropriation of $20 million to Chicago (the Yates Bill). *Id.* at 1347.

156. *Id.* at 1360.

157. *Id.* at 1349, 1360.

158. *Id.* at 1360.

159. *Id.* at 1348, based on testimony by Brady.

160. *Id.* at 1348. The program includes in-service training of the teaching staff to raise their awareness of possible racial biases with the aim of modifying biased attitudes, expectations, and behavior toward minority pupils.

161. *Id.* An account of the many activities encompassed within the Effective

Schools Project can be found in Annual Desegregation Review (1983) Part II, *supra* note 148, at 51–121. These activities are as diverse as leadership conferences for school personnel, street fairs for community outreach, development of a brochure, "Parents as Partners", to increase parental activity, and analyses of the Iowa Test of Basic Skills.

162. 621 F. Supp. at 1351–54, Findings of Fact (FF) numbers: 234, 236, 238, 242, 245, 247, 250, 252.

163. *Id.* at 1356. The court found that the Board had repeatedly sought to obtain funds from the state of Illinois, and had been repeatedly unsuccessful. *Id.* at 1368. The Board was already imposing taxes at the maximum permitted rate under state law. *Id.* at 1364. The amount set aside for desegregation activity was not cut despite strong pressure from the teachers' union, particularly in the summer and fall of 1983. *Id.* at 1368. FF. 353. Judge Shadur, in United States v. Board of Education, 567 F. Supp. 272, 273 (N.D. Ill. 1983), found that the Board had made every good faith effort to find and provide every available form of financial resource adequate to pay the cost of full implementation of the plan. Because it was never appealed, that finding is now the law of the case. 621 F. Supp. at 1369. Comparable decisions since June 30, 1983, also have found that the Board has made every good faith effort. *Id.*

164. *See* Joyce Hughes (dissenting Board member), *The Wrong Plan*, Chicago Tribune, February 1, 1982, § 1, at 13, col. 1. Joyce Hughes later resigned from the Board, complaining that the lack of clear authority lines between the Board and the mayor left her with little to contribute to the Board. Chicago Tribune, June 13, 1982, (city edition) § 1, at 3, col. 1. *See also* Chicago Tribune, February 13, 1982, § 1, at 1, col. 1, continued at § 1, at 4, col. 2. Black leaders claimed the plan continued to mask the problems of segregation and containment of minority students.

165. *Racial Busing Under Black Attack*, Chicago Sun Times, January 9, 1982, (city edition) at 17, col. 1. The attack took place at one of the public hearings of the Board held after submission of the final plan to the court.

Blacks in middle class neighborhoods, particularly on the southside of Chicago, had developed a strong antipathy to busing during the late 1960s. For example, Vrame reports that at a February 1968 Board of Education meeting, the Board was surprised to learn that a proposed busing plan was strongly opposed in the South Shore community, which was rapidly changing from white to black. Both whites and blacks from that community were angered at the plan and inflicted personal abuse upon Board members. Vrame, *supra* note 8, at 260–67. The proposal for the South Shore busing plan was tabled, nine to one, and never revived. *Id.* at 267.

166. *Poll Here Bolsters No Busing Stand*, Chicago Sun Times, February 10, 1982, at 12, col. 2.

167. *Id.*

168. Docket Item 138, filed February 12, 1982.

169. *U.S. Approval of School Plan Is Not a Surprise*. Chicago Sun Times, February 14, 1982, at 58, col. 1. "To those familiar with the Chicago desegregation plan, that description sounds familiar." This was the old neighborhood school principle working in favor of white students.

170. *Id.* The *Sun Times* described the Justice Department's response as supportive of the plan. Quoting the government response, it said:

The critical elements of the plan are those pertaining to publicity and information activities designed to recruit voluntary transfers. This campaign must be conducted more effectively than it has been in the past: we are confident that it will be. . . . If we are right, the plan will ultimately produce more desegregation in Chicago than would a wholly mandatory plan.

See also School Plan Wins Test. No Busing Provision is Accepted, Chicago Tribune, February 13, 1982, § 1, at col. 4.

171. *Id. See supra* note 141 and accompanying text.

172. *City School Desegregation Plan Hailed as "Best Hope" by U.S.,* Chicago Sun Times, April 6, 1982, at 15, col. 2.

173. Chicago Sun Times, August 17, 1982, at 12, col. 1. The solution was not busing, but improvement of the education offered in all schools.

174. Chicago Sun Times, April 6, 1982, at 15, col. 2.

175. *U.S. High on Chicago's School Desegregation Plan,* Chicago Sun Times, August 17, 1982, at 12, col. 1. "We are concerned, quite frankly, much less with student relocation than with student education."

176. In the Annual School Desegregation Review, 1983–1984, Part I, Student Assignment Appendix B (May 1984) filed with the court, racial composition breakdowns for the schools with significant proportions of white students were reported. "Significant" included schools with as small a proportion of white students as 5 percent.

177. *Id.* at 1.

178. *See* United States v. Board of Education, 554 F. Supp. 915, n. 3.

179. The educational components of the plan were addressed in a single paragraph. *Id.* at 926.

180. The first category, stably integrated schools, was exempted from mandatory student reassignment techniques, except for boundary changes, though limitations were placed on voluntary changes that would threaten the status of these schools. Various techniques were applied to the remaining two categories of schools. These included integration-enhancing transfers; boundary adjustments; curriculum changes; specifically significant educational programs; and educational teaming with other schools. *Id.* at 917.

181. This was a target that the Board failed to reach in eight schools, with one school at exactly 65 percent. Annual Desegregation Review, 1983–1984, Part I. Student Assignment, *supra* note 176.

182. 554 F. Supp. at 920. Such targets were generally met; indeed, all the schools met the 70 percent target in the fall of 1983.

183. *Id.*

184. *Id.*

185. *Id.* at 921.

186. *Id.* at 921–22, citing Board's reply memo.

187. *Id.* at 922.

188. *Id.*

189. *Id.* at 922–23. Figures for the 1983–1984 year were similar to those for the 1981–1982 school year. Indeed, these figures modestly supported an argument

that white students were being disproportionately relocated. However, it is clear that most white relocation was to the magnet schools or magnet programs within particular schools. The Urban League and others argued that it was improper to figure these educationally motivated transfers into the calculation on the same basis as other transfers. The court rejected that argument as unsound and unsupported by case law. *Id.* at 923 n. 16. In a sense, all transfers in the Chicago plan were educationally motivated; that is, parents or children seeking a better education out of district rather than in district.

190. Armstrong v. Board of School Directors, 616 F.2d 321 (7th Cir. 1980).

191. *Id.* at 321–22.

192. 544 F. Supp. at 923, citing Armstrong v. Board of School Directors, 616 F.2d at 321.

193. 554 F. Supp. at 923.

194. *Id.* at 924, citing the plan at 271. The opinion reserved, as did the Board, the possibility of compulsory busing at some time in the future if the plan did not work. *See id.* at 924, n. 17.

195. *See supra* notes 166–67 and accompanying text.

196. 544 F. Supp. at 924–25, citing the plan at 276.

197. *Id.* at 925. "[T]he Board was free to choose . . . [a plan] calculated to minimize parent resistance and thereby serve its larger goal."

198. *Id.* at 926.

199. *Chicago Upheld on School Plan Without Busing,* New York Times, January 7, 1983, § 1, at 1, col. 1.

200. Chicago Tribune, January 12, 1985, § 1, at 1, col. 4; Chicago Tribune, January 13, 1985, § 4, at 14, col. 1. Whites in the school system by October 1984 were 14.7 percent; Hispanics, 21.9 percent; blacks, 60.6 percent; and Asian or Pacific Islanders 2.6 percent. Only nine of 65 high schools were majority white schools. By 1986, only four of these 65 high schools were majority white. Chicago Tribune, January 18, 1986, § 1, at 1, col. 5.

201. From 1982 to 1983, use dropped from 239 units at 40 sites to 151 units at 26 sites, a 37 percent reduction. Annual School Desegregation Review, 1983–1984, Part I, Student Assignment at 109–10 (May 1984).

202. The number of excess students in overcapacity schools was reduced from 11,525 in 1982 to 8,988 in 1982. *Id.* at 107–08.

203. Monitoring requirements included special justification criteria for all classrooms that deviated from a standard of within a 20 percent range of white/minority enrollment for a given grade. *Id.* at 112–17.

204. The January 6, 1983, opinion mentions the reports filed by the Department of Justice on possible state liability for past segregation in the Chicago schools and on the possible existence and sources of interdistrict school segregation. "Neither report reflects any significant advance or promise of productive results." 544 F. Supp. at 927.

205. Shadur Interview, *supra* note 65.

206. These included the Citizens School Committee, the Business and Professional People for Public Interest (BPI), and the American Civil Liberties Union (ACLU). *See* discussion *supra* note 198 and accompanying text.

207. A Promise of Simple Justice in the Education of Chicago School Children? Attached as Exhibit 6 to Response of the Existing Monitoring Commission for Desegregation Implementation to the Suggestion of Commenting Organizations for Appointment of a Monitoring Commission by the Court (August 29, 1983).

208. *Id.* at 18.

209. *Id.*

210. *Id.* at 34.

211. Reply of Citizens Schools Committee, ACLU, and BPI, at 7, signed by Alexander Polkoff for BPI (September 27, 1983).

212. Three reasons were cited for this change: It would ensure independence; it would create the appearance of no possible conflict of interest in a situation where such appearance was important; and the court could shape its own requests for information as needed. *Id.* at 11.

213. The court stated at the outset it was ruling from the bench "because there has been so much paper generated on this issue as on so many other aspects of the case," at 1, entered as Docket Item No. 379.

214. *Id.* at 5.

215. *Id.* at 9.

216. Comments of the United States on the Interested Third Parties' Suggestion that the Court Appoint an Independent Commission at 5 (August 26, 1983).

217. United States v. Board of Education, 567 F. Supp. 285, 273 (N.D. Ill. 1983).

218. *Id.* at 274.

219. *Id.* at 280. "[T]his Court finds the United States has failed to use its best efforts to find and provide all available financial resources adequate for full implementation of the Plan."

220. *Id.* at 280.

221. *Id.* at 282.

222. *Id.* at 281.

223. United States v. Board of Education, 717 F.2d 378, 383 (7th Cir. 1983).

224. *Id.* at 384.

225. *Id.* at 385.

226. United States v. Board of Education, 588 F. Supp. 132 (N.D. Ill. 1984), 744 F.2d 1300 (7th Cir. 1984), *cert. denied*, 471 U.S. 1116, (1985). This district court opinion was issued on June 8, 1984, and amended July 17, 1984. The decision was immediately appealed to the Seventh Circuit, argued September 6, 1984, and decided September 26, 1984. The district court opinion was long and complicated, containing hundreds of typewritten pages.

227. 588 F. Supp. at 139.

228. *Id.* at 138.

229. *Id.* at 140. However, a fine would only move money from one pocket of the U.S. government to another. Imprisonment of the United States is impossible, and "imprisonment of defiant ranking government officials would be unseemly at best."

230. United States v. Board of Education, 592 F. Supp. 967 (N.D. Ill. 1984).

231. *Id.* at 968.

232. *Id.*

233. United States v. Lee, 106 U.S. 196 (1882).

234. 592 F. Supp. at 969, quoting from United States v. Lee, 106 U.S. at 220.

235. 592 F. Supp. at 970.

236. *Id.* at 973.

237. *Id.* For example, October 1, 1984, for school year 1985–1986.

238. United States v. Board of Education, 744 F.2d 1300 (7th Cir. 1984), *cert. denied,* 471 U.S. 1116 (1985). The case was heard and decided by the same panel—Cummings, Wood, and Flaum—that had heard it the year before.

239. *Id.* at 1306.

240. *Id.*

241. *Id.,* citing transcript of April 5, 1984, at 1416.

242. *Id.*

243. United States v. Board of Education, 621 F. Supp. 1296 (N.D. Ill. 1985), *rev'd and remanded,* 799 F.2d 281, (7th Cir. 1986). The district court rendered another monstrous opinion, 299 typewritten pages and 150 pages in print in the Federal Supplement. It was supplemented by a remedial order dated December 23, 1985. The case had been reassigned by lot, 621 F. Supp. at 1308.

244. 621 F. Supp. at 1304.

245. *Id.* at 1315.

246. *Id.* at 1314.

247. *Id.* at 1319.

248. *Id.* at 1320.

249. *Id.* at 1373. The idea of competition for excess funds is "farcical." *Id.* at 1376.

250. *Id.* at 1424.

251. *Id.*

252. *Id.*

253. *Id.* at 1426.

254. *Id.* at 1427.

255. *Id.* at 1428.

256. *Id.* at 1375.

257. The court also found that the United States had not begun to meet its fiscal responsibility under the consent decree. It therefore ordered the obligation of the United States under ¶ 15.1 to start with the 1985–1986 school year and extend for at least a five-year period. The total obligation would provide approximately $88 million over the next five years. *Id.* at 1442.

258. United States v. Board of Education, 799 F.2d 281 (7th Cir., 1986). The case had been argued June 3, 1986, and the opinion was announced August 18, 1986. The identical panel of Wood, Cummings, and Flaum heard this appeal as in the two earlier appeals. The case was ordered to be reassigned on remand pursuant to Circuit Rule 18. It appears that the original transfer of the case from Judge Shadur to Judge Aspen was because Judge Shadur erroneously believed the case was in a *remedial* as opposed to a *compliance* posture. The first appeal left it open for the government to demonstrate that it could come into compliance with its ¶ 15.1 obligations. The Seventh Circuit did not believe the district court on first remand properly viewed the case in compliance posture. Instead, the district court imposed identical remedies by finding bad faith. *Id.* at 289–90.

259. *Id.* at 294, note 13.

260. *Id.* at 297. The court cited Federal Rule of Civil Procedure 60(b) (5) that states in part, "On motion and upon such terms as are just, the court may relieve a party . . . from a final judgment, order, or proceeding for the following reasons: . . . the judgment has been satisfied, released, or discharged, or a prior judgment upon which it is based has been reversed or otherwise vacated, or it is no longer equitable that the judgment should have prospective application."

261. *Id.* at 290.

262. *Id.* at 284.

263. *Id.* at 291.

264. *Id.* Much of the court's discussion was about the November 10, 1983, plan proposed by the Department of Education. This plan provided for "competitive priority." The Board argued, and the district court found, that "top of the list priority" was a new position. The Seventh Circuit rejected the implications of both positions, for only the opinion of the Seventh Circuit, and not the oral argument, was the expression of the court. Both the lower court and the parties had improperly relied upon the oral argument in construing the Seventh Circuit's opinion. *Id.* at 284, note 3. The consent decree was entered in September 1980. The quoted text reference is a typographical error, but which year, 1980 or 1983, was intended is unclear.

265. *Id.* at 292, note 8. Another of the many ironies of the case is that the Seventh Circuit's opinion criticized the district court's extensive efforts to comply with the earlier mandates of the Seventh Circuit as too intrusive in the conciliation process, but that same Seventh Circuit opinion itself determined many specific disputes.

266. *Id.* at 292, note 9.

267. *Id.* at 293–94.

268. *Id.* at 295.

269. *Id.* Judge Aspen spoke to the same issue when he denied the Board the ability to pack the plan with irrelevant programs that turned the plan into a black hole sucking up all encumbered funds. 621 F. Supp. at 1317.

270. 799 F.2d at 295.

271. *Id.* at 296.

272. *Id.*

273. *Id.*

274. "The court must distinguish between a failure to comply through inaction or inadequate performance on the one hand, and defiant or subversive actions that constitute contempt on the other." *Id.*

275. *Id.* at 297.

276. The order should be based on appropriate factual findings concerning the Board's needs, the government's means, and the treatment of other funding priorities. *Id.* at 296.

277. The court indicated that, while "decisions of one of the signatories to ignore its obligations cannot serve as the basis for finding the decree to be impractical, the past can and should be undone where, despite good faith attempts to resolve the issue, no amount of funding sufficient to implement the Board's plan at an acceptable level can be provided." *Id.* at 297.

278. *Id.* at 297–98. The court prefaces the second option with the following: "If

there is no readily identifiable alternative to the Board's current plan, and it may be unlikely that such an alternative exists. . . ."

279. Chicago Tribune, July 14, 1987, § 1, at 1. The funding was part of Public Law 100–71, 101 Stat. 391 (signed July 11, 1987), a supplemental appropriation bill (H.R. 1827). Robert Howard, the Board's special counsel for the desegregation case, reportedly said that this bill ends the battle over the federal money. The money comes from the remaining unobligated or contingently obligated balance of appropriation for 1983–1986 that had been frozen by judicial order. It will be paid out in equal amounts over five years starting in fiscal year 1988 but will remain available until the funds are expended. 101 Stat. 391.

The legislation asserts, "[T]his $83,000,000 reappropriation constitutes full and final satisfaction of any and all past, present and future claims that the Chicago Board may have against the United States under or resulting from section 15.1 of the Consent Decree, and releases the United States from any further liability under section 15.1." 101 Stat. 421. In effect, the legislation is an offer to amend the consent decree, which must be accepted by the Board of Education and by the court.

280. The eight-page Settlement Agreement accepting the $83 million as full settlement of U.S. funding obligations under the decree is Docket Item Number 862. This was adopted in a brief unpublished minute order of December 1, 1987, after a period for comment. There were none; only the parties appeared about the matter.

281. Of course, during much of this period, the policy of the Justice Department was against busing in any event.

282. Factual Findings of the United States concerning its investigation of Interdistrict School Violations (hereinafter Interdistrict Findings) (April 4, 1983).

283. *Id.* at 1.

284. *Id.* at 2.

285. *Id.*

286. *Id.* at 4.

287. *Id.* The report referred to the separate investigation regarding state liability at this point.

288. A study done by the Board of Education indicated that, at most, two schools within Chicago could be desegregated by significant busing, given certain assumptions about the maximum length of a bus ride. 544 F. Supp. at 925. To the author's knowledge, no comparable study was ever done by the U.S. government or anyone else about the feasibility of cross-district busing.

289. The government also explored other potential areas, excepting housing and employment, which were the subjects of continuing investigation, but found no basis for interdistrict remedies in these areas. Interdistrict Findings, *supra* note 282, at 5.

290. The legal framework is set out in an Interim Report filed January 4, 1982. The Second Interim Report was filed September 14, 1982, and the Third Interim Report was filed February 25, 1983.

291. Third Interim Report, *supra* note 290, at 1. In particular, the state has refused to provide information on relevant documents that may have been transferred to storage or destroyed. Despite representations that all documents responsive to requests had been produced for the period since 1974, the Department of Justice located additional relevant material from the Office of the Superintendent of Public

Instruction in the state archives. Requests to identify lists or indices of documents that may have been stored or destroyed have been ignored. *Id.* at 2. The Chicago Board of Education produced information requested under a court subpoena dated September 14, 1982, five months later, during the week of February 14, 1983. Even then, over 10,000 pages of documents were still being reviewed to determine whether the attorney–client privilege applies.

292. *See supra* note 86 and accompanying text.

293. This includes a two-year contract with the Chicago Teachers Union negotiated in 1985. This is the first such contract in recent time, a period marked by frequent, indeed one might say yearly, teachers' strikes. "With just two weeks to go, the Chicago Teachers Union has served notice that it is willing to keep the schools closed by waging its third strike in three years." August 21, 1985, Chicago Tribune, § 2, at 3, col. 5.

294. Chicago Tribune, January 20, 1985, § 1, at 1, col. 1.

295. Chicago Tribune, February 24, 1986, § 2, at 1, col. 6.

296. *Id.*

297. Recall that a significant part of the Board's expenditures are devoted to the worst schools in the Chicago school system as defined by low educational achievement scores. Observed changes may be slowest with such targets but would be the most significant changes if achieved. Recently released Chicago school "Report Cards" give some indication of the lag in the Chicago system. Only two of the 64 public high schools reported ACT scores higher than the state average for 1985–1986. In nine schools, not even one student in the sophomore class scored in the top 25 percent nationally on one of the achievement exams. For example, at Orr High School, not one of 423 sophomores had a grade in the top 25 percent on the mathematics test, but 59.1 percent were in the bottom 25 percent. Graduation rates for 1986 were less than 40 percent in 13 public high schools. The Illinois average was 76.3 percent. The graduation rates for all-black Austin was 21.2 percent; for all-black South Shore, 23.8 percent; and for all-black Creiger, 26.9 percent. Chicago Tribune, October 16, 1986, § 2, at 2, col. 2, continued § 2, at 6, col. 3.

298. Whites made up only 16.9 percent of high school students and 13.2 percent of the elementary school population by 1985–1986.

299. Who Benefits from Desegregation? Review of the Chicago Desegregation Programs, 1980–1986, July 23, 1987, Draft, Chicago Panel on Public School Policy and Finance at 10. Not only did the percentage increase, but so did the actual number of such racially isolated students, by 1167 (from 38,574 to 39,741). The report states: "Of the 26 racially isolated high schools, 24 had at least 99 percent Black enrollment and 14 of these had 100 percent Black enrollment. Thus, while more Blacks attended desegregated high schools, others have become even more isolated within the segregated schools than they were before desegregation." *Id.* at 12. Sixty-two percent of all elementary black students were still in 100 percent non-white schools in 1985–1986. *Id.* at 20. This is a drop of 2.5 percent over six years. Modest improvement indeed!

300. The Board has also been charged with disproportionate focus of the budget upon student movement, rather than education aspects of the plan. *Id.* at 2. The union salary demand had been reduced from a first year 10 percent raise to an 8 percent raise. The union president stated that the amount required to fund the proposal

is $160 million. Chicago Tribune, September 30, 1987, § 2, at 1, col. 6. The Board will receive approximately $16.6 million per year from the federal settlement. The shortfall in plan funding will probably remain over $100 million per year. Such figures demonstrate the minimal likely impact of the federal funding on the Chicago school system.

301. A recent report indicates the overall medians of reading scores for the eighth grade class of 1986 have increased from that of the 1978 class by more than two years in over 100 schools and by more than one year at more than 100 other schools. The percentage of eighth graders reading below national grade norms has dropped from 47 percent in 1978 to 34 percent for 1986. The results, though, overstate the case. The tests have been renormed, and the differences in test administration make scores not completely comparable. As a result, the improvement in reading scores should be diminished by about one-half. Bending the Twig: The Elementary Years and Dropout Rates in the Chicago Public Schools, July 30, 1987, Chicago Panel on Public School Policy and Finance, at v, 58–59.

302. Project CANAL (Creating a New Approach to Learning) involves the creation of a training center at an underutilized school building. At least once a month, each participating school will send principals, teachers, ancillary staff, parents, and, where feasible, students for training sessions at the center. To minimize disruption, a cadre of substitute teachers will travel from school to school to replace those teachers each time they are at the training center. In the first year, 11 elementary schools and one high school will participate, and five schools will be designated as model clusters to relieve overcrowded elementary schools. Twenty-three more schools will be added starting in 1989. Additional schools may be added to the 40 schools. Project CANAL, Executive Summary at ii–vi.

303. *Id.* at ii.

304. *Id.* The first year of implementation of Project CANAL was approved by District Court Judge Charles P. Kocoras on July 14, 1988, upon a joint motion by the United States and the school Board. The program was developed under the provisions of the settlement agreement approved December 1, 1987. Under the terms of the modification of the consent decree, none of the $83 million could be used to supplant money in prior fiscal years and all money is to be used only for supplemental desegregation educational programs in the Board's racially identifiable schools. Settlement Agreement at 4, Docket Item No. 862. There were neither comments nor participation by anyone other than the Board of Education or the Department of Justice in court in connection with either the Settlement Agreement, or Project CANAL. The absence of participation by *amici* may be read as either evidence that everybody agrees with the resolutions in these matters or alternatively that the passage of time has sapped interest. Absence of newspaper coverage might suggest the latter.

305. Chicago Sun Times, December 7, 1988, at 7, col. 1. The dropout rate in 1986 for blacks was 40.5 percent; for whites, 41.5 percent; and for Hispanics, 47.9 percent. Since 1984, the dropout rate for whites has jumped almost 10 percent. Fred Hess, Executive Director of the Chicago Panel on Public School Policy and Finance, speculated that low-income and non-English-speaking immigrants account for the increase.

306. Chicago Tribune, August 23, 1987, § 1, at 1, col. 6; 18, col. 1.

307. The black high school population did increase, but the increase was matched by increases in the suburban Hispanic and Asian student populations.

308. Chicago Tribune, August 23, 1987, § 1, at 18, col. 1.

309. Chicago Tribune, July 27, 1987, § 2, at 1, col. 2. The headline was, *Illinois Schools Ranked Most Segregated.* The basis for the article was a report issued by the National Desegregation Project, entitled *School Segregation in the 1980s, Trends in the States and Metropolitan Areas,* co-authored by Gary Orfield.

310. *School Segregation in the 1980s, supra* note 309, table 2. The Illinois figure for 1984 was 16 percent. Michigan came next with 16.2 percent, and then New York with 18.5 percent.

311. The late Mayor Daley was particularly adept in financing Chicago's government. In 1971 Mike Royko (*supra* note 2 at 11), a leading critic of Daley, wrote:

> Richard Joseph Daley is in his office . . . ready to start another day of doing what the experts say is no longer possible—running a big American city. But as he, Daley, has often said to confidants, "What in hell do the experts know?" He's been running a big American city for fifteen of the toughest years American cities have ever seen. He, Daley, has been running it as long or longer than any of the other famous mayors—Curley of Boston, LaGuardia of New York, Kelly of Chicago—ran theirs, and unless his health goes, or his wife says no, he, Daley, will be running it for another four years.

Daley died in office, after another re-election.

312. *See supra* note 144 and accompanying text.

PART V

Assessment of the Court's Appropriate
Role in Education Litigation

CHAPTER 8

The View from the Bench: Judges in Desegregation Cases

BARBARA FLICKER

THE SCHOOL DESEGREGATION cases have produced profound changes in American society. The holding in *Brown v. Board of Education*[1] that separate schools are "inherently unequal" heralded the civil rights movement of the sixties.[2] The decision in *Brown II*[3] to remand the cases to the trial courts for implementation of the constitutional principles declared in *Brown I* thrust the federal district judges into an unfamiliar and unwelcome position of prominence, and often notoriety, in their communities.

Whether legal scholars label the school desegregation cases public law, institutional reform, extended impact, or frontier litigation, they agree that the cases marked the emergence of a new model of civil litigation. When a unanimous Supreme Court imposed a duty on the trial courts to fashion and effectuate remedies appropriate to varied local school problems while giving school officials "the primary responsibility for elucidating, assessing, and solving these problems,"[4] it shifted the significance of the cases from the wrong to the remedy. The focus for the next phase would be on the judge and the local officials, not the legal issues argued by the parties.

JUDICIAL ACTIVISTS

Abram Chayes, in the leading article on institutional reform cases, *The Role of the Judge in Public Law Litigation*,[5] described the prominence given to the court's decree as characteristic of the new model of civil litigation. He said:

> The centerpiece of the emerging public law model is the decree. It differs in almost every relevant characteristic from relief in the traditional model of adjudication, not the least in that it *is* the centerpiece. The decree seeks to adjust future behavior, not to compensate for past wrong. It is deliberately fashioned rather than logically deduced from the nature of the legal harm suffered. It provides for a complex, on-going regime of performance rather

365

than a simple one-shot, one-way transfer. Finally, it prolongs and deepens, rather than terminates, the court's involvement with the dispute.[6]

It is at the remedial stage of the school desegregation cases that the judges' role differs markedly from the traditional model. While a judicial finding that a local school district has practiced racial discrimination in its admission policies does not enhance a trial judge's popularity, it normally is not perceived as a personal affront to the community. The judge has been performing his or her accepted task of hearing evidence from adversarial parties and ruling on the merits of their respective positions. The objections of overreaching, of intruding in the operation of the local institution do not arise until the judge begins to issue orders that disturb the status quo.

The hundreds of judges who have been obliged to assume the unpopular role of judicial activists in order to design and implement remedial plans to achieve non-discriminatory school admissions practices are the subject of this chapter. At the time this volume on the courts' role in education litigation was planned, the author was Director of the Institute of Judicial Administration. The Institute had just completed its participation as secretariat in issuing a report on The Role of Courts in American Society.[7] As a national court organization engaged in court studies and advanced judicial education, the Institute was deeply concerned about political reactions against judges involved in institutional reform cases. Therefore, it was decided that the Institute would solicit the views of a cross-section of judges who had presided over school desegregation cases.

The results of the survey, which will be discussed in detail later in this chapter, were a great surprise. Unlike the heroic stance and near-martyrdom described in much of the literature,[8] the responding judges adopted a placid, subdued tone. Although they acknowledged a degree of initial resistance to their efforts, they emphasized their success in finding ways to secure the cooperation of the officials and other persons needed to adopt a plan. They expressed frustration at the imperfect nature of the results, citing white flight, segregated housing and zoning patterns, and insufficient funds for improved educational programs as limiting factors. But a combination of quiet pride in overcoming local problems and resignation to insuperable barriers pervaded the responses to the survey.

For example, 89 percent of the respondents found their involvement in the desegregation cases substantially greater than in comparable litigation and 92 percent monitored compliance with their orders, yet 100 percent reported compliance with their desegregation orders by the parties, 85 percent cooperation by other public officials, and 83 percent cooperation of the community, and 84 percent support from other attorneys. Only 33 percent indicated that they had observed open defiance or protest. Eighty-three percent were satisfied with the results of their cases.

If there were not sufficient evidence to the contrary, we might have assumed from the survey responses that nearly 35 years of desegregation litigation had produced a spirit of normalcy, of acceptance of court-ordered integration. Instead, it appears that resistance to the courts' intervention has moved to other venues.

The role of judges has become a heated political issue. Intense inquiry into the "judicial philosophy" of court nominees and candidates for election to state courts has produced polarized positions within the loaded concept of judicial activism, classifying judges as liberal, conservative, or moderate according to the extent to which they embrace an activist role for judges.[9]

A cogent reply to critics of judicial activism was stated by Judge Frank M. Johnson, Jr., of the U.S. Court of Appeals for the Fifth Circuit in an article entitled, *The Role of Federal Courts in Institutional Litigation*.[10] He explained that most judges would prefer to issue a simple injunction to compel government officials to correct any constitutional derelictions in the performance of their duties. But that has proved ineffective, leaving the judge with no choice but to take a more affirmative role in formulating a remedy to eliminate constitutional violations. He said:

> The remedy for judicial activism is a recognition that this trust is not one solely for the judiciary. As long as government officials entrusted with responsibility for constitutional governance disregard that responsibility, the judiciary must and will stand ready to intervene to the extent necessary on behalf of the deprived. To avoid this intervention, all that government officials need do is confront their responsibilities with the diligence and honesty that their constituencies deserve. Conscientious, responsible leadership will in most instances make judicial intervention unnecessary.[11]

The Johnson view of judicial activism is similar to the position taken by Judge Leonard B. Sand of the U.S. District Court for the Southern District of New York in a desegregation case that has provoked the most bitter contention between a federal judge and a community in recent years. In *United States v. Yonkers Board of Education*[12] the Department of Justice complaint in the first instance cited both school and housing segregation. From its inception, the case dealt with the interrelationship of school and housing segregation. Yet, the school desegregation orders were implemented successfully with relatively little community opposition, while the housing desegregation orders became the focal point of intense political obstruction that compelled Judge Sand to impose heavy fines and contempt decrees.

Nevertheless, Judge Sand rejects the notion of judicial activism in the *Yonkers* case, asserting that the extraordinary sanctions involved were efforts by the court to have the community itself fulfill its responsibilities. He said, "I am just doing what I took an oath to do." Using the example of the selection of sites for the construction of public housing, he pointed out that he did not issue an order until the community had had a full opportunity to act and failed to do so.[13]

Even among the legal scholars there is controversy over the judge in an activist role. In *The Judge as Political Powerbroker: Superintending Structural Change in Public Institutions*,[14] Colin S. Diver examined the transformation of the judge's role in institutional reform litigation. Noting that the school desegregation cases provided the ground rules for decrees in reform litigation, he cautioned against a judge's using his or her central position in a case to exercise influence beyond the boundaries of the courtroom. He contrasted the judge's adjudicative role with the political or bargaining process required in negotiating a plan for structural reform.

While conceding the necessity of departing from the judge's traditional neutrality and passivity to encourage the settlement of disputes through the consent of the parties, Diver pointed to the dangers of more aggressive use of influence. If the process of plan negotiation introduces diversity and conflict among the participants, it may reduce the prospects of consensual resolution. The court then may be compelled to impose a remedy that has weak support from the officials responsible for its implementation.

The judge intervening actively in the operational decisions of a government agency strains the limits of judicial legitimacy. Diver said, "[W]hether intrusiveness is excessive depends upon the degree to which the court has left room for the exercise of governmental choice in the remedial process."[15]

Diver is most effective in presenting the true dilemma of judicial activism, or the judge as powerbroker. The capacity of the judiciary to achieve results rests on its legitimacy as a social institution. The respect for the judiciary, its credibility, derives from the popular perception of the judicial process as reflective and dispassionate and the judge as impartial and detached. He said, "A judge's actions must conform to that narrow band of conduct considered appropriate for so antimajoritarian an institution. Whenever a court appears to manipulate the rules of litigation for the attainment of social outcomes, its authority wanes."[16]

Michael W. Combs pursued a more moderate analysis of the legal–political dilemma in judicial activism. In *The Federal Judiciary and Northern School Desegregation: Judicial Management in Perspective*,[17] he examined the influences of "the pulls and pushes of political and legal developments" on the three levels of the federal courts in school desegregation cases in Michigan and Ohio. He described the conflict between those who believe that federal judicial intervention undermines local authority and autonomy and supersedes judicial competence and those who believe the federal courts must vindicate constitutional rights when state and local officials have defaulted.

He concluded, "The underpinning of the federal courts' involvement in educational policymaking is the premise that certain rights should not be left prey to the uncertainties of majoritarian politics." [18] Contrasting the outcomes at the three levels of the federal courts, he found that

> district courts and the courts of appeals have read the remedial powers of the federal courts more and more expansively, perhaps out of frustration and a desire to dispose of these seemingly interminable cases. The Supreme Court, however, seems to have taken an opposing view, resisting broad shift of power from state and local officials to federal courts, and championing the perceived virtue of local control. [19]

In *Accommodation and Accountability: A Strategy for Judicial Enforcement of Institutional Reform Decrees*, [20] Michael G. Starr also looked at the dilemma implicit in the role of the court in institutional litigation, when local officials are unwilling or unable to make the changes required to meet constitutional standards, and suggested a method of avoiding it. He proposed that the focus from the beginning should not be on what the court can do to remedy the violation "but rather on what it can do to induce the maladjusted institution to cure itself." [21] He said, "Success at judicially managed institutional reform requires that the court attain a delicate balance: clearly and forcefully prodding the institution to make the required changes without divesting institutional managers of their sense of autonomy, control, and personal responsibility for the institutions under their charge." [22]

The inevitable deficiency in such a sensible solution to a vexatious problem is that it produces modest results. As Starr conceded, institutional litigation tends to go on indefinitely, "yet never comes close to effectuating all the changes that ideally should be made." [23] He rejected the notion that greater success would flow from more vigorous social engineering by the judges. Sounding very much like the judges who responded to our survey, he preached "prudence without resignation," contending that "there are pragmatic limits on what a court can do and jurisprudential limits on what it should undertake." [24]

The conclusion one must draw on this issue of judicial activism in institutional reform litigation, of which the school desegregation cases are a prototype, is that the Supreme Court has dictated the role of the district courts as institutional managers from *Brown II* to the present, even when it has rejected the results. The trial courts could not have done less in framing remedial plans, despite their intrusion into the distribution of political power among local officials, after the Supreme Court instructed them to eliminate obstacles to making the transition to school systems free of racial discrimination. Nor could they avoid political powerbrokering and interminable involvement in school operations when the Supreme Court expressly ordered the district courts to supervise the transition by retaining jurisdiction while the school authorities attempted to solve local problems.

The Supreme Court had other remedial choices, which were debated among legal scholars while the decision in *Brown I* was pending.[25] It could have granted minimum relief to the plaintiffs and left implementation to Congress; it could have given general relief to all persons similarly situated to the plaintiffs by specifying the remedy itself; or it could have ordered an end to discrimination in admissions to schools forthwith, declaring all state and local laws providing for separate schools or discriminatory practices invalid. By choosing to give the district courts the task of implementation through negotiation with local school authorities, it transformed traditional trial judges into judicial activists.

LANDMARK DESEGREGATION CASES DEFINING JUDGES' REMEDIAL ROLE

Beginning with *Brown II*, the decisions of the Supreme Court restricted or expanded the discretion of the lower federal courts to devise plans to overcome barriers to school desegregation. Although the actions of the legislative and executive branches were significant in their impact on the success of various remedial plans, it was the Supreme Court that provided the push or pull that propelled the district courts.

The gradualism of *Brown II*, stressing local solutions to local problems, transitional periods, and "deliberate" speed, led to a permissive period of attempting to eliminate discriminatory practices through voluntary programs, known as "freedom of choice."

In 1968 the Supreme Court abandoned deliberate speed and invalidated a freedom of choice plan that perpetuated a dual school system in *Green v. County School Board*.[26] According to Bernard Schwartz in *Swann's Way*, "When *Green* was decided, most southern school districts operated under such plans."[27]

The Court said the school boards were "charged with an affirmative duty to take whatever steps may be necessary to convert to a unitary system in which racial discrimination would be eliminated root and branch."[28] It also required a plan that "promises realistically to work *now*." The Court thereby struck down both voluntary plans and further delays, which it declared were "no longer tolerable."[29]

The Supreme Court in *Green* also firmly reasserted the long-range supervisory role of the district court, declaring that "the court should retain jurisdiction until it is clear that state-imposed segregation has been completely removed."[30]

Citing problems of dilatory tactics and resistance to implementation encountered by the lower courts during the 16 years since *Brown II*, the Supreme Court in *Swann v. Charlotte–Mecklenberg Board of Education*[31] undertook the expounding of guidelines to assist school authorities and courts. First, the Court asserted the broad scope of the district court's equitable powers to remedy past wrongs once the violation of a right had been established. It said, "In default by the school authorities of their obligation to proffer acceptable remedies, a district court has broad power to fashion a remedy that will assure a unitary school system." [32]

The Court next cautioned the local authorities and district court to "see to it that future school construction and abandonment are not used and do not serve to perpetuate or re-establish the dual system." [33]

Then the Court addressed the four issues concerning student assignment:

1. to what extent racial balance or racial quotas may be used to correct a segregated system;

2. whether every one-race school must be eliminated;

3. what the limits are on rearranging school districts and attendance zones; and

4. what the limits are on the use of transportation to correct racial school segregation.[34]

With respect to quotas to achieve racial balance, the Court held that the limited use of mathematical ratios is within the district courts' discretion. On one-race schools, the Court said the school authority has the burden of showing that assignments that would perpetuate one-race schools are "genuinely non-discriminatory." [35]

Remedial altering of attendance zones, through the pairing and grouping of noncontiguous school zones, was held to be a permissible tool if needed to achieve non-discriminatory assignments. The Court said, "In this area, we must of necessity rely to a large extent, as the Court has for more than 16 years, on the informed judgment of the district courts in the first instance and on courts of appeals." [36]

The most controversial remedial tool was busing. In *Swann* the district court found the trips for elementary school pupils averaged seven miles and took no more than 35 minutes, which the Court sustained. But the Court said, "An objection to transportation of students may have validity when the time or distance of travel is so great as to either risk the health of the children or significantly impinge on the educational process." [37] Among the factors to consider in limiting the time of travel, the foremost would be the age of the students.

Finally, the Court discussed the implications of a school system achieving full compliance, thereby becoming a "unitary" system. It held that neither the schools nor the courts are required to make yearly adjustments of the racial composition of the student enrollment once the schools are desegregated and racial discrimination through official action is eliminated. No further intervention would be necessary in the absence of a showing that a state or local agency had deliberately attempted to change demographic patterns to affect the schools' racial composition.[38]

An unresolved issue before the courts today is the effect of a finding that a school system has become unitary on the court's original mandatory injunctive orders, whether they dissolve automatically or remain in effect if the court is silent on that subject.[39] The issue will be discussed in the conclusion to this chapter.

The next landmark decision was in *Keyes v. School District No. 1*[40] in 1973. It was significant because (1) it was the first non-southern (Denver) desegregation case before the Supreme Court; (2) it applied *Brown* to official action (a systematic program of deliberate segregation by the school authorities) leading to *de facto* segregation; and (3) it recognized Hispanics as a minority group for purposes of the remedial plan. The *Keyes* case is the subject of one of the case studies in *Limits of Justice: The Courts' Role in School Desegregation*, the predecessor to this volume.[41] The progress of the case is covered in Chapter 5 in this volume.

Finally, in a major setback to district court plans to desegregate urban areas, the Supreme Court overturned a metropolitan plan in *Milliken v. Bradley* (1974).[42] It held that an interdistrict remedy could be sustained only upon proof that the suburban district also had engaged in segregative actions that had an interdistrict effect.

These decisions provide a necessary background to appreciate the context of the remarks of the judges who responded to the survey conducted by the Institute of Judicial Administration. In some instances these decisions constituted constraints on the plans the judges would have wanted to implement, especially *Milliken*; in other instances the decisions seemed to compel the judges to intervene in the school district's operations more than they would have chosen, particularly *Swann*.[43] The decision most frequently mentioned by the respondents was *Green*,[44] which supported their own inclination to take a firmer hand in moving the school system toward effective action and often precipitated a modification of the original remedial plan.

A SURVEY OF JUDGES' ATTITUDES ON THE IMPACT OF DESEGREGATION CASES

As part of the second phase of the Ford Foundation project on the role of courts in education litigation, the first of which culminated in the 1978 publication of *Limits of Justice: The Courts' Role in School Desegregation* (edited by then IJA Director Howard I. Kalodner and Associate Director James J. Fishman), the Institute of Judicial Administration (IJA) conducted an informal survey of approximately 70 judges who had presided over school desegregation cases. Most of the questionnaires were mailed out with a cover letter dated April 15, 1985, which explained that the information received would be used in a chapter on the aftermath of the desegregation cases from the perspective of the judges involved in efforts to implement desegregation orders. It also assured respondents that the confidentiality of the data provided would be preserved. A copy of the questionnaire is reproduced in the Appendix to this chapter.

Of the 70 judges in the sample, 29 judges replied in full, four returned the questionnaire but declined to answer, and at least eight judges had died. Several of the judges who returned the questionnaires but did not answer the questions in full explained that they were unable to do so because they still had jurisdiction over the cases.

The responses of judges in the survey generally reflect a deep awareness of the limited power of the court to effect change in a community that is resisting that change. Frequently politics prevailed over compliance with the court's decree. However, if desegregation were not politically unpalatable, *Brown v. Board of Education*[45] would have been self-executing instead of the beginning of a 35-year struggle to achieve implementation. Most of the judges charged with the duty to devise orders to end dual school systems learned to anticipate the obstacles they could overcome and to tolerate those beyond their authority.

Among the more illuminating answers to the questionnaire were those dealing with the judges' retrospective assessment of the results of their desegregation cases (question No. 9 under "Personal/Professional Impact" on the questionnaire). Eighty-three percent were satisfied with the results of their own cases and 78 percent said they would not have done anything differently. But only 52 percent were satisfied with the results of desegregation cases in general.

Those who were not satisfied with the results of desegregation cases in general stated a variety of reasons for their dissatisfaction. Several thought desegregation "inevitably" lowered the quality of education in public schools. One judge, referring to the problem of achieving desegregation in communities affected by white flight, saw "no apparent solution unless area-wide schools are included with desegregation plans."

Another respondent lamented the unwillingness of the parties to compromise, thereby making settlement virtually impossible. He said, "This case has been going on for over 20 years and I suspect it will go on for another 20 years." He contrasted the inadequacy of defense counsel representing the school Board with the competence and experience of the plaintiff's counsel, complaining that the defense counsel caused "needless delay, unbelievable attorneys' fees and general disaster for the community."

Another grievance frequently voiced by the judges was that there had been an assumption that the desegregated schools would be funded sufficiently to meet the extraordinary costs arising from the necessity of improving previously inadequate minority schools and other desegregation expenses. As one judge said, "They need more resources to solve the educational needs of the disadvantaged."

Only 32 percent of the judges thought litigation was the most effective solution to segregated schools and 18 percent thought that it was the only solution. Since 43 percent called it one of many solutions and 32 percent said it was an inadequate solution, the question of what they proposed as alternative remedies became significant. However, some of their recommendations were not too promising in view of the history of state and local resistance surrounding these cases. For example, one judge urged extensive negotiations prior to commencing a lawsuit and another suggested state legislation.

Other proposals were more based in reality. One judge earmarked zoning laws as perpetuating segregated housing patterns. Several respondents discussed the need for integrated housing as a precursor to desegregated schools in order to satisfy the widespread preference for neighborhood schools. One judge said, "Ultimately, I think integrated housing patterns is [sic] the solution to segregated schools. Parents, school administrators and educators favor local attendance at and control of schools. Integrated housing would promote integrated schools without sacrificing the concept of a 'neighborhood school.'"

Several respondents observed that white flight had to be taken into account in formulating a remedial plan and in adjusting the original decree.

More ambitious proposals advocated regional planning and busing, solutions expressly rejected by many respondents, but seen by their proponents as the only way to overcome the effects of white flight and segregated housing. One judge proposed the inclusion of private schools in the desegregation plans.

Another judge expressed the melancholy, but not unjustified, view that no solution could be fully successful. This was more than balanced by the welcome observation of one judge, which seemed implicit in many other responses, that the concept of unsegregated schools actually has been accepted to a large extent in this country. Nevertheless, the negative factors of white flight and resegregation were reported, with 50 percent of the respondents listing white flight as one of the community reactions to the desegregation order and 32 percent indicating the presence of resegregation.

The most unexpected result of the survey was the overwhelming proportion (over 80 percent) of denial that the judges' involvement in the desegregation case had an impact on their personal or professional relationships in the community. Their responses were contrary to the expectations we had formed in our reading of other published materials on the brave warriors of the desegregation battles, such as *Unlikely Heroes* by Jack Bass.[46] The descriptive subtitle is "The Dramatic Story of the Southern Judges Who Translated the Supreme Court's *Brown* Decision into a Revolution for Equality."

Unlikely Heroes vividly described the experiences of the judges in the U.S.

Court of Appeals for the Fifth Circuit after their decision in *United States v. Jefferson County Board of Education.*[47] Bass related numerous examples of social ostracism, hate mail, threats, abusive phone calls, isolation from colleagues, and overt attacks against the judges who defied the prevailing order by compelling local school boards to implement desegregation plans.

Similarly, Ronald J. and Margaret I. Bacigal published an article, *A Case Study of the Federal Judiciary's Role in Court-Ordered Busing: The Professional and Personal Experiences of U.S. District Judge Robert R. Merhige, Jr.,* in the *Journal of Law and Politics.*[48] They described instances of violence and vilification by the community, including death threats against the judge, the shooting of his dog, and the burning of his guest house.

Judge Merhige, who presided over *Bradley v. School Board,*[49] said, "All the controversy and hatred did change my life. I could no longer appear in public."[50]

But apparently the judges in the IJA survey did not encounter similar experiences. The violent resistance to court orders and personal harassment suffered by the judges portrayed in those and other publications were denied by the overwhelming majority of the respondents to the IJA questionnaire. They claimed compliance by the parties, cooperation by other public officials, community cooperation, and support from the attorneys. Only 33 percent acknowledged some degree of open defiance, but references to these incidents often were qualified by notations that such behavior had preceded the final order or had stopped. Only one judge reported the occurrence of violent outbursts, and another held several members of the school Board in contempt. But in general the public atmosphere conveyed by the responses was one of quiet compliance.

The overall judicial tone of the replies to the questionnaire was one of reasonableness. The judges appeared to take pride in their patient efforts to resolve the problems accompanying the involuntary desegregation of the public schools, including those produced by initial community resistance. They described their communities as civilized and pointed to workshops and other public relations activities designed to explain the court orders and the ramifications of the remedial plan to the local citizens. The judges were vigilant in modifying their decrees and adjusting their desegregation plans to allow for special circumstances as they arose. As one judge said, "I have not hesitated to revise action which did not achieve the success contemplated."

The courage and self-sacrifice of the pioneering southern judges of the 1950s and 1960s described in *Unlikely Heroes*, in *Swann's Way*, and in many other books and articles about this period,[51] appear to have been supplanted by the patience and sensitivity of the 1970s and 1980s. At first the federal district and circuit court judges had to overcome a siege mentality, apparently shared by many local judges who joined with the school officials and white citizens who were trying to find ways to evade and delay desegregation. As the concept of integration gradually became accepted, however reluctantly, the means to achieve it became the more critical issue.

Local citizen and official resistance to the prospect of sending white children to schools with predominantly black children and sending white or black children to schools out of their own neighborhoods continues to produce desegregation problems. Student enrollment in the public schools in large metropolitan areas has become so unbalanced that a racially balanced school system would be a mathematical impossibility. Plans to incorporate contiguous suburbs or counties into the design have met with fierce opposition. Voluntary transfer programs have had limited success, although they have been favored by school boards. Busing plans have been resisted violently in many communities. Perhaps the most serious impediment to effective desegregation plans has been the difficulty in obtaining funds to improve educational opportunities in the public schools. The judges in the survey discussed all of these problems.

The judicial response in the survey to the many frustrating barriers to effective desegregation typically was practical and stoical. Perseverance may be the quality that best defines the attitude of the judges. Ninety percent found their involvement in the desegregation cases substantially greater than in comparable litigation. Seventy-five percent reported that they had to modify their initial decree. Yet a stubborn optimism in the face of problems predominated.

One judge, referring to a 1967 case over which he continued to have jurisdiction, said, "Though there are still difficulties, these cases have had a profound and beneficial influence on life in this nation." He was one of those who expressed the view that litigation was a necessary but inadequate remedy for school segregation, saying, "Without litigation the problem would remain. It is, nevertheless, inadequate because additional funds are needed to improve educational facilities."

Other judges also remarked on the need for supplemental funds. But even more were frustrated by the consequences of white flight and segregated housing patterns. Their preferred solution—to expand their remedial plan to include surrounding counties—usually was rejected. Their other most favored solution—desegregated housing—has remained beyond their judicial powers. However, the *Yonkers* case,[52] in which Judge Leonard B. Sand of the Southern District of New York ordered the construction of low- and middle-income housing, will be discussed further in the conclusion to this chapter.

Because the respondents were pragmatists above all, they have turned to any reasonable remedy they could devise that might succeed in combatting school segregation. They have worked tirelessly with the parties to establish special educational centers, magnet schools, and other inducements to voluntary attendance away from segregated neighborhood schools. They have tried busing to suburban schools, redrafting of attendance zones, workshops, television coverage, and continuing refinement of their original remedial plans. Mainly they persevered. As one judge said:

> My continued presence in the case assures that there will be no receding from the successful plan and that this community can never be forced to repeat the agony involved in the establishment of the current plan. . . .
> It is impossible for a trial judge to improvise a perfect plan which would automatically satisfy the demands of problems unforeseen and yet to arise.

Other judges in the survey have sought assistance in devising a desegregation plan and monitoring compliance with their decrees. They have called upon the services of Masters, experts, law clerks, Monitoring Committees, Community Education Councils, state Departments of Education, and external auditors. In the exercise of their discretionary powers, they have enlisted any viable resource in the struggle to get the job of desegregating the schools accomplished.

The underlying theme, the consensus that can be distilled from the responses to the Questionnaire, is that litigation is not a perfect mechanism to eliminate discriminatory practices from the public schools, but it is the only remedy that seems to work. One judge summed up his viewpoint concerning the effectiveness of litigation as follows:

> I can suggest no alternative to litigation and that is the only reason that I feel it is the only solution once it is conceded that integration is necessary. In short, I feel that the courts are not well equipped to handle social plans of this nature but, inadequate as it may be I see no other alternative.

The respondent judges have labored to design creative and appropriate remedies. They have prevailed by repeatedly modifying and adapting, reducing their expectations when necessary, expanding the plan wherever possible, seeking additional funds, gradually gaining allies, and finally overseeing the best desegregation plans that their skill and imagination could devise.

SPECIFIC RESPONSES TO THE
QUESTIONNAIRE

Level of Judicial Involvement

The first part of the questionnaire dealt with the extent to which the judge was involved in framing the desegregation plan and facilitating implementation. In answer to the first question, "Did you find your involvement in the desegregation case(s) substantially greater than in comparable litigation?" 89 percent said yes and 11 percent said no.

The second question, as to how the remedy was devised, elicited a variety of answers. Twenty-five percent said they did it alone, 46 percent worked with the attorneys for the parties, 29 percent with the parties, 18 percent with a Master, and 18 percent with a task force. Other assistance came from court-appointed experts and professional consultants on education and desegregation.

The judges reported that compliance with their order was monitored in 92 percent of the cases (No. 3); and that oversight was accomplished by the judge retaining jurisdiction in 82 percent of the cases, by requiring reports in 68 percent, and by remedial discovery in 4 percent. Other oversight techniques included the use of a court-appointed Monitoring Commission, law clerks, motions by the plaintiff, a Community Education Council, court-appointed committees, semi-annual reports from the school district evaluated by a court-appointed external auditor, and field visits by the judge.

As mentioned earlier, 75 percent of the respondents modified their original order (No. 4). This was due to unforeseen developments in 56 percent of the cases, appellate review in 22 percent, and cost factors in 11 percent. Other circumstances compelling modification of the orders were the *Green* case (which declared freedom of choice plans inadequate to achieve a unitary school system),[53] demographic changes, the need for new school construction, updating the orders to build on discovered strengths or to remedy perceived weaknesses, redrawing of attendance zones, requests by the parties, efforts to reduce busing, and injunctions against dilatory tactics issued to protect school board members from political harassment.

Community Reaction

The second part of the questionnaire examined the community reaction to the desegregation cases. The relative tranquillity reflected in the judges' responses to the first question in that part—whether the desegregation orders were met with compliance, cooperation, support, or defiance —were discussed earlier in this chapter. The judges reported 100 percent compliance by the parties, 85 percent cooperation by other public officials, 83 percent cooperation of the community, 84 percent support from other attorneys, and only 33 percent open defiance from anyone.

In reply to the second question, "Has the reaction to your decision(s) substantially affected community affairs?" only 67 percent said yes. Of those who replied in the affirmative, 67 percent specified changes in race relations and in transfers to private schools. The quality of education was noted in 56 percent and flight from neighborhoods in 50 percent. The answers were split on whether the quality of education had become better or worse, but race relations were seen as improved.

The question of whether the decision has affected neighboring communities (No. 3) produced a closely divided response: Forty-six percent said yes and 54 percent said no. Several judges noted that the neighboring communities were involved in the desegregation plan, voluntarily or otherwise.

Although the percentages may indicate a majority of negative responses, we were unpleasantly surprised by the number of affirmative answers to question No. 4, "Has the phenomenon of resegregation begun in your community?" Thirty-two percent said yes and 68 percent said no.

The questionnaire inquired about the level of involvement of the attorneys in the case (No. 5). Only 54 percent of the respondents said they thought the attorneys were more involved in the desegregation cases than in the usual case.

The last questions on community reaction concerned the presence of national attorneys in the case (No. 6). Seventy-nine percent said national attorneys were involved. Of these, 90 percent said their participation did not affect community attitudes. Some of the outside attorneys were from the Department of Justice and others from the NAACP Legal Defense and Education Fund. Several comments indicated that community resentment of desegregation may have been exacerbated by the intervention of outsiders, but the majority stated a contrary view.

Personal/Professional Impact

The third part of the questionnaire inquired into the personal and professional impact of the desegregation cases on the judges. As discussed earlier in this chapter, the IJA staff was most surprised by the reported mild effect of the judges' role in the desegregation cases on their relationships with local judges, attorneys, and public officials (No. 1). Respondents reported no impact on 88 percent, 80 percent, and 84 percent of the questionnaires, respectively. The impact of the decision was a little stronger on the judges personally (48 percent yes) and on the way they view the judiciary (31 percent yes).

Fewer than half (48 percent) said the case involved an unusual amount of judicial creativity to devise the remedial plan (No. 2). Even more remarkably, only 35 percent thought the case involved an unusual degree of intervention into the operation of another agency (No. 3).

But the respondent judges reached the peak of *sang froid* in answer to question No. 4, "Did the extent of judicial activism in the case pose any unique problems?" Seventy-three percent said no. In the understated fashion that typified the responses in this survey, one judge commented that "it took a bit of original thought." Another conceded "difficulty in communicating accurate information to news media."

On a more negative note, one judge said, "I think the courts are less suited to handle these problems than I used to think before my experiences." He identified a lack of coordination with state government as a unique problem arising from his judicial activism in the desegregation case. He said that he had become less optimistic about solving social issues through legal action and that he thought that ultimately such issues must be solved by the entire community.

However, that was a minority viewpoint among the respondents. A more standard response, typically pragmatic in tone, was the following comment by another judge: "When local authorities did not want to cooperate, the plan was reduced to make cooperation possible." Nevertheless, only 58 percent thought the desegregation cases involved more discretion than other cases they have handled (No. 5).

In the same vein, 86 percent of respondents denied that their involvement in the desegregation cases made them more reluctant to take on cases involving controversial social issues, and a resounding 93 percent denied that it made them more reluctant to take on cases with few guiding precedents (No. 6).

Further, in answer to question No. 7, most said they found that public reaction to these cases did not have an impact on them personally (78 percent), on the way they viewed the judiciary (93 percent), or on the way they ultimately developed their remedial plans (89 percent).

Their responses indicated that their involvement in these cases was both less rewarding and less frustrating than the IJA staff had anticipated, with only 60 percent finding it more rewarding and 65 percent more frustrating than in other cases (No. 8).

In retrospect, a mere 22 percent said yes when asked whether they would have done anything differently and only 17 percent were dissatisfied with the results of the cases (No. 9). Yet 48 percent were dissatisfied with the results of desegregation cases in general. The implications of that disparity were discussed previously in this chapter.

Alternative Approaches

The last part of the questionnaire was designed to elicit open-ended discussion from the judges on the subject of alternative methods of dealing with the problem of school desegregation. It first attempts to promote analytical thought by offering multiple choice responses to complete the question "Do you feel that litigation to remedy school segregation is": one of many solutions (43 percent said yes), the most effective solution (32 percent said yes), the only solution (18 percent said yes), an inadequate solution (32 percent said yes).

The respondents then were asked to suggest any alternative approaches to school desegregation. The rest of the sheet was left blank to encourage unrestricted discussion. Several judges added sheets for their reply. The alternative approaches they recommended included extensive negotiation prior to litigation, state legislation, voluntary use of magnet schools, attendance at neighborhood schools if preferred, revised zoning laws to change segregated housing patterns, regional desegregation plans, and involving private schools in the remedial plans.

The judges' suggestions generally were set forth with little apparent expectation of adoption. For example, one proponent of regional planning acknowledged that treating contiguous cities and counties as one area would necessitate widespread busing, "which is not favored by anyone," he ruefully noted. Even in proposing solutions that might work if they were supported, practicality and a common sense awareness of limitations prevailed over enthusiasm or optimism among the judges who participated in the survey. In a typical exchange, the questionnaire asked, "Can you suggest any alternative approaches?" And the judge replied, "Not so long as we continue to have segregated housing patterns, enforced by zoning laws."

Almost every judge who completed the questionnaire attempted to suggest an alternative to litigation as a method of achieving desegregation. But the answer that summed it up was "No solution would be totally successful."

CONCLUSION

The intense drama that originally surrounded school desegregation appears to have subsided. The judge as hero, confronting a rebellious community, has been replaced by the judge as pragmatist, patiently negotiating a plan to achieve the maximum integration possible within a depleted public school system. Community resistance is less flamboyant and more passive, comprising delay and avoidance rather than threats and violence.

Some judges continue to battle, fighting to overcome the barriers of insufficient funds to remedy educational deficiencies, as in Chicago (see Chapter 7 in this volume), or housing patterns that are designed to perpetuate racially imbalanced schools, as in Yonkers, New York.[54]

To prove that communities are still capable of political intransigence and irrationality in the desegregation process, we need only observe the actions of the city and the district court judge in *Yonkers*, discussed earlier in this chapter. In *United States v. Yonkers Board of Education*, Judge Leonard B. Sand said, "[T]his case is not simply another in a long line of school desegregation cases. . . . No case has ever been brought in which a court was asked to determine the liability of state actors for both housing and school desegregation."[55] He found a nearly 40-year pattern of interrelated housing and school discrimination. The parties accepted a voluntary school desegregation plan in preference to a threatened mandatory busing order. But no construction has begun on the 200 to 1,000 low- and middle-income housing units that Judge Sand ordered the city to build.

His patience exhausted, Judge Sand declared a moratorium on any new development of city properties and has prohibited zoning changes, variances, tax abatements, and development bonds to assist private developers until the city complies with the housing desegregation order. An editorial in the *New York Times* entitled *When a City Defies a Judge*,[56] noted that the city had spent $15 million defending the lawsuit, which was more than construction of the court-mandated housing would cost, and was considering an appeal. However, on January 19, 1988, Yonkers officials reported to Judge Sand that they would comply with the court's order to integrate the city's housing.[57]

An ironic feature of this case is the role of the Reagan administration's Department of Justice in the historic linkage of the racial composition of the city schools with the city's discriminatory housing policies. Publication of a memo recommending withdrawal, which had been prepared by a Deputy Assistant Attorney General in 1981 as part of a review of cases that had been brought at the end of the Carter administration, produced so much political embarrassment that the department was obliged to pursue the case.[58]

Before we conclude this review of the judicial role in school desegregation cases, it might be useful to examine the current status of the cases. In a report issued by the U.S. Commission on Civil Rights in June 1987, entitled *New Evidence on School Desegregation*,[59] enrollment data were analyzed for 125 sample school districts between 1967 and 1985. The sample covered about 20 percent of 1968 public school enrollment, including nearly half of all minority enrollment.

The report disclosed that segregation had declined in 117 of the 125 districts, but white enrollment also showed a pronounced decline. Nevertheless, in 74 of the 125 districts studied, the exposure of minorities to white students increased despite the decline in the percentage of white students. The report further noted that white enrollment declined most sharply during the period of desegregation plan implementation, but the loss "tapers off" in the years following implementation.

The qualified success of 30 years of desegregation efforts and the resistance implicit in white flight, refusal to change housing or zoning patterns, and the sparseness of education funds to improve substandard schools demonstrate the strengths and weaknesses of judicial intervention.

Judges have the power to find discriminatory state action unconstitutional; they can render a decision and issue orders. They can require defendant school boards to submit remedial plans and can engage Masters to negotiate the details of the plans with all affected parties and non-parties. Judges can consult with experts. They can issue mandatory injunctive decrees prescribing specific courses of conduct to be followed by local school authorities, and they can retain jurisdiction to oversee their implementation.

But there also are limitations on what the judge can do. A judge cannot operate a school or improve the quality of the education that is provided. A judge cannot force a city or a school board to cooperate with grace or enthusiasm. A court is not a political arena and a judge is not a politician. And there is a point at which a judge has to withdraw from the supervisory role, a point at which implementation has occurred. Local officials have a right to regain control of the school system once the unconstitutional conditions that required the court's intervention have been eliminated.

The major issues in school desegregation cases today revolve around the process of finding that a school system has become unitary and that the basis for the court's jurisdiction has terminated. In *Pasadena City Board of Education v. Spangler*, the Supreme Court said, "[T]he District Court was not entitled to require the [school district] to rearrange its attendance zones each year so as to ensure that the racial mix desired by the court was maintained in perpetuity." [60]

One issue that has not been resolved is whether a district court's finding that a school system is unitary automatically dissolves the original mandatory injunctive decree. A recent Note [61] analyzes the conflicting lower court cases on this question, in both of which the Supreme Court has denied *certiorari*, *Dowell v. Board of Education* and *Riddick v. School Board*. [62] In *Dowell* the Court of Appeals for the Tenth Circuit ruled that the plaintiffs need show only a departure from the terms of the original injunctive decree. The school board then has the burden of proving that the deviation was justified and that modification or dissolution of the decree is warranted. In *Riddick* the Court of Appeals for the Fourth Circuit required the plaintiff to prove a *prima facie* case of intentional segregation to survive a motion for summary judgment.

The Tenth Circuit in *Dowell* specifically rejected the finding in *Riddick* that the unitariness finding dissolved a mandated integration plan. In each case the order declaring the school system unitary was silent on the subject of its effect on the original injunctive decree.

The Note examined Rule 60(b) of the Federal Rules of Civil Procedure on the power of the issuing court to modify or dissolve its decrees and concluded that the question should be whether a change in circumstances has rendered the relief less effective as a means of achieving the goals of the original decree. Applying that guideline to desegregation decrees, it proposed a fact-specific approach to determine the effect that should be accorded to a unitariness finding. Since *Brown II* directed the lower courts to use their equitable powers and to consider the competing interests in adopting a remedy, these same interests also must be considered at the termination stage. The Note said: "Only by considering all the concerns articulated by the Supreme Court can a lower court justify terminating the relief originally issued to combat unconstitutional segregation." [63]

If the nation is in the final stages of the school desegregation cases, its judges are no less committed to ensuring the continuing effectiveness of the remedial plans they adopted to eliminate discriminatory practices in the public schools. The unitariness cases suggest that the district court judges have one more step to take before they can walk away from their oversight role. Before they terminate their jurisdiction and restore full control to the school authorities, they must satisfy themselves that a mechanism has been established in the community to monitor and assist the school authorities in providing equal educational opportunity to all the children in the school system.

APPENDIX. Judge's Questionnaire

Name: _____

Case Name: _____

_____

Citation: _____

LEVEL OF JUDICIAL INVOLVEMENT

1. Did you find your involvement in the desegregation case(s) substantially greater than in comparable litigation?   Yes ____ No ____

2. Was the remedy devised:

    a. Yourself alone ____
    b. w/Master ____
    c. Master alone ____
    d. w/Parties ____
    e. w/Attorneys for Parties ____
    f. w/Task Force ____
    g. Other (please specify) ____

3. Did you monitor the compliance with your order(s)?   Yes ____ No ____

    If yes, how was oversight conducted:

    a. Retaining jurisdiction ____
    b. Requiring reports ____
    c. Remedial discovery ____
    d. Other (please specify) ____

4. Did you modify your initial order?   Yes ____ No ____

    If yes, was this due to:

a. Unforeseen developments ___
b. Cost factors ___
c. Complexity obstacles ___
d. Appellate review ___
e. Other factors (please specify) ___

COMMUNITY REACTION

1. Have your desegregation decisions/orders met with:

    a. Compliance by the parties?   Yes ___ No ___
    b. Cooperation by other public officials?   Yes ___ No ___
    c. Cooperation of the community?   Yes ___ No ___
    d. Support from the attorneys?   Yes ___ No ___
    e. Open defiance, *e.g.*, protests, violent out-
       bursts?   Yes ___ No ___

    Comments:

2. Has the reaction to your decision(s) substantially
   affected community affairs?   Yes ___ No ___

    If yes, did changes occur in:

    a. Housing ___
    b. Race relations ___
    c. Economic stability ___
    d. Taxing patterns ___
    e. Quality of education ___
    f. Transfer to private schools ___
    g. Flight from neighborhoods ___
    h. Other (please specify) ___

    Comments:

3. Has your decision affected neighboring communities?   Yes ___ No ___

    If yes, please specify:

4. Has the phenomenon of resegregation begun in
   your community?   Yes ___ No ___

5. Do you think the local attorneys' involvement in this case was greater than usual?   Yes ___ No ___

6. Were national attorneys involved in this case?   Yes ___ No ___

   If yes, did it affect community attitudes?   Yes ___ No ___

   Comments:

PERSONAL/PROFESSIONAL IMPACT

1. Did your involvement in this case have an impact on:

   a. You personally?   Yes ___ No ___
   b. The way you view the judiciary?   Yes ___ No ___
   c. Your relationship with other judges?   Yes ___ No ___
   d. Your relationship with other officials?   Yes ___ No ___
   e. Your relationship with local attorneys/organized bar?   Yes ___ No ___
   f. Other decisions you have made?   Yes ___ No ___

2. Did this case involve an unusual amount of judicial creativity to devise a remedial plan?   Yes ___ No ___

3. Did this case involve an unusual degree of intervention into the operation of other agencies?   Yes ___ No ___

4. Did the extent of judicial activism in the case pose any unique problems?   Yes ___ No ___

   If yes, please specify:

5. Did this case involve more discretion than other cases you have handled?   Yes ___ No ___

6. Did your involvement in this case make you:

   a. More reluctant to take on cases involving controversial social issues?   Yes ___ No ___
   b. More reluctant to take on cases with few guiding precedents?   Yes ___ No ___

7. Did public reaction to your case have an impact on:

    a. You personally?   Yes ____ No ____
    b. The way you view the judiciary?   Yes ____ No ____
    c. The way you ultimately developed your reme-
       dial plan?   Yes ____ No ____

8. Was your involvement in this case:

    a. More rewarding than other cases?   Yes ____ No ____
    b. More frustrating than other cases?   Yes ____ No ____

9. In retrospect:

    a. Would you have done anything differently?   Yes ____ No ____
    b. Are you satisfied with the results of the case? Yes ____ No ____
    c. Are you satisfied with the results of desegre-
       gation cases in general?   Yes ____ No ____

    Comments:

ALTERNATIVE APPROACHES

1. Do you feel that litigation to remedy school segregation is:

    a. The most effective solution ____
    b. The only solution ____
    c. One of many solutions ____
    d. An inadequate solution ____

2. Can you suggest any alternative approaches to school desegregation?

NOTES

1. 347 U.S. 483 (1954).
2. *See* Karst and Horowitz, *Reitman v. Mulkey: A Telophase of Substantive Equal Protection* Sup. Ct. Rev. 39, 61 (1967). Commenting on the role of the federal courts in the "Negro revolution," Professors Karst and Horowitz said, "By any test, the critical event of the early days of the Court's 'egalitarian revolution' was the decision in *Brown v. Board of Education.* True enough, the success of the judicial assault on segregation has been imperfect and partial, especially in the area of school segregation. Nonetheless, the federal judiciary's efforts have been extraordinarily successful in creating political symbols of legitimacy and justice for important and relatively rapid social change."

3. 349 U.S. 294 (1955).

4. *Id.* at 299.

5. 89 HARV. L. REV. 1281 (1976).

6. *Id.* at 1298.

7. The Final Report of the Council on the Role of the Courts (J. K. Lieberman, principal ed. 1984).

8. *See, e.g.,* Bacigal and Bacigal, *A Case Study of the Federal Judiciary's Role in Court-Ordered Busing: The Professional and Personal Experiences of U.S. District Judge Robert R. Merhige, Jr.,* 3 J.L. AND POL. 693 (1987); J. BASS, UNLIKELY HEROES (1981); J.W. PELTASON, 58 LONELY MEN (1961); and B. SCHWARTZ, SWANN'S WAY: THE SCHOOL BUSING CASE AND THE SUPREME COURT (1986).

9. *See, e.g.,* Dworkin, *The Bork Nomination,* 9 CARDOZO L. REV. 101 (1987); Gillers, *The Compelling Case Against Robert H. Bork,* 9 CARDOZO L. REV. 33 (1987); and Heymann and Wertheimer, *Why the United States Senate Should Not Consent to the Nomination of Judge Robert H. Bork to Be a Justice of the Supreme Court,* 9 CARDOZO L. REV. 21 (1987).

10. 32 ALA. L. REV. 271 (1981).

11. *Id.* at 279.

12. 635 F. Supp. 1577 (S.D.N.Y. 1986), *aff'd* 893 F.2d 14 (2d Cir. 1987).

13. Interview with Judge Sand (January 25, 1989). *See also* Lukas, *Needed in Yonkers: Old-Fashioned Politics,* N.Y. Times, August 23, 1988, at 21, col. 2.

14. 65 VA. L. REV. 43 (1979).

15. *Id.* at 92.

16. *Id.* at 104.

17. 13 J. L. AND ED. 345 (1984).

18. *Id.* at 399.

19. *Id.*

20. 32 ALA. L. REV. 399 (1981).

21. *Id.* at 401.

22. *Id.* at 439.

23. *Id.*

24. *Id.*

25. *See* Leflar and Davis, *Segregation in the Public Schools—1953,* 67 HARV. L. REV. 377, 392, cited and analyzed in T. I. EMERSON, D. HABER, AND N. DORSEN, 2 POLITICAL AND CIVIL RIGHTS IN THE UNITED STATES 1254 (Student's Ed. 1967).

26. 391 U.S. 430 (1968).

27. B. SCHWARTZ, SWANN'S WAY: THE SCHOOL BUSING CASE AND THE SUPREME COURT 58 (1986).

28. 391 U.S. at 438.

29. *Id.* at 439.

30. *Id.*

31. 402 U.S. 1 (1971).

32. *Id.* at 16.

33. *Id.* at 21.

34. *Id.* at 22.

35. *Id.* at 26.

36. *Id.* at 28.

37. *Id.* at 30, 31.

38. *Id.* at 32.

39. *See* Dowell v. Board of Education, 795 F.2d 1516 (10th Cir.) and Riddick v. School Board, 784 F.2d 521 (4th Cir.), *cert. denied* both cases 107 S. Ct. 420 (1986).

40. 413 U.S. 189 (1973).

41. Pearson and Pearson, *Keyes v. School District No. 1*, LIMITS OF JUSTICE 167 (H. I. Kalodner and J. Fishman eds. 1978).

42. 433 U.S. 267.

43. 402 U.S. 1 (1971).

44. 391 U.S. 430 (1968).

45. 347 U.S. 483 (1954); 349 U.S. 294 (1955).

46. *Supra* note 8.

47. 372 F.2d 836 (5th Cir. 1966), *aff'd en banc*, 380 F.2d 285 (5th Cir.), *cert. denied*, 389 U.S. 840 (1967).

48. *Supra* note 8.

49. 315 F. Supp. 325 (1970), *vacated*, 324 F. Supp. 456 (E.D. Va. 1971); 338 F. Supp. 67 (E.D. Va.), *rev'd*, 462 F.2d 1058 (4th Cir. 1972), *aff'd per curiam* 412 U.S. 92 (1973).

50. Bacigal and Bacigal, *supra* note 8 at 711.

51. *See* Bacigal and Bacigal; Bass; Peltason; Schwartz; *supra* note 8.

52. United States v. Yonkers Board of Education, 624 F. Supp. 1276 (S.D.N.Y. 1985).

53. *Supra* note 26.

54. *Yonkers, supra* notes 12 and 52.

55. *Yonkers, supra* note 52 at 1526.

56. N.Y. Times, November 25, 1987, at 26, col. 1.

57. N.Y. Times, January 20, 1988, at 17, col. 4.

58. N.Y. Times, January 19, 1988, at 16, col. 1.

59. Prepared by F. Welch and A. Light of Unicon Research Corporation, U.S. Commission on Civil Rights, Clearinghouse Publication 92 (June 1987).

60. 427 U.S. 424, 436 (1976).

61. Note, *The Unitariness Finding and Its Effect on Mandatory Desegregation Injunctions* 55 FORD. L. REV. 551 (1987).

62. *Supra* at note 39.

63. Note, *supra* at note 61, p. 577.

CHAPTER 9

The View from the Bar: An Examination of the Litigator's Role in Shaping Educational Remedies

PAUL L. TRACTENBERG

IN 1976, DERRICK BELL wrote a heretical article.[1] The former NAACP Legal and Educational Defense Fund (LDF) staff attorney[2] posited a dilemma confronting many plaintiffs' lawyers in school desegregation cases. Two "masters," clients and organizational employer, vied for the attorneys' loyalty.

According to Bell, in many cases these masters had conflicting objectives. Black parents wanted the best education for their children; national organizations, such as the NAACP[3] and LDF, were committed to a nationwide program of school desegregation. In Bell's view, better-funded and better-managed neighborhood schools, even if not integrated, might be preferred by some local black plaintiffs. However, such a result, he asserted, would be anathema to the national organizations.

The attorney's dilemma in such a situation is clear. Ethically, the attorney is bound to advocate zealously for the client,[4] and it is the client who must ultimately decide on the desired result.[5] The desires, or stated policies, of an organization employing the attorney should give way.[6]

Yet, in practice, the organization's policies may have great influence, in some measure because the attorney personally may be committed to them. Moreover, in many school desegregation cases the clients' wishes may not be entirely clear. Whether styled as a class action or not, the school desegregation case seeks to advance a broad constitutional and public policy end by reforming a complex public institution.[7] Those to be benefited, typically poor minority children in segregated schools and their parents, are numerous. They may lack an effective forum for expressing their views. They may not have definitive views. They may have disparate, even competing, views. In some cases, the named plaintiffs may be nominal, without significant substantive connection to the litigation.

Even where real clients, rather than attorneys or their organizations, provided the impetus for the litigation, local attorneys often lacked the resources or expertise to handle the cases completely on their own. The involvement of "national attorneys" almost inevitably affected the nature of the lawyer–client relationship and created the potential for friction between local and national attorneys.[8]

All of this Bell's article raised. That it did so in such a highly visible way, almost 25 years after *Brown v. Board of Education*,[9] is surprising. Even more surprising, though, is that since Bell's article, so little has been written focusing systematically on the pivotal role of lawyers in these monumentally important cases. By comparison, the role of judges in school desegregation litigation has been the subject of a substantial literature.[10]

This is not to say that lawyers have been excluded from the voluminous school desegregation literature. They often appear as part of the large and variegated cast, sometimes even in starring roles.[11] Occasionally, we even see school desegregation cases through the eyes and pen of a litigating attorney.[12] Most typically, these works have been fascinating and detailed narratives of the life history of a particular law suit.[13] However, there has not been a systematic effort to analyze the role lawyers have played in school desegregation litigation.[14]

This chapter is a modest first step in that direction. Barbara Flicker and I jointly selected a diverse sample of school desegregation cases for our studies. (My chapter focuses on the attorneys' perceptions of their roles and Barbara Flicker's deals with the judges' perceptions.) I then sent questionnaires[15] to all attorneys involved in those cases, as listed in the official West Reporter opinions, who could be located. This amounted to 264 potential respondents. Of those, 47 (17.8 percent) actually responded, a good rate of response for such survey research.[16] This chapter constitutes an impressionistic first report of the survey results. Much more can be done with these data, and a range of additional data should be collected. As will be evident, this report falls short of the scientific rigor necessary for a complete empirical understanding of desegregation conflicts. Nonetheless, it provides interesting and perhaps even important insights into the way a group of lawyers has reacted to the experience of litigating school desegregation cases. The questionnaires and, in many instances, unsolicited supplementary statements, convey the exhilarations and the frustrations, the certainties and the quandaries, the commitment and the vacillation of a diverse group of lawyers confronting a complex legal and social challenge.

THE RESPONDENT ATTORNEYS
AND THEIR CLIENTS

A few more than half of the 47 respondents represented defendant interests (No. 2a).[17] Twenty-one were attorneys for original or intervening defendants and five represented suburban defendants joined by court order.

The remaining 21 respondents represented plaintiff interests, 20 representcd either original or intervening parties, and one represented unnamed members of the plaintiff class.

This response pattern is interesting since almost three-fourths of all respondents and more than three-fifths of the attorneys for defendants reported that the judgments in their cases favored plaintiffs (No. 11a). My suspicion would have been that respondents would come primarily from the winning side. That is very much true of plaintiffs' attorneys who responded, but not of defendants' attorneys. In fact, some of the latter seemed to use this survey as a catharsis for their feelings of frustration and anger about the litigation and its aftermath. In the words of one who sent an especially detailed response, the questionnaire "certainly pulled my chain."

Since the prototypical school desegregation case involves parents and students suing those responsible for the public education system, defendants' attorneys primarily represented school districts and public officials, with only a few representing parents, students, or citizens/taxpayers, and one representing a state board of education. Plaintiffs' attorneys primarily represented parents and students. Four did represent organizational plaintiffs: two the NAACP, one LDF, and one a teachers' organization. Three each represented citizens/taxpayers and school districts, two represented cities, and one represented interested teachers (No. 2b).

Three-fourths of defendants' attorneys responding indicated that they became involved in the case by being employed by a party or interested organization. Plaintiffs' attorneys were equally likely to become involved through contacts by other lawyers or by legal or other organizations (No. 3).

Somewhat surprisingly, plaintiffs' and defendants' attorneys had been comparably involved, prior to their involvement in the particular school desegregation case, in "public law" cases. Plaintiffs' attorneys reported somewhat greater involvement in other school desegregation cases, other civil rights cases, and other public law or institutional reform cases. However, defendants' attorneys had been somewhat more involved in other education law cases and substantially more involved in zoning or land use cases (No. 4).

All of the defendants' attorneys, and almost three-fourths of the plaintiffs' attorneys, were in private practice when they were involved in the school desegregation litigation. Plaintiffs' attorneys tended to practice with smaller firms than defendants' attorneys. Half of the plaintiffs' attorneys, but only about one-fourth of the defendants' attorneys, were in firms of less than 15. Virtually all of the defendants' attorneys characterized their practices as "litigation" or "general." Only one characterized his practice as "civil rights." By contrast, seven plaintiffs' attorneys described their practices as civil rights and three as labor law, against six who characterized their practices as general. However, for plaintiffs' and defendants' attorneys alike the largest category was litigation (No. 5c).

Four plaintiffs' attorneys were with legal services projects and two were with government agencies, but none were employed by public interest law projects or civil rights organizations (No. 5a). Since questionnaires were sent to a considerable number of past and present attorneys with civil rights organizations, their lack of response is curious. Perhaps they are busier than those who responded, or they are more frequent recipients of information requests. Perhaps they have been involved in so many school desegregation cases that it is more difficult for them to distill from their experience responses to the questionnaire. On the other hand, I would have guessed that their commitment to school desegregation, and to racial equality in other societal spheres, would have enhanced the likelihood that they would respond. So, it is a puzzlement and a concern that these attorneys are unrepresented in the survey. Future efforts should be structured to ensure their representation, as well as to identify the sources of their reluctance to participate.

INVOLVEMENT OF ATTORNEYS AND EXPERTS IN THE SCHOOL DESEGREGATION CASE

Predictably, plaintiffs' attorneys tended to get involved in the school desegregation litigation earlier in the process than defendants' attorneys. Almost two-thirds of the plaintiffs' attorneys who responded indicated that they became involved prior to the filing of a complaint, almost half prior even to a decision to litigate. By contrast, only one-fifth of the defendants' attorneys became involved prior to the filing of a complaint (No. 6a).

The trial, appeal, and pre-trial stages of the litigation garnered the largest participation of respondents. A large number of plaintiffs' attorneys also reported being involved at the remedy stage; a smaller number of defendants' attorneys did. This may be explained by the fact that some defendants' attorneys who responded prevailed in the liability decision, and those cases, therefore, did not have a remedy stage.

Less easy to explain is the substantial fall-off of plaintiffs' attorneys' involvement in the implementation stage of the litigation. Although 16 plaintiffs' attorneys reported that they were involved in the remedy stage and the same number in the appeal stage, only 11 reported involvement in implementation. By comparison, 11 of 12 defendants' attorneys who reported involvement in the remedy stage maintained their involvement in the implementation stage (No. 6b). Perhaps this reflects, in some cases where plaintiffs prevailed, a tendency not to have an implementation stage, at least in a formal sense. This is a more likely interpretation of the data than that almost one-third of the sample of plaintiffs' attorneys who indicated involvement in the remedy stage simply did not participate in the implementation stage. In future inquiries, this hypothesis should be checked.

In the overwhelming majority of cases, including all in which plaintiffs' attorneys were involved, other attorneys were involved in representing the same client, or other aligned clients (No. 7a). For plaintiffs, the litigation team also usually included desegregation and other experts. For defendants, other experts were used about two-thirds of the time, but desegregation experts only half the time (No. 7b). The striking difference between plaintiffs' and defendants' use of desegregation experts is fascinating. It is difficult to imagine why, in complex school desegregation litigation, defendants frequently did not involve desegregation experts. The explanation certainly does not reside in inadequate resources. In most cases, plaintiffs, rather than defendants, would be burdened by resource difficulties. Two possible explanations remain: that desegregation experts tend to be more sympathetic and therefore more available to plaintiffs; or that defendants feel less need to enlist outside desegregation experts because they consider school district professional staff members to have the necessary expertise. These possibilities also should be explored further.

In general, the other attorneys or the experts used were heavily involved in the litigation, slightly more so by plaintiffs than by defendants. They also were rated as quite effective by both plaintiffs' and defendants' attorneys. Interestingly, three times as many plaintiffs' attorneys rated the other attorneys and experts in the two most effective categories as in the two least effective categories. Since the plaintiffs' attorneys represented in this sample were local as opposed to national lawyers, the favorable effectiveness ratings they gave to the other attorneys suggest that they did not experience significant friction or other difficulties with the national attorneys who participated in many of these cases.

This finding seems to conflict with Professor Bell's strong impressions about the relationships between local participants in school desegregation cases, including local attorneys, and the national attorneys. There may be several explanations for this difference. One is that Bell's observations were based solely on his own experiences, rather than on a sampling of opinion. A second is that local attorneys' views may have changed significantly over the more than ten years between Bell's study and this one, or that national organizations' policies shifted.[18] A third explanation is that the questionnaire used in this study, by being drafted consciously not to pinpoint possible friction between local and national attorneys, left respondents free to complete it without raising a potentially emotionally charged issue. The voluntary supplementary statements of at least some respondents suggest, though, that they were not reluctant to raise controversial issues in strong terms.

The explanation for this apparent shift in attitudes is another matter that should receive further scrutiny. The next cluster of findings in this chapter, relating to the litigation goals and how they were formulated, may shed additional light on this question.

Litigation Goals and Their Formulation

Plaintiffs' and defendants' attorneys agreed that integration in some form constituted the dominant plaintiffs' goal (No. 8a). Overall, integration of school buildings within a single district and integration of staff were highest-ranked. Integration among several school districts, minority hiring or promotion, and integration of classes or programs were the next cluster of plaintiffs' goals, as identified by the total respondent pool. Bringing up the rear were more explicitly educational program goals—improved or expanded educational programs, improved educational facilities, and increased educational expenditures—which were identified as plaintiffs' goals less than half as frequently as integration of students and staff. Based on aggregate responses, this seems to suggest that what Bell considered national organizational goals were the dominant plaintiffs' goals identified in this study. However, when the responses of plaintiffs' and defendants' attorneys are disaggregated, the picture looks a bit different.

Defendants' attorneys saw the primary plaintiffs' goals as integration of school buildings within a single district, integration of staff, and integration among several school districts, with considerably more than half listing each. Minority hiring or promotion was rated next, but with less than half listing it. Less than one-third listed integration of classes or programs, and less than one-fifth identified other educational program-related goals, such as improved or expanded programs, improved facilities, and increased expenditures.

A significantly different picture emerged from plaintiffs' attorneys. Like defendants' attorneys, they ranked intradistrict pupil integration and staff integration highest, with almost three-fourths and two-thirds of the respondents, respectively, indicating these goals. However, only one-third included interdistrict integration as a plaintiff goal. A significantly larger number listed integration of classes or programs, and comparable numbers listed the educational program elements, as plaintiffs' goals.

Thus, plaintiffs' attorneys were substantially more likely to see school classes or programs, or other *educational* elements, and much less likely to see integration among several school districts, as plaintiffs' litigation goals. In fact, their divergent ratings of interdistrict integration represented by far the sharpest difference in perception between plaintiffs' and defendants' attorneys. Among plaintiffs' attorneys, only one-third listed interdistrict integration, making it the next to lowest of eight choices. Among the defendants' attorneys, almost three-fifths listed it, placing it second.

The sharpness of this disparity is another matter that should be studied further. To some degree, it may be that responding plaintiffs' and defendants' attorneys were involved in different cases with different plaintiffs' goals. But it may also be that they have different perceptions and recollections of the hierarchy of goals pursued by plaintiffs.

In identifying defendants' litigation goals, a similar pattern emerged (No. 8b). Overall, maintaining neighborhood schools was seen as being a defendants' goal by almost two-thirds of all respondents, almost three-fourths of the defendants' attorneys, and more than half of the plaintiffs' attorneys. The goal that was ranked next highest—maintaining local control—garnered less than half the total respondents and fewer than two-fifths of the plaintiffs' attorneys. Overall, the lowest ranked of the three defendants' goals specified by the questionnaire—preserving the educational or employment status quo—showed another especially sharp difference among respondents. More than half the plaintiffs' attorneys listed it, compared with slightly more than one-tenth of the defendants' attorneys.

Respondent reactions to who was primarily responsible for determining litigation goals produced other interesting findings (No. 9a). A surprising number of attorneys, almost one-third of all respondents, indicated that either attorneys or interested organizations were primarily responsible. Almost twice as many plaintiffs' as defendants' attorneys identified interested organizations. Conversely, more than two-thirds of the defendants' attorneys, as compared with slightly more than half of the plaintiffs' attorneys, listed the parties as primarily responsible for determining the goals.

This last difference is understandable. Plaintiffs in school desegregation cases tend to be large and often diverse classes of people—students, their parents, and perhaps citizens and taxpayers. Organizations, local and national, may be instrumental in instigating and even financing the litigation. Attorneys come to these cases for diverse reasons and under diverse arrangements, including often *pro bono publico* commitments.

Defendants, on the other hand, are typically school districts and other public bodies or officials that maintain structured and legally enforceable decision-making processes. Their attorneys often have ongoing lawyer–client relationships with them.

Given those differences, it is hardly surprising that defendants' attorneys, much more frequently than plaintiffs' attorneys, saw decision-making responsibility resting with their clients. Indeed, what is surprising is that almost half of the defendants' attorney responses listed someone other than the party as primarily responsible for determining the litigation goals. That should not minimize, however, concern that almost two-thirds of the plaintiffs' attorney responses indicated that someone other than the client was primarily responsible. This pattern may be endemic to class action and institutional reform litigation,[19] but it nonetheless raises concerns about the decision-making processes in such litigation.

On the more specific decision-making question of the extent to which plaintiffs or their community had considered the desired remedy before the suit was filed or before a decision regarding violation was rendered, another sharp difference surfaced between plaintiffs' and defendants' attorneys (No. 9b). Two-thirds of the plaintiffs' attorneys, but only one-seventh of the defendants' attorneys, indicated that the greatest consideration had been given before the suit was filed. At the other end of the scale, nearly half of the defendants' attorneys, but less than one-seventh of the plaintiffs' attorneys, indicated that the least consideration had been given.

Regarding consideration of remedy before a violation decision was rendered, the differences were less dramatic but still substantial.

These sharp differences may result from disparate access to information or from litigator biases. They may also derive from different conceptions of the parties' role in the litigation process. In subtle and not so subtle ways, if one believes the parties' role is a secondary one, then the parties' level of participation probably will be evaluated differently.

Present Status of the Case

A considerable number of the cases in which respondents participated are still in the courts, at least through retained jurisdiction, but the bulk of the cases have had a judgment on violation and on the remedial plan (No. 10). Jurisdiction has been terminated in only a small number of the cases.

In those cases where a judgment has been entered, it favors the plaintiff almost three-fourths of the time (No. 11a). However, responding defendants' attorneys indicated that they had prevailed, at least in substantial part, almost two-fifths of the time. By comparison, about six-sevenths of the responding plaintiffs' attorneys reported that they had prevailed. As indicated previously, that means a surprisingly large number of survey respondents did not prevail in their cases.

REMEDIAL ASPECTS

Of particular interest in this study was the role attorneys played in the remedial process. Therefore, a substantial portion of the questionnaire was devoted to remedial aspects. Since most of the cases reached the remedial stage, this means a considerable body of data was generated about these matters.

In more than four-fifths of the cases with judgments favoring plaintiffs, there was a separate proceeding on remedy (No. 11b), and the surveyed attorneys were involved in nearly all of those (No. 11c).

When asked how the remedial plan was devised in their cases, the attorneys identified a surprisingly balanced array of mechanisms (No. 12a). Overall, those in which the judge was a central figure predominated. Almost equal numbers of respondents listed the following: the judge with court-appointed master or expert; the judge or master with parties; and the judge alone. A smaller, but still significant, number listed the judge or master with a task force. A very small number identified one or the other of the parties alone, a tri-ethnic commission, an ad hoc community group, or HEW.

The only significant differences in the perceptions of plaintiffs' and defendants' attorneys about how the remedial plan was devised related to the mechanisms of "judge alone" and "judge or master with the attorneys." At least three times as many defendants' attorneys as plaintiffs' attorneys reported those as mechanisms used in their cases.

Regarding review of the remedial plan before adoption, plaintiffs' and defendants' attorneys had completely consistent views (No. 12b). Each group reported that the attorneys, parties, and experts, in that order, were the primary reviewers. In descending order, about one-fourth fewer respondents identified parties than attorneys, and experts than parties. Only a small number listed the community, a task force, or any other mechanism as being involved in the review process. Only one plaintiffs' attorney listed LDF.

Overall, more than two-fifths of the respondents reported that at least part of the remedy was negotiated out of court. This included almost half of the defendants' attorneys responding, but only about one-third of the plaintiffs' attorneys (No. 12c). One-fourth of those responding affirmatively indicated that the entire remedial plan was negotiated out of court; the balance identified portions, including *Milliken II* remedies,[20] magnet schools, pairing and redistricting, and a monitoring body (No. 12d).

As to substantive aspects of the remedial plan, with some minor exceptions, plaintiffs' and defendants' attorneys agreed that a wide variety of elements were encompassed, and that the most common ones were busing, changed attendance zones, magnet schools, and teacher reassignment (No. 13). These traditional school desegregation remedies—primarily oriented toward physical mixing of the races at the student and staff levels— dominated the list. Moreover, other elements with a similar purpose—for example, creation of new or closing of old schools, reorganization of school grade levels, and interdistrict or regional arrangements—garnered considerable support. Smaller but significant numbers did identify some resource or educational quality-related remedial elements, for example, increased funding, remedial education, improved or expanded community involvement, and improved or expanded educational programs. Overall, more than three-fifths of the responses identified physical desegregation elements.

The interplay among attorneys, clients, and the broader constituency in the development of the remedy was the focus of the next set of survey questions. The attorney respondents were divided quite sharply about the degree of their personal involvement (No. 14). More than one-third reported great involvement, but almost two-fifths reported minimal involvement. The remaining one-fourth were almost equally divided among the three intermediate levels of involvement. The distribution was markedly different among the attorneys. The plaintiffs' attorneys were much more likely to rate their involvement at the highest level—one-half as compared with one-fifth for defendants' attorneys. Similarly, at the opposite end of the scale, only one-third of the plaintiffs' attorneys, but almost half of the defendants' attorneys, listed themselves as having had minimal involvement.

The primary forms of attorney involvement in development of the remedial plan were discussions with clients, review of plans developed by others, discussions with judges or court-appointed masters or experts, and consultations with experts. Regarding these relatively passive forms of involvement, plaintiffs' and defendants' attorneys reported quite similar experiences, except that defendants' attorneys reported discussions with clients half again as often as did plaintiffs' attorneys. This is consistent with an earlier finding that defendants' attorneys interacted more with clients than did plaintiffs' attorneys.[21] On the other hand, plaintiffs' attorneys reported substantially more discussion of the plan with the broader constituency or community their client represented than did defendants' attorneys.

As to the more active forms of involvement in development of the remedial plan—actual development of it or negotiation about it—defendants' attorneys reported almost twice as much involvement in negotiations, and plaintiffs' attorneys reported more than three times as much involvement in actual development of the plan. Interestingly, only one plaintiffs' attorney reported that he had developed the plan with others. Once more, this raises questions about Professor Bell's view that national attorneys played dominant roles.

The degree of clients' involvement in developing the remedial plan, as with the attorneys, tended to be rated at the extremes (No. 16). Overall, one-third of the respondents rated their clients as having had the greatest involvement, more than one-third as having had minimal involvement, and the balance—less than one-third—were divided among the three intermediate levels. Since I suspect that survey respondents, especially attorneys, would tend to select less extreme options, this finding seems significant.

Moreover, the difference between plaintiffs' and defendants' attorneys is interesting. Although plaintiffs' attorneys had been substantially more likely than defendants' attorneys to rate as "great" their personal involvement in development of the remedial plan,[22] the groups were reversed in their assessment of the extent of their clients' involvement. Almost twice as many defendants' as plaintiffs' attorneys indicated great client involvement. Curiously, an equal number of defendants' attorneys reported minimal client involvement. Once again, this may be consistent with a different defendants' attorney relationship with, or perception of, his or her client.

The most common form of client involvement in development of the remedy was discussion of the plan with attorneys (No. 17). Both plaintiffs' and defendants' attorneys gave this their highest ranking. Equally ranked by the former group, but much lower by the latter group, was discussion of the plan with the client's broader constituency or community. The opposite pattern obtained as to the most active form of involvement—actual development of the plan. Twice as many defendants' attorneys as plaintiffs' attorneys reported that their clients had alone or with others developed the remedial plan. Reviewing plans developed by others, discussing plans with a judge or court-appointed master or expert, negotiating about a plan, and consulting with experts about a plan were all identified with significant frequency by respondents.

Focusing on the role of a broader constituency or community of interest, the various techniques for obtaining its input about the remedial plan overall were identified almost equally (No. 18). To some degree, the plaintiffs' attorneys reported more reliance on small-group meetings or individual contacts, and defendants' attorneys on large-group meetings. This seems consistent with the differences, already discussed,[23] between plaintiff and defendant client communities.

Neither plaintiffs' nor defendants' attorneys considered this broader constituency or community input as having much influence in the shaping of the remedial plan (No. 19). About seven-eighths of the respondents ranked this input in the three lowest categories and almost half ranked it in the lowest. Only one of 15 plaintiffs' attorneys responding, and two of 16 defendants' attorneys, ranked it in the highest category.

The most frequently mentioned reason for this level of influence was the constituency's or community's degree of knowledge (No. 20). The degrees of these groups' consensus, political involvement, and participation were clustered at a lower level as explanations for the extent of their influence.

After the remedial plan was developed and ordered, implementation of it was the subject of a next series of survey questions. Respondents overwhelmingly indicated that compliance with the plan had been monitored (No. 22a). Typically, this had been done by the court retaining jurisdiction and, thereafter often requiring reports (No. 22b). Occasionally, the court had appointed a parent/community monitoring body or an outside auditor, and sometimes there had been remedial discovery.

The most common attorney involvement in the monitoring process consisted of appearing in court proceedings and reviewing compliance reports. Only two attorneys, one from each side, indicated that they had prepared such reports.

As to whether or not compliance with the remedial plan actually had been achieved, respondents were in striking agreement (No. 23a). Only two plaintiffs' attorneys reported that no compliance had been achieved. The other 34 respondents reported at least partial compliance, and almost three-fifths indicated that there had been full compliance. Plaintiffs' and defendants' attorneys agreed almost completely on the split between full and partial compliance.

This relatively rosy picture must be tempered, however, by some further survey results. A clear majority of respondents indicated that proceedings had been instituted in their cases to enforce the remedial orders (No. 23b) and that the most frequent result of such proceedings was more specific orders (No. 23c). Noncompliance was reported to have been found slightly more often than compliance, and one defendants' attorney reported a finding of contempt. Viewed differently, adequate compliance was found in only slightly more than one-fifth of the enforcement proceedings. There were no significant differences between plaintiffs' and defendants' attorneys' responses regarding these results.

Not surprisingly, there *was* a significant difference between these groups when they responded to the question of how defendants' attorneys saw their role regarding the remedial plan (No. 23d). All of the defendants' attorneys characterized their role as affirmative, or at least neutral, interpreting the order to their client or encouraging compliance (or figuring out how to comply).[24] Plaintiffs' attorneys had a much more mixed view. The response drawing the largest number was neutral, interpreting the order to their clients. On the more qualitative items, about two-thirds of the plaintiffs' attorneys who responded indicated that defendants' attorneys had assisted resistance or obstructed and delayed, rather than encouraged, compliance.

These results are not surprising, but they are distressing nonetheless. The role of defendants' attorneys in cases with the emotional and political impact of school desegregation litigation is no doubt a difficult and complex one. In such cases especially, defining the bounds of appropriate attorney behavior is difficult.[25] Additionally, plaintiffs' attorneys cannot be unaffected by the emotions their clients usually bring to these cases, which may influence their perception of defendants' attorneys. Still, if assisting resistance to court orders, or obstructing and delaying compliance, was practiced by defendants' attorneys in a significant number of school desegregation cases, as plaintiffs' attorneys reported, that raises serious questions for the profession.

As a result of judicial proceedings to enforce compliance with the remedial order, more than three-fifths of the respondents indicated that the order had been modified (No. 24a). Interestingly, defendants' attorneys overwhelmingly (by more than three-fourths) reported modifications, but plaintiffs' attorneys reported that to have been the case significantly less than half the time.

The primary causes of modification were appellate review, demographic changes, and unforeseen developments (No. 24b). Defendants' attorneys considered cost factors and complexity of the remedial plan as other significant causes, while plaintiffs' attorneys listed lack of cooperation in implementation. In summing up the responses to remedial and other orders in their cases, plaintiffs' and defendants' attorneys alike ranked compliance of the parties highest (No. 25). Cooperation of the community was next on both lists, but substantially lower. A significant number of plaintiffs' attorneys, but fewer than in either of the above categories, and one defendants' attorney, reported instances of open defiance. These included character attacks on the judge and plaintiffs' attorneys, withdrawal of students, and use of legal processes to delay. However, on the whole, the responses of plaintiffs' attorneys were surprisingly affirmative. More than four-fifths reflected positive reactions.

In comparable proportions, plaintiffs' and defendants' attorneys responded to whether there had been attempts to have the courts terminate jurisdiction in their cases. Overall, more than half of those responding reported such attempts (No. 26a), but jurisdiction was terminated in less than one-third of those cases (No. 26b). Interestingly, only one-fifth of the defendants' attorneys responding, but more than one-third of the plaintiffs' attorneys, indicated that the attempts in their cases had been successful.

LAWYERS' PERCEPTIONS ABOUT THE JUDGE

As a backdrop to the lawyers' views of their roles, my questionnaire asks respondents about the judges' attitudes and conduct. A remarkable consensus emerged among plaintiffs' and defendants' attorneys. Overwhelmingly, they considered the judges in their cases to be extremely active and extremely committed to desegregation (No. 21). On the active/passive continuum, about two-thirds of both the plaintiffs' and the defendants' attorneys rated the judges as most active. By comparison, only one respondent from each group ranked the judges as most passive, one-eighteenth and one-twenty-third, respectively. The picture is even more dramatic if the two most active and the two most passive categories are combined. The most active category included more than four-fifths of all respondents, eleven times as many as the most passive category.

The results are substantially the same for the attorneys' view of the judges' commitment to desegregation. More than two-thirds of the plaintiffs' attorneys and three-fifths of the defendants' attorneys, almost two-thirds overall, rated the judges as most committed. Only two plaintiffs' attorneys and one defendants' attorney ranked them in the most neutral or negative category, less than one-eighth and one-twenty-second, respectively. As with the active/passive continuum, the results for commitment to desegregation become even more dramatic when the two categories on each side of the midpoint are compared. Those attorneys who ranked their judges as committed to desegregation constituted well over four-fifths of all respondents, as compared with the one-thirteenth who ranked them as neutral or negative. Again, the former group contained 11 times as many respondents as the latter.

These extremely strong and uniform results are interesting and important in their own right. However, when compared with the quite negative perceptions the respondents had about the success of school desegregation litigation,[26] they take on additional significance. If such litigation has been a disappointment, despite the very strong commitment of judges to both de-segregation and activism, the problem must lie elsewhere, perhaps even in the intractability of the segregative situation to a litigated solution.[27]

EFFECTS OF THE LITIGATION

The survey sought to canvass attorneys' views about the impact of their school desegregation cases on directly involved and nearby communities, and on the attorneys themselves.

Two-thirds of those responding indicated that the decisions in their cases had substantially affected community affairs (No. 27a). Plaintiffs' attorneys hold this view more than their counterparts. The major areas of change identified, in order of frequency, were transfer to private schools, educational quality, race relations, and flight from neighborhoods (No. 27b). The first and last items clearly seem to be negative effects, and substantial numbers of both plaintiffs' and defendants' attorneys flagged them. The second and third items—educational quality and race relations—could be either positive or negative. In general, I would suspect that plaintiffs' attorneys who identified them would have had positive connotations in mind and defendants' attorneys negative.[28] Thus, it is interesting that for both these categories there were more plaintiffs' than defendants' attorney votes, and for educational quality there were twice as many. Nonetheless, the overall sense of the responses about the effect on community affairs tended to be negative.

More than three-fifths of the respondents, two-thirds of the plaintiffs' attorneys and somewhat fewer defendants' attorneys, reported that the decisions in their cases had affected neighboring communities (No. 27c). The responses about effect identified a mix of positive and negative results, with the negative predominating, for example, real estate steering, increased suburban smugness, and movement out of state, on one hand and stabilization of some desegregated neighborhoods on the other. Several respondents listed "other litigation" as an effect.

A much discussed aftermath of desegregation orders is resegregation.[29] The respondents to this survey strongly identified resegregation in the areas affected by the decisions in their cases (No. 28a). Almost three-fourths of all respondents, and well over four-fifths of plaintiffs' attorneys, saw this occurring. The primary causes were seen to be decreased resident white population and increased private school attendance by white students (No. 28b). A smaller, but still substantial, number saw the influx of minority population as a primary cause.

As to whether legal action had been taken or was being considered in their cases in response to resegregation, the respondents divided almost evenly (No. 28c). Almost half overall, and almost two-thirds of the plaintiffs' attorneys, indicated that legal action had been taken or was being considered. Slightly more than half overall, and more than two-thirds of the defendants' attorneys, reported that neither was true of their cases.

Where legal action had been taken, the results were quite evenly balanced (No. 28d). One-third of those responding indicated that a violation had been found, slightly less than one-third indicated that no violation had been found, and slightly more than one-third indicated that the matter was pending.

The major personal impact of the respondents' involvement in the particular school desegregation case was on the attorneys' own views and feelings (No. 29). That item drew responses from almost one-third more defendants' attorneys and almost one-half more plaintiffs' attorneys than any other. Overall, respondents ranked next a changed view of the judiciary and the judicial system. But this was identified substantially more often by defendants' than by plaintiffs' attorneys. In fact, the latter ranked the impact on relationships with other attorneys slightly higher and the impact on relationships with the community at the same level. Defendants' attorneys, too, had these next ranked in the same order. Significant but smaller numbers of respondents identified an impact on relationships with national and local organizations. Almost the same number of plaintiffs' attorneys, but only one defendants' attorney, listed an impact on the relationships with their employers.

The plaintiffs' attorney responses in this survey portion may provide some support for Bell's notion that frictions were created between local and national attorneys in school desegregation cases. After the impact on personal views and feelings (which could include views and feelings bearing on those frictions), five of the next six items plaintiffs' attorneys marked, in order, were relationships with other attorneys, with the community, with national organizations, with local organizations, and with their employers. Further information about the nature and extent of those feelings should be sought as part of a follow-up to this survey.

Overall, the respondents divided almost evenly on the question of whether or not their involvement in the particular school desegregation case had affected their willingness to take on similar cases, with only a slight margin for an affirmative answer (No. 31a). However, this balanced aggregate result masks sharply different responses by plaintiffs' and defendants' attorneys. More than two-thirds of the former, but only slightly more than two-fifths of the latter, responded affirmatively. Of those who indicated that the experience had affected their willingness to take on similar cases, a slight majority overall reported that it had made them *less* willing (No. 31b). Plaintiffs' and defendants' attorneys responded almost identically; the former split evenly and the latter favored "less willing" by a margin of one. Since plaintiffs prevailed in three-fourths of the cases, their attorneys' ambivalent response to taking on future cases suggests that winning isn't everything in school desegregation litigation, or at least that the costs of handling such cases give attorneys pause about future commitments.

The second interpretation may be supported by responses to the next question—how respondents would rate their involvement in the cases (No. 32). Slightly more than half reported that their involvement had been more rewarding than it had been in other cases; somewhat less than two-fifths indicated it had been more frustrating; and the balance stated that there had been no difference.[30] However, plaintiffs' attorneys had a substantially more favorable reaction than defendants' attorneys. Almost twice as many plaintiffs' attorneys responded "more rewarding" than "more frustrating." For defendants' attorneys, there was an almost even division.

EVALUATING SCHOOL DESEGREGATION LITIGATION

Given the considerable complexity, surprises, and even inexplicability in the attorneys' response patterns, their answers to the final evaluative questions about school desegregation litigation are especially significant.

According to more than two-thirds of those responding, their school desegregation cases involved an unusual degree of creativity (No. 30a). Plaintiffs' attorneys were especially of that view, with almost four-fifths responding affirmatively. The pre-trial, trial, and remedy-devising stages, in that order, were identified by plaintiffs' and defendants' attorneys as aspects of the case requiring special creativity (No. 30b). Monitoring compliance, on the other hand, was not identified by a substantial number of respondents as requiring special creativity.[31]

In applying hindsight to the results in their cases, the respondents produced some interesting and complex patterns. Approximately three-fourths of the respondents would not have done anything differently regarding their cases (No. 33a). Strikingly, although they prevailed much less often, defendants' attorneys registered a significantly higher degree of satisfaction with the way they handled their cases than did plaintiffs' attorneys, well over four-fifths compared with two-thirds. The small number of defendants' attorneys who would have done something differently identified pressing for prompter resolution, showing inconsistencies in plaintiffs' proposals, and placing more emphasis on the negative fiscal and educational impact of the plaintiffs' plan. The one-third of the plaintiffs' attorneys who would have done something differently identified a broader array: suing the governor and other state constitutional officers, consulting with the community about the remedy before the violation decision, clarifying the relationship with clients, being more aggressive to move the case more rapidly, bringing out more effectively the subtle racism involved, and monitoring more actively the remedy and its enforcement.

The things attorneys would have done differently fall into several broad categories: pleading or other technical legal matters (i.e., suing additional parties), litigation tactics (i.e., bringing out more of the subtle racism or of the negative fiscal and educational consequences, pressing for prompter resolution, more actively pursuing remedial monitoring and enforcement), and matters of personal style or client relations (i.e., being more aggressive, clarifying the relationships with clients, consulting with the community about the remedial plan before a violation decision).

In the final evaluative section of the questionnaire respondents were asked to assess the results in their cases and in school desegregation litigation generally, and to suggest alternative approaches to school segregation.

A slight majority of both the plaintiffs' and the defendants' attorneys expressed satisfaction with the results in their cases (No. 33b). The response of both groups is surprising. Since plaintiffs won about three-fourths of these cases, I would have expected substantially more satisfaction from plaintiffs' attorneys and substantially less satisfaction from defendants' attorneys.

The plaintiffs' attorney results may be explained by the fact that "victory" can be Pyrrhic. A court's order to desegregate does not guarantee that racially balanced, educationally effective, and harmonious schools will result. In fact, responses to this survey suggest that this is all too infrequently the result. Plaintiffs' attorneys who expressed dissatisfaction with the results in their cases explained their views by referring to the following: the remedy taking too long; too few white students to desegregate; legislative action aiding white flight and erosion of the city's tax base; and the education of black children still being second-rate.

The defendants' attorney results are harder to explain. Those who were dissatisfied with the results gave predictable reasons: more segregation than before; no real educational improvement; more money being spent on poor education; and the remedial plan's effectiveness had been compromised. However, there is no obvious explanation for the relatively high level of satisfaction defendants' attorneys expressed for the results in their cases, a substantial number of which were won by plaintiffs. Perhaps the failure of those victories to produce the results desired by plaintiffs meant that the objectives of some defendants were reached, or at least that the defendants' predictions of what would result from plaintiffs' victories were vindicated. Another, perhaps more likely, explanation is that plaintiffs' victories in some cases were not total and that attorneys representing suburban districts brought in by court order prevailed on behalf of their clients even though, in a broader sense, plaintiffs may have won those cases. Finally, it is possible that some defendants' attorneys personally subscribed to school desegregation and that plaintiffs' victories in some cases were not antithetical to those attorneys' views (or perhaps even to the personal views of their individual clients). Whatever the explanation for the respondents' evaluations of their own case results, their evaluations of the results in desegregation cases generally were quite different. Overall, almost three-fifths of the respondents expressed dissatisfaction (No. 33c), but on this question there was a sharp difference between plaintiffs' and defendants' attorneys. Plaintiffs' attorneys, surprisingly, gave school desegregation litigation generally a higher satisfaction rating than their own cases, more than three-fifths favorable. Defendants' attorneys, however, provided a strongly negative rating, three-fourths expressing dissatisfaction. They gave some interesting reasons for their dissatisfaction. Some referred to white flight and resegregation, the importance of neighborhood schools, the lack of success stories, and the abundance of disasters. Others, however, gave broader explanations. Several criticized the courts for providing remedies that exceeded the facts or for trying to impose a solution to a complex social problem. One's criticism was that the litigation reflected the political goals of the NAACP.

Some plaintiffs' attorneys shared the view that public schools in some cities under court order to desegregate had proven a disaster for the entire community. In the main, though, the sources of the plaintiffs' attorneys' dissatisfactions were different. They indicated that the remedy had taken too long, that the federal government recently had begun to play a negative role, that racism was subtle and ever-changing, and that the purposes of *Brown* had been sabotaged.

When the respondents were asked to rate litigation as a remedy for school segregation, much of the same negativity was expressed (No. 34). Of 41 responses, fewer than one-fifth ranked litigation as either the most effective or the only solution, and all of these were plaintiffs' attorneys. The remaining responses were divided almost evenly between ranking it as one of many solutions or as an inadequate solution, with several more respondents selecting the former than the latter. It was striking that plaintiffs' attorneys who picked those two responses were divided almost the same as defendants' attorneys. Two-fifths of the former and slightly less than half of the latter rated litigation as an inadequate solution. Of course, since almost half of the plaintiffs' attorneys gave litigation one of the two more affirmative ratings, overall less than one-fourth listed it as an inadequate solution. Still, a majority of plaintiffs' attorneys, and all of the defendants' attorneys, rated school desegregation litigation as, at best, one of many solutions.

Finally, the respondents were asked to suggest alternative approaches to school segregation. A wide array of suggestions was put forward, with relatively few mentioned more than once (No. 35). These included a community-based plan rather than litigation (four responses), magnet schools (four responses), statutes or regulations requiring integration (four responses), regionalization (two responses), mediation (two responses), acceptance of responsibility for the root causes by white and black communities (two responses), and state board of education leadership (two responses). Interestingly, of these seven proposed alternatives, each of the first five drew support from both plaintiffs' and defendants' attorneys. The sixth was endorsed by only plaintiffs' attorneys and the seventh by only defendants' attorneys.

Overall, the suggested alternatives fall into a number of categories:

1. Anti-desegregation (i.e., create a separate and equal system, accommodate community standards, don't try to desegregate a 20 percent–white district).
2. Break the segregation cycle at a different point (i.e., desegregate residential areas, attack the root cause of poverty).
3. Use other governmental branches or other forums (i.e., more determined political activity, state legislation or administrative regulations, mediation, community-based solutions representing the full range of interests).
4. Use specific techniques or remedies (i.e., magnet schools, regionalization, more aggressive state board of education action, meetings with school boards and other interested groups).

CONCLUSION

Out of this diverse array of survey findings, three important themes emerged. First, conflicts of goals and control between national civil rights organizations and their attorneys, on the one hand, and local attorneys and clients, on the other, which Derrick Bell described, were not directly and substantially supported by the survey data. Second, the nature of the attorney–client relationships, and lawyers' litigation-related activities, were quantitatively and qualitatively different between the plaintiffs' and defendants' attorneys surveyed. Third, despite the presence of many favorable factors, the overall response of the attorneys to the success of school desegregation litigation was at best mixed and at worst pessimistic.

Conflicts Among Attorneys

Plaintiffs' attorneys who responded to the survey were primarily local attorneys. They reported extensive involvement in their cases of other attorneys representing the same clients or others aligned with their clients. Presumably, this included "national attorneys"—those employed by or working with the national civil rights organizations. The effectiveness of outside attorneys and experts was rated very favorably by two-thirds of the plaintiffs' attorneys. Moreover, the primary plaintiffs' litigation goals and the primary focus of the remedial plans reported by plaintiffs' attorneys were aspects of physical integration. According to Professor Bell, these were the national organizations' top litigation priorities.

These survey results suggest that compatibility rather than conflict marked national–local attorney relationships. The only findings that may raise questions about this harmonious picture arise from plaintiffs' attorneys' responses to a question about the personal impact of their involvement in school desegregation litigation. Their relationship with other attorneys was the second most frequently identified effect, and relationships with national organizations also drew a significant response.

Yet, in subsequent questions, when they had the opportunity to be more specific about sources of dissatisfaction with the results in their cases or with school desegregation litigation generally, none of the plaintiffs' attorneys identified difficulties directly or indirectly traceable to national organizations or their attorneys.

Attorney–Client Relationships and Lawyer Activities

Plaintiffs' attorneys primarily represented parents and students legally challenging educational programs; defendants' attorneys primarily represented the school districts and public officials whose policies and practices were being challenged. From these basic distinctions flow several important characteristics of the attorney–client relationships I surveyed.

Plaintiffs' attorneys became involved most frequently through contacts with other lawyers or a legal organization. They tended not to have pre-existing relationships with their clients. Defendants' attorneys, on the other hand, overwhelmingly became involved through contacts by the clients, and in many cases had pre-existing attorney–client relationships.

Plaintiffs' attorneys, far more frequently than defendants' attorneys, became involved in the case prior to the filing of a complaint, or even prior to a decision to litigate.

For those reasons, and because the plaintiffs often were a large, diverse group of people, probably with a loose organizational and communications structure, plaintiffs' attorneys tended to play a much more active and influential role in decision-making than did their legal counterparts. This tendency was reflected in a number of survey findings. In reporting who was primarily responsible for establishing litigation goals, plaintiffs' attorneys listed interested organizations and attorneys almost as frequently as the parties. In fact, when the first two categories were aggregated with combinations of organizations and attorneys, they accounted for almost twice as many responses as the parties.[32]

A similar result obtained when plaintiffs' attorneys were asked to indicate how heavily their clients had been involved in developing the remedy. Attorneys were more frequently mentioned than parties as reviewers of the proposed remedial plan, and only about one-fourth of the plaintiffs' attorneys ranked their clients as having had substantial involvement in developing the remedy.

Plaintiffs' attorneys ranked their own involvement in developing the remedy as much greater. More than twice as many of them indicated that they, as opposed to their clients, had had the greatest involvement. Moreover, discussing the plan with their clients, although quite frequently listed as a form of involvement, was one of five frequently mentioned forms.

Finally, plaintiffs' attorneys and their clients apparently had substantially greater interaction than did defendants' attorneys and their clients with a broader constituency or community. Nonetheless, plaintiffs' attorneys rated input from those broader sources as having only moderate to minimal influence in the shaping of the remedial plan.

Evaluating the Success of School Desegregation Litigation

The attorneys who responded to this survey reported the presence of many factors important to the success of school desegregation litigation. Plaintiffs won about three-fourths of the time, according to the respondents. Compliance with the court's remedial plan was fully achieved more than half the time, and partially achieved in most of the other cases. According to plaintiffs' attorneys, compliance by the parties and cooperation of other public officials and the community far outweighed instances of defiance. Although a significant number of plaintiffs' attorneys indicated that defendants' attorneys had assisted in resistance to the court's order or had obstructed and delayed implementation, a greater number considered defendants' attorneys merely to have interpreted the order to their clients or even to have encouraged compliance.

In the most striking findings of the survey, both plaintiffs' and defendants' attorneys overwhelmingly characterized the judges as activist and committed to desegregation. Many more detailed survey results fleshed out and supported these characterizations. The judge was centrally involved in devising the remedial plan. In almost every case, compliance with the remedial plan was monitored, most frequently by the court retaining jurisdiction and requiring reports. In the substantial number of cases where proceedings were instituted to enforce the remedial order, more than three-fourths of the time the court took further action, including finding noncompliance and contempt. More than two-thirds of the efforts to have the court terminate jurisdiction were unsuccessful.

With all these favorable factors, however, a very somber tone surfaced in the final stage of the survey. Plaintiffs' and defendants' attorneys agreed that the decisions in their cases had substantially affected community affairs directly and in neighboring communities. Although the consequences described were mixed, they tended toward the negative. For example, the single most frequently identified effect was "transfer to private school." "Flight from neighborhoods" was also prominently identified. These consequences, plus an influx of additional minority residents, were seen as the primary causes of resegregation in the areas affected by the survey respondents' cases. Overwhelmingly, the respondents indicated that resegregation had begun, with plaintiffs' attorneys even more adamant about it than defendants' attorneys. Less than half the respondents indicated that legal action had been taken or was being considered to challenge resegregation.

On a more personal level, the attorneys reflected substantial disenchantment with school desegregation litigation. About half overall, but more than two-thirds of plaintiffs' attorneys responding, indicated that involvement in such a case had affected their willingness to take on similar cases in the future. Of those, slightly more than half (or more than one-fourth of the total) indicated that they were *less* willing to become involved in future school desegregation cases.

The group also was split almost in half over whether involvement in such a case was more rewarding, more frustrating, or no different from other cases.

When asked even more pointedly about their satisfaction with their particular school desegregation cases or with such litigation in general, the attorney respondents were still quite closely divided. A scant majority of both plaintiffs' and defendants' attorneys expressed satisfaction with the results in their cases. When asked about desegregation litigation generally, plaintiffs' attorneys were slightly more affirmative and defendants' attorneys dramatically more negative. In evaluating these responses, one has to keep in mind that (1) plaintiffs won about three-fourths of the cases covered by the survey results, and (2) both plaintiffs' and defendants' attorneys indicated by lopsided margins that in retrospect they were satisfied with how they had handled their cases.

Finally, the survey indicates that the attorneys ranked litigation fairly low as a remedy for school segregation and could not agree about promising alternative approaches. Overall, most respondents ranked litigation as either one of many solutions or an inadequate solution. One-third of the plaintiffs' attorneys did list it as the most effective solution and two listed it as the only solution; however, none of the defendants' attorneys listed it in either of those categories.

The suggested alternatives covered a considerable spectrum, but many tended to be hortatory (i.e., crucial for children to know one another, white and black communities must accept responsibility for root causes, more determined political activity, more openness to view educational ideas, better informed judges, state board of education leadership), or mechanistic (i.e., magnet schools, student reassignment, focus on affirmative action in jobs), or utopian (i.e., natural residential integration, more funding to provide equivalent programs and facilities), or buck-passing (i.e., community-based plan; mediation; school board meetings, statutes or regulations requiring integrated schools; state board of education leadership).

Institutional reform litigation, including school desegregation cases, has been justified by its capacity to alter public agendas or create leverage for change where none otherwise would exist. The results of this survey raise questions about whether attorneys who have litigated a significant number of those cases still truly believe that school desegregation litigation or perhaps even alternative forms of school improvement litigation have that potential. That dilemma, if it constitutes a fair interpretation of the survey results, would far eclipse Derrick Bell's earlier dilemma. It would require an even more fundamental rethinking of the premises upon which we have been pursuing the vindication of important civil and human rights.[33]

APPENDIX. School Desegregation Questionnaire for Attorneys

1. Please identify the school desegregation case(s)* in which you were or are involved as an attorney.

2a. Whom did you represent?

____ Original plaintiff
____ Intervening plaintiff
____ Original defendant
____ Intervening defendant
____ *Amicus curiae*
____ Other (please specify): _____

2b. Which of the following were your clients?

____ Students
____ Parents
____ Citizens/taxpayers
____ Public officials
____ School districts
____ Interested organizations (please
     specify): _____
____ Other (please specify): _____

*If you have been involved in more than one case, please underline the case you will be referring to in this questionnaire. I would appreciate responses based on all the desegregation cases in which you have been substantially involved.

3. How did you become involved in school desegregation litigation?

___ Contacted by party or *amicus*
___ Contacted by interested community or other organization
___ Contacted by other lawyers or a legal organization
___ Employed by a party or an interested organization
___ Member of an interested organization
___ Other (please specify): _____

4. Prior to your involvement in this case, did you have experience in any of the following:

___ School desegregation cases
___ Other education law cases
___ Other civil rights cases
___ Zoning or land use cases
___ Other public law or institutional reform cases
   (please specify): _____

5a. During your involvement in this case, in what setting were you practicing law?

___ Private law firm (please specify number of attorneys): ___
___ Public interest law (please specify what
   project): _____
___ Government agency
___ Legal services project
___ Other (please specify): _____

5b. In what city and state did you principally practice?

5c. How would you characterize your practice?

___ General practice
___ Litigation practice
___ Civil rights practice
___ Government agency practice
___ Other (please specify): _____

6a. At what stage did you become involved in this case?

___ Prior to decision to litigate
___ After decision to litigate but prior to filing of complaint
___ After filing of complaint (please
   specify when): _____

6b. At what stages of the case were you involved?

___ Pre-litigation
___ Pre-trial
___ Trial
___ Remedy
___ Implementation
___ Appeal(s)

7a. Were other attorneys involved in the case representing your client, or other clients aligned with yours?

___ Yes
___ No

7b. Did your legal team include:

Desegregation experts   ___ Yes   ___ No
Other experts   ___ Yes   ___ No

7c. If "Yes" to either 7a or 7b, please rate the extent and effectiveness of cooperation (circle the appropriate number, with "1" representing the highest and "5" the lowest).

Extent   1 2 3 4 5
Effectiveness   1 2 3 4 5

8a. What were the plaintiffs' goals in the litigation?

___ Integration among several school districts
___ Integration of school buildings within a single district
___ Integration of classes or programs
___ Increased educational expenditures
___ Improved educational facilities
___ Improved or expanded educational programs
___ Integration of staff
___ Minority hiring or promotion
___ Other (please specify): _____

8b. What were the defendants' goals in the litigation?

___ Maintain local control
___ Maintain neighborhood schools
___ Preserve educational or employment status quo
___ Other (please specify): _____

9a. Who was primarily responsible for determining the goals?

___ Party or parties
___ Attorney(s)
___ Interested organization(s)
___ Combination of the above (please
    specify which): _____
___ Other (please specify): _____

9b. To what extent had plaintiffs or their community considered the de-sired remedy before the suit was filed or before a decision regarding violation? (Circle the appropriate numbers with "1" representing the greatest and "5" the least.)

Before filing   1 2 3 4 5
Before violation decision 1 2 3 4 5

10. What is the present status of the case?

___ Final judgment on violation
___ Judgment upholding remedial plan
___ Judgment modifying remedial plan
___ Retained jurisdiction
___ Terminated jurisdiction
___ Case pending

11a. If a judgment has been entered, does it favor plaintiffs?

___ Yes
___ No

11b. If "Yes," was there a separate proceeding on remedy?

___ Yes
___ No

11c. Were you involved in any such proceeding?

___ Yes
___ No

12a. How was the remedial plan devised?

___ By the judge alone
___ By the judge with court-appointed master or expert
___ By a court-appointed master or expert alone

___ By the judge or master with the parties
___ By defendants alone
___ By plaintiffs alone
___ By the judge or master with the attorneys
___ By the judge or master with a task force
___ Other (please specify): _____

12b. Who was involved in reviewing the remedial plan before adoption?

___ Parties
___ Attorneys
___ Experts
___ Court-appointed master
___ Task force
___ Community
___ Other (please specify): _____

12c. Was any part of the remedy negotiated out of court?

___ Yes
___ No

12d. If "Yes," please describe the part(s) briefly.

13. What elements did the remedy include?

___ Pupil busing
___ Changed attendance zones
___ Magnet schools
___ Creation of new or closing of old schools
___ Reorganization of school grade levels
___ Changed selection for special programs
___ Interdistrict or regional arrangements
___ Teacher reassignment
___ Affirmative action in hiring or promotion
___ Human relations training
___ Increased funding
___ Improved facilities
___ Improved or expanded educational programs
___ Remedial education
___ Student discipline orders
___ Improved or expanded community involvement
___ Parental/business/university involvement
___ Other (please specify): _____

14. Please indicate the degree of your personal involvement in the development of the remedy (circle the appropriate number, with "1" representing great involvement and "5" minimal).

    1 2 3 4 5

15. What forms did your involvement take?

    ____ Developed plan alone
    ____ Developed plan with others (please
         specify): _____
    ____ Reviewed plan developed by others
    ____ Consulted with experts about plan
    ____ Negotiated with other attorneys about plan (please
         specify): _____
    ____ Discussed plan with judge or court-appointed master or expert
    ____ Discussed plan with client(s)
    ____ Discussed plan with constituency or community client
         represented
    ____ Other (please specify): _____

16. Please indicate the degree of your client's involvement in the development of the remedy (circle the appropriate number, with "1" representing great involvement and "5" minimal).

    1 2 3 4 5

17. What forms did your client's involvement take?

    ____ Developed plan alone
    ____ Developed plan with others (please
         specify): _____
    ____ Reviewed plan developed by others
    ____ Consulted with experts about plan
    ____ Negotiated with other parties about plan
    ____ Discussed plan with judge or court-appointed master or expert
    ____ Discussed plan with you or other attorneys
    ____ Discussed plan with constituency or community of interest
    ____ Other (please specify): _____

18. If you or your client discussed the remedial plan with a broader constituency or community of interest, what forums did you use?

    ____ Regular large-group meetings
    ____ Regular small-group meetings

____ Occasional or one-time large-group meetings
____ Occasional or one-time small-group meetings
____ Individual contacts
____ Other (please specify): _____

19. Please indicate the degree to which constituent or community input was influential in the shaping of the remedial plan (circle the appropriate number, with "1" representing great influence and "5" minimal).

    1 2 3 4 5

20. What accounted for the level of constituent or community influence?

____ Degree of consensus
____ Degree of participation
____ Degree of knowledge
____ Degree of political involvement
____ Degree of sophistication
____ Other (please specify): _____

21. How did the judge view his/her role in your case? (Circle the appropriate number.)

                    Active   1 2 3 4 5   Passive
    Committed to desegregation   1 2 3 4 5   Neutral or negative

22a. Has compliance with the remedial plan been monitored?

____ Yes
____ No

22b. If "Yes," how has monitoring been done?

____ Court retained jurisdiction
____ Court required reports
____ Court appointed parent/community committee
____ Remedial discovery
____ Other (please specify): _____

22c. If "Yes," what has your involvement been?

____ Prepared reports about compliance
____ Reviewed such reports
____ Appeared in court proceedings

____ Conducted remedial discovery
____ Other (please specify): _____

23a. To what extent was compliance with the court's remedial plan achieved?

____ Fully
____ Partially
____ Not at all

23b. Were procedures instituted to enforce the remedial order?

____ Yes
____ No

23c. If "Yes," what was the result?

____ Adequate compliance found
____ More specific orders
____ Noncompliance found
____ Contempt found

23d. How did defendants' attorneys see their role regarding the remedial plan?

____ Interpret order to clients
____ Encourage compliance
____ Assist resistance
____ Other (please specify): _____

24a. Has the plan been modified?

____ Yes
____ No

24b. If "Yes," what was the primary cause?

____ Lack of cooperation in implementation
____ Unforeseen developments
____ Cost factors
____ Complexity
____ Appellate review
____ Developments in the law
____ Demographic changes
____ Ineffectiveness of original plan
____ Other (please specify): _____

25. What were the responses to the remedial and other orders in your case?

___ Compliance by the parties
___ Cooperation of other public officials
___ Cooperation of the community
___ Support from the attorneys
___ Instances of open defiance (please specify): _____

26a. Have there been attempts to have the court terminate jurisdiction?

___ Yes
___ No

26b. If "Yes," what was the result?

___ Jurisdiction terminated
___ Jurisdiction retained
___ Other (please specify): _____

27a. Has the decision in your case substantially affected community affairs?

___ Yes
___ No

27b. If "Yes," in which areas have changes occurred?

___ Educational quality
___ Transfer to private schools
___ Flight from neighborhoods
___ Taxing patterns
___ Economic stability
___ Housing
___ Race relations
___ Other (please specify): _____

27c. If "Yes," has the decision affected neighboring communities?

___ Yes (please specify): _____
___ No

28a. Has resegregation begun in the area affected by your decision?

___ Yes
___ No

28b. If "Yes," what are the primary causes?

____ Influx of minority population into the community
____ Decrease of white population in the community
____ Increased private school attendance by white students
____ In-school practices that tend to separate students by race
____ Other (please specify): _____

28c. If "Yes," has legal action been taken, or is it being considered, to address the problem?

____ Legal action taken
____ Legal action being considered
____ Neither

28d. If legal action has been taken, what has been the result?

____ Violation found
____ No violation found
____ Pending

29. In which areas did your involvement in this case have an impact on you?

____ Your personal views and feelings
____ Your relationship with the community
____ Your relationship with local organizations
____ Your relationship with national organizations
____ Your relationship with other attorneys
____ Your view of the judiciary and the judicial system
____ Your relationship with your employer
____ Your future career plans
____ Other (please specify): _____

30a. Did this case involve an unusual degree of legal creativity?

____ Yes
____ No

30b. If "Yes," which aspect of the case required special creativity?

____ Pretrial
____ Trial
____ Devising the remedy
____ Monitoring compliance
____ Other (please specify): _____

31a. Did your involvement in this case affect your willingness to take on similar cases in the future?

___ Yes
___ No

31b. If "Yes," what was the effect?

___ More willing
___ Less willing

32. On balance, how would you rate your involvement in this case?

___ More rewarding than other cases
___ More frustrating
___ No different

33. In retrospect, a. Would you have done anything differently regarding this case?

___ Yes (please specify): _____
___ No

33b. Are you satisfied with the results?

___ Yes
___ No (please specify): _____

33c. Are you satisfied with the results of desegregation cases in general?

___ Yes
___ No (please specify): _____

34. How would you rate litigation to remedy school segregation?

___ The most effective solution
___ The only solution
___ One of many solutions
___ An inadequate solution

35. Can you suggest alternative approaches to school segregation?

NOTES

1. D. Bell, *Serving Two Masters: Integration Ideals and Client Interests in School Desegregation Litigation*, 85 YALE L.J. 470 (1976). This article was prepared at the

request of the Institute of Judicial Administration Project on Judicial Administration of School Desegregation Litigation and also appeared in LIMITS OF JUSTICE: THE COURTS' ROLE IN SCHOOL DESEGREGATION (H. Kalodner and J. Fishman eds. 1978). In fairness, Professor Bell's article was not the first to raise many of the troublesome issues lawyers confront in representing plaintiffs or defendants in school desegregation cases. See, e.g., Edmonds, *Advocating Inequity: A Critique of the Civil Rights Attorney in Class Action Desegregation Suits*, 3 BLACK L.J. 176 (1974); Greenberg, *Litigation for Social Change: Methods, Limits and Role in Democracy*, 29 Record of N.Y.C. B.A. 320, 331 (1974); Clark, *The Lawyer in the Civil Rights Movement—Catalytic Agent or Counter-Revolutionary?* 19 KAN. L. REV. 459 (1971); Cahn and Cahn, *Power to the People or the Profession?—The Public Interest in Public Interest Law*, 79 YALE L. J. 1005 (1970); Frankel, *The Alabama Lawyer, 1954–1964: Has the Official Organ Atrophied?* 64 COLUM. L. REV. 1243 (1964). Nonetheless, Professor Bell's article provoked a firestorm of controversy and became a focal point of the debate. See LIMITS OF JUSTICE 612–20 for excerpts from some of the letters highly critical of Professor Bell's article and from his response to Nathaniel R. Jones, then National Association for the Advancement of Colored People (NAACP) General Counsel and now a federal judge.

2. From 1960 to 1966 Professor Bell was a staff attorney specializing in school desegregation cases with LDF. From 1966 to 1968, he was Deputy Director, Office for Civil Rights, U.S. Department of Health, Education and Welfare. The LDF, originally a part of the NAACP, became a separate entity in 1939. A brief account of the split between the two organizations appears in Rabin, *Lawyers for Social Change: Perspectives on Public Interest Law*, 28 STAN. L. REV. 207, 214–18 (1976).

3. The NAACP was formed in 1909 in response to the nation's increasingly bitter interracial conflict. Although the organization's early work was mostly educational in nature, it later became increasingly involved in political lobbying and litigation. For a history of the NAACP and its involvement in school desegregation cases, see M. FINCH, THE NAACP: ITS FIGHT FOR JUSTICE (1981); L. HUGHES, FIGHT FOR FREEDOM: THE STORY OF THE NAACP (1962); C. KELLOGG, NAACP: A HISTORY OF THE NATIONAL ASSOCIATION FOR THE ADVANCEMENT OF COLORED PEOPLE (1967).

4. Rule 1.3 of the American Bar Association Model Rules of Professional Conduct (1983) provides: "A lawyer shall act with reasonable diligence and promptness in representing a client." The Comment to Rule 1.3 states: "A lawyer should act with commitment and dedication to the interests of the client and with zeal in advocacy upon the client's behalf." This superseded Canon 7 of the American Bar Association Model Code of Professional Responsibility (1969), which stated, "A lawyer should represent a client zealously within the bounds of the law."

5. According to Rule 1.2(a) of the American Bar Association Model Rules of Professional Conduct (1983), a "lawyer shall abide by a client's decisions concerning the objectives of representation . . . and shall consult with the client as to the means by which they are to be pursued. A lawyer shall abide by a client's decision whether to accept an offer of settlement of a matter." The Comment to Rule 1.2 states that the "client has ultimate authority to determine the purposes to be served by legal representation." EC 7–8 of the American Bar Association Model Code of Professional Responsibility (1969) had stated that "the decision whether to forego

legally available objectives or methods because of nonlegal factors is ultimately for the client."

6. NAACP v. Button, 371 U.S. 415 (1963), was a legal landmark establishing that the NAACP's uses of litigation and related activities were "modes of expression and association protected by the First and Fourteenth Amendments." 371 U.S. at 428–29. According to Professor Bell, however, "although the issue was raised by the state, the majority did not decide whether Virginia could constitutionally prohibit the NAACP from controlling the course of the litigation sponsored, perhaps because the NAACP consistently denied that it exercised such control [citations omitted]." LIMITS OF JUSTICE at 594. Justice White's part-concurring and part-dissenting opinion, and especially Justice Harlan's dissenting opinion, raised serious questions about whether NAACP policy required substantial departures from ethical professional conduct. 371 U.S. at 447–70.

A much more recent state supreme court decision dealt in detail with those serious ethical questions. In In re Education Law Center, Inc., 86 N.J. 124, 133, 429 A.2d 1051 (1981), the New Jersey Supreme Court stated, "The attorney–client relationship must rest upon the principle that 'an attorney owes complete and undivided loyalty to the client who has retained him.' " 86 N.J. at 133 (quoting In re Dolan, 76 N.J. 1, 9, 384 A.2d 1076 (1978)). It also stated that "the role of the public interest law firm as regards the relationship between individual staff attorneys and clients must be limited to that of 'a conduit or intermediary to bring the attorney and client together' which 'does not purport to control or exploit the manner in which the attorney represents his . . . client.' " 86 N.J. at 137–38 (quoting Touchy v. Houston Legal Foundation, 432 S.W.2d 690, 695 [Tex. 1968]; Azzarello v. Legal Aid Society of Cleveland, 117 Ohio App. 471, 185 N.E.2d 566, 570 [1962]). Several Ethical Considerations under Canon 5 of the superseded Code of Professional Responsibility also had sought to deal with the "two masters" dilemma. *See especially* EC 5–21, EC 5–22, EC 5–23, and EC 5–24.

7. For a discussion of litigation designed to reform school systems and the problems that arise in implementation of remedial decrees resulting from such cases, *see, e.g.,* L. GRAGLIA, DISASTER BY DECREE: THE SUPREME COURT DECISIONS ON RACE AND THE SCHOOLS (1976); D. KIRP, JUST SCHOOLS: THE IDEA OF RACIAL EQUALITY IN AMERICAN EDUCATION (1982); Berger, *Away from the Court House and into the Field: The Odyssey of a Special Master,* 78 COLUM. L. REV. 707 (1978).

Problems in implementation are not unique to school desegregation cases. For analyses of difficulties common to institutional reform litigation, *see, e.g.,* E. BARDACH, THE IMPLEMENTATION GAME: WHAT HAPPENS AFTER A BILL BECOMES A LAW (1977); Chayes, *The Role of the Judge in Public Law Litigation,* 89 HARV. L. REV. 1281 (1976); Diver, *The Judge as Political Powerbroker: Superintending Structural Change in Public Institutions,* 65 VA. L. REV. 43 (1979); Special Project, *The Remedial Process in Institutional Reform Litigation,* 78 COLUM. L. REV. 783 (1978); Note, *Implementation Problems in Institutional Reform Litigation,* 91 HARV. L. REV. 428 (1977).

8. Friction between local and national attorneys was a limited subtext of Professor Bell's article, but it has been more heatedly, if often informally, debated since then.

9. 347 U.S. 483 (1954).

10. This literature has dealt with the role of judges themselves in school desegregation cases (*see, e.g.*, B. SCHWARTZ, SWANN'S WAY: THE SCHOOL BUSING CASE AND THE SUPREME COURT [1986]; J. WILKINSON, FROM BROWN TO BAKKE— THE SUPREME COURT AND SCHOOL INTEGRATION: 1954–1978 [1979]; Chayes, *supra* note 7; Combs, *The Federal Judiciary and Northern School Desegregation, Judicial Management in Perspective*, 13 J.L. EDUC. 345 [1984]), and with their use of appointees, such as special masters (*see, e.g.*, Berger, *supra* note 7; Kirp and Babcock, *Judge and Company: Court Appointed Masters, School Desegregation and Institutional Reform*, 32 ALA. L. REV. 313 [Winter 1981]). It also has focused poignantly on the effects such litigation had upon the judges' personal lives (*see, e.g.*, J. PELTASON, FIFTY-EIGHT LONELY MEN: SOUTHERN FEDERAL JUDGES AND SCHOOL DESEGREGATION [1961]; T. YARBROUGH, JUDGE FRANK JOHNSON AND HUMAN RIGHTS IN ALABAMA [1981]). In many cases, the judges' involvement in these cases made them outcasts in their own communities.

11. *See, e.g.*, R. KLUGER, SIMPLE JUSTICE: THE HISTORY OF "BROWN V. BOARD OF EDUCATION" AND BLACK AMERICA'S STRUGGLE FOR EQUALITY, Vol. I, II (1975); J. LUKAS, COMMON GROUND (1985); Rabin, *Lawyers for Social Change: Perspectives on Public Interest Law*, 28 STAN. L. REV. 207 (1976).

12. For a recent example, *see* P. DIMOND, BEYOND BUSING: INSIDE THE CHALLENGE TO URBAN SEGREGATION (1985).

13. *See* R. KLUGER, *supra* note 11; J. LUKAS, *supra* note 11; B. SCHWARTZ, *supra* note 10; Lottman, *Enforcement of Judicial Decrees: Now Comes the Hard Part*, 1 MENTAL DISABILITY L. REP. 69 (1976); Olney, *A Government Lawyer Looks at Little Rock*, 45 CALIF. L. REV. 516 (1957).

14. One aspect of the lawyers' role has been considered quite frequently: the special problems associated with class representation. For a relatively recent example of that literature, *see* Rhode, *Class Conflicts in Class Actions*, 34 STAN. L. REV. 1183 (1982). That literature generally has not been based on a systematic survey of lawyer experiences. Professor Rhode did conduct seventy interviews with attorneys, judges, and social scientists involved in institutional reform litigation or related research, but her analysis does not, in her words, "purport to reflect an exhaustive survey of . . . practitioners in the field." *Id.* at 1185 note 8. Ironically, Rhode's lawyer input may have come primarily from LDF and other civil rights organization attorneys, the mirror image of my attorney input.

15. For a copy of the questionnaire, see the Appendix.

16. Based on informal conversations with several social scientists experienced in survey research, an overall response rate of almost 18 percent is considered acceptable or better. This is especially so since this survey involved: (a) a mailed questionnaire of considerable length and complexity; (b) no followup efforts; (c) a set of potential respondents associated with school desegregation cases covering a substantial time period, some as remote as the 1950s; and (d) substantial mobility in the legal profession. For information about response rates and other aspects of research based on mailed questionnaires, *see* K. BAILEY, METHODS OF SOCIAL RESEARCH 155–90 (1982).

17. All parenthetical numeric references are to the questionnaire's specific items.

18. Even at the time of Professor Bell's article, some strongly questioned whether

the desegregation–educational quality dichotomy he stressed was a real dichotomy. *See especially,* LIMITS OF JUSTICE at 615–16 (excerpts from letter by Nathaniel R. Jones, then NAACP General Counsel, dated December 8, 1976). For example, Jones asserted that "courts have included educational adjuncts and components to desegregation plans when necessary to repair the effects of past discrimination, assure a successful desegregation effort and minimize the possibility of resegregation." LIMITS OF JUSTICE at 615.

    19. *See supra* note 14.

    20. Milliken v. Bradley, 433 U.S. 267 (1977) (*Milliken II*). In Milliken v. Bradley, 418 U.S. 717 (1974) (*Milliken I*), the Supreme Court had determined that an inter-district remedy for *de jure* segregation in the Detroit school system exceeded the constitutional violation. The case was remanded to the district court, which ordered the submission of desegregation plans limited to the Detroit school system. In *Milliken II*, the Supreme Court affirmed the district court's subsequent decree, holding that, as part of a desegregation decree, a district court may order compensatory or remedial educational programs for students who have been subjected to past acts of *de jure* segregation. These programs have taken the form of remedial reading and communication skills programs, in-service teacher training, testing and counseling, among other programs. In the common parlance of the civil rights community, they are the "*Milliken II* remedies."

    21. *See* discussion at 396 *supra.*

    22. *See* discussion at 398–99 *supra.*

    23. *See* discussion at 396 *supra.*

    24. One defendants' attorney responded enigmatically that defendants' attorneys were "helpless observers."

    25. The attorney must balance his or her obligation to advocate zealously on behalf of the client (discussed at note 4 *supra* and accompanying text) with his or her role as an officer of the court. *See, e.g.,* Van Berkel v. Fox Farm & Road Machinery, 581 F. Supp. 1248, 1251 (D. Minn. 1984). That issue has been hotly contested at many points. For an especially interesting example, surrounding the Kutak Commission and attorneys' obligation to divulge client confidences, *see, e.g.,* Freedman, *Lawyer–Client Confidences: The Model Rules' Radical Assault on Tradition,* 68 ABA J. 428 (April 1982); Porter, *Lying Clients and Legal Ethics: The Attorney's Unsolved Dilemma,* 16 CREIGHTON L. REV. 487 (1983).

    26. *See* discussion at 407 *infra.*

    27. Professor Bell's article, first published in 1976, suggested variously that physical desegregation of the public schools might be unpopular with many black citizens, insufficient to improve educational quality, or perhaps even impossible to achieve. Since the Bell article, many important, revealing, and sometimes conflicting developments have occurred. The federal judiciary has been pressed to be less activist in its approach to institutional reform and to promoting racial equality, among other matters. This pressure has been partly political and partly the result of scholarly and pragmatic arguments that the courts are exceeding their areas of legitimacy and competency. Perhaps this has led to some signs of retrenchment in the federal courts (*see, e.g.,* Riddick v. School Board of the City of Norfolk, 784 F.2d 521 [4th Cir. 1986]). Conversely, some federal courts have ordered extremely broad and politically

controversial remedies (*see, e.g.*, United States v. Yonkers Board of Education, 635 F. Supp. 1538 [S.D. N.Y. 1986]). In an area analogous to school desegregation—school finance reform—this has led the plaintiffs to litigate almost exclusively in the state courts. That litigation has been quite favorable from the plaintiffs' point of view, at least as measured by judicial victories. But there, too, serious questions have been raised about whether the desired benefits for children have materialized. Some have questioned whether state courts are any more effective than federal courts at actually effecting institutional reform, or educational improvements, for poor and minority children. Since 1976, another litigation strategy has been pursued primarily in the state courts. In its initial guise, it was labeled "educational malpractice" litigation. It sought to create what Nathaniel Jones stated in 1976 did not exist—a "cause of action for educational quality per se." *See supra* note 18. Thus far, educational malpractice litigation has proven unsuccessful, even in some extremely compelling factual circumstances. *See, e.g.*, Hoffman v. Board of Education, 49 N.Y.2d 121, 400 N.E.2d 317, 424 N.Y.S.2d 376 (1979). Part of the reason is that the courts viewed education as an art rather than a science, and the educational achievement of students as influenced by a huge array of variables. An effort has been made to eliminate that objection. Drawing on the "effective schools" ideas of Ron Edmonds and others, and the claimed educational success of those ideas, a legal services attorney has sought to define another form of educational quality cause of action. For an elaborate articulation of the theory, a scathing criticism of it, and a response to the criticism, *see* Ratner, *A New Legal Duty for Urban Public Schools: Effective Education in Basic Skills*, 63 Tex. L. Rev. 777 (1985); Elson, *Suing to Make Schools Effective, or How to Make a Bad Situation Worse: A Response to Ratner*, 63 Tex. L. Rev. 889 (1985); Ratner, *Rebuttal of Elson*, 63 Tex. L. Rev. 919 (1985). With all this continuing attention to legal causes of action and the courts, several other possibilities must not be ignored. If effective schools methodology *does* work, school systems don't have to wait for courts to order them into use. And where outside impetus or resources are necessary, legislatures, state boards of education, and state education officials can provide at least some of the answers.

But, of course, this may bring us full circle. If those directly responsible, whether for educational quality or desegregation, had been performing effectively, the courts' assistance presumably would never have been sought. If the failure ultimately lies in our inability or unwillingness to cope with these problems, then the choice of a governmental or bureaucratic agency to assume responsibility may be irrelevant.

28. This assumption derives some support from the six "other" responses to this survey question, all from plaintiffs' attorneys. They indicate such positive reactions as an increased number of white students, somewhat better race relations, and increased minority representation in the work force, and in school district and municipal governance.

29. For discussions of resegregation, *see* School Desegregation: Past, Present and Future (W. Stephan and J. Feagin eds. 1980); Noblit and Collins, *School Flight and Social Policy: Desegregation and Resegregation in Memphis City Schools* 10 Urb. Rev. 203–12 (1978); M. Giles, D. Gatlin and E. Cataldo, Determinants of Resegregation: Compliance/Rejection Behavior and Policy Alternatives (Report to the National Science Foundation, 1976); C. Rossell, The Effectiveness

OF SCHOOL DESEGREGATION PLANS AS DETERMINED BY COMMUNITY RESPONSE (Report to the U.S. Commission on Civil Rights, 1985).

30. Interestingly, a significant number of respondents indicated that their involvement in school desegregation litigation had been both more rewarding and more frustrating than their involvement in other cases.

31. In one of the more interesting and thoughtful cover letters received, the writer was sharply critical of attorneys in school desegregation litigation for their failure to understand and deal effectively with the remedial and compliance stages.

32. By contrast, defendants' attorneys reported three-fifths of the time that the parties alone or with their attorneys were the primary goal-setters.

33. As a long-standing advocate of, and frequent participant in, institutional reform litigation, especially involving educational rights of poor and minority children, this concluding quandary provokes great personal concern. Surely we have won many important and hard-fought battles. Some would say that, as a consequence, we are much closer to winning the war. But others dispute that, and they despair. Many of us are in the middle (a perhaps unaccustomed position). We have come to recognize the limits of what we have been able to accomplish thus far on behalf of poor and minority children. We hope that this is not a function of the "limits of justice." Instead, we continue to search and work for better ways to convert our victorious legal battles into substantial and enduring gains for our "clients." We continue to search and work for newer and perhaps even better litigation theories and strategies. We continue to search and work for the right balance between ongoing litigation and effective political, grassroots, and other actions. As we have passed beyond three decades since *Brown v. Board of Education*, and two decades since the Civil Rights Act of 1964, we must prepare for the decades to come. The serious debate has begun. In November 1984, my own law school convened a two-day program celebrating the 20th anniversary of the Civil Rights Act and addressing the question "What needs to be done to achieve the civil rights goals of the 1980s?" For the complete conference papers and proceedings, see 37 RUTGERS L. REV. 667–1148 (1985). In October 1985, LDF sponsored an important education conference. In May 1986, the Carnegie Corporation held a conference entitled "The Role of Litigation in Meeting the Needs of Minority Children." We must broaden and deepen this debate. We must learn more about what we have done thus far and what we have yet to do by better research. Perhaps most important, we must be certain that we are intimately connected with those we seek to serve and ever mindful of our obligation actually to serve them.

CONTRIBUTORS
AND INDEX

CONTRIBUTORS

JAMES J. FISHMAN is Professor of Law at Pace University School of Law and Co-editor of and contributor to *Limits of Justice: The Courts' Role in School Desegregation*.

BARBARA FLICKER is Consulting Director and former Director of the Institute of Judicial Administration, Inc.

HOWARD I. KALODNER is Dean of Western New England School of Law and Co-editor of *Limits of Justice: The Courts' Role in School Desegregation*.

D. BRUCE LA PIERRE is Professor of Law at Washington University School of Law and former Special Master to the District Court in the St. Louis interdistrict desegregation case.

MICHAEL A. REBELL is a partner in the New York City law firm of Rebell and Katzive and author of *Equality and Education*.

ROSEMARY SALOMONE is Professor of Law at St. John's University School of Law.

ALLEN E. SHOENBERGER is Professor of Law at Loyola University of Chicago School of Law.

LAWRENCE STRAUSS is a reporter for the *Manchester Journal Inquirer*.

PAUL L. TRACTENBERG is Professor of Law at Rutgers University School of Law, and the founder and first Director of the Education Law Center, Inc.

INDEX

Greiner, Gordon, 202, 209, 211, 215, 226n.43, 230n.114
Gross, Jerry, 33–36, 38–39, 61n.68, 91
Grove City College v. Bell, 123
Grumet, Louis, 30, 56n.26

Hackworth, Ted, 196
Handicapped, education of, 6, 7, 12, 16–19
  "appropriate education" standard, 27–29
  in Boston, 16, 18, 28–29, 70–107
  compensatory services, 78–80
  decategorization, 33 34
  "educational benefits" standard, 27
  funding, 26
  mainstreaming and, 48–52
  in New York City, 16–18, 25–69
  racial discrimination, compared with, 17
  rights cases compared, Boston and New York City, 89–94
  staff, 45–48, 65nn. 116–17, 66nn. 120–27, 70, 87
  waiting lists, 38, 44–45, 48, 61nn. 65–67, 64n.107, 73–74, 97n.38, 98nn. 44, 46, 47
Hannon, Joseph P., 314–15
Hawley, Willis, 197, 210
Hill v. Gautreaux, 318
Hispanic students, 11, 21, 186, 372
  busing and, 211–12
  in Chicago, 308, 312, 315, 317, 320, 322, 323, 325–29, 339–40
  in Denver, 187, 190, 195, 197–200, 203–18, 219, 220, 221
  effect of litigation on, 218–21
  see also Bilingual education; English as a Second Language (ESL); Limited-English-speaking children
Hittman, Stephan, 47
Housing, segregated, 5–6, 20, 374

in Chicago, 8, 308, 310–11, 340
in Denver, 186–87, 200
in Yonkers, 20, 367–68, 381–82
Hughes, Joyce, 353n.164
Hungate, William L., 236, 238, 242, 277, 283n.16, 286n.48, 288n.74, 289n.93

Individual education programs (IEPs)
  Boston schools, 86, 87, 88, 103–4n.121, 104n.129
  New York City schools, 32, 40, 42, 45, 49, 50
  see also Handicapped, education of; Special education
Institute of Judicial Administration (IJA), 3, 6, 7, 19, 372, 375, 380
Interdistrict school desegregation
  in Chicago, 336–38, 372
  in St. Louis, 233–35, 242–78
  see also Suburban school systems
Interest-group mobilization, 114
Internal Revenue Service, 178n.193

Jackson, Jesse, 319
Jackson, Michael, 210, 212
Johnson, Frank M., Jr., 367
Johnson v. Board of Education, 312
Jose P. v. Ambach, 16, 28–44, 89–94, 105nn. 134, 135, 137, 106n.139
  results, 44–52
Judge as Political Power Broker, 368

Kalodner, Howard I., 3
Kennedy, Paul, 80
Keyes v. School District No. 1, 10, 187–89, 196, 197, 203, 213, 218, 221–24, 225n.24, 372
Kohn, Shalom L., 344n.31

Language problems, 11–12. *See also* Bilingual education; English as a Second Language (ESL);

DATE DUE